AMERICAN PUBLIC POLICY 96/97

First Edition

Readings from the *National Journal*

Editor

Bruce Stinebrickner
DePauw University

Professor Bruce Stinebrickner teaches American politics and chairs the Department of Political Science at DePauw University in Greencastle, Indiana. After receiving his Ph.D. from Yale University in 1974, and before going to DePauw in 1987, he taught American politics at Lehman College of the City University of New York and at the University of Queensland in Brisbane, Australia. He has a general interest in U.S. public policy and a special interest in public policies relating to children and to civil rights and civil liberties. He is currently doing research on several issues relating to child custody, including adoption, foster care, and child neglect and abuse.

Cover illustration by Mike Eagle

The Dushkin Publishing Group/
Brown & Benchmark Publishers
Sluice Dock, Guilford, Connecticut 06437

The Annual Editions Series

Annual Editions is a series of over 65 volumes designed to provide the reader with convenient, low-cost access to a wide range of current, carefully selected articles from some of the most important magazines, newspapers, and journals published today. Annual Editions are updated on an annual basis through a continuous monitoring of over 300 periodical sources. All Annual Editions have a number of features designed to make them particularly useful, including topic guides, annotated tables of contents, unit overviews, and indexes. For the teacher using Annual Editions in the classroom, an Instructor's Resource Guide with test questions is available for each volume.

Printed on Recycled Paper 

VOLUMES AVAILABLE

Abnormal Psychology
Africa
Aging
American Foreign Policy
American Government
American History, Pre-Civil War
American History, Post-Civil War
American Public Policy
Anthropology
Archaeology
Biopsychology
Business Ethics
Child Growth and Development
China
Comparative Politics
Computers in Education
Computers in Society
Criminal Justice
Developing World
Deviant Behavior
Drugs, Society, and Behavior
Dying, Death, and Bereavement
Early Childhood Education
Economics
Educating Exceptional Children
Education
Educational Psychology
Environment
Geography
Global Issues
Health
Human Development
Human Resources
Human Sexuality
India and South Asia
International Business
Japan and the Pacific Rim
Latin America
Life Management
Macroeconomics
Management
Marketing
Marriage and Family
Mass Media
Microeconomics
Middle East and the Islamic World
Multicultural Education
Nutrition
Personal Growth and Behavior
Physical Anthropology
Psychology
Public Administration
Race and Ethnic Relations
Russia, the Eurasian Republics, and Central/Eastern Europe
Social Problems
Sociology
State and Local Government
Urban Society
Western Civilization, Pre-Reformation
Western Civilization, Post-Reformation
Western Europe
World History, Pre-Modern
World History, Modern
World Politics

Cataloging in Publication Data
Main entry under title: Annual Editions: American Public Policy. 1996/97: Readings from the *National Journal*..
1. Public policy—United States—Periodicals. 2. United States—Politics and government—Periodicals. I. Stinebrickner, Bruce, *comp.* II. Title: American public policy: Readings from the *National Journal*.
ISBN 1–56134–402–8 320.6′05

First Edition

Printed in the United States of America

Editors/ Advisory Board

Members of the Advisory Board are instrumental in the final selection of articles for each edition of Annual Editions. Their review of articles for content, level, currentness, and appropriateness provides critical direction to the editor and staff. We think you'll find their careful consideration well reflected in this volume.

To the Reader

In publishing ANNUAL EDITIONS we recognize the enormous role played by the magazines, newspapers, and journals of the *public press* in providing current, first-rate educational information in a broad spectrum of interest areas. Within the articles, the best scientists, practitioners, researchers, and commentators draw issues into new perspective as accepted theories and viewpoints are called into account by new events, recent discoveries change old facts, and fresh debate breaks out over important controversies.

Many of the articles resulting from this enormous editorial effort are appropriate for students, researchers, and professionals seeking accurate, current material to help bridge the gap between principles and theories and the real world. These articles, however, become more useful for study when those of lasting value are carefully *collected, organized, indexed,* and *reproduced* in a *low-cost format*, which provides easy and permanent access when the material is needed. That is the role played by *Annual Editions*.

Under the direction of each volume's *Editor*, who is an expert in the subject area, and with the guidance of an *Advisory Board*, we seek each year to provide in each *ANNUAL EDITION* a current, well-balanced, carefully selected collection of the best of the public press for your study and enjoyment. We think you'll find this volume useful, and we hope you'll take a moment to let us know what you think.

In 1969 Professor David Easton, president of the American Political Science Association, addressed the annual national meeting of political scientists and told them that political science needed to be more "relevant" to the problems of contemporary society. Although Easton's speech was delivered at a time when most of today's undergraduate students had not yet been born, many of their political science professors were studying in college or graduate school at the time.

Easton's address was given against the background of the tumultuous 1960s. Not only were the sixties a decade of civil rights demonstrations, anti–Vietnam War protests, urban riots, and assassinations, but they also developed a widespread perception that American government was not performing well. That perception led political science professors and their students to pay more attention to public policy. Research, books, and new courses on American public policy proliferated. Already established courses such as introductory courses on American government, state and local government, and comparative politics became more likely to treat public policy issues. While in some respects public policy had always been a concern of political scientists, the focus became more systematic, more self-conscious, and more explicit.

This book is a collection of articles on American public policy taken from recent issues of *National Journal,* an important and authoritative weekly on American government and public policy. The period since Bill Clinton entered the White House has been one of intense policy discussion and debate among top American government officials as well as the public at large. While interest in public policy has been growing since the early 1960s, national elections in 1992 and 1994 may have focused attention even more. The 1992 presidential election brought Democrat Bill Clinton, a self-styled "agent of change," to the White House after twelve years of Republican administrations. The 1994 congressional elections produced a Republican Speaker of the House, Newt Gingrich, and Republican majorities in both houses of Congress for the first time in 40 years.

These recent changes in party control of Congress and the presidency occurred against the background of growing budget deficits for the national government that have caused alarm in many quarters. They have also led to serious consideration of policy changes that would have been viewed in Washington as almost impossible a few short years ago. Shift responsibility for major social welfare programs to the states? End the progressive income tax as the main source of revenue for the national government? Reduce environmental regulations and controls? Reform the U.S. health care delivery system in wholesale ways? These are just some of the ideas that have gained currency and are being seriously considered by significant numbers of Washington policymakers in the 1990s.

The organization of this book is straightforward. The first unit includes articles on recent developments in some of the institutions and processes that play important roles in making public policy in the American political system. Unit 2 treats budgetary, taxing, and spending policies of the national government, all areas that relate to the health of the national economy. Units 3 through 10 focus on different functional areas of public policy: agriculture and food (3), environment and energy (4), health care (5), social welfare programs (6), schooling, children, and child care (7), civil rights (8), crime, urban affairs, and other domestic policy areas (9), and foreign and defense policy, including trade and immigration (10). I can only agree with those readers who suggest that not all government policy making fits neatly into functional areas such as those that serve as the unit headings for this book. On the other hand, both policymakers and the general public are accustomed to thinking in terms of functional policy areas, and policy areas such as those used in this book can help focus public policy discussion and analysis in useful ways.

This book is intended to be used primarily in American public policy and public administration courses and in introductory American government courses with a policy orientation. Reactions to this new volume are especially welcome. Please complete and mail the article rating form on the last page of the book and let us know your reactions and suggestions for improvement.

Bruce Stinebrickner

Bruce Stinebrickner
Editor

Unit 1

Institutions and Processes

The selections in this unit treat major policy-making institutions of the national government, relations between the national government and the 50 state governments in the policy process, and developments in the way that constituents and interest groups try to influence elected policymakers.

The concepts in bold italics are developed in the article. For further expansion please refer to the Topic Guide and the Index.

Unit 2

The Economy, Taxing, Spending, and Budgeting

The articles in this unit cover taxing, spending, and budgeting, all parts of the public policy process that are related to the well-being of the national economy.

The concepts in bold italics are developed in the article. For further expansion please refer to the Topic Guide and the Index.

Unit 3

Agriculture and Food

This unit's focus is on public policy issues relating to food and agriculture in the United States.

Unit 4

Environment and Energy

The articles in this unit treat public policy in the related areas of the environment and energy.

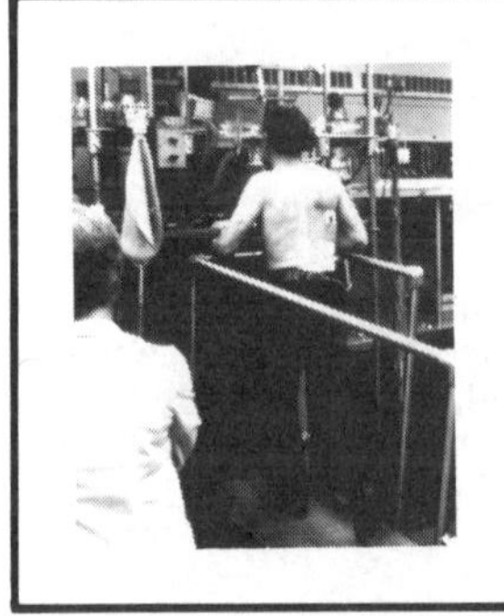

Unit 5

Health Care

The selections in this unit cover the issues of the health care delivery system in the United States.

The concepts in bold italics are developed in the article. For further expansion please refer to the Topic Guide and the Index.

Unit 6

Safety Net Programs: Social Security, Welfare, and Housing

In this unit, the selections survey social welfare public policy: the provision of subsistence levels of food, housing, and income to needy people.

Unit 7

Schooling, Children, and Child Care

The articles of this unit are concerned with public policies relating to the younger generation and public education.

The concepts in bold italics are developed in the article. For further expansion please refer to the Topic Guide and the Index.

Unit 8

Civil Rights

The status of African Americans in American society and related public policies such as affirmative action are reviewed in this unit.

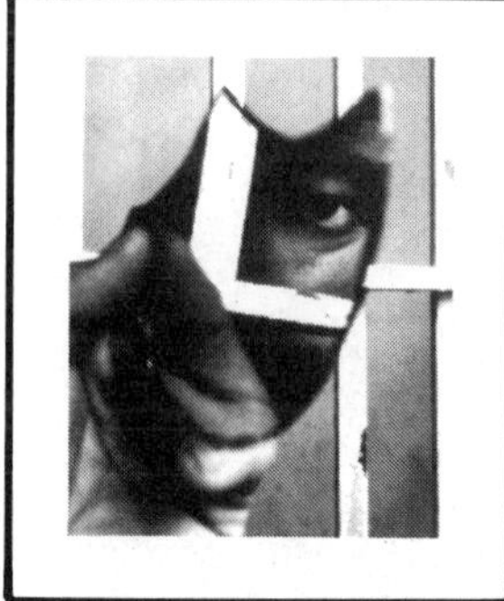

Unit 9

Crime, Urban Affairs, and Other Domestic Policy Areas

The articles in this unit treat policy problems and issues related to crime, urban life, and other areas.

The concepts in bold italics are developed in the article. For further expansion please refer to the Topic Guide and the Index.

Unit 10

Foreign and Defense Policy, Trade, and Immigration

This unit covers diplomatic and military activities as well as trade and immigration policies.

The concepts in bold italics are developed in the article. For further expansion please refer to the Topic Guide and the Index.

Topic Guide

This topic guide suggests how the selections in this book relate to topics likely to be of interest when studying public policy in the United States. The guide is arranged alphabetically according to topic, and selections that give substantial coverage to each topic are named. Articles may, of course, treat topics that do not appear in the topic guide. In turn, entries in the topic guide do not necessarily constitute a comprehensive listing of all the contents of each selection.

Institutions and Processes

As political scientist Thomas Dye has said, public policy refers to what governments do and why they do it. Governments do many things that affect the lives of citizens, and units 2 through 10 of this book treat different policy areas such as environment and energy (unit 4), agriculture and food (unit 3), health care (unit 5), and civil rights (unit 8). This unit is different in that its selections provide an overview of some of the major institutions and processes that shape public policy in the United States. Selections in this unit cover the presidency, Congress, bureaucrats, interest groups, ways that citizens can and do communicate with elected government officials, relations between national and state governments, and so forth.

One approach to the public policy process conceives of it as consisting of a number of distinct stages: identifying problems, setting an agenda for decision making, formulating and adopting policy proposals, and then implementing and evaluating policies. Although this "stage approach" can be helpful in calling attention to different steps in the policy process, the policy process in the real world seldom if ever proceeds in as neat and orderly a fashion as the stage approach suggests. One critic of the stage approach, political scientist Charles E. Lindblom, has suggested that the policy process in the real world is better viewed as a murky "primeval soup," an unordered set of overlapping events without recognizable stages. The selections in unit 1 do not explicitly address whether the "stage" or "primeval soup" model of the American public policy process is more accurate, but they do provide raw materials with which to consider the question.

The United States is, of course, one of the world's representative democracies. Indeed, Americans pride themselves on living in one of the most durable and stable democratic systems in history. The public policy process in the United States occurs squarely within the context of a representative system of government—campaigns, elections, lobbying by individuals and by interest groups, public opinion polls, protests, demonstrations, and the like.

At least some of the selections in this unit suggest that

Unit 1

outside "democratic" pressures undermine the policy-making process and the outcome of that process, public policy itself. This viewpoint is frequently voiced about the American policy process and raises an interesting question about the connection between representative government and what governments do. What role should the desires and preferences of ordinary citizens play in what "their" government does? Should public policy reflect what the citizens want, regardless of whether elected and appointed policymakers think that what the citizens want is wise public policy? These questions are as old as representative government itself and were eloquently discussed by a member of the English Parliament, Edmund Burke, in the eighteenth century.

Lindblom, the same political scientist who views the public policy process as primeval soup, believes that public policy is or would be well served by what he calls the "intelligence of democracy." At the core of his perspective is the notion that a properly organized public policy process that nurtures and capitalizes on informed and heartfelt discussion and debate among all interested citizens will result in *good* public policy.

Still another angle on the U.S. public policy process involves the notion of *incrementalism*. An incremental public policy process is one in which changes in policy tend to be relatively minor adjustments at the margins of existing policies, rather than more fundamental changes in what governments are doing. Several factors are thought to contribute to the incremental nature of public policy making in the United States: the separation of powers, the variety of demands and pressures on policy makers at any one time, and the inherent limitations on the range of factors that even wise and conscientious policymakers can take into account when reviewing a policy.

This unit does not provide definitive responses to the sorts of issues and approaches raised in this overview. Nor can they provide a comprehensive overview of the institutions and processes that anchor public policy making in the United States of America. But they should provide a useful introduction to the context in which, for better or worse, governments make policy in the American political system.

Looking Ahead: Challenge Questions

Which do you think is the more accurate reflection of how the American public policy works—the stage model or the notion of primeval soup? Why?

Do you think that representative systems of government, such as that in the United States, produce better public policy than nondemocratic systems? Why or why not?

The separation of powers is a characteristic feature of the way national and state governments are structured in the United States. Governmental powers are shared among legislative, executive, and judicial branches, and there is an elaborate system of checks and balances. In parliamentary systems such as that of Canada, the United Kingdom, and most other representative democracies in the world, effective government powers are concentrated in a cabinet made up of members of the parliament belonging to the majority party or a majority coalition of parties. There are relatively few restraints on what the governing cabinet can do, at least until voters in the next election determine whether it will continue in office. Which sort of system results in better public policy—a separation of powers system with checks and balances that often wind up hamstringing significant policy initiatives, or a parliamentary system that usually allows more drastic policy changes? Why?

Do you think that elections in the United States are much affected by policy considerations? That is, do candidates win or lose elections mostly because of the policy positions that they support? Do you think that election outcomes should be determined strictly by the policy positions of the candidates?

Do you think that a government policymaker such as a senator or the president should pay much attention to public opinion polls, what people are saying on talk radio, and what is said in communications—letters, faxes, e-mail, etc.—they are receiving from the public? Why or why not?

Do We Ask Too Much of PRESIDENTS?

BURT SOLOMON

Richard M. Nixon is dead. Jacqueline Kennedy Onassis is dead. George W. Ball is dead. A generation of American leaders is passing, as another has arrived. A generation that was forged in the clarity of World War II is being supplanted by one that was molded by the muddled lessons of the war in Vietnam.

Twenty-five years ago, when *National Journal* entered the scene, Nixon had just taken office and the world—in many ways—was a harsher but a clearer place. As the pages of this silver anniversary issue will attest, a lot has happened since then. The nation's demographics have shifted, its economic dynamics have been rearranged and its political processes are nastier and less forgiving than they were. The nation has become a harder place to govern than it used to be. It isn't likely to get any easier.

If evidence is needed, consider the past quarter-century's string of failed Presidents. Franklin D. Roosevelt, Harry S Truman and Dwight D. Eisenhower served seven terms, all told, and by most measures proved successful Presidents. It took twice as many Presidents to serve out the next seven terms—and that doesn't even count the two since.

Neither the voters nor the historians have been wowed. Only Ronald Reagan, who stuck to his guns and persuaded the public to accept his version of reality, was permitted to serve out a second term. But historians rank him between Zachary Taylor and John Tyler as below-average Presidents, according to Tim H. Blessing, a co-author of *Greatness in the White House: Rating the Presidents From George Washington Through Ronald Reagan* (Pennsylvania State University Press, 1994). The five or six Presidents who preceded the most recent five or six "will rank much higher in the verdicts of history," retired Williams College professor James M. Burns, a noted political historian, predicted.

This isn't the first time the country has suffered a run of mediocre Presidents. From the 1840s to the 1890s, only Abraham Lincoln was an obvious success. And even he had "the good luck to get himself shot," Blessing, an American history professor at Alvernia College in Reading, Pa., said in an interview. "The problem of Reconstruction was probably unresolvable."

WHEN TALENT'S NOT ENOUGH

One school of thought is that America has encountered a run of bad luck. "Basically coincidence," Everett Carll Ladd, the president of the Roper Center for Public Opinion Research Inc. at the University of Connecticut (Storrs), said of the succession of Presidents who've been found wanting. He portrayed Nixon as psychologically unsuited, Gerald R. Ford as an accident, Jimmy Carter as untested, George Bush as inattentive to the public's economic anxieties and Bill Clinton as "poorly situated" because of deficiencies in character.

But more likely, the problem hasn't been them so much as us. The particulars of the individuals who've entered the White House have paled beside the increasing demands that the public has piled on them. "There's been a lot of cranking up of expectations," Fred I. Greenstein, an expert on the presidency at Princeton University, said. Problems are expected to be solved overnight. Stephen J. Wayne, a presidential scholar at Georgetown University, reasoned that the complexity of government, along with "the recognition that certain problems are too big not to have government involvement," have combined to push more and more of the nation's troubles onto the President's desk.

Recent Presidents, by and large, have been politically and intellectually talented men. But that isn't enough anymore. "Flexible, pragmatic, capable of compromise—also firm, decisive, principled," Hedley Donovan, who'd been a White House counselor to Carter, wrote in *Time* magazine in 1982, listing 31 attributes that a President needs. "To be a 'good' President in the 1980s," he wrote, "may be even harder than to be a

Richard A. Bloom

Reagan served a full eight years . . .

Shepard Sherbell/SABA

. . . But Carter was denied reelection . . .

. . . And Bush was similarly rejected.

'great' President in the days of Antietam or Pearl Harbor."

And the criteria by which Presidents are judged—and damned—keep proliferating. Presidents must also be telegenically talented, delicately balanced in personality and pristine in private life. Thomas Jefferson, with his squeaky voice and his Deist beliefs, probably couldn't succeed in politics now. Lincoln, so prone to melancholia that he supposedly wouldn't carry a penknife, might not be trusted with his finger on the button. The wealthy FDR might be prey to a nanny problem.

More than ever, interest groups want what they want and will fight to get it, meaning that a President must mobilize unwieldy coalitions to get things done. This political task has been made harder by the social fragmentation that has turned communities with common interests—in the United States, as in the rest of the world—into competing enclaves. The political parties, internally torn, are unreliable as sources of support for an embattled President. (Ask Bush.) James David Barber of Duke University, a specialist in the presidency, noted that a President faces so many different pressures nowadays that he can't satisfy them all.

TRYING TIMES

A lot else about the times has conspired to ruin presidency after presidency. Recent Presidents haven't been fortunate in the nature of the national afflictions they've faced. "All the problems tend to run together," Henry F. Graff, a retired professor of history at Columbia University, noted. They may not be as critical as a war or an economic depression. But that only deprives the President of the extra authority and moral certitude that urgency brings. Witness the current debate over health care, which has the White House proclaiming a crisis and its opposition denying it. "The more severe the problem," Georgetown's Wayne noted, "the easier it is for a President to deal with it."

It's always been hard to govern, but now it's "super-difficult," Burns said. "Government is just much more difficult today than it used to be."

At best, technology has proved a mixed political blessing. Television, on balance, has probably bolstered presidential power. (It did for Reagan.) But having so much of what a President says stored on tape—audio or video—contributed to Nixon's downfall and has undermined his successors' chances of denying their promises and screwups. Since the Watergate scandal, when investigative reporters became the journalistic elite, the press has been prone to build up Presidents and then tear them down—a good story both times.

The advent of the media age has also turned the President into a celebrity. Stardom is tempting for a President, especially one who feels underappreciated—that is, all of them. But it's dangerous. By making Presidents so familiar, television has helped to relieve the office of its mystique. Had the public known that FDR was crippled, it would have "made him a less dramatic figure," A. James Reichley, the author of a recent book on political parties, said. He noted that the press at the time felt obliged to sustain the stature of the presidency.

Presidents have ushered the process along. Carter carried his own garment bag as part of his political strategy in reaction to Nixon's imperial pretensions. Ford toasted English muffins. Clinton, with his penchant for Big Macs and his willingness to describe his underwear, has further shrunk the President into Everyman. The recent discussion in public about Clinton's genitals smacked of the earlier talk about Michael Jackson's and may have evoked as uncomfortable a public response. No longer do Presidents grow to fit the job; they've started to seem smaller than life just as the electorate's standards have inflated.

It's no wonder that the distrust of government—and of all institutions—has climbed so much. Candidates promise more and more to get elected and seem like hypocrites all the faster when they don't deliver. The pessimism of an increasingly cynical electorate has become self-fulfilling. If people expect a one-term President, Burns said, "the prospect of presidential authority evaporates."

There's precious little reason to think that these dynamics will turn around any time soon. Expectations that the White House should try to fix whatever ails the nation aren't likely to diminish much if at all. The public's titillation with the President's personal life and its eagerness to cast judgments aren't likely to fade. The conundrums that the country faces at home and abroad aren't about to get any simpler or more susceptible to being managed one at a time. A long period of prosperity might suffice to prompt voters to ease up on their leaders, but that won't happen in a hurry.

Neither Clinton nor his successors during the next quarter-century, that is, have any reason to expect an easy time of it. "We'll continue to have vexed presidencies," Columbia's Graff prophesied. Their surest hope for success may depend on the problems they face getting worse. That way, at least, they might be given a shovel worthy of the hole they're in. History shows that it takes a great crisis, after all, to make a great leader.

Photos by Richard A. Bloom

Which predecessor will Clinton emulate?

WHEN THERE'S TOO MUCH OF A GOOD THING

RICHARD E. COHEN

The gears are jamming on Capitol Hill as more and more players, in and out of Congress, seek a piece of the legislative action. Health care reform is only the latest and most evident example as countless interest groups press their views on hundreds of Members and their aides on a seemingly inexhaustible stack of issues.

Have we created a "hyper-democracy" in which public and private-sector advocates alike have overloaded the political circuits, making it difficult for elected officials to address obvious national problems in a deliberate, thorough way? Are there so many pressures that government has gone haywire? In short, have excesses in political responsiveness produced new barriers to democracy?

Governing is inevitably messy, of course. The constitutional framers made a conscious effort to assure that the nation's many factions would have a voice. And such current-day critics of Washington as Ross Perot have won widespread applause for their contention that the Capitol is, if anything, too remote from the everyday world.

But a case can be made that the problems are just the opposite: that rising public demands for services have collided with government's eroding ability to respond, producing a form of mob rule driven by the work of lobbyists and pollsters and by pressures from a variety of interests notable for their short-term perspectives. Advances in communications have heightened the influence of organized mail and telephone campaigns, opinion polls and new forms of radio and television programming that seek to sway Congress and other parts of official Washington.

The political Left and the political Right are equally unhappy about the consequences. Liberals argue, for example, that the public makes too big an issue of the size of the national debt and that government must pay more attention to the need for increased public investment. Conservatives respond that government programs live on with little official reexamination of their premises or effectiveness, even during 12 years of Republican Presidents.

But these and other broad policy arguments tend to get lost in the fog of war on Capitol Hill. Many lawmakers complain that they have little time to think or to talk constructively with their colleagues during their often overscheduled three-day Washington workweek. And weary staffers use their Fridays and Mondays to catch their breath and to prepare for the next battle.

On health care, for example, "we put a lot of time, thought and energy into debating and pursuing proposals that are going nowhere," said Rep. Timothy J. Penny, D-Minn., who is retiring at the end of the year to co-chair a policy forum at the University of Minnesota. "I would rather have a fair fight, let the chips fall where they may and move forward. Instead, we do nothing for a long period because we are afraid of the consequences." Too much of what Members do, he added, is shaped by their reading of the opinion polls—the contemporary version of holding one's finger in the wind.

INTRUSIVE PRESSURES

Public officials have always had to reckon with the views of their constituents. In recent years, however, constituent pressures have become more intrusive.

Lobbying groups representing both broad and narrow interests have increased exponentially as the federal government's budget and regulatory reach have expanded. Meanwhile, a new class of communicators—who typically bash government and pander to public fears on both sides of such sensitive and complex issues as abortion and race relations—has relied on new phone and mail technologies to encourage a sense that "the public knows best." In the face of these pressures, many politicians have made simplistic appeals to voters that hinder public understanding or obscure the real choices on the issues.

Although populist criticisms of the governing class have long been a vital part of the American political culture, in the past quarter-century, advocates (including street protesters and talk-show hosts) have sought to apply public pressure in ways that tend to undermine the representational process and move the nation toward a town-meeting form of government.

Nostalgia for "the way we were" is endemic in Congress, which delights in paying special homage to such departed parliamentary giants as House Speaker Sam Rayburn of Texas and Sens. Everett McKinley Dirksen of Illinois and Richard B. Russell of Georgia, who supposedly cut their legislative deals while working mostly behind the scenes.

In those "good old days," though it often took several years to pass such landmark legislation as medicare and the civil rights laws of the 1960s, the public seemed to have more patience with public officials than it does today, when so much attention is focused on congressional peccadilloes.

There is no denying the hostile public sentiment displayed in recent polls. Earlier this month, a survey by the Gallup Organization Inc. for CNN and *USA Today* showed that 49 per cent of the public believes that Congress is more corrupt than it was 20 years ago. In a poll in March by the same organizations, the public, by 63-29 per cent, disapproved of how Congress was doing its job.

The public's unhappiness with Congress was evident in the 1992 House elections. The percentage of House Members who were reelected with a relatively secure 60 per cent of the vote or more nose-dived to its lowest level since 1964. From 1984-90, more than 75 per cent of incumbents—a historically high share—won with at least 60 per cent of the vote. But in 1992, only 66 per cent did that well. Many observers expect even more incumbents to fall below 60 per cent this year. *(See chart.)*

Some of Congress's woes, no doubt, have been self-inflicted or self-exacerbated. Even when Members finally act on major legislation, they tend to tie them-

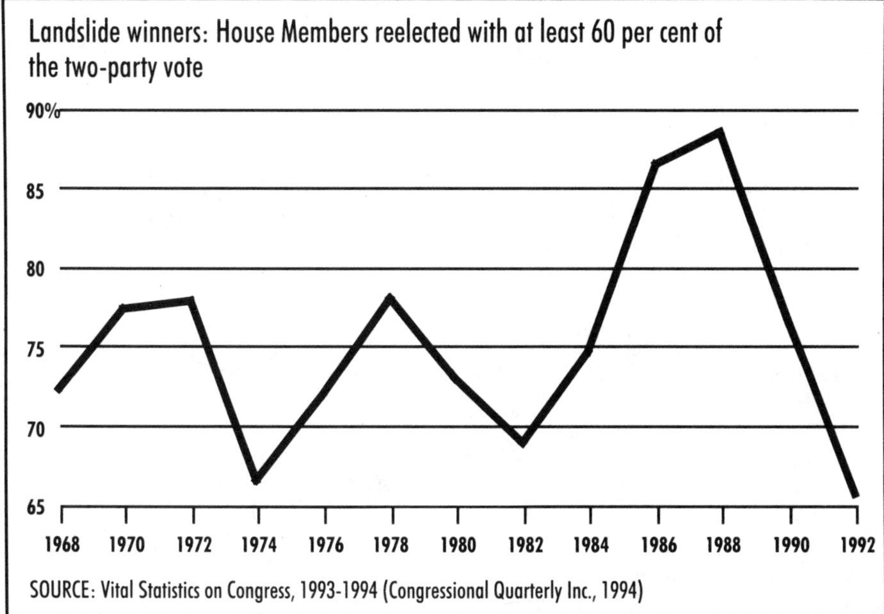

selves in knots, adding to a widespread impression of congressional ineptitude. It's become commonplace in both chambers for bills to include hundreds of pages of technical details that require the imprint of multiple committees or that demand complex procedures for floor debate.

"The nature and complexity of the issues facing Congress have changed significantly in recent years, and Congress has not kept up," said Rep. Lee H. Hamilton, D-Ind., who last year co-chaired the Joint Committee on the Organization of Congress.

Even more corrosive to public sentiment have been high-profile charges of wrongdoing against such powerful congressional figures as Speaker Jim Wright, D-Texas, and Ways and Means Committee chairman Dan Rostenkowski, D-Ill.—both of whom were forced to give up their posts because of corruption allegations.

INFORMATION OVERLOAD

Adding to Congress's collective headache have been the social, economic and technological changes in American society in recent years that have vastly increased the information and the viewpoints that inundate lawmakers.

The days when Members of Congress traveled to and from Washington by stagecoach and were out of touch with their constituents for months at a time are long gone. Now they keep in close touch with the public through frequent visits to their constituencies and regular review of polling data and communications from interest groups. But recent political events have demonstrated the perils that result from too much of a good thing.

In 1988, for example, President Reagan signed a bill providing insurance coverage to the elderly for catastrophic illnesses, to be financed out of modest tax increases on wealthy retirees. A year later, however, fringe groups within the senior citizens community used twisted facts, heated rhetoric and high-profile pressure tactics to force a compliant Congress and President Bush to repeal the legislation, despite bipartisan opposition from Members who were well-versed in the issue.

Fast-forward to 1993, when another President pressed for enactment of a tax increase as part of his bill to slice the budget deficit by a third. Even though the new taxes would fall heavily on the wealthiest, opponents of Bill Clinton's plan issued exaggerated complaints that generated millions of telephone calls to Congress in the 48 hours before the vote and added to the climate of fear among wavering lawmakers.

The bill passed, but only by the narrowest of margins, leaving the nation to wonder whether another President was teetering on the brink of failure. "There would have been disappointment and disillusion . . . if we had failed," House Speaker Thomas S. Foley, D-Wash., said in an interview the day after the vote.

Even last year's bipartisan approval of the North American Free Trade Agreement generated complaints from advocates on both sides that the debate was shallow and dominated by interest-group pressures.

HARD TO CHANGE

Prospects for changing the way that Congress addresses national problems appear dim so long as the same party holds the reins of government. After 40 years of unbroken Democratic control of the House, members of that party have grown comfortable with the procedures that they have created, especially the power-sharing reforms of the 1970s. Despite frequent grumbling and demands for additional reforms, they have found it difficult to coalesce behind changes in such areas as congressional reorganization and campaign finance.

"We refuse to admit that better internal performance could improve our image," Penny said. "Instead, leaders muzzle the critics and hope that the public will say that they like Washington. . . . We are stuck in familiar patterns."

Only one other time in the nation's history has one party (the Democratic Republicans, from 1801-25) held a House majority continuously for more than 16 years. Although quick and effective changes in congressional operations would probably be illusory under any circumstances, an overhaul would be likelier if Republicans took control of Congress. When Republicans ran the Senate from 1981-87, they instituted some procedural changes—a new budget process was the principal one—but were often stymied by the Democratic-controlled House.

Critics have proposed and won broad support for such radical changes as a balanced budget constitutional amendment and for what many critics consider gimmicks: term limits, for example, even though there is little evidence that they would achieve their professed goals.

Lawmakers' increasing willingness to challenge the President, even one from their own party, has contributed to Congress's vulnerability to outside pressures. As Presidents and Members of Congress become less dependent on their parties in seeking election than they once were, they need rely less on one another in crafting public policy. And that only raises the opportunity for private citizens to have an impact.

In his book *Demosclerosis* (Times Books, 1994), *National Journal* contributing editor Jonathan Rauch attributes many of government's problems to "the democratic public's tendency to form ever more groups clamoring for ever more goodies and perks and then defending them to the death."

Some critics challenge Rauch's premise that government has steadily lost its ability to adapt in solving problems. But few would dispute that mounting public pressures have make problem-solving increasingly difficult.

STILL TRYING TO REINVENT GOVERNMENT

Reuters/Bettmann

ELIZA NEWLIN CARNEY

Ever since Thomas Jefferson in 1801 sang the praises of "a wise and frugal government," the promise of a waste-free federal bureaucracy has enticed and eluded the third President's successors in the Oval Office.

Franklin Delano Roosevelt pledged to struggle "against confusion, against ineffectiveness, against waste, against inefficiency." Richard M. Nixon hailed a "New Federalism" that would bring government closer to the people. Jimmy Carter tackled big spending with "zero-base budgeting." Ronald Reagan promised to root out waste, fraud and abuse.

Perhaps most ambitious of all, President Clinton's National Performance Review aims, in his words, "to redesign, to reinvent, to reinvigorate the entire national government." Championed by Vice President Albert Gore Jr., the Administration's vision is lofty: to modernize government with new management techniques, cut red tape and treat each citizen like a valued customer.

Certain factors set the Clinton initiative apart from past reform efforts: It has top executive support, it was crafted in close cooperation with career civil servants and it promotes some radical notions about the way government should work.

At bottom, however, this most recent push to reinvent government suffers from the same problems that have stymied reform efforts over the past quarter-century and more. These include the lack of institutional follow-through, an obsession with public relations at the expense of meaningful investment and disregard for an essential government player—Congress.

A TOUGHER TASK?

Clinton arguably faces a tougher task than any of his predecessors. Far from trimming the federal bureaucracy, this century's political leaders have added layers with a ballooning array of programs and regulations. Early reorganization efforts, including Roosevelt's Brownlow

Richard A. Bloom

The bureaucracy has increased in complexity.

Committee and the two Hoover Commissions under Presidents Truman and Eisenhower, recognized the boom in federal programs and the need for a powerful bureaucracy to implement them.

Nixon's reform effort struggled to control this bureaucratic growth, which was accelerated by Lyndon B. Johnson's Great Society. Nixon's Advisory Council on Government Organization, known as the Ash Council (for its chairman, businessman Roy Ash), pledged to streamline management by consolidating government into four "super-Cabinet" departments.

Like previous reform efforts, the Ash Council also set out to shore up and consolidate presidential authority. Nixon succeeded in converting the old Budget Bureau into a new Office of Management and Budget and in giving OMB's director more clout.

But Congress rejected Nixon's sweeping Cabinet reorganization, and his reform plans unraveled quickly under the weight of the Watergate scandal. This failure points up an inherent problem with presidential reorganizations: Although genuine institutional reform takes a decade or more to implement, management analysts say, Presidents often last no more than four years.

Carter was equally determined to put his own stamp on government management. Reflecting the growth in popular antigovernment sentiment, Carter campaigned as an outsider and promised to reorganize the government completely. Once in office, he assigned about 300 people to work on a reorganization project housed in OMB and detailed another 160 to reform the civil service through his personnel management project.

Ironically, Carter's myriad study groups and poorly publicized recommendations reflected the very organizational problems that he said were plaguing big government. His reorganization team toiled for years but produced no public report.

Some concrete changes emerged: the creation of the Energy and Education Departments and professionalization of the civil service. Over all, however, Carter's reforms fell far short of their original promise.

Reagan accomplished even less with his Private Sector Survey on Cost Control, better known as the Grace Commission after its chairman, businessman J. Peter Grace. The Reagan reforms, long on public relations but short on actual savings, amplified the antigovernment rhetoric of the 1980s' tax revolt.

Like Clinton's National Performance Review, Reagan's reorganization promised to save the government big dollars—about $424 billion over three years. Unlike Clinton, however, Reagan stacked his commission with outsiders from the business world who had little experience dealing with federal departments.

PROMISES, PROMISES

Clinton has made the most of this contrast, noting that when the Grace Commission disbanded, its chairman went back to New York City, but that when Gore's group ended its task, the Vice President simply went back to his office down the hall.

Yet Gore's September report, "From Red Tape to Results: Creating a Government that Works Better & Costs Less," echoes the promises of previous reform proposals. As the Grace Commission did, it touts enormous savings: $108 billion from fiscal 1995-99.

It also builds on the popular theme that government is broken and needs to

Changing philosophies of government management

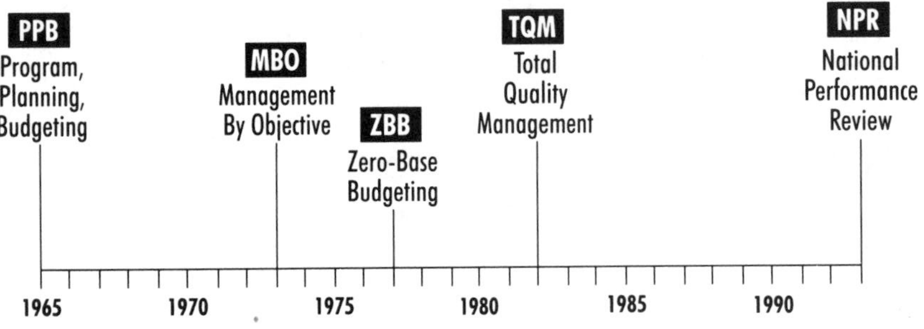

be fixed. Government programs "are being undermined by an inefficient and outdated bureaucracy," Clinton declared when he unveiled the National Performance Review; government's culture is one of "complacency and entitlement."

This focus on the culture of government—the way managers function day-in and day-out—distinguishes the Performance Review from earlier efforts that emphasized reorganization.

The political climate is also very favorable to reform. A recent ABC News-*Washington Post* poll found that 68 per cent of Americans are "dissatisfied or angry" with the way government works.

At the same time, budget pressures are forcing Congress and the executive to pare programs to the bone. With little or no resources to launch government initiatives, the pressure to shrink the bureaucracy is at a peak.

The key to achieving more with less, according to the Gore model, is new technology. Just as private companies are tightening their belts to compete in a global economy, the Gore report says, government needs to modernize. The buzzword for this decade's reforms is Total Quality Management—the philosophy of nonhierarchical management style, employee "empowerment" and customer satisfaction popularized by the late W. Edwards Deming.

The problem with this "entrepreneurial" model of government, its critics say, is that government is not and should not function like a business. Businesses respond to the bottom line; government is supposed to respond to laws written in the public interest.

The Gore report has also rung alarm bells with its promise to cut about 252,000 federal employees over the next five years, including many middle managers. (Congress has upped the ante to 270,000.) Employee cuts without structural reforms could leave government more dysfunctional than ever, perpetuating what some analysts have dubbed "hollow government."

President Nixon names George P. Shultz to be OMB's first director (1970 photo).

White House

WHERE'S THE FOLLOW-THROUGH?

For all Gore's involvement, some government management experts say, the Clinton Administration is ill-equipped to follow through on its recommendations because of changes in OMB.

By merging management and budget functions, director Leon E. Panetta has taken the "M" out of OMB, some critics say. Some of them are calling for a separate Office of Federal Management to carry out management reforms.

By giving big play to staff cuts and dollar savings, the Gore report may perpetuate a false notion that reorganization alone can realize major savings. If anything, genuine reform requires serious, long-term investment, such as on upgrading arcane data collection systems.

The National Performance Review's real Achilles' heel, some analysts say, is that it largely overlooked Congress's role. To really save money and streamline government, they say, the Administration will have to work closely with Congress to rewrite the laws that built the bureaucracy in the first place. That means going after big programs—medicare and social security, to name just two—that the public will fight hard to keep.

GOING TO EXTREMES, LOSING THE CENTER

W. JOHN MOORE

On the last day of the 1991-92 term, the U.S. Supreme Court issued perhaps its most eagerly anticipated decision of the decade, *Planned Parenthood of Southeastern Pennsylvania v. Casey*.

The Court's opinion created no legal milestone. *Roe v. Wade*, the 1973 ruling establishing a woman's fundamental right to abortion, "should be retained and once again confirmed," the Justices held. But they also said that states could impose restrictions on abortion, including a requirement that minors notify their parents before terminating a pregnancy. In short, the ruling was a compromise—one that most Americans would accept, according to public opinion polls.

Activists on both sides of the abortion debate wasted no time in attacking, though. "Don't be fooled by the Court's smokescreen. What the Court did today is devastating for women," the National Abortion and Reproductive Rights Action League (NARAL) warned on the day of the decision. "Today, the Bush Court took away a woman's fundamental right to choose and invited every politician in America to interfere in what remains of this freedom."

NARAL's bitter opponent, the Chicago-based Americans United for Life, was just as unhappy. The Court has "taken two steps backward and turned a blind eye and a deaf ear to legal protection for children before birth. We are strongly disappointed that a majority of the Supreme Court reaffirmed abortion on demand," the anti-abortion group said in a press release.

The reaction of the two antagonists symbolizes interest-group politics in Washington, where a clash of conservative and liberal agendas has destroyed opportunities for consensus sought by the broader public. Eager to attack, seldom willing to compromise, these partisans disdain moderate solutions.

"You get a polarization of debate generated by elites which ordinary citizens find neither affects their interests nor addresses their concerns," said Thomas E. Mann, director of governmental studies at the Brookings Institution in Washington. "Interest groups have discovered that they can play on fears people have as a way to advance their own agendas."

Across the political spectrum, on a host of issues, interest groups have discovered that nothing rouses the faithful like a simple message denouncing your archenemy as evil incarnate. NARAL attacks Americans United for Life. Earth First! battles the timber industry. The Sierra Club blasts leaders of the "wise use" movement, who in turn demonize Interior Secretary Bruce E. Babbitt. People for the American Way chases the Christian Right across the countryside.

Extremism in the defense of ideology is no vice. Moderation in the pursuit of donor dollars is no virtue.

"Polarized rhetoric and extreme positions help arouse the faithful and stimulate membership and contributions," said William A. Galston, deputy assistant to President Clinton for domestic policy and previously a leading light of the centrist Democratic Leadership Council. "For systemic reasons, there is more short-term mileage to be gotten in narrower-focused intensity than in a broader approach."

But the interest groups' gain comes at a cost. A public seeking solutions in Washington discovers a government held hostage at times by interest-group rhetoric.

MESSY DEMOCRACY

To some experts, the clash of ideas is democracy at work, proof positive of the beauty of pluralistic politics. University of Virginia sociologist James Davison Hunter, in *Culture Wars: The Struggle to Define America* (Basic Books, 1991), wrote that bitter disputes articulate issues at the heart of American culture. "But these differences are often intensified and aggravated by the way they are presented in public," Hunter added.

Campaign managers, political pundits, think-tank impresarios and the news media have helped perpetuate what Mann describes as an "attack on the middle."

Once upon a time, Washington think tanks went about their business quietly, with cadres of analysts using their expertise to influence policy. That kind of intellectual power remains a goal for most think tanks.

But as think tanks proliferate, the need to define an identity that's different from the competition's becomes paramount. The quest for money and attention leads to brasher statements and more-dramatic policy prescriptions, James A. Smith wrote in *The Idea Brokers: Think Tanks and the Rise of the New Policy Elite* (Basic Books, 1991). "When all of this is refracted through a media filter, it creates a perception of polarization," Smith said.

The news media, of course, thrive on conflict. There is CNN's *Crossfire*, a show based on the dubious premise that the truth somehow emerges from liberal and conservative soundbites. "For the media," Mann argues, "the road to truth is in finding two extremes and letting them clash. It is the new definition of fairness."

Hard-hitting attacks on the Clintons have helped The American Spectator and other conservative publications boost their readership.

In his influential book, *Why Americans Hate Politics* (Simon & Schuster Inc., 1991), *Washington Post* political columnist E.J. Dionne Jr. argues that conservatives and liberals have ignored the majority of voters.

"Wracked by contradiction and responsive mainly to the needs of their various constituencies, liberalism and conservatism prevent the nation from settling the questions that most trouble it," Dionne wrote. "On issue after issue, there is consensus where the country should move or at least on what we should be arguing about; liberalism and conservatism make it impossible for that consensus to express itself."

But to succeed, politicians at least must persuade a majority of voters to support them. Washington interest groups are bound by no similar constraints. In fact, many groups are established to represent the viewpoint of a tiny portion of the populace that is absolutely passionate about a single issue—whether it be abortion, guns or the environment.

What an interest group lacks in size, it can make up for with intensity. A group with an ideological agenda can't compromise without losing some of its constituents, who respond to fund-raising letters in part because they agree with the blistering rhetoric and absolutist positions staked out by the group.

"Few people are likely to send money to an organization because of its intense, flaming moderation," said R. Kent Weaver, a senior fellow at Brookings.

"A lot of this rhetoric is directed toward the 5 or 10 per cent of the people on each side who are major contributors," said Burdett Loomis, a political scientist at the University of Kansas (Lawrence).

As a result, Loomis added, interest groups succeed better at stopping perceived threats than in accomplishing legislative victories that may require compromise. The liberal People for the American Way, for example, made its name by leading the opposition to the nomination of Robert H. Bork to the Supreme Court. The group stopped Bork—and its contributions reached the highest level ever the next year.

Interest groups thrive on highlighting the differences between themselves and their foes and obscuring the similarities. The result is political discourse with all the civility of Bosnia. "The politics of bombast," as Brookings's Mann puts it.

The growth of single-issue or cause-oriented interest groups is a relatively recent development. Thirty per cent of such groups have formed since 1975; in 1986, at least 20 per cent of all interest groups and trade associations in Washington were in that category, according to an academic study that year.

Ironically, interest groups grow the fastest when their political prospects look the gloomiest. Consider the Fairfax (Va.)-based National Rifle Association (NRA), long considered the undisputed champion of single-interest groups. Last year, the NRA failed to stop legislation that established a waiting period for handgun purchases; this spring, it suffered another blow when the House passed legislation that would ban assault rifles. But since the May 16 vote, the NRA has signed up 55,000 new members.

Clinton's support for gun control, which was crucial to the defeat of the gun lobby, has become the primary focus of the NRA's membership campaign. "Make no mistake: Bill Clinton is the American gun owner's worst nightmare," the NRA warned in a letter to prospective members last year. What was possibly Clinton's worse sin, according to the NRA? The President even "kissed [gun control advocate] Sarah Brady at rallies."

THANK YOU, MR. WATT

In the early 1980s, the environmental movement found itself confronting a hostile Administration determined to ease regulations on business. But environmental activists soon discovered a silver lining in the person of James G. Watt, President Reagan's Interior Secretary. Watt "was the devil figure for the environmentalists, like Jane Fonda and Teddy Kennedy used to be for the Right," Weaver of Brookings said.

Watt's visage on mailings was a magnet for money and support. The Wilderness Society prepared an eight-pound, two-volume compendium of press clips and critical cartoons in its *Watt Book*.

"In 1982, 95,000 new members joined our ranks largely because of the anti-environmental stance of James Watt," the Sierra Club said in a fund-raising letter a decade ago. The Sierra Club doubled its membership just during Watt's tenure. And membership and contributions kept growing during the 12-year Republican reign—until the election of Clinton and Vice President Albert Gore Jr., a hero among environmentalists. In 1993, the Sierra Club's contributions dipped an estimated 6.8 per cent. *(See chart, next page.)*

Other environmental groups have experienced similar drops in donations. The economic recession was part of the reason. But environmentalists attribute much of the falloff to the Gore factor. "There is this view that because Clinton has Gore on his team that he will do the

Whether the issue is the environment or gun control, interest groups thrive on highlighting differences between themselves and their foes and obscuring the similarities. "Few people are likely to send money to an organization because of its intense, flaming moderation," an analyst says.

HCI "Go To Hell" prospect piece 6/93

Here's your chance to tell the National Rifle Association to go to Hell!

right thing on the environment. So contributions to most environmental groups have dropped or remained the same," said Graham Cox, vice president for public affairs at the National Audubon Society in New York City.

Some environmental groups have responded by discovering new enemies. The Sierra Club's latest foes are the partisans of what is called the "wise use" movement, conservative groups opposed to tough environmental restrictions on federal lands.

Environmental groups are not the only organizations that have discovered the downside to winning. After the pro-abortion rights Clinton-Gore team captured the White House, NARAL saw its monthly contributions drop by a third last year and its membership decline by 150,000.

"The worst thing that can happen to an interest group is that you win," said Ronald G. Shaiko, a specialist on interest-group politics at the American University in Washington.

Meanwhile, conservative groups have enjoyed a resurgence. The American Conservative Union now says it has 500,000 members, a fivefold increase since the 1992 election. The increase follows years of decline during the Republican years, acknowledged Jeff Hollingsworth, the group's executive director. With Reagan's election, he said, "conservative activists may have felt that the dream came true."

Now, "the shock of a Clinton-Gore Administration has brought conservatism back to life," Hollingsworth said. If many political analysts argue that Clinton has governed as a centrist, Hollingsworth disagrees. "There's plenty of evidence that Bill Clinton talks moderate and liberals get all the action," he said.

That view certainly sells with conservatives: The President and Hillary Rodham Clinton headline almost every fundraising letter mailed by a conservative organization to a carefully targeted audience. "These people are predisposed to loathing the Clintons," a conservative fund-raising expert conceded.

Opinion magazines with a conservative bent have pummeled the Clintons in story after story. Hillary Clinton graces (again) the June cover of *The American Spectator*, drawn as a witch astride a jet airplane. The story, *The Washington Post* said, is "the latest installment in that magazine's crusade to show that Hillary is the Antichrist of American politics." Inside, the subscription come-ons are even tougher.

The strategy works. According to figures compiled by the Audit Bureau of Circulations in Schaumburg, Ill., circulation at *The American Spectator* climbed from 72,468 in 1992 to 128,146 in 1993. Another conservative magazine, the weekly *National Review*, has also flourished in the Clinton year, with its circulation reaching 221,000 in 1993, up from 168,000 in 1992. Meanwhile, the left-wing bible, the *Nation*, saw its circulation drop approximately 5 per cent over the same period.

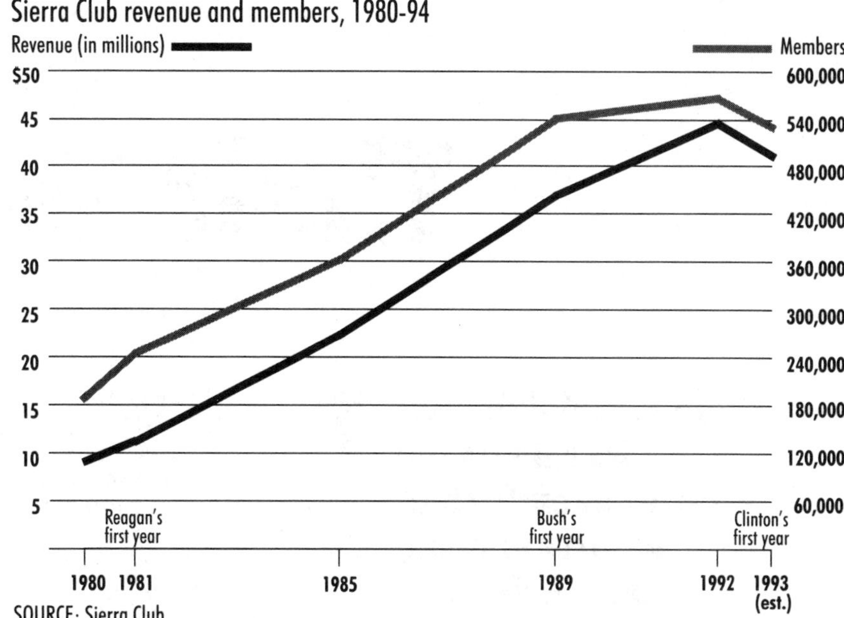

PRESS CLIPS

The mainstream news media share responsibility for catering to the extremes. Journalists often try to transform every discussion into a debate—leaving little time to analyze or provide perspective. Even shows for high-brow audiences, such as ABC News's *Nightline* or the Public Broadcasting System's *MacNeil/Lehrer NewsHour*, parade casts of dueling policy wonks. Woe to the analyst, critic or historian interested in context or complexity.

When talk radio pros decided that it was time to provide some balance to right-winger Rush Limbaugh, the man hired was lefty Jim Hightower, former head of the Texas Agriculture Commission—whose views are summed up in his immortal words, "There ain't nothin' in the middle of the road but yellow stripes and dead armadillos."

But the center is also the place to find most Americans, who are often unmoved by ideological concerns and unenthusiastic about interest groups. According to many political scientists, there is grave danger in Washington's basing policy only on pleas from ideological diehards.

"The sum of all interest groups is not the national interest," the American University's Shaiko said. "And it never will be."

Their Turn

Amid complaints that its role as the government's chief auditor is being undermined by partisan bias and misplaced priorities, the General Accounting Office is coming under serious congressional scrutiny for the first time in nearly a decade.

ELIZA NEWLIN CARNEY

The General Accounting Office (GAO), Capitol Hill's watchdog for nearly three-quarters of a century, is being measured for a shorter leash.

Amid complaints that its role as the government's chief auditor is being undermined by partisan bias and misplaced priorities, the GAO is coming under serious congressional scrutiny for the first time in nearly a decade. The House Government Operations Committee has scheduled GAO oversight hearings in late October—the first in eight years.

Separately, the Senate Governmental Affairs Committee—responding largely to Republican complaints that the GAO tailors too many of its findings to suit Democratic congressional leaders—has commissioned a $490,000 study of the GAO by the private National Academy of Public Administration (NAPA) that's scheduled to be wrapped up next spring.

"It's like Alice's Restaurant," said Sen. Christopher S. (Kit) Bond, R-Mo., one of the GAO's chief critics. "Whatever you order is what you get. It's not so much a professional, independent review as an effort to provide what those in power want to hear."

Given its far-reaching mandate—essentially to make sure that government works right—the GAO is an easy target. Since its inception in 1921, the agency has broadened its scope to include virtually everything government does. Once consumed primarily with double-checking government expense vouchers, the GAO now tackles a staggering range of issues. Its trademark blue-backed reports, which total about 1,000 a year and cover every topic from gays in the military to desert grazing fees, lead hazards in paint and food safety inspections, have become integral to daily life on Capitol Hill.

The GAO played a key role, for example, in a congressional investigation—whose findings were revealed with considerable fanfare in mid-October—that St. Louis-based McDonnell Douglas Corp. had initially billed the federal government about $30,000 for its participation in the infamous 1991 Tailhook Association convention. (McDonnell Douglas later covered the expenses.)

"The GAO threw away the green eyeshades long ago," said Robert S. Gilmour, a University of Connecticut (Storrs) political science professor and a former aide to what's now the Senate Governmental Affairs Committee. "Accountancy is no longer the dominant profession in the GAO. Today, they are political scientists; they come from sociology, history, economics. Their effort is not just to look at the books, but at how well agencies are performing in accord with congressional mandate."

The GAO's growing visibility, scope and agenda—from 1985-92, its reports to Congress surged from 457 a year to 915—have generated considerable controversy on Capitol Hill. Though the loudest criticism has come from Republicans, many Democrats agree that it's high time to take a closer look at the agency, which with its $435 million budget in fiscal year 1993 consumed approximately 6 per cent of all legislative branch spending. With just under 5,000 employees, the GAO also claims about a sixth of the legislative branch staff.

"The most frequent [complaint] that I hear is that the GAO is too dominated by various committees," said Sen. Harry M. Reid, D-Nev. "They detail people from the GAO to various congressional committees, and there are some Senators who feel that as a result of that they . . . become advocates for the committees. And they shouldn't. They should be objective."

The House and Senate are responding in part to complaints that have been piling up since roughly the mid-1980s. To some degree, the GAO has been caught in the middle of the partisan sniping that intensified in 1987 after Democrats regained a majority in the Senate and, with their colleagues in the Democratic-controlled House, sharply expanded their scrutiny, and criticism, of the Republicans who were then in charge of the executive branch. As Democratic leaders commissioned more and more GAO studies of Republican-run agencies, some Republican Members complained of a pro-Democratic bias in the agency's work.

A warning shot was fired in 1988 when the GAO presented its first "Transition Series" to the incoming Bush Administration, which included a report that struck some analysts as essentially a call for higher taxes. Republicans vigorously attacked the report, which stated that "additional revenues are probably an unavoidable part of any realistic strategy for reducing the deficit."

Aggravating the tension has been Republican resentment about the GAO detailees—specialists in subjects ranging from the defense industry to health care. Some Republicans say the detailees give Democrats too much clout and compromise the GAO's ability to undertake objective investigations. Responding to the complaints, the GAO has curbed the number of temporary assignments to Capitol Hill—these assignments have dropped from 173 in fiscal 1990 to 69 in fiscal 1993.

Congressional growling has continued. Sen. Pete V. Domenici, R-N.M., introduced legislation this year that would set up an independent committee of private auditors and outside experts to review and evaluate the GAO's work. (He introduced a similar bill in 1991.) Rep. C. Christopher Cox, R-Calif., has recommended cutting the GAO's budget to $333 million and privatizing many of its functions.

"Its original mission is a sensible one—to monitor congressional spending and reduce waste," Cox said. "The irony is that in recent years, GAO has actually grown to be a major source of deficit spending."

Some congressional leaders dismiss such criticisms as predictable partisanship. And for every GAO critic, the agency has a champion on Capitol Hill. "If there's a better agency in government, I'd like to know who they are," said Mike Synar, D-Okla., who is chairman of the House Government Operations Subcommittee on Environment, Energy and Natural Resources and who frequently calls on the GAO for help. "This may be the finest-run agency in government. They probably provide the best service, and without the GAO there is probably no way that we could make the government run in an efficient manner."

Even staunch GAO defenders, however, admit that a review of the agency's priorities is needed. In the coming months, House and Senate leaders will examine whether the GAO can step up the timeliness of its reports, which take an average of nine months and as long as two years to complete; cut back on overlap with inquiries undertaken by the executive branch's inspectors general and by other agencies; communicate better with the agencies that it audits; and improve the independence and objectivity of its reports.

At the heart of many of the questions surrounding the GAO is its credibility. In recent years, the GAO has fielded increasing congressional demands, some of them trivial, controversial or essentially subjective. At the same time, the agency has adopted a somewhat more activist approach to promoting fiscal responsibility. Some analysts wonder whether the GAO, by tackling complex policy issues, may compromise its role as an independent auditor.

"They will lose their greatest asset, which is that perception of independence and objectivity, if they jump into every controversial issue that they are asked to jump into," said a political scientist involved in the NAPA study who didn't want to be named. (NAPA is a nonprofit organization chartered by Congress to improve government effectiveness.)

John Eisele

Comptroller General Charles A. Bowsher
His agency has made lots of enemies—and a few mistakes.

A CHANGING ROLE

Under Comptroller General Charles A. Bowsher, a former managing partner with the accounting firm of Arthur Andersen & Co., who took office in 1981, the GAO has broadened its scope considerably. *(See NJ, 8/10/91, p. 1970.)* A hallmark of Bowsher's tenure has been a series of "management reviews" aimed at helping agencies identify problems and function more efficiently. Unlike the GAO's individual reports, which tend to focus on a single, narrow project or program, the management reviews offer a broad summary of how well an agency is working and where the major problem areas lie.

Launched in the early 1980s, the reviews summarize the findings of GAO reports so that agencies can make better use of them. In addition, GAO officials have worked with individual agencies—providing agency officials agree to cooperate—to target management weaknesses and recommend solutions.

Also new under Bowsher are the transition reports that the GAO—acting on its own—initiated in 1988 for the incoming Bush Administration. Designed to give an incoming Administration and Congress a comprehensive sense of the problems agencies face, the reports for the most part drew on already published GAO investigations. At the request of House and Senate leaders, the GAO prepared a new set of transition reports for the Clinton Administration.

A major Bowsher theme has been improving financial management, throughout government and at his agency. The GAO's investigations into agency financial waste helped prompt passage of the 1990 Chief Financial Officers Act, which installed a chief financial officer at each major agency.

To many congressional leaders, the agency's crusade for better savings is a model for the goals that Vice President Albert Gore Jr. outlined in his "reinventing government" proposal. The GAO's conclusions about government waste prompted some of Gore's recommendations, according to Bowsher. (NAPA, which is now reviewing the GAO, also played a role in Gore's study through its Alliance for Redesigning Government. [*See NJ, 4/3/93, p. 826.*])

Clearly, though, the GAO has stepped on some toes with its sweeping approach to fiscal problems. The 1988 transition report on the budget deficit is an example. In tackling the deficit, some Republican leaders said the GAO made an unwelcome foray into policy matters.

"The [transition] reports, not requested by any Member of Congress or the Administration, were expensive, wasteful and highly partisan," Domenici complained in June 1991 as he first introduced his GAO bill, dubbed the General Accounting Office Reform Act.

Bowsher counters that the GAO has an obligation to address such broad questions as the budget deficit if it's going to effectively reduce federal flab. "The major issues generally equate with the big dollars," he said in an interview. Bowsher noted that the GAO's 1988 warnings about the deficit are being echoed today by such watchdog groups as the Concord Coalition (headed by former Sens. Warren Rudman, R-N.H., and Paul E. Tsongas, D-Mass.).

Far more embarrassing to the agency, however, was a January 1992 report initiated by the GAO that concluded that a presidential line-item veto in place during the Reagan Administration would have produced as much as $70 billion in savings. Asked by the Senate Appropriations Committee to review the GAO's findings, the Congressional Research Service estimated the savings at just $2 billion-$3 billion or even less.

"Whatever you order is what you get. It's not so much a professional, independent review as an effort to provide what those in power want to hear."

Appropriations Committee chairman Robert C. Byrd, D-W.Va., later called the GAO report "a piece of trash," according to a September 1992 *Congress-Daily* report. Byrd also received a letter from Bowsher last July, apologizing for the report and acknowledging that a line-item veto could actually save "close to zero" or even increase spending.

The GAO may also be crossing a fine line with its agency management reviews, some analysts say. By working collaboratively with agencies to improve their management, the GAO may undermine its reputation as an outside investigator, said Paul C. Light, a professor at the University of Minnesota's Hubert H. Humphrey Institute of Public Affairs.

John Eisele

Rep. William F. Clinger Jr., R-Pa.
His Capitol Hill colleagues involve the GAO in too many "frivolous investigations."

BLAMING THE MESSENGER

The GAO's wide-ranging investigations often place the agency in a faultfinding role and invariably put some agency or official on the defensive. The GAO, required to respond to congressional requests, has been forced by its popularity in Congress to double its output in the space of eight years. In 1992, completed congressional assignments, including reports and testimony on Capitol Hill, totaled more than 1,500.

While GAO officials say they try to avoid duplication and will discourage requests that appear too narrow or too politically driven, some Capitol Hill critics wonder whether Congress tends to waste the GAO's time. Some 80 per cent of GAO reports now stem from congressional requests, compared with just 10 per cent in 1969, according to statistics gathered by Rep. Cox.

"The quality of the work, obviously, is somewhat driven by the quality of the request," said Rep. William F. Clinger Jr., R-Pa., who helped instigate this fall's House oversight hearings. "And I think Congress tends to request, probably, a lot of frivolous investigations."

With so many irons in the fire, some Members of Congress wonder whether the GAO is fully equipped to keep up. Critics complain that the quality of reports ranges from excellent to unreliable—a concern echoed by some agency heads. The volume of audits also creates a burden on agencies, according to Domenici, who's been surveying government agencies with questions on the GAO for several months.

At the Interior Department, for example, Domenici was told that the National Park Service's Concession Management Program had been audited 12 times during fiscal 1991-92. At the Energy Department, officials reported 227 "audits" or requests for information from October 1990 through September 1992.

Some criticism may be inevitable, given the GAO's watchdog role. For every GAO report that makes some government official happy, there is invariably a critic who sees the other side of the issue. There's a natural tendency to blame the messenger, say GAO defenders, who are quick to praise what they insist are the agency's impartiality and high standards.

"GAO doesn't always tell me what I want to hear," said Sen. John Glenn, D-Ohio, chairman of the Governmental Affairs Committee. "But I respect their judgment, and I have found without fail that they can back up their reports."

Notwithstanding Glenn's upbeat views, so many Members have called for investigations of the GAO that Glenn's committee had to respond with the NAPA inquiry, an aide said. For GAO advocates, concerns about the agency are far outweighed by the money it saves taxpayers.

Bowsher, testifying before the Joint Committee on the Organization of Congress in June, cited studies that led Congress to cut $4 billion from the Defense Department's inventory budget in fiscal 1992 and 1993 as a way to force the department to improve inventory management; "billions of dollars in deficit reductions" that resulted from the GAO's reporting on unnecessary health care costs; and investigations into the Energy Department's enriched uranium program that spurred the department to abandon a processing plant, saving $3.5 billion.

But Bond has sharply criticized the GAO for what he calls its unprofessional auditing procedures. Bond, a former state auditor of Missouri, said he was "appalled" by the methods the GAO used to prepare a 1992 report on drought conditions in the Missouri River Basin.

Bond contends that the GAO failed to interview experts on both sides of the issue before concluding that the Army Corps of Engineers should consider the river's recreational uses as important as its navigational uses in managing water flow. (Bond maintains that recreation should be secondary because navigational needs have historically been protected by law.) Bond also argues that the agency relied too heavily on secondary sources in conducting its research.

GAO officials stand by their findings, arguing that they interviewed a complete range of sources and can document their results. "We went back and researched the whole legislative history," said J. Dexter Peach, assistant comptroller general for resources, community and economic development issues.

But Bond, who's found fault with other GAO reports, remains skeptical. His office now has a policy of never quoting from or relying on a GAO report, even when the Senator agrees with the findings.

"It's supposed to be the independent auditing branch of government," Bond said of the GAO. "It does no good to the credibility of government as a whole when you have those unprofessional documents being foisted on a panel."

More recently, Rep. Jim Lightfoot, R-Iowa, accused the GAO of bowing to Clinton Administration pressure to tone down a September report detailing questionable payroll practices at the White House. (The report found that several White House employees drew double salaries or received retroactive pay raises early in the Clinton term.)

Though a draft of the GAO report criticized several "inappropriate and improper personnel and pay actions" at the White House, the final report states only that the GAO has "reservations about whether the broad interpretation of the [law that covers a President's appointing authority] clearly reflects congressional intent."

Richard A. Bloom

Sen. John Glenn, D-Ohio
"GAO doesn't always tell me what I want to hear."

"A lot of things in that draft [that] we thought were very strong, basically got watered down," Lightfoot said. "So that raises the question of [whether there was] political influence involved."

The GAO strongly disputes that suggestion. The key factor influencing the final report was that the GAO finally obtained a written opinion from the Justice Department's Office of Legal Counsel, countered Nancy R. Kingsbury, GAO director of federal human resource management issues.

"It has nothing to do with pressure from the White House. It has to do with a reasoned legal analysis of a very broad statute," said Kingsbury, who noted that the GAO's recent interim report on firings in the White House travel office prompted angry calls from Administration officials.

As a rule, GAO officials vehemently deny that politics plays any role in report findings. "We work very, very hard here, not only to accept the work on a bipartisan basis, but to make sure that the work is done in an independent and objective fashion," Bowsher said.

To answer Republican complaints that the GAO favors the majority party, the agency has also taken steps to improve communication with and responsiveness to Republican Members. Responding to agency officials' complaints that they are denied the chance to comment on GAO findings, Bowsher said that a formal comment period or exit interview is standard procedure for all investigations. When the GAO allows agencies to review reports in advance, Bowsher noted, the findings are often leaked to the public and the press.

Though some Members of Congress have strong opinions on the GAO's shortcomings, the agency's "problem" reports are the exception, not the rule, its advocates say.

"I think GAO has done an excellent job, by and large," Glenn said. "They have been an extremely useful arm of Congress, and if we didn't have the GAO to act as our investigating source, we'd have to invent it."

As for the GAO's policy role, some experts say the agency's move in the direction of legislative analysis may be inevitable. In addition, the GAO's many reports may do little good if the agency does not recommend solutions.

"I think that Bowsher has . . . rightly concluded that you cannot improve the management of government without dealing with some of these big structural issues like the budget deficit," the University of Minnesota's Light said. "I think we just cannot fix these things without attacking the underlying issues involving policy."

Don't look for GAO controversies to die down any time soon, however. Health care reform, Gore's program to reinvent government and ongoing defense cutbacks will all demand heavy input from the GAO, Bowsher predicted. As the pressure grows to keep costs down, Congress will also continue to look closely at GAO priorities. And whatever the agency tackles next, there's sure to be a critic in the wings.

"We're sort of in the business of faultfinding," the GAO's Kingsbury said. "And nobody likes to be at the receiving end of that—including us."

The V-Word

"Values" is the latest catchword in political rhetoric and policy debates. But people can mean very different things when they talk about values—even when they use the same words.

ROCHELLE L. STANFIELD

James Carville and fellow political consultants, take note: It's values, stupid. But which values? Whose values? Take your pick. Ambiguity is one of the beauties of the new values politics.

Webster's New 20th Century Unabridged Dictionary lists 13 definitions of the word "value." So it should come as no surprise that politicians and policy makers (and those who seek to influence them) tailor the concept to meet their own political and ideological needs.

The V-word was bandied about by candidates in the 1992 presidential campaign. And it has surfaced in recent discussions of domestic policy—on welfare reform, on health care reform and on education.

In focusing on values, politicians are reflecting the desires of the electorate. With the Cold War over and the economy relatively stable, values have become a primary concern of many Americans, according to public opinion and political specialists.

In one survey after another, "promoting more values is [one of] people's top solutions to crime, and values and improving discipline in the home is their top solution to improving education," said Celinda C. Lake, a principal in the Washington polling firm of Mellman•Lazarus•Lake Inc. who has worked for President Clinton. "When people talk about welfare reform, it isn't the money that's bothering them," but that the welfare system "seems to have the wrong values built into it," she said.

"Increased attention to values is not only a strategy for politicians but [also reflects] the deep-seated need of Americans for reassurance," said John K. White, associate professor of politics at Catholic University of America in Washington and the author of several books on politics and values.

But people can mean very different things when they talk about values—even when they use the same words.

"Emphasis on values is often used in what might charitably be called a protean way, its meaning shifting in every use," Brookings Institution scholar Henry J. Aaron and two other researchers wrote in *Values and Public Policy* (Brookings, 1994).

Consider "family values." That term "has become so effective as a catchphrase that everybody has now politicized [it] to the point that it has no meaning any longer," complained Martin J. Mawyer, president of the Christian Action Network in Forest, Va., the lobbying arm of the conservative Christian political movement that claims credit for raising family values as a political issue. Abortion-rights advocates "use the word 'family values,' and they mean something absolutely contradictory to what we mean by it," Mawyer said.

" 'Values' is another code word for 'my position'—there is some truth to that," said Frances Kissling, president of the Washington-based Catholics for a Free Choice, an abortion-rights group.

There are two main strategies for the political use of values rhetoric: the common-denominator approach and the we're-right-you're-wrong approach.

The first strategy draws on basic character traits such as industriousness, responsibility and civility to find a common ground for people whose views on economics and politics may otherwise be at odds. Ronald Reagan perfected this approach with his appeals to the values of family, work, neighborhood, peace and freedom. Political analysts give that strategy a lot of credit for his electoral landslides.

Clinton, these experts say, is an able student of the common-denominator method. He has referred time and again to three values: individual responsibility, opportunity and community. He used these themes successfully in the 1992 election; now, his Administration is employing them to advance his domestic agenda.

"The President believes that alongside of some very important differences about values are beliefs that most Americans share, and he tries to organize politics around that," William A. Galston, deputy assistant to the President for domestic policy, said in an interview.

But values can also be used to divide

people. Practitioners of this approach, who usually operate outside the political center, tend to link the values they are promoting with particular social structures or situations—and then use this narrow definition of values to drive a wedge between themselves and others. The Christian Right, for example, ties family values to the traditional two-parent family; black nationalists link racial pride to fighting the persecution of blacks by whites.

It was the us-against-them tactic, employed by presidential contender Patrick J. Buchanan at the 1992 Republican National Convention, that many political commentators believe blew up in the face of the Republican Party that year.

"Reagan always used the values strategy to broaden the Republican Party's appeal and coalition, to really enforce the identification that 'they' were somehow like 'us,' " White said. But by 1992, followers of Christian Coalition founder and 1988 Republican presidential contender Marion G. (Pat) Robertson "had made the Reagan strategy into a negative, . . . saying [to opponents], 'You're somehow un-American.' It was 'cultural wars' and 'we're not like you.' It became exclusionary, and I think that it backfired with key constituencies—for example, suburban women," he said.

While the Republicans' use of the V-word alienated some voters, the Clinton campaign presented its values rhetoric in an inclusive way. "The Democrats were very good about framing the values debate in a way that put Republicans at a disadvantage," Democratic pollster Lake said. "I think it was very clever."

A pollster for President Bush acknowledged that point. "Maybe the values weren't packaged properly," said Glenn Goulet, research director at Market Strategies Inc., based in Southfield, Mich.

If the we're-right-you're-wrong approach can sometimes backfire, it can still be a useful political tool. William J. Bennett, a conservative who served in the Reagan and Bush Administrations and is a potential 1996 presidential contender, has used such a strategy in trying to shore up his support with the Religious Right. When courting a broader constituency, he has presented himself as a seeker of common ground.

In 1992, Bennett wrote *The De-Valuing of America: The Fight for Our Culture and Our Children* (Summit Books), a bitter recounting of his years in the Reagan Administration (as National Endowment for the Humanities chairman and Education Secretary) and the Bush Administration (as drug czar). In the book, he denounced the liberal elite and said that the nation was "engaged in an ongoing and intensifying cultural war."

A year later, with his eye on the presidency, Bennett compiled *The Book of Virtues: A Treasury of Great Moral Stories* (Simon & Schuster Inc.), a far gentler anthology of classic stories and poems about values such as self-discipline, compassion and responsibility. "In teaching these stories," he wrote in the introduction, "we welcome our children to a common world, a world of shared ideals, to the community of moral persons."

The first book didn't make much of a splash outside Washington; the second has been on the *New York Times* bestseller list for 22 weeks.

Bill Clinton

RIGHTS AND RESPONSIBILITIES

The welfare reform debate provides a clear illustration of how values strategies are used in domestic policy making.

Clinton laid out a common-denominator theme in his State of the Union message on Jan. 25, when he promised to submit a plan that "restores the basic values of work and responsibility." He promised welfare recipients that the government would "provide the support, the job training, the child care you need. . ." But, he added, he would require a "simple compact": In return for this help, recipients must get a job after two years.

In the view of some analysts, Clinton's balancing of opportunity with responsibility forges a crucial political link between the rights and freedoms sought by liberals and the accountability demanded by centrists and conservatives. Public opinion expert Daniel Yankelovich terms this value "reciprocity," which he sees as a consensus-building bridge.

"There's a suspicion in the country that we've gone too far in extending individual rights," Yankelovich said. "On the other hand, people don't want to go backward and give up those rights. So they've settled on the idea of rights, yes, but you also should give something back."

Supporters of Clinton's welfare reform concept argue that it corrects a values mismatch in the current welfare system. "Welfare hasn't reinforced the right values," Lake said. "It hasn't rewarded work or initiative—or provided people with opportunity. In fact, welfare has the reverse incentive structure, where it rewards what life usually punishes."

The widespread appeal of this formulation was underscored last fall when centrist House Republicans beat Clinton to the punch and introduced their own welfare reform package, which, although tougher in the details of how the program would work, was based on the same values that underpinned the Clinton concept.

Now the right wing of the Republican Party has weighed in with a new version of welfare reform that employs the divisive values strategy by targeting illegitimacy, a bugbear of the Religious Right. Bennett, having switched back to us-against-them mode, and former Housing and Urban Development Secretary Jack F. Kemp, another 1996 Republican presidential hopeful, on April 28 joined a small group of conservative congressional Republicans in endorsing a bill that would deny welfare benefits to all unwed mothers under age 21 and use the savings to build orphanages for children whose mothers couldn't afford to care for them.

The difference in the values message is subtle because Clinton also has called for coming down hard on out-of-wedlock teenage pregnancy and irresponsible fathers who don't support their children. In his State of the Union message, he said that he would require unwed teenage mothers to live with their parents in order to qualify for assistance.

"We say in no uncertain terms that if you are biologically responsible for a child, you are also emotionally, morally and financially responsible for that child, and there can be no exceptions," Galston said.

But neither Clinton nor Galston mentioned the politically sensitive values word "marriage." The conservatives' bill makes marriage an integral part of the bargain.

"No welfare for illegitimate children and illegitimate families," said Michael Cromartie, a senior fellow at the Ethics and Public Policy Center in Washington, a think tank headed by conservative Catholic thinker George Weigel. "This will cause women to be serious and tell men, 'You don't dare, unless you marry me.' "

The question of values isn't as well articulated in the health care reform debate. Some political analysts, in fact, say that the lack of a clear statement of values by proponents of reform has contributed to the difficulties in building a consensus for legislation.

In Yankelovich's view, the Administration has depicted health care as a right, with individuals having no obligation to help control costs. "One of the reasons health care [reform] isn't getting a lot of enthusiasm is because you're really not asking people to take the kind of responsibility they should be taking," he said.

Lake disagreed. "Voters believe that welfare recipients and people in prison—the 'undeserving'—get health care, but the working poor—the people who play by the rules—don't," she said, portraying the Clinton plan as thus appealing to the values of fairness and reciprocity.

Lake and Yankelovich agree that the term "universal" health care is unfortunate because it sounds too much like a gift. Lake said she preferred "insurance that can't be taken away" to make it sound more reciprocal.

One advantage of common-denominator values rhetoric is its ambiguity. It broadens the tent by allowing in a variety of meanings.

When he talks about responsibility, Clinton usually positions himself as a centrist who's concerned about an individual's obligations. But some liberals interpret responsibility to mean communal duty.

Thus, when he was asked about the value of responsibility, Arthur J. Kropp, president of People for the American Way in Washington, talked about the Peace Corps and Clinton's national service program. "The whole concept of voluntarism [speaks to] responsibility to one's fellow man," he said. "The idea, really, is to create an ethic of responsibility to community."

DUELING OVER SCHOOLING

In the politics of values, probably no word is as laden with competing meanings as "family."

"Governments don't raise children; parents do."

"If you read through some of his statements, Clinton actually sounds like Jerry Falwell in some of his stuff," said Mawyer of the Christian Action Network.

Appropriating other groups' rhetoric may not be enough to win them over, though. "We bring to what people say about values our preconceived notion of what we already think they believe in," Kissling of Catholics for a Free Choice said. She described experiments in which people are asked whether they agree with an anonymous statement—which they do—and then are told the name of the author "and they say, 'But I don't agree with anything he says!' "

And the words that some groups use to describe their values sometimes mask what's really on their agendas.

"America is engaged in an ongoing and intensifying cultural war."

William J. Bennett

To liberals, the concept is broad. But to conservatives, a family is a pretty specific thing: a man and woman permanently bonded by church, synagogue or mosque for the purpose of raising children.

"Bill Clinton and others focus on specific behaviors and the actual functions of the family in the sense of providing a caring environment," said Jill S. Grigsby, an associate professor of sociology at Pomona College in Claremont, Calif. "The political and fundamentalist Far Right is talking about a nuclear family structure—mother, father and children—and saying that good family behavior can only take place in this kind of family."

But sometimes it's hard to tell who is talking about what kind of family when the rhetoric gets going. In his State of the Union message, for example, Clinton usurped a favorite conservative line:

When spokesmen for self-proclaimed "pro-family" organizations describe their purpose, they talk about "giving parents the ability to raise their children in strong families—that's it in a nutshell," as Mawyer put it.

But they usually go on to say that school prayer is crucial to achieving that end. School prayer "is a very important thing for religious people when they send their children to school, but it is being denied to them," Mawyer said. "These people are so committed to school prayer and the values that are being taught in public school that they are now considering school choice [vouchers for private school] as an alternative."

Most Americans say they favor allowing prayer in schools, pollster Lake said, "but their only concern is who is writing the prayer. The polling numbers on prayer in school—particularly when it's expressed as a moment of silence—[are] quite high."

Indeed, there is a movement among African-American parents of students in big-city schools to institute prayer as a way of teaching values.

To Kropp, however, the Religious Right is promoting prayer in school for a more specific purpose. "They are trying to Christianize the public schools," he said. "It really goes far beyond prayer to the abolition and undermining of public education itself."

Sex also looms large in the values politics of education policy. Jeffrey Bell, an economic forecaster in Northern Virginia, founded a conservative group, Of the People, in 1992 to promote parents' rights. He described the group's mission as "giving parents greater standing" in the schools "to oversee the upbringing of their children."

But when pressed, Bell acknowledged that his organization devotes most of its time to efforts to oppose sex education, condom distribution and curricula that discuss homosexuality.

The Christian Right's battle against sex education—generally carried out in school board elections—is long-standing and extremely bitter. The Right's point of view "is based on the idea that children ought to be protected from making sexual decisions," said David Blankenhorn, president of the Institute for American Values, a New York City think tank. "It is not developmentally appropriate for children to make decisions about having sex," and thus they shouldn't be taught about it. "This is a textbook illustration of a basic conflict," he said, where no common ground or compromise is possible.

But it is a battle that the Right almost always loses because most parents want schools to teach their children about sex. "Poll data I've seen show that 75 per cent and up of the American public want sex education in schools," Lake said. "But what's fascinating is they believe their position is not in the majority."

Whereas sex education is usually cast as a health matter, teaching about homosexuality usually comes under the rubric of teaching about diversity and tolerance.

Clinton discovered the incendiary nature of feelings about homosexuality early in his term when he tried to carry out a campaign promise to permit gays in the military. Indeed, conservatives say that his use of family rhetoric is a reaction to being burned on that issue. (Actually, he has used similar rhetoric for years.)

The big blowup over teaching about homosexuality took place in New York City in 1992, when a proposed multicultural curriculum included a book called *Heather Has Two Mommies* for primary-grade students. A ferocious campaign against the book and the curriculum contributed to the ouster of then-chancellor Joseph A. Fernandez.

Bell said that he organized Of the People in the aftermath of that fight. His group opposes teaching "that all value systems are equal and that type of relativism," he said.

Mixed into the debate over the teaching of tolerance is another thorny issue: multicultural education. Proponents such as New York State Education Commissioner Thomas Sobel say that teaching students about the contributions of different cultures will increase tolerance.

"Those men and women who founded this land made a solemn covenant that they would be the people of God and that this would be a Christian nation."

Marion G. (Pat) Robertson

Others say it will do just the opposite, sowing the seeds of ethnic conflict. Perhaps the most eloquent opponent is the historian Arthur M. Schlesinger Jr. In *The Disuniting of America: Reflections on a Multicultural Society* (W.W. Norton, 1992), he wrote: "The ethnic interpretation [of American history] reverses the historic theory of America as one people—the theory that has thus far managed to keep American society whole.... The debate about the curriculum is a debate about what it means to be an American."

In the war over values, nothing is filled with more intolerance than the skirmish over the meaning of tolerance.

On college campuses, the battle over political correctness has the Right accusing the Left of trying to deny conservatives the right to free speech.

"It seems the most intolerance is coming from the Left," Cromartie of the Ethics and Public Policy Center said. "With the 'political correctness' movement, people will tolerate every view but the conservative view."

Indeed, the Christian Right has now fashioned a new image of itself as victim. In his 1993 book, *The Turning Tide: The Fall of Liberalism and the Rise of Common Sense* (Word Publishing Co.), Robertson wrote that America leads the world because "those men and women who founded this land made a solemn covenant that they would be the people of God and that this would be a Christian nation."

However, he added: "The elites of this nation for 30 years have been carrying on an all-out assault on the people of God throughout this land, to harass them, humiliate them and strip them of their rights. (My staff gathered more than 2,000 incidents of anti-Christian bigotry in just two weeks.)"

To Kropp of People for the American Way, "This takes on an Alice-in-Wonderland kind of feel—everything is turned upside down. I read what they have to say, and it's steeped in intolerance and dividing communities; but if you criticize their movement, you're anti-Christian or anti-religious and they are the victims of intolerance."

Still, the notion that religion has been placed on the defensive has become increasingly popular. Clinton has repeated the refrain "freedom of religion doesn't mean freedom from religion" on many occasions.

"A number of people have made the argument that we ought to check our faith at the threshold," White House assistant Galston said. "This is not just the hobgoblin of the Religious Right."

And liberals are on the defensive. "When I go to a meeting, up front I have to tell people I am a person of faith, I am a member of a church and I'm very involved in it, that it is a very important part of my life," Kropp said. "I do that, but I am not entirely comfortable with doing it."

Political analysts of various stripes agree that if the economy goes sour or a foreign crisis arises, values issues would quickly fade from the political discourse. For now, though, the V-word is still hot. But as for what it means—that's still up for grabs.

Return to Sender

Congress's once-leisurely drift toward computer networking and the Information Age accelerated to warp speed when the Republicans took control of Congress in January. But the voyage isn't turning out to be as simple as many had hoped it would be.

GRAEME BROWNING

Clickety clickety click. Rep. Sam Gejdenson, D-Conn., is typing on his computer keyboard, calling up his electronic mail. And the more he sees, the crosser he gets.

"Here's one," he says, the irritation evident in his voice as he reads a message that's scrolling across the screen before him. "Comes from some college in New Hampshire. The professor must have told his class to write to all the people in Congress they could think of. But New Hampshire isn't my district."

Clickety click. "This one's written to 12 E-mail addresses in the House. And *this* guy isn't in my district, either." *Click click.* "What's this? A community . . . protection . . . initiative," he says, reading. "Who's it from? A police officer in Norfolk, Va. Well, we're just going to leave his message alone."

Gejdenson, despite appearances, actually likes E-mail. He checks it almost every day and responds to as many of his constituents as he can. But recently he asked House Information Services (HIS), the office that manages the House's computer operations, to post a notice on the official list of congressional E-mail addresses recommending that computer users send electronic messages only to their own lawmakers.

"What's happening is that with the new software programs today, 16,000 kids at a college can send me a letter with a push of a button," Gejdenson said in an interview. "I don't have the ability to go through all of that. As far as I'm concerned, the first people who deserve an answer are the people from my district."

Gejdenson is by no means the only person on Capitol Hill to find himself lost in cyberspace this way. Congress's once-leisurely drift toward computer networking and the Information Age accelerated to warp speed when the Republicans took over in January. But the voyage isn't turning out to be as simple as many had hoped it would be.

OVERCOMING TECHNOPHOBIA

The House first began experimenting with electronic communications two years ago, when Charles Rose, D-N.C., who was then the chairman of the House Administration Committee (it's now the House Oversight Committee), launched a

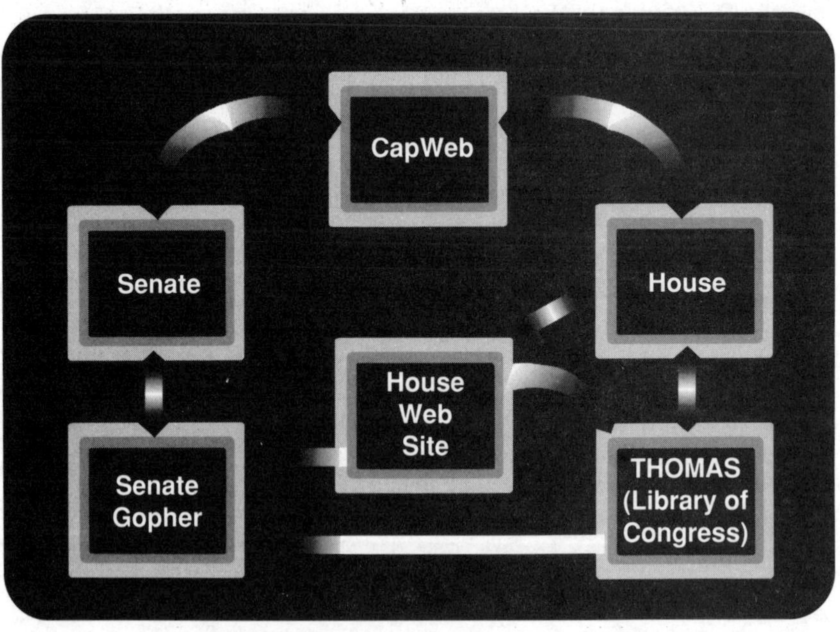

pilot program to establish E-mail addresses for Members of Congress on the Internet.

By the middle of last September, 43 House Members and 7 Senators had E-mail addresses. But most lawmakers weren't very interested in upgrading their office computer systems or in learning how to broadcast information to—or receive information from—constituents via powerful new Internet programs. Last December, even before he was sworn in as Speaker, Newt Gingrich, R-Ga., directed Rep. Vernon Ehlers, R-Mich., to organize a task force to overhaul the House's computer systems, and perhaps, in the process, to overcome the widespread Internet phobia on Capitol Hill.

Richard A. Bloom

Kenneth M. Deutsch and Sam Simon of Issue Dynamics Inc., a Washington consulting firm Their company is a pioneer in putting clients on the World Wide Web—"the Web," as it's known.

The plan has been only partly successful so far. House Members who once shied away from anything technological are now inquiring about Internet connections. For the most part, however, their aides aren't. Most congressional aides, spooked by the prospect of streams of E-mail flooding their desktop computers, don't want to join the Internet revolution.

Some congressional offices that are already "on the Net," as the term goes, have been so overwhelmed by E-mail that they have taken fairly strong measures to control it.

Gingrich's "Georgia6@hr.house.gov" Internet address, for example, received almost 13,000 E-mail messages in the first six weeks of the 104th Congress. But his staff, sources say, asked HIS in February to delete them. When HIS officials protested, Gingrich's staff revised its request. Now, every night, the Speaker's E-mail is printed on paper, downloaded to tape and deleted from his electronic in-box.

Efforts to make congressional information available electronically to the public have also snarled up.

On Jan. 5, Gingrich and William M. Thomas, R-Calif., the chairman of the House Oversight Committee, unveiled the THOMAS database of House information that's named after Thomas Jefferson and operated by the Library of Congress. But HIS continues to maintain its own Internet location, which also offers electronic access to House information. Neither system carries all the data that the other does.

The Senate maintains a third Internet location, operated on decade-old technology, and 30 Senators don't even participate in it.

CapWeb, the only Internet location that offers state-of-the-art information on both chambers of Congress, was built by two Senate aides in their spare time and operates on equipment on loan from Issue Dynamics Inc., a Washington consulting firm. *(See diagram, p. 24.)*

Ehlers, sources say, ran afoul of Thomas—who advises Gingrich on internal House matters—when the task force proposed to make HIS's Internet site the public's electronic gateway to the House. The task force has since been transformed into a subcommittee of House Oversight, and the future of HIS itself is in doubt. *(See box, p. 28.)*

These difficulties are stark reminders that the Information Age is coming to Congress a lot faster than anyone would have predicted even as recently as last year.

"Debating whether or not you want the Internet in your office is like the conversations a century ago, when people were saying, 'I don't need this gadget called a telephone that other people are hooking up in their homes,' " said Richard H. Shapiro, the executive director of the Congressional Management Foundation, a not-for-profit organization that provides management services to Congress.

Computer networks are "fast, efficient and provide instantaneous access to information," Shapiro added. "The reality is that all congressional offices will be communicating on the Internet in the near future. There will be a lot of kicking and screaming from Members, but they'll all have to do it."

HYPER OVER HYPERTEXT

There may be a subtler reason why some in Congress are so eager to be in cyberspace. The Americans who are Internet-astute also just happen to be, demographically speaking, the voters that anyone planning to hit the campaign trail next year wants to attract.

Today, more than 30 million U.S. households have personal computers, compared with 13-14 million households in the late 1980s, and that number is expected to double within just a few years.

In the past year or so, the skyrocketing popularity of a technical configuration on the Internet called the World Wide Web, and the development of increasingly powerful tools to use it, have given political communications the speed and scope that politicians only dreamed of until now.

The technology on which the World Wide Web—"the Web" for short—is based allows one computer to deliver full-color pictures or video, data and sound simultaneously to another computer. While this may not sound like much of a feat, consider that the technology on which every other Internet configuration is based delivers only text.

In essence, the Web serves up information in a format that's as close to television as computers have ever come. Web locations, or "sites," on the Internet come in all colors of the rainbow, with illustrations that range from the mundane to the miraculous. Within a week after the discovery of previously unknown prehistoric cave paintings in Combe d'Arc, France, for example, computer users could view Web pictures of the paintings that were clearer than any they could see on the nightly news.

A technology called "hypertext," however, is what makes Web sites really come alive. Hypertext, an outgrowth of graphics-based computer programs such as Microsoft Windows, is a series of location codes embedded within the text that the Internet delivers to a computer screen. In practice, hypertext is simply a mechanism to move from one Web site to another—to literally hopscotch across the Internet—with only the click of a computer mouse.

Here's how it works. It's easy to recognize a hypertext link because the topic it covers is delineated in boldface or a different color. Say you're reading the information on CapWeb, the congressional Web site maintained by Issue Dynamics and you want more information about the activities of Senate Minority Leader **Thomas A. Daschle**, D-S.D., Sen. **Patrick J. Leahy**, D-Vt., or Rep. **Peter A. DeFazio**, D-Ore.

Move the arrow on your screen to one of those names, click on it and—presto—

Daschle:
ftp://www.senate.gov/member/sd/daschle/general/daschle.html
Leahy:
ftp://ftp.senate.gov/member/vt/leahy/general/pjl.html
DeFazio:
http://darkwing.uoregon.edu/~pdefazio/index.html

a new Web site opens up. The effect is vaguely similar to reading lengthy margin notes, such as the ones in this article.

The business community has gone gaga over the Web because of its connectivity. Businesses of all shapes and sizes, from a small firm in North Carolina that airmails gourmet brownies anywhere in the world, to Sturbridge Yankee Workshop, a mail-order furniture company, have established Web sites in the past year.

"The Web is popular because it has both ease of use and a graphical interface," said Christopher M. Casey, who created the first congressional Web site for his boss, Sen. **Edward M. Kennedy**, D-Mass. "It also can point constituents to logical paths on the Internet to other information about Massachusetts or the federal government."

THE HILL AND THE WEB

The Web can do much more, as political strategists are learning. In pre-Internet days, television was the only effective way to make a powerful case on an issue to hundreds of thousands of voters. Each opportunity to make the case could cost supporters millions of dollars in production fees and airtime.

A carefully constructed Web site, or "home page," however, can present a point of view not only in a lights-camera-action mode, but also with the depth of information normally available only from magazines—at a fraction of the cost of television.

Newly evolving technology also allows sophisticated Web users to build interactive opinion polls, membership applications and comment boxes into their sites. Both Issue Dynamics and the Wexler Group, a major Washington lobbying firm, have recently built Web sites for their clients that include at least one of these options.

The key to the Web's appeal in the political realm, however, is the people it attracts.

Statistics show that Americans who regularly go on line tend to be younger and more successful than those who don't. The average head of a computer-and-modem-equipped household is 34 years old, compared with the national average of 40, and earns 77 per cent more than the average household, according to NPD Group, a market research firm.

Web users, and other Net regulars, also tend to be technically sophisticated and vitally interested in political issues. When **MacWorld**, a leading computer magazine, surveyed its readers last October about the specific services they most wanted to see offered on the Internet, being able to "vote in elections" ranked first. By comparison, "obtain video-on-demand" ranked 10th.

"Look at who's on the Internet," said Kenneth M. Deutsch, the director of information services for Issue Dynamics. "They're generally white, male and highly educated. They also don't have a high degree of party loyalty, and they're into information."

"The guys that use the Web were the swing vote in 1992," a longtime political consultant said. "Those are the people you want to reach in 1996."

Only a few Capitol Hill lawmakers have chosen so far to take the high-tech route to the Internet, via the Web. But an increasing number of House Members are choosing the low-tech route, using only the simple configurations that channel E-mail back and forth. And if their experiences with stepping onto the information superhighway are any indicator, anyone trying to persuade the rest of the House to join them may need a tow truck.

The furor on the Hill over E-mail is a

prime example. Electronic messages don't necessarily show where a sender lives. "There's an enormous resistance to E-mail on the Hill," an Internet-savvy activist said, "because the staff and the Members don't have any way to figure out where it comes from."

THE WAVES OF THE FUTURE

An extraordinarily large number of people now have the ability to communicate electronically. In an extensive survey completed last December, **Matrix Information and Directory Services Inc.**, a computer consulting firm based in Austin, Texas, estimated that the "core"

Matrix identified three concentric rings in the Internet: the "core"; another 5.7 million users who interact with the core; and an additional 14 million computer users who can exchange E-mail with other Internet users, for a total of 27.5 million users worldwide.

of the Internet consists of 7.8 million people who use computers that provide interactive computer services such as Web sites. Nearly four times that many people have E-mail capabilities of one sort or another, the firm estimated.

"The real fear Members and their staffs have is that if they hook up to the

Internet, at some point they'll really be creating work for themselves," said Shapiro of the Congressional Management Foundation. "Congressional offices are already so stretched out, and their people are so stressed out. There's the fear that this will take those offices to a whole new level of dealing with the constituent computer hacker."

That fear is not entirely without basis. It's now possible for individual computer users, with the help of relatively inexpensive new computer software, to deluge a congressional office with E-mail in much the same way that grass-roots organizations have historically lobbied Members of Congress by mobilizing letter and postcard campaigns.

While sacks of mail can be dumped in a corner of the Member's office, however, E-mail goes directly into the office's computer system, requiring a trained employee at a computer workstation to separate the wheat from the electronic mountains of chaff, according to Hill aides who have dealt with the problem.

Gejdenson, for example, tries to reduce E-mail bottlenecks by assigning an office intern to scan his messages periodically and delete repetitious ones. "Some people send you the same letter every five, six days," he said. "At some point I can't read all of them. Sometimes I want to tell people, 'You may think you're making a point, but I think you're just being annoying.' "

That sort of attitude, however, causes some in the Internet community to foam at the mouth.

"It's infuriating to notice how many of *our* representatives refuse to consider—much less respond to—communications except from their constituents," cyberspace activist Jim Warren wrote recently in a posting that went to hundreds of thousands of Internet regulars. "Their actions and votes impact *all* of us—not just those of us who can vote for them."

And even if the tactic of multiple E-mailing is annoying, there are signs that it works. Since last summer, **Internet-based grass-roots campaigns** have helped to shape a major telecommunications bill and served in several instances as the public's high-tech counterbalance to high-priced Washington lobbyists.

Members of Congress who shy away from the Internet also say that they worry about the security of information sent out over computer networks. The Senate Rules and Administration Committee and the Senate's Sergeant at Arms established a simple text-based Net site called a "Gopher" a little more than a year ago. There has been talk of establishing a Senate Web site, but "security is paramount," an aide to the Rules Committee said. "The House has chosen to go with the

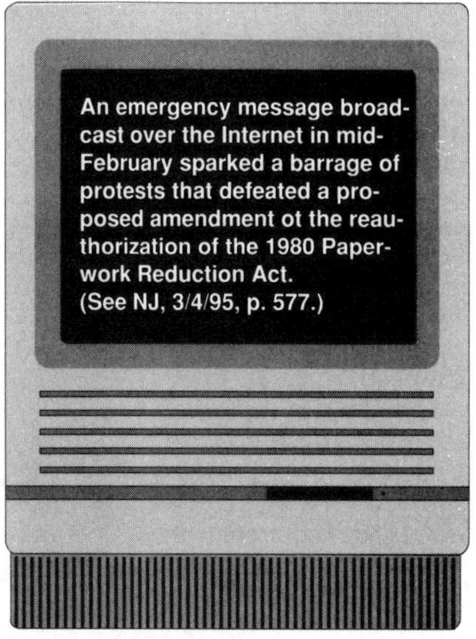

Library of Congress for its site; we would rather the Senate information be kept within the Senate itself."

What's more, some House Members have refused to establish Internet connections because they are concerned about a hacker trick called "spoofing," sources say. A spoof occurs when a hacker intercepts an electronic message, changes the wording in it and sends it on its way. Done correctly, the spoof is impossible to trace.

Rep. Norman Y. Mineta, D-Calif., drew the wrath of the Internet community on March 15, however, when his office replied to an E-mail message with an electronic form letter that said, in part: "At present there is concern about hackers intercepting and changing E-mail messages or even possibly changing the E-mail I.D. and sending out messages with my address. To ensure the security of our correspondence, I will be responding with you by [regular] mail."

Within 24 hours after Mineta's office posted its form letter, howls of protest were ringing through cyberspace. Encryption software, which rewrites electronic messages in code, makes spoofing a non-issue, Internet enthusiasts insist. A popular encryption program called Pretty Good Privacy (PGP) is even available free on the Internet.

One protest read: "Either [Mineta] has been totally scammed by the shuck-'n'-jive cracker fear peddlers, or he is saying that Congress can't figure out how to run a secure Internet site. Bull! At a minimum, [he] could simply adopt PGP and sign all msgs with his PGP key. This smells much more like this 'Representative' is simply using the vile-cracker-horror myth as an excuse for not responding to modern communications—E-mail—in a timely, modern manner."

Paradoxically, backers of greater Internet access on the Hill revel in controversies such as this. Whenever Members and their staffs are drawn into Net-based issues, Congress's comprehension of the booming electronic world grows, they say.

And the electronic venues for politics are growing day by day. Voters with access to the Internet will be bombarded by electronic political commercials and direct mail when the 1996 campaign season gets under way, Deutsch, of Issue Dynamics, predicts. Electronic town halls, on-line voting and nationwide Net-based campaigns, once considered the stuff of science fiction, could be commonplace in the presidential election of 2000, other experts say.

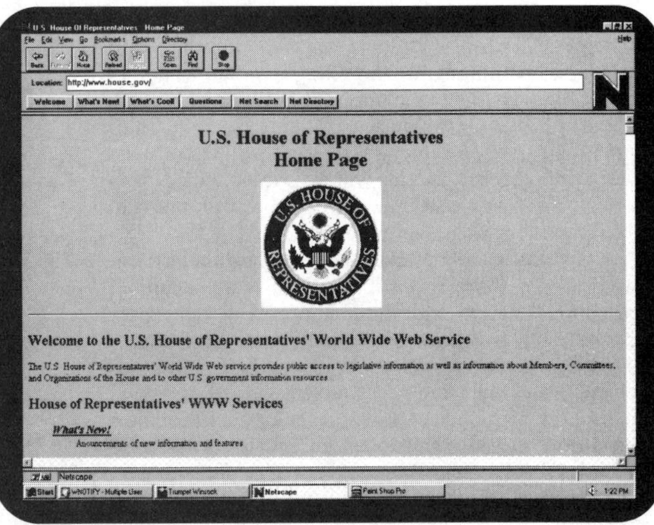

The home page of the House's World Wide Web Service

So-called intelligent E-mail systems are the wave of the future on the Hill, Casey, of Kennedy's office, said. "These systems will be smart enough to 'read' the contents of a message and bounce it to the staffer working on the problem," he said. "If you've got a person concerned about a social security check, for example, that message will go directly into the caseworker's computer queue, without anyone having to manually route it there."

All these evolutions will undoubtedly cause a profound shift in Congress's culture. Many staff members also resisted efforts in the early 1980s to convert House offices from "memory" typewriters to full-blown computer systems because they feared that computers would triple their workloads, former Hill aides say.

Congressional staff members finally began to accept computers when it became clear that the machines offered a quick, easy way to keep track of constituents' positions on issues as well as other information about them—and therefore made Capitol Hill lawmakers seem better informed and more responsive to voters than their challengers on the campaign trail. When Members and their staffs realize that Internet connections also give them a political leg up, the same turnabout is bound to happen.

SOME BUMPS ON THE SUPERHIGHWAY

For four years, Rep. Charles Rose, D-N.C., as the chairman of the House Administration Committee, ran House Information Services (HIS) with an iron hand. With Republicans in the majority and computer networks rapidly becoming central to House operations, that history may be quietly coming back to haunt the Democrats.

Rose first put his imprimatur on HIS, the office that manages the House's computer operations, in the early 1980s, when he became the chairman of the House Administration subcommittee that oversaw it. Over time, Republicans say, he transformed it into a personal fiefdom, where Members' relatives could easily find jobs. In 1991, Rose also admitted accepting more than $15,000 in campaign contributions from executives of software companies that did business with HIS.

Republicans on the committee chafed at Rose's autocratic rule—and none chafed more than William M. Thomas of California, then the committee's ranking Republican, and House Speaker Newt Gingrich, R-Ga., who was then minority whip.

When Congress convened in January, the House Administration Committee, whose members were elected by the full Democratic and Republican caucuses, was replaced by the House Oversight Committee. Gingrich appointed Thomas to be the chairman of the new committee.

HIS is now "a political minefield," a knowledgeable source said. "A number of Republicans think it should be abolished. There are a lot of strong feelings against Charlie and HIS."

Those feelings could be undergirding some recent political maneuvering over control of the electronic information that HIS gathers and makes available to the public via the Internet.

The day after the GOP's landslide victory last November, Gingrich appointed Rep. Vernon Ehlers, R-Mich., to head an independent task force whose job would be to overhaul the House's computer systems and to design an Internet location where the public could have access to a wide range of congressional documents. Ehlers, a physicist, had masterminded a similar computer conversion for the Michigan Legislature while serving there from 1983-93.

Under Ehlers's direction, HIS constructed the database of House documents that's now available on the World Wide Web. But in late December, sources said, Gingrich and Thomas abruptly shifted responsibility for a public Internet site to the Library of Congress, where congressional information is also available via THOMAS (a system named after Thomas Jefferson). Ehlers, who was home for the Christmas holidays, didn't know about the change until he returned to Washington, sources said.

Several weeks later, Ehlers's task force became a "working group" that reports to Thomas at House Oversight. HIS now reports to Scot M. Faulkner, the House's new chief administrative officer, who in turn reports to Gingrich. Ehlers "has been closed out" of the decision-making loop for both the House Web site and the THOMAS system, knowledgeable sources said. *(See NJ, 3/25/95, p. 757.)*

Meanwhile, HIS has been directed to funnel electronic versions of data—such as the texts of new bills and reports of floor action and votes—to the Library of Congress. Eventually the House's Web site will be folded into the THOMAS system, Scot Montrey, the press secretary to the House Oversight Committee, said. "The whole idea of moving this information to the Library of Congress," he said, "is to eliminate partisanship, and distance control of the database from the congressional leadership."

The *New* Federalism

Is New Federalism an idea whose time has finally come? Maybe, but figuring out what it really means or would do is about as easy as nailing Jell-O to the wall.

ROCHELLE L. STANFIELD

New Federalism is back. Again. But this time—the third try—may be the charm. New schemes to take power away from the federal government and give it to states and localities are mostly retreads from the Nixon and Reagan Administrations. It's everything else that makes this time different.

"For the last 30 years, most of the talk about New Federalism has been intellectual—the kind of thing that one-tenth of 1 per cent of the people were interested in," Lamar Alexander, former college president, Tennessee governor, Education Secretary and would-be Republican presidential candidate in 1996, said in a recent interview. "What happened on Nov. 8 was just a huge scream from the gut about the arrogance of Washington, D.C. It's moved from the head to the stomach, and therefore is something that can't be ignored."

To depict New Federalism as a primal scream may not be far off the mark. The notion of a federal system with power shared between federal and state governments is among the most basic in American politics. That's what *The Federalist Papers*—recently returned to vogue by House Speaker Newt Gingrich, R-Ga.—are all about. But what New Federalism really means or would do remains elusive. Is the purpose to make all government smaller? Or better? To make the federal government smaller by shifting responsibilities to states and localities? Or to make all government work better by clearly defining responsibilities and assigning tasks to the level that does them best?

"If you simply transfer power from bureaucracies in Washington to bureaucracies in Madison [Wis.] or Sacramento [Calif.], that is a mistake and won't satisfy people," William Kristol, the chairman of the Project for the Republican Future and one of Gingrich's top idea men, said in an interview. "People want problems addressed in new ways. They want government cut back at all levels."

Not all Republicans, though, aim simply to make all government smaller. Whatever the end, how do you get there? Everybody uses the same terms—devolution, block grants, swaps, no "unfunded

John Eisele

Rep. William F. Goodling, R-Pa.
"I'm not just for block-granting money back and saying, 'Here, do your thing.' "

[*During its first 100 Days, the Republican-controlled 104th Congress passed a so-called unfunded mandates bill that Democratic President Bill Clinton signed into law in late March 1995. The legislation makes it very difficult for Congress to pass laws that impose requirements *and* accompanying costs on states. During the same period, the House approved a constitutional amendment requiring a balanced budget, but the proposed amendment was defeated by a narrow margin in the Senate. Editor]

From *National Journal,* January 28, 1995, pp. 226-230.

mandates"—but the meaning shifts with the speaker, the context and the audience.

Most participants in the discussion agree that there are overarching national goals the federal government is obligated to seek. But whose goals—the liberals' commitment to housing integration or the conservatives' commitment to reducing illegitimacy?

These differences over practicalities are likely to slow down and complicate the process of passing New Federalism legislation, but the pervasive, gut-level feeling that something needs to be done could provide the momentum—this time—to push it through in some form.

"The point is that for the American democracy to continue in its most effective form, there needs to be a reexamination of the basic questions that were asked by Hamilton, Jefferson and Madison about who does what," Gov. Mike Leavitt, R-Utah, said in an interview. He and Gov. E. Benjamin Nelson, D-Neb., are promoting a bipartisan conference of the states to consider fundamental issues of federalism and to recommend constitutional amendments that would shift power to the states. *(See box.)*

But probably the most important factor in New Federalism's favor is the ascension of Republicans in Congress.

Most of the federal programs and approaches in question were the product of Democratic Congresses that stepped in with money and orders to meet domestic needs and demands that had been left unmet by states and localities. Regardless of subsequent state and local reforms, program obsolescence and changing times, Democratic Congresses were loathe to give up these brainchildren.

Republican control of both chambers of Congress sweeps many of those obstacles away. In his opening remarks as Senate Majority Leader on Jan. 4, Robert Dole, R-Kan., spoke of federalism and the 10th Amendment, which reserves to the states all powers not delegated to the federal government. "But there are some in Washington—perhaps fewer this year than last—who believe neither our states nor our people can be trusted with power," Dole said. "Federalism has given way to paternalism—with disastrous results. If I have one goal for the 104th Congress, it is this: that we will dust off the 10th Amendment and restore it to its rightful place in our Constitution."

In his opening speech, Gingrich alluded to federalism only indirectly—noting that "there was much to what Ronald Reagan was trying to get done; there is much to what is being done today by [various Republican governors]"—but returning power to the states is one of his frequent themes.

This time around, New Federalism isn't only a Republican thing; it's also a central feature of the New Democrat theology. Sorting out intergovernmental responsibilities is a key item on an alternative contract with America developed by the Democratic Leadership Council.

President Clinton has jumped on the bandwagon. In December, he proposed to reorganize the Housing and Urban Development (HUD) Department along New Federalist lines. The Office of Management and Budget (OMB), the White House's Domestic Policy Council and Vice President Albert Gore Jr.'s National Performance Review are looking for similar steps to take in other departments.

Richard A. Bloom

OMB director Alice M. Rivlin
"It's not easy to measure outcomes of public programs..."

OMB director Alice M. Rivlin, who wrote a book on the subject in 1992, when she was a scholar at the Brookings Institution, is one of the most enthusiastic New Federalists in the Administration. "I was persuaded early in my career, when I worked at what was then the Department of Health, Education and Welfare, that the federal government was trying to do too many different things," she said in a recent interview. "Even then, it would have made sense to rethink the relationship between the federal government and the states. I think that's even more true now."

Things are also different on the other side of the federalism equation. The November elections put 30 governorships in Republican hands—including 9 of the nation's 10 largest states (all but Florida); Republicans control both chambers of 19 state legislatures and one chamber in 13 states. The substantial influence of governors in presidential politics and the raw power of state legislatures in ratifying constitutional amendments (like one to require a balanced federal budget) dramatically increase their clout with the new Congress. On a policy level, the states have demonstrated over the past decade that they can manage programs as well as or better than the federal government. As many governors like to point out, the states have instituted both education reform and welfare reform—while balancing their budgets every year.

Meanwhile, city and county governments have also changed. Regardless of party, mayors and county officials are more businesslike. Because they can no longer rely on Congress to bail them out financially, they've begun to look to themselves, their states and to the private sector. Thus—and perhaps most important—they've decided to join forces with the states rather than fight them as they did during the previous two rounds of debate over a New Federalism.

"I was part of that whole business of dealing with New Federalism [in 1982]," Gov. George V. Voinovich of Ohio, a Republican who was the mayor of Cleveland at the time, recalled at a recent news conference in Washington. "At that time, we didn't do too well, because the organizations [representing state and local governments] negotiated individually with the Reagan Administration." After the states, counties and cities cut deals at odds with each other, New Federalism proposals fell apart.

"So we have decided," Voinovich said, "that to the very best of our ability, we're going to work together as a team." He announced the formation of a coalition of five state and local government organizations (the National Governors' Association [NGA], the National Conference of

GETTING THE STATES TOGETHER

Of the many variations on the theme of New Federalism, one is truly a back-to-basics move. Two governors, Republican Mike Leavitt of Utah and Democrat E. Benjamin Nelson of Nebraska, are promoting a "Conference of the States" to consider fundamental reforms to shift power from the federal government to the states.

"Much of the discussion about devolution is focused on rearranging boxes—which program is handled by which area," Leavitt said in an interview. "The Conference of the States is focused on the broader picture of how do we recreate that delicate balance between states and the national government." *(See NJ, 1/28/95, p. 40.)*

The proposals that Leavitt and Nelson contemplate are so basic and long-range that they're not as controversial as the New Federalism proposals for converting welfare into block grants, for example. But ultimately, they would have a far greater effect on the balance of power between the federal government and the states.

One item, for example, would make it easier for the states to initiate a constitutional amendment. Currently, the only route open to the states is to call for a constitutional convention, a politically impractical path because, some fear, such a convention could get out of hand. Another item would be to allow two-thirds of the states to kill federal legislation.

As Leavitt sees it, getting specific about such programs as welfare or such special-interest issues as abortion would destroy the effectiveness of the conference, as would partisanship. "Those three things—I call them the three deadly sins—would kill the capacity of the conference to succeed," he said.

Both the National Governors' Association and the National Conference of State Legislatures have endorsed the idea. Officials of the organizations said that most legislatures have plans to adopt a formal resolution to call the conference, which would take place by fall.

No formal role is contemplated for local governments, which are the creatures of the states and have no official status under the Constitution. And that could disrupt the newfound partnership that state and local government organizations have formed. Leavitt and others say that they want local governments to participate by bringing proposals to the conference, but not by voting in it. That may not be enough for the locals.

"We intend to have a word [in the conference]," said Mayor Victor Ashe of Knoxville, Tenn., the president of the U.S. Conference of Mayors. "We're not going to let a meeting be held and cities and counties not be represented."

State Legislatures, the National Association of Counties, the U.S. Conference of Mayors and the National League of Cities).

"I think the next couple of years are going to be the greatest opportunity to restructure federal-state relations since the New Deal," Raymond C. Scheppach, the NGA's executive director, said in an interview. "If it's done right, I think you can have a win-win-win situation for the federal government, the states and the beneficiaries [of government services]. If it's done badly, I think everybody loses."

THE DEVIL IN THE DETAILS

On the basic themes of New Federalism, everyone sings the same tune: smaller, more efficient government; less federal micromanaging; greater flexibility for states and localities. It's when you try to pin down what those concepts mean in practice—and exactly how to achieve them—that divisions appear everywhere.

Republican governors are unified in their support for a balanced budget amendment and opposition to unfunded mandates (programs that Washington has imposed on state and local governments without providing the money to pay for them), for example, but split over whether language that would prohibit unfunded mandates should be incorporated in the proposal for a balanced budget amendment.*

With their Contract With America, House Republicans appear to be a united front, marching under the flag of the Gingrich Revolution. But there are cracks in that facade.

When asked in an interview about some of the far-reaching block grants and the social agenda that some conservative lawmakers contemplate, for example, Rep. William F. Goodling, R-Pa., a moderate who chairs the Economic and Educational Opportunities Committee (formerly Education and Labor), replied, "As an authorizing committee, we will have a major responsibility in making sure that those who haven't dealt with these programs day in and day out don't make any mistakes that would come back to embarrass us."

State and local officials—Democrats and Republicans alike—insist that they will gladly exchange less federal aid for more flexibility in running the programs. But how much less and how much more? "If we get fewer dollars and we also get fewer regulations, we will be able to spend the dollars we get directly on services," Democratic state Rep. Jane L. Campbell, the assistant minority leader of the Ohio House, said in a joint interview with other legislators. "Actually, we want less federally."

But another Democratic state representative, Daniel T. Blue of North Carolina, said in the same interview: "We realize, too, that simply saying the states are going to assume greater responsibility is an empty promise if there are not resources that come with that."

And what exactly does *flexibility* mean? Everyone agrees that if Congress hands taxpayers' money to states or localities, some form of federal audit is necessary to avoid fraud and abuse. Beyond that, it gets very fuzzy.

"In areas where there is a need to have an across-the-board federal policy—safe drinking water is a good example—[the federal government could] set the standard and then let the state legislatures determine how to meet that standard," Campbell said. "If [Congress] just simply said, 'We want to make sure that children in this country don't starve and that people have a safe place to live and parents have an opportunity to be educated and trained and have child care, here's how much money there is to do it, now do it,' I think you would get extraordinarily better service. The accountability mechanism in the states is established: It's the state legislatures. We're elected by our constituents to make appropriate policy for the state."

Goodling, however, has a very different view of the extent of accountability. While he acknowledged that federal laws have "denied any local creativity" and that "we've tied the hands of local people," he said: "We should not have the right to send federal taxpayers' money anywhere unless they know what it is we expect to accomplish. I'm not just for block-granting money back and saying, 'Here, do your thing.' There has to be a purpose and goals . . . and oversight to see that's what's happening."

The Clinton Administration and the New Democrats see the federal government playing an additional role whenever it gives out money: promoting management reform. "We're really trying to reward effort," said Kathleen Sylvester, the vice president for domestic policy of the New Democrats' Progressive Policy Institute. "We've got to figure out what is the federal government's role to leverage change when there's an appropriate federal interest in something."

To some state and local officials, that smacks of the same old paternalism. "You can't just say, 'OK, this is yours, but by the way, you got to do it between A and Z,' " said New York state Sen. James J. Lack, a Republican. "Send us the unfettered authority. We'll do it. That's our job."

There's general agreement that whatever federal standards are imposed should require certain outcomes rather than set the specific practices or procedures to arrive at those outcomes. But setting outcome standards is easier said than done. "There is some glibness," Rivlin said. "It's not easy to measure outcomes of public programs, and one has to be careful not to produce counterproductive measures."

The theorists of federalism believe that the dilemma of flexibility versus accountability can be solved in the design of New Federalism legislation, and as was the case with New Federalism I and II, three general approaches are under discussion: block grants, swaps and turnbacks. But politics rarely accommodates such neat theories.

Republicans on the House Ways and Means Committee, for example, are working on a series of six block grants to consolidate as many as 300 welfare, child care, food and nutrition and other programs. But Nancy Landon Kassebaum, R-Kan., who chairs the Senate Labor and Human Resources Committee, has her eye on a swap: The federal government would take over total financing of medicaid (the states now contribute about $57 billion a year) while the states would accept total responsibility for aid to families with dependent children (AFDC), food stamps and a few small programs to make the swap at least equal and, preferably, to save the federal government money.

"It isn't just a question of sending money to the states and letting them, with a block grant, have the flexibility to run it," Kassebaum said on NBC News's *Meet the Press* on Jan. 15. "I would sever Washington's involvement."

No turnbacks have been formally introduced, but several people, including Alexander, have suggested eliminating federal elementary and secondary education programs along with a specific federal revenue source—taxes on alcoholic beverages or cigarettes, for example, which states could in turn enact to pay for the additional education expenses.

Democratic state Rep. Jane L. Campbell, the assistant minority leader of the Ohio House "The accountability mechanism in the states is established: It's the state legislatures."

"Block grants are a temptation [to Congress] to micromanage," Jeffrey Eisenach, the president of the Progress & Freedom Foundation and an adviser to Gingrich, said. "Complete devolution approaches [like swaps or turnbacks] really and truly get the federal government out of it. Once the money's in Washington, the power's in Washington, and you can't get around it."

But Eisenach acknowledged a drawback in terms of equity. Some states have a greater capacity to raise revenues than other states. "Part of the purpose of federal welfare programs, I suspect, is to hide the cross-state subsidies," he said.

For others, like Stuart M. Butler, the Heritage Foundation's vice president and director of domestic policy, the primary goal must be to reduce federal involvement. The Kassebaum swap would be "a disaster," Butler said, because the federal government would be left holding the entire bill for medicaid. "Once you've got a swap, you've got it," he said. Block grants, on the other hand, allow Congress to relinquish a program gradually. "You start by saying, 'You'll get a block grant with all the flexibility, but I'm going to cut funding by 15-20 per cent'—whatever you can get away with," Butler said. "Then the pressure is on Congress to look for ways of cutting that back further over time."

Photos by John Eisele

New York state Sen. James J. Lack, a Republican "Send us the unfettered authority. We'll do it."

Jeffrey Eisenach of the Progress & Freedom Foundation "Block grants are a temptation to micromanage."

"Everyone in state and local government knows what happens to block grants," said the Progressive Policy Institute's Sylvester. "They get whittled away and then there's less money to [provide services]."

Which is exactly why the NGA's Scheppach doubts that most governors would go along with a block grant for AFDC, food stamps or medicaid unless the grant is budgeted as an entitlement, in which the size of the grant is tied to the number of recipients. "If you're talking about a block grant that's fighting through the Appropriations Committees every year for its funding," he said, "I think that's a potential real problem."

But some governors say they want freedom so much that they're willing to risk future losses.

"I can't speak for all the governors, but I can for my governor," said Gerald H. Miller, the director of Michigan's Department of Social Services, who is handling welfare negotiations for Republican Gov. John M. Engler. "Clearly, to get the kind of flexibility we think that we need, we would be willing to give that [entitlement] up."

After meeting with House Republicans, a group of Republican governors said that they would agree to eliminating entitlements for individuals as long as Congress guaranteed that the state grants would not be reduced for five years. Republicans on the Ways and Means Committee were unwilling to make such a guarantee.

But Gov. Howard Dean of Vermont, a Democrat who's serving as the NGA's chairman this year, objected to the elimination of the entitlement. "No way, that's bad for everybody," he said in an interview.

Local officials recognize that however these proposals are structured, they ultimately will be left holding the bag. "It's the cities and counties of America where the local people will come to get help," Michael Hightower, a vice chairman of the Fulton County (Atlanta) Commission, said. "We're not saying 'Gimme, gimme gimme,' but we're also not saying, 'Give us less money.' We need the resources, because it's our hospitals and homeless shelters where the people come."

For this reason, Donald J. Borut, the executive director of the National League of Cities, sees some of these block grant proposals as "the mother of all unfunded mandates."

WHOSE AGENDA?

The flexibility of New Federalism doesn't mean abrogating national goals and principles, its exponents agree. The difficulty comes in defining just what are the nation's goals and principles.

Some are pretty generally accepted. The state and local organizations agreed, for example, to exempt civil rights from the unfunded mandates legislation. "Clearly, in the area of civil rights, I don't think anyone would even question that," said Mayor Victor Ashe of Knoxville, Tenn., the president of the U.S. Conference of Mayors. "That's basic." But some might question the definition of civil rights—whether it extends to affirmative action, for example, or to gays.

The Clinton Administration's redesign of HUD addresses the issue up front. At a news conference to explain the Administration's proposal, HUD Secretary Henry G. Cisneros spoke of "a longstanding tension between the rights of the states and the role of centralized government to deal with national goals and national ideals that the federal government has, for the last generation at least, been the protector of." Among these he listed fair housing, promoting housing mobility for the poor and attention to such special populations as the homeless, the elderly and the disabled.

Cisneros acknowledged that "in the white-hot heat of local politics, it is not possible for local government to act on these questions without some strong push from the federal government." Others argue that the results of the Nov. 8 elections call into question whether most Americans really want the federal government pushing on social welfare issues.

Nonetheless, the Administration carefully avoided using the term "block grants" to describe the three pots of money it envisions to replace 60 or so of HUD's programs. Instead, it called them "performance-based funds" to signify its "contractual agreement" with states and localities.

The conservatives also have a social agenda that conflicts with their notions of flexibility and devolution. The Contract With America, for example, is very specific on tough anti-crime legislation—traditionally the province of state government—and who should receive welfare. Left out of the contract but high on the agenda of some conservative lawmakers is a detailed list of what schools should and should not teach. This conflict shows up frequently in Republican rhetoric.

"Republicans . . . believe that our country's increasingly desperate fight against crime is an area where more freedom is needed at the state level," Dole told his colleagues on Jan. 4. And then, in the next breath, he said: "Our crime bill will impose mandatory minimum sentences on those who use guns in the commission of a crime, and make sure the jails are there to lock them up."

Similarly, on welfare reform, while contemplating the best way for the federal government to get out of the public assistance business, some Republican lawmakers insist that no money go to the illegitimate children of teenagers or to illegal immigrants.

Some conservative Republicans see a danger in this approach. "We've got to resist all these efforts that some Republicans are involved in that say we ought to fix welfare in Washington or we ought to show we're tough on crime by setting the state sentences," Alexander said. "That is absolute nonsense. The vote on Nov. 8 was about the arrogance of Washington, and the greatest danger that we have is that we'll replace their arrogant empire with one of our own."

THE NEW FIXATION OF FEDERALISM

ROCHELLE L. STANFIELD

The new political battle cry is "Get me results!" Congressional Republicans, the Clinton Administration and Sen. Edward M. Kennedy, D-Mass., all agree on one thing: What they want from federal programs is favorable results. They even concur that federal legislation should be overhauled so that programs are evaluated on "performance" or "outcome."

But accurately measuring the outcome of government programs, where profit isn't the bottom line, is a lot easier said than done. Indeed, most of the widely reviled "input standards"—which measure what goes into a program—were adopted because they were the only objective way to evaluate a program.

A public housing official can fill in little boxes on a form that totals the number of prospective tenants interviewed and the number who were given apartments, for example. But there's no form that shows, at a glance, whether the housing agency is providing safe, affordable housing—in the most efficient way possible—for those who need it.

"We've got systems now that are driven by a couple of different things," Barbara Dyer, the director of the National Academy of Public Administration's Alliance for Redesigning Government, said. "One is that we don't trust anybody, and two, because it's so hard to measure results, we use inputs and procedures because they're easier to measure as a proxy. But ultimately, nothing really matters other than the results we're intending to achieve."

Alice M. Rivlin, the director of the Office of Management and Budget (OMB), is an outspoken exponent of performance-based standards. But she also recognizes how difficult they are to do right.

Measuring the results of job-training programs is one of Rivlin's favorite examples. "The assumption is, that's pretty easy," she said in an interview. "You measure the number of people who get jobs and what their wages were, and a program is more successful if more people get jobs at higher wages."

But, she pointed out, such a standard can send the wrong signal. "If you take that as your success measure, the people who run the program are likely to select into the program people who are easy to train and are candidates for high-wage jobs," she said. "But that isn't necessarily what you want them to do. You may want them to train people who have had difficulty getting a job and for whom even a low-wage job is better than no job."

Measuring performance was a recurrent theme in the Senate Labor and Human Resources Committee's recent oversight hearings on the Job Corps, the 30-year-old residential employment training program for disadvantaged young people. Critics of the program argued that Job Corps centers have become violent and dangerous; because administrators are graded on how long participants stay in the program, they said, they don't expel disruptive or violent students.

Doug Ross, the assistant Labor secretary for employment and training, told members of the committee that he's working on the problem by tightening the anti-violence standards by which Job Corps administrators are evaluated. Organizations that operate centers where violence occurs will lose their contracts to run them, Ross promised.

But some cautioned that taking such action could have unintended consequences. The centers might stop admitting those who need the program most because they are the most likely to be violent. Or the whole character of the program could change—some organizations that operate Job Corps centers, for example, could turn their facilities into boot camps.

"How do we [achieve a] balance so we don't end up with gangs but don't end up creaming, taking only the best [potential participants] so the statistics look good?" Sen. James M. Jeffords, R-Vt., the chairman of the Labor and Human Resources Subcommittee on Education, Arts and Humanities, asked.

Oregon has been working on the development of performance standards for seven years. The effort, called the Oregon Option, is finally beginning to show results. Through a comprehensive planning process that includes neighborhoods, cities, counties and the state government, Oregon has established what it calls "benchmarks"—the results that Oregonians want to achieve from government programs in such areas as the economy, the work force, the environment and children and families. In December, the state signed an agreement with OMB and several federal departments and agencies to extend the benchmarks to federal programs in Oregon.

Those who worked on the benchmarks acknowledge how difficult it was to come up with them and then to find measurements that would accurately reflect the outcomes that Oregon residents wanted.

Ironically, Oregon's benchmark developers also found that some of the most widely criticized input standards sometimes are, in fact, reliable indicators of desired results. Connie C. Revell, a state health official on the staff of the Oregon Option, spent four years working on the benchmark that calls for reducing teen pregnancies. Because most teenage girls drop out of school and then get pregnant, Revell discovered that the old-fashioned count of daily school attendance was a very accurate guide to the status of the teen pregnancy program in different jurisdictions. "There are some wonderful, available ways to do these things," she said, "if you use some common sense."

Housing and Urban Development Secretary Henry G. Cisneros has been so impressed with the Oregon Option that he wants to consolidate 60 HUD programs into three performance-based funds with requirements modeled on Oregon's approach.

But not so fast, others say. Most other states have a long way to go before they can implement performance-based systems. "If you think about a scale of readiness that goes from 1-10," Dyer said, "Oregon is probably at a 2 and the rest of the country is at a minus-something." So even though politicians keep demanding to know what bang they're getting for the federal buck, they're going to have to wait—the one thing they hate to do—for some good answers.

From *National Journal*, January 28, 1995, p. 260.

WHO'S BEING EGREGIOUS NOW?

KIRK VICTOR

Call it a case of déjà vu. The Occupational Safety and Health Administration (OSHA) is back on the hot seat.

In a throwback to the 1970s, the business community is excoriating OSHA for a variety of "sins." Corporate lobbyists are charging that the agency is, once again, hell-bent on proposing costly regulations and on stepping up, in a combative manner, its enforcement of existing, burdensome rules.

Much of the brouhaha stems from a regulation reportedly under consideration that would require employers to examine jobs and to correct conditions that contribute to "repetitive motion" injuries. Earlier this year, OSHA took heat for proposing a virtual ban on smoking in the workplace.

But even as those initiatives attract front-page attention, another high-stakes battle is under way pitting the business community against the Labor Department. In cases wending their way through the administrative process, two companies, joined by the U.S. Chamber of Commerce, are challenging the way the Labor Secretary calculates penalties for violations of the 1970 Occupational Safety and Health Act.

In the two cases now pending before the Occupational Safety and Health Review Commission, the Secretary is being challenged for imposing multiple penalites for violations of a single regulation.

The Secretary's approach flows out of the so-called egregious penalty policy, which originated during the Reagan Administration. Rather than propose one penalty for each group of alleged violations of the same regulation, the Labor Department, on occasion, has imposed stiffer penalties on employers who have violated the 1970 Act in a particularly "egregious" way.

One of the pending cases involves Memphis-based Arcadian Corp., which ran a fertilizer plant in Lake Charles, La., where a reactor ruptured, destroying the facility, spreading debris over a 600-acre area and releasing ammonia and carbon dioxide into the air. The 70-person day shift had just left the site, limiting immediate injuries to three employees and four private citizens.

At a hearing before the review commission, a government lawyer said that the company had refused to heed "clear warning signs" that the corrosive contents had breached the lining of the reactor. Arcadian didn't shut off the reactor, despite instructions in its own operating manual requiring a shutdown when a leak was detected. "If this catastrophe had occurred just an hour earlier, it surely would have been the worst chemical disaster in OSHA history," he said.

The agency determined that 87 employees had been "willfully exposed" to the hazard by Arcadian, and the Labor Secretary issued citations to Arcadian alleging 87 separate violations of the "general duty clause," under which employers must provide a workplace free from recognized hazards that cause or are likely to cause death or serious physical harm. The Secretary proposed a penalty of $50,000 for each violation (below the $70,000 congressionally imposed ceiling), for a total of $4,350,000.

The government argued that the company owed a separate duty to each employee, justifying a per-employee citation. An administrative law judge rejected that approach and agreed with Arcadian that only one violation existed. The company argued that once an employee is exposed to a hazardous condition, the employer must correct that condition once—not 87 times—and should be penalized once.

The second case involves OSHA's citations against Hartford (Conn.)-based Hartford Roofing Co. Inc. for "willful violations" of two regulations, one that requires companies to use warning lines or a safety monitoring system or guardrails on roofing jobs and another that imposes restrictions on the use and storage of mechanical equipment.

The government charged that Hartford employees who were installing roof waterproofing and insulation last year worked without the required protection. The government alleged that Hartford had an "extensive history" of failing to provide protection for roofing work—having been cited 16 times for violations of regulations since 1982. In the past five years, at least three Hartford workers had fallen from roofing jobs. Two of them died.

Hartford responded that it had employed both an independent consultant and an in-house corporate safety manager who had inspected the site. The company said it took steps to ensure that an existing parapet wall as well as warning lines and a safety monitoring system provided sufficient protection.

The government proposed a penalty of $35,000 for each alleged violation and multiplied that by the six employees exposed to the hazards, assessing a total penalty of $210,000. But the administrative law judge found the violations to be "repeated"—not "willful"—and assessed only a single penalty of $15,000. He found that the company had engaged in a single course of conduct—not a behavior that was "individual" or distinct with respect to each employee.

The egregious penalties in both cases—multiplying the violation by the number of employees exposed—are "extremely important," Joseph A. Dear, the OSHA chief, said in an interview. "The egregious penalty multiplier enables us to create a real economic deterrent—it goes to the core of a credible and effective program."

"They are important cases because if the decisions are adverse, it would permit OSHA to propose massive penalties," Arthur G. Sapper of the Washington law firm of McDermott, Will & Emery countered. "If, for example, 100 employees pass a hazardous condition every day, the penalty under that theory could be extremely high and onerous."

But despite the business community's unhappiness, OSHA pursued only eight egregious cases in fiscal year 1994—up from five the year before, though Dear said that this year there will be a "large increase."

Also, the policy is used only in cases of "very bad actors"—companies that have engaged in willful behavior. Nonetheless, it's a good bet that come 1996 a raft of politicians running against Washington will use OSHA as a whipping boy again.

The Economy, Taxing, Spending, and Budgeting

In 1992 Governor Bill Clinton of Arkansas defeated incumbent President George Bush in his bid for reelection. Clinton's campaign centered on the state of the economy and his promise, if elected president, to focus on improving the economy while in office. His victory underscores the role that "pocketbook" issues have traditionally played in American presidential elections.

The link between the state of the economy and electoral politics in the United States should not be surprising, given corresponding links between the economic and political systems and between the economy and public policy. Both the American market economy and the American political system allocate scarce resources to more than 250 million people. In so doing, the economic and political systems significantly interact with one another. To put into effect the wide variety of public policies it has adopted, the national government annually spends an amount equal to nearly one-quarter of the nation's entire economic output. Its taxing and spending policies play a major role in shaping the nation's economy.

The size of the national government and its annual budget deficits have become more prominent policy issues in recent years, especially since President Ronald Reagan took office in 1981. Reagan ran for president in 1980 promising a balanced budget and criticizing incumbent President Jimmy Carter for sizable budget deficits in the latter years of his presidency. Once Reagan assumed the presidency, however, annual budget deficits climbed to record levels as a consequence of his taxing and spending proposals. When Reagan entered office in 1981, the national government's total debt was about $1 trillion. By 1993, after Reagan's two terms and one additional term under President Bush, who had been Reagan's loyal vice president, the national debt had quadrupled to more than $4 trillion. Against this background the central role that budgeting, taxing, and spending play in public policy today can best be understood.

Republican leader Newt Gingrich and his fellow House Republican candidates used their now-famous "Contract with America" to anchor their campaigns in the fall of 1994. One part of the contract addressed a balanced budget amendment to the Constitution. Republicans pledged to bring to a vote in the House of Representatives a constitutional amendment requiring the national government to balance its budget every year. The balanced budget amendment was passed by the House during the first 100 days of the 104th Congress, but it was defeated in the Senate a few weeks later by one vote.

The prominence of these recent events relating to a balanced budget amendment should not overshadow many other public policy decisions treating budgetary and economic matters that Washington policymakers regularly face. Selections in this unit cover many of these other policy decisions as well as discussions and debates that relate to them. One overarching public policy decision would seem to be how much to tax and how much to spend. Another would concern how to help keep the nation's economy healthy and productive. Yet taxing, spending, and keeping the nation's economy healthy are far from exact sciences, and a multitude of considerations and procedures come into play. What effect will a capital gains tax cut have on government revenues and private investment and, in turn, the budget deficit and the health of the economy? How can the so-called underground economy, that sector of the economy that regularly evades taxation, be brought to heel? If the size of the national government is reduced, what effect will such a reduction have on the economy as a whole, and how can its impact be foreseen and, if adverse, cushioned? How can the income and corporate tax codes be improved and should there be a progressive income tax that requires those with higher incomes to pay a larger percentage of their taxable incomes than those with lower earnings? How active should the government be in encouraging private investment and financing worker training and retraining schemes? These are the sorts of money- and economy-related questions that face policymakers and that selections in this unit address.

In some senses the policy issues treated in this unit subsume most of those treated in the rest of the book. As Shannon Harris, Julie McVey, and Darci Oak, three students of public policy at DePauw University, have argued, governments do next to nothing unless they spend money doing it. Sometimes a government will declare its support for some goal or condition of affairs and thus engage in what is called symbolic public policy. But the vast, vast majority of important things that governments do depend on the expenditure of material resources, or, in other words, on money. Government decisions to spend, tax, and budget are decisions to do and not do things. Just as pocketbook issues often decide the outcome of American elections, so does economic and budgetary policy mak-

Unit 2

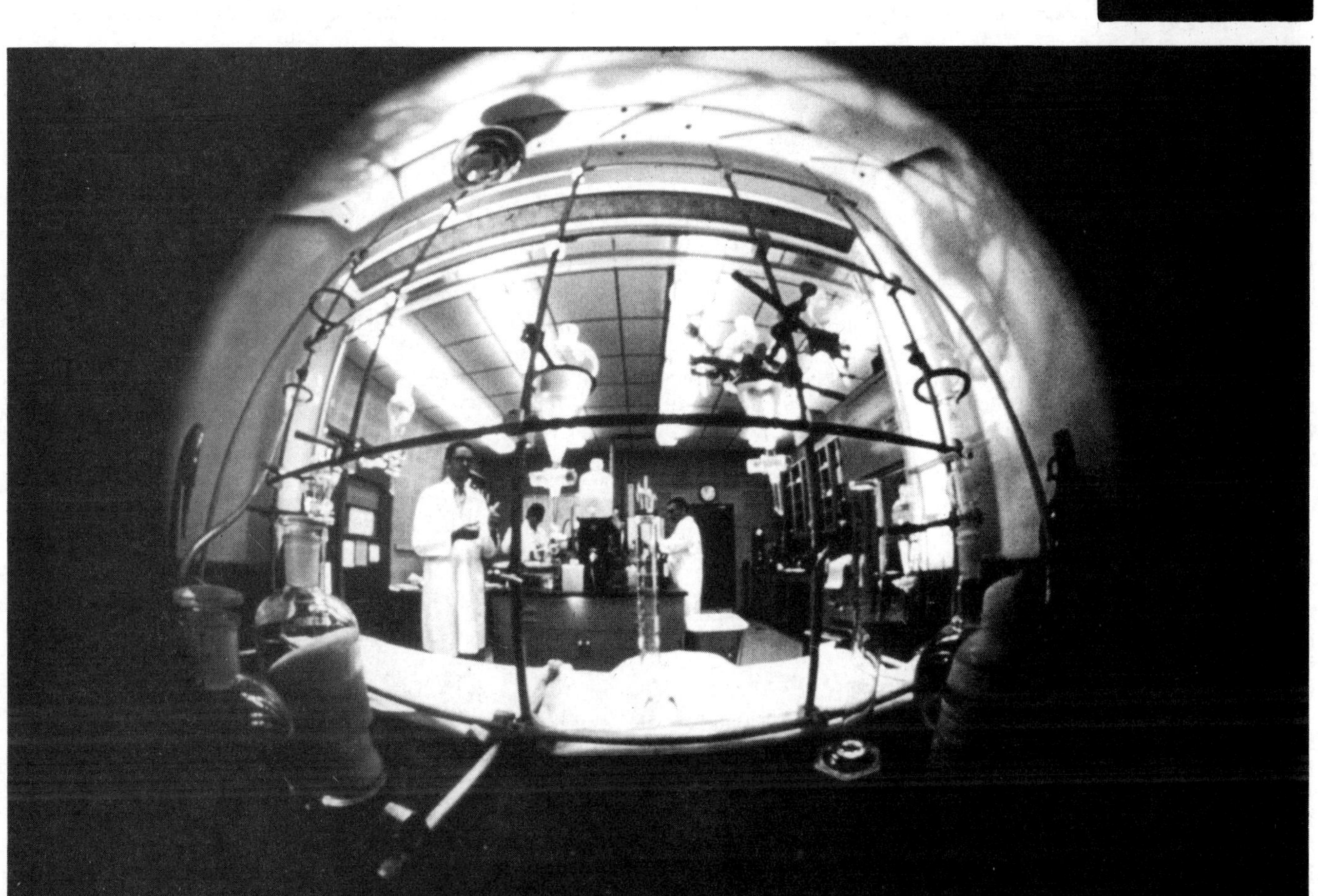

ing—the sort of policy considered in this unit—shape the entire spectrum of public policy in the United States.

Looking Ahead: Challenge Questions

The governments of most European representative democracies, such as Britain, France, Germany, Sweden, and Norway, spend a greater proportion of their nation's annual economic production than the U.S. government does. In other words, these European countries have a proportionately larger public sector than the United States and spend proportionately more on public services such as public transportation, public hospitals, the arts, and social welfare services. Even so, many, probably most, Americans think that our national government is "too big" and should be reduced in size by cutting government expenditures. Should the U.S. national government spend more, spend less, or spend about the same proportion of the gross domestic product as it spends now? Why?

The national debt has been growing in absolute numbers for most of the twentieth century, and it now totals more than $4 trillion. Nevertheless, the United States remains a stable representative democracy with one of the highest standards of living in the world and military and economic power second to none. How much attention should public policymakers pay to the total national debt and to annual budget deficits? Why?

Do you think that the U.S. government should require that those with higher taxable incomes pay a larger proportion of their incomes in taxes than those with lower taxable incomes? In other words, do you favor a progressive income tax system? Why or why not?

THE DAWNING OF THE MAKING-DO DECADE

JEFF SHEAR

In an instance of gallows humor, the stern and bespectacled chairman of the House Appropriations Committee, David R. Obey, D-Wis., launched into a budget hearing by announcing, "I've been informed by staff that the light at the end of the tunnel has been turned off until further notice."

The tunnel, of course, was the endless black hole of the federal budget deficit, which swallows about $200 billion a year—more than goes for education, science, law enforcement, transportation, food stamps and welfare.

Until the 1990 Budget Enforcement Act, Washington had little luck controlling the federal money sink. But with the passage of a second strong deficit reduction bill in 1993, the Clinton Administration can point to three successive years of decreasing costs.

There's a catch, of course. "If you deduct social security and medicare from the budget, the discretionary funds left over for the Clinton Administration [less the $200 billion needed to finance the debt] amount to about the same share of the gross domestic product as the country had in 1940," Rudolph G. Penner, a former director of the Congressional Budget Office, said in an interview.

Over the next five years, according to a recent report by the Center on Budget and Policy Priorities, "federal spending [will] constitute a lower percentage of GDP than in any other year since 1979."

The government's cupboard is plainly bare. The money available to Washington for cities, space research, defense and other so-called discretionary programs is capped. And those caps will grow tighter. At least two more hard-freeze budgets lie ahead. Congress has put a lid on the bottom line.

The 1990s are shaping up as the Making-Do Decade for Washington, a time of diminishing expectations, a zero-sum era, when government investment must be "budget-neutral." Pay as you go. To find money for welfare reform, for example, the Administration will be forced to slice into other programs.

How did we get here? The great tide of red ink began in 1981, when the federal government cut taxes by 20 per cent. According to the Office of Management and Budget, the tax cuts cost the federal government nearly $2 trillion in revenues in the 1980s.

Coupled with a splurge in military spending greater than in the peak years of World War II (about $2.6 trillion in constant 1991 dollars, according to the Defense Budget Project, a Washington-based group that tracks military costs), the nation's debt quadrupled. During the Reagan presidency, the deficit exploded from $735 billion in 1981 to more than $3 trillion in 1989, and was set on a path that has it veering toward the $5.5 trillion mark by the end of the 1990s.

HATCHET JOBS

President Reagan wasn't solely to blame. In the early 1970s, Congress used the "peace dividend" left over from the Vietnam war to log huge new social costs into the budget: an expansion of social security, the early growth of medicare. "We took that peace dividend, which was temporary, and created permanent promises," said Penner, who's now the national director for economic studies at KPMG Peat Marwick.

Those bills have at last come due, which means that federal spending will be measured out in coffee spoons. President Clinton requested $700 million for Head Start, an evergreen social program; he'll be lucky to get $250 million.

In May, Robert C. Byrd, D-W.Va., the chairman of the Senate Appropriations Committee, lamented to his colleagues, "I am not an alchemist—I cannot turn authorization wishes into appropriations dollars."

The diminished expectations on the spending side, however, don't mean that the deficit is in check. Health care and social security are outside the budget caps, and their costs are exploding. According to a 1991 study by the House Ways and Means Committee, for every $13 spent by the government on those

Richard A. Bloom

No street smarts? With deeper cuts in the federal budget, the nation's roads have fallen into disrepair. According to the House Public Works and Transportation Committee, 235,000 miles of federal highways eligible for government aid are in poor condition, as are 118,000 bridges.

Shrink rap: "There's been a 75 per cent cut in aid since the Reagan years," says Frank Shafroth, the policy director of the National League of Cities. Subsidized-housing starts, for example, are down from an average of 290,000 units in the late 1970s to about 74,000 this year.

over 65, only $1 is spent on those under 18. "We've put a hammerlock on that side of the budget that can invest in the future, and we've put no limitation on the money we will invest in the elderly," Frank Shafroth, the policy director of the National League of Cities, said.

Deeper cuts in discretionary spending will be neither easy nor popular. "There's a danger in not funding programs passed with great fanfare," Penner said. "That really is a cynical act." And one that feeds the public's distrust of government.

There is the additional concern that cuts may go too deep. "In terms of budgetary procedures, we have imposed a lot of impediments to keep us from doing things," an aide to a House committee explained. "But they may be things that we ought to do."

Reagan's philosophy that government is best when it governs least has exacerbated the problem for Democrats. Subsidized-housing starts are down from an average of 290,000 units in the late 1970s to about 74,000 this year. Roads have fallen into disrepair. According to estimates of the House Public Works and Transportation Committee, 235,000 miles of federal highways eligible for government aid are in poor condition, as are 118,000 bridges.

Cities have been whipsawed. "There's been a 75 per cent cut in aid since the Reagan years," Shafroth said. At the same time, he acknowledges a paradox. "Cities depend on the bond market," which responds favorably to deficit cutting.

At the everyday level, budget slashing will mean, for example, that lines at the passport office will grow longer and amenities offered by the national parks will disappear. The Library of Congress—the nation's (and Capitol Hill's) knowledge bank—has had to cut reading room hours by 17 per cent; its backlog for registering copyrights has grown to six months; exhibitions have been cut 33 per cent; and it's slashed jobs by 20 per cent. "Much important support for Members [of Congress] and committees [must] be delayed or scaled back," the library recently reported.

YOU CAN'T GET THERE FROM HERE

A "Dear Colleague" letter written by Appropriations chairman Obey in May neatly framed the irony. "Our future balance sheet will be determined by not only how well we do in reducing the deficit," he wrote, "but by how much of what we spend adds lasting value to our nation."

In its annual report, Congress's Joint Economic Committee pointed out that "international comparisons show that the United States has the lowest ratio of total capital investment to GDP of any of the major countries" in the Organization for Economic Cooperation and Development—among them the United States, Canada, France, Germany, Great Britain, Italy and Japan.

The situation clearly troubles Clinton. As Bob Woodward reports in his new book, *The Agenda: Inside the Clinton White House* (Simon & Schuster Inc.), Clinton angrily characterized himself as being boxed in by the budget. "We're Eisenhower Republicans here, and we're fighting the Reagan Republicans. We stand for lower deficits and free trade and the bond market. Isn't that great?"

Indeed, the Administration's signature programs hang in the budget balance: national service, reemployment and retraining, education and welfare reform.

Clinton may well feel betrayed, because the article of faith in deficit reduction has been its impact on national savings and interest rates. Lower debt means lower interest rates.

But that hasn't happened. From early February through mid-May, the Federal Reserve Board systematically raised interest rates. Today, the rates stand at the same levels as when Clinton was elected in 1992.

Why were interest rates heading back up if federal spending was going down? The answer from Wall Street is that fears of inflation were driving the Federal Reserve. If that's the case, then the effect of cutting the deficit was the opposite of what Congress intended: It spiked the recovery and triggered fears of inflation. Up went rates. That wasn't how it was supposed to work.

"The Federal Reserve's action raises the most serious questions about the viability of future policies aimed at deficit reduction," James K. Galbraith, a professor of public policy at the University of Texas (Austin) told members of the Joint Economic Committee in late May. He went on to ask: "What confidence can Congress now have that [its budget measures] will be allowed to have any positive effect on interest rates . . . ? Put another way, if the case for deficit reduction does not rest on the promise of lower interest rates, then on what premises does it rest?"

If the Fed's action adds a fast $100 billion to the 1994-98 budget deficit, as Galbraith expects, there may be little hope of light at the end of the tunnel. More likely, the Making-Do Decade will get worse before it gets better. This shortage of funds will try the Clinton Administration's ability to deliver on its promise of activist government. At the same time, it will test the Republican principle that less government is better government.

THE ECONOMY YOU CAN'T SEE

PAUL STAROBIN

Last year, the American economy produced $6.37798 trillion worth of goods and services, according to the Commerce Department's Bureau of Economic Analysis (BEA), the federal agency responsible for wrapping a tape measure around the economy.

Yeah, right. Don't be gulled: The precise-sounding number is as suspect as a Chesapeake Bay oyster left on the dock at midday. The truth is that nobody knows how big the economy is. Pressed by an interviewer, BEA director Carol S. Carson declined even to hazard a guess.

Nor does anyone know the level of family income in the United States, the extent of poverty or how many people lack jobs. And because nobody knows how much Americans earn and spend, nobody knows how much they save. Never mind that the government and others collect and publish statistics on every conceivable form of economic activity; that merely speaks to a modern society's wish for precision—or the illusion of precision. If you're looking for a reliable body of data, try baseball batting averages instead.

The main reason for the statistical squishiness is that murky mudpile known as the underground economy. BEA bean counters can count only the economic transactions that are reported to the government. That leaves out the zillions of transactions for which there isn't a paper (or electronic) trail. These include illegal activities, such as drug-peddling, as well as legal ones, such as babysitting, on which taxes or regulations are frequently evaded.

The underground sector wasn't born yesterday: Before America was even America, pirates were running West Indies rum past the colonial customs authorities. Tax evasion has been around as long as the tax man has—and prostitution and illicit gambling longer still. Nevertheless, there are many reasons to think that over the past quarter-century, the underground economy has grown at a faster pace than the above-ground economy has, and there's almost no reason to think this trend will slacken over the next 25 years.

Seismic changes in the nation's economy and its culture—such as a shift from manufacturing to services and increased popular discontent with government—favor the continued growth of the underground sector. This may be an uncomfortable truth for an often-moralistic society, but an underground economy has become a permanent fixture of post-industrial American capitalism, as much a part of the economic infrastructure as Wall Street's gleaming skyscrapers. It's as if a seedling from Nairobi or some other Third World spot has taken root in the sidewalk cracks of the world's most sophisticated economy.

A SAFETY VALVE?

If the underground economy is viewed as some sort of out-of-control dandelion, then the solution might be to redouble enforcement efforts to eradicate tax dodging and the like. But aside from certain predatory activities, such as drug dealing, the shadow sector may not be all bad. Many analysts are coming to view it as a safety valve, a generator of jobs and business opportunities that holds frayed communities together.

In a public housing tenement on the South Side of Chicago, for example, welfare mothers get together on Sunday nights and bake breakfast rolls for sale to schoolchildren. They don't declare the income to Uncle Sam because if they did, they wouldn't get their welfare checks, according to John Kretzmann, a Northwestern University social policy analyst who has surveyed the housing project residents about their off-the-books-activities. "Almost everybody has some [underground] economic activity going on," Kretzmann said. "I think it's absolutely necessary for people's survival that they have these activities."

As usual, California seems to be leading the way. A recent study by economists at San Francisco-based Wells Fargo Bank concluded, "California's underground economy has taken its place with foreign trade, biotech, entertainment and health services as one of the few growth industries during the worst recession to hit the state since the 1930s."

New York, however, probably isn't far behind. Last year, a six-part series in *The New York Times* revealed a dizzying breadth of underground activities in New York City—such as illegal immigrants peddling T-shirts and mood rings on the sidewalks in front of the Immigration and Naturalization Service office in lower Manhattan.

The United States has plenty of company: Shadow economies are flourishing in Eastern Europe and in such supposedly law-abiding places as Canada, where a surge in tax cheating and cigarette smuggling has ignited a national soul search on the ethics of economic disobedience. Canada's finance minister, Paul Martin, recently declared: "The underground economy is not all smugglers. . . . It's hundreds of thousands of otherwise honest people who have withdrawn their consent to be governed, who have lost faith in government." Sound familar?

Common sense suggests that data on the reported economy not only understate the true scale of U.S. economic output, but also overstate the amount of unemployment. If nearly everyone on government relief earns off-the-books income, then alarmist reports on a widening income gap between rich and poor may need to be toned down—except, of course, if the wealthy are heavily misreporting income. No doubt there are plenty of fat cats who don't report capital-gains income on some spectacular investments. (Illegal misreporting shouldn't be confused with legal tax avoidance, everyone's favorite sport in America.)

But don't put much stock in any of the estimates of the size of the underground economy. After all, secrecy and disguise are its defining characteristics.

The Wells Fargo analysis pegged California's underground sector at 18 per cent of the state's above-ground economy—but the author of the study, economist Gary Schlossberg, confessed in an interview that that number was no more than "a conjecture" based on a very crude analysis of the level of cash transactions in the economy. (Drug dealers, prostitutes and off-the-books carpenters usually don't take MasterCards.)

Using the same rubbery yardstick, Schlossberg estimated the national underground economy at about $1 trillion in 1993; that's nearly 17 per cent of the officially reported gross domestic product. Over the past two decades, other economists have produced guesstimates of the underground economy ranging from 1.4 per cent of the reported economy to 28 per cent. *(For a range of such estimates, see table.)*

The Internal Revenue Service (IRS) has thrown up its hands. Asked for an estimate of the underground economy, a spokeswoman said the IRS had long ago stopped trying to make any calculations. (Back in 1976, the IRS estimated the shadow sector at 8 per cent of reported economic output.) "It's too nebulous," the spokeswoman said. "You can't get a figure on it." One number that the IRS does spit out is the so-called tax gap—an estimate of the difference between what taxpayers should pay if they fully report all income from legitimate activities, and what they actually pay. For 1992 alone, the gap was pegged at $90 billion. (The BEA takes account of this estimate when it comes up with its economic-output calculation.)

THE PAPER MONEY TRAIL

With all the fuzziness, why do many analysts say the underground economy has grown rapidly over the past few decades? And why is it widely assumed that this trend will accelerate?

One clue is the curious staying power of paper money, just about the only acceptable means of payment, other than barter, in the underground economy. A little more than a decade ago, experts were hailing the arrival of the cashless society: "Paper currency will give way to electronic impulses," a soothsayer predicted. And in fact, the proliferation of plastic-money credit cards and bank debit cards now allows consumers to fill their carts at the grocery store and their cars at the service station without ever removing a bill from their wallets. But cash hasn't disappeared: In fact, on a per person basis, paper-money holdings rose from $179 in 1950 to $1,142 in 1990, a 538 per cent increase that surpassed the 440 per cent increase in inflation over this period. The underground economy isn't the only reason for the persistence of cash—some people just can't leave their homes without that $10 bill in their side pocket—but it is certainly a very prominent one. The illegal drug economy alone probably accounts for a good deal of the continued popularity of $100 bills.

And how could the numbers racketeers ply their trade without cash? Despite the spectacular growth of legal gambling outlets all over the country, many people still prefer to take their winnings in nontaxable form. A few months ago, Manhattan prosecutors busted "Spanish Raymond" Marquez—a legendary numbers king with a fiefdom of 41 betting parlors that reportedly grossed $30 million annually.

Another spur to the underground economy is illegal immigration. Illegals are heavily employed in activities that can easily be conducted off the books, such as peddling, taxi driving, day care and construction work. In New York City alone, unregulated garment sweatshops, drawing on a pool of cheap, often illegal immigrant labor, have multiplied from the hundreds to the thousands over the past 20-odd years, according to labor union estimates.

Then there are the changes that have rippled through the economy over the past quarter-century. The most important trend is a shift away from the production of tangible goods, such as automobiles and screwdrivers, toward the production of not-so-tangible services, such as business consulting and health care. It's usually easier for service providers than it is for manufacturers to conduct business without leaving a paper or electronic trail. (An important exception is financial services, which often do leave a trail.)

And with the decline of a manufacturing-based economy has come the decline of labor unions, which historically have offered protections against off-the-books business operators. What's more, jobs in the economy have been shifting away

THE SIZE OF THE UNDERGROUND ECONOMY

Estimates of how large the underground economy is vary widely, as shown by this comparison of studies over the past two decades by the Internal Revenue Service (IRS), academic economists Edgar L. Feige and Vito Tanzi, Federal Reserve Bank of Philadelphia economist Joel F. Houston, the Commerce Department's Bureau of Economic Analysis (BEA), U.S. Trust Co. economic consultant James J. O'Leary, author Harry I. Greenfield (from his book *Invisible, Outlawed and Untaxed*), the Labor Department and Wells Fargo Bank.

Study	Estimate (in billions)	Per cent of GNP*	Year of estimate
IRS	$145	8%	1976
Feige	600+	27	1979
Tanzi	118-159	4.5-6	1980
Houston	400	14.7	1980
BEA	184	5.4	1983
O'Leary	432	15.2	1985
Greenfield	350	6.7	1990
Labor	500	10	1992
Wells Fargo	1,000+	16.8	1993

***all estimates stated as a share of gross national product except Wells Fargo's, which is a share of gross domestic product**

SOURCES: Federal Reserve Bank of Philadelphia (except for Wells Fargo data)

from large firms to small ones, including sole proprietorships, that can more easily disguise their books.

SORRY, BIG BROTHER

Also nurturing the underground economy is the growth of a postindustrial regulatory regime that has put all sorts of business activities under some form of government control. Keep in mind that some economic actors operate underground principally to escape burdensome requirements—restrictions against pollution, for example.

The tighter the clamps, the greater the incentive for underground activity. Many analysts predict that increased government controls on the health care sector, now being considered by Congress, will spur the growth of off-the-books activities by doctors and others subject to new rules.

The White House has tried to deal with this possibility by calling for tough penalties—including prison terms—for doctors and patients who don't abide by new regulations. And yet, the Congressional Budget Office (CBO) didn't address the potential resort to underground activities as part of its economic and budgetary analysis of the Administration's health care bill. "I don't have any idea what the magnitude of this incentive might be," CBO director Robert D. Reischauer told a researcher for the Federal Reserve Bank of Minneapolis who recently published a lengthy piece on the underground economy.

Likewise, efforts to set tighter controls on the gun market could drive a lot of the activity underground—and not necessarily prevent criminals from getting their hands on weapons.

For evidence of the power of economic incentives—the law be damned—consider the drug trade. The inner-city toughs who peddle crack cocaine are, in a sense, following a basic law of economics. "Returns in the regular [legal] sector can't match the returns in the illegal sector," observed economist Harry J. Holzer of Michigan State University, who has long studied the employment market for minority youths. "These people are making a fairly straightforward economic calculus." A rational actor, of course, might also weigh the short-term rewards against the long-term odds of survival. But the dealers behave according to a famous maxim of British economist John Maynard Keynes: In the long run, we're all dead.

Although the drug trade has thwarted every attempt to eradicate it, there's not much popular support for legalizing drug use. Nor does there appear to be much support for legalization of prostitution—a first step toward bringing it into the above-ground economy.

Many analysts and ordinary citizens say that the solution to evasion of taxes on legitimate activities is stepped-up enforcement by the authorities. And why not crack down on all those unlicensed peddlers in New York City?

But before the enforcement squad is doubled and given loads of fancy new equipment, the side effects should be contemplated. "A world of perfect enforcement could be an intolerable place," economist Frank A. Cowell warned in an essay published last year by the Washington-based Institute for International Economics. Think of the shadow sector, Cowell suggested, as "an economic ventilation shaft to enterprises in danger of suffocation. Plumbing, decorating and vehicle repair jobs may get done that would otherwise be unprofitable under an inappropriately austere tax regime."

On the principle that it is more difficult to disguise spending than to disguise income, Uncle Sam may want to consider a shift away from the income tax to a value-added consumption tax. Some economists already back this step as a way to encourage more saving. If the underground economy can't be legislated, moralized or otherwise Big Brothered into oblivion, maybe it's time to reconcile ourselves to its stubborn presence.

THE DOWNSIDE OF DOWNSIZING

LOUIS JACOBSON

As Congress debates big cuts in the federal budget, some economists are quietly wondering how to trim government spending without triggering hardship for the rest of the economy.

The federal government directly accounts for about 4 per cent of America's gross domestic product, more than agriculture or communications. More important, its cash benefits, procurement orders and payroll checks ripple outward, multiplying in impact as they disperse. And so when cuts are made, people and companies are left with less money. For example, proposals to convert the food stamp program into block grants to states—which would cut $31 billion over five years—could endanger as many as 128,000 farm and food-processing jobs, according to the Agriculture Department.

With interest on the national debt now devouring $300 billion a year, virtually everyone agrees that spending cuts are necessary. But cutting astutely, not recklessly, is difficult. Many economists warn that programs with a small "multiplier effect" should be the first to go and that investments that boost the nation's long-term competitiveness should be spared. And cutting too much at the wrong time, some argue, could rapidly worsen an economic downturn.

First, the big picture. Economist Dean Baker of the Economic Policy Institute said that budget cuts and tax increases since 1992 haven't hurt the economy too much, partly because of the general economic recovery and partly because a period of low interest rates impelled many Americans to refinance their mortgages, leaving their cash flows unusually healthy.

The mortgage refinancing cushion won't last long, Baker said, and a recession could come before 2002. These conditions, he said, could double the normal drag on economic growth caused by spending cuts.

How bad it might get depends on how much is cut, and how fast. Daniel E. Sichel, an economist at the Brookings Institution, said that if Congress simply trims enough to offset its proposed tax cuts, the economy will probably create enough jobs and income growth to balance the federal downsizing, especially if the Federal Reserve Board jiggles interest rates accordingly.

But such cuts would not trim the deficit ($203 billion in fiscal 1994). If Republicans in Congress want to balance the budget by 2002, as their constitutional amendment proposes, much deeper cuts will be needed. These would have "a notable depressing impact," Sichel said. "If we're in a period where the economy is generally growing well, a cut of that magnitude, offset by the Fed, would not by itself generate a recession. But if for some other reason growth is slower, could that put the economy over the edge? Possibly." Even worse, he said, would be for politicians to procrastinate, forcing them to make massive cuts overnight in 2002.

Any economist's predictions, of course, are based on models that presume "all other things being equal"—a condition that never occurs in the real world. Oil shocks, recessions or sudden wars can throw forecasting models into disarray. On the upside, it's entirely possible that the economic benefits of tax cutting that supply-siders tout could dwarf any dampening impact.

The kinds of cuts also matter. Some cuts—reducing subsidies to industries, for instance—are likely to cause short-term misery in narrow sectors but, in the longer term, would make markets more efficient. Such cuts might even spur the kind of industrial shakeout that improves competitiveness and, ultimately, boosts long-term tax revenues.

Other cuts, such as trimming the bureaucracy, may not provide such measurable benefits, but their impact and duration may be limited because in time many laid-off employees will return to the private sector. (The impact, of course, would be uneven: Washington, for example, could lose 10,000 federal and local government jobs in 1995 alone.)

The most damaging cuts—as illustrated in a (perhaps somewhat self-serving) report by the House Transportation and Infrastructure Oversight Subcommittee—are those that weaken America's wealth-producing infrastructure, from roads and bridges to communications networks and education. To be sure, individual programs may be pork, and thus fair game for budget hawks. But on the whole, cutting sensible infrastructure programs, unlike eliminating subsidies or bureaucracy, may cause long-term, cumulative damage to the economy.

One of the complications is figuring out how much of what the public sector casts off will be picked up by the private sector. Historically, Baker said, when federal medicare spending has been cut back, private insurers have tended to increase their outlays—meaning that medical providers were spared immediate and serious economic pain. How a newly cost-conscious medical sector—or, for that matter, any private industry—will respond to cuts in federal spending is anybody's guess.

Perhaps the most intriguing issue is whether duties shed by the federal government will wind up at the state or local level instead. Ironically, for all the talk of "devolution" and a "new federalism," and for all the anger at government intrusion into Americans' lives, there are more than four times as many state and local employees (or "bureaucrats") as there are in the federal sector. The state and local government work force is almost 20 per cent bigger now than it was in 1980; the federal government's is only 5 per cent bigger.

Devolution to local and state authorities may make government more responsive and may reduce over-all employment costs. Perhaps even more important, said Gail Fosler, the vice president and chief economist at the New York City-based Conference Board, this is the first time in decades that the federal government has rethought its mission—a valuable exercise.

But while an expansion of state and local government would help cushion the macroeconomic effects of federal spending cuts, it probably won't reduce the size of government. And at the moment, it's not clear which goal is more important to American voters. "The real test," Fosler said, "is how happy people will be in two years, at election time."

CRITICS DOWN ON THIS LEVY

LOUIS JACOBSON

Few proposals are as likely to kick off the mother of all statistical food fights as the coming congressional battle over a capital gains tax cut. Because the outcomes of recent studies have differed wildly on the question of how such a cut might affect both economic activity and tax burdens, almost everyone can point to research that justifies his or her view.

TAXES

"No debate in public policy is more laden with the values of the participants than capital gains," said Ken Hagerty, a Washington lobbyist whose Coalition for American Equity Expansion is pushing for a capital gains cut.

Advocates of a cut have long argued that setting the capital gains rate closer to—and preferably below—the tax rate on ordinary income would get rid of an economic inefficiency, encouraging capital that's sitting in old assets to be shifted to newer and more-useful investments. Lowering the rate, they argue, could also eliminate what amounts to a double tax on corporate profits and might reap taxes that otherwise would have evaporated were the asset holder to die without selling (because many capital gains taxes are waived at death).

Opponents don't necessarily doubt this logic, but they do raise some contentious questions. First, can the benefits of a capital gains cut be had at a relatively low cost to the Treasury? If not, another mix of tax cuts might accomplish more good for less cost. And second, are taxpayers across the economic spectrum going to benefit? These are the questions that hinge on those complicated statistical models.

With so much disagreement, it would be helpful if the government spoke with a unified voice. But with capital gains, that's not always the case. The government's biggest tax policy shops—including the Treasury Department's Office of Tax Analysis, Congress's Joint Committee on Taxation, the Congressional Budget Office (CBO) and the Congressional Research Service (CRS)—sometimes "score" various aspects of the tax proposals differently.

While each office's techniques are justifiable on economic grounds, the arcane calculations have a track record of confusing far more tax novices than they enlighten. And independent tax specialists say that since the 1980s, each office has periodically made technical changes, some of which produced estimates more favorable to the view of the party that controlled their branch of government.

The two tax offices deny allegations of political influence. Other experts chalk up most differences to honest economic disagreements rather than conspiracies. "The staff doesn't cheat with the numbers—it's all done with integrity," said C. Eugene Steuerle, a senior fellow at the Urban Institute and a columnist for *Tax Notes*. The offices "often haven't been far apart in their estimates, but there have been periods in which their net cost for a capital gains cut becomes positive or negative depending on relatively small differences."

There's plenty of research to justify any point of view.

Here's why. Most economists agree that during the first year after any capital gains tax cut, a surge of Americans will sell (or, in the jargon, "realize") a lot of long-held assets. But just how big this "unlocking" will be—and how long this surge in "realizations" will last—is open to disagreement.

If the surge is big and long-lived—as capital gains advocates argue that it will be—the Treasury's revenue stream will not be gravely hurt, and might even increase for a while. (Even though a lower tax rate would be assessed, more items would be sold, helping make up the revenue shortfall.)

But many deficit hawks and populists argue that the level of asset sales will not remain high enough to make up for the revenue shortfalls caused by lower rates—and that could affect the government's ability to pay its bills. Opponents insist that lawmakers weigh the shortfalls of these "outyears" even though they may extend beyond the five-year budget "windows" that lawmakers typically use to weigh fiscal policy changes.

Into the statistical fray have stepped several federal offices. Gerald Auten, a Treasury specialist, said that his office and the Joint Tax Committee agree generally that the "unlocking" would increase revenues immediately after a cut is passed; they also agree that next would come a period when over-all revenues fall to 60-80 per cent of their prior level. Because there's "a lot of uncertainty," he added, the two offices' estimates currently differ by $8 billion-$10 billion.

Competing green eyeshades are also being donned elsewhere in the government. Jane G. Gravelle, the CRS's senior specialist in economic policy, has been a particular thorn in the side of capital gains advocates, who grilled her (politely) at a Senate Finance Committee hearing in February. She sided with those who predict lower levels of realizations than proponents would like to see and drew upon two scholarly papers (one by her, one by a pair of specialists now at the CBO) that she said used newer and more precise realization models.

Gravelle also cited another factor affecting the cost of a capital gains cut: indexing. With indexing, an asset holder would pay tax only on that portion of the increase in an asset's value that had nothing to do with ordinary inflation—potentially a big saving for asset holders and an equally big drain on the Treasury. Further obscuring the issue is the fact that revenue losses to indexing tend to be greatest in the outyears, where they may not necessarily be weighed by lawmakers working with a five-year window.

Cost isn't the only issue in dispute. The other big battleground is "distributional"—that is, which taxpayers benefit most from a capital gains cut. Capital gains advocates have so far had only limited success in fighting the perception that their proposals would benefit the rich, who disproportionately own the kinds of assets affected by a cut. But Margo Thorning, the chief economist at the American Council for Capital Formation, says that opponents often fail to point out that many middle-income Americans would benefit, too, including the employee-shareholders that Hagerty's group is trying to represent.

Proponents of a capital gains cut are pleased by statistics that take behavioral changes into account (sometimes called "dynamic" models). The big increases in realizations shown by dynamic models imply that higher tax bills will be paid in any given year (especially in early years) by the more affluent owners of capital—an indication that they're not getting a free ride.

By contrast, anti-capital gains forces favor a "static" approach that measures distributional effects without showing a jump in asset sales. Such models ascribe apparently lower tax bills to the rich—a factor that opponents could exploit in a public debate. Indeed, opponents like to argue that it's a bit disingenuous for advocates to suggest that people who clearly benefit from tax cuts are in fact shouldering a heavy, new tax burden.

On the distributional issue, the Joint Tax Committee and Treasury also disagree. The committee, which in the 1980s was devoted to a static model, now uses a dynamic system for distributional studies (a system adopted when the Democrats still controlled the committee). Treasury, after flirting with a dynamic model in the Bush Administration, has returned to a static model.

In the meantime, advocates of a capital gains cut aren't exactly thrilled with one of the few approaches that both the joint committee and Treasury agree on. In their technical assessments, neither office explicitly considers the long-term economic benefits of a capital gains cut, such as lower costs of capital, which some mainstream economists say could drop by 4-8 per cent.

Thorning, who supports a capital gains cut, acknowledges that estimating the impact of that kind of benefit is an imprecise endeavor. But, she added, it's also illogical to completely ignore it. "At least we could have competing estimates and see the figures side by side," she proposes. A reasonable suggestion, many would agree. But its ironic side effect would be to remove one of the last areas of simplicity in a maddeningly complex debate.

Takin' on the Bacon

Last November, Labor Secretary Robert B. Reich challenged Washington's think tanks to take on "corporate welfare." Now everyone's asking, What hath Reich wrought?

KIRK VICTOR

When Labor Secretary Robert B. Reich ended a speech to the Democratic Leadership Council last November by challenging Washington think tanks to come up with examples of "corporate welfare," he had little idea that his dare would set off such a fierce debate.

"I didn't expect the explosion that ensued," Reich said in a recent interview. "It's a vitally important debate to have at this point in the nation's history. Some business leaders, executives, called and warned me against using such provocative language. Their calls confirmed my suspicion that I was onto something."

In his speech, Reich pointed to a list compiled by the Progressive Policy Institute (PPI), a group affiliated with the Democratic Leadership Council, of subsidies and tax breaks for specific industries that will cost the Treasury $111 billion over the next five years. In a more recent study, PPI identified 120 programs and tax subsidies to "powerful industry groups" that, if eliminated or reduced, would produce $265 billion in savings over five years.

"I invite the other great think tanks of this city—the Heritage Foundation and the Cato Institute, to pick two at random—to add to the list their own examples of business subsidies that don't make sense," Reich said in the speech. "Since we are committed to moving the disadvantaged from welfare to work, why not target *corporate* welfare as well, and use the savings to help all Americans get better work?"

Jerry J. Jasinowski, the president of the National Association of Manufacturers, blasted Reich for using what he sees as a pejorative, misleading phrase. "The scrutiny is appropriate, but people ought to not be stupid about mislabeling what should be analyzed," he said in an interview. "I am tired of putting up with gross distortions of the facts in order to paint business in black hats. I mean, that's what this is all about, and it's stupid—plain old stupid."

Jasinowski said that there's a big distinction between tax provisions that benefit corporations and laws that govern welfare programs. Corporations have "to do something in order to achieve those benefits, which is not the case with respect to welfare," he said. "It is inaccurate and irresponsible to label any of these provisions corporate welfare."

But if Reich had chosen some less provocative phrase—"industry subsidies,"

John Eisele

Labor Secretary Robert B. Reich "I didn't expect the explosion that ensued."

say—the red-hot debate that's unfolded may never have gotten off the ground, Robert J. Shapiro, PPI's vice president, said in an interview.

The war over corporate welfare isn't simply a shoot-it-out story that pits the hired guns of corporate America against reformers of various ideological stripes. It's also another chapter in the never-ending tale of Washington hypocrisy. Some of the politicians who are now eagerly lining up to take a whack at corporate pork have, in the past, either encouraged such government booty or looked the other way as it was doled out.

"The dirty secret in this town for a long time is that both parties have been protecting subsidies for industries that have inordinate influence in this town, that fund people's campaigns," Shapiro said on CNN's *Crossfire* on the day of Reich's speech, Nov. 22. "It's not partisan. It's not ideological. It's not liberal or conservative or Democratic or Republican."

Reich's challenge, in fact, didn't just sting business lobbyists. Other top officials of the Clinton Administration seemed blindsided or peeved that Reich had helped ignite a heated squabble that could affect programs on their turfs. Indeed, because the notion of corporate welfare means different things to different people, the debate has sometimes veered considerably from the path that Reich presumably had in mind.

Critics of the Clinton Administration have used it as a vehicle to attack Democratic initiatives. "That speech that Reich gave was fine, but he should really be introduced to [Commerce Secretary] Ron Brown because Mr. Brown is Mr. Corporate Welfare," Stephen Moore, the director of fiscal policy at the libertarian Cato Institute, said in an interview.

The Cato Institute is one of the growing number of groups that responded to Reich's challenge. *(See box, next page.)* Its study identified 125 programs that subsidize businesses at a net cost of more than $85 billion a year, including 9 at Commerce that, if cut, would save well over $2.3 billion. (Of all the Cabinet departments, only Agriculture and Defense had a greater number of programs on Cato's hit list.)

Asked about the idea on the day of Reich's speech, Brown told a reporter: "I have not heard about that proposal; I'm not aware of it. As far as I know, it has not been discussed at the highest level of the Administration." When pressed as to why Reich would have advanced the proposal before a discussion of it within the Administration, Brown said, "I have no idea—I don't know the proposal about which you're speaking."

Despite repeated requests for Brown's current views on the issue, the Commerce Department's press office, which isn't known for being bashful in its dealings with the news media, provided no additional comment.

Then-Treasury Secretary Lloyd Bentsen was also dismissive of Reich's idea when he was asked about it on CBS News's *Face the Nation* a few days after the speech. Bentsen said that he hadn't been consulted about the proposal in advance. As for whether there was anything appealing about proposals to cut programs that assist corporations, Bentsen said, "I didn't find myself very excited about them, no, I didn't."

That Bentsen and Brown would be skeptical of Reich's idea surprises few of those who have worked on the issue. They invariably note, while asking for anonymity, that Bentsen, who became known as "Loophole Lloyd" while he was the chairman of the Senate Finance Committee from 1987-92, had led the fight for many of the tax breaks now being scrutinized and that Brown had lobbied to preserve the breaks as a top gun at the Washington firm of Patton, Boggs & Blow (now Patton Boggs).

Richard A. Bloom

Jerry J. Jasinowski of manufacturers' association "It's stupid—plain old stupid."

But the Clinton Administration is hardly alone in finding the issue a difficult one on which to be pure. Some of the leading Republican presidential contenders also either eagerly helped or didn't utter so much as a peep of protest as Congress passed legislation with subsidies for various companies and industries.

Sen. Phil Gramm, R-Texas, for example, didn't hesitate a second in adding his voice to the chorus of those calling for aggressive action to cut such subsidies. "The time has come in America to ask the 40 million people riding in the wagon on welfare to get out of the wagon and help everybody else pull, and I think the time has also come to ask corporate America to get out of the wagon and to end government subsidies to corporate America," he said in response to Reich's speech.

Gramm has even issued his own hit list—$217 billion in spending cuts over five years—to pay for the promised $189 billion in tax cuts that grew out of the GOP's Contract With America.

But critics point out that this is the same Phil Gramm who favored mohair subsidies, who fought for the superconducting supercollider and who supported spending taxpayer dollars on projects that reek of corporate pork—mesquite and prickly pear research, for example, and a plant stress lab.

Gramm was aggressively quizzed about those positions on NBC's *Meet the Press* in March. "Whenever we've decided how much money we're going to spend on agriculture research, I'm a Senator from Texas, and part of my job is representing my state," he said. "If we voted in the Senate to—on the issue of building a cheese factory on the moon, I would vote against it; I would fight against it. But if we decided to do it, I would want a Texas firm to do the engineering, I would want a Texas firm to construct the plant. I would want to use milk from Texas cows. . . . But I am—am I for the cheese factory on the moon? No."

Senate Majority Leader Robert Dole, R-Kan., has been conspicuously silent on the corporate welfare issue. His critics are quick to point out that like virtually all other congressional power brokers, he's been showered with lots of loot from businesses that are big beneficiaries of the kind of special breaks that are now the targets of intense scrutiny.

Take Archer-Daniels-Midland Co. (ADM). The Decatur (Ill.)-based agribusiness behemoth has made more than $150,000 in political contributions to Dole over the years, according to Cato. When Dole's wife, Elizabeth, left her post

SOME CHOICE CUTS OF PORK?

At least five organizations from across the ideological spectrum have weighed in with various prescriptions to reduce what Labor Secretary Robert B. Reich has branded "corporate welfare." The libertarian Cato Institute, the conservative Heritage Foundation, the moderate Progressive Policy Institute and an amalgam of groups that includes the conservative National Taxpayers Union and the liberal Friends of the Earth Inc., as well as the heavily labor-backed Citizens for Tax Justice and the Ralph Nader-affiliated Essential Information, have all put their stamps on the debate.

Here are some "choice cuts" drawn from the reports of these organizations and, where estimated savings have been included, the applicable dollar amounts:

Repeal the "section 936" tax credit. Many pharmaceutical companies and other firms benefit from this tax credit, which exempts a large chunk of the income they earn on their operations in Puerto Rico and other U.S. possessions. Repealing it would generate $19.7 billion in added revenues over five years.

Charge airlines and owners of private planes user fees to pay for all operations of the Federal Aviation Administration—including air traffic control—or privatize nonsafety services. This proposal would save $11 billion over five years.

Stop spending money on highway demonstration projects. Rescinding funds for demonstration projects that don't qualify for federal support under state transportation plans or highway grant programs would save $2.6 billion over five years.

End subsidies to large electric utility cooperatives. These subsidies—low-interest loans—have been criticized for benefiting ski resorts in Aspen, Colo., and luxury hotels in Hilton Head, S.C. Eliminating them would save $2 billion a year.

Repeal the 1872 General Mining Law. Signed by President Grant, this law permits mining companies to extract about $3 billion worth of minerals each year, royalty-free, from federal lands. Its repeal would generate as much as $1 billion in added revenues a year.

Eliminate the federal price support program for sugar. The General Accounting Office (GAO) has estimated that 42 per cent of this program's benefits have gone to 1 per cent of the nation's sugar farms. By propping up the price of domestic sugar, the GAO has found, the program costs U.S. consumers $1.4 billion a year in higher grocery bills.

Eliminate subsidies to the timber industry. The Agriculture Department's Forest Service builds roads in national forests—some 340,000 miles in the past 20 years—primarily to help private logging companies remove timber from the forests. The Forest Service also subsidizes such companies through below-cost timber sales. Eliminating these subsidies would improve the federal balance sheet by $700 million over five years.

as Labor Secretary to head the American Red Cross in 1991, Dwayne O. Andreas, ADM's chairman and chief executive officer, whipped out his checkbook and sent the organization $500,000, the San Jose *Mercury News* reported. (In the next two years, he sent similarly hefty donations to the Red Cross, where his wife is now a board member.)

ADM was cited in Cato's report as the chief beneficiary of two tax breaks for producers of ethanol, a gasoline substitute. The report states that the justification for the special treatment—reduced pollution and less U.S. dependence on foreign oil—is contradicted by an Agriculture Department study that called the $500 million subsidy "an inefficient use of our nation's resources." ADM declined to comment.

The *Mercury News* also reported that Dole went to bat for ADM as early as 1978, when he introduced a bill that exempted ethanol from the federal highway tax on gasoline—a subsidy that's cost taxpayers more than $4.6 billion, according to the Transportation Department.

"There's a direct connection between unwarranted tax breaks and the problems that we have in our current system of campaign finance and lobbying," Reich said in the interview. "Ninety per cent [of corporate welfare], if not 100 per cent of it, is a result of lobbying and campaign donations by particular companies and industries. It's potentially embarrassing for the Republicans because they are dependent on a lot of this money and they espouse a free-market ideology while distorting the market through unwarranted subsidies and tax benefits. You can't have it both ways."

But the Clinton Administration has been just as eager to please ADM as have others. Andreas, after all, has been decidedly bipartisan in dipping into his deep pockets and spreading his and ADM's wealth. He forked over $100,000 at a Democratic Party fund-raiser in June 1994 and, from July 1992 through March 1994, ponied up $270,000 in "soft" money to Democrats, according to a study by Common Cause. *(See NJ, 7/2/94, p. 1577.)*

Andreas and his company were handed some more good news by the Administration when the Environmental Protection Agency required that renewable fuels—such as corn-based ethanol—make up at least 30 per cent of the gasoline blend mandated for the nation's most polluted cities by 1996. (A federal appeals court recently struck down EPA's rule.)

Of the current crop of presidential candidates, PPI's Shapiro said, Richard G. Lugar, R-Ind., the chairman of the Senate Agriculture, Nutrition and Forestry Committee, has the best record on attacking corporate welfare. "He is not playing interest-group politics," Shapiro said. "He's playing idea politics."

Ralph DeGennaro, who's setting up a new group to fight government waste, agreed with Shapiro's assessment. "What Lugar did on farm subsidies is to show that political courage isn't dead in Washington," DeGennaro said. "He said let's phase out most agricultural commodity subsidies."

BIG MAC ATTACK

Sen. Richard H. Bryan, D-Nev., can't for the life of him figure out why such hugely profitable companies as McDonald's Corp. and ConAgra Inc. should be getting a stash of taxpayer money to boost the overseas sales of their products—from Big Macs to Peter Pan peanut butter. Bryan sees it as a prime example of corporate welfare run amok.

But in trying to end the program that dispenses public funds to boost corporate advertising, Bryan found that the politics of business subsidies aren't drawn along party or ideological lines. Some of those speaking most vehemently against his initiative were fellow Democrats.

Just before Congress adjourned for its spring recess, Bryan teamed up with Sen. Dale Bumpers, D-Ark., to try to kill the marketing promotion program, through which the Agriculture Department enters into cost-sharing agreements with nonprofit trade associations, farmer cooperatives and other groups to promote U.S. food and agricultural products in foreign markets, where competition is often subsidized. Bryan skewered the program as providing "the equivalent of food stamps for the largest corporations in America."

"You've got some of the largest businesses in America—good companies, nothing against the companies—that are receiving American taxpayer dollars to supplement advertising budgets that in some instances are tens if not hundreds of millions of dollars," Bryan said in an interview. "It just doesn't make sense to me at all. It's indefensible."

Cato's report also lambasted the program as a prime example of corporate pork. "In 1991, American taxpayers spent $2.9 million advertising Pillsbury muffins and pies, $10 million promoting Sunkist oranges, $465,000 advertising McDonalds' Chicken McNuggets, $1.2 million boosting the international sales of American Legend mink coats and $2.5 million extolling the virtues of Dole pineapples, nuts and prunes," it said of the $100 million program. *(See box, this page.)*

HOW SWEET IS IT?

Through its marketing promotion program, the Agriculture Department doles out dollars to boost the advertising budgets of some of the biggest exporters in the United States. Here are the top 10 beneficiaries:

Sunkist Growers Inc.	California	$6,611,500
E&J Gallo Winery Inc. (wine)	California	4,315,162
Sunsweet Growers Inc.	California	2,381,268
Brown-Forman Corp.	Kentucky	1,147,055
American Legend Cooperative (mink)	Washington	883,559
Dole Fresh Fruit Co.	California	820,022
Dole Dried Fruit & Nut Co.	California	757,840
Sun-Maid Growers of Calif.	California	736,000
Jim Beam Brands Co.	Illinois	713,000
E&J Gallo Winery Inc. (brandy)	California	630,140

SOURCE: Compiled by Essential Information, based on fiscal 1993 data from the the Agriculture Department

In the debate on the Senate floor on April 6, Bryan cited several other examples. He noted, for example, that since 1986, Omaha-based ConAgra has received $826,000 under the program. The company, which produces a slew of goods with household names (among them Butterball, Chun King, Country Pride and Wesson), racked up net profits of $462 million in 1994, Bryan said.

ConAgra's annual advertising budget is $200 million, Bryan said, and its chief executive officer made more than $1.2 million last year. "How in God's world do we justify . . . spending taxpayer dollars to supplement this program?" Bryan asked. "They can effectively handle their own advertising and promotion budget."

Bryan was no less bowled over that since 1986, $1.6 million in taxpayer money has gone to Oak Brook (Ill.)-based McDonald's Corp., which earned $1.2 billion in 1994, she said, and paid its chief executive officer nearly $1.8 million. The company's advertising budget, Bryan said, was nearly $700 million. A McDonald's spokesman did not respond to repeated requests for comment.

Lynn Phares, ConAgra's vice president for public relations and community affairs, noted that her company doesn't get federal money directly but through cooperative groups that allocate funds to firms that sell particular commodities in overseas markets. "It's not a very big part of a program that is budgeted at something like $100 million," she said. "Neither is it a very big part of our export business.

"This program is aimed at opening or expanding markets—it is not aimed at all at increasing market share of a particular brand," Phares said. "We have never lobbied on behalf of this program, but that doesn't mean that we don't believe it serves a valid purpose. I think the purpose it serves is to open markets for U.S. agricultural products."

"It's very easy to attack [the program]," Timothy J. Galvin, the associate administrator of the Agriculture Department's Foreign Agricultural Service, said. "They [the critics] don't understand the nature of the competition we face. The bottom line is not who we're subsidizing, but are we going to compete?"

That argument was echoed during the Senate debate by Barbara Boxer, D-Calif., who argued that "to cut a program that is working to increase our exports when we are approaching the 21st-century mark and exports are crucial to our economy—and promoting those exports is certainly crucial to that—I think it would be a very radical move."

Boxer's outspoken support isn't surprising, considering that California is by far the program's biggest winner of all states. Firms there collected nearly $21 million in fiscal 1993. Far behind, in second place, were New Jersey-based companies, which received $2.2 million. (By contrast, companies in Bryan's home state of Nevada got nothing.)

Sen. Thad Cochran, R-Miss., as staunchly conservative as Boxer is firmly liberal, joined her in defending the program. "Putting the sign of McDonald's on the floor of the Senate and suggesting this program is designed to subsidize McDonald's or any other particular firm is an outrageous distortion," he said during the Senate debate.

The Bryan-Bumpers initiative was rejected, 37-61. Of the four Senators who are seeking the GOP presidential nomination, only Lugar voted for the proposal. "The sacred cows of American agriculture continue to be protected," Bryan said in the interview. "This is kind of an 11th commandment of American agriculture that these programs are part of the Holy Grail. It [the vote] certainly shows the power of parochial politics."

THE PORCINE TRIANGLE

The debate over corporate welfare boiled over shortly after the conservative National Taxpayers Union (NTU) and the liberal Friends of the Earth Inc. joined forces in issuing a report that recommends cutting 34 federal programs to save $33 billion over the next 10-15 years.

Twenty-one Republican House Mem-

Richard A. Bloom

Progressive Policy Institute's Robert J. Shapiro "It's not partisan. It's not ideological."

Sen. Richard H. Bryan, D-Nev., a foe of the government's marketing promotion program "The sacred cows of American agriculture continue to be protected."

bers, including Majority Leader Richard K. Armey of Texas and Majority Whip Tom D. DeLay of Texas, signed a "Dear Colleague" letter that decried the NTU as a once-friendly organization that was now "serving as a front for the extreme environmental movement."

"What's happening is, there are vestiges of politics as usual and business as usual," said Jill Lancelot, the NTU's director of congressional affairs. "We very rarely agree with the environmentalists, but [the report] was a place of common ground. We want to cut wasteful spending, and environmentalists want to cut harmful [environmental] programs, so our goal is the same."

Pointing to the defeat of the Bryan-Bumpers proposal to end the marketing promotion program, Lancelot said that the only way to make headway in attacking corporate pork is with a broad, bipartisan coalition.

Activist Ralph DeGennaro "Political courage isn't dead in Washington."

In response to the "Dear Colleague" letter, James D. Davidson, the NTU's chairman, wrote to the 21 lawmakers who'd signed it and reminded them that 10 of them had been endorsed by the NTU Campaign Fund and that the NTU had just spent $200,000 on radio and television advertisements to support the passage of a balance-the-budget constitutional amendment—the No. 1 item in the Contract With America.

"We remain friends," Davidson wrote. "Friends enough to tell you when we think you are wrong and to hope that you will recognize your error and apologize for it."

But after attending a heated meeting of the Western Caucus in April, during which lawmakers blistered his group's role in the report, David Keating, the NTU's president, suggested that the experience may bring about a rethinking of the organization's strategy.

"There may be a strategic advantage to doing things differently," Keating said in an interview. "These [environmental] groups are so hated in certain parts of the country that it may not add anything to any effort [for reform] to do things jointly."

DeGennaro, who had been at Friends of the Earth and was a co-author of the report, had a different take. "I expect the western Members who have mining, grazing and water interests to stick up for their brand of welfare," he said. "What surprised me was that Armey and DeLay put the stamp of the Republican leadership on it. That shows that the Republican Party is not serious. They hate environmentalists more than they hate the deficit."

But some recently elected Republicans seem ready to seek cuts in corporate subsidies. "What it seems to me has happened is that a business-government complex has developed, similar to the military-industrial complex that President Eisenhower talked about," freshman Rep. Sam Brownback, R-Kan., said in an interview.

When questioned about the recent flap over the NTU's calls for reform, Brownback acknowledged that the outburst by his colleagues caused him some heartburn. "I can see some potential for a generational split on it [corporate welfare]," Brownback conceded, adding that he and several other lawmakers are working to put recommendations together, as is John R. Kasich, R-Ohio, the chairman of the House Budget Committee. "If we are ever going to solve this budget crisis—and we will—we've got to take on things like this. It's just too big an issue, too big a target, too important."

PPI's Shapiro agrees. "Over time, there will be a general disposition to find resources not only from social programs but also from special spending and, I hope, tax provisions for business. And you'll get a kind of accretion, so they'll knock off a couple each time they need some money. The most influential corporations will be able to retain theirs and others will lose. . . . If you do it on a piecemeal basis, then the weakest claims will go first—so you would expect Archer-Daniels-Midland to hold on to theirs for a while, for example, despite the fact that, perhaps, it is the single most egregious."

The other alternative, Shapiro said, is to get a consensus by creating a process—a nonpartisan commission, for example, like the one that has been used to close military bases—to enable an all-out attack against corporate pork.

Without such a commission or some other mechanism to provide political cover, corporate America's allies on Capitol Hill don't seem likely to suddenly switch sides. At the end of the day, bipartisan support for attacking what Reich calls corporate welfare may well be more illusive than real.

A CAPITAL IDEA, OR A FISCAL SAND TRAP?

LOUIS JACOBSON

Given the political fallout from the Senate's failure to approve a balanced budget amendment, capital budgeting—an approach that 47 states use to keep their budgets squarely balanced—might seem like a godsend. After all, setting up a separate budget for capital investments—which, depending on how you define the term, can include everything from bridges to educational grants—could theoretically help Members of Congress erase much, if not all, of the apparent federal deficit.

A small, bipartisan group of Members—mostly on the public works panels—continues to battle for capital budgeting. Yet the notion remains so enigmatic that a slew of ordinarily self-assured economists and think-tank specialists remain agnostic, perplexed at how an idea with such intuitive economic appeal can also open budgeting to so many perils.

State specialists say capital budgeting has worked outside the Beltway. But would capital budgeting be good for the federal government? The upside is clear enough. "There's a lot of myopia in government budgeting," said Roy T. Meyers, a former Congressional Budget Office analyst who is now a political scientist at the University of Maryland (Baltimore County). "One reason to do capital budgeting and planning is to look toward the future."

Capital budgeting does this by forcing legislators to think about how much they are spending on future investments, rather than current consumption. "More important than the size of the deficit is what expenditures go for," said Robert Eisner, a Northwestern University economist. "Congress is saying we should reduce the deficit to protect our grandchildren, when in fact . . . the way to protect the future is to invest."

BUDGET

At the same time, capital budgeting would rid current budget rules of a nagging economic implausibility. Current rules force long-term capital projects to be paid off in a lump sum in year one, even though their benefits will accrue for many years. Most proposals would allow highways and other such items to be paid off in small annual charges during the investment's normal life, much as a family might pay off a house or a company would depreciate the cost of a factory.

But while capital budgeting might foster wise federal investments, it would also open a Pandora's box. Among the problems:

- "Making policy for 40 years down the road," a private budget expert argued, "may not be a good idea." As poorly as the current system treats long-term investments, some economists fear capital budgeting might push the pendulum too far in the opposite direction, socking future taxpayers with the costs of programs they don't want—and never had any say about. For instance, if decades-old investments in hydroelectric dams had been made under capital budgeting rules, today's generations would be stuck not just with the ecological damage the dams caused but also with an annual assessment for the original construction costs.

Agreeing to expenses decades in advance could also tie the hands of future legislators who might have different preferences. This could be most damaging if old commitments prevented Congress from dealing with short-term ecomomic crises.

- Deciding what is and isn't an investment can be a challenge. Clearly a highway, a building or a pipeline is a capital investment. But a computer? A chair? A paper clip? What about a highway that turns out to be useless, or an expensive chandelier in a courthouse?

There's more. Should maintenance be included in a project's capital cost? Maintenance looks suspiciously like consumption, yet a highway or a building would be useless without it—and in the long term, maintenance can cost more than construction. There's no simple answer.

Even if a good definition of capital investment could be found, depreciation could still prove tricky. Should the government depreciate existing assets or only new ones? How about objects the federal government doesn't own (such as state infrastructure built with federal grants)? And if such intangibles as education or training are included, how does one depreciate them?

"Accountants can't make these judgments," a budget expert said. "Only Members of Congress can." But leaving it to them, most analysts agree, would be like turning 535 kids loose in a candy store.

- In the rush to eliminate current disincentives, capital budgeting might create new ones. For instance, if legislators reject the broader definition of investment and limit it to brick-and-mortar projects, legislators might choose to pay for more school buildings at the expense of teachers' salaries.

Worse, when governments no longer need to pay a project's full costs up front, a big deterrent to hyperspending is lost. (Unlike the federal government, states are constrained by the need to maintain good bond ratings.) In this way, a device designed to curb uncontrolled spending might unintentionally encourage larger deficits than ever.

- Because federal capital outlays are a small part of the budget, the deficit savings from pushing investments into a separate account may be underwhelming. Estimates of exactly how much vary based on the definition used. In 1995, the federal government will spend only $20 billion directly, plus $38 billion in state and local grants, for big, tangible projects. That's less than a third of the entire federal deficit, or 4 per cent of all federal outlays. (Defense Department capital projects, which many economists would bar from capital budgets, add $60 billion.)

Only after broadening the definition to include research and development ($69 billion, including defense) and education grants ($47.2 billion) is it large enough to wipe out the deficit completely. But defining capital investment so broadly is sure to be controversial. And if lawmakers decide to depreciate old assets as well (which would be the most honest course) the deficit changes might well cancel one another out.

So is capital budgeting worth it? The General Accounting Office advocates joint congressional-executive branch targets for long-term productivity investments (using a definition that allows various types of infrastructure, research and education outlays). But the agency rejects a separate capital budget, a new depreciation policy or a decision to explicitly permit deficit financing for capital projects.

And as much as both political parties would like lower budget deficits and higher investment, key deficit hawks are wary of capital budgeting's pitfalls. As a congressional aide said, "It will be a very uphill climb."

MARKET BASKET MIXUP?

PAUL STAROBIN

Thanks to a few decades of government regulation, Americans these days drive cars loaded with safety and antipollution devices ranging from air bags to catalytic converters. As anyone who has bought a car recently can testify, this stuff ain't cheap.

But according to the government, the cost increase caused by these devices has not been a *price* increase. That's right: For the purpose of calculating the inflation rate—the rate at which prices for the same basket of goods and services change over time—these mandates are treated by government calculators as quality improvements. Tell that to consumers who grumble about having to pay for the equipment.

Welcome to the strange world of the consumer price index (CPI). Federal Reserve Board chairman Alan Greenspan recently sparked a rip-roaring debate by suggesting that the CPI overstates the true increase in the inflation rate and thus the cost of living. The budget deficit can be greatly reduced, Greenspan told Congress, if entitlement and tax benefits pegged to the CPI are adjusted downward.

Analysts inside and outside the government agree that certain aspects of the CPI calculation method overstate the inflation rate. For example, there is the substitution effect: When the price of a product rises, consumers tend to look for cheaper substitutes. However, a switch to substitutes isn't factored into the monthly changes in the CPI, which is calculated by civil servants at the Labor Department's Bureau of Labor Statistics (BLS).

Then there is the new-goods problem. A fancy piece of, say, audio equipment, makes its first appearance on store shelves for a price of $1,000. A year later, improved production methods push the price down to $650. The price decrease may never be captured in the CPI because of a lag in incorporating new goods into the market basket examined by BLS price-watchers.

But, as with the automobile, there are also calculation methods that understate the inflation rate. Thus the great debate: On balance, does the CPI overstate or understate inflation?

There is a fellow in Washington whose expertise on this question is probably unsurpassed: Jack E. Triplett, chief economist of the Commerce Department's Bureau of Economic Analysis, which is charged with computing the size of the economy. Back in the mid-1960s, Triplett did his doctoral thesis at the University of California (Berkeley) on the question of how so-called quality changes in goods and services can be measured by price indexes. He has worked at the BLS and has written numerous research papers on the CPI controversy. One of them, published in 1988, declared, "I suspect that the CPI has, if anything, understated inflation in the last several years."

Asked in an interview for his current assessment, Triplett tactfully said that the CPI measurement issue was fraught with uncertainty, and he was reluctant even to speculate on the politically sensitive matter. He also noted that since 1988, the BLS has adjusted a few measurements that tended to understate inflation. But, he said, he's still not convinced that the CPI currently overstates inflation.

The measurement problems in a postindustrial economy are staggering. Consider medical prices. The point of the CPI is to measure changes in a fixed set of goods and services. But technology is rapidly changing the nature of drugs, medical equipment and treatment procedures. Although many researchers suspect that the CPI overstates the rise in medical prices, some suspect an understatement. Who can say with certainty?

And yet, on Jan. 10, in prepared testimony to a joint hearing of the House and Senate Budget Committees, Greenspan suggested that the CPI may overstate inflation by "perhaps 0.5 per cent-1.5 per cent per year. . . . Removing the bias in the CPI would have a very large impact on the deficit," he added. Greenspan is right about that: If cost-of-living adjustments in the tax code, social security and other federal programs were reduced to 1 percentage point below the change in the CPI, the federal government could save $150 billion over five years, according to Fed calculations.

Picking up on the Greenspan message, House Republican leaders said that the "technical" adjustment should be quickly made; House Speaker Newt Gingrich of Georgia even suggested that the jobs of BLS bureaucrats should be eliminated if the adjustment wasn't forthcoming. Lost in the shouting was this statement to reporters by BLS commissioner Katherine Abraham, a former economics professor: "It's not impossible that the CPI in total understates inflation."

Where did Greenspan get his numbers? They come from a paper prepared by a trio of staff economists—David E. Lebow, John M. Roberts and David J. Stockton—in the research and statistics division of the Federal Reserve Board. The economists reviewed the scholarly literature on measurements of the level of prices. They did no field research; they didn't, for example, go to auto manufacturers or physicians for price data. And they couched their findings in tentative language. "These estimates are by necessity extremely rough," they said.

Greenspan had suggested in earlier forums that the CPI might overstate inflation—as had the Congressional Budget Office. But the Fed chief had never before put a deficit-savings number on the table. (And, in fact, the paper makes no effort to calculate possible deficit savings. The researchers didn't begin with the deficit in mind; they were wondering whether the Fed could declare victory in its quest for price stability even if the CPI continued to increase.)

So what's going on? "Greenspan is very concerned with budget issues here," said Patrick Jackman, an economist at the BLS who specializes in the quality-measurement CPI issue. As ever, policy makers are desperately looking for painless deficit cuts, Jackman said; "it would be beneficial for them to say that BLS overstates inflation."

But would it be honest? The BLS hopes to convene a commission of outside experts to study the matter. Given the uncertainty and the pressure for politically correct numbers, that sure sounds like a good idea.

Weak Link

Reducing the federal budget deficit will free up credit and spur private investment. That's the conventional wisdom in Washington and the battle cry of a growing national grass-roots movement. But many economists aren't sure there's a strong connection between deficits and investment.

PAUL STAROBIN

It's been said a million times: The budget deficit is a drain on the pool of national savings available for investment—a sponge that soaks up scarce economic resources. Cutting the deficit will thus boost the productive capacity of the economy and better the living standards of the American people.

As conventional economic-policy wisdoms go, this one appears impregnable. In Washington, virtually all of the opposition to deficit reduction stems from the unwillingness of politicians to risk raising taxes or cutting spending. Although there is an understanding that fiscal sacrifices may cause some immediate economic pain, hardly anyone questions the chain of logic that leads from deficit reductions to more factories getting built to greater economic growth over the long haul.

Last year, this was the Clinton Administration's cornerstone argument for its big deficit reduction package; now, it's employed by proponents of a balanced budget amendment to the Constitution that the Senate is expected to vote on shortly.

Washington reporters, too, treat the deficits-curtail-investment proposition as something akin to a Newtonian law of physics. In a recent column bemoaning the modesty of President Clinton's deficit reduction program, *The Washington Post*'s David S. Broder wrote, "Clinton is planning to borrow at least $200 billion each year for the foreseeable future, draining the pool of investment capital."

But if policy makers and journalists assume that their beliefs rest on established tenets of economic science, they are wrong. The connection between deficits and investment has never been a matter of agreement among economists. Though their voices may be hard to hear over the din of cut-the-deficit cries, plenty of economists aren't convinced that the current budget imbalance is (to invoke another metaphorical cliché about the deficit) eating away, like a pack of termites, at the foundation of our economic house.

Economist Robert S. Chirinko of the University of Illinois (Urbana-Champaign) has surveyed some 75 years of studies on the question of what drives investment. He found, he said in an interview, that "there really isn't any" evidence that deficits curtail investment. "Whether deficits impale our children on the cross of debt is a big debating point" among economists.

For example, Washington's conventional wisdom holds that reductions in the deficit lead to cuts in interest rates that lower the cost of capital for businesses and thereby boost investment.

But according to economist Robert S. Pindyck of the Massachusetts Institute of Technology, "lower interest rates don't always lead to more investment." Pindyck and Princeton University economist Avinash K. Dixit, two of the economics profession's biggest wigs, are the authors of *Investment Under Uncertainty* (Princeton University Press, 1994), a book that fellow research economists are hailing as groundbreaking. Its main theme is that investment decisions are driven principally by perceptions of a stable, predictable business climate.

Also cutting against the grain is a new study by economist Steven M. Fazzari of Washington University in St. Louis. Fazzari looked at capital investments by major manufacturers from 1971-90 and found that investment was influenced quite a bit by a firm's sales and cash flow—and not much at all by interest rates. "So deficit cutting is not likely to stimulate investment through the interest-rate channel," Fazzari said in an interview.

In *The Misunderstood Economy*, to be published shortly by the Harvard Business School Press, Northwestern University economist Robert Eisner scolds journalists and others for their unblinking acceptance of the deficit reduction gospel. Eisner, long a vocal critic of deficit doomsayers, argues that increased government savings resulting from deficit reduction steps may be more than offset by shrinkage in savings by households and businesses. Therefore, deficit reduction won't necessarily increase the total pool of savings available for investment.

The prospect of increased capital investment isn't the only reason given for reducing the deficit, of course. Many fiscal conservatives believe that the government is simply spending too much on programs that don't work; many policy makers and analysts bemoan the budgetary burden of paying interest on trillions of dollars of federal debt.

And as the surprisingly strong performance of Ross Perot in the 1992 campaign suggested, deficit reduction has finally developed a grass-roots political constituency. Despite efforts by liberal Washington think tanks to promote a "public investment" agenda of government expenditures on roads, bridges, schools and the like, deficit hawks have controlled the political initiative since Clinton's election. Clinton was forced to scale back his campaign promises to expand public investment, and he has appointed fiscal conservatives to key economic policy posts.

As Chirinko noted, opposition to the deficit "has multiple facets to it, as well as a lot of political appeal. An individual can't run a deficit successfully, so how can a government? That has a great soundbite quality to it."

Moreover, many economists say that even if a link between deficits and investment is only a theory, it's a theory that makes a lot of common sense and has certainly not been disproved. In an interview, Harvard University economist Dale W. Jorgenson, a pioneer of the mainstream "cost-of-capital" theory that views interest rates as a powerful determinant of investment decisions, dismissed Fazzari's study as "advocacy stuff." He noted that Fazzari's work has been sponsored by the Economic Policy Institute, a liberal Washington think tank with close ties to organized labor and a frequent publisher of contrarian views on the deficit.

"I'm a deficit hawk," Jorgenson added. The 1980s was "a tremendous catastrophic era in fiscal policy; we have to correct that."

CAUSE AND EFFECT?

In theory, the relationship between budget deficits and fixed investment—new factories and equipment—works like this: The federal government competes with private-sector borrowers in the credit markets for a scarce pool of savings. Because the government always gets the funds it needs (investors know Uncle Sam won't default), an increase in its borrowing tends to crowd out private borrowers, forcing them to pay higher interest rates if they want funds. That increases the cost of capital to a business. As a result, fewer ventures are projected to be profitable, and fewer factories get built.

Likewise, a reduction in government borrowing is supposed to lower interest rates and thus the cost of capital by dampening competition for funds in the capital markets.

But skeptics say they have located weak links in this chain of logic.

Ohio State University economist Paul Evans, a self-described Republican conservative, has pored through data on budget deficits and interest rates during the 1980s and other periods, not only in the United States, but also in Canada, France, Germany, Japan and the United Kingdom. His conclusion? "You can pick your period, and you won't find any strong relationship between budget deficits and interest rates. . . . I really don't know exactly why," he said in an interview.

Evans's findings place him well within the mainstream of the economics profession; Chirinko wrote recently in a letter to this reporter summarizing his survey of 20th-century economic research that "the deficits-interest rate link has been the subject of much debate, and the empirical evidence studied by academics has been inconclusive."

Paul Starobin

Are lower budget deficits the key to greater investment in new factories and equipment? Or are other factors, such as perceptions of a stable business climate, more important?

A possible explanation, according to Evans, is that the capital markets are so huge that even changes in government borrowing patterns aren't all that important. Another possibility is that interest-rate changes are mitigated by international capital flows. As Chirinko suggested in his letter, "To the extent that funds flow across national borders, the higher interest rates induced by government deficits would attract foreign funds, replacing the funds lost to the government and lowering interest rates toward their previous level."

Hold on. Didn't interest rates start dropping as soon as Clinton began talking seriously about a deficit reduction package?

Since the November 1992 election, the interest rate on 30-year Treasury bonds has fallen by nearly 2 percentage points—a significant drop for which the Clinton Administration has claimed credit, on the theory that the prospect of lower future deficits led bond-market investors to expect less competition for private savings.

But economists caution that there may be other explanations. Bond-market investors may also have been reacting to expectations of lower inflation or continued slow economic growth. And now that the economy is picking up steam, interest rates may start to rise just as the deficit reduction legislation kicks in.

Most economists attribute a portion of the interest-rate decline to the Administration's deficit reduction program—but not necessarily the lion's share. Gordon Richards, the chief economist for the National Association of Manufacturers (NAM), said the Administration could legitimately claim credit for about a third of the decline in the 30-year Treasury bond since the election.

Whatever has caused the drop in interest rates, they are now very low. Won't this spark a boom in investment? Common sense suggests that if you cheapen the price of a product, more of it will be consumed. It is clear, for example, that the past year's boom in home mortgage refinancings and residential construction was triggered by a sizable drop in mortgage rates.

But if economists can easily agree that the housing sector is extremely sensitive to interest-rate changes, there's quite a bit of disagreement about the interest-rate sensitivity of decisions to build factories and undertake other long-term business investments that might substantially increase productivity and growth.

In the early 1960s, Harvard's Jorgenson wrote a seminal paper that provided a mathematical method for relating changes in the cost of capital to changes in investment. He found that the cost of capital—which includes interest rates—had a great deal to do with investment. A great many economists and business-school professors have followed in his wake, creating a powerful school of "cost-of-capital" adherents who tend to believe that deficit reduction will have a big impact on investment. (Some of them are also fervent advocates of reducing the capital gains tax rate as an investment spur.)

In *Investment Under Uncertainty*, economists Dixit and Pindyck offer a new take on cost-of-capital theory. They argue that investment decisions by businesses cannot easily be reversed but can usually be postponed. Therefore, there may be a financial value in waiting for better information about the economic environment before committing to a major investment. The key role for government policy makers, they argue, is to help reduce uncertainty by promoting a stable climate for investment, including a clear sense of economic policy direction.

Although Jorgenson said that he hasn't revised his view that the cost of capital is "still an extremely important consideration," he called the Dixit and Pindyk book "the most important work in this area in the last six decades."

According to Pindyk, controlling the deficit may make for "a more stable economy" by reassuring jittery bond investors who sometimes worry that the government will take rash action, such as printing truckloads of new money, to get out from under debt. But he doesn't see much of an investment bang from lower interest rates. "There's a long history of attempts to build econometric models of investment," Pindyk said, and the model builders "have always been surprised that interest rates have never seemed to have that big an effect on investment. The only sectors where interest rates do seem to matter is housing and maybe automobiles."

Pindyk suspects that uncertainties over the prospects of various Clinton Administration initiatives—particularly its health care reform proposal—are delaying corporate investment decisions.

Another challenge to the cost-of-capital model comes from economists who contend that investment is driven principally by a firm's financial health and strategic vision and by the over-all strength of the economy. Many of these economists are disciples of John Maynard Keynes, the British economist who advocated deficit spending as a means of stimulating economic activity.

Economist Fazzari, an unapologetic Keynesian, analyzed the capital-spending patterns of some 5,000 U.S. manufacturing firms that accounted for nearly half of U.S. fixed capital investment from 1971-90. His goal was to measure the sensitivity of investment to three variables: a firm's growth in sales, a firm's internal cash flow and change in the cost of capital.

"What I find," he said in an interview, "is that the sales and cash-flow variables have very strong effects on investment, while the interest-rate variables have weak if any impact on investment. I'm not saying that when government borrowing increases, interest rates don't go up—they might—but the higher interest rates don't have the expected negative effect on investment."

Fazzari doesn't expect that the Clinton deficit reduction program will yield much of an investment bonus, and he's not alone. "In reality, investment is far more of a strategic decision than a financial one," said David A. Levy, director of economic forecasting at the Jerome Levy Economics Institute of Bard College in Annandale-on-Hudson, N.Y. The Levy Institute is a sponsor of Fazzari's research.

Some business executives agree. "I think interest rates are kind of a second-order discussion item," said George Sollman, president of Centigram Communications Corp., a midsized telecomunications firm in California's Silicon Valley. "In our class of business, the issues of quality management, strategic planning, product positioning, will probably be more important than interest rates."

And Philip Caldwell, the former chief executive officer of Ford Motor Co., said: "The first factor, of course, is, why do you want to make the investment in the first place? What are your hopes and aspirations? Interest rates, present and forecast, are one of the economic factors that are typically built into the analysis. . . . I don't think it is necessarily the determinant factor."

George Sollman, who heads a telecommunications firm Interest rates are secondary to other considerations.

A POLITICAL STEAMROLLER

Let's go back to basics. As every first-year economics student learns, there is a fundamental identity between savings and investment: The level of investment is equal to the level of savings.

There are three basic components of national savings: the savings of the government, the savings of households and the savings of business, including profits. A budget deficit represents, in this sense, "dissavings"—money that is not being saved for investment. So, if the deficit is reduced, then the national savings pool is expanded, right?

This is the source of all the deficit-as-a-drain metaphors that have been employed by analysts and news organizations. As White House adviser David R. Gergen wrote in a 1992 *U.S. News & World Report* editorial in support of a balanced budget amendment to the Constitution, "Federal deficits have sucked in roughly two-thirds of our private savings," and "as a result, our rate of gross investment has been too low."

But as Eisner points out in *The Misunderstood Economy*, this is too simple a picture. What is often not taken into account is the possibility that a reduction in the deficit will trigger offsetting reductions in the savings of businesses and households. For example, a tax on corporate profits could reduce business savings, and a cut in government entitlement programs that reduced the income of beneficiaries could reduce their household savings.

Among sophisticated economists, the real debate is over the size of the offset. At one extreme, a group led by Harvard's Robert Barro argues that the offset is 100 per cent—that changes in the deficit have no effect on total savings. The idea is that taxpayers are super-rational creatures who match their level of savings to the government's. Suppose, for example, that the government decided to borrow $1 billion more in the credit markets. In Barro's way of thinking, taxpayers will increase their savings by that sum in the expectation that they will eventually have to pay higher taxes to finance the government's increased borrowing.

Many economists view this theory as nutty; lots of deficit hawks argue that every dollar of deficit reduction yields a 70 or 80-cent increase in the pool of national savings.

Not all deficit reduction dollars may be alike in their impact on investment. The central element of the 1993 Clinton package was an income tax hike on the wealthy that Treasury has projected will raise $125 billion over five years. But how will the rich pay for the tax increase: by cutting into their savings or by paring back their consumption?

John Eisele

Van Doorn Ooms of the Committee for Economic Development Deficit reduction "remains our most powerful policy tool."

Notwithstanding their professed optimism about the long-term economic benefits of the deficit reduction plan, Administration policy makers privately acknowledge that nobody really knows the answer. "We hope that it won't all come out of savings because then you don't increase investment," an Administration economist said. "On the other hand, we hope that it doesn't all come out of consumption because the economy is not yet that strong."

Jorgenson predicted a sharp drop in savings by wealthy taxpayers who, he pointed out, are the principal savers in the household sector of the economy. The Clinton plan "is not going to make a heckuva lot of difference" to investment, he suggested. Other economists expect that about half of the new tax bill will be paid from savings and the rest from reduced consumption.

Economist Van Doorn Ooms of the Committee for Economic Development, a business-supported research group that has long championed deficit reduction as a spur to investment, says the Clinton program is working just as the conventional "crowding out" theory predicts. Even with all the "slippages," deficit reduction "remains our most powerful policy tool for trying to increase long-term income and living standards in the United States," he said.

Current data on business investment certainly don't contradict Oooms. Capital spending on new plant and equipment increased by 7 per cent in 1993 on the heels of a 3.4 per cent increase in 1992, according to the Commerce Department. A Commerce survey of business plans forecast a 5.4 per cent increase in 1994.

But some economists attribute the capital-spending boom not so much to deficit reduction as to the surge in the stock market, which makes it cheaper for companies to raise capital, and to cyclical factors rooted in the economy's recovery from the 1990 recession. If the recovery slows in the latter half of 1994, as some economists predict, then capital spending could drop sharply.

Although plenty of economists entertain doubts about the alleged connection between deficits and investment, Eisner has been almost alone in waging a high-profile war against it—to the point that some analysts, such as Richards of the NAM, write him off as an ideologue. The news media, meanwhile, have showered attention on deficit hawks such as investment banker Peter G. Peterson, author of *Facing Up: How to Rescue the Economy From Crushing Debt and Restore the American Dream* (Simon & Schuster Inc., 1993) and the subject of a recent profile on CBS's *60 Minutes*.

It may be that cautious economists prefer that policy makers err on the side of deficit reduction; maybe it won't cause a big investment boom, but the experiment is worth trying. It may also be, as Levy suggested, that many economists simply don't like seeing the government awash in an ocean of red ink.

And now that deficit reduction finally seems to be developing a grass-roots constituency—mobilized by Peterson and such groups as the Concord Coalition, the Washington-based lobby started by former Sens. Warren Rudman, R-N.H., and Paul E. Tsongas, D-Mass.—some economists may be hesitant to throw themselves in front of a political steamroller. "The deficit has become a metaphor in people's mind for everything that is wrong with the economy and the government," Levy said. "There have been hard times for a lot of people, and this has become the embodiment of what they're angry at."

Anger over fiscal laxity is one thing. But how will the citizenry feel if the sacrifices that experts urge to reduce the dreaded deficit fail to produce the promised economic payoff? Some years down the road, the economics profession may find itself ducking for cover.

Thrift Begins at Home

In the view of some economists, the answer to ruinous budget deficits may lie in forcing Americans to put more of their own money into savings. Not surprisingly, the idea hasn't caught fire with politicians.

PAUL STAROBIN

If the government can't save money, why not make the people do it? In despair over the prospects of coming to grips with the budget deficit, a small band of intrepid idea merchants is suggesting that a mandatory private savings program may offer a way out of the economic calamity threatened by the tidal wave of government red ink.

The real problem with the federal budget deficit, they say, is that it soaks up the pool of national savings available for investment. If steep tax hikes and deep spending cuts are unacceptable to politicians and the public—and would anyone like to argue to the contrary?—then citizens should be forced to tighten their belts and provide the savings themselves.

"I firmly believe this," said Robert E. Litan, who recently joined the Justice Department but before that, as a Brookings Institution economist, solicited support for a proposal he had crafted that would require taxpayers to save a certain percentage of their incomes each year.

"I think of it as less instrusive than a tax increase," said Paul M. Romer, an economics professor at the University of California (Berkeley) who has been touting mandatory savings to groups including the National Governors' Association, whose members include his father, Colorado Democrat Roy Romer.

Also endorsing a form of mandatory savings is economist Barry P. Bosworth of Brookings.

Although Litan, Romer and Bosworth are well-respected mainstream economists, they walk the mandatory-savings plank at their peril: Romer got a letter from an outraged citizen branding him a Communist, and Litan had his proposal labeled "sick and wrong" by a fellow economist. Never mind that Romer is a card-carrying free-marketer who trained in the University of Chicago's economics department, which is as committed to capitalism as the Vatican is to Catholicism.

Mandatory savings hasn't won support from politicians, either. But others are intrigued. Romer has piqued the interest of the business-supported Committee for Economic Development (CED), a New York City-based research group that has long warned of the link between continued deficits and the shrinkage of the savings pool. The CED plans to explore mandatory savings as part of a broad study of savings and pension plan issues.

"We're starting to think the unthinkable," said Van Doorn Ooms, the CED's research director and a former chief economist of the House Budget Committee. "A very interesting idea," said Bill Beeman, the CED's director of economic studies. "From my personal perspective, the major economic problem in this country is low savings."

The data certainly look dark. The national savings rate—total savings by households, corporations and the government as a share of economic output—plunged from an average of about 8 per cent in the 1960s and 1970s to 4 per cent in the 1980s and 0.6 per cent in 1992.

Mainstream economists almost universally agree that the single best step toward boosting the rate would be another major round of deficit reduction. But the cause of deficit reduction seems politically exhausted. Congress removed the boldest aspects of the deficit reduction plan proposed by President Clinton earlier this year, and his health care reforms—although billed by the Administration as a deficit cutter—contain costly new entitlements.

Perhaps the happy coincidence of self-interest and public interest that's generally required to close deals in Washington will be found on Wall Street, whose mutual fund managers and stockbrokers stand to reap fees from a program that would fatten the accounts of their customers. Securities firms have long been cheerleaders for tax breaks to spur private savings, and sure enough, Litan's proposal has stirred interest from several brokerages.

Marc E. Lackritz, the president of the Securities Industry Association, said in an interview that mandatory savings was a "provocative idea" but that he wasn't quite ready to climb onto this bandwagon. "Personally, I get worried about gov-

From *National Journal,* October 30, 1993, pp. 2592-2594.

ernmental mandates about almost anything—particularly with respect to individual behavior," Lackritz said.

But as Romer sees it, mandatory savings would reinforce the conservative ethic of personal responsibility.

Many Americans aren't saving enough for retirement and can't expect to live well on social security alone, he said. So, unless they're forced to save, they're bound to come clamoring to the federal government for help. "What's really at stake here is that we're moving into a system in which large numbers of people in the United States consume their paycheck and expect the government to take care of all of their needs after they retire," Romer said. "My argument is that individuals really need to take responsibility for themselves. You can't just free-ride on the safety net."

Darn right, Bosworth seconded: "People are too myopic. . . . Society has a right to require them to save more for their retirement than they would want to."

Of course, additional private savings might be encouraged by the creation of voluntary programs, along the lines of individual retirement accounts. But mandatory-savings advocates say that such initiatives wouldn't do much to bolster the national savings rate because they generally rely on tax breaks that deprive the Treasury of revenues.

John Eisele

Economist Robert E. Litan
Mandatory savings beats having "your benefits cut [or] your taxes increased."

MAKING IT WORK

There are many ways to construct a mandatory savings plan—and the architects are still grappling with difficult design problems.

Romer would start with the adjusted-gross-income line on the individual income tax return. From that number, which represents income before personal deductions and exemptions, the taxpayer would subtract $20,000. From the amount that's left, the taxpayer would have to set aside some portion—say 10 per cent—in a government-approved savings vehicle, such as a stock or bond mutual fund, from which the money could not be removed until retirement. What if you contributed less than 10 per cent to the account? The Internal Revenue Service would dun you for the shortfall.

But Romer's is a gross savings plan; a taxpayer conceivably could meet its requirements without saving more money, simply by shifting assets from an existing account or investment into a government-approved account.

To counter that problem, Litan would go a step further and impose a net savings requirement. Under his plan, as laid out in a new article in *The Brookings Review*, co-authored by Brookings economist William G. Gale, taxpayers would have to calculate how much money they've saved by subtracting sales of assets from their purchases during the year. For example, a person who invested $10,000 in a mutual fund and sold $3,000 worth of stock would show a net savings of $7,000.

The savings requirement would be progressive: A taxpayer might be required to have a net savings of 4 per cent of income between $20,000 and $40,000, 6 per cent between $40,000 and $60,000 and so on. Withdrawals would be permitted for retirement and perhaps also for contingencies such as large health care expenses and college bills.

And the payoff? In their *Brookings Review* piece, Litan and Gale calculate that a broadly defined net savings requirement could boost the household savings rate by an amount equal to 4.1 per cent of economic output. "Perhaps more important," they write, "the estimated increases are roughly in line with projected future deficits, suggesting that the effects of deficits on national savings could be largely offset by net savings requirements."

A net savings plan raises formidable administrative obstacles, though. Not least, taxpayers would have to produce reams of documents on their purchases of assets. So many basic questions remain to be answered that Gale—unlike Litan—isn't willing to endorse a net savings proposal at this point. "This is not a proposal that we can walk down to the Hill and say, 'We can do this now,' " he said in an interview.

Bosworth recommends a third approach: He would require employers to deduct a portion of an employee's gross wages—about 10 per cent—and put the funds into a pension plan. In effect, this would be a return to a system of employer-sponsored pension plans that many firms have abandoned in recent years in favor of voluntary 401(k) plans and the like, which permit workers to make tax-deferred contributions to retirement funds, typically bolstered by company matching contributions.

The problem with the 401(k) type of plan, Bosworth said, is that it's not compulsory, and so many workers either don't participate or make only a small contribution. And many workers, particularly in the higher income brackets, use the plans as a tax-avoidance scheme. He frets, for example, about "liberal conditions under which you can remove your money when you change jobs." And he is worried about new data indicating that lower-income workers aren't taking much advantage of 401(k) plans.

Hold on, says Boston University economist Laurence J. Kotlikoff: "We already have a forced, mandatory savings program—it's called social security."

The difference, of course, is that the payroll tax every worker must pay into social security doesn't go into a private savings account of the sort contemplated by Romer. The money is used partly to meet the program's obligations to the current generation of retirees and the rest, in effect, to finance the government's spending habits.

If we're going to have a debate about mandatory savings proposals, Kotlikoff said, "we ought to consider seriously" schemes for privatizing social security—that is, funneling the cash from payroll taxes or some other financing device into private retirement accounts. Kotlikoff, who offered pointers to the Clinton campaign, is currently doing a study for the

John Eisele

Committee for Economic Development's Van Doorn Ooms "We're starting to think the unthinkable" about savings.

World Bank on privatized social security plans.

Chile has made the switch from a social security-type plan to a scheme under which workers must place 10 per cent of their monthly earnings into private savings accounts managed by a government-approved and regulated financial intermediary. "Half of Latin America appears to be going this route," economist Peter Diamond of the Massachusetts Institute of Technology said in an interview. "The catch is, in most of these other countries, it is done in the context of a bankrupt social security system. We don't have a bankrupt social security system."

Among conservatives, the idea of privatizing social security is not so new. Back in 1985, analyst Peter J. Ferrara edited a volume for the libertarian Cato Institute in Washington in which he called for a radical reform to permit workers to contribute up to 20 per cent of their social security taxes to "Super IRA" savings accounts.

WORRYWARTS?

Litan isn't convinced that mandatory savings is a political impossibility, given the even-greater unattractiveness of the alternatives. Before he joined Justice, he gave numerous speeches to outside-the-Beltway audiences on mandatory savings. " 'You can either have your benefits cut, your taxes increased, or the government can force you to save more,' " he said he told them. Put that way, the listeners "all liked the mandatory requirement."

But politicians haven't exactly jumped on this bandwagon. Litan thought he had a taker in Sen. Bill Bradley, D-N.J., who hasn't hesitated to talk about the need to sacrifice sacred cows, such as the mortgage interest tax break, on the altar of reducing the deficit and boosting national savings. Earlier this year, the economist took a seat next to Bradley on an airplane and filled his ear with mandatory-savings talk for nearly an hour. Bradley took "detailed notes," Litan recalled, and not long afterward, Gerald F. Seib of *The Wall Street Journal* wrote a column that seemed to put Bradley on board.

"Do you want tax-and-spend or save-and-invest?" Bradley was quoted as asking. Money in a mandated savings account would be "available for whatever banks and financial institutions are going to use it for, which means they're going to put it back in the economy, maybe by financing equipment, maybe by financing college educations," he told Seib.

But Bradley now seems to be backing off. In an interview, he said *The Journal* "exaggerated" his enthusiasm for mandated savings. "I've got too much to do now to work through the intellectual traps," he said.

And when House Democratic Caucus chairman Steny H. Hoyer of Maryland heard the pitch for mandatory savings, he "did not like it," Litan said. "He thought it was politically unrealistic."

That's practically an endorsement compared to the criticism that has been offered by economist John H. Makin of the American Enterprise Institute for Public Policy Research. *New York Times* columnist Peter Passell quoted Makin as labeling the Litan proposal "sick and wrong" and "a major invasion of personal liberties."

More temperately, Boston University's Kotlikoff said that he's not averse to requiring workers to put 10 per cent of their salaries into a retirement account—but he would prefer that the government first try a voluntary approach. Every worker, Kotlikoff suggests, should get a report from Uncle Sam that lays out what can be expected from social security and what the worker should be trying to save on his or her own, with an accompanying letter from the President urging people to save.

It could be that worrywart economists are too anxious about the savings situation. Maybe the government will bite the bullet on the deficit. Maybe the baby boom generation isn't fated for hardship in retirement: A new study by the Congressional Budget Office says that contrary to popular wisdom, baby boomers are busy accumulating wealth and will have higher retirement income than older people have today. Although many boomers aren't saving at the same rate their parents did, many are making more than their parents ever did. Also, more women will be eligible for their own social security and pension benefits. And—thanks, Mom and Dad!—the boomers may inherit the acorns of wealth squirreled away by their parents.

Even assuming that economic policy wonks could solve the design problems, there remain lots of ways that a mandatory savings program could backfire. Bosworth wouldn't put it past schizophrenic policy makers simultaneously to require households to increase their savings and to offset those increases with a new spurt of spending. The government might say, "It's OK to borrow more—there's plenty of savings," he speculated.

Washington economist Sylvester J. Schieber of the Wyatt Co., which specializes in retirement plan consulting, is worried that any serious push for mandatory savings might ring new alarm bells in Congress over the adequacy of social security and lead to another increase in the payroll tax—money that, he said, would probably not be saved for future retirees but squandered on current government programs.

The promoters of mandatory savings readily acknowledge the political improbability of their proposals and say that part of their aim is simply to wake up Americans to the ruinous consequences of sky-high deficits and a plummeting national savings rate. Although many Americans are worried about the deficit, it seems to disturb them more as a symbol of government excess than as a grave economic ailment. "Sometimes it helps to shock people," Romer said. With the slow progress on the deficit-and-savings front to date, many more buckets of cold water may be needed to roust people out of bed.

RETHINKING WORKER RETRAINING

LOUIS JACOBSON

Long before he became Labor Secretary, Robert B. Reich says, he knew America needed to cope with technology by retraining its work force. "Unlike past economic recoveries, where people were called back to their old jobs, a large portion of unemployed workers today need to get new jobs," he said in a recent interview. "The old rules for getting your job back don't apply."

Some economists say that reinventing the labor force will be impossible without reinventing training programs. The narrow skills taught in today's programs quickly become outdated. With diverse companies demanding a wide (and ever-changing) variety of skills, how can anyone know what skills should be taught?

Take computers. Should we be teaching IBM or Macintosh? Windows or DOS? Databases, word processing or desktop publishing? Microsoft Word, Word Perfect or MacWrite? And what happens in a few months when an update comes out? Many of these skills are both detailed and, alas, mutually exclusive. Perhaps computers are an extreme example, but other, lower-tech jobs, from die-pressing to filing patent applications, need highly specialized skills or change rapidly—or both.

Lacking a crystal ball, the government is bound to sponsor many useless training efforts. For one thing, many recently trained workers won't discover any jobs in their new field—perhaps, in a worst-case scenario, because of competition with fellow newcomers. Such a model seems alarmingly like old Soviet central planning, a reality that has been overshadowed by the popularity of the push to retrain.

Some experts prefer a program modeled on the GI Bill, enabling workers, rather than the government, to choose the skills they want to learn. While this would eliminate central planning, it fails to address a more basic dilemma of chicken and egg. How can companies hire workers if they aren't sure the new hirees have the exact skills the company needs? And how can workers retrain themselves without knowing who will hire them, and in what capacity?

It may have been different in the 1940s, when many ex-soldiers and sailors simply went to college or graduate school. But today, workers are scarcely able to direct their retraining dollars better than bureaucrats can. No worker can possibly know which cutting-edge skills in far-flung careers are in demand this month—even if he or she scans the help-wanted ads.

Offering general education—reading, writing and arithmetic—is part of the answer, because these skills are always useful (and, today, too few workers have a good command of them). But there's something else, a neat little trick to use the vaunted invisible hand of the market to match workers and firms. The idea is both old and unloved by economists. It's called wage subsidies.

The skepticism that has dogged wage subsidies has more to do with their practice than their theory (more on that later). In theory, wage subsidies have been called, not incorrectly, that rarest of economic miracles: a free lunch. The idea is simple and compelling: give workers a voucher worth a portion of their unemployment benefits, applicable to their next job's salary. Workers will have an incentive to seek work, and even to settle for a lower-paying job. And because the workers would cost the firm less than a full salary, employers will have an incentive to hire them.

Because the vouchers amount to less than the workers' unemployment benefits, the program would require little new expenditure, even allowing for administrative costs and other inefficiencies. Such a program might even save money—all while turning workers from benefit-drains into taxpayers.

Dennis Snower, an economist and unemployment expert at Birkbeck College in London, has added some twists to this old recipe. He argues that firms should be able to draw subsidies only if they retrain their hirees, so that firms would have an incentive to keep employees for the long haul. Presumably firms that have invested time and money in training subsidized workers would be less likely to dump them when the subsidy runs out, as it eventually must.

Happily, this requirement also solves the dilemma that plagues other retraining schemes. Namely, workers need not guess what skills they should learn, and firms need not rely on the government's hit-or-miss training system. Firms, which know their needs best, would retrain workers exactly how, and when, they want them. The government would reward these companies for their efforts, spending its money only when the workers benefit. The unspent balance could finance continuing, non-vocational education. Who knows, maybe wage subsidies would also reduce the general level of unemployment.

There are good reasons for economists' historical skepticism. While test efforts have shown that subsidies place workers in jobs, such efforts can be "leaky"—that is, expensive and inefficient. Workers who might have found jobs without a subsidy might be paid one anyway; companies might fire current workers and replace them with subsidized hirees; workers might feel stigmatized when interviewing with a voucher in hand. Snower has ways to attack each of these drawbacks, though each of his responses spawns problems of its own.

Still, though the perfect wage-subsidy plan will always be elusive, there may be no better time to try the idea than now. Here's why: In the old days, wage-subsidy advocates prescribed their idea only as a way to lower unemployment. Given the leakiness of early trials, cooler heads concluded that the alternative—doing nothing—was safer, perhaps even benign.

But now the policy landscape has shifted markedly. The question, as Reich suggests, seems to have gone beyond whether there will be a massive, government-sponsored retraining effort and on to when and how. Snower and others contend that instead of weighing wage subsidies against the easy alternative of doing nothing, officials should perceive wage subsidies as a way of avoiding an expensive and possibly wasteful retraining initiative. For once, wage subsidies might do the job more cheaply and more effectively.

Unequal Shares

The 1980s ended with wage-and-salary earnings more unequally divided than at any time since 1939. Since then, the gap's gotten wider. It's a trend—driven by basic economic and technological changes—that may have disturbing political and social consequences.

PAUL STAROBIN

Worried about an unequal division of the economic pie? You've got good reason to be. But don't blame Ronald Reagan for the problem. Instead, evidence is mounting that the real culprit is a hodgepodge of changes in the basic structure of global capitalism. And that means that governments might not be able to do much to reverse the trend.

The 1980s ended with wage-and-salary earnings more unequally divided than at any time since 1939. Over the first third of the 1990s, earnings fell for high-wage and low-wage workers alike, but the drop was greater for low-wage workers, according to a new analysis of Bureau of Labor Statistics data, timed for release on Labor Day, by Lawrence Mishel of the Economic Policy Institute.

So the earnings gap seems to have widened—and it might not narrow any time soon. "The trend is in the same direction and, if anything, may accelerate" over the rest of this decade, said economist Gary W. Loveman of the Harvard Business School.

"A lot of people are terrified," Loveman added, referring to himself and his Harvard colleagues. "It really has the potential of being one of the major social issues of the next 10 years." Although he acknowledged that the fallout was difficult to predict, he speculated: "I can't but imagine that these trends exacerbate the sense of hopelessness and lack of prospect of good fortune" in America's inner cities and other deteriorating areas.

Not everyone's so gloomy. Some economists expect that the natural push and pull of forces in the labor market will start correcting for the inequality problem. But not even the optimists are predicting a rapid and substantial reversal of this deeply rooted trend.

Although earnings inequality accelerated in the 1980s, it was also growing in the 1970s. Its continued growth in the 1990s has both liberal and conservative analysts convinced, more than ever, that the trend has very little to do with the role of government policy, including the zigs and zags of tax policy. Reagan, who made deep cuts in the top marginal tax rate, is off the hook; Bill Clinton, who just persuaded Congress to raise the top rate on the rich, probably won't much change things.

"Reagan's tax policies don't have much to do with wage inequality," said economist Mishel of the Economic Policy Institute, a Washington-based liberal think tank that's partly financed by organized labor. "I don't think they were the main thing behind income inequality, either. Most of the income inequality that occurred was before taxes." (Job earnings compose by far the biggest chunk of family income, the distribution of which also became more unequal in the 1980s.)

"The main reason that inequality increased [in the 1980s] was for economic factors that were outside the control of the government. And those, I think, are still largely outside the control of the government," said liberal economist Gary Burtless of the Brookings Institution. Economist Paul Krugman of the Massachusetts Institute of Technology (MIT), another liberal who has written widely about inequality, agrees with Burtless.

Although they are confident about their measurements, the analysts don't know precisely what to blame for the earnings disparity. But the hunch that the villain is global capitalism is buttressed by data showing an increase in earnings inequality throughout the advanced-industrialized world. "No advanced economies show declining wage inequality during the 1980s," University of Chicago economist Steven J. Davis reported last year in a study by the National Bureau of Economic Research in Cambridge, Mass. Moreover, Australia, Canada, Great Britain and West Germany experienced a surge in inequality on the order of the sharp increase in the United States. Inequality rose even in Sweden, a bastion of social-welfarism.

Many economists point a finger at the so-called reengineering of the workplace by firms in the United States and elsewhere. Using new technologies and management methods, many large firms have reorganized the production process in ways that have increased demand for a relatively small cadre of well-skilled, well-educated workers—and reduced demand for the much larger cluster of low-skilled workers. It's a trend that began in the manufacturing sector, which has become increasingly automated, and has now spread to the service sector.

Analysts also speculate that growth in international trade has bid down wages by exposing low-skilled manufacturing workers in advanced capitalist nations to more intense competition. Another possible culprit is the influx of Third World immigrants into the advanced countries—a trend that may be widening inequality by expanding the available pool of low-skilled workers. Low-wage earners may also have lost ground because of the steady decline in unionization across the industrialized world.

There's even blame assigned to the so-called superstar effect. Economists have long been intrigued by the ability of the best athletes, movie stars, opera singers and others to command stupendous salaries that far outstrip the earnings of their only-slightly-less-talented peers. Now they're finding signs of a similar, if less dramatic, pattern, in such professions as the law. "Thanks to computers and faxes and Federal Express," Krugman said, "the most productive people," the sharpest operators, can more easily dominate a line of business.

Because so little is known about the causes of the earnings inequality gap (and because few have much confidence in the problem-solving ability of the government), many economists are hesitant to offer policy prescriptions. The safest and wisest course, most analysts say, is for the nation to invest heavily in improving the educational system. The changes in the global economy "favor people who use their minds rather than their hands," Davis said in an interview.

BRAVING THE '90S

The new data analyzed by Mishel suggest that earnings inequality grew from 1989 through the first half of 1993 but at a slower pace than in the 1979-89 period. From 1989-91 (no data are yet available on 1992 and 1993), the gap in income inequality narrowed slightly. Perhaps because of a drop in interest income on stock-and-bond holdings and the like, the share of aggregate income held by the top 5 per cent of households dropped from 18.9 per cent in 1989 to 18.1 per cent in 1991, according to the Census Bureau.

According to Mishel, the lead author of *The State of Working America*, a well-respected publication updated every other year by the Economic Policy Institute, the recent trend has been for a worsening of real (inflation-adjusted) earnings for workers at virtually all points of the spectrum. While the highest-paid workers are getting poorer, the lowest-paid are getting poorer faster.

There are different ways to measure earnings—Mishel's numbers, for example, don't include nonwage fringe benefits—and not all economists agree that the average worker fared quite so poorly during the 1980s. There is general agreement, however, that the past 20 years or so have seen a flattening of earnings gains of workers in the immediate post-World War II period.

This is how Mishel analyzes recent history. From 1979-89, he plots a 0.4 per cent decline in the real hourly earnings of a worker at the 80th wage percentile—a worker, that is, whose hourly earnings exceeded those of 79 per cent of all other members of the labor force. Over this period, a worker at the 60th percentile experienced a 4.5 per cent earnings decline. The drop for a 40th-percentile worker was a steeper 7.1 per cent; and for a worker at the 20th percentile, it was 11.8 per cent. These are the statistics that led many analysts to worry about a vanishing middle class in America.

In his new Labor Day analysis, Mishel found that from 1989 through the first six months of 1993, an 80th-percentile worker suffered a 0.6 per cent real wage loss. The drop was 2.4 per cent for a 40th percentile worker and a less steep 0.7 per cent for a 20th-percentile worker. Earnings for a worker at the 90th percentile fell by 0.3 per cent.

Richard A. Bloom

Economic Policy Institute analyst Lawrence Mishel
The highest-paid workers are getting poorer, but the lowest-paid are getting poorer faster.

Mishel also found that earnings inequality had continued to grow in the 1990s across other dimensions, including college-educated workers versus those who went no further than high school. He gloomily predicts "a continuing erosion of wages and job prospects for the vast majority of Americans."

A bright spot is the earnings of women. Although they continue to earn less than men at virtually all points of the wage distribution, the gap is narrowing. And even though the earnings gap between females is widening, most women are still making real-wage gains. Analysts speculate that more well-educated women are entering the work force than before and that many women are employed in growth sectors of the economy. There are relatively few women, by contrast, in the declining manufacturing sector.

An important caveat: The Mishel data don't tell us anything about the mobility of workers or households. The data, in other words, don't track how a particular worker or family fared over the course of the 1980s or even from 1989-93; all that's provided is a snapshot of the earnings distribution at different points in time. There's disagreement among analysts about the degree of mobility in America; some conservatives, including economist Marvin H. Kosters of the American Enterprise Institute for Public Policy Research (AEI), argue that many workers and families were able to seize on opportunities and greatly improve their material lots in the 1980s. In this important respect, they say, the American dream remains very much alive.

What is not seriously contested within the economics profession, however, is a long-standing growth in earnings inequality going back at least to the early 1970s. "It's persistent," said Gary Becker, the free-market-leaning, Nobel prize-winning economist at the University of Chicago. "There's no denying that."

Richard A. Chase

Harvard economist Gary W. Loveman
The trends "exacerbate the sense of hopelessness."

DON'T BLAME REAGAN

Are Reagan and George Bush really not to blame for growing inequality? If they aren't, then one of the more resonant liberal themes of the 1990s—appropriated by Clinton and just about everyone else in or connected to the Democratic Party—is a myth fit for history's dustbin.

Here's how it looks to most analysts. Reagan's 1981 tax cuts, which reduced the top marginal tax rate from 70 per cent to 50 per cent, were regressive. The 1986 Tax Reform Act, which among other things expanded the earned-income tax credit (EITC) for the working poor, was progressive. Bush's 1990 tax bill, which also expanded the EITC and also increased tax rates on the rich, was progressive. The result? From 1980-91, there was "almost no change in the effective tax rates of almost all income groups," Urban Institute analyst C. Eugene Steuerle declared in *The Tax Decade*, published by the Urban Institute Press last year.

Clinton's new economic package, which once again expanded the EITC and hiked tax rates on the rich, is also progressive. But the rate hikes affect only the wealthiest 1 per cent or so of taxpayers, and the EITC affects only the working poor. The legislation "will affect the posttax income distribution, but not very much," said labor economist Lynn A. Karoly of RAND, a Santa Monica (Calif.) think tank. One problem is that the rich can be expected to change their financial behavior to try to evade the higher rates. *(See NJ, 8/14/93, p. 2016.)*

The larger point is that—fiscal policy aside—the distribution of pretax income has also been growing increasingly unequal. It's the uneven distribution of pretax pay that has so many economists worried.

Of course, governments can attempt to influence pretax pay. For example, a case can be made that the rapid growth in earnings inequality in the 1980s could have been forestalled by aggressive applications of policies, such as a higher minimum wage, to which Republicans were hostile but which were favored by many Democrats and their core constituents in the ranks of organized labor.

The minimum wage remained fixed at $3.35 per hour from 1981-90—which meant that its after-inflation value declined quite a bit. (The hourly minimum was increased to $3.80 in 1990 and to $4.25 in 1991. About 6 per cent of the labor force is paid the minimum wage or lower.) By contrast, in France, which experienced considerably less wage inequality in the 1980s, the real value of the legal minimum wage increased. According to a recently published study by economists Loveman, Lawrence F. Katz (currently a top adviser to Labor Secretary Robert B. Reich) and David G. Blanchflower, the increases in the French minimum wage, coupled with tough wage bargaining by entrenched unions, appeared to slow an erosion in real wages at the low end of the French wage distribution.

But the French also experienced much higher unemployment among youth compared with other industrialized countries—in 1984, youth unemployment was 26 per cent. Some economists speculate that France essentially paid for more wage equality among active workers with higher unemployment. The French experience may be worth pondering for the Clinton Administration, which is considering a proposal, backed by Reich, for raising the hourly minimum wage from $4.25 to $4.50 and then indexing the wage to inflation. Clinton favored a proposal along these lines during last year's campaign.

The 1980s also saw a decline in the manufacturing sector's share of total employment in the United States and just about all other industrialized countries. Some analysts argue that a shift from well-paying factory jobs to lousy service-sector jobs helps to explain the increase in earnings inequality—and perhaps could have been forestalled in the United States by an activist Administration willing to adopt an industrial policy to protect the manufacturing base. To Reagan and Bush, of course, industrial policy was anathema.

But economists who have studied the manufacturing-to-services shift, including RAND's Karoly, say that deindustrialization hasn't much contributed to the growth in earnings inequality. The telling sign, according to Karoly, is that widening inequality took place *within* both the goods-producing and services-producing sectors of the U.S. economy. This finding suggests that government policies to bolster the manufacturing sector—to which the Clinton Administration is sympathetic—may help the firms but won't necessarily do much to reverse the pattern of inequality.

DAMN COMPUTERS!

When economists don't have the foggiest idea of how to account for their observations, they often point the finger at technology—a convenient black box that seems to be affecting everything happening in society. But in this case, technology may deserve the blame.

The Information Age has dramatically reshaped everything from the method of making cars to the method of publishing newspapers. The growth in inequality over the last 20-odd years, meanwhile, neatly corresponds to the widespread introduction of computers and related products to every nook and cranny of the industrialized world.

In a 1991 study of 1984-89 data for the National Bureau of Economic Research, Princeton University economist Alan B. Krueger found that workers who used computers on the jobs earned a 10-15 per cent higher wage rate than otherwise similar workers. On the basis of this study, Microsoft Corp., the software giant, ran advertisements in *Time* magazine and elsewhere declaring, "We make it easier to get a 15 per cent raise."

Although Krueger wouldn't necessarily go that far, his findings appear to make a lot of sense for certain occupations, such as clerical work. Temporary-employment agencies, for example, typically offer higher pay for computer literacy.

In an interview, Krueger said it was possible that the increasing supply of computer-knowledgeable workers may dampen the computer's contribution to wage inequality. But referring to the constant changes in computer software, the economist said it was also possible that the demand for ahead-of-the-curve computer-savvy workers might continue to outpace the supply.

Wage gains experienced by computer users also seem to reflect the growing advantages of education and flexible skills in the postindustrial economy—or, put another way, the growing disadvantages of not being well educated and flexibly skilled.

Paul Swaim, an MIT-trained labor economist at the Agriculture Department's Economic Research Service, has found in his research that the investments that employers make in training their workers tend to reinforce the "inequalities," as he put it, of the entering personnel. "Workers who come into the job with a college education tend to get a lot more training than those who don't, which tends to amplify the differences in earnings over the pattern of a career," Swaim said.

Well-educated, adaptable workers appear to be the prime beneficiaries of the "reengineering" craze that has taken hold at firms in the United States and elsewhere. Basically, companies have pushed for efficiencies by overhauling their practices in ways that typically give a fortunate cadre of workers more responsibility and more pay. A quick-learning factory hand at a paper mill, for example, may be given additional responsibilities for operating computerized machinery. Or, as recounted in a case study used at the Harvard Business School, Taco Bell Corp. reorganized its operations to increase demands on its store managers, who were also given much higher salaries.

John Eisele

Brookings Institution analyst Gary Burtless
Inequality increased in the 1980s because of factors "outside the control of the government."

The downside to reengineering is that a lot of workers get pink slips or are shunted to low-skill jobs. And in America and elsewhere, the economy isn't generating a lot of demand for low-skill workers. There's something of a paradox here: The problem maybe isn't that the economy has too many "bad" jobs, but not enough, say many economists. Low-skill workers would get paid more if they were in greater demand. But these days, "the economy in the international marketplace is enhancing the demand for skill," Loveman said.

The growth in earnings inequality over the past 20-odd years corresponds to the introduction of computers and related products.

It is possible that the labor market will mitigate the problem on its own. Tomorrow's crop of wage earners, alerted to the increasing return on earnings to a good education, may take greater care to get a good education. (And, in fact, college enrollment rates among high school graduates are higher now than they were in the 1970s.) As the wages of college graduates rise, meanwhile, employers may start to make wider use of the more cheaply available pool of workers who didn't go to college.

"There are a lot of labor-market forces that tend to be self-correcting," the AEI's Kosters said. He foresees a narrowing of the earnings-inequality gap over the remainder of the decade.

Suppose he is wrong, however. Unless there is another spasm of social unrest on the scale of last year's Los Angeles riots—and maybe not even then—the safe bet is that inequality will not move to the top of the national policy agenda. In both parties, the No. 1 objective is economic growth.

In an anemic economy, growth is a perfectly understandable objective. Only the very envious would find comfort in an economy in which everyone was getting poorer—but the rich at the fastest rate. But growth is not always a rising tide that lifts all boats. After all, the 1980s saw a spurt in inequality notwithstanding the longest peacetime economic expansion since the Second World War. The one mitigating factor—the factor that perhaps keeps a lid on public discontent over the increasingly unequal division of earnings—is mobility. Americans seem willing to tolerate wide gaps between rich and poor so long as as they view the door of opportunity as open.

The Visible Hand

The Clinton Administration is doing industrial policy, all right—and it's going to great lengths to succeed where its predecessors have failed. But perils are already in sight.

JONATHAN RAUCH

Remember those smart sick-bay cots in *Star Trek*—the ones that read your vital signs after you get phasered? Well, you may not have to wait until Stardate Whenever to see one. James Genova, an enterprising high-technology type with Alexandria (Va.)-based Raven Inc., is working on the ultimate whoopee cushion. Put it on a wheelchair or a mattress, and it monitors a patient's pulse and breathing. Better still, it sends the information straight to a computer, which can tell doctors by telephone how their patients are doing or summon parents and paramedics if a baby stops breathing.

Sounds pretty good. But, like most new things, it's risky. And so Genova and Shea Smith, a business consultant, have turned up at a Holiday Inn in Gaithersburg, Md., to hear federal officials brief several hundred potential applicants about an apple of the Clinton Administration's eye. Called the Advanced Technology Program (ATP), it's an initiative to subsidize high-risk, high-tech commercial research that's deemed to offer potentially large economic returns.

The program has spare change in its pocket: $200 million this fiscal year. That's three times its budget of a year ago and 20 times its budget in fiscal 1990, back when the Republicans were in charge—and even this year's appropriation is a fraction of the $744 million that the Administration plans to be dropping into the program by 1997. But only 1 in 10 research proposals will land government aid. How to choose? Program officials leave little doubt what they're after: It's the economy, stupid.

"Remember, the ATP is here because we're trying to stimulate economic growth," one of the officials tells the 300 or so high-tech types assembled in the Holiday Inn ballroom. "Our mission," another declares, "is to achieve economic growth by funding R&D projects." A third is bluntest of all, saying that the goal is "to try to make industry rich—if you all don't prosper as a result of this, then we haven't done our job."

Welcome to the brave but not entirely new world of industrial policy, Clinton style. Although the "industrial policy" tag is both recent and controversial, the practice of subsidizing so-called key industries and technologies is not. Government has been in this business since the 1789 Tariff Act first bestowed protection on the U.S. maritime industry.

Under Clinton, however, industrial policy is neither anathema nor stepchild, as it was in the Reagan and Bush years. Rather, the Administration touts its microeconomic agenda—that is, its attempts to increase over-all U.S. economic performance by aiding particular sectors and technologies *within* the economy—as central to its plans to create good jobs and raise productivity.

"I think it's important," Laura D'Andrea Tyson, who chairs Clinton's Council of Economic Advisers, said. "It's part of the growth agenda." At the National Economic Council in the White House, deputy director W. Bowman Cutter said of the microeconomic initiative, "I think we think of it as a major effort." Clinton himself, he said, is specifically aware of the Advanced Technology Program and its siblings: "He feels very strongly about it. These were things *he* wanted to do."

Actually, the microeconomic agenda appears to have become a higher priority than the Administration intended. In the 1992 presidential campaign, Clinton's linchpin economic proposal was a federal investment program scaled in the hundreds of billions of dollars. Congress and the federal budget deficit pitched that plan into the trash. The President's economic stimulus plan likewise got flushed. His big national service plan emerged as a pea-sized version of itself. His deficit reduction plan passed, but considering that it looked pretty much like President Bush's deficit reduction package, only smaller, it was hardly an activist economic program.

With most of the macroeconomic program fallen off the tracks, what remains is mostly micro: job training and a clutch of critical-technology programs. Programs to subsidize cleaner-running cars, flat-panel electronic displays, information centers for manufacturers and software for the health care industry may be less than visionary, but they do have the advantage of being cheap. In theory, the key is smart targeting: Smallish subsidies for carefully chosen projects will yield large returns for the economy.

That's the theory, anyway. The hard part is making it work.

A SIX-RING CIRCUS?

Anyone who sifts through the Administration's microeconomic proposals is likely to wind up feeling both impressed and confused. With the possible exception of its $1 billion attempt to create a flat-panel display industry, the Administration mostly shuns grand, big-money gestures in favor of a chocolatier's assortment of bite-sized programs.

"The thing is more like a six-ring circus," said Max B. Sawicky, an economist with the Economic Policy Institute. "That's not to demean it, but there's not a consistent worldview throughout. It's pretty eclectic." *(For details, see box.)*

Richard A. Bloom

Laura D'Andrea Tyson, who chairs the Council of Economic Advisers Subsidizing certain technologies is "part of the growth agenda."

None of the numbers involved is staggering. "Remember," Tyson said, "we're starting small." Nor are the ideas themselves new. Today's federal budget is littered with subsidies for sectors once deemed critical: maritime subsidies from the days of the Founders, farm subsidies from the 1930s, economic development subsidies from the 1960s, energy subsidies from the 1970s and so on.

"Every Administration has tried to do a little something in civilian technology, and none of them has ever been very satisfied," said Bruce L.R. Smith of the Brookings Institution, the author of *American Science Policy Since World War II* (Brookings, 1990). A partial list includes the 1965 Technical Services Act under President Johnson, the New Technology Opportunities Program under President Nixon, the Cooperative Automotive Research Program under President Carter, the Sematech semiconductor consortium under President Reagan and, under President Bush, the seeds of many of the programs that Clinton is now cultivating: the Advanced Technology Program, the Manufacturing Extension Partnership, the Technology Reinvestment Project and others.

What is new is the Clinton Administration's determination to do better than its predecessors. There is room for improvement, to say the least. "The record should make us very skeptical, and it's not as though we have a surplus of resources," said Robert J. Shapiro, an economist with the Progressive Policy Institute who was a principal economic adviser in Clinton's 1992 campaign.

There was, for example, the unsuccessful effort to develop synthetic fuels from coal, which cost $2 billion from 1970-84. "The entire program," write Linda R. Cohen and Roger G. Noll in *The Technology Pork Barrel* (Brookings, 1991), "had a quality of madness to it." And the Clinch River breeder reactor, a newfangled nuclear technology that, Cohen and Noll write, "was the quintessential example of a technological turkey by the time it was mercifully put to rest in 1983." And the supersonic transport, which cost nearly $1 billion over 10 years and wound up, economist Susan A. Edelman concludes in the same book, "a costly and dismal failure." Not to mention the wool and mohair subsidy program, an Eisenhower-era industrial policy for textiles that had lost its rationale by 1960 but wasn't ended until last year. And many, many others.

Everyone agrees that markets are imperfect where technology is concerned. The private sector underfinances basic research, may overlook or delay useful technologies and often doesn't take into account environmental costs and defense needs. But correcting those flaws is inherently difficult. Attractive as selective high-tech subsidies may look on paper, the obstacles in practice are formidable. A skeptic's basic checklist would include:

Misguided Premises. The need for industrial-technology subsidies is unproven at best. It's unclear that the United States has any problem with lagging research or technology that needs solving. "Even if defense R&D is subtracted from total U.S. research spending," writes Smith of Brookings, "the United States still has a dominant position" relative to other nations. It's true that U.S. productivity growth has been sluggish for two decades, but some economists view the current preoccupation with high-tech manufacturing as barking up the wrong tree. "Service productivity matters more than manufacturing productivity," economist Paul Krugman argues in his new book, *Peddling Prosperity: Economic Sense and Nonsense in the Age of Diminished Expectations* (W.W. Norton & Co.). Because the service sector is so much larger, he says, "a percentage-point gain in service productivity is worth about three and a half times as much as an equal gain in manufacturing."

Subsidies Make You Lazy. There's also little evidence that selective subsidies—as opposed to spending on basic infrastructure, such as roads and education—will actually produce broad economic benefits. Many nations have tried to subsidize their way to prosperity but succeeded only in strangling their economies. "The only force we know that drives innovation is competition," Shapiro said, "and all these subsidies reduce the effects of competition." He and others advocate fewer, not more, targeted subsidies as the key to raising productivity.

CLINTON'S HIGH-TECH TO-DO LIST

Here are the most prominent items on the Clinton Administration's list of technology policy and industrial policy programs:

Advanced Technology Program (ATP). Matching grants for companies developing broadly applicable, cutting-edge manufacturing technologies aimed at the commercial market. First authorized in 1988 and began operation under President Bush; now being rapidly expanded. Financing: $200 million in fiscal 1994; $451 million proposed for fiscal 1995. Administered by the Commerce Department's National Institute of Standards and Technology (NIST). *(See NJ, 12/11/93, p. 2952.)*

Cooperative Research and Development Agreements. Joint research and development agreements between industry and the 726 federal labs. A long-standing program that the Clinton Administration is expanding. Combined public and private spending under these agreements is $1.5 billion in fiscal 1995, with 3,211 agreements in effect. Administered by various government agencies and labs.

Flat-Panel Display Initiative. Matching R&D grants for companies that will build high-volume factories for the commercial production of flat-panel displays, which are used for computers and other advanced instruments and which the Administration views as vital for defense. The goal is to create a U.S flat-panel industry, serving both defense and commercial needs, with four plants and 15 per cent of the world market by 2000. Financing: $587 million over the first five years, up to $1 billion over a decade. Administered by the Defense Department.

High-Performance Computing and Communications Program. Finances R&D into more-powerful computers and software. Created with the support of then-Sen. (now Vice President) Albert Gore Jr., D-Tenn., in 1991; began operating in 1992. Financing: $936 million in fiscal 1994; $1.2 billion requested for fiscal 1995. Conducted by various government agencies and overseen by the White House's National Science and Technology Council.

Manufacturing Extension Partnership. Plans to establish 100 centers—35 have been created so far—to assist small and medium-sized manufacturers with new technologies and methods. First authorized in 1988, with seven centers open by the end of President Bush's term. Financing: $30 million in fiscal 1994; $61 million proposed for fiscal 1995. Receives additional financing from the Technology Reinvestment Project (see below). Administered by NIST.

Partnership for a New Generation of Vehicles ("Clean Car" program). Ten-year collaborative research program with the three major U.S. automakers to develop vehicles that are three times more fuel-efficient than today's models. Total budget not yet announced. Administered by the Commerce Department with support from the Energy Department and other agencies. *(See NJ, 5/21/94, p. 1176.)*

Technology Reinvestment Project. Matching grants for companies proposing to develop "dual-use" technologies (those with both defense and commercial applications); also finances competitive grants to university engineering programs and manufacturing extension centers. First authorized in 1991 for fiscal 1992 but didn't begin operating in its current form until last year. Financing: $554 million in fiscal 1994; $652 million proposed for fiscal 1995. Administered by the Pentagon's Advanced Research Projects Agency.

Wrong Choices. Just which are the "key" industries and technologies? "The technologies identified as critical," Smith writes, "are almost coextensive with the entire economy." So how to choose who gets government's help? There's little need to subsidize a marketplace winner, but if you pick a marketplace reject, you're likely to bet on a dog. Sure, many innovations—almost all of them, in fact—create side benefits for society as a whole, but in advance, Shapiro said, "it's virtually impossible to identify which technologies or firms will produce sufficient positive externalities to justify government support." Worse, what if government subsidies lead industry on a wild-goose chase? That's what happened with Japan's botched effort to promote high-definition television.

Permanent Pork Barrel. It is all but impossible to measure the success of programs that carry such broad mandates as "creating jobs" or "increasing economic competitiveness." In the absence of any clear goalpost, programs go on and on, fiercely defended by their clients and staffs. "Targeted" subsidies become permanent entitlements for the lobbies that defend them, or pork barrel grants spread across every congressional district. "It is virtually impossible," Shapiro said, "to conduct a policy of public, taxpayer support for commercial technology that is not interest group-dominated."

Enter the Clintonites. That they are doing industrial policy isn't news. What is news is that they are intensely, almost obsessively, determined to learn from past mistakes and get it right. They are aware of the odds but believe they can beat them—or die trying. "Unless these things are structured properly, they run the risk of becoming subject to congressional pressure and the possibility of using the expenditures in wasteful ways," Tyson said. "We realize it's very important to make sure the program is structured in a way to enhance the prospects for success, to reduce the odds of failure as much as we can."

To remedy the Wrong Choices problem, the Clinton people rely on industry to decide which technologies are important, and they insist on stiff, expertly judged competitions to decide who finally gets government money. To remedy the Permanent Pork Barrel problem, they call for rigorous program evaluations and time-limited grants. To remedy the Subsidies Make You Lazy problem, they demand that industry match federal subsidies, risking stakeholders' own money rather than letting businesses ride sleepily atop taxpayers' shoulders.

Will it work? Industrial policy, however defined, inevitably requires that government make choices about what to subsidize and on what terms. If you're sympathetic, you call this process "merit-based competition with rigorous evaluation." If you're unsympathetic, you call it "bureaucrats picking winners." Either way, it comes to much the same thing: betting that folks like Steven R. Ray and Barbara L. Maia Goldstein can succeed where others have failed.

GETTING DOWN TO BRASS TACKS

To meet Ray and Goldstein, drive out to the grassy campus of the National Institute of Standards and Technology (NIST) in Gaithersburg, Md., where deer loll on the lawn in midafternoon and hundreds of government scientists toil in their labs. Walk down endless metal-walled corridors, past dozens of orange doors, and at last you're in Ray's small office. Steel shelves bulge with thick files and two video monitors enjoy pride of place atop the desk.

Here Ray and Goldstein, both career NIST employees in their 30s, talk about their work as co-managers in the Advanced Technology Program (which

Richard A. Bloom

W. Bowman Cutter, the deputy director of the National Economic Council "You have to retain considerable skepticism and a capacity for oversight."

NIST runs). He is a mechanical and aerospace engineer, she a mathematician on detail from the electronics and electrical engineering lab. As part of the ATP's mission to find and support promising but risky research that companies cannot or will not finance on their own, they are running a project on computer-integrated manufacturing.

Manufacturers today rely on computers for everything from design to shop-floor scheduling. But getting the different kinds of computers to talk to one another isn't easy. "Companies today spend millions of dollars trying to get their software systems to work together," Ray said. Most manufacturers have to design their own software systems, a slow and cumbersome process.

That's where the Advanced Technology Program comes in. The ATP is looking to spend about $100 million over five years on matching grants for companies and joint ventures that develop commercial software for electronics manufacturing. The selection committees will pick through piles of detailed grant proposals, up to 70 pages each, in search of possible breakthroughs.

Why this project? Why not any of a thousand others? Part of the answer is in the chart that's reprinted on this page. The ATP folks see a potentially rich economic payoff in the computer-integrated manufacturing project. That's what their chart shows. Assuming that better software is developed and that 10 per cent of the nation's biggest electronics companies adopt it, those companies' revenues will grow an additional $205 billion over five years, with a $230 billion gain for the U.S. economy. Multiply these kinds of numbers by the ATP's many research grants, and you derive the program's claim that "the ATP is expected to generate hundreds of thousands of jobs in the long term."

To which prediction Smith, the Brookings Institution's science policy expert, replies, "Gimme a break." Shown the chart on this page and another like it, he said: "This is just complete rubbish, these kinds of inventions. Fantasies." No one, he said, knows in advance which technologies will produce how many jobs. At the Progressive Policy Institute, Shapiro had a similar reaction. "There's no serious basis for any of these projections," he said. "They make up assumptions and then project them."

Actually, the ATP didn't just make them up. "These charts were provided by industry," George A. Uriano, the program's director, said. "This is what industry thinks the future looks like."

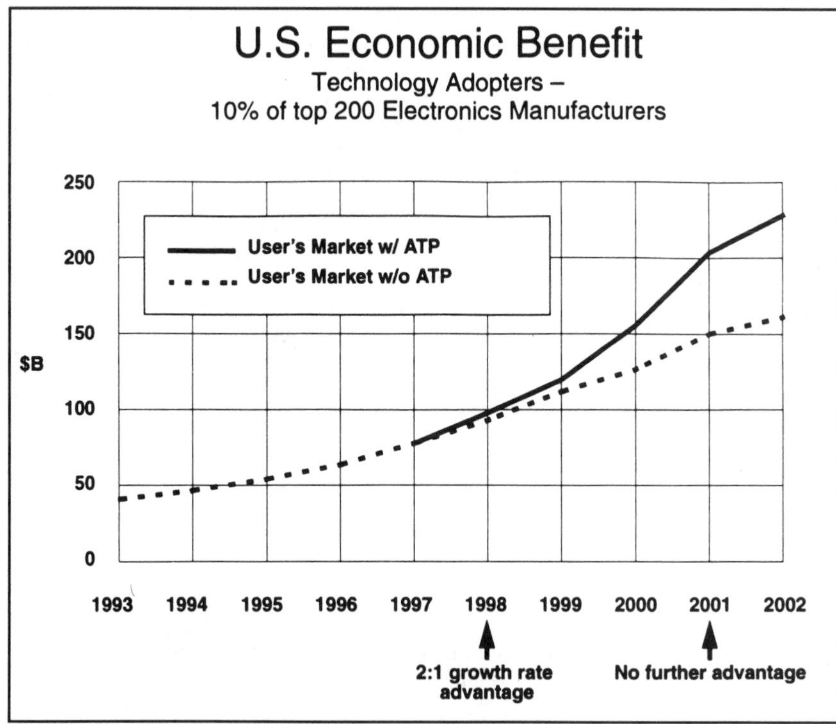

Why subsidize the development of computer software for manufacturing? This chart, from a briefing packet prepared by the Advanced Technology Program, shows projected economic gains if research leads to successful commercialization.

Susan M. Muniak

Bruce L.R. Smith, a science policy specialist at the Brookings Institution
No one, he says, knows in advance which technologies will produce how many jobs.

That, of course, doesn't make the projections wrong. But it does point up a potential difficulty for this program and others like it. To avoid pouring federal money down ratholes, the new-style technology policies are "industry-led." That is, they rely on companies in the marketplace—which, after all, know best—to guide federal dollars to the worthiest projects. Then, to prevent rampant pork barreling, they require the industry to match federal money. Both points are emphasized again and again by Administration officials high and low. As one ATP official told potential applicants, "Whatever we do, it's because you people in industry think it's important to do it."

The upside of this approach is that it's more likely to produce the kind of business-government cooperation that supposedly has worked well in Japan and elsewhere. "Part of what feels very new to me is the idea of listening to industry and partnering with industry, rather than being in an adversarial mode," Arati Prabhakar, NIST's director, said. "Absolutely, every 10 seconds we get input from industry about what are the best ways to focus our program."

The downside, however, is that it's not necessarily easy to distinguish the new-style, industry-led subsidy programs from the old-style, interest group-led ones. Indeed, in justifying its computer-integrated manufacturing project, the ATP points to strong support from the American Electronics Association (AEA)—the high-tech industry's trade group, which played a big part in lobbying to start the ATP to begin with and then lobbied hard to expand it. "Many AEA members have already benefited from the ATP," the association boasts in one of its pamphlets.

"The goal is ultimately to have an industry-led technology policy," said Jon E. Englund, the AEA's director of technology. To that end, the association has put together an Advanced Technology Coalition that's made up of groups, companies and individuals that support the Advanced Technology Program. Meanwhile, the aide who handles the ATP and other technology issues at the White House's National Economic Council, Thomas A. Kalil, is a former lobbyist who counted the Semiconductor Industry Association among his clients.

THIS TIME, FOR SURE

How to keep such a program from turning into a feeding trough for industry lobbyists?

The Administration is building some imposing defenses. As a bulwark against industry goody-hunting, the ATP sends every grant proposal to at least three scientific experts and at least another three business specialists. Panelists are asked to consider not just technical plausibility, but each applicant's business plan, finances and likelihood of producing a broadly useful commercial product, plus benefits for the economy as a whole.

That's just the sort of thing, of course, that private investors and financial analysts do for a living, and it might work for the government. Yet the dilemma remains: To choose well, the ATP must rely on the expertise and support of the very companies that stand in line for federal money. That doesn't mean the safeguards won't work, but it does pose a constant risk of turning the ATP into the latest corporate handout.

So far, attempts to keep lobbyists and politicians at bay seem to have succeeded. Program officials say, for instance, that congressional letters plugging favorite projects are politely acknowledged but are never seen by grant evaluators. But then the ATP is a new program, and it takes time—though not much time—for a program's clients to build protective walls around their benefits. The Pentagon's Advanced Research Projects Agency complains that 70 per cent of its budget is restricted by congressional earmarks, resulting, director Gary L. Denman testified recently, in "a significant loss in flexibility."

With the Advanced Technology Program, the Administration is betting that NIST's scientific culture can tame Washington's pork barrel culture. Equally possible, however, is that Washington culture will finally tame NIST instead. Next year, ATP grants are expected to account for about half of the NIST's budget. That's a juicy target for the hungry interest groups and eager Members of Congress that circle every federal honey pot.

The program's managers are well aware of the danger. "This problem never goes away, and as the program expands, it becomes a more and more tempting target," said NIST's Prabhakar. So what's the plan? "Eternal vigilance is the only thing I can offer," she said.

Susan M. Muniak

Arati Prabhakar, the director of the National Institute of Standards and Technology "Part of what feels very new to me is the idea of listening to industry . . ."

A larger question remains: How can anyone tell whether the program as a whole contributes enough to the economy to justify its cost? "The problem for all of these is it's very hard to evaluate in simple ways whether a program is successful or not successful," Tyson said. "But I think everyone recognizes that, and we're all working on it."

Within the Administration, NIST appears to lead in the search for ways to measure success on the industrial policy front. Recipients of federal funds are required to report back on their progress quarterly and annually over the life of their grants, and then biennially for six years after that. Where most programs spot-check final outcomes, the ATP plans to generate a detailed case history for every grant it makes, all to be compiled for use in evaluating the program's success. Few if any federal programs have ever gone to such lengths to assess whether they work.

So far, so good. But once the data are gathered, then what? Every subsidy generates some success stories, but gauging the impact on the nation's economy is a contentious, murky task. Moreover, the ATP sets no clear, measurable goal for itself.

"It's not sensible to say a particular number is some magic achievement," Prabhakar said. "The bottom line, in my view, is that it comes down to a judgment. What we're going to try to do is try to provide as many of the measurements as possible to illuminate the judgment."

Richard A. Bloom

Robert J. Shapiro, an economist with the Progressive Policy Institute "The only force we know that drives innovation is competition . . ."

Even if the program is judged to be a loser, how do you pull the plug? "I think it's a problem," said the National Economic Council's Cutter. "It's one of these things you have to be extremely aware of. You have to retain considerable skepticism and a capacity for oversight." Maybe, but when it comes to extending programs, Washington is a surpassingly unskeptical place. Many is the federal program that has been assessed and found wanting, yet lives on anyway.

That the Clinton Administration is further along than its predecessors in grappling with these problems seems clear. Equally clear is that so far the Administration has more determination than hard answers. "I really think everybody feels this is our chance to show that this *is* possible in the American context," a White House official said of the Administration's microeconomic effort. Skeptics will wish him luck, but they will also recall what Bullwinkle, the moose of cartoon fame, said to Rocky when he tried for the umpteenth time to pull a rabbit out of a hat: "This time, for sure."

A NEW WAY TO BUDGE THE BUDGET

JEFF SHEAR

Leaders of the National Taxpayers Union Foundation (NTUF) will soon announce their plans to unleash the personal computer as an incendiary device. They say that the hot new software they're about to introduce will prove to be the Molotov cocktail of the interactive set. This may be the true dawning of the age of cyberpopulism.

Within weeks, when "VoteTally" becomes available over CompuServe, the nation's most popular public on-line service, the wheels of revolution aimed at budget-busting legislators will turn and the barricades will be mounted across the "information superhighway." Big spenders on Capitol Hill may already be running for cover.

"This program will be the end of special-interest power as we know it in Washington," Paul Hewitt, the NTUF's vice president for research, said.

What the program does, according to Hewitt, is to fix like the "Hubble space telescope" on how much each Member of Congress proposes to spend each year, by totaling the tabs for bills they propose, sponsor, co-sponsor or vote for.

As the organization put it in a press release, the "NTUF obtains independent cost estimates for each vote, which are periodically cross-indexed with each Member's voting record and tallied in accord with accounting rules designed to ensure that no spending increases or decreases are double-counted." The NTUF says that its spending figures have nearly total acceptance by Members of Congress. At the top of the House in spending in the first session of the 103rd Congress was Del. Eleanor Holmes Norton, D-D.C., who proposed legislation that would cost some $673 billion. Daniel K. Inouye, D-Hawaii, led the Senate with a $561 billion tab. Both have topped the congressional dollar pile two years running.

In use since 1991 by journalists and other moths round the Capitol flame, VoteTally, formerly known as the Congressional Budget Tracking System, was available only in hard-copy form. But it drew wide attention from the press. The NTUF says that its reports, which appeared two or three times a year, were credited in at least 1,500 news stories and editorials. (Updates are now promised 10-20 times a year.)

Renamed VoteTally for personal-computer use, the service will be on-line free of charge. It will allow users to group congressional spenders by state, by region, by party and by political slant. Charts will illuminate the analyses.

Hewitt boasts that the NTUF's database has already produced dramatic results. In the first nine months of the 102nd Congress, only one lawmaker had a record of sponsoring more spending reductions than increases. Two years later, when the database's information began appearing in the press, 209 lawmakers showed a newfound interest in spending-reduction bills. In 1991, spending bills outnumbered reduction bills 49-1; now, they hold a mere 6-1 edge.

Part of this trend-shift certainly was the increased national focus on the parasitic federal budget deficit, but the NTUF should not go without credit, if for no other reason than having made Capitol Hill lawmakers squirm.

Hewitt calls VoteTally an effort at "taxpayers' consumerism," adding: "You no longer have to listen to what your Representatives say, you can see for yourself what they're doing. If you give these Congressmen a speedometer, they can obey the speed limit, and the public can enforce it."

Until now, sorting out congressional spending has been a haphazard and perilous journey through procedural arcana. There are, for example, 19 ways to vote spending measures in Congress. The NTUF calls this "complexity by design."

By submerging the real spending action in procedure, Members are able to hide their votes from public view. Often, they have been accountable to the leadership for their votes, making them vulnerable to varieties of political arm-twisting. The sponsors of VoteTally say that they have sorted through the procedural fog by testing each measure for its actual impact on spending.

"Legislators today are more accountable to organized constituencies on specific votes than they are to the general public for the totality of the budget actions," according to one of the NTUF's press releases. "One result is that at the point of decision, pressures to spend inevitably exceed those to cut."

Will turning such information over to personal-computer users usher in a return to representative government? "Lobbying today is the art of achieving undemocratic outcomes on the back of the democratic process," Hewitt said, noting that lawmakers are more accountable to interest groups than they are to their parties. "Now, with a home computer, we can go around those interest groups."

VoteTally, however, is far from perfect. An obvious flaw is its proclivity for inflating actual spending figures. VoteTally adds a dramatic and significant fudge factor by counting bill sponsorship, which represents the raw material of legislation, not the dollars and cents of enactment.

What impact the meeting of computers and politics will have on the information superhighway remains to be seen.

Adlai E. Stevenson once joked that newspapers separate the wheat from the chaff and print the chaff. No such criticism can be leveled at the on-line databases, which are veritable silos of information. The "White House Forum" operated by America Online, for example, allows subscribers to search official documents by key words. A search of the term "welfare reform" turned up 146 entries, including President Clinton's "New Directions" speech to Congress. All this and more for less than $10 a month.

Many folks, though, may see as much gridlock on the information superhighway as they see in Washington. In two of three attempts to pull up the welfare reform-related documents, America Online, in the manner of a bureaucrat with better things to do, simply hung up. Such roadside kills are unfortunately commonplace along the Infobahn, but they may be a small price to pay for the promise of powerful new interactive connections to the political process.

Agriculture and Food

So essential is food to human existence and, by extension, to the nation's well-being that a considerable proportion of American public policy addresses the nation's food supply and the quality thereof. Government involvement ranges from regulations aimed at ensuring that food purchased by consumers is minimally safe to eat, all the way to subsidies and trade policies designed to ensure a secure, steady food supply for the American people.

In recent years American consumers have demanded more and more precise labeling of the ingredients of processed and prepared foods of all kinds. As people have become more concerned with food-related health problems such as heart disease, diabetes, and hyperactivity, governments have responded by requiring labels that inform consumers in appropriate and detailed ways. This preoccupation with labeling food seems to give rise to new policy questions almost continuously. One of the selections in this unit treats the issue of whether genetically engineered foods need to be labeled as such before being sold.

A wholly different area of agricultural and food policy involves government activities designed to guard private producers from variations in prices and production costs over time. Government subsidies are supposed to make it more likely that there will always be a satisfactory supply of certain commodities such as corn, wheat, sugar, and soybeans, even if the government sometimes pays what seem to be outlandish subsidies to wealthy producers. What has evolved is a fairly complicated and expensive policy of farm subsidies that is the object of considerable scrutiny and criticism.

Related to domestic subsidies are issues of international trade policy. The shift to freer movement of goods across international borders is now proceeding at a steady pace, and there are few areas in which the stakes are higher than food and food products. Determining and implementing a coherent set of farm subsidy and food trade policies are not easy tasks, especially in a representative democracy whose elected leaders are subject to seemingly never-ending electoral considerations and constituent demands.

The controversy over the national government's food stamp policy in the first 100 days of the 104th Congress is another example of the importance of public policy as it relates to food and agriculture. Initial proposals to shift some responsibility for helping needy people to get enough food from the national to state governments were strongly contested. Opponents argued that the national government should continue to provide a nationwide program that guarantees subsidies for food purchases by those who would otherwise go hungry.

While developments in food and agricultural policy do not occupy the front pages of the newspapers on a daily basis, the selections in this unit provide a sample of recently arising issues that illustrate the importance and complexity of this policy area.

Looking Ahead: Challenge Questions

Should government be involved in regulating, managing, and ensuring the nation's food supply? Or should the marketplace of potential buyers and sellers be allowed to function without government restriction or involvement? Why?

Should producers of a food product be required by government to list its ingredients on the product label? Why or why not?

Should the government pay producers or potential producers of a particular food crop not to produce as much of the crop in a given year?

Do you think that the importation and sale of foreign food products in the U.S. should be restricted or prohibited? Defend your answer.

Unit 3

Genes in the Bottle

Western crops and agriculture methods may have reached their limit in terms of helping farmers in the Third World produce more food. Is biotechnology—"genetic engineering"—a panacea or a Pandora's box?

GRAEME BROWNING

In the Aquaculture Research Center at Fells Point, a gleaming new laboratory near Baltimore's Inner Harbor that's been built by a unit of the University of Maryland, scientists are juggling fish chromosomes like silver balls.

The researchers pluck the gene that produces the growth hormone for trout out of a trout's cells, multiply the gene in test tubes and insert the results into carp and catfish embryos in the hope that the fish will grow bigger, faster. If this nature-defying act succeeds, the scientists say, it could eventually pump more protein into the diets of millions of hungry people in the Third World.

Biotechnology, or genetic engineering—the scientific process of rearranging the core genetic material in plants and animals, including microorganisms—has made headlines in the United States since the late 1980s by producing promising drugs for such diseases as cystic fibrosis, diabetes, hepatitis and leukemia. But supporters of this new-wave science say that it has a much more compelling destiny to fill outside U.S. borders in the coming century.

The world's population, even by conservative estimates, is expected to grow nearly 50 per cent in less than two decades. Nine of every 10 people in the new multitudes will live in developing countries where food resources are scarce. Western crops and agricultural methods have reached their limit in terms of helping farmers in the Third World produce more food, some experts say. The only option left is biotechnology.

Most of the research on genetically engineered plants and animals—which is usually lumped together under the heading of "agricultural biotechnology"—is being financed with private, not public, money. Because the corporations financing the research recoup their investments by charging relatively steep prices for their products, most farmers in developing countries can't afford them.

But if governments in the industrialized world—and the United States in particular—were to pour more public money into research on agricultural biotechnology, the swollen bellies and glazed eyes of starving children would no longer haunt Western consciences, biotechnology advocates say.

"Biotechnology, including the genetic engineering of higher-yielding, pest-resistant rice, corn, vegetables and other crop plants, . . . will give us the opportunity to banish hunger from even the poorest nations of the Third World," Dennis T. Avery, the director of the Center for Global Food Issues at the Indianapolis-based Hudson Institute, a conservative think tank, recently wrote. "In the decades ahead, our children and grandchildren will be able to enjoy bountiful harvests, even though the number of mouths the world has to feed will double . . . ."

At the same time, however, what was once only a small ripple of voices protesting the unrestricted sale of genetically engineered crops in developing countries is swelling into an international chorus. Since September, three organizations—representing government officials, scientists and activists in the United States, Europe and Asia—have called for moratoriums on government approval of, and trade in, crops and food products produced through biotechnology.

On Dec. 20, in the most recent protest, the Washington-based Union of Concerned Scientists released a report in which it called for the United States to bring the regulatory approval process for genetically engineered crops to a temporary halt until federal officials have a reliable way to control the ecological risks that such crops might pose to the world's environment.

"Genetic engineering is an unsettling technology that has elicited concern—and in some cases outright opposition—in countries around the world," Margaret Mellon and Jane Rissler, two biologists for the scientific group, wrote in the report, *Perils Amidst the Promise: Ecological Risks of Transgenic Crops in a Global Market*. Mellon and Rissler also cautioned, "U.S. approval of a [genetically engineered] crop does not assure its safety outside the United States."

Just 20 years ago, the science—or art, if you will—of gene splicing didn't exist. But today, scientists in laboratories all over the world are mixing and matching chromosomes with an eye toward producing improved seeds, pesticides and veterinary medicines; better food additives and more-efficient food processing enzymes; and more-nutritious crops.

It is a testament to the potency of this new technology, however, that even with its short history, scientists are already debating whether genetically engineered crops will turn the tillable acreage of the world into a new Babylon—or a wasteland.

THE MARCH OF PROGRESS?

Modern farming methods, fertilizers, chemical pesticides and hybrid crops have helped American farmers to double their per-acre yields since 1940, according to a 1991 study by Congress's Office of Technology Assessment (OTA). In the years after World War II, many of these techniques and products were transferred to developing countries, ushering in a "green revolution" of higher crop quality and yields.

But the farming revolution in the Third World is hardly comparable to the boom in cheap, abundant foods that industrialized nations have come to enjoy.

The National Academy of Sciences, for example, recently concluded that developing countries lose more than 100 million tons of cereals, vegetables and starchy staples such as sweet potatoes every year because of pre-harvest ravages by diseases and pests, and post-harvest problems with transportation, storage and food processing.

The human cost of these losses is staggering. The academy estimated that the lost foodstuffs would provide the minimum energy requirements for about 300 million people each year.

Meanwhile, as the third millenium approaches, Third World farmers face increasing pressures to produce bigger crops to feed more people. Asia, for example, has more than half the world's population and more than 70 per cent of the world's farmers, but only 25 per cent of the world's arable land, according to estimates of the World Health Organization (WHO), a Geneva-based agency of the United Nations. At the beginning of the 21st century, it projects, China will have less than a fourth of an acre of arable land per person and India slighly more than a third.

"The only pathway open to countries like China and India for feeding their growing human populations is continuous improvement in yield," the Food and Agriculture Panel of the WHO Commission on Health and Environment reported in February 1992. "The tools of biotechnology can help in raising the productivity of major crops, thus increasing their economic value."

Few Third World countries, however, have the financial resources or the scientific expertise to conduct their own research in agricultural biotechnology. Only 10 developing nations have any agricultural biotechnology programs at all, for example.

Some European governments are trying to fill that void. The Agricultural Research Department of the Netherlands, for example, is developing low-cost, biotechnology-based kits for Third World farmers to use in detecting disease and parasites in their crops and animals. The Belgian government is financing biotechnology research at the University of Leuven that's aimed at banishing pests and disease from bananas, which are a staple crop for almost 400 million people around the globe.

The U.S. Agency for International Development, the World Bank and private charitable groups such as the Rockefeller Foundation have also invested money in programs that are designed to train Third World biochemists and molecular biologists in agricultural biotechnology.

Still, most of the crucial work in this scientific arena is being conducted in corporate laboratories in a handful of industrialized nations.

Only a fraction of the field testing conducted each year on genetically engineered crops, for example, occurs outside the United States, the European Community and Canada, according to the OTA's report, *Biotechnology in a Global Economy*.

According to the Rome-based Food and Agriculture Organization (FAO), five multinational corporations with interests in the sale of agricultural chemicals underwrite most of that research: E.I. du Pont de Nemours & Co., based in Wilmington, Del.; Monsanto Co., based in St. Louis; Sandoz Corp., a subsidiary of Kalamazoo (Mich.)-based Upjohn Co.; Imperial Chemical Industries PLC, the British chemical firm; and Ciba-Geigy Ltd., the Swiss pharmaceutical giant.

John Eisele

Madilyn Fletcher of the Aquaculture Research Center Biotechnology could revive Maryland's fish industry.

PANACEA OR PANDORA'S BOX?

To activists, the portrayal of biotechnology as the answer to starvation in the Third World is merely a smoke screen used by corporations that hope to make genetically engineered foodstuffs palatable to wealthy consumers elsewhere.

"I don't want to claim there will never be a genetically engineered product anywhere that won't help at least somebody," Mellon said in a recent interview. "I'm just saying that to fix on biotechnology as the lodestar, to think that somehow if only you allow people to move genes back and forth you can solve the world's problems, that's overselling. And overselling this stuff is very wrong and very dangerous."

Mellon's view is shared outside the United States. In early September, for example, a panel of 33 agriculture experts convened by the Nairobi-based U.N. Environment Program (UNEP) called for an international treaty to prevent industrialized countries from transferring potentially hazardous products of genetic engineering into developing countries.

The panel recommended that the proposed treaty include a "prior informed consent" clause, which would require a country that exports a biotechnology product to secure the official consent of the recipient country before a transfer

Richard A. Bloom

Margaret Mellon of the Union of Concerned Scientists "Overselling this stuff is . . . very dangerous."

takes place. A similar clause was adopted in the 1989 Basel Convention on Transboundary Movement of Hazardous Wastes and Their Disposal, which was signed by 20 countries in May 1992. The Senate ratified U.S. participation in the treaty in August 1992.

A few weeks after the UNEP meeting, agriculture officials, scientists and activists from 14 Asian countries threw their weight behind those recommendations by petitioning the FAO to convene its own panel of experts to study the impact of biotechnology on farming in developing countries. According to press reports, the Asian groups also urged the Rome-based organization to establish a treaty that would govern the transfer of genetically engineered products.

Some scientists and activists also fret that no matter how far agricultural biotechnology advances, the developing countries that need it the most won't have access to it because Western corporations will hang too high a price tag on it.

Money from philanthropic foundations and governments of developing and industrialized countries alike helped make green revolution technologies available to farmers all over the world, the WHO Food and Agriculture Panel wrote in its report.

But "the gene revolution technologies associated with biotechnological research may not be so available, since they owe their origin mainly to investments made by private companies and may be protected by patent right," the report continued. "Where should the line be drawn between private profit and public good, particularly in a world characterized by glaring economic inequities?"

Other analysts and scientists, however, consider such arguments pure Pollyanna.

"The societies that pioneered high-yield agriculture are now suggesting that the Third World reject it, and reject biotechnology as well," the Hudson Institute's Avery said in a speech to the McLean (Va.)-based Agriculture Research Institute in September. "But if we raise yields more, we can have more forest and more wildlife. If you're going to farm the damn acre, farm it for all it's worth."

"Public-interest groups are always railing at corporations for picking things that make money," Nina Federoff, a research scientist at the Carnegie Institution of Washington's embryology department and an expert on molecular genetics, said in an interview. "That's like railing at somebody for breathing. Companies don't exist for the good of humanity; they exist to make a profit."

THE PRICE OF KNOWLEDGE

There is also a strong sense among many researchers that pushing the envelope on agricultural biotechnology has merit on its own, no matter who benefits.

"I cannot overemphasize the importance of marine biotechnology," Rita R. Colwell, the president of the University of Maryland's Biotechnology Institute, which built the Aquaculture Research Center, said at a hearing held last April by the House Merchant Marine and Fisheries Subcommittee on Oceanography, Gulf of Mexico and the Outer Continental Shelf. "It is one of the most exciting areas of the new scientific frontier, if only for the sheer raw potential of the great diversity of marine organisms within the world's oceans, which constitute 75 per cent of the earth's surface."

In addition to the research on carp and catfish, scientists at the center are also trying to clone growth hormone genes for Chesapeake Bay oysters and reproductive hormones for striped bass, Madilyn Fletcher, the center's director, said in an interview. Both the oyster and the striped bass are crucial to Maryland's commercial fish industry, which has declined sharply in the past decade.

Fletcher contends that genetic engineering will improve not only the growth rate of commercially bred fish, but also their tastiness and their resistance to disease. "I don't think the United States yet has fully recognized the significance of this area, in terms of its own competitiveness and its ability to feed its people and protect its environment," she said.

Perhaps not. In fiscal 1994, for example, only $234 million of the $4.3 billion the federal government is expected to spend on biotechnology research will go to research on all types of genetically engineered crops and food animals, officials of the Agriculture Department say. In comparison, Japan invests $180 million each year in marine biotechnology research alone, according to testimony before the House Merchant Marine and Fisheries Committee.

Representatives of the U.S. biotechnology industry don't find those figures threatening. Japan uses much more fish than the United States does, they say. Besides, U.S. firms have received government approval to field-test a wide range of genetically engineered crops, while Japanese firms so far have gotten the official go-ahead for only four genetically engineered plants.

"No other nation on earth is at the stage we're at in terms of testing and getting approvals for food and agricultural biotechnology products," Richard D. Godown, a senior vice president of the Washington-based Biotechnology Industry Organization, said in an interview. "We've got the undisputed lead in the United States."

But as long as corporations in the United States and other industrialized nations bear the brunt of paying for biotechnology advancements, scientists say, it's unlikely that they will be willing to freely share the knowledge they have gained.

Federoff noted, for example, that the Agriculture Department has stored thousands of pages of valuable information on farming methods in a computerized database at its National Agricultural Research Library. Farmers from around the world can tap into the database for tips on how to improve their cultivation methods.

"That database was supplied with taxpayer money," Federoff said. "It's easier to be generous to other countries in a situation like that. The same is true with agricultural biotechnology research. If it's paid for by public dollars, it's more likely that it will be made available at a decent cost to international partners."

Food Fight

Thanks to advances in biotechnology, scientists have managed to genetically engineer a tomato that resists rotting up to a month longer than its conventional cousins. But for now, at least, the Food and Drug Administration doesn't require genetically altered foods to be so labeled. Consumer activists are crying foul, and the biotech industry is fighting back.

GRAEME BROWNING

The Manhattanites who frequent New York City's trendy and expensive Water Club restaurant demand that their chicken be free-range, their tuna dolphin-safe and their raspberries grown without pesticides. So you'd think that Rick Moonen, the restaurant's executive chef, would welcome tomatoes that stay ripe and juicy for weeks on end.

Any day now, the Food and Drug Administration (FDA) is expected to approve just such a tomato, called the Flavr Savr. Scientists at Davis (Calif.)-based Calgene Inc. have managed to rearrange the tomato's DNA—the core genetic material in its cells—so that the Flavr Savr resists rotting up to a month longer than ordinary tomatoes.

Moonen isn't sure that he wants to use the Flavr Savr in his kitchen. "I believe you're better off leaving some things to Mother Nature," he said in a telephone interview from the Water Club, which overlooks the East River.

But he may have no choice. Once the Flavr Savr has been approved for sale, food-processing companies may mix it into soups and sauces, and pack it whole in cans along with ordinary tomatoes. And Moonen—or any other cook, for that matter—won't be able to distinguish a can of ordinary tomatoes from a can of genetically engineered tomatoes, because the FDA doesn't require the food industry to disclose that information on product labels.

That policy angers Moonen, who belongs to the Washington-based Pure Food Campaign. Food processors "are going to start sending us tomatoes with God knows what in them, and no labels so you know what you're getting," he said. "But what really worries me is that once the FDA approves this tomato, a lot of other [genetically engineered] products out there won't go through as tough a scrutiny."

More and more Americans are beginning to agree with him. For more than a decade, the evolving science of biotechnology—or genetic engineering—has existed almost exclusively in pharmaceutical laboratories, where it has contributed to the discovery of new drugs. Now, however, this brave new world is on the verge

Richard A. Bloom

Daniel J. Barry, the executive director of the Pure Food Campaign
Labeling products as genetically engineered, he said, gives consumers "an informed choice."

of expanding into the consumer marketplace. And once it does, genetic engineering could ultimately become a key ingredient in our daily bread.

That's why the battle over how to regulate genetically engineered foods has been turning increasingly bitter. Food-safety activists, who insist that the federal government must closely monitor the new foods, and the biotechnology industry, which believes that too much regulation and supervision will choke off promising discoveries, offer arguments to support their positions.

In essence, though, the debate reflects the same clash of interests that's surrounded many scientific and technological innovations since the mid-1980s. Science by its very nature demands the freedom to explore. The public, on the other hand, has become wary of the prospect of technology run amok.

DESIGNER GENES

The FDA lit the fuse on the latest round of controversy in May 1992, when it announced that it would take a relatively lenient approach to regulating genetically engineered foods.

In a set of broad guidelines published in the *Federal Register*, the FDA said that it would not require food companies to notify the agency every time they put a genetically altered food on the market. The agency also said that it would not require food producers to add the words "genetically engineered" to the label of every item in whose production gene splicing played a part.

Under the FDA's 1992 guidelines, producers must reveal the presence of genetic engineering on a label only when the substance added to the original food might cause an allergic reaction or when the original food's nutritional value has been changed. Shellfish and peanuts, for example, are "known," or common, allergens. If a company adds shrimp or peanut genes to catfish eggs, and sells fillets from the resulting fish, its label must notify consumers that the catfish "contains shrimp protein" or "contains peanut protein."

By the FDA's count, consumers wrote 3,000 letters of opposition to the new policy in the three-month comment period that followed the 1992 announcement. Many of the letters came from the Pure Food Campaign, which had been founded earlier in the year by Jeremy Rifkin, a longtime crusader against genetic engineering.

Rifkin's group contends that allowing genetically engineered foods to be sold without strict government regulation is tantamount to opening Jurassic Park on the shelves of local supermarkets. The group estimates that hundreds of genetically engineered foods, plants and animals are now under development in laboratories across the nation.

"Scores of companies are now using [genetic engineering] to produce absolutely unprecedented genetic combinations, [including] cantaloupe and yellow squash containing bacteria and virus genes; potatoes with chicken and waxmoth genes; tomatoes with flounder and tobacco genes; corn with firefly genes; even fish and pork with human genes," a Pure Food Campaign handout warns consumers. "Many of these genes and genetic combinations have never before been part of the human food supply [and] virtually none . . . have relevance to improved nutrition."

Rifkin and other consumer activists insist that all genetically engineered foods, regardless of whether they carry allergens or not, must be labeled as such. Only in this way, they say, will consumers be able to make what Daniel J. Barry, the Pure Food Campaign's executive director, calls "an informed choice."

Richard A. Bloom

Biotechnology Industry Organization's Richard D. Godown "Science doesn't deal in absolute certitude. . . ."

"Consumers have become used to judging the feel, the smell and the color of foods to tell if they're fresh or not," Barry said in an interview. "Unlabeled genetically engineered foods . . . have the potential of presenting a product that looks fresh but may actually be carrying food-borne diseases and be reduced in its nutritional value."

THE FEAR FACTOR

Consumer activists also argue that without mandatory labeling—and in some cases, government testing—industry can be expected to scramble plant and animal genes indiscriminately, without regard to consumers' health and safety or to the long-term impact on the world's food supply. *(See box, next page.)*

A broad array of chemical manufacturers, food processors and agribusiness concerns—from Monsanto Co. and Hunt-Wesson Inc. to seed giant Pioneer Hi-Bred International Inc. and the Maine Potato Board—consider that argument, however, to be simple fear mongering.

Providing complex and confusing scientific information on food labels is not only useless but possibly destructive, industry contends. Labels will only frighten consumers away from a new technology that has the potential to lend infinite variety and choice to their diet and, ultimately, to increase the worldwide food supply.

"What [consumer activists are] asking for is absolute certitude, and science doesn't deal in absolute certitude—science deals in probability," said Richard D. Godown, a senior vice president of the Washington-based Biotechnology Industry Organization. "It is the willingness to go forward that has produced the major advances of our civilization, after all. Wilbur and Orville would still be standing on the cliffs at Kitty Hawk wondering 'Will this thing work?' if it were otherwise."

The Wright Brothers, however, couldn't afford to build anything more than test craft until they won a contract in 1908 to provide planes for the U.S. War Department. So it is with genetic engineering. Scientists may tinker with tomatoes all they want, but until those tomatoes are selling by the trailer-truckload they remain simply objects of curiosity sitting on a laboratory counter.

Biotechnology companies make no bones about their financial stake in the success of the Flavr Savr and its cousins. The worldwide tomato market, for example, is worth $5 billion each year. Compa-

TOWARD A MORE PERFECT COW?

Anti-biotechnology crusader Jeremy Rifkin and his followers have a nightmare vision of the genetically engineered future. It's called bovine somatotropin (BST). Cows naturally produce small quantities of BST, a hormone, to stimulate their production of milk. Farmers have administered booster shots of BST to their herds for years. Until a decade ago, however, the only way to produce BST was to butcher cows and collect their pituitary glands.

In 1982, genetic engineers discovered how to mass-produce synthetic BST by splicing cow genes with the genes of *E. coli* bacteria. St. Louis-based Monsanto Co. expects to win the approval of the Food and Drug Administration (FDA) for its genetically engineered hormone any time now.

Milk from cows injected with synthetic BST should be clearly labeled, the Pure Food Campaign, a Washington-based activist group founded by Rifkin, insists. Test usage of synthetic BST has produced some of the horrors that Rifkin and his allies fear from unrestricted genetic engineering: infections and deformities in cows, milk overproduction and a boom in the drugs and antibiotics needed to counteract its side effects. "BST is a bellwether," said Daniel J. Barry, the Pure Food Campaign's executive director.

Maybe. And maybe not. Scientists agree that BST-treated cows don't pass on any more of the hormone in their milk than untreated cows. And BST differs from genetically engineered foods because it goes into the cow that produces the milk, not into the milk itself. "I don't think BST is really a biotechnology product in terms of what drives the labeling debate," said Jerold R. Mande, the FDA's acting associate commissioner for legislative affairs.

"The bellwether is going to be the successful marketing of genetically engineered products, regardless of what they are," Richard D. Godown of the Biotechnology Industry Organization said. "After the first two, or three, or four, or five products have been accepted, there probably won't be any more discussion."

nies developing genetically engineered tomatoes, Godown said, "are trying for a share of that market."

Investment analysts suggest that success in the marketplace could also boost the value of biotechnology stocks, which have slumped on Wall Street in recent months. Even the U.S. economy stands to gain, the industry argues.

Last year, the U.S. biotechnology sector sold $5.9 billion worth of products and generated 79,000 jobs for American workers, industry representatives say. If regulatory snarls over labeling hinder the sale of genetically engineered foods, the United States may lose not only jobs and tax revenues, but also its current undisputed lead over Japanese and European biotech competitors, the industry contends.

John Eisele

Michael Taylor, the Food and Drug Administration's deputy commissioner for policy "The questions will be resolved before these folks cross the line to the market."

The biotechnology community bristles at the activists' suggestion that the industry is more interested in making a profit than it is in protecting the public from a future where a family sitting down to dinner finds animal, vegetable and mineral all jumbled together on the plate.

"There is, and has been, and will continue to be, a considerable amount of thought given to the long-term consequences of genetic engineering," Godown said. "To presume that any health or safety considerations are being subsumed into [the industry's] financial decisions is, first, to betray ignorance about how the federal regulatory system works. And two, it simply ain't true."

ALTERATION ALTERCATION

When it comes to genetic engineering, the federal regulatory system seems to be in something of a quandary.

Rifkin and his allies expected the FDA to crack down publicly on genetically engineered food products after the Clinton Administration came to town. To the activists' surprise, however, the Administration has adopted a conciliatory approach to the biotechnology industry and its agribusiness and food-processing supporters.

In late April, the FDA took the unusual action of holding a second comment period on its genetic engineering guidelines; FDA officials estimate that most of the 700 letters they received during the second period fiercely opposed mandatory labeling.

"Genetic engineering is merely an extension of traditional [plant-breeding] techniques that is more precise (and therefore likely to be on average less risky) than the more 'scattered-shot' techniques of crop modification that have been in use up to now," the Bethesda (Md.)-based American Society of Biochemistry and Molecular Biology wrote. "There is no scientific basis for labeling foods simply because they have been genetically engineered."

FDA officials also have yet to clarify how wide a range of allergens its 1992 labeling guidelines encompass.

The FDA guidelines may require a label when a genetically engineered food contains a known allergen (nuts, shellfish or wheat, for instance), but what about allergens outside the "known" range, consumer activists ask. Scientists have already developed a tomato that carries genetic material from a flounder to protect it from cold growing conditions. Wouldn't someone who happens to be allergic to flounder deserve to know about that when he or she tops off a hamburger with a thick slice of genetically altered tomato?

The issue is tricky, FDA officials concede. "If you take all the vitamin C out of oranges, that would be a clear change in attribute," Michael Taylor, the agency's deputy commissioner for policy, said in an interview. "But if you cross species lines, from animals to plants, is that the kind of change that is important enough to be disclosed on a label? I will admit to everybody we don't know the answer to that."

The FDA will hold a public hearing next spring to address all the ramifications of the allergenicity question, Taylor said. Biotechnology companies, however, have already begun to complain that the longer the agency takes to make up its mind on such issues, the harder—and costlier—the process of getting their products to market becomes.

"I don't blame them for wanting to know the answers to these questions," Taylor said. "They've invested a whole lot of money in developing these products, so it's fair to want answers. [But] they ought to rest assured that we have a public process in place to resolve these questions. And the questions *will* be resolved before these folks cross the line to the market."

IT'S ONLY NATURAL—OR IS IT?

With the Flavr Savr tomato just around the corner from your neighborhood supermarket, the confusion over what's "natural" seems to be increasing. Thanks to advances in biotechnology, in fact, genetically altered foods may be the new and improved natural foods of the future. So what's *really* natural—and what's not?

Take ordinary tap water, for instance. It's treated with chemicals and additives to make it safer to drink. And what about spring water? It contains benzene, a cancer-causing agent that must be filtered out before the water is safe to drink.

And what about such hybrid fruits and vegetables as tangelos (a cross between tangerines and oranges) and broccoflowers (a cross between broccoli and cauliflower)? Richard D. Godown, a senior vice president of the Washington-based Biotechnology Industry Organization, said that genetically engineered plants are just as natural as the hybrid variety. "The genetically modified plant is when a plant is modified through recombinant-DNA technology instead of being produced through traditional means of crossbreeding," he said in an interview.

The meat industry has used steroids, growth hormones and artificial insemination for a long time. But now, with genetic engineers able to clone cattle and other animals (reproducing any number of identical specimens from a single embryonic cell) or even to splice genes from other species into them, consumer activists say that the line between what's natural and what's not may soon get even fuzzier.

Natural is what "takes place in nature," said Michael Sligh, the director of the Rural Advancement Foundation International's Sustainable Agriculture Program. "A lot of mutations take place in nature, but they take place within a species." With genetic engineering, "that paradigm no longer exists," Sligh explained. "If human genes can be used to make leaner pork, it makes me wonder when pigs will start talking."

—Vanessa B. White

THE RACE TO REGULATE

State and local governments might beat the FDA to the punch. Last March, longtime consumer activist Mark Green, then New York City's consumer affairs commissioner and now its public advocate, proposed a city ordinance that would require genetically engineered foods to be displayed for sale separately from other foods and to be identified by a conspicuous sign. The New York City Council is still debating the measure.

On Aug. 4, the Windy City went the Big Apple one better when the Chicago City Council unanimously passed an ordinance requiring grocery stores and restaurants to display signs proclaiming "This Food Product Has Been Genetically Engineered" over products that meet that description. The law carries fines of $25-$500.

Even though the ordinance officially went into effect on Oct. 3, it has yet to be enforced. The Chicago Department of Consumer Services, which is in charge of enforcing the ordinance, is still "in the process of researching and developing rules and regulations," Constance Buscemi, a spokeswoman, said in an interview.

The biotechnology industry isn't impressed. The Chicago ordinance, Godown said, "is a tempest in a midwestern teapot."

"Chicago has set a very important example, and we want to follow their lead," the Pure Food Campaign's Barry said. His group is contacting about 1,800 local lawmakers nationwide to encourage them to introduce Chicago-style ordinances in their own cities.

There's also a chance that the entire controversy over genetically engineered food could end up in Congress's lap.

In the 102nd Congress, Rep. Gerald D. Kleczka, D-Wis., introduced legislation that would force the FDA to require any genetically altered foods to be so labeled. The bill went nowhere, but Kleczka reintroduced it in May.

The Consumer Federation of America and the Environmental Defense Fund, Kleczka said in an interview, are considering supporting the bill. "Besides, the labeling issue won't go away," he added. "It will only become more evident when these foods go on the market."

The FDA also hints that it might ask Congress to expand its statutory authority so that it can require "premarket notification" from companies that are planning to introduce genetically engineered foods into the marketplace.

Under the 1938 Food, Drug and Cosmetic Act, companies must obtain a license from the FDA before they can sell drugs of any kind. But because the law doesn't require a license for food products, the FDA has no way to keep track of foods that contain altered genes.

The Pure Food Campaign is pushing the FDA to registry of genetically engineered foods so that the agency can track down a food's producer if problems occur.

At the moment, Calgene, Monsanto and the handful of other biotechnology companies with products already in the regulatory pipeline are working hand in glove with the FDA. Calgene has even offered to provide informational pamphlets to accompany Flavr Savr tomatoes sold whole in produce sections.

FDA officials are clearly worried that biotechnology companies will become less compliant over time. But they are reluctant to press the point. "We are considering the possibility either administratively, or even conceivably legislatively, of creating a premarket regime that would make more formal the consultation that is currently going on," Taylor said, choosing his words carefully.

"Industry would be very, very concerned about any change in the Food, Drug and Cosmetic Act," Godown responded when told of Taylor's comment. "We can't conceive of any possible need for new authority for the FDA in order for it to regulate genetic engineering."

In other words, if the newest round of the old science-versus-the-public debate goes to Congress, look out for a food fight.

The Big Harvest

Corn growers, midwestern politicians and Archer-Daniels-Midland Co. lobbied relentlessly for an Environmental Protection Agency ruling that guarantees ethanol a major share of the reformulated-fuels market.

PETER H. STONE

Last November, a small group of midwestern lawmakers huddled with presidential adviser Bruce R. Lindsey in the offices of Sen. Thomas A. Daschle, D-S.D. The Congressmen reminded Lindsey that Bill Clinton had pledged during his 1992 campaign to help midwestern farmers and to boost the use of ethanol, a corn-based automotive fuel. A pro-ethanol policy would buoy Democratic political fortunes—presidential and congressional—in the Midwest, they argued.

That wasn't the last that the White House would hear from the ethanol lobby. Soon afterward, it was deluged with postcards and letters from midwestern corn growers urging that the government adopt a mandate requiring that ethanol be included in reformulated gasoline, which oil companies must start selling in 1995 to comply with the 1990 amendments to the Clean Air Act.

And when the Democratic National Committee (DNC) scheduled a major fund-raising dinner in Washington in June, Dwayne O. Andreas, the chairman of Archer-Daniels-Midland Co. (ADM)—which produces about 70 per cent of the nation's ethanol—agreed to be a co-chairman of the event and chipped in a $100,000 donation. Andreas, renowned for his large contributions to Republicans as well as Democrats, gave more than $200,000 to Democratic Party organizations in the 15 months preceding the dinner.

The ethanol lobby's persistence paid off. About two weeks after the fund-raising gala, the Environmental Protection Agency (EPA) issued a regulation essentially requiring that by 1996, 10 per cent of the gasoline sold in the United States contain ethanol.

"This was a steamroller, and it ran over everybody," said Fred Craft, the president of the Oxygenated Fuels Association, which represents makers of fuel additives that use ethanol and its chief market rival, methanol. "It had to do with money, politics and the White House." Craft's group opposes special breaks for either additive.

Although Clinton had been an ethanol enthusiast since his days as governor of Arkansas, he faced considerable pressure on the reformulated gasoline issue. Oil and natural gas interests—which produce methanol—argued that ethanol should not be given favored treatment. Joining them were environmental activists, who argued that MTBE (methyl tertiary butyl ether), a methanol derivative, would be more effective in reducing toxic air pollutants. Before EPA issued its final decision, 51 Senators and more than 120 House Members wrote to EPA administrator Carol Browner, urging her to abort the ruling.

Critics contend that increased ethanol use could lead to increased pollution and would not, as ethanol advocates maintain, significantly reduce U.S. dependence on imported oil. They also argue that EPA lacked authority to take such action under the Clean Air Act.

The fight isn't over. Sen. Bill Bradley, D-N.J., has introduced a bill that would largely phase out other major government subsidies for ethanol. Sen. J. Bennett Johnston, D-La., is pushing legislation that would cut off EPA funds to implement the rule.

And earlier this month, the American Petroleum Institute (API) and the National Petroleum Refiners Association filed a lawsuit in the U.S. Court of Appeals for the District of Columbia Circuit, seeking to have the rule set aside.

"It's blatantly illegal and irrational," said Charles J. DiBona, the president of the API, which has promoted petroleum-based fuels such as methanol. "The EPA does not have the authority to redistribute income."

THE FARM TEAM

The Administration worked hard to avoid such a backlash. When the EPA ruling was announced, Clinton issued a statement touting its potential to boost demand for corn by 250 million bushels a year and to provide "thousands of new jobs for the future. . . . This policy is good for our environment, our public health and our nation's farmers—and that's good for America," he said.

The ruling implements a provision of the Clean Air Act amendments stipulating that the gasoline sold in the country's most-polluted cities must contain a smog-reducing renewable oxygenate by 1995. In effect, that mandates the use of ethanol because—unlike most methanol—it is made from a renewable product, and it is the only renewable additive available in large quantities.

As of next Jan. 1, gasoline sold in those cities must contain at least 15 per cent ethanol; a year later, the percentage is to rise to 30 per cent, giving ethanol an estimated 10 per cent share of the nation's automotive fuel market.

Ethanol improves combustion and limits carbon monoxide emissions. But critics point out that it makes gasoline evaporate faster, which adds to smog problems. To help curb smog in summer—when the problem is worst—the EPA rule would permit ETBE (ethyl tertiary butyl ether), an ethanol derivative that's less prone to evaporation, to be substituted for ethanol during the summer months. But critics say that remedy is insufficient.

The EPA's decision followed a lengthy Administration debate about how to help ethanol producers—and cultivate the midwestern electoral base—without antagonizing environmental activists, the oil industry and their congressional allies.

When Clinton took office, ethanol producers were pushing aggressively for a waiver that would allow ethanol-blended gasoline to exceed federal pollution-control standards.

But the Administration was wary of this proposal because of its environmental risks. (A variation on the waiver idea was backed by the Bush Administration, but was never implemented.) Even ethanol advocates were divided. Some Senators, including Democrats Paul Simon and Carol Moseley-Braun of Illinois and Republican Charles E. Grassley of Iowa, supported the proposed waiver. But another bloc of midwestern legislators—including Daschle and Democratic Sens. Tom Harkin of Iowa, Robert Kerrey of Nebraska and Paul Wellstone of Minnesota—argued that a less-risky avenue should be found to spur ethanol use.

In May 1993, several midwestern Senators met with Browner and Vice President Albert Gore Jr. to press the Administration about what it would do to promote ethanol. Gore made supportive comments about ethanol, but he made no commitments and voiced concerns about the proposed waiver. He also said that he would like to see some independent scientific studies to support ethanol's benefits.

Proponents of the waiver tried to allay Gore's concerns by citing a study by the Chicago-based Council of Great Lakes Governors that stressed the advantages of using ethanol. The report concluded that fuel containing 10 per cent ethanol would be as effective as MTBE in reducing urban ozone pollution. Although the report was viewed skeptically even by some lawmakers sympathetic to ethanol, it was widely distributed to Administration officials and to corn state Senators as lobbying ammunition.

In the meantime, ethanol advocates had found an ally in the Administration: Agriculture Secretary Mike Espy. Espy, concerned that the proposed waiver was not environmentally defensible, floated a proposal during the summer of 1993 that called for reformulated gasoline to contain 30 per cent ethanol.

Keith Heard, the Washington lobbyist for the National Corn Growers Association, said that ethanol makers' efforts to capitalize on the Clean Air Act amendments were starting to flounder until Espy became active. "Espy made his play with a proposal similar to what EPA came out with," Heard said. "Espy was very important."

Congressional ethanol boosters stepped up the pressure, too. Kerrey asked the Agriculture Department last November to analyze the economic impact on corn growers if ethanol was not given a "meaningful" share of the reformulated gasoline market. The study forecast big reductions in the amount of corn used for ethanol and warned that this could increase government subsidies to corn growers.

During October and November, Daschle had at least two discussions with then-White House chief of staff Thomas F. (Mack) McLarty III about the need for fast action. Ethanol enthusiasts "talked extensively to Gore, Browner, McLarty and to anyone who would listen," Daschle said in an interview. "Our message was that this was good for farmers, for the environment and for the budget."

Archer-Daniels-Midland chairman Dwayne O. Andreas
Behind-the-scenes lobbying—and $300,000 in "soft" money—helped ADM win big.

Other political pressure came from the Governors' Ethanol Coalition, a group of about 20 mostly midwestern governors. The group, founded about three years ago, was one of the first and most visible proponents of setting a mandatory minimum ethanol content for reformulated fuels. And it had special cachet with the Administration because Clinton had been among its first members; before his election as President, he had been slated to head the organization in 1993.

Another key ingredient in the lobbying effort was the clout of corn growers. The National Corn Growers Association boasts that during April and May of this year, its members sent about 15,000 tags from corn seed bags to the White House. The tags were addressed to Clinton in care of Marion Berry, a special assistant to the President on agriculture who has offices in the White House and at the Agriculture Department.

So effective was the effort that an

Energy Department official advised a meeting of oil lobbyists at the API last spring that "if they wanted to turn this around" they should emulate the growers' tactics.

State farm bureaus also flexed their muscle. The Illinois Farm Bureau estimates that it helped generate 12,000 letters from Illinois farmers to Administration officials in support of the ethanol mandate after EPA first proposed it last December.

Bill Burton, a former top aide to McLarty who is now a partner in the Austin (Texas) office of Jones, Day, Reavis & Pogue, the Cleveland-based law firm, recalled that McLarty's office earlier this year "received a tremendous number of postcards, letters and phone calls from the Midwest" in favor of a mandate. In particular, Burton cited large quantities of preprinted yellow postcards from farm groups addressed to the President.

DWAYNE'S WORLD

Less visible, but no less effective, was a quiet lobbying campaign by ADM and allied ethanol trade groups.

ADM, a giant grain company headquartered in Decatur, Ill., is known for getting political favors by working behind the scenes in Washington. Ethanol enjoys two tax breaks: a credit for companies that blend ethanol and an exemption from federal excise taxes. No other motor fuel enjoys such treatment. And ADM has successfully lobbied for sugar import quotas, which lead to higher prices for corn sweeteners that the company makes.

It's estimated that the ethanol excise tax exemption costs the Treasury about $550 million annually. The increased use of ethanol under the new rule could cost taxpayers an additional $340 million yearly.

Ethanol advocates, aware that the Administration didn't want to appear to be giving ADM another subsidy, urged company officials to keep a low profile. "Our message to ADM was just try to stay out of it," Daschle said. "We didn't want people to point to ADM and say that ADM was the driving force behind this effort." (Andreas and other ADM executives declined to be interviewed for this article.)

METHANOL POISON

THIS IS A TRUTH ALERT.

American Petroleum Institute (API) with an $80 million annual budget and 450 propaganda specialists at its disposal has disseminated a barrage of false information about ethanol.

WHY? Because their objective is to substitute foreign Methanol for Ethanol. Methanol is a dangerous, poisonous material. Ethanol is pure grain alcohol, like you drink when you drink Vodka.

Gasoline with 10% Ethanol is proven to reduce carbon monoxide from automobile emissions by 25% or more, saving millions of people from lung damage.

Methanol on the other hand as advocated by API is deadly poison. It was called wood alcohol on your mother's shelf in a bottle with skull and bones on the label.

One ounce of it will make you permanently blind—2 ounces will kill you as it has thousands of people around the world who drank it by mistake.

Fumes from your gas tank contain ... Methanol can make you sick. When ga... tions in Alaska used MTBE; made fro... Methanol, so many people went to th... pital that the government banned it ... their state. Other states, such as New ... have had equally bad experiences.

TRUTH In 1989, before his constituents decided to use this poisonous toxic material on a large scale because it is so cheap, the Vice President of American Petroleum Institute (API), Mr. O'Keefe said, **"The inhalation of Methanol vapors can be fatal... Methanol fuel raises serious public health concerns because it is highly toxic. Small amounts either ingested or absorbed through the skin can cause blindness, permanent neurological damage and death."**

Moral of this story: Believe Mr. O'Keefe who told the truth in 1989.

ALSO, Charles J. Dibona, President of the American Petroleum Institute, summed it up best in his March 1991 testimony before the U.S. Senate Committee on Energy and Natural Resources: "Growing dependence on oil imports from insecure sources...threatens energy security, undermines the U.S. economy, and costs ...

"Thumbs Up" For Ethanol!

We are governors who believe a new federal program that creates jobs for Americans, cleans our air, stimulates the economy and reduces oil imports is a great idea.

The U.S. Environmental Protection Agency has designed this program under guidelines of the Clean Air Act. It will use fuels such as ethanol which cut dangerous carbon monoxide and other pollutants when mixed with gasoline sold in our smoggiest cities.

Ethanol is a renewable product, today made primarily from Midwest corn. But it can be produced throughout the nation from other grains and, potentially, all forms of biomass such as switch grass, sorghum, sycamores, poplars and even waste paper.

Our Governors' Ethanol Coalition estimates that the program will stimulate the investment of as much as $3 billion in capital in ethanol plant construction. And, up to 75,000 jobs can be created every two years in the next decade as the demand for ethanol expands.

As several U.S. Senators put it in a recent letter to their Capitol Hill colleagues, the EPA initiative "will benefit national taxpayers by reducing farm support payments, and generating economic activity nationwide."

Of course, the more we can rely on a "home grown" renewable fuel, the less foreign oil we will have to import from abroad.

We are confident that our nation's agriculture and petroleum industries—whose technical, research, manufacturing and transportation capabilities are the envy of the world—can deliver new fuels to American motorists by the government's 1995 timetable.

And, the members of the Governors' Ethanol Coalition give our "thumbs up" for ethanol.

The fuel of the future.

GOVERNORS' ETHANOL COALITION

Nebraska Governor
E. Benjamin Nelson
Chair
Governors' Ethanol Coalition

Wisconsin Governor
Tommy G. Thompson
Vice Chair
Governors' Ethanol Coalition

Arkansas Gov. Jim Guy Tucker
Iowa Gov. Terry Branstad
Montana Gov. Marc Racicot
Colorado Gov. Roy Romer
Kansas Gov. Joan Finney
New Mexico Gov. Bruce King
Hawaii Gov. John Waihee
Kentucky Gov. Brereton Jones
North Dakota Gov. Ed Schafer
Illinois Gov. Jim Edgar
Michigan Gov. John Engler
Ohio Gov. George Voinovich
Indiana Gov. Evan Bayh
Minnesota Gov. Arne Carlson
South Dakota Gov. Walter Dale Miller
Missouri Gov. Mel Carnahan

Ethanol advocates advertised heavily. But some of their rivals cried foul.

Still, Andreas had multiple avenues for getting his message to Washington. He is good friends, for instance, with former DNC chairman Robert S. Strauss, a name partner in the Washington office of the law firm of Akin, Gump, Strauss, Hauer & Feld. Strauss sits on ADM's board, and his firm represents the company.

Last year, when Strauss helped the Administration in its fight for approval of the North American Free Trade Agreement, he called on Andreas for assistance, and ADM lobbied aggressively for the pact.

Strauss's law partner, Vernon E. Jordan Jr., is a Clinton confidant and chaired the DNC fund-raising dinner in June. It was Jordan who solicited Andreas's $100,000 contribution, Strauss said in an interview. Although Andreas didn't attend the dinner, he was listed as one of five co-chairmen of the event.

Political contributions have long been a central part of Andreas's modus operandi. During the Reagan and Bush Administrations, he was a leading Republican Party donor; during the 1992 election cycle alone, Andreas and ADM kicked in about $1.1 million in "soft" money to Republican Party organizations. (Soft money, although it can't legally be spent on federal campaigns, can be used for state and local campaigns and for get-out-the-vote drives and other party activities.)

But Andreas has always been adept at spreading his capital around to hedge his political bets. As the 1992 campaign drew to a close and Clinton looked like a winner, he started upping his gifts to Democrats. During the past 18 months, Andreas and ADM have given more than $300,000 in soft money to Democratic groups—roughly six times what they have contributed to Republicans.

Andreas and ADM have also been liberal contributors to Members of Congress, especially midwesterners. In the 1992 election cycle, the leading recipients of donations from ADM executives, their families and the company's PAC were Daschle and Grassley, who got $10,000 apiece, and Sens. Christopher S. (Kit) Bond, R-Mo., and Byron L. Dorgan, D-N.D., who got $8,000 each, according to the Center for Responsive Politics, a nonpartisan Washington group that tracks campaign spending.

In June, ADM vice president Howard Buffett visited key lawmakers on both sides of the issue. He was accompanied by Fred Potter, an Arlington (Va.)-based publisher of three alternative-fuels newsletters who supports wider use of ethanol. Potter recently was retained by ADM as a Washington consultant.

Earlier, Simon hosted a meeting for Energy Secretary Hazel R. O'Leary with Buffett and Martin L. Andreas, Dwayne's nephew and assistant, in which the ADM duo pitched the merits of the company's products.

The Renewable Fuels Association, an ethanol trade group that is dominated by ADM, also lobbied Congress and the Administration for the mandate.

ADM and its allies also mounted an advertising blitz proclaiming the virtues of ethanol and warning darkly of risks from competing alternatives such as methanol. The company helped organize a group called Agriculture for Clean Air that ran anti-methanol advertisements in several large publications. Larry Quandt, the president of the Illinois Farmers Union, a leading member of the group, said that the ads cost more than $200,000 and that ADM was instrumental in financing them.

The Governors' Ethanol Coalition also ran advertisements in five Washington publications. And Nebraska Gov. E. Benjamin Nelson, who heads the group, wrote pro-ethanol op-ed articles for *The New York Times* and met with presidential aide Lindsey.

Some of the advertising seems to have backfired, though. Shortly before EPA issued its decision, the American Methanol Institute filed a complaint with the Federal Trade Commission alleging that two of the ads—including one entitled "This is a Truth Alert"—were "blatantly false and misleading." The complaint said that the ads would dissuade consumers from buying fuel containing methanol-derived MTBE, an additive used to make gasoline cleaner.

The Truth Alert ad, which appeared in Congressional Quarterly Inc.'s *Weekly Report*, *National Journal* and *The Washington Post*, called methanol a "dangerous, poisonous product" but didn't note that gasoline mixed with ethanol is also toxic and dangerous, the complaint said. And it said the ad failed to point out that methanol and MTBE are generally safe when used appropriately.

The complaint also charged that the ads falsely described methanol as an "imported" product, when 93.5 per cent of methanol used in the United States is produced domestically, according to Commerce Department statistics.

Methanol advocates countered the ethanol industry attack with their own advertising campaign. Although their advertising budget was smaller, they went for the jugular, too. "EPA's plan is bad for the environment, bad for taxpayers, bad for consumers," proclaimed an ad that the American Methanol Institute helped underwrite.

ANOTHER TAX BREAK?

Critics of the proposed ethanol mandate also worked hard on Capitol Hill; they were instrumental, for example, in generating the congressional letters of protest to Browner. The ethanol debate helped create an informal—and unusual—alliance of oil companies and such major environmental groups as the Sierra Club and the Natural Resources Defense Council Inc.

But ethanol had the upper hand. "This is an issue that the agriculture industry cares passionately about," said A. Blakeman Early, a lobbyist for the Sierra Club who fought hard against the mandate. "But it's only one of many issues that the oil industry has on its agenda. These are important political states. The oil industry was unable to stop this."

"I've never seen such a successful lobbying campaign that persuaded people in the White House to do something when there was no underlying reason to do it other than politics," Craft of the Oxygenated Fuels Association said.

Craft and other critics are especially peeved at the Clinton Administration for abandoning an agreement that EPA announced in 1992 after it oversaw lengthy negotiations between oil, ethanol and environmental interests. The agreement gave oil companies considerable leeway to formulate cleaner-burning fuels, without specifying what kind of additives they should use.

"This is the biggest gasoline change in the history of America," Craft said. "What the hell is all this about? It has to do with market share. [Ethanol interests] don't want the risks of the marketplace influencing their profits."

Environmental activists cite a recent Energy Department study suggesting that the EPA rule could lead to a slight increase in pollution because of ethanol's volatility. And some state environmental officials testified at congressional hearings last spring that the mandate could worsen air quality and contribute to an increase in greenhouse gas emissions.

Requiring the use of less-volatile ETBE during the summer could make the situation worse, Early said. ETBE is relatively untested and is more expensive than ethanol, and refiners would have an incentive to load up their fuel with ethanol during the spring and fall so they could minimize their use of ETBE and still meet the over-all 30 per cent minimum, he said.

John Eisele

Sen. Bill Bradley, D-N.J.
He wants to eliminate tax credits for ethanol makers.

Consumers may also be hurt. Sen. Bradley has estimated that ethanol-blended fuel will cost at least 3-7 cents a gallon more than regular gasoline.

Bradley, who represents a state that's home to major oil refineries, has gone on the offensive, introducing legislation that would phase out ethanol tax credits. "From my standpoint, they already have too many subsidies through the tax," he said in an interview. "They don't need a mandated market. It makes no economic sense and no environmental sense."

And Johnston, whose state is also home to major oil-industry interests, has introduced legislation that could be acted on by the end of July, to prohibit EPA from spending funds to implement the rule.

EPA officials vigorously defend their decision. "I believe we succeeded in crafting a rule that achieves the maximum environmental benefits," Mary Nichols, the assistant EPA administrator for air and radiation, said. Fuel containing 30 per cent ethanol emits 15 per cent fewer toxic and smog-causing pollutants than regular fuel does, she said.

Nichols acknowledged that there were divisions within the Administration. "I'd say there were varying degrees of enthusiasm at EPA and [the Energy Department] about the rule," she said. Asked whether there was White House pressure to issue the rule, Nichols said that she was "aware that the President had made a commitment to the role of ethanol in the reformulated gas program."

Burton, the former McLarty aide, said that the Administration tried its utmost to avoid making a decision that appeared to benefit ADM. "The conventional wisdom on this is wrong," Burton said, referring to press coverage that linked the ruling to ADM's political contributions. "It's an important rule that affects a lot of people. Ethanol is good for farmers. [The Agriculture Department] was one of its biggest proponents."

Meanwhile, the ethanol industry is seeking additional tax breaks. Daschle has introduced legislation that would extend the ethanol tax credit to cover ETBE, and ethanol interests are lobbying the Treasury Department to extend the tax credit by administrative action.

Ironically, much of the pressure for the expanded credit is coming from ARCO Chemical Co., a unit of the oil giant Atlantic Richfield Co. ARCO produces ETBE, but it's also the biggest manufacturer of the methanol derivative MTBE.

Like the cornfields of the Midwest, the ethanol lobby just seems to keep rolling along.

Plowing a New Field

Ideological battle lines are being drawn, and this year's farm bill will provide a test of Republicans' appetite for radicalism.

JONATHAN RAUCH

This time, it's war. "All or nothing," Thomas A. Hammer said. "No more Mr. Nice Guy. We're talking about a floor fight for the whole bag of marbles."

Hammer is president of the Sweetener Users Association, which represents soft-drink companies, chocolatiers, bakers, ice cream manufacturers, confectioners. All have in common their dislike of the federal sugar program, which props up sugar prices by restricting imports and regulating domestic supplies.

In the 1990 farm bill, the sweetener users lobbied for lower price supports on sugar. Instead they got their heads handed to them: Congress reaffirmed the existing price level and, to maintain it, authorized mandatory federal controls on how much sugar producers can sell. "The government tells us who we can buy from and at what price," Hammer said. "In our opinion, it's horrible."

Now comes the 1995 farm bill, and this time the sugar users are going for broke. "We've been at the business of trying to reform this program for decades, and it hasn't gotten better, it's gotten worse," Hammer said. "A decade is long enough to work for reform. You've got to get rid of the program."

Hammer is making a bet: that the new Republican Congress is in a revolutionary mood and the old rules are out the window. "I don't think a business-as-usual type of solution is going to fly," Hammer said. "If Congress doesn't do anything about the sugar program, this Congress is going to look very much like the old Congress."

Across town, Luther A. Markwart is not trembling. Cool as the proverbial cucumber, Markwart is chairman of the American Sugar Alliance, which represents sugar growers and other beneficiaries of the current program. Abolition? "I don't think so," he said with smiling assurance. "I feel confident it will be renewed."

The General Accounting Office says that the sugar program costs Americans $1.4 billion a year, a number that Markwart disputes. Underlying his confidence, however, is a number accepted by all sides: zero. Because it relies on supply controls rather than subsidy payments, the sugar program costs the Treasury nothing. "If you're a taxpayer looking around saying, 'We've got to find places to save money,' this is not one of them," Markwart said. In the standard playbook, no-cost programs don't get whacked.

But this may not be a standard year. The sugar dispute is more than a lobbying war. Like the farm bill debate generally, it's a microcosm of a defining battle for the Republican soul. On one side is fiscalism; on the other, radicalism.

Fiscalism is about reducing the budget deficit. Under fiscalism, the deficit defines and drives change: First you pick a deficit reduction goal, then you get there with as little structural change as possible. Across-the-board freezes, payment-formula adjustments, benefit-payment delays and accounting tricks are the preferred methods; eliminating or radically changing programs is avoided except where absolutely unavoidable.

Radicalism, by contrast, is about reducing the government. Curtailing, privatizing or killing programs may or may not save a lot of money, but for radicals that's a secondary issue. The main thing is to cage the gorilla in Washington. If replacing welfare, reducing tariffs or killing the sugar program carries some up-front costs, so be it.

Fiscalism has dominated, indeed obsessed, Washington since the early 1980s. But radicals think the election gave them a mandate. William Kristol, a leading Republican strategist, scoffs at the notion that the sugar subsidy is off-limits just because it's budgetarily invisible. "I don't think that'll wash. People are more sophisticated today, and it isn't just a budgetary matter. It really is a matter of limiting government interference in both society and the marketplace."

Tom Hammer is betting on radicalism and Luther Markwart has his money on fiscalism. Old farm-bill hands favor Markwart to win. But this year, they hasten to add, could bring the farm bill that upends all the rules.

From *National Journal,* January 28, 1995, pp. 212-216.

A BLUNDER'S LEGACY

In 1981, President Reagan sent up a farm bill calling for deep reductions in spending; Congress, waving it aside, instead passed a bill that set high support prices for commodities. That turned out to be one of the decade's great policy blunders. The government supports commodity prices by buying crops from farmers when market prices fall below a specified level. The 1981 support prices turned out to be so far above market prices that the government ended up buying much of the country's crop.

As grain poured into government warehouses instead of into foreign and domestic markets, program costs soared and U.S. exports crashed. From 1980-86, U.S. agricultural exports declined by half, after inflation. Meanwhile, the farm sector fell into a profound recession, the worst since the 1930s. "It was a traumatic decade," said Neil E. Harl, a farm economist at Iowa State University. In Iowa, farmland values declined by a dizzying 63 per cent.

The story of U.S. agriculture since then has been one of slow, aching recovery, both for farmers and for federal farm policy. The farm sector is mostly back on its feet, if still a bit wobbly. Farm policy has steered a corrected, though not reversed, course.

In the 1985 farm bill, Congress set out to right what had gone so far wrong. Support prices were reduced sharply, so that farmers would sell their crops on the market instead of to the government. But to prevent farmers' income from crashing as prices fell, cash subsidies (known as deficiency payments) were increased.

The new program succeeded in moving U.S. crops back into the marketplace, but it was expensive. So the 1990 farm bill began whittling. It stayed the course set in 1985, but reduced payment levels and cut back on the number of subsidized acres. In effect, the 1990 policy was less of the same.

There were three problems with that approach. First, it didn't keep the deficit wolf away from the door. Farm programs are entitlements whose costs depend on the vagaries of world market prices and crop yields, and so their costs have a way of running ahead of expectations. Farm program costs have declined since the crisis years of the 1980s. But they've also been well above the level that Congress thought it approved in 1990. *(See table, this page.)*

Second, one way in which farm programs support commodity prices is by inducing farmers to take land out of production; in an average year, about one of every seven acres is idled. The trouble is that agriculture is now a hotly competitive world market, and when the United States sells less, other countries gleefully snap up additional market share. And, in fact, the U.S. share of grain trade has been tending downward. *(See chart, p. 88.)* Many economists believe the farm programs have contributed to that trend.

Third, along with farm subsidies come strings. Environmental rules. Land conservation rules. Rules on what you can plant and how much of it. As subsidy levels are reduced, the incentive for farmers to join the programs and put up with all those headaches diminishes. Robert E. Young, an agricultural economist with the Food and Agricultural Policy Research Institute at the University of Missouri, calculates that by the turn of the century, wheat farmers will be getting a return of only about $20 an acre from the farm program, down from $50 in 1990—and that's under current policies. Another round of reductions would only steepen the drop.

"You do get to the stage where what you're getting inside the program is about the same as what you get outside it," Young said. "Why not say forget it?" That's one reason some reformers argue for a total overhaul. Continued budget cutting, they say, eventually drives the programs to irrelevance.

A "PROFOUND" DEBATE?

Nonetheless, until last November the shape of the 1995 farm bill looked pretty clear. President Clinton and the congressional Budget Committees would seek to whittle down farm programs, and farm-state legislators would grumblingly comply. The result would be a rerun of 1990: more cost cutting without fundamentally altering the government's role. In other words, fiscalism.

Smart money is still betting on that kind of farm legislation. So are the old-line farm lobbies. "The conventional wisdom before the election—and still in aggie-land—is that there will be a little bit of a cut and basically the same programs we had before," said Kenneth A. Cook, the president of the Environmental Working Group, a Washington research group that works for environmentally friendly farm policies. "But I think there's going to be a much more profound debate."

This year, two factors could break the farm bill debate wide open: first, the rise of radicalism—or at least of radical talk—on Capitol Hill; second, the emerging organizational strength of farm subsidies' opponents.

At an orientation seminar for new Members of Congress in December, a roomful of freshmen listened as John Frydenlund of the Heritage Foundation explained that all farm subsidies should be phased out over five years. By conventional standards, that's a pretty shocking idea. Even Heritage, the most conservative of Washington's major think tanks,

EXPECTATIONS V. REALITY

Farm spending and the 1990 farm bill (billions of dollars, by fiscal year)

	Actual spending	Predicted for 1990 farm bill
1982	$11.7	—
1983	18.9	—
1984	7.3	—
1985	17.7	—
1986	25.8	—
1987	22.4	—
1988	12.5	—
1989	10.5	—
1990	6.5	—
1991	10.1	$ 7.1
1992	9.7	8.5
1993	16.1	8.8
1994	10.3	10.2

SOURCES: Agriculture Department; Senate Agriculture, Nutrition and Forestry Committee

John Eisele

Thomas A. Hammer, president of the Sweetener Users Association
"A decade is long enough to work for reform. You've got to get rid of the program."

had never dared such a proposal until now; throughout the Reagan and Bush years, it settled for demanding reforms and reductions.

So were the incoming Members shocked? To the contrary, many thought Heritage was too tame. "There were a number of Members who thought, if we're talking about reforming welfare in two years, why in the world would it take five years to do agriculture?" said Frydenlund, who directs Heritage's agricultural policy project. "I'm really not a liberal, but there were some there who thought I was more of a liberal or a moderate."

The 1995 farm bill will say volumes, perhaps more even than the vaunted Contract With America, about whether the Republican revolution really is one.

As with welfare reform, so with farm programs: In the past few months, the radical has become thinkable. "I don't think we consider our proposal to be radical anymore at all," Frydenlund said. "The election has put us in a whole different realm."

Among Gingrichites, indeed, talking tough about farm subsidies has become a badge of commitment, a fact that causes no end of exasperation for the programs' proponents. "Everyone's saying cutting agriculture is a test of Republican seriousness," said Rep. Charles W. Stenholm of Texas, a conservative Democrat. "That's ridiculous."

Ridiculous or not, it is reality. "I wouldn't know a soybean from a—whatever," said Kristol, who grew up in Manhattan. But farm programs have become caught up in conservatism's larger quest for moral legitimacy. Conservatives are well aware that Democrats and liberals want nothing more than to portray Republicans as attacking the poor rather than dismantling Big Government. "If we cut welfare, why not farm subsidies?" said a *Wall Street Journal* editorial this month.

"The Republicans need to prove to a skeptical electorate that they're a different kind of politics," said David Frum, a conservative writer whose recent book, *Dead Right* (New Republic Books, 1994), is influential in Republican circles. "In order to do that, they need to pick out some of the most worthless programs that people would think Republicans would want to defend and ceremoniously have them decapitated. It's important as a test of whether you really believe in something."

Also as a test of seriousness about change. Just before Christmas, Kristol met with Pat Roberts, R-Kan., the new chairman of the House Agriculture Committee, to urge major cuts in farm programs—preferably the elimination of some. "The press is going to look at farm programs as a test of our willingness to cut government—and rightly so," Kristol said in an interview. "If the Republican Congress ends up producing a farm bill identical to the one a Democratic Congress produced, we will have failed."

UNPREDICTABILITY

Thus, to a unprecedented extent, this year's farm bill has been radicalized and nationalized, much as the 1994 elections were. That doesn't guarantee radical results, but it does create a whole new element of unpredictability. Adding to that unpredictability are new House rules that will make it easier to attack farm programs on the House floor, as the sugar program's opponents plan to do. Plus there's House Majority Leader Richard K. Armey of Texas, a free-marketer who for years has crusaded against farm programs; typical Armey-grams have called the peanut program, for instance, "wasteful and disgusting," "unfair" and "feudal," among other things. And then there's Sen. Richard G. Lugar, R-Ind., the wildest card of all.

Lugar is hardly wild in temperament or style. He is a farm owner from a farm state, and on most issues he is thought of as a conservative but no revolutionary. On agricultural policy, however, his free-market bent and his hawkish anti-deficit views have radicalized him. In the past, he has led quixotic efforts to kill the sugar and peanut programs. Now he is chairman of the Agriculture, Nutrition and Forestry Committee. And this Agriculture Committee chairman is talking about abolishing the agriculture programs.

His goal: "Moving very resolutely in the five-year period to the end of subsidies," he said in an interview. "Why should taxpayers subsidize farmers when they do not subsidize other small businesses that have failure rates often approaching 50 per cent?" Asked how he would feel about another 1990-style farm bill—one providing less of the same—he gave an emphatic reply: "I think that would be a very unsatisfactory situation for American agriculture. All of the distortions will have been confirmed."

Lugar has issued a long list of scorching questions about farm subsidies, to be the subject of Senate hearings starting probably in February. ("What is the ratio-

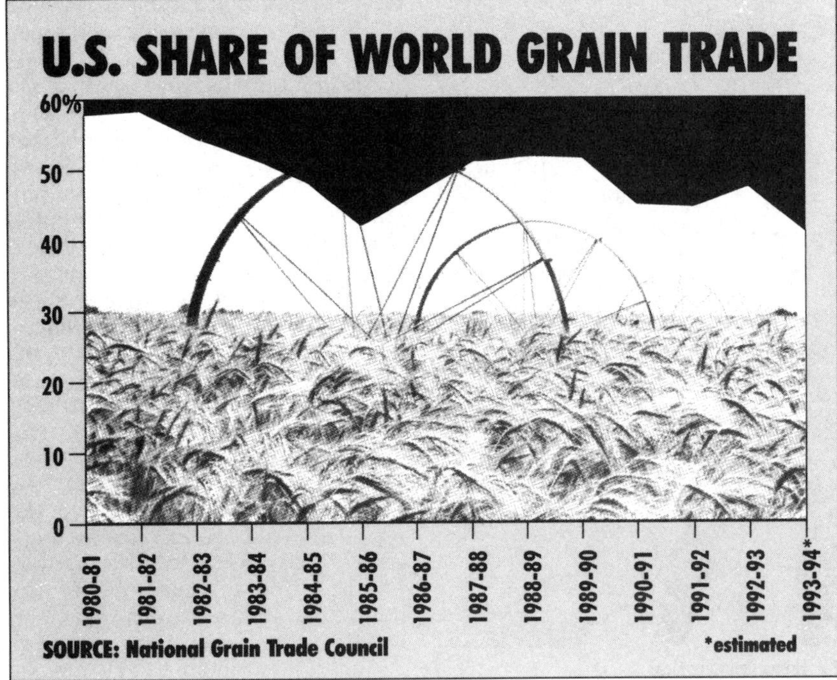

nale for transferring public funds from taxpayers, most of whom have moderate incomes, to all farmers, including those whose incomes and wealth are substantially above the national average?") He is demanding a "bottom-up" reappraisal of all farm programs and, what's more, speaks of ending the programs' entitlement status. "We must reform agricultural programs in such a way that spending has limits," he told Senate Budget Committee chairman Pete V. Domenici, R-N.M., in a December letter.

True, every farm bill is harder to pass than the last, partly because of the dwindling number of farmers. (Today less than 2 per cent of the population lives on farms, and most of those people are part-timers.) This year's bill, however, figures to be the most embattled yet. "It's very clear to me that this is going to be an extremely tough sell," Stenholm said. "Yeah, I would be worried."

WOULD-BE REVOLUTIONARIES

In the lobbying world, a different threat is emerging. Mention agriculture, and people will naturally assume you're talking about farms. A new group is seeking to change that.

At the center of this would-be conceptual revolution is Robert R. Petersen. He's president of the National Grain Trade Council, but his larger claim to fame may be his work as a ringleader and organizer of the Coalition for a Competitive Food and Agricultural System.

"Current farm programs," said Petersen, "do a lot of nasty things and harm a lot of people." Last June, he and three other lobbyists for companies that buy or trade grain met over lunch to talk about the 1995 farm bill. Inspired by the effort on behalf of the North American Free Trade Agreement, they started calling companies and trade groups that believe they pay through the nose for farm subsidies.

By now the coalition has more than 80 members, from the National Pasta Association and the Association of American Railroads to General Mills Inc. and the Indiana Port Commission—and, for that matter, Tom Hammer's group, the Sweetener Users Association. It relies on its members for volunteer staff.

"This group is *not* advocating a complete dismantling of the farm programs," said Brian Folkerts, a lobbyist for the National Food Processors Association, a coalition member. Actually, it isn't clear what the group is advocating; its membership is too diverse to allow easy agreement on program specifics. Its main interests, however, are two.

First, cut commodity prices and reduce government intervention in agriculture markets. "We are supportive of having better access to all available sources of our inputs and at lower cost," Folkerts said. Translation: Farm programs shouldn't restrict supplies or jack up prices.

Second, and what may be more important: Change politicians' notion of who makes up the farm programs' constituency. "It's about educating Members of Congress that agriculture doesn't begin and end on the farm—an attempt to define agriculture more inclusively," Petersen said. The agriculture sector, he argues, accounts for 16 per cent of the economy, but only about an eighth of that amount comes from farms. The rest is generated by agribusinesses ranging from fertilizer makers to grain shippers to biscuit companies.

"When farm bills were written in the past, the primary focus—if not the sole focus, actually—has been on assisting the farmers," Petersen said. The new group preaches that if a farm policy helps farmers at the expense of other agriculture

John Eisele

Senate Agriculture Committee chairman Richard G. Lugar, R-Ind. His goal: "Moving very resolutely [over five years] to the end of subsidies"

Robert R. Petersen, president of the National Grain Trade Council "Current farm programs do a lot of nasty things and harm a lot of people."

interests, it isn't good for agriculture. Message: The farm bill isn't just for farmers.

"We think it's time for bold reform," Petersen said. Failure to produce a farm bill that relies more on markets and less on government, he said, would be a historic opportunity lost. "We'd be saying we're satisfied with the status quo. And that would be a sad conclusion to come to."

Whether the new coalition will make much of a difference in 1995 remains to be seen. Still, its potential for shifting the dynamic of the farm debate is apparent. In the past, farm bills were dominated by commodity groups such as wheat and sugar growers, and opponents would swing in to lobby on issues of immediate concern and then disappear again. The new coalition, by contrast, figures to be a standing counterweight to the traditional farm lobby. "I see it as part of a continuing thing," Petersen said.

Yet the old farm politics remains potent. Roberts, the chairman of the House Agriculture Committee, hails from a Kansas district that is a veritable magnet for federal farm dollars. No one expects him to take kindly to dismantling the country's farm programs. And Lugar is a legislator first and a crusader only second. "I'll be very surprised if there are major differences between Congressman Roberts and Sen. Lugar," said Stenholm, who knows both.

Then there is that enigma, the Clinton Administration. If it proposes an incrementalist farm bill, it risks looking timid in the face of Republican activism; but it is nowhere near a consensus on any kind of radical reform. In fact, it is nowhere near much of anything on farm policy. Last summer and fall, a bevy of task forces drawn from the Agriculture Department and other agencies developed farm-bill proposals for review by higher-ups. Then came Nov. 8, and everything ground to a halt. "The election changed the whole character of the discussion," an Agriculture Department official said.

The farm bill was put on hold while the department went looking for budget savings to help pay for the President's proposed tax cuts. Meanwhile, Agriculture Secretary Mike Espy was leaving office under an ethical cloud; his nominated successor, former Rep. Dan Glickman, D-Kan., has yet to be confirmed. Department officials guess it will be March at the earliest before the Administration produces its farm policy. Meanwhile, on agriculture, the Administration occupies what has lately become its accustomed position in Washington: on the margins.

"What's the farm policy?" Stenholm asked. "After two years, not a clue."

The initiative belongs to Congress. And there, for all the brave talk of long knives on Capitol Hill, some would-be Republican revolutionaries seem of two minds about drawing blood. Take Rep. Thomas W. Ewing of Illinois. As chairman of the Agriculture Subcommittee on Risk Management and Specialty Crops, he oversees the sugar, peanut and tobacco programs. "I'm a conservative in philosophy," he said. "I believe we have too much government and it's costing us too much, as does the Heritage Foundation."

So what about eliminating the sugar or peanut program, both of which slap mandatory government controls on production and imports? Not so fast. "I am a free-enterprise person," Ewing said, "but I also recognize that free enterprise has to have some controls and regulations on it. I say if [the programs] work for sugar and for peanuts, we should not, just because they may not be philosophically pure, throw those ideas out."

Sympathetic listeners might call this a statement of principle leavened with pragmatism. Critics might call it mush. Either way, the 1995 farm bill will say volumes, perhaps more even than the GOP's vaunted Contract With America, about whether the Republican revolution really is one.

House Agriculture Subcommittee head Thomas W. Ewing We should go slow on discarding programs that work.

Environment and Energy

For some observers, the year 1970 signaled the beginning of a more environmentally conscious era in the United States. In that year the first Earth Day was celebrated amidst considerable fanfare and popular support and the Environmental Protection Agency (EPA) was established in the executive branch of the national government. Along with the EPA came landmark environmental enactments by Congress that the EPA had the responsibility to enforce—the Clean Air Act of 1970, the Clean Water Act of 1972, the Safe Drinking Water Act of 1974, the so-called Superfund law of 1980, and so forth.

The celebration of the 25th anniversary of the first Earth Day was accompanied by a growing feeling among both policymakers and the public that public policy related to environmental concerns needed reviewing and revamping. While all public policy decisions require trade-offs among competing values and scarce resources, it seems that such trade-offs are writ especially large in the environmental sphere. For example, how much more should consumers be asked to pay for cleaner-burning fuels? How should policymakers decide whether hydroelectric energy, which often involves flooding acres of land and upsetting natural fish habitats, is to be preferred to alternative sources of energy that do less damage to the land but cause more air pollution? To what lengths and costs should governments go to try to save an endangered species?

Environmental public policy has strong intergenerational implications. As with the budget deficit, future generations are said to have a direct and important stake in today's public policy decisions shaping the environment. When a species becomes extinct, a productive and picturesque valley is flooded by a dam, a wetlands and its inhabitants are eliminated, the ozone layer is diluted or destroyed, or a Pacific Ocean atoll is subjected to high doses of human-made radiation, many future generations of people can be affected. Similarly, in the energy realm, depletion of Earth's supply of fossil fuels is for all practical purposes an irreversible process.

Some public policy decisions concerning land use also run afoul of traditional notions of private ownership. Suppose the owner of a large tract of land engages in strip mining as the cheapest way to mine coal? Suppose the owners of oceanfront properties do not want others using "their" beach? Suppose the owner of a stand of timber cuts it all down to maximize immediate profit at the cost of longer-term ecological imbalance? Economists' notion of "externalities" helps justify governmental regulation in such circumstances, legitimizing restrictions that reduce air pollution caused by industrial smokestack emissions or bans on homeowners burning leaves from their property.

Selections in this unit suggest that the public policy pendulum on environment and energy issues may have reached one end of its swing and be about to begin its swing back to an era of less direct national government regulation. The selections treat proposed changes in public policy that range from a variety of free market approaches to a shift in environmental responsibility from national to state level.

Looking Ahead: Challenge Questions

Species have come and gone during the history of Earth. In recent decades American public policy has protected endangered species, sometimes at great cost to governments and private individuals. Why not just let nature take its course and, if a species cannot survive changes in its environment, let extinction occur as a matter of course?

The economy of the United States depends on industries that use great amounts of energy. But all known sources of reasonably priced energy have adverse environmental consequences. Fossil fuels are increasingly difficult to extract and, when burned, pollute the atmosphere and contribute to potentially dangerous global warming. New sources of hydroelectric power usually require flooding countless acres of land and are also likely to upset natural fish habitats. Nuclear energy creates wastes whose disposal can be an environmental nightmare and also contributes to so-called thermal pollution of nearby water sources. Not only do industrial economies consume energy in alarming quantities, but economic growth seems tied to even more energy consumption. Should governments shape public policy so as to discourage economic growth in favor of legitimate environmental concerns, even if this means a leveling off of Americans' standard of living? Why or why not?

Past generations did not seem to be much concerned

Unit 4

about the environmental heritage left to future generations. Forests were cut down, farmland was cultivated until its nutrients were exhausted, rivers were dammed for a variety of questionable reasons, and natural waterways were polluted by what would seem, by today's standards, unconscionable amounts of wastes. Do you think that the environmental and energy interests of future generations should be important considerations in making public policy today?

What kinds of government policies are likely to be most effective in making citizens more environmentally conscious and careful? Fines and other penalties for environmentally destructive behavior? Rewards for environmentally sound practices? Educational programs in public schools? Educational campaigns for the general public in mass media? If you wanted to get ordinary Americans to be more environmentally conscious, what public policy steps would you take?

THE GREENING OF ENVIRONMENTAL REGULATION

MARGARET KRIZ

In the early 1970s, William D. Ruckelshaus, the first administrator of the newly created Environmental Protection Agency (EPA), was called on the carpet by a top executive of U.S. Steel Corp., who then proceeded to scold him like a schoolboy.

"He said, 'Not only are we not going to pay any attention to your stupid agency, we're going to get you,' " Ruckelshaus recalled in a recent interview. "My response was 'Stand in line.' "

U.S. Steel wasn't the only company to take a hard line against the environmental movement in the late 1960s and early 1970s. "Industry's original approach to the environmental issue was to hope that if they resisted it, it would go away," said Ruckelshaus, who served as EPA's administrator in the Nixon and Reagan Administrations and is now the chairman and chief executive officer of Houston-based Browning-Ferris Industries Inc.

But recalcitrant industries met their match in the emerging environmental movement. Strengthened by spirited public support, environmental activists pushed Congress to write a series of tough laws aimed at cleaning up the nation's air, water and land.

EPA administers 10 major environmental protection laws and has additional pollution control responsibilities under 40 other statutes. *(See timeline.)*

Instead of fading away, the environmental movement forever changed the way corporate America does business.

Today, Ruckelshaus observed, environmental laws are much like worker safety and tax laws. "It's one of the conditions," he said, "of companies staying in business."

But the environmental laws that shook, rattled and roiled U.S. companies also had some fundamental flaws that have often undermined EPA's best efforts to curb pollution.

The problems stem from initial assumptions written into the laws, Ruckelshaus said. Lawmakers assumed, for example, that scientists knew what levels of pollution caused specific health and environmental problems. They also had faith that corporations had or could easily develop relatively inexpensive technologies to abate the problems.

And the laws were written with the notion that pollution was the fault of industry, which should therefore be punished for its misdeeds, he said.

"Under that set of conditions, all you needed was clear environmental standards and a will to enforce them to succeed," Ruckelshaus said. "Well, it turned out that none of the assumptions was right."

A MORE HOLISTIC APPROACH?

On the positive side, the laws ended some of the nation's most obvious pollution problems, cleaning up such national embarrassments as Ohio's Cuyahoga River, which in 1969 caught fire because it was so polluted.

But the laws frequently failed to target the underlying causes of pollution. They hamstrung regulators by imposing different regulatory schemes, depending on whether pollution went into the air, water or land, EPA administrator Carol Browner pointed out in an interview.

"We wanted to get the pollution out of the rivers, and the solution was that we put it in landfills," she said. "Then we found out that the landfills leaked, so we built incinerators. We just kept moving the problem around. In the meantime, we now generate double the amount of garbage we did then."

The environmental laws also perpetuated the adversary relationships of the early 1970s between industry, environmental activists and government, triggering protracted legal battles and often delaying significant environmental improvements.

Ruckelshaus said he recognized some of the flaws in the laws shortly after he began his first term at the agency. "When I set the clean air standards, the roof fell in and I began to look at some of the complexities involved in the equation," he said. "It was clear that determining whether these pollutants caused health effects was nowhere near the exact science we thought. And it was expensive as hell to clean all of this stuff up.

"Every EPA administrator I've ever talked to has gone through the same sort of metamorphosis. They say: 'God, we spend so much money on things that don't make much difference. Here's a whole environmental problem over here that we ought to be addressing, and I don't have any authority to do it.' "

In the past five years, however, the federal government's environmental protection strategies have begun to undergo a dramatic transformation.

Rather than imposing prescriptive pollution control requirements on industry to reduce emissions of greenhouse gases, for example, EPA regulators leaned on companies to take voluntary action. A surprisingly large number of them, wary of seeing a return to the draconian laws of the past, are accepting the challenge.

Industry, the environmental community and government regulators are trying experimental partnerships aimed at reforming such troublesome laws as superfund—the 1980 Comprehensive Environmental Response, Compensation and Liability Act.

EPA is also employing risk assessments and other economic tools to target the nation's most critical environmental problems and maximize its regulatory muscle. And Browner is championing new, more flexible environmental programs to reduce regulatory burdens and compliance costs while targeting the severest pollution problems.

EPA, for example, plans to select several key industries and develop a comprehensive regulatory program for the unique pollution problems each faces. The agency also plans to design pollution control plans for river watersheds and to work with companies and communities in those geographic regions to target the worst pollution problems.

"The culture of the agency is more mature and sophisticated than it has ever been," former EPA administrator William

K. Reilly, who's now a visiting professor of international studies at Stanford University, said. "The respect for science and for economics is more profound."

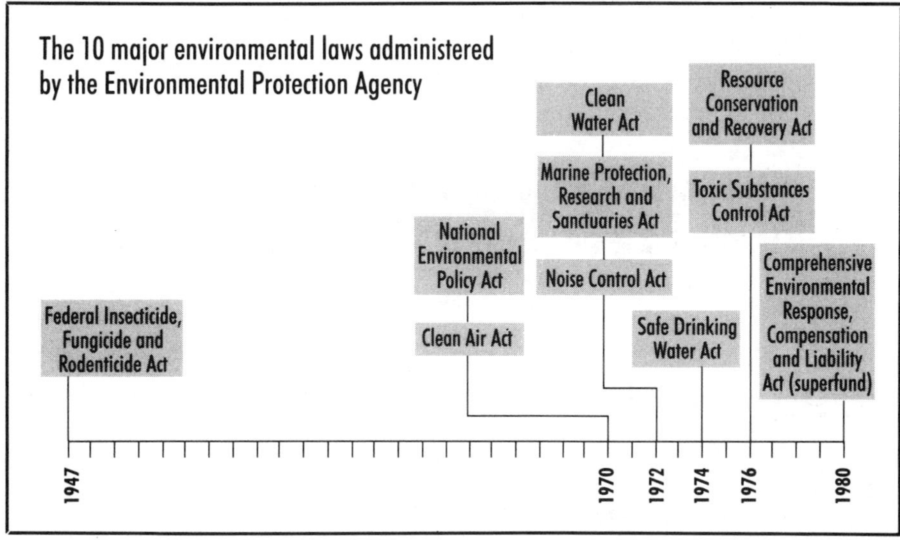

THE BACKLASH

The seeds of change were first sown years ago. In 1983, Ruckelshaus began his second term at EPA with a stirring speech to the National Academy of Sciences in which he called for a greater reliance on science in assessing environmental risks and for setting priorities to tackle the nation's pollution problems.

That attempt to move away from the narrow pollution control laws wasn't well received, however, largely because Ruckelshaus was replacing Anne Gorsuch Burford, who favored dismantling many federal environmental protection programs.

"I can remember when I went to EPA for the second time, talking to the Members of Congress, some of whom I'd known for 20 years, and saying, 'Look, you've just got to give me more flexibility,' " Ruckelshaus said. "You can't write the level of specificity in the laws that Congress was imposing and have it apply across a country as complex and vast as this without causing some tremendous distortions. Their response was, 'We trust you all right, but how do we know who's coming next?' "

President Reagan recognized a public demand for change but misread his mandate, Ruckelshaus said. "What the public was saying was, 'Let's try some more-efficient ways to protect the environment,' " he said. "They did not say, 'Abandon the goals of clean air and clean water.' "

The public suspicion of EPA had not completely disappeared by 1989, when Reilly, who came from the environmental movement, began his stint as its administrator. He created a voluntary pollution control program under which 1,246 companies from coast to coast agreed to reduce their chemical pollution by a third.

The response wasn't uniformly positive. "One reporter said: 'Don't you know your job is to kick ass and take names? What are you doing getting into bed with these people?' " Reilly said. "A lot of people in my own agency didn't think it was quite legitimate."

The response from industry, on the other hand, was gratifying, Reilly said. "The companies cut their emissions of toxics by 400 million pounds in a year and a half," he said. "I couldn't have gotten that with any law that I'd administered. And I knew that if it worked, it would change the culture of the agency and make it more receptive to these kinds of voluntary industry approaches."

While some industry executives were working more closely with government, resistance to strict federal environmental mandates was growing within certain quarters.

Farmers and other landowners, for example, opposed wetlands protection laws that restricted the use of their property. Local government officials objected to the costly environmental measures required—but not paid for—by Congress. Various business and conservative organizations pressed for a law that would require EPA to guarantee that the benefit of an environmental regulation outweighs the cost.

That backlash is gaining support in Congress, where conservative groups are angling to rewrite several of the most problematic environmental laws, including the 1972 Clean Water Act and the 1974 Safe Drinking Water Act. Such wholesale change is opposed by environmental activists, federal regulators and powerful lawmakers on Capitol Hill.

"The idea that you could require the agency to issue a cost-benefit analysis to justify every wetlands regulation or a decision to protect the visibility in, say, the Grand Canyon is implausible," Reilly said. "These groups are doing it to throw a log in front of an agency they see as out of control."

But Browner said the fact that the backlash movement is gaining momentum proves that the federal government, environmental activists and industry need to take more-innovative approaches to protect the environment.

"We can't just continue to put out the same old environmental regulations and expect to get solutions," she said. "We need to change the process. We need to convince people that this is a democracy, and we need to trust each other. It's scary. But the alternative is that we will not get the level of environmental protection that we want."

STIRRING THE POT

Ruckelshaus said that the Clinton Administration is in a unique position to usher in a new generation of environmental policy that attacks the nation's worst pollution problems.

"This Administration has a grand opportunity to rationalize this whole process if it wants to," he said. "But the President would have to put it up higher on his priority list. And he apparently sees it like the Republican Presidents did, as a political problem: The more you stir it, the worse it gets, so the thing to do is to leave it alone."

That's not to say that environmental protection depends solely on the whim of the White House, Ruckelshaus said. Americans may not rank the environment as a pressing political issue these days. But if politicians ignore the nation's environmental problems, public environmental fervor will rise again, he predicted.

"The environment is very much an issue driven by public opinion," Ruckelshaus said. "Whatever clean water and clean air mean to the American people, it means something way down in their stomachs; it's very important to them. It's going to be part of our lives from here on, and we're going to have to pay more attention to it. The important question is, how do you pay more intelligent attention to it."

THIS LAND IS WHOSE LAND?

MARGARET KRIZ

Economist Terry L. Anderson likes to talk about his hunting group, which leases the right to hunt elk on a large tract of privately owned forest in Montana. The leasing fees, he says, give the landowners a long-term financial incentive to protect the forest habitat, rather than allowing timber companies to clear it.

Speaking at an October conference sponsored by the Political Economy Research Center, a Bozeman (Mont.)-based think tank, Anderson cited the arrangement as an example of how private property rights—rather than restrictive government mandates such as the 1973 Endangered Species Act—can be used to preserve sensitive ecosystems.

By taking a property-rights approach, the federal government can protect water flows in prime fishing streams and curb logging and grazing on federal lands, according to Anderson, a senior associate with the research group who is also an economics professor at Montana State University and co-author of *Free Market Environmentalism* (Pacific Research Institute for Public Policy, 1991).

For example, Anderson said in an interview, individuals and groups that have an interest in protecting environmentally sensitive lands could buy permits giving them logging and grazing rights on those lands—and then choose not to exercise those rights. (Currently, that's not possible because the government sells permits only to people who plan to use the land for logging and grazing.)

Anderson's is one of several public policy doctrines that are attracting a following among the growing ranks of corporations and state and local governments stung by the high costs of environmental protection.

A 1990 Environmental Protection Agency study calculated that by 1994, the cost of implementing federal environmental mandates will reach $103 billion annually. Of that, private industry will bear 57 per cent, local governments 24 per cent, the federal government 15 per cent and states 4 per cent.

As the expense mounts, so does pressure to curb federal laws or to find less-expensive ways to protect the environment. In late October, for example, the U.S. Conference of Mayors and several other local government groups held a rally in Washington to protest what they described as "unfunded mandates"—environmental protection requirements that the federal government has imposed on local governments but has not fully financed.

In the view of some critics, whoever wanted these environmental laws in the first place should darn well have to pay for them. In other words, if the federal government wants communities to clean their wastewater before dumping it into rivers, then it should pay for new sewage treatment plants.

In the same vein, property-rights groups argue that environmental laws are effectively reducing the value of some privately owned land by limiting its use and that landowners are entitled to compensation. These groups contend, for example, that if the government wants to protect endangered waterfowl living on prime beachfront property, then it should pay landowners not to develop those sites.

Environmentalists and some government officials worry that the unspoken goal of these critics is to eliminate important environmental laws. For example, they cite a campaign waged by several property-rights groups to severely restrict the scope of the National Biological Survey, which aims to catalog plant and animal life in the United States. (*For details, see NJ, 10/30/93, p. 2597.*)

"It's a cleverly contrived campaign to get at the heart of some of these environmental statutes," House Merchant Marine and Fisheries Committee chairman Gerry E. Studds, D-Mass., said. Interior Secretary Bruce E. Babbitt described the attack on the survey as a "dress rehearsal" for the groups' ultimate aim of gutting the Endangered Species Act.

Most environmental advocates say that they are all for giving companies and property owners incentives to protect the environment. But they maintain that the incentives should be backed by strict mandates.

"Unfunded mandates are a serious problem," the Environmental Working Group, a Washington-based research group, noted in a recent study, "Costs of Pollution." "But any solution that requires the repeal or weakening of environmental protection laws would be a disaster for the health and safety of the U.S. population and the preservation of our natural resources."

Richard L. Stroup, director of the Political Economy Research Center, takes issue with the notion that existing environmental laws are preferable to a private property-rights system. Stroup argues that federal mandates contain a perverse incentive to save even the most marginal lands. "When somebody else pays for preservation, the people who want to preserve the land are going to want to save a lot of land," he said.

But environmentalists say that it's dangerous to force the federal government to take full responsibility for protecting sensitive lands. For one thing, because of the budget deficit, the government can't afford to buy much property. And it's unrealistic to expect that private groups such as Anderson and his fellow elk hunters will take up the slack because not all sensitive ecosystems have an obvious market value.

"The basic operating principle behind a 'free-market society' is an anti-democratic one: that people's preferences, whatever they may be, should be accepted and given an importance in proportion to the dollars that back them up," Thomas Michael Power, chairman of the University of Montana economics department, and Paul Rauber, associate editor of the Sierra Club's magazine, *Sierra*, write in the magazine's November issue.

The current system of environmental protection laws was written in response to public demand for higher "moral and social values," Power and Rauber write. But 20 years after many of the nation's environmental laws were written, a public debate is heating up over who will pay for achieving those lofty goals.

From *National Journal,* November 13, 1993, p. 2750.

The Conquered Coalition

The Republican landslide on Nov. 8 transfigured the politics of environmental policy and could usher in a radical reexamination of federal environmental laws. In the aftermath of the GOP's takeover of Congress, environmental activists are looking for ways to rebuild their movement.

MARGARET KRIZ

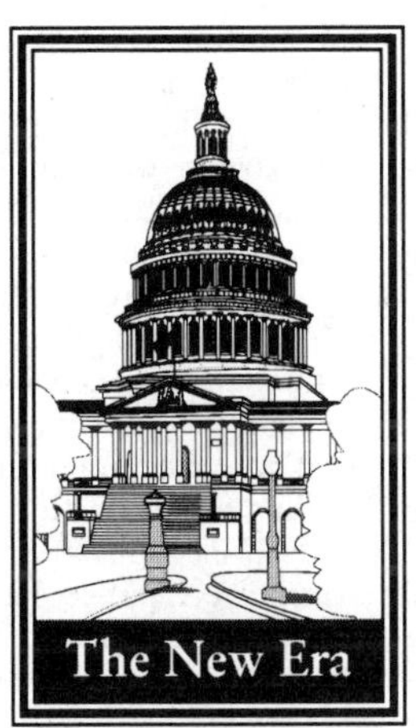

Expectations were running high on Nov. 16 as Vice President Albert Gore Jr. was to give his first speech on environmental issues since the Republican Party's landslide victory in the midterm elections.

Long before the election, Gore had agreed to be the featured speaker at a gala dinner to celebrate the Environmental Law Institute's 25th anniversary and to honor Senate Majority Leader George J. Mitchell, D-Maine, who's retiring at the end of this term.

Now Gore faced more than 800 environmental activists, lawyers and others who were crowded into the grand ballroom of the Washington Hilton, nibbling salmon and Ben & Jerry's ice cream and swapping the latest rumors on who's in and who's out.

Those who were expecting Gore to issue a rousing call-to-arms, however, were quickly disappointed by his subdued performance. After running through the now-standard jokes about his Achilles tendon operation, Gore made a passing reference to the election's impact on environmental policies and programs, observing only that "those of us who care deeply about this struggle must redouble our efforts."

Mitchell, on the other hand, warned of disaster in his impassioned address. If conservatives implement policies of "unrestrained economic growth and disregard for the natural environment," he said, the nation could become as environmentally devastated as Eastern Europe. "No matter what happened in the election," he said, "we've got to stand up and fight for the protection of the American environment."

The two speeches were evidence of the formidable struggle that's going on within the environmental movement in the aftermath of the Nov. 8 elections. Environmental activists in government and in national advocacy organizations are spending long hours debating how they should react to the Republican takeover of Capitol Hill.

One thing they all seem to agree on, however, is that the elections transfigured the politics of environmental policy and could force a radical reexamination of federal environmental laws.

Environmental activists argue that the elections were not a referendum on the American public's commitment to environmental protection and therefore shouldn't be seen as a mandate for Republicans to overhaul environmental and natural resource programs.

But they admit that they will have far fewer friends in the next Congress than they have now. In the Senate, one of their allies, John H. Chafee, R-R.I., will become the chairman of the Environment and Public Works Committee if he survives a strong conservative challenge. And the Appropriations Subcommittee on Energy and Water Development is likely to be chaired by Mark O. Hatfield, R-Ore., one of the original authors of the 1973 Endangered Species Act.

Chafee and Hatfield, however, are likely to have precious few Republican Senators on their side to help them protect the nation's environmental laws.

More dramatic are the changes in the House, where such environmental pit bulls as George Miller, D-Calif., the chairman of the Natural Resources Committee, and Henry A. Waxman, D-Calif., the chairman of the Energy and Commerce Subcommittee on Health and the Environment, will move to the minority. (Another, Rep. Mike Synar, D-Okla., lost his Democratic primary election earlier in the year.)

In their places will be Republicans who voted "green" only 7 per cent of the time in the 103rd Congress, according to the League of Conservation Voters.

Republican leaders in the House say that their top priority during the first 100 days of the 104th Congress will be their "Contract With America," a 10-point legislative agenda that promises, among other things, to protect the nation from environmental regulations run amok.

The contract, which says nothing about environmental protection, places a new importance on defending private property rights. Some key Republicans on Capitol Hill, in fact, are trying to set up new

From *National Journal,* December 3, 1994, pp. 2824-2829.

subcommittees on regulatory reform specifically to safeguard property rights.

The contract would also require regulators to balance the economic costs of a new regulation against its benefits. And it would stop the federal government from adopting environmental programs that have to be implemented and paid for by the states.

During the past two years, lobbyists for the nation's largest environmental organizations fought tooth and nail to block all property-rights, cost-benefit analysis and "unfunded mandates" proposals, which they said were being used by conservatives and business interests to overturn existing environmental controls.

In the process, however, the environmental activists unwittingly helped to kill legislation that would have also strengthened existing environmental laws.

"It is very convenient to say that the environmental bills failed because the Republicans blocked them," Peter L. Scher, the staff director of the Senate Environment and Public Works Committee, said in an interview. "But that's only part of it. The environmental community wouldn't recognize that there are legitimate complaints about the way these laws operate and that these problems are not going to go away."

Two years after they celebrated President Clinton's election with an environmental inaugural ball and bold promises to strengthen federal environmental policies, environmental activists pushed only one major new law through Congress: the California Desert Protection Act. The chairman of the House Energy and Commerce Subcommittee on Energy and Power, Philip R. Sharp, D-Ind., who's retiring at the end of this term, recently described the 103rd Congress as "the nadir of the political influence of the environmental movement in the Congress." *(See NJ, 10/29/94, p. 2545.)*

Little wonder that some of the nation's leading environmental organizations are rethinking their past political stands and legislative tactics. In devoting too many resources to building their images and lobbying firepower in Washington, they now recognize, they didn't tend to their grass roots. A sign of the neglect: declining membership rolls.

Virtually everyone in the environmental movement is looking for new political strategies, and some are seeking to work with the Republicans to shape a more moderate approach to environmentalism.

First and foremost, however, the nation's big environmental organizations want to regain the trust of the American public. Having barely survived the earthquake, they're looking for new ways to rebuild the House of Green.

THE FORK IN THE ROAD

Ever since the environmental movement came of age with the birth of the Environmental Protection Agency (EPA) in 1970, Democrats have controlled the House and usually controlled the Senate. Even when the Republicans seized the Senate in 1980, a team of powerful moderate Republicans were there to defend federal environmental protection laws.

Today, all that's changed. Conservative Republicans in the House and Senate have taken charge; moderates are few and far between. And environmental leaders on and off Capitol Hill are understandably baffled about how to react.

"The heyday of the old-style environmental movement is over," Robert W. Hahn, a resident scholar at the American Enterprise Institute for Public Policy Research (AEI), said in an interview.

Environmental activists are considering two different strategies to respond to the Republican landslide. They can attack the GOP's new leaders as radical ideologues who are out of touch with the American mainstream, they said. Or they can work with the Republicans to develop less punitive environmental controls. But the smart money says that most environmental groups will do a lot of the former and only some of the latter. *(For more on one group's strategy, see box, next page.)*

The wheels are already in motion within several environmental organizations to wage a negative campaign that portrays the new Republican leaders as modern incarnations of former Interior Secretary James G. Watt. During the early years of the Reagan Administration, Watt's ultraconservative policies and antagonistic rhetoric triggered a public backlash that helped the environmental groups to attract millions of dollars in contributions and thousands of new members.

John Eisele

G. Jon Roush, the president of the Wilderness Society
"We shouldn't let people cast us as regulatory zealots. We have to seize the center."

In a similar way, the environmentalists aim to capitalize on the rise to power of the pro-industry lawmakers who are taking the reins of several key environmental committees. Their primary targets will be Alaska Republicans Frank H. Murkowski, who's in line to be the chairman of the Senate Energy and Natural Resources Committee, and Don Young, who's in line to be the chairman of the House Natural Resources Committee. Environmental activists are tagging them as right-wing extremists.

The environmental activists are also calling attention to several of the more radical Republican proposals that in the 1980s were particularly unpopular with the American public. Some Republicans have suggested, for example, that the federal government sell off some national parks as well as some lands controlled by the Bureau of Land Management.

Lobbyists for environmental organizations warn that they will declare war on Congress if the Republicans try to implement that plan or try to fulfill their promises to dramatically rewrite the Endangered Species Act and the wetlands protection provisions of the 1972 Clean Water Act. They're also launching a massive public relations effort to educate the American public about the GOP's property-rights campaign.

In particular, they're taking aim at legislation introduced in the 103rd Congress by Sen. Phil Gramm, R-Texas, that would have required the federal government to compensate property owners when an environmental regulation reduces the value of their land. Environmental activists argue that Gramm's proposal would force the government to compensate corporations that are required by law to install pollution control equipment.

"The property-rights people are not unbeatable," said Brock Evans, the National Audubon Society's senior vice president for national issues. "I'd love to force their agenda into the public eye."

Such a politically combative posture could have the added benefit of boosting the ailing bottom lines of many environmental groups. During the past five years, the nation's 10 largest environmental organizations have seen their memberships fall off and revenues decline or stagnate.

Since 1990, for example, Greenpeace has seen a 40 per cent drop in membership, the Wilderness Society a 35 per cent decrease and the National Wildlife Federation a 14 per cent decrease. In October, the Sierra Club announced that it was cutting its 1995 budget by $4 million and eliminating 40 jobs.

Some argue that the Republicans' strong rhetoric could be just what the doctor ordered to revive the sagging environmental movement. "The next Con-

THE THREE Rs: RETRENCH, REGROUP AND RETHINK

In mid-November, as the environmental community was still reeling from the Republican takeover of Congress, employees of the Sierra Club suffered another blow. Officials of the San Francisco-based environmental organization announced that they would eliminate 40 jobs and slash their budget in an attempt to grapple with a $2.9 million debt.

Times are not good for the Sierra Club, which was founded 102 years ago by John Muir, the legendary naturalist. But Carl Pope, its executive director, is hoping that his organization, and indeed the entire environmental movement, can turn the tide of misfortune by putting its resources into three ambitious campaigns.

"The first thing we need to do is organize around the environment instead of organizing around specific pieces of legislation," Pope said. "We need to go back to the basics, reminding people that we're still losing ecosystems, we still can't drink the water in some areas and we are still paying a phenomenal amount of money for subsidies to people who abuse our lands and water."

Persuading the American public that the nation needs better environmental protection will not be difficult, he said. "We know how to do that—we've done it many times before," he said. "We clearly took our eye off the basics in the last two years, and now we need to go at it again."

The next push, according to Pope, is to take on the property-rights movement. "We need to make it clear what the consequences would be of adopting these glib approaches to private property rights, unfunded mandates and risk assessment," he said.

Environmental activists have successfully fought back property-rights campaigns on the state level. Arizona voters, for example, rejected a ballot initiative that would have expanded the right of property owners to be compensated when environmental controls reduce the value of their land. Environmental groups in the state blasted the proposal as a threat to public health and the environment and argued that it would create layers of burdensome government regulations. The initiative went down, 40-60 per cent.

The third—and most ambitious—crusade in Pope's plan is to reestablish the respectful relationship between the American public and the federal government. "We need to restore the public trust in government and make government more worthy of that trust by cleaning up the political process," he said. "We need to make the American people realize that if they walk away from democratic government, they are walking away from environmental protection. It's simply not possible to leave this task of protecting the environment up to the marketplace."

Carl Pope of the Sierra Club
"We need to go back to the basics."

To that end, the Sierra Club plans to promote congressional campaign reform and to encourage environmental activists to get involved in government by voting and by working on local environmental campaigns. "We are not advocates of bigger government," Pope said. "We are advocates of more-accountable government, government that listens to what the average voter wants instead of listening to what the average campaign donor wants."

Pope acknowledged that the environmental movement is fighting an uphill battle to reeducate the American public. Although public opinion polls all show that voters think of themselves as environmentalists, their support for specific environmental programs tends to be shaky. When asked to rank their top 10 concerns, voters usually put the environment behind such issues as crime, education and jobs.

But Pope and other environmental leaders are warning Republicans on Capitol Hill not to mistake the election returns as a mandate to back away from environmental protection. "Once people get a look at the specifics of some of these proposals, they'll be saying, 'Wait a minute, this is not what we voted for,' " Pope said. "Our job is to remind people that if they don't hold government accountable, they're not going to have a decent planet to give to their grandchildren."

gress is going to be almost as good for the environmentalists' direct-mail solicitations as James Watt was," Robert N. Stavins, an associate professor of public policy at Harvard University's John F. Kennedy School of Government, said in an interview.

But Carl Pope, the executive director of the Sierra Club, warned that the cure might be worse than the illness. The potential fund-raising benefit "certainly doesn't help enough to make up for the damage done by having two Republican Senators from Alaska in charge of the nation's land use policies," Pope said. "It's not good news."

SEIZE AND DESIST

While some environmental activists are eager to go on the attack, others want to negotiate with the new Republican leaders of Congress to "reinvent" more-moderate environmental policies.

Officials of the Environmental Defense Fund (EDF), for example, say that the Republican victory is a sign that the American public, while supporting a clean environment, wants less government control and more incentive-based regulations.

"The message from the election is that people are angry about the government and they're tired of programs that don't work," Fred Krupp, the EDF's executive director, said in an interview. "They're concerned about the intrusiveness of government."

Krupp said that the public—and a majority of Capitol Hill lawmakers—want government-industry partnerships and regulations that provide incentives, tax credits and market-based systems for protecting the environment.

Krupp's organization is the environmental movement's most enthusiastic supporter of such approaches. The EDF helped to craft the market-based acid rain reduction system that President Bush included in his proposal to rewrite the 1990 Clean Air Act, and it supports similar techniques for cutting other types of pollution.

"These are the ideas that will capture the center," Krupp said. "I can see both Republicans and Democrats now being open to using more economic incentives and less command-and-control-style regulations. We need to mandate tough results, but we can afford to be far more flexible about the means."

An increasing number of environmental leaders are also voicing tentative support for industry-friendly environmental controls. "We have to look at a whole new generation of market-based incentives," said Jay D. Hair, the president of the National Wildlife Federation, "but we're always going to need some semblance of command and control."

EPA administrator Carol Browner championed flexible regulations and negotiated agreements with industry during the 103rd Congress. She was instrumental, for example, in getting environmental activists to sit down with representatives of the chemical and insurance industries to craft compromise legislation to overhaul the superfund program.

Browner said that the issues of property rights, risk assessment and unfunded mandates need to be addressed head-on next year, before any other environmental legislation can be handled. "Certainly these issues cast a shadow over environmental legislation," she said in an interview.

In the past, environmental activists sought to dismiss the three issues by disparaging them as the "unholy trinity," and later as "the three pigs" of the right wing. No more.

"We accommodate the ideologues on the Right when we say we're going to draw a line along these code words and show our teeth every time we hear them," Jim Maddy, the director of the League of Conservation Voters, said. "We shouldn't have done it in the last Congress, and we'd be even more foolish to do it in the next Congress."

Instead, some environmental activists are looking for ways to acknowledge the validity of the public concerns about the three issues and to recast the debate with an environmental slant.

"We're for property rights, but not irrational property-rights legislation," G. Jon Roush, the president of the Wilderness Society, said. "There's room for some rationality, and environmentalists should not deny that. We shouldn't let people cast us in the position of being regulatory zealots. We have to seize the center."

Susan M. Muniak

Myron Ebell, the Washington representative of the American Land Rights Association
"As long as those laws are on the books, the environmentalists are going to lose ground."

FIGHTING FOR THE WHITE HAT

Even before the Republicans won control of Congress, no one had to measure the coat of the woolly caterpillar to conclude that the environmental community was in for a long, cold winter.

In the weeks before the election, a wind shift was apparent throughout the nation's capital. Environmental activists who once belittled their colleagues for working with industry lobbyists to rewrite the superfund law suddenly were preaching the virtues of such cooperation.

Melancholy Democratic aides on Capitol Hill began quoting from President Nixon's 1970 State of the Union address, in which he described clean air and open spaces as "the birthright of every American."

Storm-weary Democratic House leaders alerted lobbyists for environmental organizations to don their flak jackets in preparation for Republican attacks in 1995.

The truth was, the 103rd Congress was almost a total loss for the environmental movement, and the 104th doesn't look much better.

What went wrong? For one thing, environmental organizations lost many of their most respected leaders to the Clinton Administration as Gore helped to pepper the executive branch with his supporters. The environmental activists left behind were spread thin. Rather than focus on one or two major campaigns on Capitol Hill, however, they promoted dozens of large and small legislative programs. *(See NJ, 9/10/94, p. 2108.)*

Many environmental organizations pursued their own pet projects and were unable or unwilling to help one another. Several of the biggest were more interested in getting credit for their own accomplishments than in getting behind a united agenda, according to insiders.

In trying to protect their past gains, environmental activists also fell into the trap of defending big government and its cumbersome regulatory structures. They were loath to accept, for example, that the laws protecting endangered species and wetlands have been unevenly enforced, have hurt some landowners and need to be reformed. They were also unwilling to admit that federal drinking water programs were strangling local governments with high costs and unnecessary red tape.

The environmental movement's unyielding defense of several troublesome laws hurt its cause, argued Myron Ebell, the Washington representative of the American Land Rights Association, a conservative advocacy group. "As long as those laws are on the books," he said, "the environmentalists are going to lose ground and we are going to gain converts, because those laws cause people pain."

When lobbyists for environmental organizations pushed a legislative initiative, they often wanted Congress to impose the traditional command and control methods of regulation. In their proposals to strengthen the Clean Water Act, for example, they sought to punish farmers who pollute rivers with chemical-laden runoff from their fields. Farm groups wanted to develop incentive programs that would gradually phase in new farming practices.

"What governor is going to ask the legislature to authorize a program that imposes penalties and jail terms on farmers and ranchers?" asked Tom Curtis, the director of the National Governors' Association's natural resources group. "That would not have been politically salable. The environmentalists are so caught up in the notion that you've got to stick it to the regulated community if they don't comply."

Richard A. Bloom

Peter L. Scher, an aide to the Senate Environment Committee "The whole dynamic is very different now."

In the battle over rewriting the Clean Water Act and the 1974 Safe Drinking Water Act, the environmental activists also found themselves clashing with the nation's mayors and governors. "In the early '70s, it was the environmentalists on one side and it was industry on the other side," said Scher of the Environment and Public Works Committee. "The whole dynamic is very different now."

And Congress listens when governors and mayors come to Capitol Hill to oppose ambitious environmental laws that must be implemented and paid for by local governments.

When votes were counted in the House and Senate, the environmentalists found themselves totally outgunned. Not only did they lack the stature they once had as the only voice for the public interest, but they also lacked the grass-roots muscle needed to push their legislative proposals over the top.

Administration officials and Democrats in Congress begged environmental organizations, for example, to unleash a grass-roots blitz to pressure Congress into passing their rewrite of the Safe Drinking Water Act. But the extra help never came.

"We've done a miserable job of organizing our supporters into a political force," said Maddy of the League of Conservation Voters. "Organizing is unglamorous and expensive. To organize, you need thousands of poorly paid young people. Environmentalists are a little bit like bureaucrats. They prefer a smaller number of highly paid specialists."

In the final calculation, lobbyists for environmental organizations came across as representatives of just another special interest rather than protectors of a sacred public trust.

"There are new constituencies that have an arguable claim to the white hat," AEI's Hahn said. "They're vying for power with the environmentalist community, and they're winning."

"OUR TIME TO MAKE HAY"?

What route the national environmental organizations take next year will depend a great deal on the agenda and tactics adopted by Congress's new Republican leaders.

The early statements of House conservatives seem to foreshadow a year of ideological warfare between the environmental community and Congress. The environmental movement engaged in a similar struggle with the Reagan Administration in the early 1980s, when Watt and EPA administrator Anne Gorsuch Burford tried to roll back several major environmental laws.

"We could have a return to the Reaganesque environmental policy," said Jonathan H. Adler, the associate director of environmental studies at the Competitive Enterprise Institute. "The problem with that type of a policy is it sows the seeds of its own defeat because it is purely negative."

The new Republican leaders, like the environmental activists, have two options for the next Congress: They can try to quickly rewrite major environmental laws, which would trigger battles and possibly gridlock on Capitol Hill, or they can work with some compromise-minded environmental groups and with free-market-oriented think tanks to develop new approaches to protecting the environment.

House Republicans undoubtedly will try to fulfill their promises under their Contract With America by bringing legislation to promote private-property rights and risk assessment to the floor.

"We will do everything to ensure that property rights is on an equal level as environmentalism," said Nancie G. Marzulla, the president and chief legal counsel of Defenders of Property Rights. "We are going to win big in the 104th Congress. This is our time to make hay."

But the Republican leadership, which will have its hands full with other parts of the GOP's wish list, isn't likely to give other environmental legislation as high a priority.

Even if they wanted to dismantle 25 years of environmental legislation, Republicans don't have a comfortable majority in either chamber of Congress. Just as Democrats in the 103rd Congress didn't have the votes to strengthen the environmental laws, Republicans in the 104th probably won't have the votes to gut the programs, according to lobbyists for both sides. Only moderate proposals that capture Congress's elusive center are likely to become law.

In addition, the new Republican leaders may be reluctant to take up the environmental laws, which tend to be complex and overwhelming. With nearly half of all House Members in their first or second terms, the collective learning curve will be especially steep.

Consequently, Adler and other conservative activists are pushing the Republican leaders to consider a longer-term, free-market approach to environmental policy that would, among other things, promote private-sector incentives and move more control over environmental protection laws to the states.

Adler said that there's plenty of room for compromise, recalling the unlikely coalition of conservative and environmental groups opposed to legislation that would have allowed local governments to require all local garbage to be processed at a designated facility. The coalition argued that the measure would hinder market-driven recycling efforts and create a government monopoly.

Among those joining that campaign were representatives of Clean Water Action, the Competitive Enterprise Institute, the National Taxpayers Union and the Atlantic chapter of the Sierra Club.

Maddy predicted that the House Speaker-in-waiting Newt Gingrich of Georgia and other Republican leaders may be willing to work with environmental organizations to make needed changes to the Safe Drinking Water Act and the superfund. "Gingrich doesn't want dirty air and dirty water to become his 'gays in the military,' " Maddy said, referring to the public relations debacle that Clinton faced shortly after his election.

But all hell could break loose if conservatives try to eviscerate federal laws that protect endangered species, public lands and wetlands, he said.

"It's the public lands issues where we will fight the hardest for a filibuster," Maddy said. "Failing that, we'll hold midnight vigils around the White House begging for a veto."

And Republicans on Capitol Hill may not have a large window of opportunity to pass environmental legislation before the debate is overwhelmed by the onset of the 1996 presidential campaign, the National Wildlife Federation's Hair predicted.

The 1996 race is also certain to affect the White House's handling of environmental protection legislation, Hair said. "I would guess they'll put effort into anything that will raise the popularity of the President," he said. "And if it is perceived that the environment won't do that, they won't play that card."

Instead of turning automatically to Congress, representatives of national environmental groups say that they'll increasingly look to federal departments and agencies to strengthen environmental protection programs. They're also forming coalitions with smaller environmental organizations to tackle regional problems. The National Wildlife Federation, for example, is putting more resources into a program to improve water quality in the Great Lakes region. American Rivers and other national groups have joined with environmental activists in the Midwest and the South to create the Mississippi River Basin Alliance.

Environmental activists hope that working with the regional groups on regional problems will help them rebuild their grass-roots support and their power base in Congress.

For the environmental movement, the journey into 1995 comes with no road maps and no guarantees. Its top activists may try to shape government policy by reverting to the movement's old alarmist tactics or by settling for something less than the punitive environmental laws of the past. No matter which way they turn, however, the future is politically uncharted terrain.

Richard A. Bloom

Jim Maddy, the director of the League of Conservation Voters
"We've done a miserable job of organizing our supporters into a political force."

Cutting the Strings

The movement to curb "unfunded mandates"—programs that Washington has imposed on state and local governments without providing the money to pay for them—may be on the brink of revolutionizing the relationship between the federal government and the states. And it's picking up steam on Capitol Hill.

MARGARET KRIZ

Michael J. Pompili, the assistant health commissioner of Columbus, remembers the final straw—the project that caused the city's top officials to take a stand against the federal government.

It was 1991, and the city was planning to clean up the site of the old Short Street municipal garage. Over the years, the garage had suffered its share of paint and solvent spills, resulting in a serious pollution problem.

But not in their wildest dreams—or nightmares—could the city officials have guessed the initial estimate for complying with federal pollution cleanup laws: $2 million to remove 2.6 million pounds of dirt—enough to make the land as clean as neighboring sites.

"We had a meeting to talk about how to come up with this $2 million," Pompili recalled in an interview. "And after a while, I mentioned that we weren't just talking $2 million, we were talking $65 million. And their mouths just dropped open."

That was Pompili's rough estimate of how much the city would have to spend to comply with the flood of new federal environmental regulations pouring into his office. Washington was ordering the city to do everything from inspecting leaking underground storage tanks to overseeing asbestos cleanup programs in schools and other public buildings.

Anxious about Pompili's math, city officials asked him to assess the costs of complying with all federal environmental "unfunded mandates"—programs that Washington has imposed on state and local governments without providing the money to pay for them.

"The report blew us away," Pompili said. "We found that over the next 10 years, we'd spend $1 billion on unfunded federal mandates. We had no clue that was true." In 1991, costs associated with unfunded mandates made up 10 per cent of Columbus's operating budget; by 2000, the city estimates, they will eat up nearly a fourth of the city's budget.

Word of the Columbus study spread like wildfire through statehouses and city halls. Before long, dozens of other governors and mayors had ordered similar studies. In October 1992, Gregory S.

John Eisele

Sen. Dirk A. Kempthorne, R-Idaho
He's heading the GOP's drive in the Senate against unfunded federal mandates.

[*During its first 100 Days, the Republican-controlled 104th Congress passed a so-called unfunded mandates bill that was signed into law by Democratic President Bill Clinton in late March 1995. The legislation makes it very difficult for Congress to pass laws that impose requirements *and* accompanying costs on states. **Editor**]

From *National Journal,* January 21, 1995, pp. 167-171.

Lashutka, the mayor of Columbus, rallied public support by holding an "Unfunded Mandates Day" and began flying a red flag outside of city hall that reads "Stop Unfunded Mandates."

"I don't know of any mayor who is against the environment," Lashutka said in an interview. "We champion the environment as much as the environmentalists do. Unfortunately, the environmentalists don't have the responsibility for fighting crime in the streets or for putting emergency vehicles on the road. They don't have to repave the streets. They can very easily look through a soda straw at one part of life. But that's not how our cities and regions operate."

Richard A. Bloom

Frank Shafroth of the National League of Cities "We want accountability."

The angry city officials in Columbus aren't alone. The movement to curb unfunded mandates is sweeping the nation and may be on the brink of revolutionizing the relationship between the federal government and the states.

In the process, governors, state legislators, mayors and other local officials have gained unprecedented political clout. The groups that represent them in Washington—"the Big Seven," as they're known—are being hailed as the voice of the people by the new Republican leaders of Congress.

Legislation to stop new unfunded mandates, which came close to passing in the 103rd Congress, is speeding through the Senate and House like greased lightning. House and Senate passage is eminent. The Senate Budget and Governmental Affairs Committees approved the measure on Jan. 9. The House Government Reform and Oversight Committee approved a similar measure the next day, despite complaints from Democrats that the Republicans refused to hold hearings on the issues. Republicans rejected nearly all amendments, mostly on party-line votes.

House Speaker Newt Gingrich, R-Ga., predicted that an unfunded mandates bill will be on President Clinton's desk by late January. Despite complaints that the legislation has been rammed through Congress without careful consideration, Clinton, a former governor of Arkansas, has promised to sign an antimandates measure.

THE FAST TRACK

It's called the Job Creation and Wage Enhancement Act, and it's one of the 10 sweeping tenets of the House GOP's Contract With America. But the Republicans are packaging the proposal as the "Get Government Off My Back Act." The proposed legislation is designed, in part, to ease regulatory burdens on state and local governments and on industry. *(See NJ, 1/14/95, p. 123.)*

At first, the ban on new unfunded mandates was part of the Job Creation and Wage Enhancement Act. But Republican leaders, looking for a fast victory on Capitol Hill, developed separate legislation on unfunded mandates and introduced it as the first bill in the Senate and the fifth bill in the House.

The unfunded mandates legislation would force Capitol Hill lawmakers to publicly acknowledge the costs and red tape that go along with new measures they want to impose on state and local governments.

The legislation would require the Congressional Budget Office (CBO) to file a detailed report on any legislation that would impose $50 million or more in costs on state and local governments. If Congress finances the mandate, lawmakers would have to identify where the money would come from; if Congress doesn't finance the mandate, any lawmaker could demand a separate vote on the measure. The legislation would exempt bills covering constitutional and civil rights, emergency relief and national security.

The legislation could theoretically force the federal government to pick up the tab for all new programs prescribed by Congress. But with lawmakers groping for ways to cut the federal budget deficit, it would more likely stop Congress from passing new health, safety and social welfare laws.

In addition, the law would kick in whenever Congress makes major changes to existing laws that increase the regulatory burden on state and local governments. As a result, nearly all environmental, health, labor and other social welfare laws could fall under its umbrella within the next decade; if a law were simply reauthorized without major changes, however, the mandates legislation wouldn't apply.

On the environmental front, for example, the 104th Congress may rewrite the 1972 Clean Water Act, the 1973 Endangered Species Act, the 1974 Safe Drinking Water Act and the 1980 Comprehensive Environmental Response, Compensation and Liability Act (superfund). If the unfunded mandates legislation is enacted, the federal government would have to fully finance them.

Critics worry that the process of analyzing the cost of every proposed "mandate" will be costly and time-consuming for Congress, delaying or killing vital legislation. Some Democratic lawmakers also warn that the unfunded mandates measure would undermine Congress's ability to set national policy.

"We could no longer pass essential laws to address urgent social problems or to protect human health and the environment," Rep. Henry A. Waxman, D-Calif., who's championed many health and environmental laws, argued at a Jan. 10 meeting of the Government Reform and Oversight Committee.

But supporters of the legislation argue that the change is needed because Congress rarely has any idea of how much federal mandates cost state and local governments. "When the Brady [gun control] bill passed, everybody talked about whether or not it would result in a reduction of violent crimes," said an aide to Rep. Rob Portman, R-Ohio, a leading opponent of unfunded mandates. "No Member had any information about what the Brady bill would cost in the way of unfunded mandates on the states and local governments."

Some lawmakers want to go a step further by limiting federal laws that affect corporate America. That effort is opposed by organizations that represent local governments, which worry that such a move would divert attention and support from their anti-mandates agenda.

In its current form, the legislation would require the CBO to analyze any legislation that would impose costs of $200 million or more on the private sector. But lobbyists for the business community say that it needs more relief. They argue that the legislation would discriminate against private industry because it would limit federal mandates on state and local governments while continuing to impose them on the private sector.

And that would give a wide range of government-owned entities—from hospitals to landfills to power plants—a competitive advantage over their private competitors, Richard F. Goodstein, the vice president of government affairs at Browning-Ferris Industries Inc., argued in a Dec. 16 letter to Congress.

Similar concerns have been expressed by the U.S. Chamber of Commerce, the Edison Electric Institute and trade associations that represent bus and water companies that compete with local governments. Republican lawmakers, however, are pressuring business lobbyists to mute their criticisms and support the Republican agenda.

Richard A. Bloom

Dawn Martin, the director of the American Oceans Campaign's Washington office
"There is not going to be enough time and thoughtful debate" before Congress votes.

THE BIRTH OF A COALITION

The unfunded mandates issue burst on the scene during the 103rd Congress when local government officials, complaining that federal laws were diverting funds from crucial local services, found a champion for their cause in Sen. Dirk A. Kempthorne, R-Idaho. Kempthorne, who is heading this year's drive in the Senate against unfunded mandates, had been the mayor of Boise for seven years before he came to the Senate in 1992.

During the 103rd Congress, a compromise bill developed by Kempthorne and John Glenn, D-Ohio, then the chairman of the Governmental Affairs Committee, nearly passed in the Senate. Their measure was endorsed by the Clinton Administration but roundly criticized by public-interest groups, which helped to block passage of the measure on the Senate floor.

This year, however, the public-interest community's allies in Congress don't have the votes to amend, let alone kill, the unfunded mandates legislation. After the November elections, environmental and public-interest groups were slow to gear up for battle. As a result, they've all but ceded the issue to the Republicans and concentrated on trying to block broader regulatory reforms in the Contract With America.

As the 104th Congress opened, the unfunded mandates issue rose to the top of the GOP's agenda for three big reasons: It had the unified support of the state and local government groups, it had unified Republican support (it's one part of Gingrich's contract that Senate Majority Leader Robert Dole, R-Kan., readily supported) and it also had the tacit consent of the White House.

Gingrich tapped Portman to write the unfunded mandates provisions of the Contract With America and to lead the campaign to enact them. Portman, a second-termer who worked in the Bush White House, is part of the Ohio contingent that's on the front lines of the unfunded mandates campaign.

Meanwhile, Glenn is heading up a Democratic working group on unfunded mandates. Gov. George V. Voinovich of Ohio has been one of the most prominent advocates within the National Governors' Association (NGA) and the Republican Governors Association. In addition, Senate leaders assigned Republican Mike DeWine of Ohio, a former lieutenant governor, to serve on its working group on unfunded mandates.

For the coalition of state and local government groups, this campaign is its second major foray into influencing federal policy on mandates. During the 103rd Congress's debates over rewriting the Safe Drinking Water Act, the groups stopped an effort by national environmental organizations to tighten the regulation of municipal drinking water systems.

Local government officials wanted to ease expensive water testing require-

Richard A. Bloom

Consumer activist Ralph Nader
"These laws have tremendous benefits for the public."

ments, which they argued were unnecessary. They also wanted greater flexibility to waive federal requirements and wanted to force federal regulators to prove that the benefits of environmental mandates outweigh the costs. The national environmental organizations and their allies in Congress contended that such changes would undermine public health protections.

Waxman, who then chaired the Energy and Commerce Subcommittee on Health and the Environment, tried to forge a compromise bill with the NGA's lobbyists, but they wouldn't go along with the measure without support from others in their coalition.

the Republicans make good on their promise to pass a constitutional amendment that would require a balanced federal budget, many federal programs will be shifted to the local level at the same time that the federal purse strings are becoming even tighter.

After a Jan. 6 meeting with Republican governors, Gingrich agreed to hold hearings and schedule a vote on a separate constitutional amendment that would bar unfunded federal mandates on states.

"We know there are not going to be streams of federal dollars flowing to the state and county and city governments anymore," Larry Naake, the executive director of the National Association of Counties (NACo), said. "And the people at home are not interested in raising taxes. In that case, mandates steal dollars from local programs."

John Eisele

Rep. William F. Clinger Jr., R-Pa.
He wants Congress to sort through existing mandates and target some for elimination.

"The defining moment to me came late in the Safe Drinking Water Act battle," Frank Shafroth, the director for policy and federal relations of the National League of Cities, said. "The people from NGA said they had an agreement with Waxman that NGA could live with. But they would not sign off unless we gave them the green light. That kind of unified position had never, ever happened before. It was an extraordinary gesture."

In the end, Shafroth and representatives of other local government groups weighed in against the Waxman compromise, and the legislation died. But the move solidified the commitment and resolve of the coalition of state and local organizations.

"No one is saying we want the federal government to go away," Shafroth said. "We want accountability. There should never, ever be a mandate imposed by the federal government that hasn't been labeled up front."

Local government officials worry that if

For NACo's members, that translates into a $33.7 billion tab for unfunded mandates during the next five years, according to a study by the organization. Most of the costs would come from complying with federal immigration laws and the 1972 Clean Water Act's wetlands protection mandates.

But environmental activists argue that the NACo study and other cost surveys conducted by the state and local organizations vastly overestimate the expense of federal laws and neglect to take into account the federal aid that cities and towns receive.

A report completed last June by the staff of the Senate Environment and Public Works Committee said that NACo's estimates included the full cost of local programs that would exist even without the federal requirements, such as drinking water treatment plants and garbage dumps. In addition, the committee's staff said, the local governments didn't acknowledge that they receive billions of dollars for such things as sewage treatment plants.

Consumer activist Ralph Nader argues that the unfunded mandates legislation fails to acknowledge that the public receives something in return for the federal laws: health and safety protection. Automobile safety requirements, for example, have translated into fewer deaths and injuries, he said at a Jan. 10 press briefing. "These laws," Nader said, "have tremendous benefits for the public."

HOW FAR IS FAR ENOUGH?

Just how far an unfunded mandates law should go is open to debate within Congress and even within the state and local government organizations that are pushing for such legislation.

Conservatives want an outright ban on unfunded mandates. Rep. William F. Clinger Jr., R-Pa., the chairman of the Government Reform and Oversight Committee, also wants to create a commission that would sort through existing mandates and target some for elimination.

Republican staff members who helped to craft this year's unfunded mandates legislation said that House conservatives fought for a ban on unfunded mandates, but that Republican Senators wouldn't go that far. The Republican Senators argued that most of the 67 co-sponsors of the Kempthorne-Glenn measure are still in office and support a moderate approach.

City officials who are struggling to pay for the structural changes that are needed to comply with the 1990 Americans With Disabilities Act, for example, would prefer to meet with local activists to set priorities for their spending, said Shafroth of the League of Cities. "My guess is that local groups would say: 'We understand you don't have enough money. Here are the most important actions the city could take to serve groups with disabilities.' But cities can't do that now. There is no flexibility in the law."

Public-interest groups worry, however, that existing public health and safety programs will be the first casualty of the unfunded mandates crusade.

"It sounds great in the press to say they're going to eliminate unfunded mandates," Pam Goddard, an associate representative on the Sierra Club's environmental quality team, said. "But they don't say how they're going to continue programs that protect all of us. I don't think the average citizens would say, 'Let's not have safe drinking water or worker safety laws anymore.' "

Some state and local officials are willing to defend federal health, safety and environmental protection laws. They are far more critical, however, of the red tape that has engulfed the laws.

"We want to get rid of all those prescriptive bureaucratic kinds of requirements that have been building up over the last 15 years," Gov. Howard Dean of Vermont, a Democrat who chairs the NGA, said. "But we don't want to get rid of the fundamental environmental standards. If you do that, the Midwest will be dumping acid rain on us again."

Public-interest groups also warn that leaving state and local governments responsible for protecting public health and safety would lead to uneven standards.

"I think that sets a really dangerous precedent," Dawn Martin, the director of the American Oceans Campaign's Washington office, said. "The rich states are going to be protected, while the poor states and the poor people who live in them won't get the same kind of attention."

UNCHARTED TERRITORY?

Fern Shepard is one of many environmental activists who worry about the consequences of putting state and local governments in charge of protecting health and the environment. Shepard, a lawyer with the Sierra Club Legal Defense Fund, spends much of her time trying to get states to comply with federal laws that protect children from exposure to lead.

The Centers for Disease Control and Prevention ranks lead poisoning as the most serious environmental problem facing America's children. And according to the Environmental Protection Agency, one in every six children has blood levels of lead high enough to cause significant harm to neurological development. Studies show that more than two-thirds of all inner-city black children have lead levels high enough to impair their IQs, hearing and growth.

Yet states have been slow to implement federal laws that would prevent lead poisoning, Shepard said. The Sierra Club Legal Defense Fund and other groups have sued several states to force them to implement federal medicaid laws that require doctors to test low-income children for lead exposure. Shepard has also taken states to court to force them to test water at school and day care centers for lead.

"This is something that stays with the child," Shepard said. "And we are paying for it, believe me, in medical care, education, probably in crime. We know how to prevent this in the first case. We know how kids are being poisoned. But some of the states aren't doing anything about it."

Some state officials have defended their noncompliance with federal lead exposure laws, Shepard said, by arguing that the testing requirements are unfunded mandates and therefore illegal.

In this era of Republican rule, the health and environmental activists who blocked unfunded mandates legislation in the 103rd Congress don't have the votes to stop or change it this time around. They are about to announce the formation of a coalition of more than 200 public-interest groups from coast to coast that are planning a coordinated attack on the Contract With America. But they weren't prepared for the GOP's fast footwork on the mandates bill.

As a last stand, the groups hope to amend the legislation to exempt health and safety laws, which, they say, could include many environmental and worker safety laws.

Richard A. Bloom

Larry Naake of the National Association of Counties "Mandates steal dollars from local programs."

"We'll take it to the floor," the Sierra Club's Goddard said. "And if the Members of Congress want to vote against health and safety, let's get them on the record. We know we can't operate with blank checks, but at the same time, we can't do away with laws that protect people."

LAW OF UNINTENDED CONSEQUENCES

The major obstacle for opponents of the unfunded mandates legislation is time.

Republican leaders in the Senate and House made unprecedented progress on the legislation in the first three weeks of the session. That's given the new Congress—including the half of all House Members who have been in office for two years or less—little time for studying and debating the probable effects of the revolutionary approach to federalism.

"There is not going to be enough time and thoughtful debate," Martin of the American Oceans Campaign said, "to be able to understand what effect it would have on the local health and safety programs."

Environmental activists are rushing to remind new Members that the American public still supports strong federal environmental protection laws. According to a December survey by Peter D. Hart Research Associates for the National Wildlife Federation, 62 per cent of Americans favor existing or stronger environmental protections. "Anyone who thought this election was a mandate to undo 25 years of environmental protection had better think again," Jay D. Hair, the federation's president, said.

Longtime government regulators warn the conservative Republicans that they could trigger a powerful backlash if they use the unfunded mandates campaign or other regulatory relief efforts to undercut existing health and safety protections. One recalled that the Reagan Administration's drive to cut environmental laws ignited a public outcry that resulted in more-stringent pollution control laws, including the 1990 rewrite of the 1972 Clean Air Act.

Many state and local officials say that it will take more than a few weeks in early 1995 to redefine the relationship between the federal government and its state and local counterparts. As Tom Needles, an aide to Gov. Voinovich of Ohio, put it, "I think this is going to be the issue of the '90s."*

A New Shade of Green

Radical theories for controlling pollution and protecting the environment are gaining support among the new breed of conservative Republicans in Congress who are pushing for dramatic changes in the way the federal government operates. But is the nation really ready for such a revolution?

MARGARET KRIZ

Imagine, for a moment, life without federal environmental laws. Richard L. Stroup, a professor of economics at Montana State University, can. Stroup, a senior associate at the Political Economic Research Center in Bozeman, Mont., is one of a cadre of increasingly influential scholars who advocate scrapping the current maze of expensive federal statutes and returning to the principles of common law for controlling pollution and protecting the environment.

Under the centuries-old common-law approach, citizens have an inherent legal right not to be harmed or threatened by pollution—much as they have a right not to be mugged. Citizens who can prove that they've been harmed can sue the company or individual whose pollution "trespassed" on their property. Or they can sell their "property rights" to the polluter.

Instead of the laborious system of cleaning up thousands of hazardous waste sites overseen by the Environmental Protection Agency (EPA), for example, the common-law strategy would have allowed landowners near Love Canal, N.Y., to immediately sue Hooker Chemical Co. (now Occidental Chemical Corp.) when the long-buried chemicals trespassed on their property, Stroup said.

Likewise, common law could be applied to save natural resources, according to Jonathan H. Adler, the Competitive Enterprise Institute's associate director of environmental studies. Adler advocates privatizing federal lands and regional fisheries, thereby giving the new owners greater incentive than federal regulators to protect the resources. "In England," he said, "private fishing clubs own the rights to fish along some rivers, so of course they are quick to respond to pollution threats."

Opponents worry that common-law environmentalism would take health and safety decisions out of the hands of scientists and regulatory experts and move them into the courts, where, critics say, most landowners would have a difficult time fighting large corporations.

"It's true that juries and judges are not scientists," Stroup said. "But we trust our lives to them all the time. If you compare the regulatory process against the flaws of courts, I'll take my chances on the courts."

Common-law environmentalism has long been embraced by libertarians and others who favor infusing more free-market incentives into government. Now the radical theories are gaining support among the new breed of conservative Republicans in Congress who are pushing for dramatic changes in the way the federal government operates.

The advocates of such common-law philosophies are among the many policy wonks who are jockeying for the right to play Professor Henry Higgins to EPA's Eliza Doolittle.

Several serious proposals to change not only the way EPA walks and talks, but also its fundamental mission, are gathering momentum in Washington.

Industry officials, state and local leaders, political activists and think-tank intellectuals agree that the nation is on the brink of a revolution in federal environmental policy. Many of the new approaches are far less sensational than the common-law system. But even defenders of existing environmental laws admit that a new day is dawning.

Even the White House has come up with a dramatic approach to environmental law that tries to reward companies for being environmental "good guys" and to reduce the regulatory burden on small businesses. President Clinton was scheduled on March 16 to unveil a plan that would give companies greater flexibility in complying with environmental regulations if they cut their pollution even more than federal law requires.

"For 25 years, our solutions to very serious environmental problems have been regulatory solutions, and we've made significant progress," said Jonathan Lash, the president of the World Resources Institute and a co-chairman of the President's Council on Sustainable Development. "Then, in order to address more-serious problems, we added in more-specific requirements and tighter command and control by government. That isn't going to happen anymore. We've reached the end of the regulatory era."

AN ARRAY OF APPROACHES

Most of the new blueprints for reconstructing federal environmental policy go far beyond the regulatory reform proposals in the House GOP's Contract With America. The contract's proposals, while extraordinary in their own right, primarily reshape the way regulators handle existing environmental laws.

Nearly all the new paradigms, however, would require fundamental and in some cases jolting changes that go to the heart of federal environmental law.

If the common-law theory of law is too extreme, for example, consider a more modest proposal from Jerry Taylor, the director of natural resource studies for the Cato Institute. Taylor suggests returning all environmental protection duties to the states—no mandates, no strings, no federal support.

Under such a system, state and local governments could decide how to handle—and pay for—the hazardous waste sites now regulated by EPA. "It might well be that a community would fence off the site and spend its money on something else," Taylor said.

The toss-it-back-to-the-states approach appears to have the support of Sen. Robert C. Smith, R-N.H., who chairs the Environment and Public Works Subcommittee on Superfund, Waste Control and Risk Assessment. Smith will preside over this year's debate in the Senate over rewriting the 1980 Comprehensive Environmental Response, Compensation and Liability Act, better known as superfund.

The nation's governors, however, have their own ideas. Gov. E. Benjamin Nelson, D-Neb., for example, is promoting a new model under which the federal government would write broad environmental goals and help the states to set local priorities. Beyond that, the states would be free to design their own solutions to their pollution problems. "For too long, I've felt like branch manager for the federal government," Nelson said at a Feb. 16 forum on reinventing EPA that was organized by the National Environmental Policy Institute.

Unlike Taylor's proposal, however, Nelson's calls for federal block grants to help underwrite the state programs.

Richard A. Bloom

Terry Davies of the Center for Risk Management EPA "is driven by statutes."

The new proposals for revamping environmental law all have one thing in common: They reject the vision of EPA as the strict federal command-and-control cop charged with cleaning up the air, drinking water, rivers and waste dumps.

Some new policy schemes would send federal regulators to sensitivity training sessions in the hope of transforming them into flexible big brothers to states and to corporate America. Others, such as the common-law approach, would simply euthanatize the agency.

Proposals to overhaul the federal environmental infrastructure have been debated in the abstract for years. The theoretical discussions became more serious, however, as state and industry officials struggled to comply with an ever-increasing mountain of federal environmental regulations.

In previous Congresses, any attempt to challenge the status quo was considered political suicide. The reigning Democrats were quick to defend the laws that they had written and had strengthened over the years. The national environmental groups, then considered a powerful force in national politics, labeled as "anti-environment" anyone who wanted to make environmental law more flexible.

But the political dynamics shifted dramatically in November, when the Republicans took control of Congress. Now a host of conservatives, industry coalitions and research groups are moving into the breach.

Some hope to pass sweeping legislation as soon as this year. Others predict that the emerging debate to transfigure federal environmental law will become a key issue in the 1996 presidential campaign.

All of them agree that the prospects for change have never been better.

THE STREAMLINERS

In the early 1980s, officials of the Conservation Foundation held a long-term strategic planning session to choose the group's next big mission. The result was a remarkable campaign to create a new government model for protecting the environment.

Although the existing environmental laws were making impressive progress in cleaning up the nation's waterways and the urban air, "the kind of discontent that exists now was detectable even then," said Terry Davies, a former executive vice president of the foundation who now directs the Center for Risk Management at Resources for the Future Inc. "People were getting fairly fed up with laws that nobody could understand and a framework that nobody could begin to follow."

The Conservation Foundation recommended a holistic approach to protecting the environment that would address all of a company's pollution sources under one permit. Existing environmental laws tend to attack air, water and land wastes separately. As a result, companies were known to cut their water pollution levels by, say, diverting toxic waste to a landfill.

That piecemeal approach to environmental laws was an unintended consequence of the national pressure for fast federal help. "Historically, environmental regulations were created on an emergency basis," EPA administrator Carol Browner said at the National Environmental Policy Institute's forum.

In 1969, when Ohio's Cuyahoga River became so polluted that it caught fire, for example, congressional activists began work on the 1972 Clean Water Act.

By 1980, when Congress's environmental law machine finally stopped pumping out new statutes, EPA found itself in charge of 16 laws overseen by more than 70 congressional committees and subcommittees.

Congress embraced strict command-and-control techniques to reduce pollution for several good reasons. For one thing, many companies weren't willing to voluntarily control their pollution. Indeed, many corporate executives scoffed at the environmental movement as a passing phase.

For an anxious American public, the prescriptive federal laws offered some certainty that air and water pollution would be reduced—or that the polluter would be held accountable.

Richard A. Bloom

Carol Browner, the administrator of the Environmental Protection Agency "The laws are probably more flexible than people have tended to think they are."

"If you look at the successes of the last 25 years, the things we are proudest of occurred when we as a nation were willing to say: 'No more. We are going to take lead out of gasoline. We are going to take benzene out of drinking water. We are going to ban DDT,' " Browner said in an interview. "These are protections that the American people have every right to expect from their government."

But those protections came at a price.

The traditional policy tools, such as prescriptive technology standards and strict pollution limits, were expensive for government to implement and for industry to adopt. And they provided little or no flexibility for companies or for regulators.

Little wonder, then, that industry officials were intrigued by, though cautious about, the Conservation Foundation's recommendations for a unified environmental statute.

"We kept running into the criticism that there would be no way you could combine all of these environmental laws," Davies said. Out to prove the critics wrong, he drafted the "1988 Environmental Protection Act," though it was never meant to be seriously considered by Congress.

The unified statute was designed to replace nine federal pollution control laws. Under the proposal, regulators would issue a single environmental permit for each facility. EPA would train inspectors in the strengths and weaknesses of pollution control approaches for each industry.

Davies's work was revolutionary for the 1980s. Today, however, the draft statute is being taken off the shelves around Washington. For many industry and think-tank analysts, the proposal has become the starting point for reconstructing environmental law.

"Part of the election message was the fact that big government bureaucracies don't work anymore," said former Rep. Don Ritter, R-Pa., who's now the chairman of the National Environmental Policy Institute. "The command-and-control nature of environmental law is not the optimal system of the '90s, let alone the 21st century."

BENDING THE RULES

In the early 1990s, executives of St. Paul-based Minnesota Mining & Manufacturing Co. (3M) faced a dilemma. Seeking to expand their line of new products, they set a goal of achieving 30 per cent of the company's annual sales from new products.

But there was a daunting obstacle in the way of following through on new product ideas: the 1970 Clean Air Act. Under that law, a company needs an EPA permit before it can make a major change in its production processes.

"Getting these products out of the lab, through the regulatory process and to the marketplace is critical," Thomas W. Zosel, the manager of 3M's pollution prevention programs, said in a recent interview. "When we have to wait nine months for a regulatory permit, that's too long."

In 1993, the company sought to clear the roadblock for a new facility in St. Paul by entering into a bold experiment with state and federal environmental officials.

3M promised that the new plant would generate no more than half of the air pollution emissions allowed by federal law. In return, federal and state environmental regulators agreed not to micromanage the company's production line. Specifically, 3M can make many routine changes in its production processes without getting state or federal approval. "This is the greatest degree of flexibility allowed under current EPA regulations and policy," Zosel said.

Having alleviated its problems for one plant, 3M undertook a far more ambitious task: reforming federal law.

Early last fall, Zosel began circulating draft legislation that would provide regulatory relief to companies that are willing to cut their emissions of pollutants to no more than 75 per cent of the levels permissible under federal law. In return, the firms could sidestep many of the onerous requirements of the Clean Air Act, the Clean Water Act and the 1976 Resource Conservation and Recovery Act, which governs the disposal of solid and toxic wastes.

"We believe that companies that have been superior environmental performers need to be recognized and rewarded," Zosel said. "They don't need the time delays of paperwork."

Some industry officials contend, however, that 3M's approach retains too many paperwork requirements. They lean toward a regulatory proposal put forward by General Electric Co., under which a company's executives could negotiate a covenant with a mayor or county to limit the over-all pollution emissions allowed at a facility. Each company and community could draw up its own set of environmental priorities to address local needs.

At the same time, EPA is promoting its own innovative program for increased regulatory flexibility. Under the plan, dubbed the "common sense initiative," regulators and officials of six "volunteer" industries are working with outside groups to streamline complicated regulations and to eliminate inconsistent requirements.

Along the same line, Browner is attacking regional environmental cleanup problems by negotiating settlements with local citizens, industries and government officials. In January, for example, EPA announced a new program that will allow cities to begin redeveloping former superfund sites and returning them to productive community use without having to eliminate all pollution at the sites.

Since she took office two years ago, in fact, Browner has proselytized about the need to overhaul EPA's operations. She maintains that most of the troublesome environmental regulatory hurdles can be overcome through negotiations.

John Eisele

Former Rep. Don Ritter, R-Pa., of the National Environmental Policy Institute
Part of the election message: "Big government bureaucracies don't work anymore."

"I think that the laws are probably more flexible than people have tended to think they are," she said. "I don't know that you need to rewrite every single environmental statute to achieve a new paradigm of environmental protection."

But some industry officials complain that EPA's attempts to put new flexibility into the environmental laws have been slow to get off the ground. They also argue that any innovative agreements with industry could be challenged by national environmental organizations—an argument Browner disputes.

"If we're able to agree on a blueprint for how best to manage each of these industries in a way that does the job cleaner and cheaper, and there's an agreement reached with the environmental community, the state, the EPA and the industry, who's going to object?" she said.

But unless federal laws are changed, EPA doesn't have the authority to lift statutory requirements, Davies, who did a tour of duty as assistant EPA administrator for policy, planning and evaluation early in the Bush Administration, said. "The agency is driven by statutes. Anything you do that doesn't have a statutory backup has to be done by consensus, and that gives everybody involved veto power over what happens. The administrator is finding the same problems that all the administrators before her have found in trying to provide flexibility."

CARROT V. STICK

When industry officials complain about EPA's intransigence, discussion often turns to the Amoco Yorktown experiment. In 1992, Amoco Oil Co. and EPA released the results of a two-year, $2.3 million environmental audit of the company's oil refinery in Yorktown, Va.

The study concluded that Amoco was required by federal law to spend more than $40 million over a four-year period to reduce hydrocarbon emissions at the plant. It also concluded that Amoco could have reduced emissions by nearly the same amount at a cost of $10 million if it had been allowed to adopt alternative—but not federally mandated—pollution control programs.

In releasing the study, EPA and company officials agreed that the audit was evidence that federal environmental laws need to be rationalized.

But the story comes with a bitter epilogue. Even though the company was working in good faith with the federal government to improve conditions at the Yorktown facility, EPA was quick to hit the company with a $5.5 million fine when an unrelated violation at the same refinery was uncovered.

And despite the audit's conclusion that expensive new wastewater treatment equipment wasn't needed at the Yorktown facility, EPA wasn't able to waive the law's legal mandate that the equipment be installed.

Industry officials see the Amoco case as evidence that EPA simply doesn't have the ability to develop a more flexible regulatory atmosphere without major changes in federal law.

Everyone agrees that companies should be encouraged to find and fix their environmental problems, not punished when they don't meet the letter of the law.

"The bottom line is, we've got to recharge the search for environmental innovation," said Bruce W. Piasecki, the director of Rensselaer Polytechnic Institute's environmental management program and the author of *Corporate Environmental Strategy* (John Wiley & Sons Inc., 1995).

There are several examples of such programs. Hundreds of companies have cut pollution as a result of a federal law that requires companies to let the public have access to information about a plant's annual emissions of certain toxic chemicals, Margaret Rogers, the environmental policy manager of Dow Chemical Co.'s government relations office in Washington, said.

Too often, "the agency's actions appear to be driven by the desire to punish all, including inadvertent violators of minor paperwork rules," Rogers said. "The focus should be on environmental performance."

Other corporate executives express skepticism that EPA regulators, reared on a steady diet of strict command-and-control laws, could implement a flexible approach to environmental protection, even if Congress embraced such a program.

William J. Mulligan, who is the manager of federal relations for Chevron Corp., suggested that a different regulatory body, not EPA, might be needed. "The EPA bureaucracy is capable of suffocating a new regulatory regime," he said. "Regulators are capable of making a program so good, so tight and so predictable that in the end you don't want to be a part of it."

HOW CLEAN THE SWEEP?

With revolution in the air, suspicion is rampant on all sides of the environmental policy debate.

The Clinton Administration and the public-interest community are at war with the Republican leaders of Congress over their efforts to win fast passage of the regulatory reforms in the Contract With America.

Browner accused the Republican leaders of being more interested in tearing down existing environmental protections than in crafting a better federal environmental policy.

"I'm more than happy to have a conversation with anyone who's willing to take the time to seriously analyze the environmental successes of the past and build to meet the challenges of the future," she said. But the measures in the House GOP's contract, she added, "are not about creating a more creative, flexible system—they are dismantling public health and safety laws with no public debate."

Escalating tensions from that battle could make it difficult for all sides to cooperate when the discussion eventually turns to fundamental changes in environmental law.

Even industry officials are critical of how the Republicans have handled legislation that's part of the contract. "It's an abrupt change to the way we've done things," Mulligan said. "You know how you would react if someone tried to force-feed you. We're dealing with something that you have to go a little more slowly with."

Gov. E. Benjamin Nelson, D-Neb.
He's felt "like branch manager for the federal government."

Fred Krupp, the president of the Environmental Defense Fund, who's been the environmental community's most aggressive supporter of partnerships with corporate America, warned industry leaders that provisions of the House GOP's contract could hinder future cooperation. "Let's not jeopardize the good faith and dialogue we have established over the last few years," Krupp said at the National Environmental Policy Institute's forum.

Outside of such warnings, however, the major national environmental organizations have not actively participated in the emerging debate over reinventing national environmental policy.

"I think there's a lot of openness to serious new ideas within the environmental community," said the World Resources Institute's Lash, whose résumé includes stints as an environmental activist and as a Vermont environmental regulator. "But it's hard to have that discussion from the bunkers."

Busy fighting the Republican proposals, most environmental activists continue to be skeptical that industry can solve its environmental problems. And many worry that state and local governments will cave in to industry demands for weaker regulations unless Uncle Sam acts as the national enforcer.

Gov. Nelson of Nebraska bristles at such mistrust. "Out in the hinterlands, the mentality that somehow states can't be trusted is called 'the [Capital] Beltway mentality,' " he said at the National Environmental Policy Institute's forum. "If I'm not worried about the quality of water in the state of Nebraska, then I'm a fool, because I have to drink it."

Despite the discord, the outlines of a new generation of environmental laws are beginning to emerge.

Most academic and industry analysts support a system under which the federal government would establish pollution control goals for states and for industry and give them wide berth in deciding how to meet them. States would also be allowed to rank their environmental problems, accelerating work on their most pressing problems and delaying compliance with other laws. EPA would be responsible for monitoring specific environmental benchmarks and collecting scientific data on pollution problems.

That would be a dramatic shift from current environmental laws, which prescribe pollution control technologies and set strict compliance deadlines.

Any comprehensive or revolutionary changes in environmental regulation, however, won't happen overnight. Industry officials suggest that a flexible environmental program similar to the one that Clinton has proposed could be incorporated into regulatory reform legislation that's pending in the Senate.

The next step might be for Congress to add flexibility to environmental laws as it rewrites them. Topping the agenda for action in the 104th Congress are the Safe Drinking Water Act, the Clean Water Act and superfund.

Ultimately, however, Congress is likely to take up a more sweeping reexamination of environmental law. Such a reexamination might be triggered by a long-awaited report by the National Academy of Public Administration, which is expected to recommend bold changes in EPA's mission, structure and legal authority. Ordered by Congress in 1993, the study could be issued in early April.

How far might Congress go?

"It may be time to move on to a new era," John H. Chafee, R-R.I., the chairman of the Senate Environment and Public Works Committee, said at the National Environmental Policy Institute's forum. "But it is important to remember that we have experienced some real achievements under our current laws."

Even supporters of the common-law, free-market approach concede that their proposals for a wholesale transformation of environmental law aren't politically feasible—yet.

"The freshman class and a fair number of the sophomore congressional class are fairly hard-core about the idea that the federal government has encroached on their lives," John Shanahan, an environment and energy policy analyst for the Heritage Foundation, said. "That idea drives this movement to dismantle the environmental laws. But the political reality is that this is not a conservative Republican President and our majorities [of conservative Republicans] are too thin without the White House."

Ritter, the chairman of the National Environmental Policy Institute, said that his group is developing a bipartisan "reinventing EPA" project. "Let's get this out on the table for all sides to take on and let the presidential candidates take a look at it," Ritter said. "We'd like to have it ready for the presidential debates."

Dozens of industry lobbyists, academics and Washington policy analysts are joining the movement to create the next generation of environmental protection. "The sum total, all the ingredients, are on the street today," Mulligan said. "But this mosaic has not been assembled into a clear picture yet."

Burial Insurance

Nuclear power plants are running out of space to store their radioactive waste, and a federal plan to bury the waste in the Nevada desert has run into roadblocks. Utility executives and state regulators are trying bolder tactics to address the problem in the courts and on Capitol Hill.

MARGARET KRIZ

The nation's commercial nuclear waste program has taken on the atmosphere of a three-ring circus lately, with James J. Howard, chairman and chief executive officer of Minneapolis-based Northern States Power Co., more often than not in the spotlight.

Early this year, Howard persuaded the Minnesota Legislature to let his company build additional waste storage space at its Prairie Island nuclear power plant. Otherwise, Prairie Island would probably have been forced to close in 1995, when it was projected to run out of storage space.

Reluctant legislators sought to prevent Prairie Island from becoming a permanent waste site, though. They forced Northern States to scale back its construction plans and allowed the company to build only enough storage to house spent nuclear fuel rods through 2002.

Dissatisfied, Howard moved to the national arena.

On June 20, Northern States joined 13 other utilities and 20 state governments in a lawsuit charging that the Energy Department is trying to renege on its legal obligation to take possession of the 22,000 tons of nuclear waste building up at the nation's 110 commercial nuclear power plants.

The suit came in response to Energy Secretary Hazel R. O'Leary's comment that although her department has a "moral obligation" to claim ownership of the waste, she isn't legally bound to take possession until the agency completes work on its long-delayed repository in Nevada. Until then, the states are on their own.

Utility executives and state regulators strenuously disagree. "We signed a contract with the federal government, and for that they were to take our spent nuclear fuel beginning in 1998," Howard said in an interview. "We've sent them a lot of money—my company over $200 million, [the nuclear power] industry about $8 billion."

While pursuing the lawsuit, Howard is making a separate attempt to ensure his company's nuclear future. Northern States and 34 other utilities are negotiating with the Mescalero Apache tribe to build a privately financed temporary nuclear waste storehouse on Mescalero lands in New Mexico. The companies promise to help underwrite the unprecedented facility, which proponents say would hold nuclear waste for 40 years at a small fraction of the price that it would cost the federal government.

A tentative contract with the Mescaleros is expected to be completed this month; it will be put to a full tribal vote later this year. New Mexico elected officials are united in opposition to the proposal and are considering federal legislation to block it. But Howard sees the project as nearly a done deal.

"I can't see anything that could stop it," he said. "The federal government could try, but they would have to go way out of their way to do it. And the question is, why? If you do that, you may as well shut the nuclear program down in this country."

Some congressional leaders, however, view the lawsuit and the attempt to privatize the nation's nuclear waste facilities as a distraction from the main event. Next year, according to staff aides, Congress will concentrate on making it easier for the federal government to build a long-term waste facility. And there's widespread agreement among congressional aides, federal officials and industry officials that legislation is inevitable.

A POLITICAL MINEFIELD

O'Leary's clash with Northern States has an ironic edge. Before becoming Energy Secretary, she was the company's executive vice president for corporate affairs and lobbied on nuclear waste issues in Washington. But for Northern States and other electric utilities, time is running out.

The electric power industry is drowning in nuclear waste. At least 23 utilities will run out of storage space for their spent fuel by the turn of the century. With the federal government unable to guarantee when it will take possession of

From *National Journal,* August 6, 1994, pp. 1852-1854.

the waste, state regulators and utility executives are trying bolder tactics.

The recent lawsuit "raises the issue on the political radar screen," Howard said. "There are a lot of things going on in the world right now, but everybody's lights are on and their air-conditioners are working. Nuclear waste is such a long-term issue. This does tend to put a bit more of a sense of urgency on the issue."

The increased pressure could force a reluctant Congress to step once again into the political minefield that surrounds nuclear waste issues.

James J. Howard of Northern States Power Co. It's time for "a sense of urgency on the issue."

Congressional leaders acknowledge that they postponed until next year any substantive debate on the question, in part because of the congressional elections this fall. Sen. Richard H. Bryan, D-Nev., a leading critic of the proposed nuclear waste site beneath Yucca Mountain in his state, is up for reelection.

And House Energy and Commerce Committee chairman John D. Dingell, D-Mich., a major player in the debate, has been focused on health care reform. About the only thing Congress has been willing to consider this year is increasing the Energy Department's budget for preparing the Yucca Mountain facility.

The Senate, at the urging of J. Bennett Johnston, D-La., who chairs the Appropriations Subcommittee on Energy and Water Development, passed a fiscal 1995 appropriations bill that would provide $533 million for the program. That's a $150 million increase over the current budget. A House-passed measure would deliver $434 million, or a $50 million increase. A House-Senate conference committee will settle the difference. In both bills, the additional funds would come at the expense of other Energy Department programs.

Johnston, who also chairs the Energy and Natural Resources Committee, has vowed to increase funds for the program to $700 million for fiscal 1996.

Next year, however, Congress is destined to tackle several more-controversial nuclear waste problems, according to federal regulators, congressional aides and industry officials.

Lawmakers are likely, for example, to consider building a temporary facility to house nuclear waste in Nevada until the Yucca Mountain repository 100 miles northwest of Las Vegas is completed.

Some pro-nuclear lawmakers also want to reevaluate the health and safety standards that the Yucca Mountain project is required to meet. Nuclear energy proponents say that the standards—one of which requires the Energy Department to prove that the material will be safe for 10,000 years—are impossible to meet and could doom efforts to use deep geological disposal technologies envisioned for the site.

The health and safety standards are set by the Environmental Protection Agency. In the 1992 Energy Policy Act, however, Congress asked the National Academy of Sciences to reconsider the standards and suggest changes. That report is due out at the end of this year.

Environmental activists contend that it's unsafe to house nuclear waste at the Yucca Mountain site for the long haul. They note that the region has endured two earthquakes in the past two years, including one that measured 5.6 on the Richter scale and caused $1 million in damage to nearby Energy Department facilities.

"Sen. Johnston realized that his preferred site didn't meet the health and safety standards. And so he's going to try to change the standards rather than change the site," said Bill Magavern, director of Public Citizen Inc.'s Critical Mass Energy Project, a Washington lobby group that is calling for nuclear power to be phased out in the United States.

Utility executives and state regulators worry that Congress, faced with opposition from environmental groups, may not have the political will to sort through the highly technical and politically contentious arguments surrounding the issue. "The longer you delay, the greater the cost of handling this nuclear waste," warned Michigan utility commissioner Ronald Russell, one of the state regulators who sued the Energy Department.

"If we don't resolve this issue now, no one will want to deal with this politically in 1996 when you get into the presidential elections," Russell said. "Then it'll be '97 before you have an opportunity to address this. One of two things will happen: It will cost a lot more money to build the repository, or nothing will be completed and dozens of nuclear power plants will be forced to shut down."

BUDGET SHELL GAMES

In 1987, Members of Congress thought they had solved the nation's nuclear waste problems when they passed a law requiring the Energy Department to build a storage facility deep beneath Yucca Mountain.

Since then, however, the disposal effort has bogged down in a sea of lawsuits filed against the federal government by Nevada state officials who don't want the waste in their backyard.

Margaret Kriz

Michigan utility commissioner Ronald Russell Dozens of nuclear plants may have to shut down.

The project also stalled each time a new Energy Secretary took office and attempted to redefine the mandate. As a result, Yucca Mountain is substantially over budget and behind schedule.

On the positive side, scientists have completed some technical studies on the site. A specially built tunnel-boring machine is poised to dig shafts into the mountain to permit analyses of the mountain's geology, the movement of the local groundwater and potential seismic and volcanic activity.

But after spending $3.8 billion on the waste site, the Energy Department still hasn't decided whether Yucca Mountain can safely house the stuff.

There's also a problem of financing. The department has received nearly $8 billion from the utility industry to build the waste storehouse. That money goes into a trust fund within the department's general budget.

Congress has doled out some of the funds for examining the site. But the rest remains on federal budget ledgers—and is used in the ongoing shell game to offset budget deficit numbers.

To put an end to the charade, Johnston and industry officials want to move the fund off-budget. Legislation to create a separate trust fund account is expected to be offered next year.

In the meantime, a chronic shortage of funds is slowing progress at Yucca Mountain, according to Dan Dreyfuss, director of the Energy Department's civilian radioactive waste management office.

"The schedule and the budget that were a matter of record when I came here were obsolete and impossible to achieve," he said in an interview. "They anticipated, for example, that in 1994, we'd be spending $700 million. Instead, we're spending something like $250 million."

If Congress grants the increased funds that he requested and that the Senate adopted, Dreyfuss said, the department will know by 1998 whether there is any technical reason to disqualify the Yucca Mountain site. If scientists give the site a green light, the department would complete environmental impact studies and apply to the Nuclear Regulatory Commission for an operating license. Under that scenario, Yucca Mountain could take fuel by 2010, he said.

To meet that timetable, Dreyfuss has redesigned the site study plan, consolidating research and scaling back the amount of tunneling that will be done.

But Dreyfuss worries that the rigorous health and safety standards being applied to the site may be nearly impossible to meet. "It's pretty tough to make projections of what can happen over 10,000 years, to contemplate whether or not there would be earthquake activity, project the disintegration of waste packages and therefore the rate of release of radio nuclides into the repository," he said. "That's a pretty speculative deal."

In fact, in a 1990 study, the National Academy of Sciences suggested that no amount of research could guarantee that a nuclear waste site would be safe for 10,000 years. "Basically you're stretching the data and the analysis beyond its useful limits," Dreyfuss said.

John Eisele

Dan Dreyfuss, head of the Energy Department's civilian radioactive waste office
The remaining questions about the Nevada disposal site are political, not technical.

FORCING THE ISSUE

When the Clinton Administration took office, environmental and antinuclear activists called for a complete reexamination of the federal nuclear waste disposal program, particularly the Yucca Mountain project. Instead, Congress is pouring more money into it.

"This is the kind of thing that happens only in Washington," Magavern said, "where when a program is flawed and is spending money unwisely, the response is, 'Let's spend more money.' "

Dreyfuss argues that the Yucca Mountain site has been studied to death. The pending questions about the site aren't technical, he said. "I don't think blue-ribbon committees thinking about it are going to get us there. This is really a public policy issue."

Mary Olson, a staff biologist for the Nuclear Information and Resource Service, a Washington-based antinuclear group, noted that the utilities complaining the loudest about their nuclear waste problems are the ones that most want to continue generating the waste.

"Unless we tackle the question of whether we should be generating this material, they are doing nothing more than operating a shell game to enable continued production," she said. "Putting this radioactive material in the ground is an effort to move it out of sight and out of mind. It's not a guarantee that it will remain isolated."

Olson said that some citizen activists are urging her group to intervene in the states' and utilities' lawsuit against the Energy Department. The aim would be to force a national debate on the federal government's continued support for nuclear power, which has not waned in the Clinton Administration.

But even if antinuclear groups don't take part in the suit, the continuing nuclear waste disposal problems are serving their ends.

If utilities run out of storage space, nuclear plants could be forced to close and state utility commissions would be reluctant to allow companies to build new ones.

Michigan regulator Russell complained that the nation is backing into a new policy. "We as a country need to face the issue of nuclear power, not to create a policy by default, because it's costing too much money," he said.

Indeed, the nation is beginning a de facto nuclear phaseout, Magavern said. "It would help if we could arrive at a national consensus on managing the decline of the nuclear era. That would require the industry to give up on the fantasy that they're going to build new plants or extend the lives of the current ones. Then they would get the cooperation of citizens groups in dealing with the disposal problem."

Political leaders in Washington don't share that vision, though. And they'll be calling the shots when the issue is taken up by Congress.

"Whether or not anybody ever builds another nuclear reactor is an interesting sidelight to this, and it does change the volume of nuclear waste," Dreyfuss said. "But it doesn't change the fundamental need to solve this problem. We have got to do it."

Health Care

In running for president in 1992, Bill Clinton linked reform of health care delivery in the United States to improving the nation's economic health. He made health care reform one of the pillars of his presidential candidacy, and toward the end of his first year in office he proposed a major health care reform package designed to contain costs, improve efficiency, and extend health care insurance to all Americans.

Less than a year after being introduced in late 1993, President Clinton's health care reform package was declared dead on Capitol Hill. The Clinton proposals were attacked from all sides. Critics favoring a more radical proposal, a so-called single-payer plan similar to that used in Canada, said that Clinton's plan was a bureaucratic nightmare concocted to avoid antagonizing the powerful health insurance lobby. Conservative critics said that Clinton's plan would intrude on the all-important doctor-patient relationship, prevent Americans from choosing their own physicians, and introduce the functional equivalent of socialized medicine. The American Medical Association opposed the plan on the grounds that it would restrict doctors' professional autonomy as well as their relations with patients.

Bill Clinton was the not the first president to address the need for reform of the nation's health care delivery system. In 1969 Republican president Richard Nixon warned of a "massive crisis" in health care and his Department of Health, Education, and Welfare outlined plans for a "revolutionary change" in the nation's health care delivery system. But little more was heard of Nixon's warning or his revolutionary plan.

While Clinton's 1994 reform plan may be dead, his focus on the nation's health care delivery system has had considerable effect. For one thing, Americans have had their attention called to various problems in the system, and an attentive minority have become acquainted with different proposed solutions. Policy debates over proposals for more "managed care" and "portability" and on "how to save medicare" have served to educate the general public as well as policymakers themselves. In addition, partly in response to increased awareness among the public and government policymakers and partly in response to mounting financial pressures, cost containment and other reform measures have been introduced in the health care delivery system in attempts to improve some of the worst features of the current system. At the very least, President Clinton has served to put health care reform squarely on the policy-making agenda, and it seems that his efforts have touched off significant changes that are already occurring and will continue to occur in the near future.

Selections in this unit can, of course, offer no closure to what now seems likely to be an on-going process of incremental change and reform in the U.S. health care delivery system. But they can serve to introduce the reader to such central health care issues as "managed care," the problems that the entire medicare program is facing, and the possibility of giving state governments a bigger role in shaping the health care delivery system, especially for the needy. They can also acquaint readers with the rather complicated policy arguments and problems that can arise in connection with any number of proposed reforms.

Looking Ahead: Challenge Questions

Americans spend a greater proportion of their nation's gross domestic product on health care than any other industrialized nation in the world. Yet the United States does not have the best record on some critical health indicators such as life expectancy, incidence of birth defects, and so forth. Many policymakers, President Clinton among them, think that containing or reducing the overall amount of money that Americans spend on health care is an important goal, not the least because high health care costs disadvantage U.S. manufacturers and producers in competition with manufacturers and producers from other countries that spend less. Others say that if Americans want to spend relatively more on their health care, that is their choice and it is not an unreasonable one. What do you think about these facts and points of view?

Medical doctors are among the highest paid of all

Unit

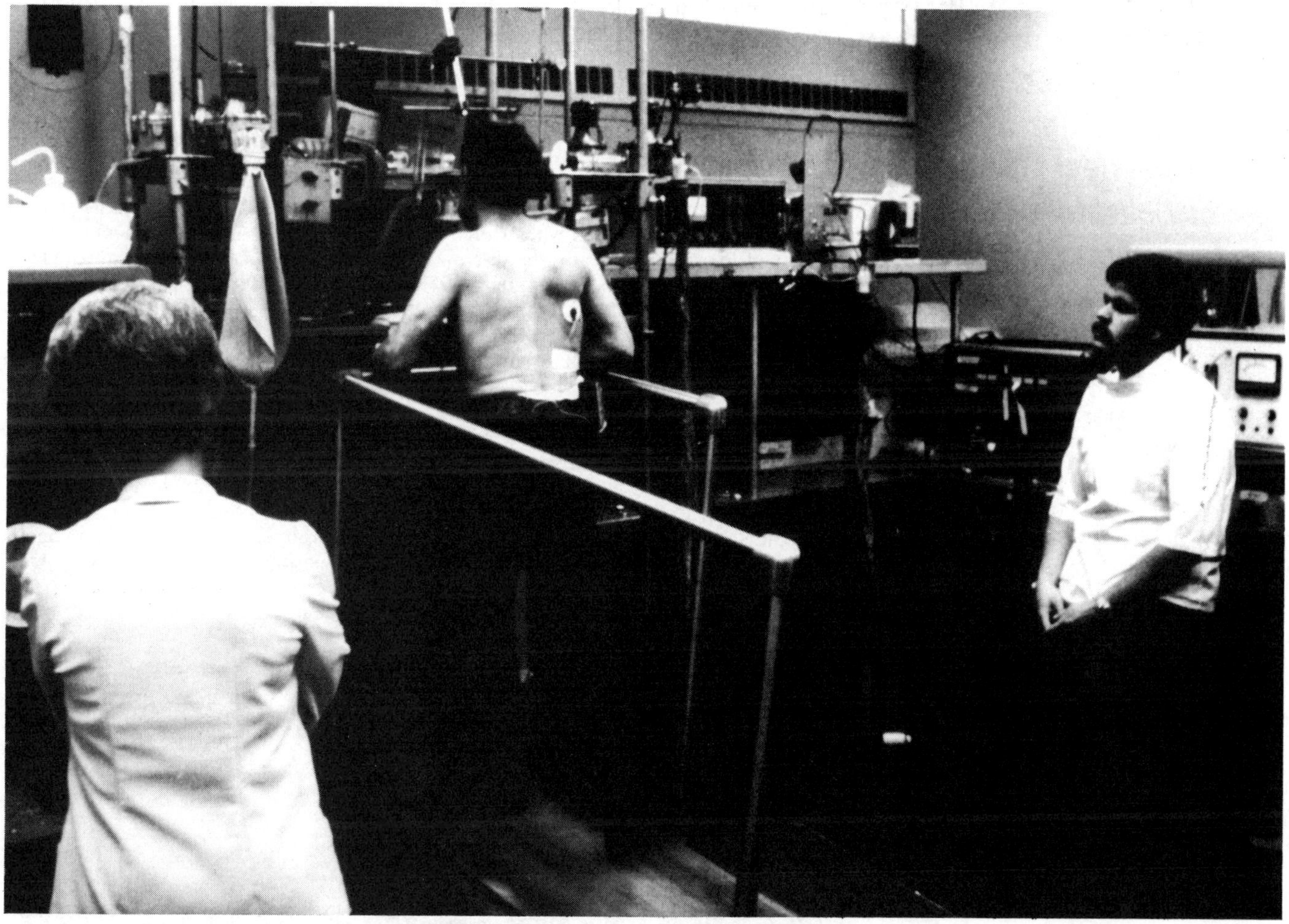

professionals in the United States and earn average annual salaries well in excess of $100,000. They also enjoy a social status and a security of income unmatched by almost any other professional group. Compared to doctors in most other countries, American doctors are very well off. Do you think that health care reforms should include measures whose effect would be to limit or reduce doctors' earnings and in that way cut overall health care costs in the United States? Why or why not?

Do you think that elderly and seriously injured people should be kept alive at all costs, even if society as a whole (through medicare) is footing the bill? Or do you think that there should be fairly rigorous cost limits on how much medicare money is spent to keep a person alive?

Unmanaged Care?

Changes in the health care marketplace have outpaced many of the laws and regulations that were intended to protect patients. Consumer advocates want new safeguards, but employers and the managed care industry warn that could raise the cost of coverage.

JULIE KOSTERLITZ

Florence Corcoran checked out of the hospital after learning that her health insurance wouldn't pay for her to stay there during a troubled pregnancy. A "utilization review" company hired by her employer to police insurance claims had decided that she didn't need hospital care and arranged for her to be hooked up to a fetal monitor and cared for at home by a part-time nurse. Thirteen days later, when the nurse was off duty, Corcoran's unborn fetus died.

The utilization review company had acted against the advice of her physician and a second doctor whose opinion her employer had solicited. But when Corcoran sued for wrongful death, she discovered she had virtually no rights of redress. In a decision that sent shock waves through the legal community, the U.S. Court of Appeals for the 5th Circuit ruled in 1992 that because Corcoran was covered by her employer, she was not entitled to sue under state tort laws. Employer-sponsored health plans, the court found, are the exclusive province of the 1974 federal Employment Retirement Income Security Act (ERISA).

And ERISA, which applies to the 140 million Americans in employer-sponsored health plans, offers them virtually no protection in disputes over their coverage. Corcoran had "no remedy, state or federal, for what may have been a serious mistake," the 5th Circuit said in its ruling.

As Corcoran discovered, the transformation of the nation's health care marketplace has outpaced many of the laws and regulations that were intended to protect consumers. The consumer safety net—long a confusing web of state and federal law—has in recent years been frayed beyond usefulness by the explosive forces of the health care revolution.

Under pressure from employers fed up with runaway costs, health plans have been transformed from passive bill-payers to aggressive overseers. Under the rubric of "managed care," they are using a wide variety of techniques to constrain costs.

Few observers would disagree that cost consciousness in the health care marketplace is long overdue. And many health care experts contend that managed care has the potential to improve care as well as restrain costs.

Yet consumer advocates remain concerned that some health plans are stinting

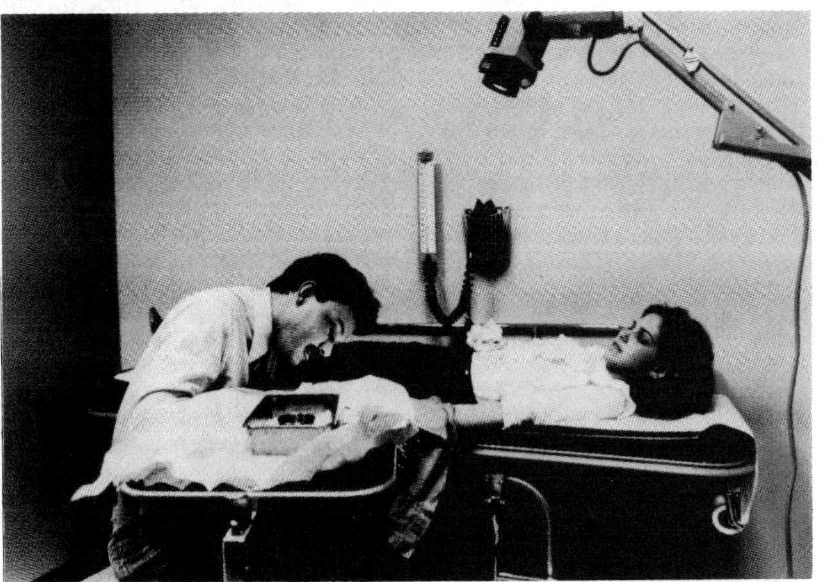

Richard A. Bloom

Consumer groups worry that managed care encourages doctors to stint on treatment.

on care. "We apply code words like 'managed care,' when in fact there is such a range of animals in that zoo," said Stan Jones, a health care policy consultant who works for several charitable foundations. "Some of them I think we should be concerned about. Others, I think, are stellar. So far, we haven't helped [consumers] get very sophisticated in telling one from the other."

Not only are consumers poorly equipped to judge their health plans; they're also losing the ability to protect themselves when they suspect they aren't getting the care they need.

Richard A. Bloom

Health policy consultant Stan Jones
Patients don't get much help in telling good health care plans from poor ones.

For starters, their ability to vote with their feet has been greatly limited. Most managed care plans limit patients' choice of doctors and hospitals. And some studies suggest that employers are increasingly limiting their employees' choice of health plans.

Government protections are eroding, too. State insurance regulators are often ill-equipped to keep tabs on the new breed of health plans. Employer-sponsored plans face little regulation under ERISA, and a spate of recent court cases has narrowed the legal remedies available to enrollees in these plans.

Working Americans and their families have even fewer protections than the elderly do. The federal medicare program provides an array of oversight and appeal procedures for beneficiaries enrolled in health maintenance organizations (HMOs), including ombudsmen to help patients steer their way through these often Byzantine organizations.

"Many people say we need more protections for the medicare population," said Geraldine Dallek, executive director of the Center for Health Care Rights, a Los Angeles-based nonprofit group that contracts with the state of California to act as an ombudsman for medicare patients. "The issue that nobody's looking at is [that] there is this huge working population enrolled in managed care plans who are often given no choice of plans at all, or forced into a plan because it's the cheapest, and they have very inadequate protections."

Consumer advocates took a stab at beefing up protections for managed care enrollees during the debate over health care reform, but the issue got lost in the tussle over larger and more-contentious matters. The demise of comprehensive reform and the advent of a more-conservative Congress—for which new regulations are likely to be anathema—make prospects for stand-alone consumer legislation uncertain.

Some large employers and the HMO industry have shown interest in having Congress set uniform standards for health plans—in part to head off a possible regulatory backlash. But they're adamantly opposed to some items on consumer advocates' wish list. Employers, for example, don't want to augment the legal remedies available to workers under ERISA. That, they argue, could make it harder for health plans to hold down costs and could jeopardize employers' ability to continue offering health benefits.

"Employees in particular, and the American public in general, have a notion that health care should be provided for free," said Mark J. Ugoretz, president of the ERISA Industry Committee, a trade group for managers of large corporate benefit plans. "It isn't free, it's very expensive. Those who are paying for it believe they have an obligation as well as a right to organize it so they get the best possible benefit for an affordable cost."

USER-UNFRIENDLY

During congressional deliberations over health care reform, insurance industry advertisements suggested that requiring health plans to operate under a budget set by the government might lead to rationing. But in the absence of government-driven reform, decisions about trimming costs are being made anyway—by employers and health plans.

Most managed care plans have set out to reverse the financial incentives built into traditional fee-for-service medicine, which is widely believed to encourage doctors to provide too many services.

Some plans still use fee-for-service medicine but insist on discounted fees from doctors and hospitals while using administrators, known as utilization review or claims review personnel, to police spending.

Other plans reward doctors or hospitals for being conservative in their use of resources. Some, for example, require providers to stay within a fixed budget; others offer bonuses to physicians who keep a lid on spending.

Still others say that they try to reward physicians for good medical practice and consumer satisfaction. "We pay doctors more if they do a better job," said Neil Schlackman, medical director and president of quality assurance program at US Healthcare, a rapidly expanding for-profit HMO company based in Blue Bell, Pa. "We look at things we think can be measured," he said, including ease of patient access to doctors, the quality of the services rendered and patient satisfaction as measured by detailed surveys.

But the managed care revolution is increasingly raising the question that dogged health care reform: Are health plans cutting costs by becoming more efficient or by stinting on patient care? To date, the debate has been fueled mainly by theory and anecdote.

Advocates of managed care argue that creating incentives to be cost-conscious doesn't hurt patients. HMOs, which charge patients a flat fee for providing all their medical needs, are "the only system with every incentive to keep people healthy, whether that means we prevent disease in the first place, treat problems early or take charge of the management of chronic diseases," says Susan Pisano, a spokewoman for the Group Health Association of America, the leading trade association for HMOs. "People who function poorly cost more to the [health plan] and to society."

US Healthcare's Schlackman says that his company's centralized tracking of medical records allows it to identify, for example, all patients who are diabetic. It shepherds all these patients in for annual eye examinations, helping to prevent the deteriorating eyesight that often afflicts diabetics.

But it's not hard to find horror stories. In July, Karin Smith, a 28-year-old accountant, testified before Congress about how her Milwaukee-based HMO failed to diagnose her cervical cancer, and how her pap smears and biopsies were misread by an overworked technician at the laboratory that the HMO contracted with. The lab owner, Smith testified, sat on the HMO's board of directors and was given advance access to bids by competing labs that wanted the contract.

Smith sued for malpractice in state court and reached a $6.3 million settlement with a dozen defendants, including the lab and the HMO. (Unlike Corcoran, Smith wasn't covered by an employer plan, and her case involved poor care, not a denial of benefits.)

Many HMOs save money by coming up with "a variety of ways to make the system user-unfriendly, making it difficult to get in [to see a doctor], speeding up the doctors and telling them to see patients at required rates, of [so many] per hour, and telling them to follow the pace or suffer penalties," said Quentin Young, a Chicago internist and activist with Physicians for a National Health Program, a group that favors a government-financed health system. "The inevitable tendency is to avoid giving care or to make it difficult for those in their care to get attention."

A MATTER OF CHOICE

But there's no definitive research on how managed care affects patient care. "I can't cite a study that tries to quantify the amount of difficulties people are having with managed care because these studies aren't taking place," said Rand E. Rosenblatt, professor of law at Rutgers University Law School and co-chairman of the Society of American Law Teachers Committee on Access to Justice in Health Care Reform.

What research there is paints a mixed picture. An Aug. 18 article in the *New England Journal of Medicine* reported that people covered by traditional health insurance were 20 per cent likelier to suffer a ruptured appendix than were patients who are members of prepaid health plans such as HMOs. The HMOs promoted earlier treatment of appendicitis by removing financial barriers to patients seeking early care and by assigning patients to a specific physician or clinic—thus eliminating confusion about where to seek care. But the Oct. 27 issue of the *Journal* reported that generalist physicians provided poorer care to heart attack patients than specialists did, raising concerns about the tendency of managed care plans to limit patients' access to specialists.

Sara Rosenbaum, a researcher at the George Washington University Center for Health Policy Research who is studying the legal contracts between health plans and physicians, says that some of the contracts are worrisome for doctors and patients. "Some of these arrangements put doctors at massive legal risk and enormous financial risk," she said.

A basic feature of managed care is that it constrains patients' choice of doctors. HMOs typically require enrollees to use only in-house physicians; other plans sometimes allow patients to use outside doctors, but often at a substantially higher cost. That lets health plans exert more control over the cost and quality of care that patients receive.

"With the fee-for-service system, [consumers] did have one extra protection," Dallek said. "If they felt they were getting poor-quality care, they could go elsewhere." Doctor shopping by patients, she acknowledged, drives up health care costs

John Eisele

ERISA Industry Committee's Mark J. Ugoretz
Employers have a right to seek "the best possible benefit for an affordable cost."

The doctors are "seriously underpaid to take on all the service and referral obligations the plan gives them. They become mini-insurance companies, but their caseloads are too small" to adequately spread the financial risk.

Such arrangements, Rosenbaum said, could force doctors to choose between their professional judgment and their financial solvency. "It puts them in an ethical bind of unimaginable proportions."

Concerned about the potential impact of such contracts on medicare recipients, Congress voted in 1989 to prohibit HMOs serving medicare patients from paying bonuses to physicians who limit care, or from putting doctors at "substantial financial risk" if they run up higher-than-expected costs in treating patients. A congressional aide called that measure only a partial solution, but it's more protection than most Americans have.

What troubles consumer advocates such as Dallek is that consumers have few tools for evaluating health plans or for protecting themselves when they believe that they are being shortchanged.

and may not be the most sophisticated way to police the quality of care. But it was "a protection which they don't have anymore."

Moreover, many people don't have a choice of health plans. According to a survey by the accounting and employee benefits consulting firm of KPMG Peat Marwick, 45 per cent of Americans who get their health insurance through their employers are offered only one plan. Some employee benefits experts dispute these numbers, though.

BURDENING THE STATES

Government safeguards against abuse are also eroding. In many states, responsibility for oversight of health plans is split between several agencies. Insurance companies are supposed to be scrutinized by the insurance commissioner, while credentialing and disciplining of doctors falls to state licensing boards. Some states specifically police HMOs, often through their health departments.

Few state agencies are equipped to

police some of the newer hybrid plans that combine insurance and health care delivery. "The line is really blurring between what constitutes an insurance company and a health maintenance organization, and there's considerable opportunity for mischievious characters to fall between the regulatory cracks," said Rep. Ron Wyden, D-Ore., who held hearings on ERISA in November.

Richard A. Bloom

Sara Rosenbaum of George Washington University Some doctors face enormous legal and financial risks.

Even before the managed care revolution, states varied widely in their ability and willingness to scrutinize health plans. A General Accounting Office report issued earlier this year found that state insurance offices spent only a fourth of their operating funds on health insurance regulation and were ill-equipped to monitor the solvency of health plans. Nine states, the report said, didn't police plans' marketplace conduct—such as denial of patients' claims—at all.

In California, Dallek said, the Corporations Department is required to scrutinize each HMO only once every five years, and it fails to do even that in 10 per cent of cases. It's difficult and costly for consumers to get copies of audits, she said, and the audits lack information on patient complaints and other issues. What's more, the public seldom knows it when regulators give an HMO poor grades, Dallek said; the company can have critical comments expunged by certifying in writing that a problem has been corrected.

State regulators acknowledge their limitations. "Nobody's finding it easy" to keep pace with changes in the marketplace, said Dixon F. Larkin, Utah's deputy insurance commissioner and chairman of a National Association of Insurance Commissioners (NAIC) working group on health care accountability.

The group is trying to write model legislation offering basic protections—against health plan bankruptcies, for example. "The big thing you worry about is that they go out of business and people are left high and dry," Larkin said, "or that plans change benefits in midstream." But the NAIC is only beginning to discuss ways to keep health plans from arbitrarily limiting patients' access to care, he said.

Even if the NAIC comes up with a set of crackerjack laws, and even if every state adopted them and enforced them vigorously, Americans with employer-provided coverage would not benefit at all because of the ERISA exemption for employer-sponsored plans.

The federal law, which was intended to guarantee that employers deliver on their benefits promises, focuses mainly on pensions and has little to say about health plans. When it was enacted in 1974, "the health care cost issue just was not significant, and health care was not an important benefit, so these issues just weren't contemplated at the time," said David M. Certner, senior coordinator for economic issues at the American Association of Retired Persons (AARP) and chairman of a Labor Department advisory council on ERISA.

As employer-sponsored managed care plans start cracking down on use of health care services, consumers are beginning to discover the law's limitations. They can complain to the Labor Department, which oversees ERISA. But the agency can do little more than send out a brochure informing workers of their limited rights of appeal. They have 60 days after a claims denial to file a written appeal with the health plan. Then they are entitled to a review and an explanation of the plan's final decision within 120 days. But the review is handled at the plan's discretion; the law gives the department almost no power to oversee the process or mediate disputes.

ERISA allows aggrieved workers to sue in the federal courts. But a series of court decisions in recent years has made it progressively tougher to get redress. The rulings have put a high burden of proof on plaintiffs and have dramatically narrowed the remedies available to those who prove they were unfairly denied a benefit. In a 1987 ruling, *Pilot Life v. Dedeaux*, the Supreme Court ruled that consumers were not entitled to damanges for loss of life, health or property, or for emotional distress when their health plans acted in bad faith.

The most that consumers can hope to recover, legal experts say, is the cost of the service originally denied them. Thus—in a hypothetical example often used by consumer advocates—if a woman proves that her health plan failed to detect her breast cancer at an early stage because it wouldn't pay for a mammogram, the plan would probably be liable only for the cost of the mammogram, even if the woman can show that the cancer cost her tens of thousands of dollars in lost wages and foreclosure on her home.

"In some worst-case examples, if the consumers die, there is no benefit to be paid at all," the AARP's Certner said. That sends a message to "the employer and insurer that there is nothing to be lost in denying a benefit claim, except for the cost of litigating if they actually go to court," he said.

In light of the court rulings, few consumers and lawyers pursue such cases. Lawyers, who often take liability cases on a contingency-fee basis, say that ERISA cases tend to be money-losers for them, although the law gives the courts discretion to pay lawyers' fees.

Under ERISA, "there is no forum for evaluating actions by utilization review or managed care companies, which arguably have caused great harm," law professor Rosenblatt said. What's more, "you have no place to develop the rules of the game, because access to the state courts is gone, and ERISA is being interpreted so narrowly that consumers are not able to litigate, and because no regulatory apparatus exists" to set standards for patient care.

REPORT CARDS

Consumer advocates not only want ERISA's legal remedies expanded, they also want other safeguards that might keep complaints from ending up in court.

In their view, consumers should have access to more information about health plans and should be entitled to speedy independent review of disputed decisions.

Rosenblatt argues that consumers need someone to help them thread their way through the bureaucracies of managed care plans, just as the government provides ombudsmen for medicare recipients dealing with HMOs. "Most people don't have the personal skills or funds to pursue claims themselves or hire an attorney, and this is especially true when people are ill—no matter what their income," he said.

Some of the health care reform proposals debated this year included new consumer safeguards. The Clinton Administration, for example, would have required all employers to offer at least three health plans and would have created regional purchasing cooperatives to police health plans. "Report cards" for each plan and information about malpractice judgments against doctors would have been available. The Administration also wanted to provide ombudsmen to help consumers with grievances and to set up a review and mediation process. The House Education and Labor Committee and the Senate Labor and Human Resources Committee passed reform measures that would have expanded legal remedies for consumers in employer-sponsored plans.

But with the demise of comprehensive reform, consumer advocates will have to start from scratch. Most of the Members interested in expanding consumer protections have been Democrats; a Republican-controlled Congress may be less enthusiastic.

Still, Congress may face pressure from a variety of interest groups to set standards for health plans. Some state governments want to regulate plans now covered by ERISA as part of state health reform efforts; they are pressing Congress to make exceptions to ERISA. To head off such a move, some large employers and the managed care and insurance industries are talking about beefing up federal standards for all health plans. The HMO industry, which faces heavier state and federal regulation than most other managed care plans do, would like to see uniform standards to level the playing field. The American Medical Association and other physician groups want Congress to legislate greater protections for doctors who contract with managed care plans.

Employers and health plans, however, are adamantly opposed to key elements of the consumer reform agenda. Wyden, for example, has offered a proposal that would require HMOs to let patients use outside doctors. HMOs oppose that idea, saying it would hurt their ability to control costs."That's an issue very much on our mind," said Karen M. Ignagni, the Group Health Association of America president.

Employers have vigorously lobbied against broader legal remedies for consumers enrolled in the health plans they sponsor. The ERISA Industry Committee's Ugoretz argues that complaints about managed care stem from patients' dislike of any constraints on their use of care. Many of the lawsuits brought against employers' managed care plans, he said, are for benefits not explicitly promised, such as experimental therapies or custodial care.

"There has been no showing ever, in the past 10 years, that there is a problem of employer plans improperly denying [promised benefits]," Ugoretz said. Employers have no incentive to deny benefits, he said. "They're not providing these plans for profit, they're providing them as a benefit to their employees. They can't afford, for the sake of employee morale, to improperly deny benefits. It just isn't happening."

Enhancing consumer remedies under ERISA, Ugoretz said, would encourage lawsuits—driving up employers' legal and health care costs "without improving care or even providing greater benefits."

John Eisele

Rep. Ron Wyden, D-Ore.
He'd require HMOs to let patients use outside doctors.

Federal judges—who typically don't hear the garden-variety consumer lawsuits handled by state courts—also worry about the impact. In August, the Judicial Conference of the United States, the top policy-making body for the federal courts, warned that some of the consumer protections in many of the health care reform plans would "generate a flood of litigation by people trying to enforce new rights to medical benefits and insurance payments."

Employers and the managed care industry argue that the marketplace will take care of many problems that consumer advocates complain about. In fact, many of them argue, the private sector is already policing itself: The National Committee for Quality Assurance, a private body governed by employers, managed care industry officials, organized labor and a consumer representative, is developing voluntary standards of quality measurement and accreditation for HMOs. And a few employers, such as Xerox Corp., are already requiring such accreditation from the plans they use.

Consumer advocates applaud such efforts, but they aren't satisfied. Some question whether a committee dominated by employers and health plans will safeguard consumers' interests. Others note that the science of quality measurement is in its infancy.

"There's lots going on that's very positive: report cards, and businesses demanding accountability," Dallek said. "But these efforts are just at their start." They're no substitute, she said, for an appeals system that offers immediate and independent review of patient complaints.

Such measures, Dallek added, are in the best interests not only of patients but also of employers and managed care plans. "Employers are paying lots of money to cover health care for employees. They ought to really make sure they're getting bang for their buck." And managed care plans "won't have humongous litigation if there are better appeals rights," she said. "It seems to me [they] should be in favor of this."

Managed Medicare

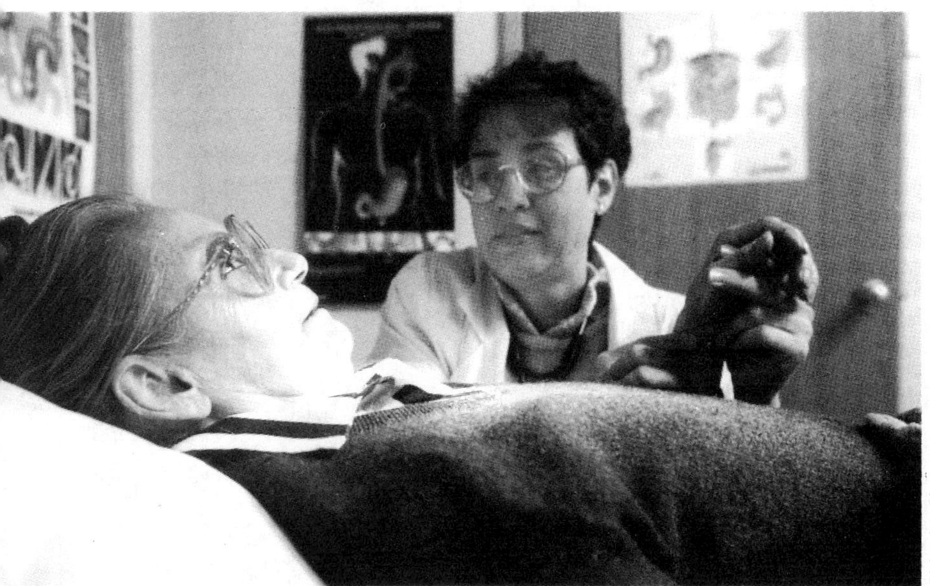
Richard A. Bloom

It's time for elderly Americans to join the managed care revolution that has become a way of life for their children and grandchildren, many congressional Republicans say. But attempts to put medicare patients into HMOs have run into trouble.

MARILYN WERBER SERAFINI

As painful as they may seem, cuts in the medicare budget this year won't provide a lasting cure for what ails the program. Unless medicare is overhauled, this money-hungry dinosaur will continue to eat huge holes in the Treasury, and its hospital insurance trust fund will go broke in about five years.

That's the emerging consensus among key congressional Republicans who are contemplating sweeping changes in medicare. Their chief goal: to shepherd the program's 34 million beneficiaries into health maintenance organizations (HMOs), preferred provider organizations (PPOs) and the other managed care structures that have become a way of life for the children and grandchildren of elderly Americans. Many lawmakers also want to offer medicare beneficiaries a choice of options for their health coverage, including vouchers and medical savings accounts.

Medicare has changed little since its creation in the 1960s. Most care is provided on a fee-for-service basis—an arrangement that many private-sector health plans now shun because of its reputation for encouraging higher costs and overuse of services. Medicare costs are rising by 10.9 per cent a year—compared with an over-all health care inflation rate of about 6.7 per cent.

"What we're doing is fundamentally reconceptualizing the whole approach to seniors and medicine," said Rep. William M. Thomas, R-Calif., who chairs the Ways and Means Health Subcommittee.

Sound familiar? It does to Harris Berman, president of the Tufts Associated Health Plan, a Boston-based HMO. In the mid-1980s, Tufts was one of more than 100 HMOs that contracted with the Health and Human Services Department's Health Care Financing Administration (HCFA) to serve medicare beneficiaries. The contracts required the HMOs to provide medicare recipients with comprehensive care for a set monthly fee—an arrangement known as risk contracting.

Some of those ventures succeeded and are still flourishing. But plenty more collapsed quickly, offering a cautionary tale for those who prescribe managed care as a miracle cure for medicare.

Tufts, already well established in New England, had no problems attracting medicare patients. The challenge was caring for them on the budget provided by the government. Too late, the HMO discovered that the kind of care its medicare recipients required was different from what its other enrollees needed. "We managed these patients the same way we managed our commercial population," Berman said. "As a result, hospital utilization was enormous. On that we lost our shirts." Three years and $5 million later, Tufts hoisted the white flag and retreated from medicare.

As Republicans seek to bring medicare into the world of managed care, they will have to grapple not only with complaints from HMOs about inadequate government payments, but also with resistance from senior citizens who have long-standing relationships with doctors and hospitals. What's more, studies have found that the medicare managed care plans haven't saved the government a penny so far.

Members of Congress say they are crafting proposals that would fix some fundamental problems in risk contracting and provide incentives for participation by medicare beneficiaries and managed care plans alike.

And despite its rocky introduction to medicare, the managed care industry appears eager to tap the market. HMOs already provide care for 50 million Americans; medicare is the next logical step.

"It's the realization of the maturity of the managed care market," William L. Roper, senior vice president and chief medical officer of the Prudential Insurance Co. of America and a former HCFA administrator, said, explaining why Prudential last year opened its HMOs to medicare beneficiaries. "I believe the time is right now for a substantial push into managed care."

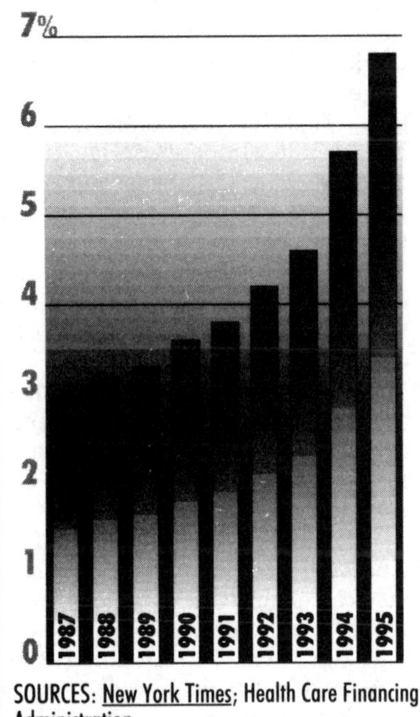

EFFICIENCY GETS PUNISHED

Still, medicare is likely to bring up the rear of the managed care revolution until some problems are fixed.

Foremost, HMOs want Congress to change the way HCFA pays them under medicare risk contracts. The payment rate varies widely according to location. HMOs in the Miami area get a monthly fee of $615 per participant, for example, while those in the Minneapolis area get only $362.

"In many urban areas and most rural areas, the . . . payments to managed care organizations are not sufficient to cover the costs of caring for an older person," K. James Ehlen, the president of the Minneapolis-based Allina Health System said in recent testimony before the House Budget Committee.

HCFA sets a payment rate for each county, based on the average cost of treating medicare beneficiaries who are not in managed care plans. HMO operators complain that the system punishes efficiency. When HMOs began accepting medicare patients in the mid-1980s, Ehlen said, the payment rate in Minnesota was high enough for HMOs to offer generous benefits, including prescription drug coverage that is unavailable to most medicare beneficiaries. "Seniors flocked to the program," he said.

But at about the same time, health care cost inflation in the Minneapolis area began to slow dramatically, thanks to a surge in local enrollment in managed care plans that, experts say, also curbed the prices charged by doctors and hospitals outside those plans. As a result, HCFA's monthly medicare payments in the area leveled off for several years; many local HMOs curtailed their benefits packages, and some stopped accepting medicare beneficiaries. Meanwhile, though, the rates continued to rise in cities where fee-for-service medicine prevailed.

The same pattern has occurred across the country, Ehlen said. "Seniors enrolled in HMOs in some high-payment areas can receive coverage which often includes prescription drugs for zero premiums per month," he said. But those in lower-payment areas, "if they have access to HMO coverage at all, are unlikely to have such benefits and may pay premiums of $40-$60 per month, and some over $100 a month."

In Minneapolis, most HMOs no longer accept a monthly fee for medicare patients. Instead, they have reverted to a fee-for-service approach in which HCFA reimburses them for services provided. HCFA officials say they want to move away from this arrangement because it offers no incentives for efficiency.

But lawmakers contend that HMOs will not accept a set monthly fee unless the payment system is improved. Some have suggested basing the payment calculation on a wider geographic area. Others—including House Budget Committee chairman John R. Kasich, R-Ohio—are interested in a modified form of competitive bidding, in which each HMO in an area would tell HCFA what it considered a fair monthly fee for treating medicare patients. The agency then would set a fee based on an average of the bids submitted.

HCFA is also contemplating some form of competitive bidding, although it may not want to move as quickly as congressional Republicans do. The agency has contracted with New Jersey-based Mathematica Policy Research Inc., to help prepare a proposal. Mathematica is expected to complete its report later this year. "We want to look at more delivery systems, what types of geographical areas we should be in, what type of premiums should be involved, so we can be prepared to deal with competitive bids," said Rodney C. Armstead, director of HCFA's office of managed care. "Republicans don't have the information to do it now."

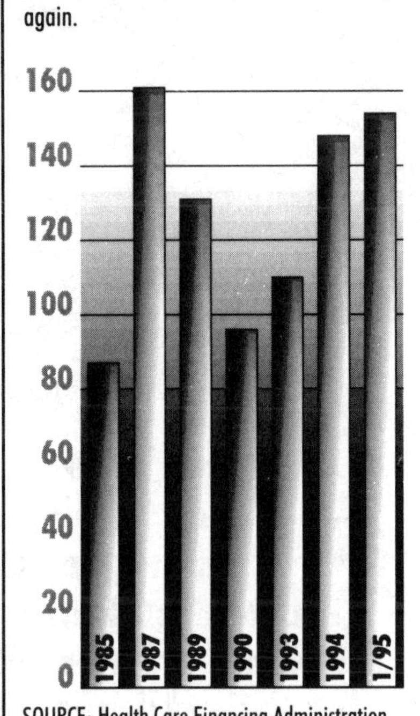

But Thomas is impatient. "We've got a bureaucracy dragging its feet," he said.

Like other Republican lawmakers, Thomas envisions a revamped medicare program in which beneficiaries could choose among several options.

They might be given vouchers to buy HMO coverage, for example. Although some senior citizens' groups have criticized that idea, Thomas said, "simply giving people a check and putting them into the cruel world of HMOs to be battered about in the wind isn't exactly what we have in mind." Beneficiaries would use the vouchers to enroll in plans that have contracts with HCFA, he said, and the plans could not turn them away.

Thomas is also exploring the idea of allowing medicare beneficiaries to stay in employer-sponsored health care plans. Under this approach, employees who turn 65 could remain in their employers' plans, even after they retire. Medicare would reimburse employers for their monthly premiums; the employers might get a tax break as an added incentive. The idea is to keep elderly people in a pool with younger, healthier people, to lower the cost of coverage and allow them to stay in a plan they're familiar with.

Thomas and many Republicans also want to expand a demonstration project now under way in 15 states that allows PPOs to sign up medicare beneficiaries for portions of their coverage. The project, known as Medicare Select, generally works like a traditional fee-for-service plan, however. HCFA pays the PPOs on a per service basis, and they offer discounted prices because patients agree to use certain medical providers.

Sen. Judd Gregg, R-N.H., wants medicare beneficiaries to be able to choose from a variety of plans, with those who choose lower-cost plans being allowed to pocket the savings. "I think there will be as many new ideas for packages as the marketplace can create," he said. "There will be a variety of add-ons and price mechanisms used to tailor health care plans to seniors in the community."

Many Republicans would also like to see medical savings accounts made available to medicare beneficiaries. Under that approach, the government would provide catastrophic coverage with a high deductible; HCFA would put enough money into a savings account for each beneficiary to cover the deductible each year; and the beneficiary could keep any money left over in the account at the end of the year. *(For more on medical savings accounts, see NJ, 4/1/95, p. 804.)*

Costly hospital stays were a big problem for HMOs that ventured into medicare. More recently, HMOs have learned that elderly patients who see their doctors frequently are less likely to be hospitalized.

Richard A. Bloom

MOVING INTO THE MARKET

Even if Congress does nothing, HMOs are gearing up to enter what many view as the final frontier in the health care market.

In a recent survey by the Group Health Association of America, the major HMO industry association, roughly three-fourths of HMOs said they were interested in expanding access to the medicare population, Karen Ignagni, the group's president, said.

"It's an enormous market," said Westcott W. Price III, the chief executive of California-based FHP International Corp., one of the largest HMO medicare providers. "If you're not in the medicare business, you're not really in the health care delivery business. Fifty per cent of health care dollars in the country are spent on people aged 65 and older."

"The seniors are becoming a larger population. Don't ignore it. Start working with it," said Fred A. Jacot, the chief executive of the Spokane-based Medical Service Corp. of Eastern Washington, a Blue Shield plan that is preparing to begin a medicare risk contract with HCFA. "If you don't do it, somebody else will," Jacot added.

Already, more than 150 HMOs have risk contracts with HCFA, and 78 proposals are pending for new or expanded contracts. Almost 7 per cent of medicare beneficiaries have signed up, and HCFA predicts a 20-25 per cent increase this year. In some areas, such as Portland, Ore., and San Diego, more than half of medicare recipients are in HMOs.

Even Tufts is rejoining the movement. Last year, it teamed up with PacifiCare Health Systems Inc. of Cypress, Calif., one of the largest medicare HMOs, which has begun selling its technique for managing elderly patients. In essence, Tufts has a PacifiCare franchise. Berman sends doctors to a PacifiCare facility in Texas for a crash course on the most efficient ways to coordinate care for seniors. There's another class for marketing.

Although Tufts is not making money on the enterprise yet, Berman said, it appears to be a promising line of business.

Craig S. Schub, PacifiCare's senior vice president for medicare, couldn't agree more. PacifiCare has moved its medicare venture, known as Secure Horizons, into a half-dozen states since 1985 and is talking about partnerships with other HMOs.

What separates HMOs such as PacifiCare from those that failed in medicare contracts? The secret is in treating elderly people like elderly people, Schub said. "When the population ages, you have little things that don't kind of work perfectly," he said. "They're not life-and-death, but they happen every day. Their need for care from the system is not so much high-powered and onetime, but every day."

PacifiCare provides comprehensive

care, coordinated by a primary care physician. Doctors see medicare patients more frequently and try to catch problems early. They try to keep patients out of the hospital or shorten stays by using home health care. By using this method, PacifiCare has made its medicare managed care plans as profitable as its commercial plans, Schub said.

Costly hospital stays were a major problem for Tufts, which saw its hospital usage rate grow tenfold when medicare beneficiaries joined the HMO. But by following PacifiCare's model, the HMO has seen remarkable results, Berman said. In the first five months of its new medicare venture, hospital usage for elderly enrollees was about the same as for younger ones. "The key is doing what needs to be done in the appropriate location," he said. "Don't just send them to the hospital because that's where old people should be."

In addition, Tufts doctors have a financial stake in keeping hospital stays down. Tufts sets a target for hospital stays for each doctor's patients. If the patients use fewer days, the doctor gets to keep the savings. If they use more, the doctor pays the extra cost.

But such financial incentives worry the American Association of Retired Persons (AARP) and Families USA, a Washington-based advocate of comprehensive health reform. "It's a classic conflict of interest," Families USA executive director Ron Pollack said. "When a patient sees a doctor, that patient has reason to expect that doctor will make a decision based on one factor and one factor only—what's in the best interest of the patient."

There's another factor restraining HMOs' entry into the medicare market. Under federal law, medicare and medicaid patients cannot make up more than 50 per cent of any HMO's total enrollment. An HMO must develop a commercial base in each market before it can get medicare contracts, and that can take years. That's why HMOs such as PacifiCare are looking for franchise-style arrangements in which they team up with other HMOs.

TERRIFIED SENIORS

Moving medicare into managed care will be no easy task, though. For one thing, there's no evidence that existing medicare managed care plans are saving the government money.

In fact, the Mathematica consulting firm concluded in a 1993 study for HCFA that the agency was overpaying HMOs with which it had signed medicare risk contracts. The youngest, healthiest medicare recipients tend to choose HMOs, the study found, while payments to the HMOs are pegged to the average cost of treating all medicare patients in a given geographic area.

Although some critics have questioned the study, the Congressional Budget Office in February released a report supporting its premise. "Medicare's costs generally increase for each enrollee who switches to an HMO under the current payment system," the report said. "This happens because medicare's per capita payment to the HMO—which is based on what enrollees cost in the fee-for-service sector—does not adequately reflect the generally healthier population that chooses the HMO option."

The GOP also faces a political complication. Many senior citizens are terrified that Congress will force them into health plans they don't want. And the elderly represent a growing proportion of the GOP's voter base; in the November elections, elderly voters reversed a long trend by casting more ballots for Republicans than for Democrats in congressional races.

The last thing seniors want is to be pushed, a spokeswoman for the AARP said. "Managed care isn't for everybody, and people need to feel comfortable with changes." The AARP says that it favors making managed care available to medicare beneficiaries, but that no one should be forced to join a managed care plan.

John Eisele

Rep. William M. Thomas, R-Calif.
"We've got a bureaucracy dragging its feet."

Although no Member of Congress has talked about requiring beneficiaries to sign up, there is "more than one way to be forced in," the AARP spokeswoman said. "If what really happens is that fee-for-service becomes so expensive, that's not a real choice anymore."

The American Medical Association (AMA), which has resisted the move to managed care, has also argued that safeguards are needed to protect consumers. "People who get into managed care should be informed of what they're buying, what's covered, what hospitals they can go to, so they can make an informed decision when they decide how to choose," Thomas R. Reardon, an AMA trustee, said.

House Speaker Newt Gingrich, R-Ga., is showing some sensitivity to the AMA's concerns. In a recent speech to the group, he called for congressional hearings on managed care. But he and other GOP lawmakers still consider managed care the long-term solution to medicare's problems.

Thomas argues that Congress should act soon on overhauling medicare. "We have to get it done fairly quickly" because the hospital trust fund is expected to run dry about 2001 or 2002 if costs continue to rise at the present rate. Growing enrollment is fueling the sense of urgency about revamping the program.

Initially, Thomas and other Republicans had talked about delaying action on medicare reforms until after they complete work on the budget. But there's increasing discussion about attaching a medicare overhaul package to the budget reconciliation bill—on the theory that longer-term changes in the program might make short-term budget cuts more politically palatable. The question, though, is whether seniors will accept the deal.

No Strings Attached!

Many governors want to convert medicaid to a block grant and do away with the myriad federal rules that have vastly expanded the program's reach in recent years. Congress may oblige them. But groups that fought for the rules aren't going to sit still.

MARILYN WERBER SERAFINI

Carol, a 50-year-old single mother in New York City, is going back to work. After eight months on welfare, she says she's thrilled to begin a job as a part-time special-education teaching aide, earning $160-$240 a week.

Were this 1987, Carol would have refused the work. The moment she left the welfare rolls, her medicaid health benefits would have vanished, and her wages wouldn't have been enough to buy private insurance for her and her son, both of whom have chronic medical problems.

"Whoo, whoo, I hate to even think about [the cost]," Carol said. "I try to go to clinics so the expenses are lower, [but] without getting my medication, without my doctor visits, I would just have to be at home."

Fortunately for Carol, Congress voted in 1988 to require states to keep providing benefits to medicaid recipients for two years after they leave welfare and enter the work force. The idea was to make medicaid available to the working poor—so they could work.

But today, that vision may be threatened. Congressional Republicans are trying to slash the federal budget deficit, and medicaid, the joint federal-state health care program, is a prime target. Federal and state spending on medicaid has more than tripled since 1985, in large part because of expanded coverage and services mandated by Congress. Medicaid now accounts for 18 per cent of all state spending.

Governors are clamoring for flexibility in administering their medicaid programs, and many say they are willing to accept less federal money—if they can have it with no strings attached. The requirements imposed by Washington "are terrible," said Gov. Howard Dean, D-Vt., the National Governors' Association (NGA) chairman. "They cost us a fortune." The idea of a no-strings-attached block grant appeals to many Republican lawmakers, too, because it would mesh with the GOP's push to eliminate "unfunded mandates."

Many congressional Republicans want to convert medicaid to a block grant, with a cap on annual federal expenditures and only minimal requirements placed on the states. "There need to be some checks and balances to make sure the states do not use the money to pave roads," J. Dennis Hastert, R-Ill., the chief deputy House majority whip, said. But, he said, the federal government should place no requirements on medicaid eligibility or scope of services.

The groups that fought for expansion of the medicaid program aren't going to sit still for such changes, though. In their view, federal medicaid regulations are a guarantee that states won't neglect some of their neediest citizens. Their first choice would be to kill the block grant concept altogether; in its pure form, a block grant would erase medicaid as an entitlement and re-create it as an optional state program. Nonetheless, many see block grants as inevitable, and they are fighting to keep some federal mandates in place to ensure minimum eligibility standards and benefits.

Advocacy organizations ranging from the Children's Defense Fund to the American Association of Retired Persons (AARP) are suiting up for battle. Together and independently, they're aggressively working the grass roots, lobbying Congress and planning advertising campaigns.

Medicaid advocates, fearing that the public views medicaid as an extension of welfare, want to show that the program also helps working families and the elderly and disabled. Indeed, elderly and disabled people account for nearly 60 per cent of medicaid spending.

"I'm a 70-year-old grandmother," begins a radio advertisement that the AARP and the Coalition for America's Children, a Washington-based advocacy group, have been airing in 20 markets around the country. "My daughter Sue is a waitress. She needs medicaid to cover her family's health costs. Without medicaid, my grandson won't get the asthma medication he needs. And my bill for home care would cost more than my rent. Without medicaid, Sue couldn't work; she'd have to care for me. What the

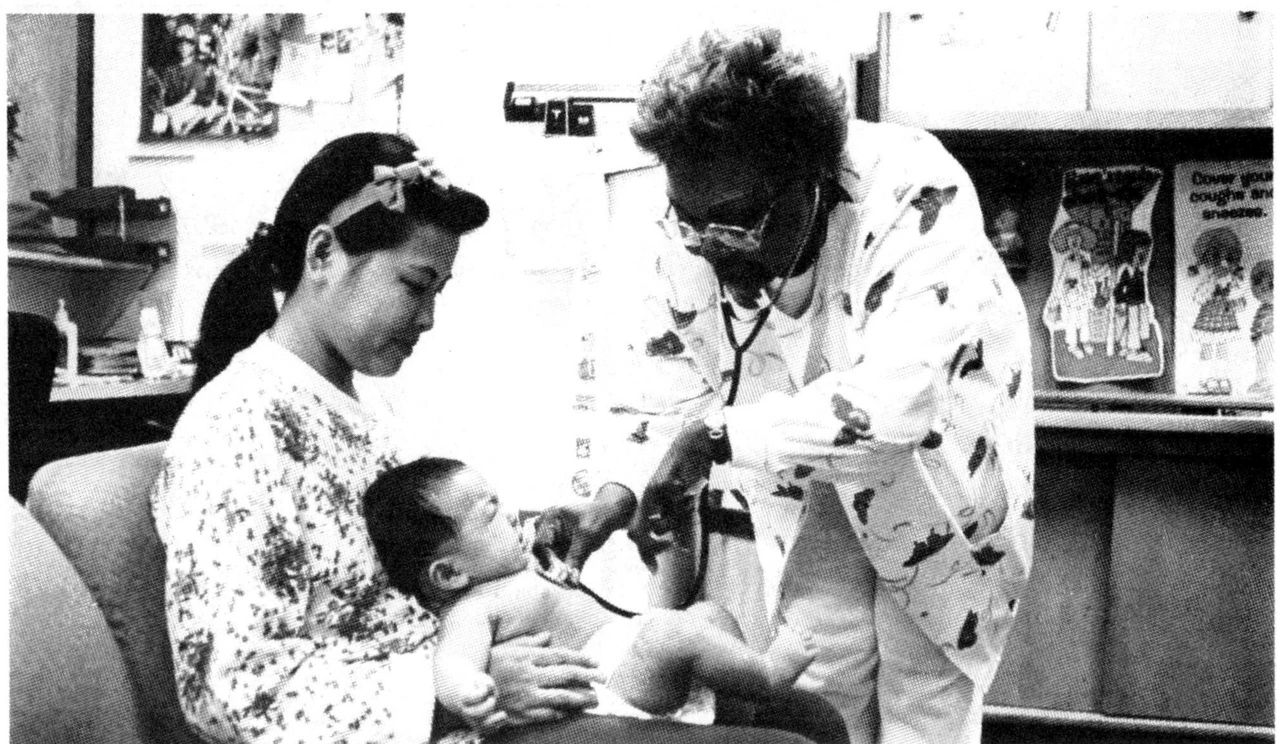
John Eisele

Children's hospitals and clinics depend heavily on medicaid, which now covers a quarter of all Americans under age 18.

politicians won't tell you is that cuts in medicaid will hurt families. Medicaid works so families can work."

WIDENING THE NET

When medicaid was established in 1965, it was billed as a partnership: The states were to design their own programs under broad guidance from the federal government, which would provide slightly more than half the funds through a matching arrangement based on each state's poverty rate. Medicaid was closely tied to welfare; eligibility was limited to recipients of aid to families with dependent children (AFDC).

But in the early 1980s, some Members of Congress—joined by Reagan Administration officials—began arguing that medicaid should be made available to low-income working people, to encourage welfare recipients to enter the work force.

Congress began passing laws almost yearly that required states to expand medicaid eligibility and add services. In 1984, it required states to begin offering medicaid coverage for a limited period to people who lost their eligibility for AFDC because they took jobs.

The next year brought a requirement for states to begin covering adoptive and foster children with special medical needs, regardless of the incomes of the families who took them in.

In 1986, states were told to start covering some disabled people who formerly received supplemental security income (SSI) benefits but were able to return to work. The states also had to cover emergency care and pregnancy services for legal and illegal aliens.

In 1988, Congress told states to cover all pregnant women and children in households below the poverty line and to keep AFDC recipients on the medicaid rolls for at least two years if they went to work.

The next year, states were required to provide medicaid benefits to all children under age 6 and pregnant women if their family's income was less than 133 per cent of the poverty line. Children also got expanded benefits for early health care screening and diagnostics and for medically necessary treatments—even if those treatments weren't otherwise covered under medicaid.

In 1990, Congress told states to start phasing in coverage of children up to age 18 whose families are below the poverty line. It also extended maternity care to cover the postpartum period and required states to establish convenient sites to process applications.

And in 1993, Congress required states to cover all nurse-midwife services and to establish a program to distribute pediatric vaccines furnished by the federal government.

From 1989-93 alone, the medicaid rolls grew from 24 million to 32 million; critics and advocates agree that much of the growth was related to added federal mandates.

Congress also changed some of the ground rules for medicaid reimbursement. Particularly irksome to the governors is the so-called Boren Amendment, passed in 1980 and renewed in 1987, that requires states to reimburse nursing homes and hospitals at rates adequate to cover the costs incurred by "efficiently and economically operated facilities." Although it was intended as a cost-saving measure, the amendment spurred a host of lawsuits by hospitals and nursing homes seeking higher reimbursement. To date, those institutions have won 27 such cases.

"They'll get very little cooperation from us if they don't get rid of the Boren Amendment," Gov. Dean said.

At a recent House Budget Committee hearing, Gov. Tommy G. Thompson, R-Wis., said that the Boren Amendment has added $120 million to his state's medicaid costs over the past three years. The amendment has forced states "to pay hospitals and nursing homes higher rates than to other medicaid providers, and at rates increasing much higher than inflation," he said. "It also forces Wisconsin and other states to maintain extraordinarily complex payment systems and an elaborate bureaucratic process to track the adequacy of payments to hospitals and nursing homes."

Another costly mandate requires the states to cover co-payments, deductibles and premiums for low-income medicare beneficiaries.

The NGA has not taken a formal position on medicaid block grants, and its members sharply disagree on how medicaid funds should be divided among the states. *(See box, this page.)* But there is virtual consensus when it comes to liquidating federal mandates. "The governors realize what a terrible threat this poses to their budgets," Dean said. "It's in everyone's interest to work out a common position, and we're going to try to do that."

YOUNG AND OLD

As Congress has extended medicaid coverage to millions more Americans, it's also provided a major infusion of funds to hospitals, nursing homes and clinics. Many of these institutions fear that without federal mandates, states would begin to restrict medicaid eligibility or change their reimbursement practices.

Children's hospitals could be among the institutions most affected. Sixteen million children—a fourth of all Americans under age 18, and a third of all infants—are now covered by medicaid.

"There's no other single payer of care that comes close to being as significant to touching as many children's lives," said Peters D. Willson, vice president for public policy of the National Association of Children's Hospitals and Related Institutions (NACHRI)

Likewise, nursing homes and home health care agencies rely heavily on medicaid, which now pays for half of all nursing-home bills. Private long-term care insurance has never sold well, and the high costs of nursing home care drive many middle-income seniors onto the medicaid rolls. "Many people don't realize medicaid's crucial role in long-term care," said John C. Rother, legislative director of the AARP. "But when mom gets hit by Alzheimer's or has a stroke and needs round-the-clock care, and when her life savings are all gone, it's the only place families can turn for help."

Medicaid also covers 4.9 million blind and disabled persons, most of whom are eligible because they receive SSI payments. Advocates for the disabled argue that it would be prohibitively expensive for disabled people to buy private insurance, if they could get it at all.

The threat of reduced medicaid coverage has spurred a wide variety of lobby groups to join forces. Families USA, a Washington-based group that advocates comprehensive health care reform, is spearheading an informal coalition of more than 70 groups, including the American Geriatrics Society, the American Nurses Association, the NACHRI and the Planned Parenthood Federation of America Inc., that holds regular strategy sessions and lobbies to retain medicaid as an entitlement.

The Coalition for America's Children, an alliance of about 250 organizations

A NEW WAR BETWEEN THE STATES?

Many governors say they'd like to get medicaid funds in block grant form, even if it means their states would get less money than they used to. But how much should each state get? And would all states suffer equally if Congress places a cap on increases in medicaid spending?

Federal support for medicaid now varies widely from one state to the next. Funds are distributed according to formulas based on each state's poverty level. A relatively poor state might get 70 per cent of its medicaid budget from Washington; a more affluent state might get only 50 per cent.

The picture is complicated further because not all states offer the same medicaid coverage and benefits—and the federal government pays a fixed share of each state's costs, no matter how generous its program.

What's more, states receive extra money, known as "disproportionate-share payments," to compensate hospitals with relatively large medicaid patient loads.

In the 1980s, some states were criticized for cooking up elaborate schemes to inflate their medicaid reimbursement. Hospitals in some states were asked to make special donations to state medicaid coffers; state officials then applied for federal funds to match this money, which ostensibly was to be spent on caring for medicaid beneficiaries. But when the aid arrived from Washington, the state government returned the hospitals' donations and kept the federal money.

States that have struggled to make their medicaid programs more efficient complain that they would be penalized if the present system is used as a baseline for block grants. California, for example, spent about $2,801 per medicaid beneficiary in 1993, well below the national average of $3,895. "A block grant that locks California into this base would put the state into a deep fiscal hole for the foreseeable future," Rep. Henry A. Waxman, D-Calif., said in a recent speech.

"There's a whale of a problem," said John H. Chafee, R-R.I., a Senate Finance Committee member who is a major player on medicaid. "What do you use as a base for the amount you give each state on medicaid?"

"If you lock in existing funding disparities, depending on how you structure a block grant, you can be rewarding states that have abused the system and punishing those that kept to the straight and narrow," said Stan Dorn, a managing attorney in the Washington office of the National Health Law Program.

Although Senate Budget Committee chairman Pete V. Domenici, R-N.M., and House Budget Committee chairman John R. Kasich, R-Ohio, have proposed medicaid block grants, so far no lawmaker has put forth a specific plan for distributing funds among the states.

There's also concern that an annual cap on growth in federal medicaid spending would hurt some states disproportionately. Domenici and Kasich both have proposed a 4 per cent annual cap that would be phased in. "If you're in a state that anticipates growth rapidly, a one-size-fits-all cap will hurt you worse than your sister states," Dorn said.

A recent study by the Henry J. Kaiser Family Foundation found that if Congress capped medicaid growth at 5 per cent annually, and if states continued to use existing eligibility and benefits standards, the effects would vary dramatically. At one extreme, Florida, Montana, North Carolina and West Virginia would lose 23-24 per cent of their federal medicaid contribution by 2000; at the other, New Hampshire would lose only 2.3 per cent. In absolute dollars, New York would lose the most—$18.45 billion by 2000—followed by California, which would lose $14.23 billion.

Another factor that could amplify differences between the states is the recent movement by a handful of states to move participants into managed care plans. These states may be reluctant to accept block grants with federal spending caps because they have already negotiated arrangements with the federal government allowing annual increases of as much as 21 per cent.

That helps to explain why the National Governors' Association is having difficulty coming to consensus on block grants. "The issue transcends party lines," Dorn said. "Both Democrats and Republicans are worried they might get the short end of the stick."

formed in 1991 that was active in last year's health care reform debate, has collaborated with the AARP on radio advertising; the two groups are looking for other ways to work together on the medicaid issue.

Also lobbying on medicaid is Maternal and Child Health Advocates, a coalition formed about eight years ago whose members include the March of Dimes, the NACHRI and the National Education Association.

Still another player is the Consortium for Citizens With Disabilities, which represents 125 organizations. It is creating educational materials to emphasize the disabled community's reliance on medicaid, according to Kathy H. McGinley, assistant director of government affairs for the Arc, a member of the consortium that represents retarded citizens.

Foremost, children's groups want to ensure that medicaid eligibility coverage remains tied to income levels, not to the receipt of welfare benefits. Now children up to age 6 and pregnant women are eligible if their family's income is below 133 per cent of the federal poverty line (about $16,745 for a family of three).

The NACHRI is particularly concerned about children over 6 whose families are below the poverty line because their medicaid coverage is still being phased in. "In the block grant context, all bets are off," said Gregg H. Haifley, senior health associate at the Children's Defense Fund.

The NACHRI also wants to retain the mandate that children covered by medicaid be screened regularly for health problems and that they receive medically necessary care even if the treatment would not otherwise be covered. And the group wants to keep a mandate requiring medicaid to reimburse pediatricians and obstetricians at rates comparable to those in the private sector.

"We spent a long time trying to build a certain safety net for children's benefits," said Edwin K. Zechman, president of Children's National Medical Center in Washington. "For children, there is absolutely no other safety net."

Meanwhile, nursing homes are fighting to retain legislation enacted in 1987 that provided more generous medicaid reimbursement to them. The law included an update of the Boren Amendment as well as a provision requiring states to subsidize some nursing-home staff training. "Mandates are interesting things. Sometimes they tell people to do what they should have been doing in the first place," said Paul R. Willging, executive vice president of the American Health Care Association (AHCA). "You'd think [the Boren Amendment] is this monster from hell. It's only two lines that says that the state—those poor guys—have got to pay the costs of the efficient and economically operated facilities."

The Long Term Care Campaign, an alliance of 141 organizations spearheaded by the AARP, has produced state-by-state projections for lost benefits under a block grant. Republican budget proposals, the group contends, could lead to the loss of long-term care for 1.74 million people by the end of the decade.

The AARP is lobbying to preserve another provision in the 1987 law that protects elderly people from having to deplete all their savings before their spouses can qualify for medicaid. "It was designed to protect an amount of income and assets so a person at home could remain independent with some dignity and not have to draw welfare benefits," said Patricia Smith, AARP's senior coordinator for health issues. Before the legislation was enacted, she said, "people were getting divorced. They had been married 50 years, one spouse was going into a nursing home and they couldn't afford it. It was creating some heart-wrenching circumstances."

Richard A. Bloom

Paul R. Willging of nursing-home group
Long-term care belongs with medicare, not medicaid.

Medicaid advocates are closely watching the Senate Finance Committee, which has jurisdiction over medicaid—and has only an 11-9 GOP majority, so that a single Republican vote could kill the block grant idea.

They have found a sympathetic ear in Finance member John H. Chafee, R-R.I., who has been a leader of efforts to ex-

John Eisele

Peters D. Willson of children's hospital association
"There's no other single payer of care that comes close" to medicaid.

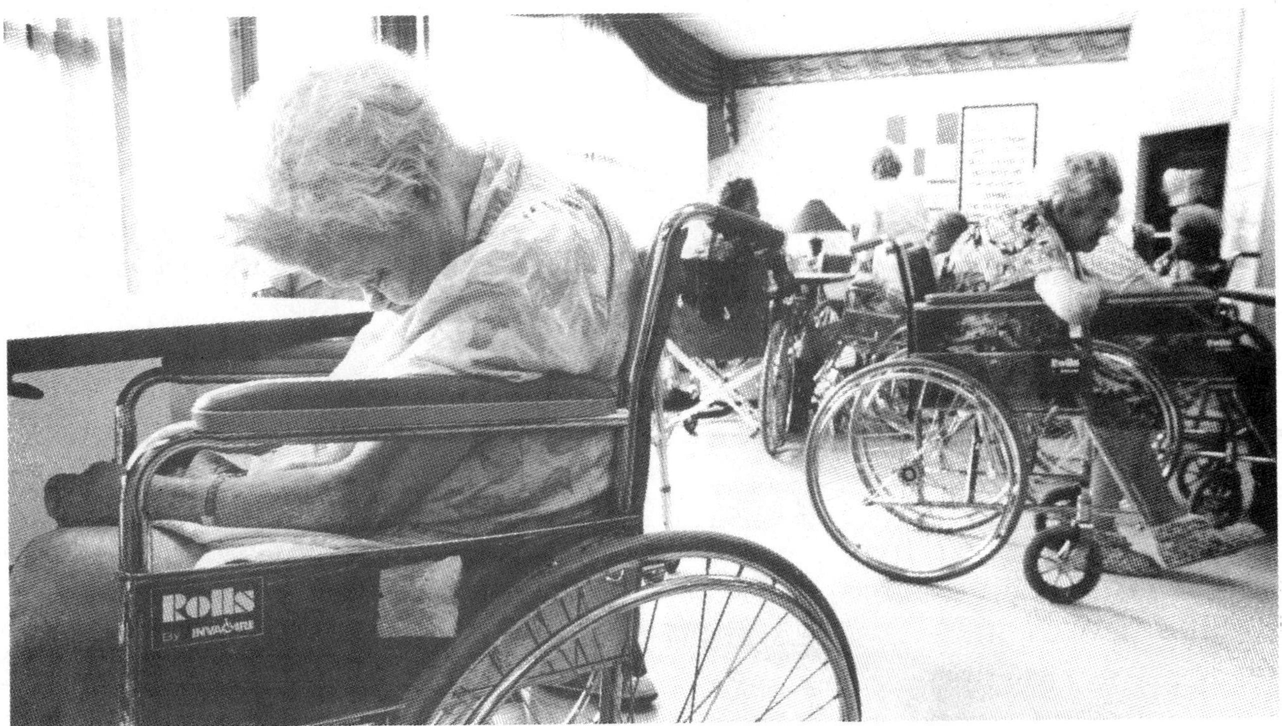

Richard A. Bloom

With half of all nursing-home bills paid by medicaid, advocates for the elderly are lobbying against proposed cuts.

pand medicaid coverage. "The mandates are very important," Chafee said in an interview. "We gradually extended the age of mandatory coverage for children, and every report indicates health is improving. I'd hate to have a situation where we back away from all that." If federal medicaid payments to the states are reduced, states may not be able to absorb the loss without cutting people from the rolls, curtailing benefits or both, he said.

Bill Bradley, D-N.J., another Finance member, predicted that the committee would attempt to please both sides by approving block grants but keeping some strings attached. "We'll have some compromise to get some requirements," he said.

Even Senate Budget Committee chairman Pete V. Domenici, R-N.M., who has introduced a medicaid block grant proposal, said that he would support a mandate that would force states to provide coverage to children meeting certain eligibility standards.

Chafee has proposed an alternative to the block grant arrangement that would allow states to enroll medicaid recipients in managed care plans, bypassing the current process of applying to the Health and Human Services Department (HHS) for waivers. HHS has already granted waivers to a handful of states that are trying to reduce costs and expand enrollment. *(For details, see NJ, 2/4/95, p. 294.)*

Chafee also wants to change a formula by which the federal government provides extra funds to states to help compensate hospitals with high medicaid traffic. States have been criticized for skimming money from that program and using it for other purposes; Chafee wants to make payments directly to hospitals that need extra help, a move that he says could save as much as $50 billion over five years.

Rep. Henry A. Waxman, D-Calif., the past chairman of the Energy and Commerce Subcommittee on Health and the Environment who was the leading force behind expansion of medicaid during the 1980s, predicts that block grant proponents will fail. "They may be able to [win] in the House, but they won't get away with it in the Senate, and I certainly hope President Clinton won't sign it."

DISCORDANT NOTES

If advocates for children, the disabled and the elderly are mostly singing in harmony about preserving medicaid, some discordant notes are creeping in.

Children's groups are suggesting that if reductions are inevitable, children should not take the first hit; elderly people, they note, at least have medicare coverage, while poor children have no other source of health care benefits.

The NACHRI's Willson notes that although children and their mothers make up 73 per cent of medicaid enrollment, only 30 per cent of medicaid dollars go toward their care. Only 12 per cent of medicaid recipients are elderly, and another 15 per cent are disabled, but these groups together account for 59 per cent of medicaid spending.

The nursing-home lobby, in turn, wants long-term-care coverage moved out of the medicaid program and perhaps made a part of medicare—a program that enjoys much broader public support. The AHCA's Willging argues that nursing-home patients don't really belong in medicaid; they've been put there only because medicare doesn't cover long-term care. Willging advocates connecting long-term care to medicare and possibly requiring patients to make additional contributions to offset the costs.

The AHCA has done most of its medicaid lobbying independently. "Sometimes it's better to have diverse voices arguing the same point," Willging said. "If they hear it from one group, it's easier to dismiss than if they hear it from 250 groups."

Nursing homes are in the best position politically to weather possible cuts in medicaid under a block grant arrangement, Waxman said. "Nursing homes are a strong lobby, but more importantly the frail elderly are often from middle-class backgrounds," he said. "Elderly people are more likely to vote, especially those who are middle-class. Their adult children are more likely to vote."

In addition, Waxman said, most Americans are sympathetic to the needs of the elderly. "They see themselves getting old and needing long-term care. Most people won't make that same identification with a poor woman and her child." That's all the more reason, he said, to keep some federal strings attached to medicaid to guarantee coverage of poor families and children.

A Medicaid Miracle?

Tennessee is drawing national attention for an overhaul of its medicaid program that greatly expanded coverage while putting a lid on state spending. But the reforms have sparked plenty of controversy at home.

STUART SCHEAR

Stuart Schear is a media fellow of the Henry J. Kaiser Family Foundation, which financed his travel for this article.

NASHVILLE—While the debate over comprehensive health care reform lumbered on in the nation's capital last year, Tennessee finance and administration commissioner David L. Manning gambled with his state's health care system and his career. Manning set up TennCare, a program with two seemingly contradictory goals: expanding medicaid coverage for the poor and disabled while capping state spending on the program.

In some respects, the gamble paid off. Within a year, Manning extended coverage to an additional 418,000 Tennesseeans, channeled recipients into cost-conscious "managed care" plans run by private companies and established a firm limit on medicaid spending.

But Manning's policies and tactics—particularly an alliance that he forged with consumer activists and the state's largest insurer—so rankled Tennessee's doctors that Republican Don Sundquist, who was elected governor on Nov. 8, made a campaign pledge to replace him. TennCare will survive his departure, though, and its track record has already become the subject of a debate among would-be reformers from other states.

As the prospect of comprehensive national health care reform fades, the focus has shifted to the states. And for many states, fixing medicaid is a top fiscal priority. The joint federal-state health insurance program is breaking state budgets across the nation. Costs skyrocketed during the late 1980s and early 1990s; in 1993, the federal and state governments spent $131.8 billion on medicaid, up from $54.3 billion only five years earlier. In Tennessee, the annual increases topped 20 per cent. Although the increases have moderated somewhat, cash-strapped governors are still demanding savings.

Reforming medicaid has bipartisan appeal; Republican governors have placed it close to the top of their post-election wish list. And medicaid reform is one of the few arenas in which the White House still wields power to reshape the health care system; states wishing to overhaul their medicaid programs must obtain waivers from the federal Health Care Financing Administration (HCFA). *(For details, see box.)*

Increasingly, would-be medicaid reformers are turning to the managed care models now dominating the private sector. These range from preferred provider organizations (PPOs)—networks of doctors and hospitals working for discounted fees—to traditional health maintenance organizations (HMOs) that use "gatekeeper" physicians to direct patients' care.

Dozens of states have introduced managed care into their medicaid programs; according to the Health and Human Services Department, 23 per cent of the nation's 34 million medicaid beneficiaries were enrolled in some kind of managed care plan in 1994, up from 14 per cent the year before. But Tennessee, which received a five-year waiver from HCFA to operate TennCare as a demonstration project, has the nation's most aggressive and farthest-reaching program.

After months of negotiations, HCFA gave Tennessee the go-ahead in November 1993. On Jan. 1, 1994, the state began moving its nearly 900,000 medicaid enrollees from the old fee-for-service program into managed care plans and started expanding coverage to the previously uninsured. A year later, all former medicaid enrollees and another 418,000 people—the vast majority of all Tennesseeans who lacked health coverage a year earlier—were covered by TennCare plans. The program grew so rapidly that the state froze open enrollment of the uninsured working poor in January 1995 to ensure adequate funds to cover those already enrolled.

Everyone agrees that the pace has been breathtaking. "You can probably implement programs like this faster than we had thought possible, but not as fast as Tennessee decided to do it," without encountering serious disruption, HCFA administrator Bruce C. Vladeck said in an interview.

Tennessee "created a number of enemies" by moving so quickly, said Sara Rosenbaum, co-director of the George Washington University Center for Health

Policy. Doctors complain that they have been coerced into treating TennCare patients; hospitals and community health centers say that the program has placed them in a dangerous financial squeeze. These groups have filed a flurry of lawsuits against TennCare and are lobbying hard in the state capital to revamp the program. Sundquist appears receptive to many of their arguments.

And TennCare will be under growing pressure to rein in costs. Under its agreement with HCFA, the state got a hefty increase in federal medicaid funds during TennCare's first year. But increases in federal spending are to be sharply restricted during the next four years of the program. And if TennCare's total costs exceed $12.16 billion over five years, HCFA will not help pay for the excess. (Now, federal funds cover about two-thirds of TennCare costs, and the state picks up the rest.)

There are signs of trouble already: On Jan. 30, the Sundquist administration announced that TennCare ran a $99 million deficit during its first year.

Stuart Schear

David L. Manning, Tennessee's finance and administration commissioner, so rankled the state's doctors in setting up the program that the new governor made a campaign promise to fire him. Manning is unapologetic. "I plead guilty to managing costs," he said.

TURKEYS AND LIFE INSURANCE

To get TennCare up and running, state officials pooled their medicaid funds—including special payments to hospitals serving the poor—with other state and federal funds dedicated to public health services. The consolidated $3 billion budget was used to pay for expanded coverage and to gain enough leverage in the market to wring out deep discounts in the fees charged by providers.

TennCare expanded coverage to include low and moderate-income people who previously were uninsured, as well as "uninsurable" people with preexisting medical conditions. And by all accounts, it drove down the price of care.

At the center of TennCare's structure are 12 managed care organizations, known as MCOs, that provide care to all enrollees. The MCOs, which vary in size and structure, have established networks of participating health professionals, hospitals and clinics. Two operate statewide; the others serve regional markets. Each must provide a standard package of benefits mandated by the state, including prescription drugs, in exchange for a fixed annual payment from the state for each enrollee.

TennCare's goal is to "empower consumers," Manning said, by letting them choose an MCO. Once a year, there is an open-enrollment period during which they may switch plans. That, Vladeck said, is consistent with the principle of "managed competition," allowing consumers to vote with their feet if they are dissatisfied with the care they are getting.

During the initial sign-up period last year, MCOs offered potential enrollees incentives ranging from fresh turkeys to $10,000 life insurance policies. Dr. Russell Adcock, a family physician in the small town of South Pittsburgh who sees many TennCare enrollees, said that these goodies enticed many of his patients to sign up for plans that didn't serve them very well. State authorities responded by issuing rules to limit such incentives.

How well is TennCare working for patients? Trips to doctor's offices, clinics and hospitals serving low-income patients turn up contradictory information.

Jeremy Nance, a quadriplegic 16-year-old from rural central Tennessee, has been a winner. Jeremy, who is confined to a wheelchair and breathes with the aid of a respirator, was disabled in a car accident nearly seven years ago. His private insurance ran out; his multiple surgeries and ongoing rehabilitation cost far more than the $1 million limit under his family's policy. TennCare now covers all his care.

But the program's cost-consciousness proved nearly fatal for Mary Milburn, an elderly woman in Nashville. Milburn, who had been successfully treated for high blood pressure under medicaid, discovered that her MCO would not pay for her expensive medicine and was forced to take another medication. Her blood pressure shot up and down, causing several visits to the local hospital and a couple of close calls with death.

Despite TennCare's promise that every MCO provides essentially the same care, clear disparities exist. In the waiting room of a Memphis clinic for people infected with the AIDS virus, a young man reports that his MCO consistently provides him with everything his doctor has ordered, including 10 prescription medications. But a man sitting next to him complains that his MCO won't approve the only drug he needs at the moment: a new antidepressant.

The greatest gap between TennCare's promise and its performance results from the unpreparedness of its provider networks. In the intensive care unit of the Regional Medical Center in Memphis, a man tells how his son was injured in a car accident. The son, in his mid-30s, was already disabled from severe diabetes and was covered by an MCO. But when he was taken from the scene of the accident to a nearby hospital, it would not admit him because no doctor affiliated with his MCO was on staff. The operator on the MCO's toll-free line told the father to transport his son to a hospital 100 miles away.

There have been administrative snafus, too. Annie Watkins, a longtime employee of a Memphis hospital, enrolled her grandparents in an MCO formed by the hospital. But her grandparents received a letter of acceptance from another MCO that they hadn't applied to join. And they were sent membership and billing cards by yet another MCO. Now Watkins is not certain where they should seek care.

Despite such complaints, Tennessee officials say that TennCare's framework is sound and that its problems can be resolved. Gordon Bonnyman, a veteran legal aid lawyer in Nashville who has sued the state dozens of times over expanding access to health care for the poor, said that fixing TennCare's problems is "simply a function of time and political will."

And the Tennessee Health Care Campaign, a coalition of advocacy groups that operates a state-financed telephone hotline to help Tennesseeans navigate the new system, reports that the volume of calls has dropped markedly in recent months and that many callers' problems are easily resolved.

Stuart Schear

Tennessee Medical Association vice president Warren McPherson TennCare's policies are so coercive that doctors have become "state employees."

"If enrollees call MCOs, they often don't know the buzzwords and what will work," said Patricia Whitewell, a patient advocate who works with the hotline. "You have to know how to cut through." Patient advocates often speak directly with the MCO staff and sometimes file appeals with MCO medical directors. If they aren't satisfied with the response, they can file a complaint with the medical director of the state's TennCare bureau, the final arbiter of disputes. Only 26 such cases arose during TennCare's first year.

MCOs are budget-driven. The state pays a flat fee, averaging $1,507 annually, for each enrollee. The MCO is expected to economize by negotiating discounted fees with doctors and hospitals and squeezing out unnecessary care. If an MCO fails to live within its budget, the doctors and hospitals affiliated with it must accept reduced payments. State officials say that under TennCare, nonemergency visits to emergency rooms by poor people have dropped by close to 40 per cent, and that the amount of inpatient care has declined.

The state recognizes that some plans may attract an unusually large number of high-cost enrollees, such as patients with cancer or the AIDS virus. The state has set up a $40 million account that can be drawn upon to ease the burden on any MCO that has enrolled a disproportionately large number of patients requiring unusually expensive care. No payments are to be made from the account until HCFA approves the state's method for deciding which plans deserve aid.

A BOON FOR THE BLUES

Some MCOs operate as HMOs, requiring their members to select a primary care physician who oversees their care. Others function as PPOs, looser networks of health professionals who are willing to accept discounted payments in exchange for a guaranteed flow of patients.

The quality of the MCOs is uneven. One of the two statewide plans, Access Med Plus, is notorious for requiring patients to travel long distances to see physicians and for being slow in making payments to physicians and hospitals. While some MCOs seem to function well in regional markets, TennCare's anchor has been Tennessee Preferred, a statewide PPO put together by Blue Cross and Blue Shield of Tennessee.

Finance commissioner Manning knew that a statewide network was essential to TennCare's success. Realizing that starting from scratch would be impossible, he turned to Blue Cross, the state's largest insurer. Several years earlier, Manning and Blue Cross officials had worked together to build the Tennessee Provider Network, a PPO for state employees.

But, in a move that still angers many Tennessee doctors, Blue Cross told doctors in the Tennessee Provider Network that if they wished to continue participating in that plan, they would have to take TennCare patients.

Doctors quickly dubbed that requirement the "cram-down" rule. Some doctors feared that the presence of medicaid patients in their waiting rooms would scare away private patients. Many, including Tennessee Medical Association vice president Warren McPherson, argued that the policy was so coercive that it made doctors into "state employees."

Rather than accept TennCare patients, nearly half of the 7,000 providers in Blue Cross's private network (which serves 220,000 state employees and one million other customers) dropped out of both plans. Mayhem ensued; many of Blue Cross's TennCare patients, as well as middle-class patients in its private plan, had trouble finding doctors.

But Blue Cross stuck to its guns, and in time, providers began to make their way back into both networks. Doctors discovered that they could not maintain their practices without conducting business with the state's largest insurer. By August, Blue Cross had regained virtually all of its original network.

Blue Cross's steadfastness was hailed by consumer activists who wanted equal treatment for the poor. But Blue Cross senior vice president Glen Watson said that although the company believes in taking all comers, the decision was based on business considerations. According to Watson, Blue Cross determined that it could deliver care and thrive financially within TennCare.

Some observers conjecture that Manning played hardball, telling Blue Cross that its continued participation in the state employee plan might hinge on its cooperation in TennCare. Others argue that Blue Cross needed no prodding because it viewed TennCare as an opportunity to increase its market share. Blue Cross has captured 50.6 per cent of the TennCare market. A Nashville health lobbyist, who didn't want his name used, said that providers fear Blue Cross's growing power, viewing it as tantamount to that of a state single-payer system.

The most rancorous opposition to Blue Cross's role has come from the Tennessee Medical Association. In sharp contrast with the American Medical Association, which initially was receptive to comprehensive national health reform, the state association immediately took a firm stand against TennCare. The doctors' group used a lawsuit, intense lobbying, political campaigning and a public relations drive to try to weaken, delay or stop TennCare.

Although its lawsuit stalled in the state courts, the association's political strategy was more successful. Its political action committee and an overwhelming majority of its members contributed heavily to the campaign of Gov. Sundquist, who is establishing a committee to review TennCare. According to an aide, Sundquist has no plan to scrap TennCare but wants to "fix" it. He has promised to end the cram-down rule and "wants to bring providers to the table," the aide said.

PUSHING FOR CHANGES

Even TennCare's sharpest critics concede that it is here to stay. The action now centers on reengineering the program. Some of the same health care interest groups that lobbied heavily in Washington last year are now at work in Nashville, pressuring Sundquist's administration to change TennCare according to their specifications.

The insurance and hospital lobbies, often at odds with physicians, have found common ground with the Tennessee Medical Association. All three groups complain that the state's annual payments to MCOs are too low.

Sundquist has promised a review of the rates, but if he decides to increase them, he would probably have to slow down enrollment in TennCare or reduce the services that enrollees receive. (He has ruled out any tax increase to raise revenues for the program.)

Manning, a budget hawk, forged an unlikely alliance between consumer advocacy groups and the administration of Sundquist's predecessor, moderate Democrat Ned R. McWherter, whose top priority was avoiding a looming state budget shortfall. Tony Garr, executive director of the Tennessee Health Care Campaign, said that McWherter helped keep opposition in the legislature at bay. Twenty bills were introduced to break up Blue Cross's network, Garr said, but McWherter made sure they never got out of committee.

Now, consumer advocates are worried. Garr said he fears that the state will no longer support the advocacy phone line. As for the new governor's commitment to end the cram-down rule, Garr said, "Sundquist made a promise to the [Tennessee Medical Association] that he would break up the network, but one of the admirable things about TennCare was that the poor could see the same doctors" who cared for middle-class patients.

Hospitals and community health centers that have traditionally provided care to the poor are also pushing for changes. Until last year, 126 Tennessee hospitals received special payments from HCFA to help compensate them for treating a disproportionate share of uninsured patients. Under TennCare, the payments ended; instead, the funds were used to pay MCOs to provide coverage to the uninsured.

Manning reasoned that hospitals would benefit because patients who enrolled in MCOs would be less likely to visit hospital emergency rooms for routine care. He and other state officials also set $100 million aside in a transition fund that could continue to make some payments to hospitals to cover their care of the uninsured.

But the situation for some hospitals is more complicated. Consider the Regional Medical Center in Memphis, known locally as the Med. Until recently, virtually all of the area's poor came to the Med, which has a policy of accepting all comers. Although many of the Med's patients are now covered by TennCare, their MCOs pay the hospital far less than it received for treating medicaid patients in the past. MCOs also refuse to cover some services that medicaid once paid for routinely.

What's more, hospitals complain of patient dumping by MCOs. For example, officials at the Med say that Access Med Plus has directed its patients to the Med even though the hospital is not part of the MCO's network.

Charlotte Collins, the Med's senior vice president for policy and chief legal counsel, said that the hospital has been forced to eliminate 250 of 2,800 staff positions, primarily because of TennCare. She bristles at Manning's argument that hospitals such as the Med must learn to compete in the market. Nonetheless, Collins has helped the Med form its own MCO.

TennCare has also placed competitive pressures on Tennessee's federally financed community health centers. They complain that MCOs pay them far too lit-

Stuart Schear

Legal aid lawyer Gordon Bonnyman
TennCare has hurt some hospitals and clinics. But more people are getting care.

USHERING IN REFORM THROUGH THE BACK DOOR?

Tennessee is far from alone in its endeavor to revamp medicaid. Six other states—Florida, Hawaii, Kentucky, Ohio, Oregon and Rhode Island—have won waivers from the Health Care Financing Administration (HCFA) to enlarge their medicaid programs and in many cases to steer participants into managed care systems. HCFA recently gave South Carolina a tentative approval, and nine more applications are pending.

With at least a dozen other states contemplating similar requests, policy makers are beginning to wonder whether the waivers, which are supposed to let states operate short-term demonstration projects to test theories about medicaid efficiency, aren't bringing about a fundamental restructuring of the program that merits a closer look in Washington.

"When you have a million and one demo projects, they're no longer demo projects," said Rep. Michael Bilirakis, R-Fla., who chairs the Commerce Subcommittee on Health and the Environment, which has jurisdiction over medicaid. Congress will have to make a broader policy decision about the future of medicaid, Bilirakis said.

Should medicaid be expanded—and if so, how? Can the costs to the federal and state governments be controlled? Should states be allowed to force recipients to enroll in managed care plans?

With congressional Republicans eyeing medicaid cuts to help finance deficit reduction, those questions may have to be addressed soon. The Senate Finance Committee has already begun discussions about reforming medicaid in the context of welfare reform, a top priority for the GOP.

For now, many in the Administration and Congress want to continue granting waivers to states to encourage them to experiment. Judith Feder, the principal Health and Human Services deputy assistant secretary for planning and evaluation, said it doesn't matter whether the state programs are real demonstration projects, as long as the results are positive. "States are making use of the process for a wide array of activities," she said. The Administration is considering restructuring the waiver process, though.

But Bilirakis questioned why states should have to obtain federal waivers if they want to expand coverage and save money at the same time. He favors giving states medicaid block grants to use as they wish.

Gov. Howard Dean, D-Vt., the National Governors' Association chairman, said that he and other governors are talking with the House Republican leadership about legislation that would do away with the waiver process.

The waivers now are granted for five years, during which HCFA may pay a state more for medicaid than it paid previously. But at the end of five years, HCFA will stop paying for recipients who were added to the rolls during the demonstration project. The question is whether states by then will have realized enough savings from managed care to pay for the expanded coverage.

Members of the Physician Payment Review Commission, which advises Congress on physician reimbursement under medicaid, have suggested that Congress should examine the issue more closely. "This one here is a large political question," said Princeton University professor Uwe E. Reinhardt, a commission member. "If we expand the waiver authority beyond research, is this a backhand way of reforming medicaid?"

—**Marilyn Werber Serafini**

tle for their services. Alarmed that other states will follow Tennessee's example, the National Association of Community Health Centers is suing the federal government to halt the medicaid waiver program under which TennCare and six other state programs are operating.

James Feldesman, the association's counsel in Washington, said that community health centers are trying to form a national network that could compete effectively with commercial insurers in caring for medicaid patients. Building such a network will take time and capital, though, and the centers need federal aid to survive the newly competitive market engendered by medicaid reform, he said.

Feldesman noted that President Clinton's proposed Health Security Act would have furnished community health centers and other "essential community providers" with the kind of protection that HCFA has refused to grant them in medicaid reform: a five-year transition period. When it comes to health care reform, he said, medicaid waivers are now "the only game in town, and . . . we would like to be given a chance to win."

Legal aid lawyer Bonnyman, who has filed an amicus brief opposing the community health centers' lawsuit, acknowledges that TennCare has hurt some institutions that traditionally cared for the poor. But, he said, a more important point is that TennCare is covering hundreds of thousands of previously uninsured people.

Still, the reaction of health care providers remains a big stumbling block for TennCare, and their political influence appears to be growing. The Tennessee Medical Association's McPherson denounced TennCare as "managed costs and not managed care;" Collins of the Med, ordinarily no friend of the doctors' group, called TennCare "fiscal reform and not health reform."

"I plead guilty to managing costs," finance commissioner Manning responded. "I don't mean to be critical of health care providers. They just responded to the bad incentives that were out there. . . . We believe that the health care system has far too long been organized and judged by the levels of satisfaction providers have had with the system as opposed to consumers. . . . We want to make sure that consumers are served by the system."

James Blumstein, a Vanderbilt University law professor who has been a leading advocate of health care market reforms, contends that providers' complaints are proof that TennCare has brought real reform. "The old view was that there was a single right way to deliver care, and that was an old-fashioned and very paternalistic view," he said. "The bottom line on TennCare is that it is changing the way services are delivered."

Rosenbaum of George Washington University takes a more critical view. "It is never possible to make change without making a lot of people angry," she said, but "it is my sense from some of the architects of TennCare that they hate health care providers."

Bonnyman remains optimistic about TennCare, although he warns that the state's "political will" is essential to its continued success. "Squirreled away in Dogpatch, U.S.A., this state has covered 400,000 people," he said. "Now, one state in the country has the possibility of tying its spending to the health needs of the public—what a radical concept!"

LONG-TERM PROBLEM

LOUIS JACOBSON

One of the many ironies of health care reform is that even as 9 of every 10 Americans tell pollsters that they want coverage of long-term care for the elderly and the disabled, these benefits seem further than ever from squeezing their way into a congressional reform package. Like the weather, long-term assistance to people in nursing homes or at home seems to have become an issue that everybody talks about but no one can do anything about.

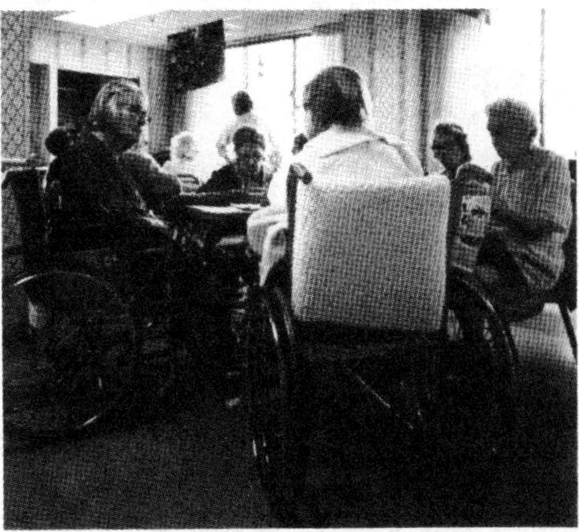
Richard A. Bloom

Lawmakers are in a bind. On one hand, some important constituents —namely, the lobbying powerhouse for older Americans, the American Association of Retired Persons (AARP)—might not support health care reform if it lacks long-term care benefits. John C. Rother, the AARP's top lobbyist, says that if the final bill does not contain such coverage, "it would be almost impossible to imagine us doing anything to support such a plan; it would be a question of how hard we fight against it."

But lawmakers also know that long-term care is extremely expensive. Joshua M. Wiener of the Brookings Institution estimates that with the graying of baby boomers, providing care for the elderly and disabled in nursing homes and at home will cost $168 billion a year in 2018—more than twice the level today—unless the current system is changed.

The congressional committees overseeing health care have kept symbolic long-term care benefits in their bills, although some would provide even less than President Clinton wants. His reform proposal would provide states with capped budgets to cover home care for the severely disabled.

Valerie S. Wilbur, a lobbyist for the Coalition on Long Term Care Financing, a group of care providers and insurers, estimates that Clinton's plan would provide about $53 per patient each week. A proposal by House Ways and Means Committee acting chairman Sam Gibbons, D-Fla., would offer $30-$40 a week. That would not even cover a single home visit by a professional caregiver; such visits, Wilbur estimates, average $78.

The legislative fudging has much to do with money. The three main financing options for health care reform—an employer mandate, restrictions on medicare and an increase in tobacco taxes—are all under attack. But there's also a problem of policy-wonk paralysis—and that paralysis is delaying some reforms that many advocates say make an awful lot of sense.

The problem, as a private-sector health care analyst put it, is that "long-term care is a real can of worms because it's nearly impossible to estimate its real impact."

Medicaid, the federal-state program for the poor, covers nursing home care but not cheaper, less-intensive alternatives such as home care or adult day centers. Families coping with an aging, chronically ill family member face an unappetizing choice. They can deplete the family member's savings until he or she qualifies for medicaid benefits (and with nursing-home care averaging $37,000 a year, that may not take long). Or they can care for the person themselves.

The second option can cost a family $15,000-$30,000 a year in expenses and lost wages, but most choose it anyway: About 90 per cent of chronically ill patients receive some care from their families; two-thirds are cared for exclusively by their families.

It seems to make economic sense to offer cheaper alternatives for the people who now receive—but don't need—nursing-home care. But in the world of long-term care, such common sense is flipped on its head.

Agreeing to pay for less-intensive services would spur demand that is now invisible—at least on the government's ledgers—according to most long-term care experts. The added cost would, in all likelihood, more than wipe out any savings on nursing-home expenditures.

There is a historical precedent for such induced demand. A late-1980s change in medicaid rules, including the lifting of a requirement that patients spend three days in a hospital before qualifying for nursing-home coverage, helped boost spending fourfold. "When you look at these figures, it shows how expensive it can be if it's not carefully controlled," Wilbur said.

Wilbur favors targeting benefits to the poorest Americans. So does Mark R. Meiners, associate director of the University of Maryland's Center on Aging, who praised the Clinton plan but said that "it would have been better to acknowledge the [financing] fears. . . . It's not as sexy as universal coverage for everyone, but it's a practical attempt to deal with the reality."

The pesky problem of induced demand (as well as a political imperative to focus on the acute-care system) has spooked legislators, leaving them afraid even to experiment with some of the innovative and potentially money-saving ideas being floated by scholars and practitioners.

Burton V. Reifler, chairman of the psychiatry and behavioral medicine department at Wake Forest University, advocates centers where elderly people can be cared for during the day but returned to their families at night. Such care costs only a fourth to a third as much as nursing-home care, but it is not reimbursable by the government today, and bringing it under medicaid appears unlikely for now. Efforts to expand meals-on-wheels programs and provide transportation and shared domestic help for the elderly and disabled are also going nowhere fast.

"What frustrates me is that the opportunity to struggle with it has been [lost] for the simple fear of costs," Meiners said. "I fully recognize that there are real cost concerns and that we need to come up with good solutions. But we need to be working on it, not [ruling out] experimentation."

Indeed, solving the problems of long-term care may prove to be a task even more Byzantine than fixing the acute-care sector. "It's not like there's a well-developed system, as there is with hospitals and doctors, that you can twitch" with new federal policies, Meiners said.

It's no surprise, then, that after more than a decade of debate, few have any illusions that the process will be fast or easy. "I think it's a gradual education process," said Gail Shearer, who analyzes health care for Consumers Union of United States Inc. "I don't think it's close to being resolved."

Safety Net Programs: Social Security, Welfare, and Housing

In modern industrial societies, governments have assumed responsibility for providing assistance to the needy, a task that in a bygone era would have been seen as the responsibility of family and local community members, church groups, or other voluntary associations. The term "welfare state" reflects this new and burdensome role that governments have assumed in recent times.

In the United States, the national government dramatically moved into this area of public policy during the 1930s under the auspices of President Franklin Roosevelt's New Deal. A cornerstone of the New Deal was the Social Security Act of 1935, which required regular deductions from wage earners' paychecks in order to provide guaranteed benefits ("entitlements") to those same people in old

Unit 6

age, after the death of the head of their household, or in case of permanent disability. The Social Security Act also established Aid to Families with Dependent Children (AFDC), a program through which the national government makes money available to states to provide assistance to poor families—usually single-parent households—with young children. The term "welfare" is often used pejoratively in this country to refer to AFDC payments to undeserving recipients.

In the 1960s, President Lyndon Johnson and a cooperative Congress added a number of "Great Society" programs to complement Roosevelt's New Deal. As a result of these and other legislative additions since the 1930s, American national and state governments today operate programs that help provide millions of needy individuals with access to sufficient food (food stamps, school breakfast and lunch programs), housing (public housing and housing subsidies), and medical care (Medicaid for the poor, medicare for the elderly). (medicaid and medicare are treated under health care in unit 5 of this book, but they constitute part of the idea of a welfare state.)

For all the programs and all the dollars that the national government spends on helping the needy and the elderly, the United States stands out in comparison with other industrial democracies such as Canada, Britain, Germany, and Norway. No other government of an industrialized country spends as small a proportion of its nation's resources on social welfare programs as do the state and federal governments in the United States. And problems of poverty, homelessness, and the like seem to afflict American society to a greater extent than they do in Canadian, Japanese, and comparable European societies.

Economic circumstances and presidential leadership in the 1930s (the Great Depression and President Franklin Roosevelt) and the 1960s (prosperous times and President Lyndon Johnson) facilitated passage of the New Deal and the Great Society. In the 1970s and especially the 1980s and 1990s, the same two factors stimulated popular demands that social welfare programs be reformed and cut back. The Arab oil embargo of 1973 sent shock waves through the American economy, which both increased global competition and the aging of the U.S. industrial infrastructure, and also contributed to a decline in the nation's economic position relative to other nations. President Ronald Reagan assumed office in 1981 committed to reducing domestic spending, and social welfare programs were among his primary targets. He told stories about "welfare queens" (that is, female AFDC recipients) who drove Cadillacs, thus helping to legitimate the notion that the social welfare programs of the Roosevelt and Johnson administrations had run amuck. Perhaps most important, Reagan pushed through Congress a significant reduction in income tax rates that made budget deficits rise dramatically, thus creating a climate of opinion among policymakers and the public alike that made spending reductions seem a necessity.

The selections in this unit can serve to introduce the reader to some of the intricacies of today's policy debates and problems involving social security, AFDC, and various government housing programs. As will be seen, these debates and problems are inevitably related to economic and budgetary policy concerns (treated in unit 2) and to the health care delivery system, especially as it applies to the elderly and the needy (treated in unit 5).

Looking Ahead: Challenge Questions

Some observers believe that the relative stinginess of the U.S. state and federal governments in social welfare spending helps account for the high levels of crime that plague the country. Some suggest that if the poor, who are disproportionately racial minorities, were given decent levels of public assistance, they would have less need to engage in street crime. What do you think?

Do you think that old-age Social Security payments, AFDC payments, and medicaid assistance should be "entitlements"? That is, should every needy person who meets specified legal requirements be guaranteed government assistance, regardless of the total cost to taxpayers in a given year? Defend your answer.

Do you think that local governments, state governments, or the national government are best suited to run welfare programs for the needy? Why?

STRAINING THE SAFETY NET

JULIE KOSTERLITZ

In 1969, Congress celebrated the 30th birthday of social security—the largest and most significant social welfare program in the history of the nation—with a bidding war.

Designed to assure against loss of income in retirement, the program had proved enormously popular. The question was whether it was generous enough.

In the House, Democrats Claude Pepper of Florida and Edward I. Koch of New York stood up to plead for more benefits. Koch decried the Nixon Administration's request for a mere 10 per cent increase, saying it would mean "an endless perpetuation of poverty" for the old. In the end, Congress approved a 15 per cent increase. Three years later, it locked in this generosity by guaranteeing that benefits would keep pace with inflation.

Those gestures, in hindsight, represent the end of an era for social security and the assumption on which it was built: that each generation ought to be better off than the next.

The economic boom of the 1960s gave way in the early 1970s to oil price shocks, periodic recessions and bouts of inflation. Even when sustained growth returned in the 1980s, the rising tide did not lift all boats: Wages stagnated or fell for workers at the low end of the income scale—principally the less-educated and those with young children.

By 1989, poverty rates stood at 12.8 per cent—well above the historic low of 11.1 in 1973. Over 25 years, the burden of poverty had shifted dramatically: The poverty rate for the elderly was cut nearly in half, to 12 per cent, but for children, it nearly doubled, to 22 per cent.

Those statistics aren't merely a worry for do-gooders. Economists recognize that today's children (and there are fewer children than in the preceding generation) are the people whose skills and productivity society is counting on to fulfill its promise of support for tomorrow's elderly.

The growing gap between the incomes of the well-educated and the less-educated will also leave a legacy of more-pronounced income differences within the ranks of tomorrow's elderly.

A DEMOGRAPHIC REVOLUTION

The concepts of retirement and old age have been radically altered by changes in life expectancy and work patterns. When social security began, men could expect to live roughly 12 years after reaching age 65; women, about 13.5. Today the figures are about 15 and 19.

But while Americans are living longer, they're retiring sooner. Over the past 25 years, the share of men in the work force has dropped from 80 per cent to 77 per cent—in large part thanks to the availability of early-retirement plans and a change in the law allowing receipt of reduced social security benefits at age 62. (The vast influx of women into the work force has masked the trend—but it can't keep doing so for long.)

Increased longevity and early retirement have transformed social security from a safety net for those who can't work to a baseline of support for a population that can expect to spend about a third of its life span not working.

The two trends have had a massive impact on goverment policy. Social security has risen from less than 5 per cent of federal spending in 1950 to 21 per cent today. Throw in medicare and other health and retirement programs targeted mainly at the elderly, and you're looking at an increase from 11 per cent to nearly half of all domestic spending.

If Congress is chafing at the share of the budget devoted to entitlements mainly benefiting the elderly, imagine its chagrin when that share jumps to 52 per cent by 1998.

And all of this will have occurred *before* the true demographic revolution has begun: Starting in 2011, the gargantuan baby boom cohort will swell the ranks of the elderly. Not only is the baby boom generation bigger than its predecessor, the boomers live longer than their parents did. And the declining

Photos by Richard A. Bloom

Will low-wage workers fork over an ever-growing share of their paychecks to support the elderly?

From *National Journal,* June 18, 1994, pp. 1452-1454.

Expenditures for social security, medicare and other elderly programs account for nearly half of domestic spending. And that's before the true demographic revolution—the aging of the baby boomers—has begun.

birthrates that followed the baby boom will deplete the ranks of working folks.

Although the social security trust fund is now building up substantial surpluses, in less than a decade it will begin spending more than it gets in revenues. From that point, according to the government's best estimates, it will be about 16 years before it's bankrupt—unless something is done to bail it out.

When the fund starts drawing down its surplus, Congress could find itself in a mess. That's because the surplus isn't sitting in a bank collecting interest. The government has used the money to meet other expenses, promising to repay it as needed. But meeting that promise will require raising taxes or cutting spending. By 2030, the combined cost of social security and medicare could require the equivalent of a 71 per cent increase in individual income taxes, Urban Institute researchers C. Eugene Steuerle and Jon M. Bakija say.

TIME FOR AN OVERHAUL?

Politicians already confront a growing belief among workers that the government won't honor its promise of retirement security. And academics warn that staving off disaster requires a long lead time so that the public can adjust its expectations and its financial planning.

Although gadflies have long proposed radical changes to the social security system—from doing away with it to converting it into a welfare program for the poor, the rumblings are beginning to show up in serious legislative proposals. In 1990, New York Sen. Daniel Patrick Moynihan, now the Finance Committee chairman, proposed rolling back social security tax rates to do away with the illusion that today's workers are setting aside funds for their own retirement. The mounting trust fund surplus, he argued, masks the extent of the federal budget deficit—compounding the burden on tomorrow's workers to see the baby boomers through retirement.

Others are floating proposals that are bound to provoke controversy. Rep. Dan Rostenkowski, D-Ill., has introduced a bill to address the trust fund's long-term insolvency by reducing cost-of-living increases and speeding up a planned increase in the age at which full benefits can be collected. He'd raise payroll taxes and trim benefits for the wealthy, too—but that wouldn't start until well into the next century.

Where once America worried about rescuing the elderly from poverty, today it worries about keeping its promises to tomorrow's elderly without bankrupting the young. The political and economic makeup of the nation 25 years hence will depend a good deal on how bravely and skillfully it faces the future now.

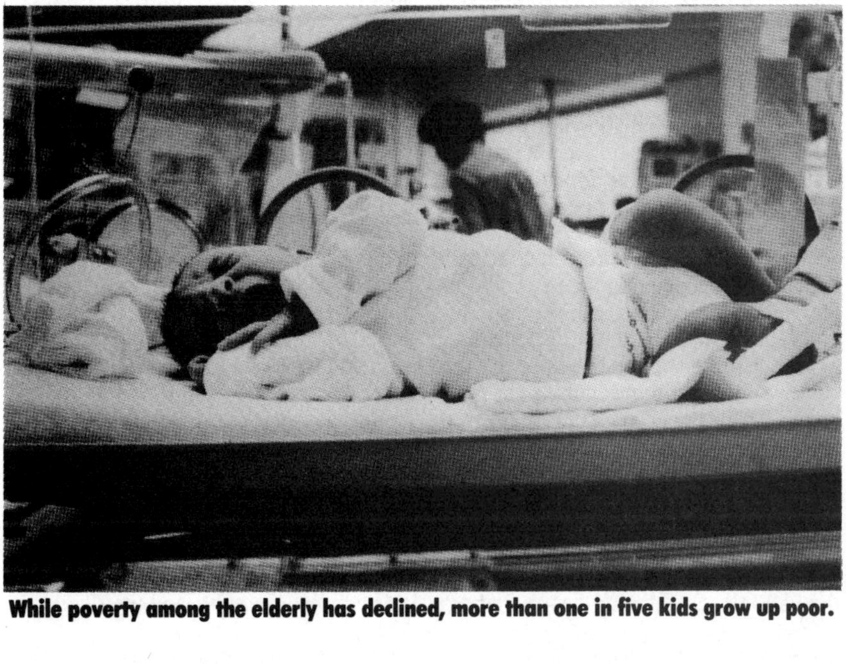

Richard A. Bloom

While poverty among the elderly has declined, more than one in five kids grow up poor.

Photos by Shepard Sherbell/SABA

Legitimate Questions

The emotionally charged issue of illegitimacy and teenage births has been thrust into the forefront of the welfare debate. Abortion may be the wild card in the legislative deck.

ELIZA NEWLIN CARNEY

Ask 18-year-old Felicia Easton if cutting cash welfare benefits would discourage her and other teen mothers from getting pregnant, and she shakes her head impatiently.

Easton, who's enrolled in a job-training program for teen mothers at the Greater Washington Urban League, answers in a single breath: "No, because some teenagers have children to keep the male friend that they're with. Other teenagers have children because they feel that they want something that'll love them back. Other teenagers have children to be accompanied by another person. It's not for the money."

Many researchers contend that Easton is right. Although welfare costs and out-of-wedlock births have both risen sharply in recent decades, there's little conclusive evidence that the cash ushers in the babies. And while some analysts place the blame for illegitimacy squarely on welfare, others point to cultural and economic factors.

But House Republicans drafting this year's welfare reform legislation have little doubt about what's amiss. Their bill fingers welfare as the principal cause of the nation's skyrocketing out-of-wedlock birthrate and targets cash cutoffs as the remedy.

This approach has thrust the emotionally charged issue of illegitimacy into the forefront of the welfare debate. More than any other issue that's central to welfare reform, illegitimacy is a subject that produces broad disagreement and extreme rhetoric on both sides.

Liberal critics have attacked the Personal Responsibility Act, the welfare reform bill that House Republicans have included in their Contract With America, as a mean-spirited and moralistic attempt at social engineering. Reductions in cash aid would do virtually nothing to reduce out-of-wedlock births, the bill's opponents say, but could force millions of children into poverty. Some have warned that a cap on aid to welfare recipients based on family size violates the Constitution and could land the law in court. *(See box, "New Jersey's Family Cap".)*

Republican governors have also resisted mandates that penalize unwed mothers as examples of federal micromanagement. The Republican bill would bar states from boosting cash aid to women who bear another child while on welfare. It would also cut off all cash benefits to unwed minor mothers and their children,

Teenage MOTHERS AND WELFARE IN AMERICA

1. The international picture

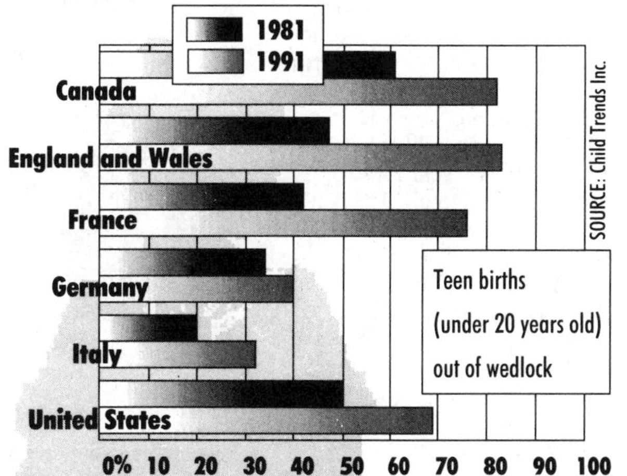

2. Teenage mothers

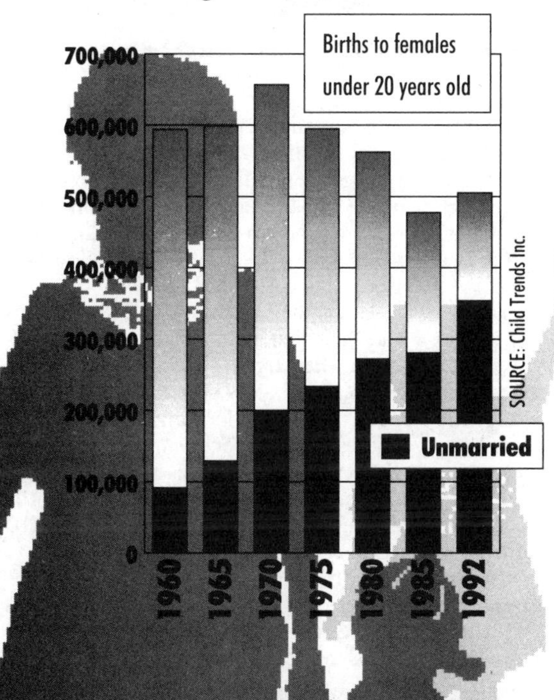

3. Unmarried mothers and AFDC

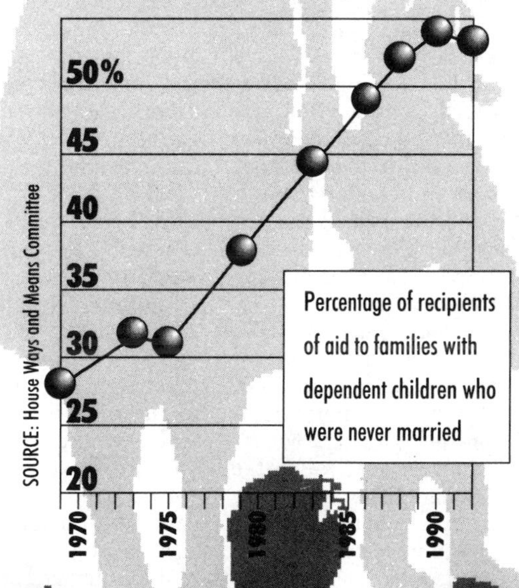

4. Poverty and single mothers

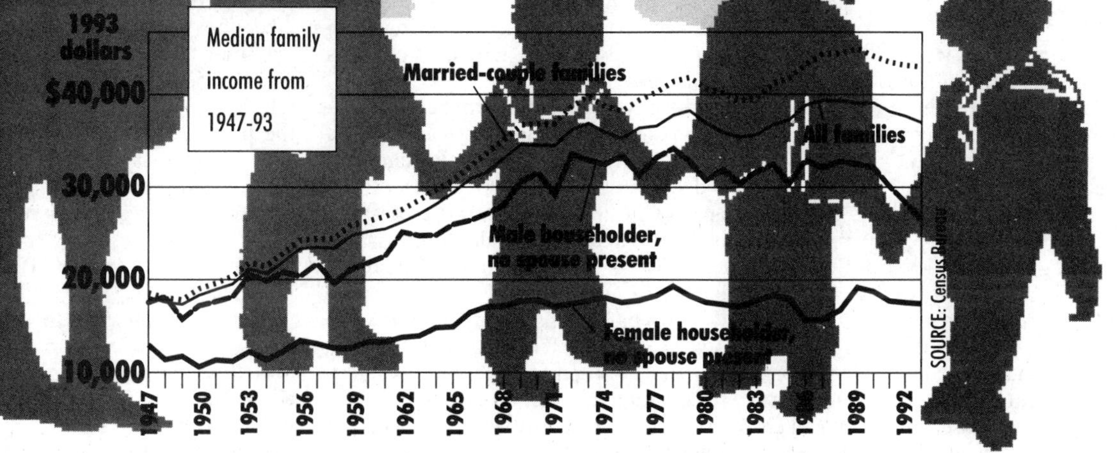

Phyllis L. Maringer

though it would leave them eligible for food aid.

Some leading Senators on the welfare issue have promised to fight the cutoffs, setting the stage for a clash over illegitimacy as the welfare debate progresses. The issue invariably raises controversial questions about sex education and abortion, and has polarized welfare reform advocates on Capitol Hill who otherwise share common ground.

Most divisive for Republicans bent on reforming welfare this year is the opposition of anti-abortion groups. The National Right to Life Committee and its allies have moved aggressively to kill proposed reductions in cash aid to unwed mothers, particularly the so-called family cap, which they argue would increase the abortion rate.

"National Right to Life believes that it is wrong to increase the number of deaths by abortion now, based on an unproven theory that this policy will somehow subsequently lead to less sex and therefore less abortion in the future," David N. O'Steen, the committee's executive director, said.

But Republican congressional leaders argue that welfare reform will have accomplished little if it doesn't address what many experts consider the core cause of poverty in the United States: an out-of-wedlock birthrate that's 30 per cent of all births and climbing. What harms children, the Republicans say, are welfare policies that effectively reward young mothers with cash for staying unemployed and unmarried.

"Birth out of wedlock is an issue whose implications are just becoming clear for our society," said Rep. Nancy L. Johnson, R-Conn., a leading welfare reform advocate who sits on the Ways and Means Committee. Teenagers need to get the message that having a baby is no easy street, she said. "To give a kid under 18 an income when she has shown that she can't manage her life is ludicrous."

REVERSING THE TREND

In tackling out-of-wedlock teen births head-on, Washington policy makers are breaking new ground in welfare reform. Until recently, most attempts to help welfare-dependent adolescent mothers have focused on education, training and family-planning services offered *after* the baby is born. By that point, even the most successful programs have lost half the battle and yield only mixed results. *(See NJ, 7/23/94, p. 1728.)*

The Republican bill, scheduled for floor action later this month, aims to *prevent* adolescent births—a tall order that's eluded social scientists and policy makers for decades. Yet even the legislation's

Some critics would restructure welfare as an employment program for both parents.

harshest critics agree that the nation's out-of-wedlock birthrate is out of control.

President Clinton, in this year's State of the Union address, called the epidemic of teen pregnancies and out-of-wedlock births "our most serious social problem" and urged community leaders to join in a national campaign to halt it.

Out-of-wedlock births to women of any age surged from 5 per cent to 30 per cent of all births from 1960-92, according to Child Trends Inc., a Washington research group. For African-Americans, the rate was 68 per cent in 1992; for whites, it was 23 per cent. By some estimates, the overall rate will climb to 40 per cent by 2000.

The trend is most dramatic among teenagers. In 1992, 70 per cent of all teenagers who gave birth that year were unmarried. In 1960, only 15 per cent were unmarried.

And while teen mothers have only 30 per cent of all out-of-wedlock births, they account for more than half of all *first* births to unmarried women, according to the Congressional Research Service (CRS). In other words, a substantial percentage of women who are giving birth out of wedlock had their first child as teenagers.

These statistics ring alarm bells for policy makers struggling to overhaul the nation's poverty programs. Researchers widely blame rising poverty rates on the upsurge in single-parent families because of divorce and out-of-wedlock births. *(See chart No. 4, p. 141.)* Children in single-parent families are likelier than those with two parents to grow up poor, to drop out of school, to have problems with the law and to become single parents themselves, numerous studies suggest.

Conservative advocates of welfare reform have zeroed in on these data, and on studies that link rising illegitimacy with burgeoning welfare rolls.

That welfare costs are up is undisputed. Aid to families with dependent children (AFDC), the nation's principal cash welfare program, served 14.1 million people in 1993—a 91 per cent increase over 1970—at a cost of $22.3 billion.

Almost half of those AFDC recipients had their first child as teenagers, according to the General Accounting Office. More than half—53 per cent in 1992—were never married, up from about 28 per cent in 1969. *(See chart No. 3, p. 141.)* A CRS study concludes that never-married mothers accounted for most of the 27 per cent increase in the AFDC caseload from 1987-91.

For most House Republicans, welfare's impact on illegitimacy is self-evident. E. Clay Shaw Jr., R-Fla., who chairs the Ways and Means Subcommittee on Human Resources, likens the existing welfare system to "federally funded child abuse." In an interview, he said that "the primary reason" for the rise in out-of-wedlock birthrates is that "welfare has taken the place of the male in the family."

Earlier this year, a parade of Republicans testifying before Shaw's subcommittee drew the same conclusion. "I think the policies of our federal government have been causing not only our teenage pregnancy problems in this country, but are also causing enormous growth in poverty," said Rep. Jan Meyers, R-Kan., who sits on the House GOP's welfare reform task force.

If young women got the message that the government cash spigot was being turned off, "fewer teenagers would make the decision to become unmarried moms," Rep. James M. Talent, R-Mo., a principal architect of the Personal

NEW JERSEY'S FAMILY CAP: A RELIABLE MODEL?

New Jersey's get-tough "family cap" law may be the nation's best-known welfare reform experiment, but it's also among the most controversial.

State officials have hailed the so-called child exclusion law as an obvious success. Enacted in 1992 as part of a broader welfare reform package, the law ends monthly benefits increases for mothers who give birth again while on welfare.

Births to welfare recipients dropped by 13 per cent in a 10-month period after the law's enactment, the state's Human Services Department maintains. This much-publicized drop has sparked a flurry of copycat child exclusion laws, which are now in effect in Arkansas, Georgia, Indiana and Wisconsin.

Seven more states have sought federal approval to enact similar laws, and House Republicans propose a family cap in their welfare reform bill.

But New Jersey's 13 per cent figure has been assailed by researchers who say that the numbers don't add up. Civil liberties and women's groups have sued the federal government on behalf of 23 low-income individuals for allowing New Jersey to enact the cap. The suit, which is before a U.S. district court judge in New Jersey, may pave the way for a constitutional challenge if Congress approves a national family cap.

The law violates the Constitution's equal protection and due process clauses, said Martha Davis, a senior staff lawyer with the New York City-based NOW Legal Defense and Education Fund, which is a party to the suit. (New Jersey abortion opponents filed a friend-of-the-court brief.)

The cap "is a government attempt to coerce women to forgo childbirth, and if they do conceive, to have an abortion," Davis said. It violates the equal protection clause because it treats women on welfare "differently from all other women," she said, and it denies due process to children affected by the cap by punishing them for parental behavior over which they have no control.

The Supreme Court has rejected similar attempts to penalize children born out of wedlock, according to a recent statement signed by 470 law professors concerned about the Republican welfare bill. Child exclusion provisions "appear to raise equal protection concerns," the statement said.

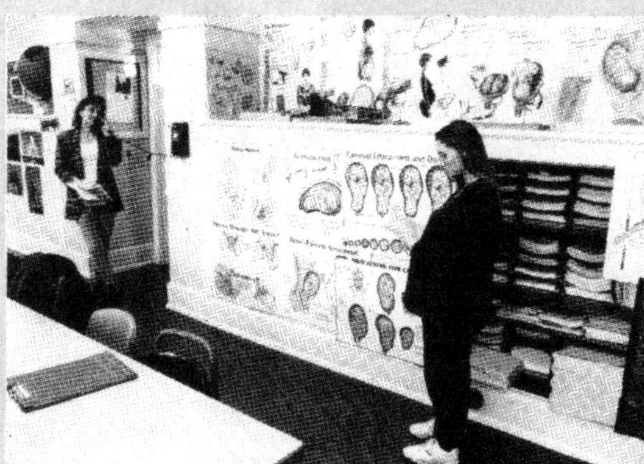

Is denying aid to repeat mothers unconstitutional?

The Health and Human Services Department, in a brief, denied that New Jersey's law violated the Constitution.

New Jersey, in bragging about the 13 per cent reduction in births to welfare mothers, ignores the law's effects on welfare recipients whose birthrates have not declined, child welfare advocates say. They warn that the bulk of families on welfare now face greater hardship.

New Jersey officials caution that numbers showing a 13 per cent birthratedrop are not conclusive and may reflect other factors. "This is raw data; it is preliminary," state Human Services Department spokeswoman Jacqueline Tencza stressed.

Much of the reduction may actually be due to a parallel birthrate decline in New Jersey's general population, according to a study made public last year by Michael C. Laracy, who was then a fellow at the Center on Budget and Policy Priorities. (A former policy director for New Jersey's Human Services Department, Laracy is now a senior program associate at the Annie E. Casey Foundation in Baltimore.)

Laracy also questions a more recent, higher estimate by Robert Rector, a senior policy analyst at the Heritage Foundation who helped to write the Republican welfare reform bill. In a paper made public last month, Rector projects New Jersey's birthrate reduction at a dramatic 29 per cent.

That estimate is based on data that June O'Neill, at the time a professor of economics and finance at the Baruch College of the City University of New York, prepared as an expert witness in the New Jersey lawsuit. O'Neill, who declined to comment, is now director of the Congressional Budget Office.

Laracy argues that Rector has "totally distorted" O'Neill's findings, in part because New Jersey officials are sticking to the 13 per cent estimate for now. The Rutgers University School of Social Work is evaluating the law's impact at the state's request, but those results are not yet available.

Rector defended O'Neill's findings, but he said that even if the birthrate reduction hadn't shown up, the policy would be justified. "I support the family cap simply because it's morally correct," he said in an interview. "You need to send a message of moral responsibility that says, 'We will not give you more welfare if you become a larger burden on society.'"

Tencza concurs. "The family cap wasn't necessarily meant to reduce births to women on welfare," she noted. "The intent of it was to send a responsibility message."

Responsibility Act, said. In his testimony, he also underscored the issue's moral dimension:

"As a society, we ought to begin to move toward stigmatizing behavior. And I think there's a way we can do that without stigmatizing people."

To carry out the contract's promise "to diminish the number of teenage pregnancies and illegitimate births," the Republican bill would ban cash welfare for children of unmarried women 17 and younger. (States could still offer assistance through their own funds.) As introduced, the legislation would have made the ban permanent for the child's lifetime, but the Ways and Means Committee, under pressure from critics, voted to remove the prohibition when the mother turns 18.

The measure would also reduce cash benefits for a mother who has not identified her child's father, impose tough new child support provisions and—perhaps most controversial—cap cash benefits for welfare recipients who bear more children while on welfare.

NOT SO SIMPLE

But if curbing teen births were as simple as withholding cash, it would have been done long ago, child welfare advocates say. If welfare plays a role in out-of-wedlock births, they argue, it's a marginal one. The primary factors, they say, are cultural and economic.

Changing mores in the past three decades have dramatically driven up out-of-wedlock births for middle-income Americans as well as for the poor. Out-of-wedlock births are also rising in industrialized nations worldwide, and some European countries top the United States in the percentage of teen births that are out of wedlock. *(See chart No. 1, p. 141.)*

Meanwhile, a shifting industrial base that has gutted the low-wage job market has dimmed the marriage prospects for many low-income women.

Teen birth statistics, moreover, tell a complex story. The actual teen birthrate has, in fact, declined in recent decades. Teenagers 25 years ago weren't having fewer children than they are today; they were just likelier to get married before giving birth. *(See chart No. 2, p. 141.)* In the meantime, middle-class women have been delaying marriage and having fewer children. That means that even if out-of-wedlock teen births had remained static for 30 years, they'd still represent a larger percentage of all births today.

"The argument that teenage childbearing is caused by welfare suggests that these girls are on some level planning their pregnancies," said Kristin A. Moore, executive director and director of research for Child Trends Inc. "And study after study shows that they don't."

Though welfare costs and out-of-wedlock births are soaring, there's little firm evidence that the cash ushers in the babies.

Children who have children are likely to be failing in a wide range of other areas, specialists who work closely with adolescents say. Many lack firm goals or a sense of hope for the future. A startlingly high number report having been abused at home or coerced into sex by men in their 20s, suggesting that incentives aimed at women miss part of the picture.

Nevertheless, social scientists acknowledge that cash-based penalties may, in fact, cause a modest dip in the out-of-wedlock birthrate. Some studies conclude that welfare does have a small but significant impact on illegitimacy, particularly among white and Hispanic women. But family caps and cash cutoffs could also drastically increase poverty in the welfare population, critics warn.

The "suitable home" rules enacted in the 1950s and early 1960s also sought to discourage illegitimacy and unwed live-in arrangements, but to disastrous effect, children's advocates say. Nine states, most of them in the South, adopted laws that denied aid to children living in homes deemed "unsuitable" for a variety of reasons, including promiscuity and the birth of an illegitimate child.

Thousands of children were dropped from the rolls, and the hardship that excluded families felt was so severe that the federal government stepped in, according to an account by Winifred Bell in *Aid to Dependent Children* (Columbia University Press, 1965); it cut off federal welfare grants for any state that sought to deny benefits to a child "because of the behavior of his parent or other relative."

This year's Republican bill would make five million children ineligible for welfare, the Center on Budget and Policy Priorities estimates. The bill's proposed cash penalties "essentially say that there are some poor children for whom the federal government will withdraw a safety net," center research associate Sharon Parrott said. "There is very little evidence that this will have any kind of large impact on out-of-wedlock childbearing and very significant evidence that it will cause a tremendous amount of hardship among very poor families with children."

ABORTION WARS

Some conservatives agree. The Republican welfare bill has driven a wedge in conservative ranks by mobilizing anti-

Opposition of anti-abortion groups hurts Republican welfare reformers this year.

abortion activists who warn that cash penalties will encourage abortions.

"We think it's implausible that a change in welfare law will decrease teen sexuality while you have abortion-on-demand available, and while other cultural factors—the content of television, movies, music, value-neutral education, etc.—remain in place," the National Right to Life Committee's O'Steen said. "It just doesn't seem to make sense to us."

Key anti-abortion lawmakers on Capitol Hill, including Republican Reps. Henry J. Hyde of Illinois and Christopher H. Smith of New Jersey, have also denounced the bill's cash cutoffs. Smith is working closely with the Right to Life Committee, the U.S. Conference of Catholic Bishops, Catholic Charities USA and Feminists for Life to galvanize anti-abortion voters.

The last two organizations have also formed an uncharacteristic alliance with abortion-rights groups through the Child Exclusion Task Force, a lobbying coalition co-chaired by the American Civil Liberties Union (ACLU) and the NOW Legal Defense and Education Fund, both based in New York City. The task force has assisted in a legal challenge to New Jersey's family cap and is fighting the cash penalties in the Republican welfare bill through the ACLU's Washington office.

Anti-abortion forces have targeted 40 freshman Republicans whom they've identified as abortion opponents—more than half the freshman Republican class—in a bid to sway the bill's key support bloc.

They have an ally in Rep. Jim Bunn, R-Ore., who refused to sign the Contract With America because its proposed cutoff of cash welfare for unmarried mothers raised abortion concerns. Welfare reform "must not push young women to undergo abortions, in my opinion the ultimate denial of personal responsibility," Bunn said in testimony before Shaw's subcommittee earlier this year.

Ways and Means Committee members who marked up the bill tied themselves in knots in an attempt to defuse the abortion controversy. The committee wrote a complex formula into the bill that would effectively offer cash bonus rewards to states that reduce both out-of-wedlock birth and abortion rates.

But abortion opponents warn that the formula could backfire and abortions could go up anyway because adolescents are unlikely to know or care about state bonuses.

"We don't think that the government should be in the business of coercing women into abortions that they wouldn't otherwise have, because of economic pressures," said Sharon M. Daly, deputy director of Catholic Charities USA.

The Ways and Means Committee's bill aims to encourage adoptions through a $5,000 tax credit and an easing of restrictions on interracial adoptions. But Daly warned that funds available for adoption are likely to shrink because of the plan to roll the money into capped block grants that wouldn't rise with inflation or increased demand.

COMMON GROUND

If social scientists are correct that welfare curbs won't do much to change teen behavior, these abortion fears may be overstated. But the House Republicans' focus on illegitimacy, some on Capitol Hill complain, diverts attention from work requirements and other less disputed reforms.

In the Senate, cash penalties for unwed minor teens are controversial and likely to meet resistance. The two influential Kansas Senators, Majority Leader Robert Dole and Nancy Landon Kassebaum, who chairs the Labor and Human Resources Committee, have criticized penalty-based approaches.

Likelier to win broad consensus are incentives that would deny teen mothers benefits unless they stay in school, live at home or under adult supervision and identify the father. Although no state has sought federal approval to cut off cash aid to unwed minors, several have imposed sanctions aimed at discouraging teenagers from dropping out or living on their own.

Clinton's welfare reform bill, the 1994 Work and Responsibility Act, would also have imposed stay-at-home and other conditions on teens seeking cash benefits. It would also have made family caps a state option; many on Capitol Hill say that the Republican bill should do the same.

"Let the states wrestle with it," said Sen. Charles E. Grassley, R-Iowa, who has introduced welfare reform legislation that would reward states that reduce their out-of-wedlock birthrates with unrestricted block grants. "It is the states, not the federal government, that [have] the proven track record."

Tougher child support laws, another cornerstone of Clinton's bill, have also won broad bipartisan support. (This year, Clinton has sought to reclaim the issue with a crackdown on "deadbeat" federal employees.)

"We want this bill to be every bit as tough on men as it is on women," Rep. Johnson said. Adolescent males would be less eager to father children, she argues, if they knew that they'd be forced to support them. Less than a sixth of mothers on welfare report receiving formal child support.

Johnson and a coalition of moderate women, including Rep. Barbara B. Kennelly, D-Conn., helped to push through a package of sweeping child support amendments to the Ways and Means bill. But the committee rejected a Kennelly amendment that would have allowed states to withhold driver's and professional licenses from deadbeat parents. Kennelly will work to attach the amendment to the bill when it reaches the House floor, an aide said.

Johnson, too, advocates job training and placement for adolescent fathers who may have the will but not the means to support their children. She has urged that

In tackling out-of-wedlock teen births head-on, Washington policy makers are breaking new ground in welfare reform.

the bill include school attendance and work requirements for adolescent fathers as well as mothers.

Helping adolescent men is a key to reducing out-of-wedlock births, welfare policy experts say. As long as welfare remains a program primarily for single mothers, some analysts say, it will implicitly condone families with a missing father.

A better approach would be to restructure welfare as an employment program for both fathers and mothers, said S. Anna Kondratas, a senior fellow in the Indianapolis-based Hudson Institute's Washington office. Kondratas is working with Wisconsin legislators, who have agreed to abolish AFDC by 1997, on an alternative model built on work-based programs for both parents.

BEYOND WELFARE

But for all the attacks on the House Republicans' approach to illegitimacy, critics have been slow to formulate alternatives.

Democratic leaders have denounced the Republican bill as soft on work requirements and hard on children but have yet to introduce their own bill. (The Democratic alternative, which party leaders have said is in the offing, is expected to build on last year's Clinton bill in its approach to teen pregnancy.)

Child-welfare advocates tend to tout programs that assist teen mothers after the fact. And traditional liberal solutions that emphasize family planning and birth control, child care, health care and job training have lost political credibility now that conservatives control the welfare debate.

"The liberal thrust has always been that cash and services take care of these things, and they have continuously failed," said Patrick F. Fagan, a senior policy analyst at the Heritage Foundation who specializes in family and community issues. "And to this date, the liberal critique and the liberal counterproposal is an expansion of cash and services. There's no reform there."

Part of what's stumping the critics is that the teen pregnancy debate goes far beyond welfare policy. It's about good schools, safe neighborhoods and a strong job market. In developing countries, teen births go down when young women's educational and economic options go up, family-planning experts say. They maintain that this applies in the United States as well.

"It's been said that the best contraceptive device is a job," Jodie Levin-Epstein, senior state policy analyst at the Center for Law and Social Policy, said.

Congress may be prepared to tackle education, crime and economic policy too, but not in the context of welfare reform. In the meantime, advocates on both sides of the issue applaud Clinton's promise to use the White House as a bully pulpit in a campaign against teen pregnancies.

Ironically, the President had hoped that obstetrician-gynecologist Henry Foster Jr., his nominee for Surgeon General, could lead the campaign against teen pregnancies. Foster has won national attention for his abstinence-based "I Have a Future" program at Nashville's Meharry Medical College. But Foster is under attack for performing abortions and for alleged lapses in medical ethics—underscoring how easily the teen pregnancy debate lands in controversial territory.

But Clinton's call for a private-sector mobilization against teen pregnancy has been taken up by corporate lawyer Jodi Greenstone. Greenstone, a former special assistant to Clinton and deputy to ex-White House counselor David R. Gergen, recently began recruiting business, community service, news media, religious and education leaders to help spearhead such an effort.

Greenstone envisions a campaign modeled after the Partnership for a Drug Free America that would discourage teen pregnancy through public service announcements, act as an information clearinghouse and possibly offer grants for community-based programs.

Welfare reform advocates on the Left and the Right agree that the message to teens must be clear: Don't bring a child into the world whom you can't support. It's a message that Felicia Easton may wish she had heard more clearly before she had her son last year.

"Before I got pregnant, I was going into the military," she said. "I was going to establish myself a career in the military. But when I had my son, I just knew all that was going down the hill."

Test Drive

Welfare reform will undoubtedly be a hot-button issue in the 104th Congress. But while Washington talks, governors and state legislatures from coast to coast have been aggressively experimenting with reforms. So far, though, the view from the states is disappointingly hazy.

ELIZA NEWLIN CARNEY

DETROIT—Every day Kiki Joyce, 19, makes her way through a neighborhood of boarded-up houses and trash-strewn parks to attend class at a big, modern school building downtown.

Joyce has long wanted to earn her general educational development (GED) degree—her high school education was interrupted by her two children, now 4 and 5—and get off welfare.

But right now Joyce's class time isn't filled with multiplication tables, history or grammar. She's learning how to dress for a job interview, express herself clearly and get places on time, along with 20 or so other welfare recipients in her class, which is run by CareerWorks Inc., a Detroit-based job-training firm.

Joyce still hopes to get her GED. But new welfare rules in Michigan require that she work at least 20 hours a week or lose her benefits, and Joyce has caught on quickly. "I know that getting a job is first," she said. "Education will always be there."

Joyce is one of thousands of welfare recipients in Michigan who are being funneled into jobs, job placement and training as part of the state's most recent welfare reform effort—aptly dubbed "Work First." The program, which is one element of a reform package that was launched statewide in 1992, has drawn fire from advocacy groups worried that the new rules will in fact prevent young mothers such as Joyce from completing their educations.

But Republican Gov. John M. Engler has trumpeted the state's reform experiment as a national model. Engler says that Michigan's reforms have saved taxpayers $22 million, reduced the number of families seeking assistance and boosted the percentage of welfare recipients who are working from 15 per cent to more than 24 per cent.

Engler isn't alone. From New Jersey to Oregon, governors and state legislatures have embraced welfare reform experiments with gusto. Many are well into approaches that still are just rhetoric in Washington, among them work incentives, penalties for parents whose children don't attend school and two-year time limits for welfare benefits.

Some advocates for low-income families fear that state experiments have gone too far, creating a hodgepodge of poorly monitored programs that will put children at risk. More-conservative critics say that the reforms don't go far enough, amount to little more than public relations and are tinkering at the edges of a badly broken welfare system.

Whatever their pet solutions to the welfare crisis, Engler and other governors are eager to take the ball and run with it. At the Republican Governors Association meeting in Williamsburg, Va., last month, GOP governors issued a clear warning to Washington on welfare reform: Leave the states alone.

"The states should be freed to experiment with welfare reform in 50 different state laboratories," Engler said in an interview. "One strategy dictated from Washington and micromanaged by the federal bureaucracy simply will fail."

State legislators may not win the freedom they seek, but they've promised to resist any legislation from Washington that ties their hands too tightly. Either way, state welfare reforms are providing both an inspiration and a reality check for lawmakers on Capitol Hill.

CARROTS AND STICKS

So far, the view from the states is disappointingly hazy. Most of the experiments are too young to have yielded concrete results. Although states have long been able to test new approaches to welfare, the state reform craze didn't hit its stride until the 1990s. Evaluations have barely begun, and many states are pursuing so many tracks at once that clear results may prove elusive. *(See box.)*

States have been on the welfare system's front lines since 1935, when the Social Security Act established aid to dependent children—now aid to families with dependent children (AFDC)—as a way to give cash assistance to families without fathers.

In addition to administering a host of

REFORM ROULETTE: WHAT THE STATES ARE DOING

Welfare reform is still just talk on Capitol Hill, but it's already well under way in the states, where virtually every governor has pledged to radically overhaul public assistance.

Welfare experiments are in progress in more than 40 states, although most are too new to have yielded clear results.

Just what are the states up to? Here's a look at what some are doing:

California: Regarded as one of the most successful state welfare experiments, California's Greater Avenues to Independence (GAIN) program, launched in 1989, is a mandatory welfare-to-work program that combines education, training and job search services. The program emphasizes basic mathematics and reading for high school dropouts. Other reform experiments under way in California include a requirement that teenage mothers who haven't completed high school attend the state's "Cal Learn" education program, with a $100 reward for grades above a C and a $100 penalty for D's or F's.

Colorado: A pilot project in five counties requires mothers to immunize children under 2, and offers a $500 reward for a high school diploma or a general equivalency degree earned while in the program. Participants get to keep the first $120 of their monthly earnings, plus 58 per cent of any additional earned income. Able-bodied parents are required to work or attend job training after two years. Food stamps, cash grants and child care are rolled into a monthly payment, with the aim of teaching money management.

Florida: Florida's Project Independence, a statewide job-training program initiated in 1989, mandates immediate entry into the work force or job training, even for single parents with pre-school-age children. Also in the works in Florida is a two-county demonstration project that limits families to two years of benefits, requires dropouts under 18 to attend high school, offers training as an alternative to cash assistance and allows families to keep up to $5,000 in savings.

Iowa: Iowa is encouraging welfare recipients to work and build up savings through "individual development accounts," from which they can make withdrawals only to start a business, buy a home, pursue education or job training or take care of a family emergency. The state also requires participants to sign an agreement that identifies the date on which they'll leave the aid to families with dependent children (AFDC) program.

New Jersey: New Jersey faces a lawsuit from state advocacy groups for its "family cap" provision, which denies additional benefits to mothers who have a child while receiving AFDC. The state also allows welfare recipients who are working to keep a higher percentage of their earnings than allowed under current law. A welfare parent who gets married does not lose benefits, even if the spouse is working.

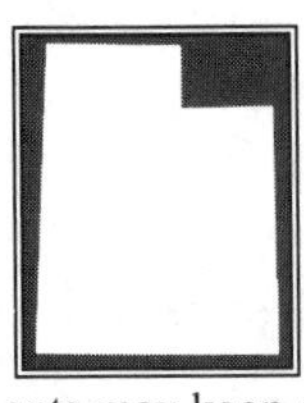

Utah: Utah requires all able-bodied AFDC parents and children older than 16 to participate in activities designed to get them ready for jobs. Recipients may keep a larger portion of their earned income and still receive benefits. AFDC applicants with good job prospects may receive a onetime cash grant, and short-term medical and child care, in lieu of permanently joining the welfare rolls.

Vermont: In an experiment that mimics the two-year time limit in President Clinton's welfare reform bill, Vermont has launched a statewide pilot project that limits participants to 30 months on AFDC. After that, they must go to work or take a government-subsidized community service job. Teenage recipients with children must live with their parents or in a supervised setting.

Wisconsin: Wisconsin is testing a host of reforms, including a family cap, a two-year time limit, a 20-hours-a-week work requirement and different benefit levels for residents moving in from another state. A pilot project would allow up to $10,000 in a restricted savings account. The Legislature has also agreed to abolish AFDC by 1999 and replace it with a new welfare program now in the planning stage.

complex programs, states are required to help pay for AFDC and medicaid. (Food stamps are federally financed.) The state share of AFDC and medicaid ranges from 20-50 per cent.

As caseloads and costs have burgeoned in the past two decades, states have grappled with the welfare monster up close. The number of AFDC recipients surged from 7.4 million in 1970 to 14.1 million in 1993, an increase of 91 per cent. AFDC expenditures (adjusted for inflation) went up 44 per cent in that time, from $15.5 billion to $22.3 billion.

Governors have technically had room to experiment since 1962, when an amendment to the Social Security Act gave states permission to seek waivers of the federal rules to conduct welfare pilot projects. But the state reform movement didn't start percolating until the 1980s, when President Reagan launched a push for work-based reforms and Congress granted states new leeway to impose job requirements on welfare recipients.

The resulting welfare-to-work programs formed the basis of the most recent welfare overhaul, the 1988 Family Support Act, which sought to redefine welfare as a transition to work through the Job Opportunities and Basic Skills (JOBS) program.

JOBS was supposed to move welfare recipients into the work force through government-financed placement, education and training programs. But tight budgets in the 1980s prevented states from fully matching federal funds for JOBS, and results have been spotty. That's led states to seek a host of other solutions, spurred in part by easier access to waivers during the Bush Administration.

Since President Clinton took office, the stream of waiver applications has swelled to a flood. The Clinton Administration has granted waivers to 20 states for welfare demonstration projects, from school attendance requirements in Arkansas for AFDC parents under 16 to a cash bonus in California for teenage mothers who get good grades. All but two states now are conducting some form of welfare experiment.

While it's too early to draw sharp conclusions, some points of consensus have emerged. The biggest barriers to work, many state legislators agree, are federal welfare rules that reduce benefits dollar-for-dollar against earnings. (Under current rules, welfare recipients generally may keep $30 of earnings a month for the first year on assistance.)

Accordingly, states are testing a host of incentives that attempt to "make work pay" by letting welfare recipients keep more of what they earn, build up their savings and own a better car. (Current rules prevent AFDC recipients from having more than $1,000 in savings or owning a car that's worth more than $1,500.) Some states are experimenting with restricted savings accounts that encourage recipients to invest in education or work training.

Also widely tested are measures aimed at eliminating what amounts to a marriage penalty: the current federal regulations that require two-parent households to be dropped from public assistance if one member of the family works more than 100 hours a month. Many states are also experimenting with new techniques of wringing child support from "deadbeat" spouses and providing extended child care and health care services to welfare recipients who work.

More controversial are a number of penalty-based reforms, including the two-year time limit that is the centerpiece of the Administration's welfare reform bill (the 1994 Work and Responsibility Act) and sanctions for behavior disapproved by the state. Some waivers—including a cap on family size in New Jersey and laws in California and Wisconsin that pay different benefits to recipients who move in from out of state—have even drawn court challenges.

To Republican leaders on Capitol Hill, the most sweeping state reforms are the most promising. The Personal Responsibility Act, the welfare reform bill proposed in the House GOP's "Contract With America," builds on the concept of the family-size cap to tackle what many Republicans see as the heart of the welfare problem: illegitimacy. Much in the Republican bill, however, goes far beyond what states have sought to test.

The legislation would end aid to most noncitizens, would require mothers to establish paternity as a condition of receiving AFDC and would cut off benefits to the illegitimate children of minor mothers. It would also allow states to spend welfare money on adoptions, orphanages and supervised group homes for teen mothers.

John Eisele

Mark Greenberg, a senior staff attorney at the Center for Law and Social Policy
It's not "a matter of federal indifference whether a state assists poor families."

Such proposals have rung alarm bells among advocates for low-income families, and even among many governors. State legislators argue that noncitizens or young mothers cut off from welfare will simply turn up elsewhere in the system, taxing state programs that serve the hungry, the homeless and abused or neglected children.

On the flip side, the Republican plan would allow states to opt out of AFDC altogether and instead craft their own welfare programs, which would be financed by fixed annual block grants. The proposal echoes the approach taken in Wisconsin, which, in addition to an ambitious series of welfare reforms already under way, plans to abolish AFDC by 1999 and replace it with a brand-new system.

Some on Capitol Hill see state autonomy as the key to welfare reform. Sen. Nancy Landon Kassebaum, R-Kan., has introduced legislation that would effect a "swap" between the states and the federal government. The federal government would take over medicaid; states would take over the cost and responsibility for administering AFDC.

"Much of the framework for welfare [reform] is in place," Kassebaum said. "And each state, and state legislators, are going to feel some responsibility for making sure that it's working."

Democrats, too, are warming to the idea of state autonomy. Inspired in part by his state's approach, Sen. Herbert H. Kohl, D-Wis., has introduced legislation that, like the GOP's Personal Responsibility Act, would block-grant AFDC and most food stamp money to the states. (Food stamps for the disabled and the elderly would stay in place, and the supplemental feeding program for women, infants and children would be expanded.)

"If we simply design another federal program, one size fits all," Kohl said, "the danger is awfully great that we will be right back where we are now in a few years, trying to fix the welfare program."

Not everyone agrees that states should have free rein. Many experts argue that full state autonomy would be a backward-looking reform and would create drastic variations in welfare benefits from state to state.

Economic downturns, some advocates for the needy fear, could tempt state legislators to sharply reduce public assistance. States also might compete to have the least-generous program to discourage low-income families from moving in from other states, they warn.

"There's an important distinction between trying to encourage state creativity in welfare reform efforts and saying that it's a matter of federal indifference whether a state assists poor families," said Mark Greenberg, a senior staff attorney at the Center for Law and Social Policy.

The Administration, too, favors national legislation as a way to ensure a minimum standard of help for needy families. At the same time, though, its reform bill also puts a premium on state flexibility. The bill would set aside money for state demonstration programs and give states the freedom to pursue a host of rule

Richard A. Bloom

S. Anna Kondratas of the Hudson Institute "You can't have AFDC reform working in a vacuum . . ."

changes, including caps on family size. It's this philosophy of state freedom that's led the Administration to approve so many waivers.

"What the waiver demonstrations represent is a recognition on the part of the states, just as there is a recognition on the part of the federal government, that there need to be some pretty dramatic changes in the welfare system," said Mary Jo Bane, the assistant Health and Human Services (HHS) secretary in charge of the Administration for Children and Families.

Advocates of state flexibility argue that the states are in the best position to fix welfare: Reforms that work in New York, they say, will have little application in Wyoming, and vice versa. Governors won't want to put families in jeopardy, the argument goes, because if they do, it's the states that will have to pick up the pieces.

"It's easy to be concerned that somehow states will go the wrong way," Sheri E. Steisel, the human services committee director of the National Conference of State Legislatures, said. "But it's not in states' interests to suddenly have a group of people who are homeless. It's not in states' interest to have a group of children who are in foster care. Foster care is more expensive than AFDC."

To hear the governors tell it, welfare reform in the states is one success story after another:

- In New Jersey, state officials point to nearly a 10 per cent reduction in the number of children born to AFDC families following implementation of the 1992 "family cap" law, which prohibits additional benefits to welfare mothers who have more children.
- In Iowa, a statewide reform package has reduced the average monthly size of AFDC grants from $374 to $249 since 1993, state officials maintain. Among other reforms, Iowa requires AFDC recipients to sign and stick to a "family investment agreement" that maps out steps to employment. Its reforms are also credited with lifting the percentage of two-parent families on AFDC from 7 to 10 per cent.
- In Utah, a demonstration project aimed at putting families to work and boosting family incomes has reduced the AFDC caseload by as much as 30 per cent in some areas, state officials say. Utah legislators also point to a rise in the number of AFDC clients who are working, from 18 to 25 per cent. (The national average is about 8 per cent.)

"There's been a real culture change," said William S. Biggs, the coordinator of the Single Parent Employment Demonstration Program at Utah's Human Services Department. "The line staff feel that they're really helping participants. They see participants moving into jobs. They see participants having increased income."

CAUTIONARY TALES

But many welfare policy analysts are skeptical of the states' success claims. The reform efforts tend to be long on public relations, they say, and short on public policy. New Jersey's reduction in the AFDC birthrate, for example, has been questioned by researchers who point out that the state has seen an over-all decline in family size.

The biggest problem facing state legislators is that it remains tremendously costly, in time and in money, to get young mothers with infants into the work force. Ironically, it often proves cheaper to simply write a welfare check than it does to furnish welfare recipients with day care, transportation and training.

"Every state runs its 'gee whiz' training programs, and every single one of them is a flop," said Robert Rector, the senior policy analyst for welfare issues at the Heritage Foundation, a conservative think tank.

Liberal critics are just as unhappy. Advocates for low-income families complain that the Administration has granted a plethora of waivers with little opportunity for public comment and with little thought to the impact on children of such controversial reforms as family caps and rigid time limits.

"Welfare reform is happening all over the country without Congress having held one markup session, and it is proceeding in a very chaotic and uncoordinated way," said Jennifer A. Vasiloff, the executive director of the Coalition on Human Needs, a group of liberal advocacy organizations.

HHS's Bane countered that the Administration has been careful to approve only waivers that are consistent with its welfare reform bill, that retain a safety net for families and that promise to yield concrete results. Federal rules require state waiver demonstration projects to be cost-neutral and to incorporate control groups.

But the sweeping approaches to welfare reform in the states may make credible evaluations virtually impossible, said Gary Burtless, an economist and senior fellow at the Brookings Institution who specializes in labor and social policy issues. Indeed, some states are carrying out as many as 40 waiver experiments at once. Too many variables, Burtless argues, make it impossible to isolate the approaches that work. "We are left with a laboratory," he said, "in which all results are inconclusive."

Not all welfare experiments, however, have been conducted in a vacuum. Those with the most concrete results are the early pilot projects initiated in the late 1980s, including California's Greater Avenues to Independence (GAIN) program, the nation's largest JOBS program, and a similar welfare-to-work program in Florida called Project Independence.

Evaluations by the New York City-based Manpower Demonstration Research Corp. (MDRC), a not-for-profit organization that field-tests public programs, found that both programs boosted the number of welfare clients in the work force, improved recipients' earnings and reduced their dependence on public assistance.

But as in other state experiments that MDRC has studied, welfare caseloads were not reduced dramatically, and costs remained high. Even in California, which is widely cited as a welfare success story, savings were not across-the-board. The

GAIN program more than paid for itself in two of six counties studied and broke even in a third over a five-year period. But in the other three counties, GAIN failed to save money. *(For more on GAIN, see NJ, 1/15/94, p. 111).*

Some experts point to measurable successes in California and Florida as evidence that the JOBS program is working and argue that it should be fully financed before policy makers launch into a whole new round of reforms. Indeed, most state welfare experiments build heavily on the training and education infrastructure created by JOBS.

THROW IT OUT

There's a growing impatience on Capitol Hill, though, and even in some state legislatures, with reforms that fail to drastically overhaul the system. Critics of state JOBS programs complain that they invest heavily in education and training with only a 10-15 per cent reduction in caseloads.

"One of the most important lessons we've learned [from the states] is the limits of the work-oriented approaches that have been tried up to now," Burtless said. "We haven't discovered penicillin. We've discovered aspirin, I suppose."

And for welfare reform advocates on Capitol Hill, especially Republicans, aspirin isn't enough. Among their most popular models is Wisconsin, which has attracted national attention because of Republican Gov. Tommy G. Thompson's promise to get rid of AFDC entirely by 1999.

Wisconsin already has waivers to test several approaches, including a two-year time limit, a cap on benefits for AFDC parents who have more children and a two-tiered benefits system based on residency. Now Thompson wants to scrap the whole system and start again.

"Anything you do is going to be an improvement," Thompson said in an interview. "And the more radically you try to change it, the better off you are going to be for the recipient, [and] for the state."

With the help of the Indianapolis-based Hudson Institute, Wisconsin is laying the groundwork for a host of new public assistance rules, some of which are being tried in other states. These include more partnerships with local businesses to train and place workers and the consolidation of job-training programs.

More broadly, Wisconsin is considering a redefinition of the welfare population to include not just single mothers with children, but also anyone who needs assistance. The idea would be to avoid government rewards for single-parent families. Like several other states, Wisconsin is also looking at ways to bring health care, child care, job training and other public assistance programs under a single roof.

"You can't have AFDC reform working in a vacuum in areas that are severely distressed," said S. Anna Kondratas, a senior fellow in the Hudson Institute's Washington office.

Among other provisions, the state requires all families receiving welfare to sign a "social contract" in which they pledge either to work, go to school or volunteer in the community for at least 20 hours a week. Recipients who refuse to participate are phased off welfare.

For applicants entering the welfare system for the first time, the rules are even stricter. Able-bodied new recipients must work at a private-sector job paying the minimum wage for at least 20 hours a week. An early result, according to Michigan caseworkers, is that some prospective recipients are calling up to cancel interviews with the news that they've already found work. Other welfare seekers are showing up at state agencies dressed for job interviews.

Eliza Newlin Carney

Gerald H. Miller, the director of the Michigan Social Services Department "Conservative micromanagement is just as bad as liberal micromanagement."

Some policy makers are hoping that Wisconsin will become a national model for welfare reform. Those who want Congress to turn the welfare system on its head, however, may meet their strongest opposition in the states. State legislators have criticized the bills on Washington's table so far, whether Democratic or Republican, as overly complex, bureaucratic and intrusive.

Many governors see Clinton's proposal to cut off aid to welfare families after two years as too rigid. States with poor economies could be left holding the bag, they argue. At the same time, Republican proposals to cut off most noncitizens and minor mothers of illegitimate children have drawn fire from state legislators as overly proscriptive.

"Conservative micromanagement is just as bad as liberal micromanagement," Gerald H. Miller, the director of the Michigan Social Services Department, said. "The issue here in welfare reform is to get people a job and off of public assistance."

From Miller's point of view, contentious debates over illegitimacy simply divert attention from the primary focus of welfare reform, which is to get people working. In Michigan, legislators say that their statewide experiment, which combines incentives and penalties for welfare families, is doing just that.

"We'll stand by our results," said Miller, who questions whether a two-year time limit on welfare would work in Michigan. "You have to recognize the reality of the economy we live in. If you go over to Wal-Mart now, you know what you're going to get offered? You're going to get offered 19 1/2 hours a week. And you know why? Because they don't want to have to pay benefits. That's the real world."

Whatever Congress may do, Michigan legislators want the freedom to complete the welfare reform experiments that they've launched. That would suit Kiki Joyce just fine. She has no complaints that the state forced her into job-training classes, and she has high hopes for a career in nursing.

"They're giving us a chance," Joyce said. "And if you don't take that chance, you will be one of the ones left without anything."

THE GOOD, THE BAD AND THE UGLY

ROCHELLE L. STANFIELD

The good news is that most poor people live in relatively decent housing these days. The bad news is that many of them have to pay more than half their incomes for rent. And the ugly bottom line is that despite the expenditure of $26 billion a year, federal housing programs reach only 16 per cent of the nation's neediest households.

At a time when homeownership opportunities for the middle class are better than they've been since the halcyon days of the 1950s, the housing problems of the poor have gone from discouraging to dismal.

Two new reports depict these stark contrasts in housing fortunes.

The first report, from the Housing and Urban Development Department (HUD), shows that the number of households with "worst-case" housing needs grew by 8 per cent—to 5.3 million—from 1989-91, after declining over the previous four years.

Meanwhile, Harvard University's Joint Center for Housing Studies issued an upbeat assessment of the nation's progress toward the dream of homeownership, especially for young families, immigrants and minorities. If current trends continue, the center predicted, the nationwide homeownership rate could reach an all-time high by 2000.

"The 1990s could be a dynamic decade for single-family housing and homeownership," William C. Apgar Jr., the center's executive director, said in an interview.

But despite its optimistic tone, the center's report—like HUD's—concludes on a somber note: "Unfortunately, progress for those who can make the transition to homeownership does not translate into gains for those who cannot. As a result of growing income inequality and persistent discrimination, many households—including many minorities and new immigrants—still cannot secure decent and affordable housing."

HUD's report focuses on the 13.2 million households counted by the Census Bureau's American Housing Survey in 1991 whose incomes were less than half local medians and who lived in rental housing. All these households were eligible for federal housing assistance, but only 3.3 million of them—a fourth of those eligible—actually got it. A lucky 1.4 million additional poor households spent no more than 30 per cent of their incomes on rent and lived in decent, uncrowded dwellings. That left 8.5 million households with some kind of housing problem. Of those, 5.3 million had the worst-case needs. Half of the worst cases were families and a fifth were elderly.

Nearly all the worst cases—94 per cent—spent more than half of their incomes on rent in 1991. Indeed, for 74 per cent, that crushing financial burden was their only housing problem; the other 20 per cent also lived in dilapidated, crowded or otherwise substandard conditions.

"Over the last several decades, we've gone in a positive direction on the quality front—reducing substandard housing—but in a negative direction on the affordability front," Robert Greenstein, the director of the Center on Budget and Policy Priorities, a Washington think tank that does research on poverty, explained in an interview.

Money isn't the only answer to the housing problems of America's poor. The housing situation is so complex because different areas of the nation have sharply varying amounts of housing stock in sharply varying conditions. Much of the rental housing stock needs to be rehabilitated; much of it needs to be torn down and replaced.

For five million-plus poor American families, however, money would be a giant step toward adequate housing. But it's an answer that isn't on the horizon.

Housing is the only basic human need that federal law doesn't consider an entitlement. If you are poor and hungry, the federal government will give you food stamps. If you are in poor health, medicaid will provide for a doctor's care or a stay in a hospital. If you have children, you are entitled to receive aid to families with dependent children (AFDC), and your children are entitled to a free or reduced-price lunch at school. But chances are that you'll be placed on a very long waiting list to receive housing assistance.

The Census Bureau's Current Population Survey estimated that about 37 million Americans were below the poverty line in 1992. Of them, 56 per cent lived in households that received medicaid benefits, 51 per cent in households that got food stamps and 43 per cent in households that received cash assistance. But only 18 per cent lived in public or subsidized housing. "We don't pay attention to housing," Greenstein said.

Why? One reason is that because housing assistance is costlier than other forms of federal aid, it requires a long-term commitment by the government.

The 3.9 million worst-case households whose only housing problem is that they have to spend more than half of their incomes on rent could really use section 8 housing certificates—vouchers that guarantee HUD will pay the difference between 30 per cent of a recipient's income and the rent charged by a private landlord. In the late 1970s, HUD added 400,000 certificates each year. It currently finances about three million certificates.

But in its budget for the fiscal year that begins on Oct. 1, HUD asked for enough money to add only 79,000 new certificates. The House, which approved its version of the HUD appropriation on June 29, added about 10,000 certificates. The Senate Appropriations Committee cut the number to 66,000 certificates in the version it passed on July 15.

Harvard's Apgar sees a need for a variety of housing programs to meet different needs in different areas. Nonetheless, he said, "If you told me you were going to have a universal coverage program in which everybody who is a worst-case need got something and if that something were a voucher, I'd say fine." The problem is, he continued, "HUD is penned-in in terms of money."

From 1989-91, the incomes of poor Americans went up by 5.6 per cent while their rents rose by 9 per cent. If that trend continues—and assisted housing remains on the back burner of the Administration and Congress—the worst-case housing needs of the nation's poor could go from worse to impossible.

Big Money in Low Rents

Federal low-income-housing tax credits now finance 94 per cent of all new or renovated rental apartments for the poor and near-poor—about 100,000 units a year. But who gets more from the tax credit—the nation's low-income people or well-heeled corporate interests? Nobody knows.

ROCHELLE L. STANFIELD

Jeffrey V. Gibney first stepped into the mind-numbing world of low-income housing tax credits in 1989, on a road trip out of South Bend, Ind., his home base.

" 'I hate this shit!' I kept yelling to my co-worker, who was driving," Gibney recalled in a recent interview. "I threw the tax credit handbook into the back of the car several times. I said, 'It's just too complex for a small group like ours.' "

Gibney is the executive director of the South Bend Heritage Foundation, a not-for-profit community development corporation that, with a nine-member staff, develops low-income housing and runs other community projects in South Bend, a declining midwestern city of 106,000 residents.

But Gibney kept retrieving the handbook and studying how to use the tax credits because, he said, he had no other source of funds for housing projects. He eventually concluded that despite some drawbacks, the credits were a pretty good deal.

"The tax credit program can bring about 50 per cent of the equity you need [to finance a project] to the table," Gibney said. "That was enough of an incentive for us to work through the process." South Bend Heritage Foundation is about to undertake its third—and largest—tax credit project.

Federal low-income-housing tax credits now finance 94 per cent of all rental apartments for the poor and near-poor that are being built or rehabilitated across the nation—about 100,000 units a year.

A provision of the 1986 Tax Reform Act—made permanent by Congress in the 1993 Omnibus Budget Reconciliation Act—allows corporations to take a tax credit for the money they invest in low-income rental housing. A company that puts up $1 million for a housing development, for example, can subtract the full $1 million from the federal income tax it owes.

Big corporations love the tax credit because they can reap returns of 16-20 per cent on their investments.

Lawyers and accountants do, too, because the complexity of the tax credit deals often guarantee them huge numbers of billable hours. When Gibney closed on his first project—the rehabilita-

John Eisele

Norman M. Dreyfuss, a real estate developer in Maryland "The tax credits, quite frankly, are worth a lot."

tion of 15 apartments—14 lawyers sat around the table. Legal and accounting fees and other nonconstruction costs consumed 40 per cent of the project's total budget.

Members of Congress like the tax credit because they don't have to appropriate large sums of money for something as controversial as housing for the poor.

And many advocates of subsidized housing for the poor support the credit—or don't actively oppose it—because it's all they've got.

"Is it the most efficient way" for the federal government to subsidize new housing for the poor, F. Barton Harvey III, the chief executive officer of the Enterprise Foundation in Columbia, Md., asked rhetorically. "Right now, it's the only way." The foundation's Enterprise Social Investment Corp. is one of two giant not-for-profit syndicators of the tax credits. (Syndicators raise money from public and private investors and act as their investment managers.)

"If Congress repealed the tax credit, there wouldn't be any low-income-housing construction," added John McEvoy, the executive director of the National Council of State Housing Agencies in Washington.

But is it the best expenditure of federal housing dollars? A bewildering antiphony of pros and cons precludes an easy answer to that question.

Because most tax credits are syndicated, and their value discounted in the process, the federal government spends about a dollar in tax credits for each 50 cents that goes into construction. Some critics see that as a rip-off of taxpayers.

Even so, that dollar goes a lot further than a dollar spent on public housing. That's because the federal government foots the entire bill for the construction of public housing, while many sources help to finance a typical tax credit project.

The $425 million in tax credits allocated in 1993 are expected to produce about 100,000 housing units. By contrast, the fiscal 1994 appropriation of $559 million for public housing is expected to yield fewer than 7,000 new units.

It takes only three federal bureaucrats in the Treasury Department and the Internal Revenue Service (IRS) to administer the tax credit program. The federal government is thus spared large administrative costs, and tax credit projects are spared heavy-handed regulation by the Housing and Urban Development (HUD) Department. At the same time, though, they are also freed from having to conform with such HUD policies as serving the neediest people first and allocating housing fairly across a whole city.

Some of the rules designed to prevent the misuse of the tax credit by businesses—such as allowing tax credits only on individual apartments rented to the poor, not on entire housing developments—inadvertently contradict national housing policy goals, chief among them economic integration.

Regardless of the policy implications, the biggest worry for both community activists and housing developers is the potential for scandal in a program that offers rich returns of public dollars to private investors.

"I think the tax credit could become the scandal de jour of the late 1990s, when someone wakes up to the fact that the money is going to well-off people and corporations and very little of it is getting into the ground," Richard West, a consultant to the National Low Income Housing Coalition, said in an interview. "That could cancel the program with nothing to replace it."

"I think the tax credit could become the scandal de jour of the late 1990s, when someone wakes up to the fact that the money is going to well-off people and corporations and very little of it is getting into the ground."

—Richard West, a consultant to the National Low Income Housing Coalition

DOING WELL AND GOOD

The low-income housing tax credit "is attractive politically because it allows corporations, as *they* say, to 'do well by doing good,' and it's not demanding a financial sacrifice from anybody—except the public sector," Jennifer A. Miller, the manager of community development for the Illinois Housing Development Authority, said in an interview. "But it is not the most efficient way" to subsidize housing for the poor, she added.

"The tax credits, quite frankly, are worth a lot," Norman M. Dreyfuss, a for-profit real estate developer in Montgomery County, Md., said. Dreyfuss's company, IDI Md. Inc., used tax credits to convert a decaying, frequently empty hotel in the suburban Washington community of Wheaton into 162 modern efficiencies and one-bedroom apartments.

"We're serving a very needy group of people," Dreyfuss said. "Not only do we have a place that a lot of people who need housing can live in, but we took something that was deteriorating and improved it, so it became an asset to the community instead of a deteriorating liability. So, it's like win-win."

Because the tax credits allow developers to get smaller mortgages, they can charge lower rents. Thus, Dreyfuss can rent his efficiencies for $445 a month, the one-bedrooms for $621. Unsubsidized rents would be a third or half again as much.

The Internal Revenue Code requires that tax credit apartments be leased to households whose annual income is no more than 60 per cent of the area's median income and that rents be no more than 30 per cent of that income. In the case of Dreyfuss's project, that's about $18,000-$25,000 a year in income. Gibney, whose housing in South Bend is in an area with lower median incomes, must work out deals so that he can rent two-bedroom apartments for $300 a month and three-bedroom apartments for $400 a month.

To put his deal together, Dreyfuss went to the Maryland Community Development Administration, which is in charge of allocating the tax credits. Based on its population, Maryland is permitted to allot about $10 million in tax credits every year.

Dreyfuss got a total of about $3 million in tax credits, but not all up front. Because the credits are parceled out over 10 years, Maryland used up only about $300,000 of its annual allocation on the deal. Dreyfuss, in turn, sold the tax credits directly to First National Bank of Maryland for about $1.5 million, also over 10 years.

In most cases, developers don't go directly to investors, but to syndicators. For-profit developers such as Dreyfuss usually go to such private syndicators as New York City-based Related Companies Inc.; Boston-based Boston Capital

Inc.; and Greenwich (Conn.)-based Richman Group Inc. Not-for-profit developers such as Gibney usually go to such not-for-profit syndicators as Harvey's Enterprise Social Investment Corp. or the National Equity Fund of the New York City-based Local Initiatives Support Corp. (LISC).

But Dreyfuss got a better deal by going directly to the bank. "We got roughly 50 cents on the dollar," he said. "We looked into using a syndicator, but we would have gotten only 35-40 cents on the dollar."

The bank got a pretty good deal, too. Not only will it get to shelter its profits, but it will also get credit under the 1977 Community Reinvestment Act for investing in the local community. "They got a double bang," Dreyfuss said.

But buyers of the tax credits are quick to point out that it's not all gravy. Investors must put their money in for at least 15 years, and in many cases 30 years. "It's not like buying a Treasury bond, where they can call up and sell the bond in 10 minutes," said Richard P. Richman, the president of the Richman Group, which invests in credits in Maryland and other states.

And they don't get the credits unless a project is built and fully rented to eligible tenants. "It's really almost an all-or-nothing type of return," George A. Lambert, the First National Bank vice president who worked out the deal with Dreyfuss, explained. If the project goes bad after a few years, the tax credits stop.

And unlike someone who holds a mortgage on a property that can be resold after a foreclosure, the tax credit investor gets nothing if the project goes sour. "You have no legal status other than as a limited partner," Lambert said. "You are subject to losing your position if other people don't do what they're supposed to do."

For that reason, the investors usually insist that a deal be structured very conservatively, with ample reserve funds. "Because the private sector is investing, there's a discipline that's built into the investment process so the projects will work for the 15 years," Harvey said. "That's a very good and positive discipline" that often isn't present when the federal government simply allocates funds directly, he added.

John Eisele

Benson F. Roberts, a Washington-based official of the Local Initiatives Support Corp. "The tax credit turns out to be a terrific deal for the feds . . ."

But structuring the deal so that investors are comfortable increases its complexity and raises the legal and accounting fees. So do the facts that tax credits alone often aren't sufficient to lower rents to the required level and that they must be used in conjunction with state and local subsidies. Dreyfuss, for example, received below-market loans from the state and additional subsidies from the county. In one of Gibney's projects, he had nine sources of funds.

To make the apartments affordable to poorer people—30 per cent or 40 per cent of median income, say, rather than 60 per cent—requires even more subsidies and a still more complex deal. "Groups that really want to serve the homeless and the poorest end up with the highest transaction costs and the most complicated projects," Michael A. Stegman, HUD's assistant secretary for policy development and research, said. "That's been a problem with the tax credit, and it remains a problem."

Nevertheless, "the tax credit turns out to be a terrific deal for the feds, who are getting very long term use out of the housing stock," Benson F. Roberts, LISC's Washington-based director of policy and program development, said. "It's run through the IRS. They know where to find you and won't take no for an answer, but [the actual administrative work] is done by tax professionals. The states do some of the monitoring, and there is a whole private-sector monitoring process. I think it's a great deal."

HOW GOOD FOR THE POOR?

No one, however, knows exactly how good—or bad—a deal the low-income-housing tax credits are for the general public or for the nation's poor. While the IRS makes sure that the investors don't defraud the government, no one keeps complete records of just who gets housing, where it is built or at what price.

"We don't even know how many tax credit units there are," Stegman said. "We know the dollar volume of tax credits that are allocated, but not always whether they're used."

The National Council of State Housing Agencies keeps some figures on the use of the tax credits and, as a result of new requirements in the 1993 law, will begin keeping more as states do more-thorough reviews of the housing built. But most of what is known about the program is anecdotal.

The council estimates, for example, that about 600,000 housing units have been built or rehabilitated since 1987. "That's a very large segment of our assisted housing inventory that we need to know more about so we can preserve it," Stegman said.

Since he arrived at HUD, Stegman said, he's wanted to develop a comprehensive database for the tax credits. "But that's not cheap to do, and the wheels have run slower than I had hoped," he said. By this time next year, he said, he expects to have such a database up and running.

That should please low-income-housing activists, who've had a lot of questions about whom the program really serves. Some of them, in fact, had urged Congress to postpone a permanent extension of the credit until an in-depth study could be completed. In the clamor for permanent extension by both corporate and housing interests, however, their pleas were ignored.

"There are a lot of questions that have to be answered, but we could never find people to fund an in-depth study," Charlotte B. Sobel, a housing specialist at the Washington-based Center for Community Change, said. "For example, our instincts tell us that the credit is never going to serve the truly poor, the people most in need of housing. We need an analysis to examine that."

Projects in which LISC's National Equity Fund invests, Roberts said, rent housing to households whose annual incomes are only 40-45 per cent of the area's median income. And most of the projects need another form of subsidy, usually from the state or local government.

To make the apartments affordable to even-poorer people is likely to require additional federal subsidies, such as section 8 certificates. Those are given to tenants, not apartment units, and HUD pays the difference between 30 per cent of household income and the apartment rent. The drawback is their scarcity. The fiscal 1994 appropriation provides for fewer than 40,000 new certificates. What's more, there's no coordination between the section 8 program and the tax credit program.

Some housing officials contend that the tax credit isn't the appropriate mechanism for subsidizing the truly poor. "You're going to need tenant services for a project like that," Candy McKinney-Coates, the chief development officer in Florida's Housing Finance Agency, said. "You'll need a lot of money thrown at a 30 per cent [of median] deal, and the tax credit was not designed to do that. It's not the vehicle. You can't put this round peg in a square hole."

The problem, low-income-housing activists point out, is that no other federal source of funds of this scope exists to meet that need.

The tax credits also make it more difficult to encourage mixed-income neighborhoods. The federal housing policies of the 1980s resulted in the concentration of the poorest of the poor in festering inner-city ghettos. To correct that situation, the Clinton Administration wants to mix income levels within neighborhoods.

Because a tax credit is allowed only on apartments that are rented to poor tenants, investors generally insist that all units in a development be designated for the poor to maximize their return.

"I think this is a terrible problem," said Judith S. Siegel, the president of Landex Corp., a national for-profit developer of low-income housing based in Warwick, R.I. "We can do mixed-income, but generally it's economically infeasible, and so we're creating social problems."

But not all tax credit developers see it that way. "You have to look at the neighborhood and know your market," South Bend's Gibney said. "Our neighborhoods are exclusively poor, and middle-income people aren't going to come here to live. If we did a mixed-income project, it would go belly-up."

In the absence of hard facts about tax credit projects, critics make a lot of assumptions about where the projects are built and by whom. Because of the large so-called transaction costs (legal and accounting fees and so forth) and the complexity of layering several subsidies, it's proportionately cheaper to do larger projects in which the apartments will be rented to households right at or under 60 per cent of median. That would mean suburban development, and many critics of the tax credit assume that suburbs are where most tax credit dollars go. Nobody knows for sure.

Richard A. Bloom

Charlotte B. Sobel of the Center for Community Change "There are a lot of questions that have to be answered . . ."

The Federal National Mortgage Association (Fannie Mae), for example, is probably the largest investor in tax credits. It is very profitable and has a lot of income to shield from income taxes. Wendell L. Johns, Fannie Mae's vice president for housing investment, who supervises the tax credit program, said that most of the tax credit purchases are in urban areas. He couldn't say, however, whether they are in cities or suburbs. But the kind of projects he described as typical Fannie Mae investments are more likely to be found in suburbs than in inner cities.

The Maryland Community Development Administration, which has considerable state subsidies to hand out, doesn't encourage the use of tax credits for small projects in city neighborhoods. "You have to recognize that tax credits are not for every low-income development," Nancy S. Rase, its deputy director, said. "For small inner-city low-income housing projects, we don't use tax credits. We discourage the sponsors from doing that, and we do it with state and local funds."

But state and local funds are scarce in some places, notably Indiana. And so not-for-profit developers in Indiana have found a way to make the tax credits work for city projects. Dennis J. West, the president of Eastside Community Investments Inc. in Indianapolis, is an old hand at tax credit deals, with 11 projects under his belt. For his latest two projects, he's taken two smaller, newer, less experienced and less sophisticated not-for-profit developers under his wing and negotiated a larger tax credit deal to cover the projects of all three organizations.

Stegman said that a lot of the problems with the tax credit can be worked out—once he has reliable data. "It is very important for the department to play a role [in the program]," he said, "and when there is discussion about the tax credit for the [HUD] Secretary to be at the table."

But that's exactly what a lot of investors and developers don't want.

"The perfect system would be one in which a god of government sat behind a desk and you brought him or her your project and he or she would say, 'I'll give you a cash subsidy,' " McEvoy of the state housing agencies council said. "You wouldn't have any investors taking a piece of the action. You wouldn't have any salesmen selling it. You wouldn't have any corporations demanding a high rate of return. The trouble is, that isn't reality. That won't happen."

And so, until a perfect system comes along, investors, developers and housing activists continue to make do with the low-income-housing tax credits—and continue to hope that a scandal won't end this one and only source of funds for building rental apartments for the poor.

Vouching for the Poor

Public housing has become so unpopular that the Democratic Clinton Administration is pushing an old Republican idea—rent vouchers for the poor.

ROCHELLE L. STANFIELD

RICHMOND, VA.—Gilpin Court in this city's Jackson Ward is not a pretty place. "It looks like public housing," Richard C. Gentry, executive director of the Richmond Redevelopment and Housing Authority, which runs the sprawling project, acknowledged during a recent tour.

With 783 cookie-cutter garden apartments for families and a 200-unit high-rise residence for the elderly, Gilpin Court accommodates about 3,000 people and is the largest public housing development between Baltimore and Atlanta. "It should never have been built that way," Gentry said.

The spartan apartments lack air-conditioning, and grass doesn't fare well under the pounding feet of hundreds of children. But trees shade the buildings and the grounds are immaculate. The plumbing works, and the roofs don't leak. Not a single unit is boarded up.

And while it may be homely, Gilpin Court has been a godsend to Elaine R. Taylor and her three children. A practicing crack addict at the time who was subsisting on aid to families with dependent children (AFDC), Taylor brought her family to Gilpin Court four years ago. "I came in on my knees and fell on my face," she recalled recently.

The project provided the family a safe haven for $68 a month; the housing authority supported Taylor with a range of services to help her pull back from the brink. Three years ago, she entered a drug treatment program and has been clean since. She took part in a community leadership training program last year that led to a paying job with the housing authority.

"I've straightened up. I'm standing tall, and I want to move on," said Taylor, now 39. But she's stuck.

Federal law requires that public housing tenants pay 30 per cent of their income as rent. So when Taylor took a job,

Rochelle L. Stanfield

Elaine R. Taylor, a resident of Gilpin Court public housing in Richmond, Va. She complains that the system discourages her from moving into private housing.

her rent shot up to $330 a month. Now she wants to get a second, part-time job to pay off debts she incurred in her drug-using days, clear her credit record and thus obtain the references necessary to move into private housing.

"But a second job is considered income, and my rent would go up again," she said. "So I'm kind of stuck between a rock and a hard place. Why are they penalizing me for trying to do better for myself and my family?"

A rent structure that discourages work is just one manifestation of the disrepair of federal public housing policy. Dozens of other federal requirements—many of them at odds with one another—have combined to turn much of public housing into warehouses for the poorest of the poor. The Housing and Urban Development (HUD) Department calculates that the annual income of public housing families averaged $6,228 in 1994, only 16 per cent of the $39,900 national family median. In 1980, the figure was 33 per cent of median income.

Public housing—built with federal money and to federal specifications but for the most part owned and operated by local housing authorities—is the oldest form of federal housing aid, dating from the 1937 Housing Act. Over the years, the federal government has invested about $90 billion in this housing stock. Last year, Congress appropriated $8.4 billion for public housing during the current fiscal year, but now is considering rescinding as much as a third of that amount.

Shepard Sherbell/SABA

Dozens of federal requirements have turned much of public housing into warehouses for the poorest of the poor.

The 1.4 million units of public housing across the country represent less than a third of the 4.7 million housing units that are now subsidized by the federal government. About 1.8 million dwellings are privately owned and subsidized under a variety of federal programs. And about 1.5 million households receive vouchers to help them pay for rent on private housing.

Unlike other forms of welfare, housing assistance has never been an entitlement. Because this form of assistance is so expensive and so unpopular in Congress and with the public, only about a fourth of the 18 million eligible households get aid.

Public housing has a bad reputation, even though most of it—like that in Richmond—is well managed. While much of the public housing inventory is in small developments that blend into their neighborhoods, the public image remains of decrepit, foul-smelling and crime-ridden inner-city high-rise complexes that give all public housing a bad name, encourage the imposition of red tape and discourage generous federal appropriations.

The dollars for public housing are likely to be reduced again in the fiscal 1996 appropriations, but for once, the rules and regulations may shrink as well.

The Clinton Administration, congressional Republicans, conservative think tanks, housing authority representatives and low-income housing activists are all rushing out plans to transform the public housing program.

"There are as many plans as players," John McEvoy, the executive director of the National Council of State Housing Agencies, said. "This is a case where you can't tell the program without the players because there are so many points of view, even among the Republicans."

Indeed, the public housing question has divided the Republicans, split the Democrats and provoked conflict within the low-income-housing lobby. Common to each proposal is the rhetoric of deregulation, devolution and individual empowerment. But the practical consequences for the housing authorities and for the residents remain in doubt. It's not at all clear, for example, how Elaine Taylor would fare under the different schemes.

Senate Majority Leader Robert Dole, R-Kan., along with the House Republican freshmen and a collection of other congressional conservatives, wants to abolish HUD. Dole and the others haven't yet spelled out what would happen to public housing in the process, but a favorite notion is to combine housing assistance with a general welfare block grant to the states. Presumably, the states could provide vouchers for housing or add the money to cash assistance.

Taylor, who has worked her way off welfare but who still needs housing assistance to squeak by, would probably lose her housing aid. And without federal aid for operating expenses, Gilpin Court would deteriorate.

Sen. Christopher S. (Kit) Bond, R-Mo., the chairman of the Appropriations subcommittee that oversees HUD's budget, and Rep. Rick A. Lazio, R-N.Y., who chairs the Banking and Financial Services Subcommittee on Housing and Community Opportunity, are both drafting public housing block grants.

That notion, favored by the public housing authorities that would administer the block grant, would eliminate most federal regulations—presumably including the 30 per cent of income rule. Taylor would benefit from such a plan because Gentry, the Richmond public housing chief, has in mind a rent structure that would give residents the incentive to work. Without some sort of rent ceiling, however, public housing authorities in other localities might have to price their apartments out of reach of the neediest families if drastic reductions in aid accompanied the block grant.

The Administration plan—officially called the "blueprint"—is the most fully evolved and, surprisingly, the most radical. The Administration would convert the public housing program to a voucher system. HUD would give local public housing authorities funds with which to provide vouchers to public housing tenants. The tenants could stay where they are and pay the rent with the vouchers or could use the vouchers to rent private housing.

The voucher would be valued at the difference between 30 per cent of income and the total rent—up to a ceiling on the rent. The HUD blueprint calls for work incentives, but it's not clear how they would relate to the 30 per cent rule. So HUD's voucher plan would help Taylor move out of public housing but—depending on the fine print—might not help her work herself off her dependency on housing assistance.

"HUD's blueprint is designed to save HUD, not to make the programs better," Robert L. Armstrong, president of the Omaha Housing Authority, said in an interview.

VOUCHERIZE!

HUD's voucher plan has split the Democrats and wedged moderate Republicans such as Bond and Lazio in between.

Shepard Sherbell/SABA

A rent structure that discourages work contributes to the disrepair of public housing policy.

As HUD officials explain their proposal, vouchers would empower public housing residents and impose market discipline on the public housing authorities.

"We're here to serve residents, the program participants," Joseph Shuldiner, assistant HUD secretary for public and Indian housing, said in an interview. "So rather than giving money to buildings or governments or institutions, we're going to give the money directly to participants."

Michael A. Stegman, the assistant HUD secretary for policy development and research, who helped to draft the plan, added, "When you give tenants the power to say, 'I'm not getting value for my money and I'm going to see if I can make a better deal somewhere else,' you discipline the system that has not really been attuned to those kinds of market choices that most housing consumers have."

Liberal Democrats in Congress don't buy those arguments. Rep. Barney Frank, D-Mass., denounced the voucher plan at an April 6 hearing by Lazio's subcommittee as "morally, the worst job of blaming the victim. People are in public housing because that's the best housing they can find."

"You can't condemn people to choice when, in fact, they will have no choice at all," Frank's fellow Massachusetts Democrat, Joseph P. Kennedy II, said at the same hearing. "You will create homelessness."

Some HUD officials concede that the blueprint was an act of political desperation in response to a White House assault on HUD in general and public housing in particular after the Democrats' drubbing in last November's elections.

"The public housing program is so discredited nationwide with the population that we couldn't get our own Administration to put money in it for the 1996 budget," Shuldiner said. "So we needed to come up with, in effect, a new product to sell to get the money."

As a political tactic, the voucher proposal might help the Democrats because it places moderate Republicans in the uncomfortable position of opposing a quintessentially conservative Republican notion. The voucher system that's already in place, the so-called section 8 certificate program, was established by the Nixon Administration in 1974. The Reagan Administration tried to extend housing vouchers and use the concept for education. So Republicans don't dismiss the idea out of hand while condemning the Administration's heavy-handed approach to it.

"It's not to say that vouchers wouldn't work," Bond said in an interview. "But I'd like to test them in [different kinds of] communities first."

"I'm not less committed to vouchers," Lazio agreed in a separate interview. "I think they are a good idea for situations in certain neighborhoods, and they are a necessary alternative in some areas, but I am more cautious about it than the Administration is. In that sense, I share some of the concerns of some of the people on the Democratic side."

Practitioners and low-income housing advocates, who rarely find themselves on the same side of the table as the Republicans, agree with Bond and Lazio. They like vouchers, but only as one component of a multifaceted housing policy.

"Vouchers are a fundamental building block of a comprehensive housing policy," Robert J. Adams, president of the National Low Income Housing Coalition, said. "At least in theory, they provide a choice for low-income families in terms of type of unit and location. In theory, they provide opportunity. In theory—there's the rub."

The HUD blueprint contemplates a six-year transition from the current hyper-regulated conglomeration of public housing provisions to a housing block grant and eventually to vouchers. Federal construction aid over that period would enable public housing authorities to rehabilitate and upgrade their developments to make them attractive places to live. Complexes that are beyond repair, in bad locations or simply redundant would be demolished—a step that is very difficult for housing authorities to take under current federal law. But the House has already voted to subtract $1.1 billion in modernization funds from the fiscal 1995 budget; the Senate has voted to cut $615 million.

At the end of the transition period, HUD would provide funds to public housing authorities to administer a single

Shepard Sherbell/SABA

voucher system, combining the current section 8 certificate program with the new public housing voucher. HUD would not send vouchers directly to recipients.

If a tenant uses a voucher to move out of public housing, the housing authority would be able to rent the apartment to an unassisted family. Because most authorities don't have mortgages on their developments and don't pay taxes, they could price the apartments competitively. The unsubsidized families moving in would have higher incomes than those who move out. They would most likely be working families with fewer social problems than typical public housing tenants and thus would serve as role models for those who stay in public housing.

"We'll only provide assistance to the very, very poor, but we may be helping house people who are better off in attractive housing that's affordable to them," Shuldiner said.

A rosy picture but, critics grumble, an unrealistic one. "The public housing program wasn't put together or managed or designed or funded to be a sleek, mean, competitive real estate fighting machine," said Gordon Cavanaugh, a Washington lawyer who represents the Council of Large Public Housing Authorities. "A good portion of it was built to be cheap because it was for 'those people,' so the inventory is just not something that is going to attract people who aren't subsidized."

Richmond's Gentry foresees a grim future under the voucher plan. His current tenants pay, on average, $125 a month for rent, but it costs him $375 a month to operate each unit. HUD makes up the $250 gap in the form of an operating subsidy.

"If I lose that family and the subsidy that goes along with them, and I can't find somebody who can pay a $375 rent, then I'll lose income," Gentry said. "Since maintenance is my biggest controllable expense, I'll do less maintenance, and the property will deteriorate. Therefore, I'll have something that's less marketable, so more people will move out and create a vicious spiral down."

HUD officials acknowledge that their blueprint won't work without substantial deregulation. "The first thing we have to do is deregulate," Stegman said. "Otherwise, it would be a disaster."

But critics contend that HUD would lay down just as many new rules as it would eliminate and merely change the label to "performance standards."

"What they are deregulating with one hand they are reregulating with the other," Richard Y. Nelson Jr., executive director of the National Association of Housing and Redevelopment Officials, said. "Their performance standards spell out all of these things that the housing agencies would have to do, and who they would have to serve. They're still telling agencies where to go."

For example, Congress and HUD have required housing authorities to give preference to specific classes of public housing applicants, such as the homeless. HUD's blueprint calls for removing those preferences, but it would replace them with guidelines such as these: Half the new tenants should be working or "work-ready"; residents who don't work or aren't preparing themselves to work must do community service; and 10 per cent of the apartments should be reserved for applicants on "special-purpose waiting lists."

The ultimate question for the HUD blueprint, however, is whether vouchers will meet the tenants' needs. HUD officials insist they will; just about everybody else has doubts. A HUD study showed that 80 per cent of the people in large urban areas who received rent certificates under the section 8 program last year were able to rent in the private market. A new HUD survey says the proportion is now up to 87 per cent.

But in tight, high-priced markets such as New York City, the proportion is only 62 per cent. In addition, the elderly—who represent about 40 per cent of public housing residents—and the disabled are less mobile and find rental vouchers much harder to use. Furthermore, HUD plans to reduce the value of the vouchers. Section 8 certificates currently pay the difference beween 30 per cent of the tenant's inome and a rent that's no more

As a political tactic, the proposal for a housing rental voucher system might help the Democrats because it places moderate Republicans in the uncomfortable position of opposing a quintessentially conservative Republican notion.

Photos by John Eisele

Sen. Christopher S. (Kit) Bond, R-Mo., and Rep. Rick A. Lazio, R-N.Y. They are drafting bills to provide public housing block grants to the states.

than 45 per cent of rents in the area; the blueprint would lower that ceiling to 40 per cent.

"You would have more vouchers floating around but no more buildings available or landlords willing to rent at the price those vouchers are good for," said Evan Lewis, the housing law staff lawyer at the Virginia Poverty Law Center in Richmond. "So you would have more competition for the same level of housing."

HUD officials say that their plan would open up additional housing by loosening the regulations that now govern section 8, thus making vouchers more attractive to landlords. Critics are skeptical.

"You have to add in things like discrimination in the housing market," said Rachel G. Bratt, a housing policy professor at Tufts University in Medford, Mass. "You have no guarantee that folks, particularly families of color, will be treated fairly."

"There's an argument that vouchers would work," Gentry said. "My argument is that I don't think they will."

BLOCK THAT GRANT!

Gentry and other public housing officials share with moderate Republicans such as Bond and Lazio the view that a public housing block grant is preferable to HUD's voucher proposal.

"If we took a lot of the constraints off public housing, put funds for public housing in a block grant and only retain post-review in HUD to deal with those who aren't doing the job, and let public housing administrators at the local level make the decisions, we could get a lot better quality of housing for the people who live in public housing," Bond said.

"To me, it's not the decision that's made that is as important as who makes the decision," Gentry said. He and his fellows want to be the ones to make the decision.

That would mean putting a lot of trust in local officials who may not always have the best interests of the tenants in mind, HUD officials and housing advocates for the poor counter. Most federal housing regulations—whatever their consequences—responded to local misdeeds, they say.

"People look at the public housing program and say, 'Look at this federal failure that got us these huge projects built in impoverished neighborhoods,' " low-income-housing advocate Adams said. "Well, the truth is, that wasn't a federal requirement; the land use and location of housing was a local choice.

"So we need to be careful about simply rolling all of the decision making down to the local level and remember why it was that the federal government got involved in the first place," he continued.

"There is a reason for having a federal housing department," Shuldiner said. "Civil rights, the protection of vulnerable populations, those are the kinds of things we really can't trust to the locality."

The other big problem with block grants, in the view of housing advocates for the poor, is the underlying assumption that they would cost less than the current system.

"There is a degree of naïveté and wishful thinking about how much you can cut the present federal level of effort financially" and still provide assistance to those who now get it, McEvoy, the director of the state housing agency organization, said. "Some people in positions of leadership on the Hill are talking about 20 per cent efficiency cuts by just getting rid of the federal superstructure. Well, that just isn't true."

"The dollars I think we'll have will certainly be less," Lazio conceded in an interview. Congress is in the process of rescinding previously appropriated funds. HUD programs, and public housing in particular, have taken the lion's share of these cuts. Of the $17.3 billion in rescissions voted by the House, $7.3 billion would come out of HUD, including $4.2 billion from public housing programs. The Senate approved $16 billion in rescissions, including $4.8 billion from HUD, with $2 billion of that sum from public housing.

"Even after the rescissions, I think HUD will be asked to make some other contribution toward deficit reduction," Lazio said.

Regardless of the form that housing assistance takes, it has to mean less help for fewer people. "Housing costs money," said Dennis W. Fricke, assistant director of the housing and community development issues staff at the General Accounting Office. "There's no cheap fix."

As Bond and Lazio search for what they recognize will have to be a complex solution to federal housing problems, their colleagues on the political Right see the answer in starker terms. "Abolish HUD," Sen. Lauch Faircloth, R-N.C., demanded at a March 20 hearing of the Banking, Housing and Urban Affairs Committee. "HUD has failed to do what it set out to do—promote homeownership—and we can't afford not to abolish HUD."

"There's not an inconsiderable number of people in both the House and the Senate who say, 'Let's just toss the whole thing [HUD] out,' " Bond said in the interview. "But I don't know how you do that in a program like this."

If Congress doesn't just try to walk away from public housing, it is likelier to enact a block grant than HUD's voucher plan. What would that really mean for people like Elaine Taylor in Richmond's Gilpin Court?

"I'm determined not to go back," she said. "I want to live in a house with my own backyard and a dog that runs around—and I'm determined to find a way." The real question is how determined Congress and HUD are to find a way to help her do it.

Schooling, Children, and Child Care

Governments in the United States enact and implement a great number of public policies directed at children and their well-being. These include policies that regulate children's activities by making it illegal for children to engage in activities in which adults are allowed to freely engage and policies that subsidize or provide goods or services for children that are not provided to adults, or at least not provided to them so readily. Examples of regulatory children's policies include child labor laws, compulsory schooling laws, and restriction of children's access to tobacco, alcohol, and pornography. Examples of government policies that, in effect, provide or subsidize goods or services for children at government expense include Aid to Families with Dependent Children, government subsidies or tax breaks for child care, public elementary and secondary schooling, and government vaccination programs.

In the American political system, state and local governments play relatively large roles in public policy relating to children, while the national government, which is the dominant public policymaker in so many policy areas, assumes a relatively smaller part. That having been said, the national government is hardly insignificant when it comes to regulating and providing for children's welfare. Moreover, children and children's welfare have become a prominent topic in national political rhetoric since Bill and Hillary Clinton became national figures during the 1992 presidential campaign.

School desegregation cases are, of course, one way that the national government has become heavily involved in public schooling and thus the lives of children in the United States. But only relatively recently have federal courts been rendering decisions that go beyond mere racial composition of student bodies. One selection in this unit addresses the effect of federal court intervention in school desegregation cases and the way that some recent decisions have also included directives that can help improve the quality of education in concrete ways above and beyond racial desegregation.

In most industrialized democracies, there are few, if any, private colleges or universities. Instead, national governments typically operate a single university system that is responsible for all or almost all postsecondary education and professional training in the nation. In the United States, by contrast, virtually all colleges and universities either are private institutions or are operated by a state or local government. Nevertheless, the national government is involved in important ways in higher education, especially through research or program grants that help pay for operating colleges and universities and an extensive program of student loans and other forms of student financial assistance. The policy issues that federal student loan programs raise, especially in a time when college tuition is increasing at rates faster than inflation, are the subject of one of the selections in this unit.

The remaining selections in this unit treat child care and the way that children and children's welfare have found their way into political rhetoric in recent times. While the vast array of children-related and education-related public policies can hardly receive comprehensive coverage in this unit, the selections can provide some insights into the issues that can arise in these policy areas.

Unit 7

Looking Ahead: Challenge Questions

In some countries where governments operate all or most colleges and universities, no tuition is charged. That is, just like elementary and secondary public schooling, attendance is free, although only the better students who want to pursue their studies beyond high school are admitted. Do you think that it makes sense to provide free public education through grade 12, and then charge for college? Or does the system of free or nearly free higher education used in many other countries make more sense?

Some people say that parents ought to be responsible for the care of their children, and not government. Others say that it is up to governments to ensure that children are properly fed, clothed, and educated. On which point of view do you think public policy related to children should be based? Defend your opinion.

Governments in the United States play no role in screening people to be babysitters. If parents want to hire young, inexperienced, inattentive babysitters to mind their children, government does not interfere. Why, then, do you think that governments should or should not play a role in regulating and licensing child care centers?

A few years ago the Swedish parliament passed a law that forbade anyone, including parents, from using corporal punishment on children. That is, striking a child, even a parental spanking for disciplinary reasons, was declared illegal. Do you think that governments should outlaw corporal punishment of children? Why or why not?

Reform by the Book

Court-supervised settlements in scores of school desegregation cases around the nation may offer an additional route to achieving meaningful education reform—a route that doesn't depend on Washington's legislative cartographers.

ROCHELLE L. STANFIELD

Theresa C. Henderson walked into the middle of a mess in the fall of 1984, when she took over as the principal of Hoffman Elementary School in Cincinnati.

Student achievement at the very poor, nearly all-black school was in the cellar. Suspensions for misbehavior were through the roof. Teachers transferred out as soon as they could get a new assignment. Books were old and shabby, equipment scarce and the building a cheerless dump.

"My feeling was the first thing we had to do was change the climate," Henderson recalled in a recent interview. "You can't get to academics without going through other things, and one of the first things to get through was discipline."

Working with a rejuvenated staff and as many parents as she could corral, Henderson put together a school-wide discipline plan.

"I want the children to come into a very caring environment, so we hug them and accept them," Henderson explained. "At the same time, we have rules and regulations. The adults must follow them, and the children must follow them. And if we don't, there are consequences."

What followed is the stuff of legend: Hoffman has become an award-winning model. Its students' math scores compare favorably with nationwide averages. Suspensions are among the lowest in Cincinnati. There's practically no turnover on the teaching staff.

Much of Hoffman's transformation can be traced to the sheer force of Henderson's personality. But she also carries a big stick that, she says, has helped her immeasurably in accomplishing change: the court-supervised 1984 settlement agreement in a 19-year-old racial desegregation suit, *Bronson v. the Cincinnati Board of Education.*

The settlement has given Hoffman money for extra staff, teacher training, equipment, supplies, library books and other essentials that poor schools can rarely afford. It's also given Henderson leverage with the school board and a freer hand to launch some of her reforms.

Now *Bronson* rides again. In October, the plaintiffs and the school board reached a new settlement, which will usher in a variety of far-reaching improvements, including the requirement that all public schools in the city adopt a radical new approach to discipline—a scheme similar, in many respects, to the plan that Henderson pioneered at Hoffman.

To civil rights lawyers and education reformers, the recent *Bronson* agreement illustrates a potentially new life for old desegregation cases—a vehicle for achieving the kinds of school reform that the Clinton Administration, governors and education reformers are clamoring for.

"It certainly is a way to give [reform] more of a sense of urgency," said Robert W. Evans, a former assistant state superintendent of public instruction in Ohio and the court-appointed facilitator of the Cincinnati settlement. "I suspect that Cincinnati has done some things a lot quicker because of *Bronson*."

Indeed, *Bronson* and cases like it may provide new common ground for the separate, often warring, national education camps: those who demand equity and those who seek excellence. Studies of what happens in schools as the result of desegregation cases demonstrate a point that also emerged from the debate this summer over President Clinton's Goals 2000 education reform legislation: You can't have one without the other. *(See NJ, 7/3/93, p. 1688.)*

"This development in school desegregation law offers some very interesting connections with school reform," David S. Tatel, a civil rights lawyer in Washington who litigates school desegregation cases around the nation, said in an interview. "There are a lot of cases where advocates of school desegregation are working very closely with advocates of school reform."

Some education improvements have been part of many desegregation decisions since 1977, when the Supreme Court ruled against city-suburban busing in Detroit but ordered extra support for the city schools to wipe out inequities caused by segregation.

At first, the court-ordered improvements consisted mainly of extra funds for a few special programs. Over the past few years, however, they have taken an increasingly reformist turn. The new *Bronson* agreement builds in higher standards, teacher accountability and a new emphasis on results—the same ideas embodied in the six national education goals.

But some civil rights lawyers caution against high hopes for these agreements, pointing to the decidedly cool attitude of many federal judges toward continuing court involvement in old desegregation cases. In the past few years, the Supreme Court has relieved several school districts—including DeKalb County, Ga., and Norfolk, Va.—of the need to comply with old desegregation plans.

Recycling desegregation cases for school reform "is all for the good where you can do it," Phyllis McClure, the director of policy and information in the Washington office of the NAACP Legal Defense and Educational Fund Inc., said. "But it's probably going to happen only on an ad hoc basis when the circumstances are just right."

Even in Cincinnati, where enthusiasm is high over the new settlement agreement, those involved in reaching it have taken off the rose-colored glasses.

"It's a very promising step, and I expect to see more of this kind of thing," William L. Taylor, the Washington lawyer who negotiated the Cincinnati settlement, said. "But there's also a big step between writing this on paper and actually doing it."

IT TAKES TWO TO TANGO

Most civil rights activists and school reformers have come to agree that achieving excellence in education calls for financial equity and racial equity as well as better teaching methods. Higher standards won't make a dent in achievement scores at substandard schools. But neither desegregation nor more money will automatically create better schools.

In the nine years that the original *Bronson* settlement has been in effect, Cincinnati's school system has been desegregated. The public school population is now about 62 per cent black, and most schools have a mix of black and white students. There are very few Hispanic or Asian children in the system.

A handful of schools remain overwhelmingly black. One of them, ironically, is Hoffman, where there are only 2 white children among 472 kindergarten-to-6th graders. Hoffman also remains predominantly low-income: 96 per cent of its students qualify for free or reduced-price lunches, the proxy for poverty used by the federal government.

"The settlement mandated a specific level of desegregation objectively computed, and basically, that was achieved," said Robert S. Brown, a Cincinnati lawyer who chairs the 14-member community-wide task force that monitors the settlement. As to the educational improvements required by the settlement, however, Brown said somewhat vaguely, "Progress has been made in all those areas."

Susan M. Muniak

Washington civil rights lawyer David S. Tatel
School desegregation cases and education reform are connected.

Evans's assessment is much harsher: "Access [to integrated schools] for minority kids is better," he said. "Whether it's better [access] to a better product is the question."

That question was the major impetus for negotiating the new settlement agreement. Court supervision of the 1984 agreement was scheduled to expire in 1991 when U.S. District Court Judge Walter H. Rice extended it for two years because of lagging progress in the educational improvement standards.

In 1984, the court had identified eight schools, most of them predominantly black, in which student achievement was abysmal. They became the "Coalition of Innovative Schools" and received extra funds to bring them up to speed. Of the eight, only Hoffman has made appreciable progress. The new settlement agreement requires the eight schools to institute all-day, all-year preschools, nongraded primary grades, new forms of assessments and high standards for all students, among other specific steps.

"We're not moving away from [an emphasis on] racial discrimination as such as much as we're trying to identify barriers to poor, minority kids and find ways to overcome those barriers," Taylor said.

Scholars who study school desegregation and student achievement aren't surprised at the lack of progress in Cincinnati's poor schools. Gary Orfield, a professor of education and social policy at Harvard University's School of Education who was involved in a desegregation-school improvement case in San Francisco, has found that the best way to raise the achievement of poor, minority students is to transfer them to middle-class schools.

"But we found that if you desegregated and didn't produce that kind of social class change, you didn't get any real gains unless you did radical school reform," he said in a recent interview.

The San Francisco case generally parallels Cincinnati's. A 1982 consent decree to settle a desegregation suit required desegregation and school improvement. The state pumped in millions of dollars to ease the politically delicate job of desegregation. Schools that simply got infusions of money, Orfield discovered, made little or no progress. But the consent decree also authorized a very bold experiment at six schools.

"We totally emptied out those schools and created basically new schools in the old buildings," Orfield said. "We removed the entire staff. New principals were appointed, and they were allowed to recruit outside the union contract from anywhere in the country. The new staff was committed to certain principles of educational reform and equity."

Voilà: The six schools showed dramatic improvements, proving what Henderson showed mostly by chance at Cincinnati's Hoffman Elementary School. Now the San Francisco school district has agreed to begin "reconstituting" all of its schools.

GETTING THERE

As logical as the reform steps may appear to be, getting there is no cakewalk.

None of the improvements contained in the Cincinnati settlement is a bolt from the blue. All have been tried successfully in schools around the nation. But that doesn't make it any easier or faster to institutionalize a whole package of reforms in a big-city school system.

That's where some of the players see the school desegregation cases coming into play, inasmuch as they can proffer carrot and stick simultaneously.

"Court supervision of a settlement agreement is an ideal structure to introduce change that might otherwise be unpopular," Brown, the Cincinnati lawyer, said. "It creates the drive on the part of the school board to get out from under court supervision, so they try to make things happen. And the fact that it is a settlement [as opposed to a decision after a trial] lets everybody walk away claiming that to some extent their viewpoint got reflected in the settlement."

In fact, just obtaining sufficient goodwill to negotiate a settlement is a major first step. The pessimism that McClure of the NAACP's Legal Defense Fund expressed about the widespread use of desegregation cases as a springboard to reform stemmed in part, she said, from the difficulty in finding school boards willing to settle and federal judges amenable to extending court supervision for years into the future.

"We just lost a big case in Oklahoma City, for example, where we were completely shut out [in both the federal district and circuit courts]," she said.

In Cincinnati, the *Bronson* negotiations were tough from the beginning. Observers and participants who spoke on the condition that their names not be used say that the school board came to the bargaining table kicking and screaming. School superintendent J. Michael Brandt—who assumed that position in 1991 after court supervision of the 1984 agreement was extended—is generally viewed as a constructive factor in the most recent process. But even he expressed some resentment over the outside forces that have been compelling the school district to act.

"Federal intervention generally is not understood very well in [school] districts, and most of the inside people saw it as a negative," Brandt said in a recent interview. "It would be very difficult, in my professional opinion, to have this type of federal intervention drive the reform. I think it would be like shoving it down people's throats."

Once reform policies are in place, resistance can take subtle and indirect forms that may be just about impossible to prove. A case in point is the problem of disciplinary suspensions in Cincinnati's school system.

In 1991, when the parties to the *Bronson* settlement were trying to figure out what to do about the impending end of court supervision, the plaintiffs noticed a tremendous increase in suspensions from school, particularly in the desegregated schools. What's more, black students were twice as likely to be suspended as white students.

Richard A. Bloom

Washington lawyer William L. Taylor
"We're trying to identify barriers to poor, minority kids."

And so both sides agreed to hire Junious Williams, a civil rights lawyer in California who specializes in discipline codes. "I told them at the outset that trying to sort out what was causing the disparities would be very difficult," Williams said in a recent interview.

And sure enough, while Williams could prove that there were disparities, he couldn't show definitively that teachers and principals were deliberately discriminating against black students by throwing them out of school. So instead of assessing blame, Williams came up with a set of recommendations for a new approach to behavior management that eventually was included in the new settlement agreement.

Meanwhile, in 1991, the Cincinnati Federation of Teachers (CFT) had won the inclusion in their contract agreement of a stiffer discipline code for the school system. The code expanded the range of offenses that would trigger automatic suspension—the use of profanity directed at a staff member, for example. No surprise: Suspensions skyrocketed throughout the system.

The discipline code in the new settlement agreement, however, goes out of its way to avoid suspensions. The code will direct each school to develop a schoolwide "behavior management plan" and to train teachers in conflict resolution. It also holds teachers accountable for their disciplinary actions.

Each time teachers send a student to the office, for example, they'll have to fill out a form that includes the student's name and race. Teachers whose classes are deemed good learning environments can win cash awards; those whose classes are a shambles and who send a lot of students to the office will receive extra training. If that help doesn't reduce the problem, Taylor (who negotiated the agreement) said, the offending teachers could eventually lose their jobs.

Teachers, however, are very wary. "Our worst fear is that teachers and principals alike will read this settlement as a retreat from maintaining good standards of behavior," Thomas J. Mooney, the CFT's president, recently told a reporter for *Education Week*. "Schools operate on middle-class norms of behavior, and frankly, we get a lot of students, black and white, who don't know anything about those norms."

Obviously, Mooney's view doesn't prevail throughout the system. At Hoffman, Henderson and her teachers successfully instituted an approach similar to Williams's and taught children who didn't understand "middle-class norms of behavior" to abide by and respect those norms.

"In America, we too often equate kindness with weakness," Henderson said. "I wanted to show the children that kind people can be very, very strong."

And so the Cincinnati experiment is about to take off in a new direction. So is the use of the desegregation consent decree to overhaul San Francisco's schools. Other such efforts are under way in Cleveland, Kansas City, Mo., St. Louis and Yonkers, N.Y. Civil rights lawyer Tatel suggested that "hundreds of [desegregation] cases around the country" could spawn similar initiatives.

Tatel may be overly optimistic. Just the right conditions are required for reform to move from the courtroom to the classroom. But for all their limitations, recycled desegregation cases offer an additional route to achieving meaningful school reform—a route that doesn't depend on Washington's educational cartographers.

Price War

For years, the government has responded to rising college bills by doling out more student aid. The Clinton Administration may tackle the problem from the other side, by pressuring schools to rein in costs.

ROCHELLE L. STANFIELD

Still breathing hard from its slugging match over student loans and a national service program, the Clinton Administration is loading up for a wider attack on the escalating cost of higher education.

"We're not averse to a good fight. We just engaged in one," David A. Longanecker, the assistant Education secretary for postsecondary education, said in an interview. "But we'll only fight when we think we've got a very good case."

Congress has adopted scaled-back versions of two Administration initiatives for postsecondary student aid: a plan to switch from federally guaranteed private loans to a direct government loan program and a proposal to establish a national service program that would provide student aid in exchange for community service work. *(See box.)*

Now, President Clinton is pressing on. By next year, as part of his fiscal 1995 budget proposal, he may propose a package of sweeping reforms in the financing of postsecondary education. The plan probably won't please a lot of folks in the education business, though.

One reason is that rather than seeking more money for student aid, budget-conscious Administration officials want to take the unprecedented step of tackling affordability from the other side: applying pressure to colleges, universities and trade schools to trim their costs. The plan might, for example, establish "reasonable" cost standards for institutions. Government aid would pay only for schooling priced within those guidelines.

In addition, the Administration may split off postsecondary vocational training from the student aid program for colleges and universities. Private vocational schools are certain to fight such a move because it inevitably would entail more restrictions than existing student aid programs do. Colleges and universities aren't likely to be happy either, because some money would probably be sliced out of the student aid pie and earmarked for vocational training.

Administration officials also want to consolidate and streamline the hodgepodge of programs that now provide about $27 billion annually in aid to nearly 7.1 million students. But even that could

Richard A. Bloom

Assistant Education secretary David A. Longanecker
Under existing aid programs, "if we give money away, that's considered a success."

provoke a battle because each of the programs has developed its own political power base.

Those obstacles could make for a tough fight on Capitol Hill. Democratic leaders on the House and Senate education committees have been eager to accommodate their Education President but find many of his ideas anathema.

"My observation over 20 years of this is that the executive branch doesn't matter very much in this business," said David W. Breneman, a former president of Kalamazoo College in Michigan who's now a visiting professor at Harvard University's Graduate School of Education and a visiting fellow at the Brookings Institution in Washington. "Congress has really got a lock on what happens in higher education."

Still, Members of Congress and representatives of colleges, universities and trade schools agree, something has to be done. The current system of financing higher education, they concede, is a mess. For more than a decade, college costs have skyrocketed, and federal aid has not kept pace.

From 1980-90, the price tag for a college education rose 126 per cent, twice the rate of inflation—and even more than the 117 per cent increase in health care costs. The median income of families headed by 45-54-year-olds (the age group most likely to have children in college) increased by only 73 per cent during the period. And federal spending on student aid rose only 47 per cent. The result: The proportion of college costs covered by federal aid declined over the decade from 18 per cent to 11 per cent.

Since 1965, the government has created a bewildering, multilayered array of grants, loans and work-study programs, each with its own eligibility requirements and application forms. Although many programs are supposed to target needy students, the proportion of low-income students enrolled in colleges and universities has not increased substantially.

Efforts to ease the burden on some students and families often have made the situation worse. For example, last year Congress made it easier for middle-income students to qualify for grants and at the same time tightened some eligibility requirements for low-income students—thereby squeezing out some of the poorest students.

AID PLANS GET A BUMPY RIDE

The Clinton Administration is claiming victory in its fight for two student aid initiatives this year. But it had to struggle each step of the way for compromises that fell considerably short of the initial proposals.

The Administration wanted to transform the student loan program—which now relies on federally guaranteed loans by private lenders—into a program of direct government loans to students. The plan was to be administered by the Education Department and phased in over five years; advocates said it would save the government $4.3 billion during the period by eliminating subsidies that lenders now receive.

The House bought the idea, but the Senate didn't. Many Senators questioned whether the Education Department was up to the job of administering direct loans. Their opposition was fueled by heavy lobbying by private lenders and financial middlemen such as the Student Loan Marketing Association. The Senate voted to cap the proportion of direct loans at 50 per cent.

During negotiations on the budget package, House and Senate conferees hammered out a compromise that would phase in direct loans over five years, with direct loans accounting for at least 60 per cent of lending at the end of that period. Schools would have the option of switching entirely to direct loans after two years.

President Clinton's proposal for a national service program followed a similarly bumpy path. The House, essentially adopting the President's plan, agreed to provide educational aid of $4,725 a year, plus minimum-wage stipends and health and child care benefits to young people who devote up to two years to community service.

But the five-year price tag—estimated at more than $10 billion—was too high for Senate Republicans, who filibustered that chamber's version down to $1.5 billion over three years. The House accepted the Senate version.

WHAT'S "REASONABLE"?

The traditional approach to dealing with rising college costs—providing more student aid—is no longer in the cards. And so, higher education finance experts are beginning to look at the other side of the equation: cutting costs.

"I think cost containment is going to be the issue of the '90s in higher education," Jamie P. Merisotis, who was executive director of the congressionally chartered National Commission on Responsibilities for Financing Postsecondary Education, said in a recent interview. He now heads the private Institute for Higher Education Policy in Washington.

"Rather than try to provide more and more aid, which you never really catch up on and which we don't have the money for, it behooves policy makers to create incentives—not regulations—for cost containment," Arthur M. Hauptman, a Washington-based education consultant, said.

Existing federal student aid programs take the opposite tack. In calculating the aid for which a student is eligible, they simply take the school's price tag and subtract a portion that the student is considered able to pay. If the institution raises its price, the aid for which the student is eligible goes up. (Because Congress usually appropriates far less money than it authorizes for student aid, however, students often don't get all the assistance for which they are eligible.)

In its final report issued early this year, Merisotis's commission called for establishing a per-student ceiling on federal aid. The Education Department would set the ceiling, based on what it determines is the average cost of educating a student at a U.S. college or university. The maximum would be the same, no matter whether a student went to a local state college or to an exclusive private institution. (The commission figured the current amount would be $14,000 per academic year.) Students attending relatively inexpensive schools would get less than the maximum; those attending higher-priced schools would have to look for aid from other sources.

Clinton Administration officials say they like the concept, although they talk about setting different standards for different kinds of institutions and services. For example, there might be a higher ceiling for students at a research university than at a liberal arts college. Also, the government might cover the cost of housing in a dormitory room shared by two students—but require students who wanted the relative luxury of a single room to pay the differential out of their own pockets. And in calculating the "reasonable" cost of a college education, it might exclude institutions' expenditures for expensive recreation facilities and other nonessentials.

"This approach says, 'This is what it reasonably should cost to provide this service. If you provide it at a higher cost than that, that's your business. But we aren't going to recognize that,' " Longanecker said. "I'm sort of intrigued with that concept because it allows us to give some signals that are important."

Longanecker is confident that some of these changes could be accomplished without too much trouble. As a state higher education official in Minnesota and Colorado, he participated in efforts to set reasonable cost standards for public colleges and universities under his jurisdiction. His new boss, Education Secretary Richard W. Riley, has enthusiastically embraced the notion of cost standards. And the President responded favorably to the idea when it was presented to him.

In fact, Riley would like to go still further and develop performance standards for institutions receiving federal student aid, to make sure that students and the government are getting their money's worth.

"Look at the Goals 2000: Educate America Act and the kind of expectation on outcome performance stipulated there," Longanecker said, referring to the Administration's proposed elementary and secondary school reform package that would codify national education goals and set standards for achieving them. "You can imagine where we might be headed for postsecondary education."

To participate in federal aid programs, institutions have to be accredited by private accrediting organizations, but the government does not try to measure how well institutions educate their students.

In the $6 billion-a-year Pell grant program, the chief aid program for low-income students, "if we give money away, that's considered a success," Longanecker said. "We don't look to see if students complete their programs, or if they do complete the program, whether they get jobs in the field for which they've prepared. I think a focus on performance standards will become much more significant." Any attempt at setting performance standards is bound to be controversial, though, given the long tradition of academic autonomy in the country.

Cost standards would probably engender opposition, too, once they are spelled out in legislative detail.

Susan M. Muniak

Jamie P. Merisotis, who directed a commission on higher education finance His group recommended an aid ceiling, based on the average cost of educating a student.

Major higher education groups endorsed the Merisotis commission's recommendation for a student aid ceiling. "Great piece of work," said Robert H. Atwell, president of the American Council on Education, the Washington-based umbrella organization for higher education. "Sooner or later we're going to have to address some of these problems."

But the Administration's talk of setting different ceilings for different kinds of institutions may not sit well with education groups. Some liberal arts colleges, for example, rank among the nation's most expensive institutions, while some state-supported research universities have relatively low tuitions.

And education groups fret that the process of determining what costs are "reasonable" could lead to government intrusion into universities' budget decisions.

Higher education organizations insist that colleges and universities are tightening their belts already without any prompting from the federal government. "Cost containment is happening in the private universities because of the market," Atwell said. "It's a little more complicated at the publics," because of state laws and restrictions on state colleges and universities.

Indeed, in the past few years, tuition and fees at state schools have risen faster than at private institutions because the public schools have had to make up for cuts in state appropriations.

But James B. Appleberry, president of the American Association of State Colleges and Universities, insisted that his member-institutions also have been cutting costs. "When the state budget shortfalls began, the institutions took the budget cuts that were opportune. They cut the support budgets, maintenance, trimmed back administration," he said. "This has gone on so long that [savings from such reductions] are gone, and now they're cutting into the academic areas like books and libraries and degree programs."

Higher education financial analysts contend that colleges and universities can squeeze out more savings with technology, efficiency measures and restructuring—the same approach that has been used in industry.

"Higher education is in the world of the mom-and-pop store," Stephen J. Carroll, a senior researcher at RAND, a Santa Monica (Calif.)-based think tank, complained. "You've got one on every corner, and each one has a meat department, a grocery department and so forth. And we can't afford it."

He envisions greater specialization within university systems. For example, introductory courses might be taught at a state college and more-advanced courses at a research university.

Carroll and other analysts also call for a greater use of technology. "We've done very little in the way of substituting capital for labor in higher education," he said. But colleges have been loath to go the technology route. They rarely switch from live instruction to videos, for example, because they say that detracts from a shared learning experience.

Appleberry sees a much larger role for technology in instruction. But there's an immediate obstacle: Institutions can't afford the initial capital investment. "In the long range, they may work their way out of [their fiscal bind] through technology," he said. "But in the short range, that means a further diminution of resources."

TRADEOFF

Would-be reformers are also taking a hard look at the student aid dollars that now pay for vocational training at for-profit trade schools and community colleges. During the 1980s, the proportion of federal grant money spent at for-profit trade schools more than doubled; such schools now account for about a fourth of the money spent by the Pell program.

Analysts argue that the current student aid program doesn't work effectively for short-term occupational training, especially for disadvantaged students who make up a disproportionate share of enrollment in vocational programs. For-profit schools can set tuition as high as the market will bear and will still be reimbursed. There is scant quality control; students have complained that instruction is poor at some schools and that they can't find jobs after completing their training.

Many critics contend that the government shouldn't provide loans to students at for-profit trade schools. The loan default rate at such schools is six times the rate at private four-year colleges, five times the rate at public universities and more than twice the rate at two-year colleges.

"These people are not getting jobs [and are] not able to repay their loans, so you're subjecting them to a set of conditions which makes their life chances a lot worse rather than better," consultant Hauptman said.

The solution, many analysts say, is to set up a separate system for financing vocational training.

But if the Administration decides to go this route, it will have to do so carefully. The issue of trade school participation in student aid has been a political minefield for years.

Merisotis's commission tiptoed very lightly over the question, in part because it is so emotion-laden. "The commission felt [the report] would not be taken seriously" if it included a recommendation to split off vocational training, Merisotis said. "All the attention would focus on that and not on the broader agenda."

Indeed, when Congress last year reauthorized the 1965 Higher Education Act, House Education and Labor Committee chairman William D. Ford, D-Mich., a fervent supporter of vocational training, flatly refused to consider any proposals to treat trade schools differently from colleges and universities.

"Do you think that a young black or Hispanic woman in New York City who is going to a six-week course for elementary office skills should get as much attention from us as somebody going to MIT to become a nuclear physicist?" Ford asked in a 1991 interview. "That's the basic philosophical underpinning of this program, that we don't try to elevate one educational goal over another."

What has been missing in the past, some analysts say, is for proponents of a separate program to come up with a plan that would not treat vocational training as a stepchild.

"I suspect many Members of Congress would be much more willing to consider an alternative if it was packaged within a very serious policy initiative with some reasonable expectation for support," said Brian K. Fitzgerald, staff director of the Advisory Committee on Student Financial Assistance, a permanent agency set up by Congress to give technical assistance to Congress and the Education Department.

That's exactly what Administration officials say they will do. "What we'd be looking for is ways to basically assure better customer service," Longanecker said. "Logically, the money currently being spent [on aid to vocational students] would flow with those students."

But that wouldn't please colleges and universities. They have tried for years to divorce vocational training from the student aid program—but only on the condition that most of the money would stay in the collegiate aid pot, which Administration officials say isn't likely to happen. Splitting off vocational training "is not going to be a panacea for higher education," Longanecker said.

Two approaches are in circulation. The more popular, albeit more expensive, would be to transfer vocational training programs to the Labor Department as part of a comprehensive school-to-work plan. The department would contract with schools to offer specific courses and would monitor instructional quality and the employment prospects for graduates. Part of what makes that approach attractive in the education community is the interest taken in vocational education by Labor Secretary Robert B. Reich.

The other route would be to set up a separate loan program for vocational training that would provide intensive counseling for students and that would make the amount of their loan repayments contingent on their future incomes. "I think that's wrongheaded," Hauptman said. "For that to work, you'd have to have a high degree of quality control so you're not providing for useless or poor-quality training." Education Department officials say, though, that any new proposal for financing vocational training will include quality-control measures.

Critics also assail the proliferation of grant, loan and work-study programs, which has generated huge amounts of paperwork and administrative costs—and has created so much confusion that students may not obtain all the aid for which they're eligible. Merisotis's commission recommended streamlining the system by creating a single grant program, a subsidized loan program for lower-income students, an unsubsidized loan program for more-affluent students and a single work-study structure.

As logical as that sounds, it's also likely to be controversial. Consolidation is never easy. For student aid, it is likely to be even harder because Members of Congress and interest groups have pet programs that they see as unique.

Richard A. Bloom

American Council on Education's Robert H. Atwell
Colleges are already having to tighten their belts.

For example, the Administration this year proposed reducing spending on three relatively small programs in which the government gives aid to colleges and lets them distribute it to students. Higher education groups went on the warpath, and the House rescued the programs.

Whatever the Administration plans to do, just about everybody agrees, it is going to have to consult early and often with Congress. Longanecker says the Education Department plans to do that, but congressional committee aides say it hasn't happened yet.

Many observers don't expect a major overhaul any time soon. They look at the divisive battles over direct loans and national service and conclude that a consensus for change is missing both in Washington and across the country.

John Eisele

The Kiddie Card

Click on C-SPAN these days and you're all but certain to find a politician talking about the pressing needs of America's children. Beyond all the warm, cuddly rhetoric, however, lurks a nasty reality; it's still politically safe to cut children's programs but dangerous to reduce those of the elderly.

ROCHELLE L. STANFIELD

Children can't vote. They don't write checks to election campaigns, and they rarely form pressure groups to storm Washington with their demands. But they're cute. They melt your heart with their vulnerability. They represent the best and worst of society and—most important—they symbolize the future.

Those are some of the reasons why children long have served as a potent rhetorical device in politics. They provide an excellent vehicle for promoting policy goals with little threat of retribution should promises not be kept.

So, it's no surprise that House Speaker Newt Gingrich, R-Ga., is selling the balanced budget amendment and other items in his party's Contract With America as a way to ensure the future of the nation's children. President Clinton explains his New Covenant with the American people by referring to its impact on children.

Behind the rhetoric, however, the reality of children's policies confronts politicians with a nasty dilemma. Politically, it is safe to cut children's programs but dangerous to reduce those of the elderly. Thus, social security, an entitlement for the elderly, has been taken off the budgetary chopping block while programs under which children are substantial beneficiaries—aid to families with dependent children, food stamps and medicaid—are under the ax.

In practice, however, children's programs are much cheaper than programs for adults. And, in terms of long-term investment, they are a real bargain. A dollar spent on childhood immunization saves up to $30 in health care bills later, the Children's Defense Fund estimates.

If George Washington didn't surround himself with children on the campaign trail, his successors certainly have. Even somber Abraham Lincoln carried in his pocket a letter from 11-year-old Grace Bedell that he often quoted.

"I think all these references to children are largely gratuitous and to some extent calculated," acknowledged a political pollster who didn't want to be identified. "But it's not like this is anything new."

"It is a quintessential way to say you're not being political right now," added Celinda C. Lake, a Democratic pollster and partner in Mellman • Lazarus • Lake Inc., the Washington-based political consulting firm. "It makes you long-term rather than short-term, interested in the next generation rather than the next election."

But something more profound is going

on than reliance on an old political gimmick. Many Americans are angry and confused and worried about the future and about how well their own children will do in their later lives. By focusing on children, the politicians are able to capture these immediate concerns and speak more abstractly about the long term.

So play the kiddie card, public opinion experts advise politicians, but do so carefully. People are serious about children and suspicious about what politicians say about them. An offhand remark about children can easily backfire, as Gingrich found when he suggested building orphanages for illegitimate children of teenage welfare recipients.

Wherever they stand in the real priorities of the President and the new Republican Congress, children are front and center in their speeches.

In his third State of the Union address on Jan. 24, Clinton used references to children to define his centrist "new social compact" between a smaller but still activist government and individuals who must exercise personal responsibility.

Government does have a role to play, he insisted, and some spending programs can't be cut. Why not? "Our young people," he said. "We should think of this when we cut. Our young people hold our future in their hands."

But he warned that the future will be bleak if adults don't teach children to take responsibility. "Too many of our children don't have parents and grandparents who can give them those experiences that they need to build their own character and their sense of identity," he said.

Three weeks earlier, when the Republicans took charge of the House after 40 years, they symbolized their new order by bringing their children to opening day.

As he made his inaugural address as the newly sworn-in Speaker, Gingrich acknowledged the children present. "The young people you see around you are really what, at its best, this is all about," he said. And as for the importance of his legislative agenda, he went on, "the ultimate reason for doing that is these children and the country they will inherit and the world they will live in."

EVERYBODY'S DOING IT

Gingrich and Clinton have lots of company in playing the kiddie card. Just about every politician and public policy organization is doing it. And if talking about children is good, showing pictures of them is a thousand times better.

The National Governors' Association (NGA) has adopted the Governors' Campaign for Children as its yearlong theme. So the glossy brochure announcing the NGA's late-January winter meeting in Washington featured large pictures of children, two smiling white tots on the cover, a pensive black toddler inside.

The Citizens' Commission on Civil Rights, a private watchdog organization, recently issued its evaluation of the Clinton Administration's civil rights record at midterm. Though the report covered such adult topics as job discrimination, fair housing and fair lending practices, the front and back covers depicted smiling little kids at play.

Susan M. Muniak

Rhetoric about children is commonplace in the capital.

But in a word-driven town, children's rhetoric is the most common ploy.

Nowhere is this more the case than in the ongoing debate over welfare reform. In a policy statement, the NGA on Jan. 31 demanded utmost flexibility for states in whatever Congress ends up doing but acknowledged that "the governors believe that children must be protected throughout this process."

E. Clay Shaw Jr., R-Fla., chairman of the House Ways and Means Subcommittee on Human Resources, which will write his chamber's version of welfare reform, sought to calm gubernatorial anxieties over the harshness of some proposed Republican remedies by saying, "We're not going to let babies starve."

Meanwhile, Clinton has demanded that Congress adopt legislation that "lifts people up without punishing children."

But child chatter doesn't begin and end with welfare. In exhorting his colleagues to vote for the balanced budget amendment on Jan 26, House Majority Leader Richard K. Armey, R-Texas, said, "This moment is about the future of our children in this great nation."

Earlier, John H. (Jack) Gibbons, the director of the White House Office of Science and Technology Policy, opposed the balanced budget amendment and other provisions in the Contract With America for the same reason. "Our initial interpretation of proposals to fund the Contract With America raises our concerns that we will not be able to develop and disseminate the education technologies our children will need to compete in the global, knowledge-based economy," he told the House Science Committee. At the same hearing, Environmental Protection Agency administrator Carol Browner denounced the regulatory risk assessment provisions of the contract as delaying "actions needed to protect the public health of our children."

And Clinton relied on kids to illustrate how much safer the world is today. "This is the first State of the Union address ever delivered since the beginning of the Cold War when not a single Russian missile is pointed at the children of America," he said.

But the prize for the most blatant use of children's images goes to both sides in the fight over the Corporation for Public Broadcasting (CPB). Conservative Republicans consider the CPB unnecessary in an age of cable, an inappropriate object of taxpayer spending, to say nothing of a nest of liberal elitists. Democrats defend it as an electronic haven from crass commercialism and a crucial niche for innovation.

But those aren't the arguments that the two sides have been using in the scrap over CPB's annual $285.6 million appropriation. Instead, the corporation and its supporters trotted out characters from its two most popular, and uncontroversial, children's shows, *Sesame Street* and *Barney and Friends*.

Rep. Nita M. Lowey, D-N.Y., waving puppets of *Sesame Street* characters at a House Appropriations Committee hearing on Jan. 19, said: "Make no mistake. This debate is about Big Bird and Oscar the Grouch and Barney and Kermit. The new Republican majority has put them on the chopping block."

"The American people do not have to come to the forefront necessarily and underwrite Big Bird and Barney," Rep. Bob Livingston, R-La., committee chairman, responded, alluding to the profitability of those two programs. "They can shift for themselves."

The current proliferation of children's images in the dialogue of politics and policy appears to go beyond simple reliance on a political sure thing, many analysts say. "Obviously, there is an opportunistic side to all of this in that it's always great to use children as a foil for one's policy preferences," said Chester E. Finn Jr., a former Education Department official who's now a senior fellow in the Washington office of the Indianapolis-based Hudson Institute, a conservative think tank. "But there's something bigger and more honorable going on, too." Finn is the director of a Hudson Institute project on the American Dream, whose goals include decentralizing the government.

"An important part of the American Dream is the belief that one's children will fare better in life than oneself, an idea of intergenerational progress," Finn explained. "For the first time in American history, people say they don't believe their children will be better off than they are."

Nearly four-fifths (78 per cent) of the American people believe that the American Dream will be harder to attain for future generations, according to a survey conducted late last summer for the Hudson Institute project by Frank I. Luntz, who heads Luntz Research Cos. in Northern Virginia and is Gingrich's favorite pollster.

Thus, Republican Gov. William Weld of Massachusetts was right in step with the public when he devoted his second inaugural address, on Jan. 5, to his commonwealth's children. "Too many children today do not look to life with the same great expectations that we held for ourselves," he said. "*Our* challenge is to ensure that their lives can be as full and rewarding as the lives of their parents and grandparents."

A Weld spokesman acknowledged that the concept behind the speech was to look future-oriented. Weld spent his first term "with a fiscal nightmare we had to clean up," said John C. Brockelman, the spokesman. "Now we can look to the future, and the future is our children—they are a symbol for this."

BUT DON'T OVERDO IT

Despite its venerability as a political tool, the children's ploy is a strategy that must be applied with care, public opinion experts warn. References to children, made either insensitively or with too great abandon, can backfire. Indeed, the kiddie card seems to work better when it's employed to try to change party or political stereotypes rather than to reinforce them.

> Most people fear that the American Dream will be harder to attain for future generations, according to a recent survey.

When Republican politicians mention children, middle-class voters think of their own children and react positively, experts have discovered, but when Democratic politicians do the same—especially if they talk about "programs for children"—the public thinks of government largess for welfare and minorities and responds negatively.

For Republicans, "it is a tactic to demonstrate compassion," said a knowledgeable Republican who didn't want to be identified. "We've always had the image of the green eyeshade, of supply-side economics. People don't think we care about people. Well, we can show we do care by talking about our children and our families."

But, unless they're careful, Democrats can turn voters off when they try to do the same thing. "Increasingly, voters think that when Democrats and progessives talk about children, they mean only poor children," Lake said.

To counteract that image, Lake recommends that Democrats do what Republicans do—talk about their own children, about education and other universal children's topics that apply to the middle class.

Republicans have been able to capitalize on two children's subthemes—crime and family values.

Violence among children "has become a kind of metaphor for what's breaking down in our society," Lake said. "People are very concerned about how young and how violent offenders have become. It's a way real people are thinking through the cultural crisis that they feel in our country."

Many of last fall's successful Republican gubernatorial candidates concentrated on the youth crime issue. George W. Bush in Texas and Pete Wilson in California made particularly effective use of this ploy. But there's hardly a politician—Republican or Democratic—who hasn't referred to the small child pushed to his death by other children from a Chicago public housing project to dramatize the urgency to take whatever action they're promoting.

In his State of the Union message last month, the President turned the crime image around when he defended the ban on assault weapons. "A lot of people laid down their seats in Congress," Clinton said, "so that police officers and kids wouldn't have to lay down their lives under a hail of assault weapon attack."

Republicans have also found children a good euphemism for family values. "It allows us to talk about using government to promote our values without using the phrase 'family values,' which tends to get you into a little bit of trouble and does not seem to make the connections that we want to make," the knowledgeable Republican explained.

The phrase doesn't seem to confront Democrats with the same problem. Clinton peppered his State of the Union address with the "V" word, and other Democrats have taken to using it.

Indeed, there doesn't seem to be a simple set of rules on how best to employ children in political rhetoric. Perhaps that's because attitudes toward children are inconsistent.

Despite the public's disdain for welfare programs and adult recipients, surveys show genuine concern for the plight of poor children. While 68 per cent of the public favored ending welfare payments to grownups after two years and making able-bodied adult recipents get a job, a late-December poll conducted for the Kaiser Family Foundation and Harvard University showed that only 26 per cent approved of doing so if it meant the family head couldn't support his or her children. And 66 per cent of the respondents opposed ending welfare benefits for unmarried women if their children would be sent to group homes or orphanages as a result.

Those findings might provide Democrats ammunition for attacking provisions of the Republican welfare reform proposals, but not for striking at the Republicans themselves, pollster Lake discovered.

The Children's Defense Fund and the Center on Budget and Policy Priorities each came out with a report analyzing the welfare reform proposals in the Contract With America and concluding that five million-six million children would be greatly harmed if those provisions were adopted.

Democratic politicians used those findings to mount an attack on the contract and its backers, which didn't work. "Nobody really believes that anyone is anti-kids," Lake said. "So when you see language like 'Republicans are going to victimize children' or 'five million children are going to starve'—people just don't believe that."

Richard A. Bloom

The political reality for kids' programs is quite stark.

RHETORIC AND REALITY

Glowing rhetoric about the need to help children may reverberate in congressional speeches, but the political reality for children's programs appears to be quite stark.

Programs aimed at children are likely to be cut, yet those that benefit the elderly are expected to remain untouched. Undoubtedly, politics is not the only reason for that. Social security is viewed as efficient, unlike some of the children's programs that have been discredited by critics. And even though most recipients of social security are paid out of current taxes, the program is considered an insurance program, not a handout like programs for poor children.

Nonetheless, politics looms large in this calculation: Children have no real clout. The younger they are, the poorer and less likely to vote their parents are, while the elderly not only vote out of proportion to their numbers but the senior citizen lobbies in Washington are also very effective.

Congressional Republicans "are terrified of [lobbyists for elderly Americans], and I think we all better stop being terrified," Democratic Gov. Howard Dean of Vermont, the current chairman of the NGA who chose the children's theme, said in an interview. "I think it's perfectly ludicrous."

Nonetheless, the David and Goliath image extends even into the ranks of children's advocates who insist that they don't want to start intergenerational war in the next breath after they point out the difference in treatment between programs for children and those that are intended for the elderly.

"I think one of the real dangers in any discussion like this is to pit children against the elderly," said a children's advocate who asked not to be identified. "I think it's very important for us not to do that."

If it weren't for politics, children's programs might be much more appealing from a practical standpoint: They are much cheaper than programs for the elderly or for adults in general.

There's growing momentum among would-be health care reformers—including the President, as he made clear in his State of the Union speech—to begin an incremental approach with a children's program.

Analysts say such a program would cost only a small fraction of a program for adults because children rarely have serious illnesses and almost never require long-term care, the two big-ticket items of health care.

"Health care for kids is nickel-and-dime," said Robert J. Blendon, a professor of health policy at the Harvard School of Public Health. "You can sound like you have a program and not spend much money."

Families with children under age 18 account for only 34 per cent of the nation's households. So granting new tax credits only to families with children, as both the Contract With America and Clinton's proposals would do, dramatically reduces the cost.

"Just by limiting it to families with children, I limit the amount of money I'm giving away, so this becomes a cheap program," Blendon said.

Over the long term, programs for children have even greater payoffs. Most economists concur that investments in children—whether it's prenatal care, immunizations or preschool—pay off later in greater productivity and lower societal costs (such as for welfare and crime).

Dean said that's the practical consideration behind a package of children's programs that he has promoted in Vermont and that formed the impetus for his NGA campaign.

State spending on corrections programs has been one of the fastest growing elements in the Vermont state budget. "The only way to deal with things like corrections is to invest money 15 years earlier in children," Dean said.

In an ironic twist, Dean has done a reverse on the kiddie card to promote his children's package at home. "There are a lot of voters out there who may not have the interest in children that I do, but they almost all have an interest in their pocketbooks," he said. "So I like to sell this stuff as a business proposition."

But just about every other politician in the country is following the age-old rhetorical gimmick of clothing business propositions in the cute garb of adorable tykes.

WHEN A PENNY SAVED IS A DOLLAR SPENT

ROCHELLE L. STANFIELD

Welcome to the topsy-turvy world of child care economics. You get what you pay for, but because almost no one is able or willing to pay for quality, children—middle class and poor alike—suffer.

You could say that the free-market system has worked in child care. Over the past three decades, as greater proportions of mothers of very young children went to work outside the home, the number of child care providers increased to meet the need. The marketplace created a variety of child care arrangements: nannies in the home, family day care in the provider's home and public, nonprofit and for-profit day care centers. Because the supply kept going up, the cost remained pretty stable.

Now, about 3 million day care workers—97 per cent of them women—take care of 10 million children. More than half of mothers with children under 1 year old are in the workplace; nearly half of all children under 3 years old are cared for by someone other than their mothers.

But capitalism didn't triumph in this case. The result wasn't a better mousetrap; it was questionable care.

"Most child care is mediocre in quality, sufficiently poor to interfere with children's emotional and intellectual development," according to "Cost, Quality, and Child Outcomes in Child Care Centers," a study by researchers at four prestigious universities that was published in January. "Market forces constrain the cost of child care and at the same time depress the quality of care provided to children."

That probably shouldn't come as a big surprise. Parents with young children tend to be young themselves, still starting out on the career path. The median income of families with children under 6 years old is $32,215, according to the Census Bureau, while that of families with children 6-17 years old is $39,359. The median income of female-headed households is only $17,443.

Because child care is a very labor-intensive industry, pay and benefits for child care workers is pitiful. On average, they earn only $11,725 a year, according to one study, about half the $21,747 average of all women in the civilian labor force. Fewer than a fifth of all child care centers provide health insurance for their employees; family day care providers are on their own.

As a result, the most qualified child care workers can't afford to stay in the business if they depend on it for their livelihoods. Claudia E. Wayne, the executive director of the National Center for the Early Childhood Work Force, has dozens of anecdotes like this one: A child care center recently lost two of its top teachers when a supermarket opened nearby. It couldn't compete with the wages and benefits paid to grocery baggers.

High turnover—which averages a third of a center's staff a year—is bad for the emotional security of the children, every study of child care has concluded.

The quality of day care can be improved easily and dramatically, two new studies by the New York City-based Families and Work Institute show. But to do so requires two things nobody wants to talk about: more money and more government regulations. One study showed remarkable improvement in the emotional development of children in family day care in California, North Carolina and Texas after their child care workers received special training. (A control group without specially trained workers didn't improve.) That costs money.

The other study, conducted in Florida, showed that new state requirements for higher staff levels at day care centers and more training for staff resulted in marked improvements in the quality of care.

As they have for the past four years, child care workers protested their economic situation with Worthy Wage Day on April 27. Their fortunes, though, haven't gotten much better. Now they are likely to get even worse because of proposed congressional cuts in day care assistance for the poor.

As part of welfare reform, the House approved legislation that would consolidate nine federal child care programs into a single block grant to the states, ending the current entitlement to child care aid and capping the appropriation at $1.9 billion, the combined level of the nine programs for fiscal 1994.

Consolidation is probably a very good idea. State and local government officials universally complain about the regulatory maze and the paperwork headache caused by the current patchwork of child care programs.

But capping the funds means denying child care to as many as 400,000 children just as welfare reform will require their parents to go out and get jobs. And blocking the funds means removing a 5 per cent set-aside for quality improvement that has enabled child care programs to invest in some training for their staffs.

A study of a multiyear Florida welfare reform initiative, recently completed by New York City-based Manpower Demonstration Research Corp. (MDRC), eerily foreshadows what might happen. The 1988 Job Opportunities and Basic Skills Training Program (JOBS) offered funds to states to provide employment and training programs for welfare mothers. Part of the deal was that the state had to provide child care for the participants' preschool children.

Florida's program was called Project Independence. MDRC began studying it in 1990. For a variety of reasons, in 1991 much of the child care money was diverted as the economy declined and welfare caseloads grew. As a result, MDRC discovered, many mothers of preschoolers couldn't take advantage of training opportunities and thus were less likely to become independent than mothers of school-age children.

Pointing up the shortsightedness of it all, MDRC found that for every dollar the state spent on services for welfare mothers with older kids, it got back $1.85 in lower welfare costs; but for the mothers of preschoolers, the state got back only 55 cents.

Congress may be about to learn for the umpteenth time that there's no such thing as a free lunch. The easy part is toting up how much can be saved now by denying child care to hundreds of thousands of families. The tough part is figuring out how much society will ultimately be forced to spend as a consequence of its indifference.

Civil Rights

In 1619 the first African slaves were brought to what is now the United States. Slavery became an essential component of the economy of the South as well as a highly controversial practice that led to the Civil War. In 1863 President Abraham Lincoln issued the Emancipation Proclamation, which declared all slaves in the Confederacy to be free. Immediately after the war ended, the Thirteenth, Fourteenth, and Fifteenth Amendments, aimed at regularizing the status of former slaves as citizens and voters, were added to the Constitution.

These new constitutional provisions did not usher in an era of racial equality in the South. Racial segregation became the norm in schools, public transportation, eating establishments, hotels, and other such settings. In *Plessy v. Ferguson* (1896), the U.S. Supreme Court ruled that racial segregation of the sort practiced widely in the South did not violate the Constitution, even though schools, accommodations, and public conveyances available to African Americans were substantially inferior to those available to others.

In *Brown v. Board of Education of Topeka* (1954), the Supreme Court in effect reversed its ruling in *Plessy* and declared racial segregation of public schools unconstitutional. Coming after several earlier Supreme Court decisions sympathetic to the plight of African Americans and President Harry Truman's post–World War II order to desegregate the armed forces, the *Brown* decision touched off years of litigation and controversy. By the 1960s, the Civil Rights movement, aimed at securing for African Americans the range of rights and opportunities that European Americans enjoyed, was in full swing.

By the late 1960s and early 1970s the Supreme Court had followed through on its original *Brown* decision in ways that made racial desegregation a reality in many school systems across the land and in other facilities such as public libraries and public swimming pools. The Civil Rights Act of 1964, pushed by President Lyndon Johnson and passed by Congress, extended the drive for equality beyond programs and facilities run by governments to private accommodation and private employment. The Voting Rights Act of 1965 was intended to prevent the abridgement of voting rights in the Old South and, like the Civil Rights Act, was successful in many respects. In a variety of matters affecting African Americans, public policy was having its desired effect, although American society remained far from color-blind.

At first, the term "affirmative action" referred to rather tame attempts by employers and others to advance the cause of African Americans' civil rights. For example, an early version of affirmative action consisted of advertisements for vacant government jobs carrying the disclaimer that neither race nor religion would be used to disadvantage an applicant. Soon another variant of affirmative action appeared, one in which minority applicants were aggressively recruited for jobs and educational openings for which they might not otherwise have competed. "Goals" for minority and female job hiring and school admissions were yet another affirmative action development, and employers and educational admissions officers were required or at least well-advised to keep careful statistics about the race and gender of applicants. Finally, there were "quotas," whereby a certain proportion of

Unit 8

vacancies were to be filled by specified categories of candidates (for example, African Americans, women, or Hispanic Americans). Affirmative action in its more extreme form became controversial, and pronouncements on various affirmative action plans by courts, legislatures, and executives served sometimes to clarify, sometimes to muddle, and sometimes to enrage.

The selections in this unit treat only selected aspects of public policy relating to civil rights. As the reader will see, American society is far from color-blind, and civil rights remains a difficult and complicated area of public policy.

Looking Ahead: Challenge Questions

If two candidates for a job or a college are equally qualified, do you think it is justified for preference to be given to a member of an historically disadvantaged group (African American or females, for example)? Do you think that it is appropriate for any of the following to provide the type of preference just described: the government? a private employer? a college admissions office? Why or why not?

Do you think that the United States will ever be a fully color-blind society? Why or why not? What, if any, public policies might be helpful in achieving such a goal?

Do you relate differently to people of your own race than to people of another race? Do you think others do? What, if anything, might governments do to reduce racial tensions in American society?

The Split Society

Some 30 years after the civil rights movement's march on Washington, segregation has all but disappeared as a pressing issue on the national agenda, despite evidence that the chasms between black and white may be growing wider.

ROCHELLE L. STANFIELD

"This is America, and there is racism in this country," Delores A. Irvin said matter-of-factly. "Being black in America has been—and still is—very hard."

Irvin runs a program in Chicago that helps poor black families from the city's public housing projects rent apartments in its predominantly white suburbs. She ostensibly was describing her program, but the subtext was clear: For blacks, regardless of income, segregation driven by racial animosity remains an immutable fact of life.

While Irvin may be the image of a middle-class professional, "if I went to certain of these areas, I would get rebuffed," she said. "Being an African-American, it goes with the territory."

It's been 40 years since the Supreme Court declared that separate education for blacks isn't equal, and 30 years since Congress passed the 1964 Civil Rights Act. But integration is still a fragile exception; segregation the sturdy rule. The desegregation of America's public schools, which continued through the 1980s despite the hostility of the Reagan Administration, has now reversed. Residential integration, for the most part, has hardly happened at all.

"If you thought that segregation of blacks was a problem in 1960, the numbers you're seeing today would indicate that it's still a problem," Roderick J. Harrison, chief of the Census Bureau's racial statistics branch, said. "If you were hoping that civil rights, fair-housing laws, the growth of the black middle class would, over a 20-30 year period, really change the picture, I think everybody would agree" that they haven't.

For more than two decades, Presidents did little to push for the vigorous enforcement of antidiscrimination laws. Desegregation became a word rarely, if ever, spoken in public, regardless of the race of the speaker or the audience.

"We don't talk about race anymore," Mayor Sharpe James of Newark, N.J., acknowledged at a recent question-and-answer session with *National Journal* reporters. "We don't understand that it's as fundamental as motherhood and apple pie, and we will never be a great nation until we recognize the fact that our diversity is our strength." *(For more on that session, see NJ, 3/26/94, p. 726.)*

Not all black leaders agree with James. Indeed, black nationalists and some black politicians see advantages in racial concentration. But surveys show that an overwhelming majority of blacks desire integration.

For the first time in decades, a President and some members of his Cabinet are talking about desegregation. So far, however, their rhetoric speaks louder than their deeds.

It started with Housing and Urban Development (HUD) Secretary Henry G. Cisneros, who, from virtually his first day on the job, began speaking openly and passionately about desegregating housing, especially in cases where federal policies caused the segregation in the first place.

"This is offensive wherever it occurs," he said recently, referring to segregated HUD-owned housing. "It is just wrong."

Cisneros has promised to desegregate HUD housing programs and has made the enforcement of fair-housing laws a high priority. He's even backed up the rhetoric with some money to establish programs similar to the one Irvin runs in Chicago.

Next came Attorney General Janet Reno. She quietly began beefing up the housing section of the Justice Department's Civil Rights Division when she arrived in Washington. In December, she spoke out on the subject of fair lending, telling leaders of financial institutions that they must stop their long-standing, subtle but pervasive discrimination in making mortgage loans.

Together, Reno and Cisneros—with the cooperation of Eugene A. Ludwig, the Comptroller of the Currency—engineered a fair-lending agreement between the two departments and eight other federal bodies that regulate financial institutions. On March 8, the top officials of all 10 entities stood before a jam-packed press conference to announce, in effect, that they would for the first time consistently enforce a law that's been on the books for 26 years.

"It restates the current law, so there's nothing new in that," Roberta Achtenberg, the assistant HUD secretary for fair housing and equal opportunity, acknowledged in an interview. "But it's pretty remarkable in the annals of banking history."

As for President Clinton, civil rights activists praise him for talking about integration. To commemorate Martin Luther King Jr. Day on Jan. 17, Clinton signed an executive order to create a Cabinet-level interagency council on fair housing and ordered it to get moving on antidiscrimination initiatives.

Eight days later, in his State of the Union message, Clinton said, "We must continue to enforce fair lending and fair housing and all civil rights laws, because America will never be complete in its renewal until everyone shares in its bounty."

Civil rights activists said that they couldn't recall the last time a President made such a specific plea about civil rights enforcement in a State of the Union speech—at least not since President Johnson's 1965 message.

But Clinton has been very slow to act. An assistant attorney general for civil rights has just been confirmed, and other key civil rights posts in the Administration have gone unfilled. Vacancies remain at the Equal Employment Opportunity Commission, which continues to tread water as it has for 12 years.

Despite the promises, strong policy directives and personal intervention of Cisneros and Achtenberg, however, civil rights activists complain that much of HUD's bureaucratic machinery has yet to gear up to implement fair housing.

And desegregation seems to have missed the elementary and secondary education arena altogether. At Justice's Civil Rights Division, the education section remains a backwater.

And Education Secretary Richard W. Riley has been silent on the subject, though he's pushed for higher standards at urban schools where minority youths are concentrated. That is somewhat of a surprise because Riley has one of the strongest civil rights backgrounds in Clinton's Cabinet. In 1970, as South Carolina's governor, for example, he took an active role in promoting school desegregation in Greenville.

School desegregation activists haven't complained too bitterly, however, taking some comfort in the renewed drive for fair housing. "We've gone from full reverse to neutral," said Gary Orfield, a professor of education and social policy at Harvard University who has designed school desegregation plans ordered by the courts. "And that's some progress."

LIVING ARRANGEMENTS

The post-World War II civil rights drive started with the schools and got its first big push with the Supreme Court's 1954 ruling in *Brown v. Board of Education*. But if American society is ever to become racially integrated, activists and researchers agree, it will have to happen by desegregating housing. That's still a long way away, even though Congress passed the Fair Housing Act in 1968 and strengthened it 20 years later.

Richard A. Bloom

Assistant HUD secretary Roberta Achtenberg "Sometimes HUD has been the problem."

Some progress on the integration front, however, is under way.

Reynolds Farley, a professor of sociology at the University of Michigan, created a mild flurry of excitement in civil rights circles in February when he reported "modest" but "pervasive" declines in residential segregation across the United States in the 1980s. He looked at Census Bureau data from the 232 metropolitan areas in which blacks make up at least 3 per cent of the population and found a decrease in segregation in 194 of them.

Farley also highlighted a trend that may augur significant future declines in segregation. He found the biggest upticks in integration in small but growing metropolitan areas in the South and West—Orlando, Fla., and Riverside, Calif., for example—where a large proportion of the housing was built after the 1968 Fair Housing Act and not subject to the segregated patterns set in northeastern and midwestern cities before World War II. *(See box.)*

But even Farley, who's among the most optimistic of the researchers who follow these trends, acknowledged that the changes were far from dramatic. "It is a small movement that is creeping along," he said in a recent interview.

And it doesn't really affect most blacks where they live now, which is in the large metropolitan areas of the old Industrial Belts of the Northeast and Midwest, the most segregated places in the nation.

Douglas S. Massey, a professor of sociology at the University of Chicago, and Nancy A. Denton, an assistant professor of sociology at the State University of New York (Albany), examined segregation in the nation's 30 largest metropolitan areas, where 60 per cent of urban blacks reside. They found very little change in the past 20 years; most of the decline that did take place occurred during the 1970s.

In six major metropolitan areas (Chicago; Cleveland; Detroit; Gary, Ind.; New York City; and Newark, N.J.) in 1990, for example, the average black family lived in a highly segregated neighborhood (one in which at least 80 per cent of the black households would have to move to predominantly white neighborhoods to achieve full integration). The biggest sustained drops over the two decades were in Boston and Los Angeles, but by 1990 both metropolitan areas were still highly segregated.

Researchers have also found that black residential segregation is fundamentally different from that of other racial and ethnic groups. Blacks are more concentrated and isolated in center cities (many would have to go clear across the city to find a white family, for example), a condition that Massey and Denton call "hyper-

MOST AND LEAST

The greatest segregation of blacks occurs in the old industrial centers of the Northeast and Midwest, where segregated housing patterns were established before World War II and not broken, according to Reynolds Farley, a sociologist who's studied patterns of segregation in 232 metropolitan areas with substantial black populations. The least segregation is in newer, generally smaller, metropolitan areas in the South and West, particularly in communities that have big military bases or universities. This table lists the 15 most segregated and least segregated metropolitan areas in 1990, and the percentage of black households that would have to move to predominantly white neighborhoods to achieve full integration.

Most Segregated

Gary, Ind.	91%
Detroit	89
Chicago	87
Cleveland	86
Buffalo, N.Y.	84
Flint, Mich.	84
Milwaukee	84
Saginaw, Mich.	84
Newark, N.J.	83
Philadelphia	82
St. Louis	81
Ft. Myers, Fla.	81
Sarasota, Fla.	80
Indianapolis	80
Cincinnati	80

Least Segregated

Charlottesville, Va.	45%
Danville, Va.	45
Killeen, Texas	45
San José	45
Tucson	45
Honolulu	44
Anaheim, Calif.	43
Cheyenne, Wyo.	43
Ft. Walton Beach, Fla.	43
Clarksville, Tenn.	42
Lawrence, Kan.	41
Fayetteville, N.C.	41
Anchorage	38
Lawton, Okla.	37
Jacksonville, N.C.	31

SOURCE: Reynolds Farley, Population Studies Center, University of Michigan

segregation." Neither Hispanics nor Asians live in hypersegregated neighborhoods.

At the current rate of integration, the Census Bureau's Harrison predicted, it could take as long as 100 years for black segregation to fall to the level of Hispanic segregation.

During the 1980s, the segregation rates for Hispanics and Asians increased because immigration was so great and the first stop for most newcomers is a neighborhood settled by their compatriots. But as soon as Latinos or Asian-Americans assimilate and acquire some money, many move into majority-white neighborhoods. That's not the case with African-Americans.

"Levels of segregation for the black nonpoor are very close to those of the black poor," Harrison said. "In most other groups, there is a sharp difference in segregation, with the poor being much more segregated."

Even when blacks move into the suburbs, most of them end up in predominantly black enclaves. The close-in Washington suburb of Prince George's County, Md., for example, became 51 per cent black in 1990. But the distribution was far from even. Bowie remained 94 per cent white, for example, while Hillcrest Heights was 88 per cent black and Suitland was 84 per cent black.

Perhaps such statistics show that blacks prefer to live in segregated communities, some observers have suggested. After all, there's been a rise in black nationalism with the increasing prominence of the Nation of Islam. Black politicians cultivate predominantly black cities and congressional districts. And on many university campuses, black students are demanding their own African-American dormitories.

There's even a name for new middle-class black suburbs and neighborhoods: "zones of emergence." The phrase was coined by Richard P. Nathan, a longtime urban researcher who's now the provost of the Rockefeller College of Public Affairs at the State University of New York (Albany).

"There is something of a movement in the African-American community away from integrationist perspectives," said David A. Bositis, a senior research associate at the Joint Center for Political and Economic Studies, a Washington think tank that's devoted to African-American issues.

If there is such movement, however, it apparently hasn't touched most blacks. Polls consistently show that the overwhelming majority of blacks would prefer to live in an integrated neighborhood. A recent survey for the National Conference of Christians and Jews, for example, showed that although blacks, Hispanics and Asian-Americans had little good to say about one another or about whites, most of them—including 71 per cent of the blacks—supported "full integration."

Farley studied the housing preferences of blacks and whites in the Detroit area—the second-most-segregated metropolitan area in the nation, with a long history of bitter racial animosity—in 1976 and 1992. In both years, the vast majority of the blacks opted for integrated neighborhoods, with a 50-50 ratio their ideal. Most blacks ranked an all-black neighborhood very low on their preference list, and only 25 per cent said that they would be willing to move into such a neighborhood.

In the 15 years between the studies, whites became much more accepting of integration, but not to the point, apparently, of a 50-50 mix. In 1992, 56 per cent said they would be comfortable living in a neighborhood that was a third black, up from 43 per cent in 1976. In 1992, 53 per cent of the white respondents said that they would try to move out of a majority-black neighborhood, down from 64 per cent in 1976.

So, if everybody is for integration, why doesn't it happen? Government officials and civil rights activists answer in unison: Discrimination in the housing industry is remarkably tenacious.

"Markets, when left alone, don't generate integrated outcomes very often, even when there are people out there who would prefer them," John Yinger, a professor of sociology at Syracuse University who conducted housing discrimination studies for HUD in the late 1980s, said.

Yinger and most of his colleagues argue for a concerted policy to speed racial integration.

"I would hate to see us move toward a separate but equal society, even if it were possible to have that equality," said George C. Galster, a visiting senior research associate at the Urban Institute who has written extensively about desegregation. "I think that's a lousy public policy goal."

"You can't attack urban problems unless you come to terms with segregation and the forces that produce it," Massey said in a recent interview. "Whatever you try to do in the realm of education or job training or community investment is going to be overwhelmed by these disastrous neighborhood conditions, which follow fairly axiomatically from segregation."

Florence W. Roisman, a longtime civil rights activist who now teaches law at Georgetown University, had a direr prediction. "I think integration is an idea whose time must be now," she said, "because if it isn't, what happened to what used to be Yugoslavia is going to happen to us."

TAKING ACTION

If Cisneros and Reno have their way, the federal government will aggressively promote housing integration. That would reverse decades of practice because, despite the fair-housing laws on the books, the federal government itself has erected some of the highest barriers to housing desegregation for both the middle class and the poor.

"Sometimes HUD has been the problem," Achtenberg said. "We are not the cause of all segregated housing patterns in America today, but we have all too often played some role even by virtue of the way we have allowed our programs to reinforce racially restrictive neighborhood patterns."

Nowhere is that truer than in the suburbs, which since the early 1950s the Federal Housing Administration (FHA) has helped to build and finance as white necklaces around increasingly black cities.

In FHA-assisted projects, developers are required to search out minority buyers but rarely do.

"HUD is doing zip, *nada*, nothing," Roisman said. "HUD's own studies show that a lot of the projects that are supposed to have affirmative fair-housing marketing plans don't have them and even when they have them, they're not followed and the people who work there don't know about them or laugh them off."

Acknowledging that "the affirmative marketing requirements are quite minimal," Achtenberg said that HUD is "in the process of revising the entire affirmative marketing program."

As long as many middle-class black families can't get mortgages, however, no amount of marketing will help. That's where the new fair-lending agreement should come into play.

"We're devoting a lot of resources to obtain voluntary compliance [by the financial institutions]," said Paul F. Hancock, the chief of the Civil Rights Division's housing section at the Justice Department. "But we're also telling the industry that for those that don't get the message and continue to discriminate, we will use the full extent of our enforcement powers."

Hancock's office has already begun to do so. In the past 18 months, it has taken four banks to court and in several cases obtained settlements of about $1 million.

"The statistics on fair lending are easy to show," John P. Relman, the director of the fair-housing project of the Washington Lawyers Committee for Civil Rights and Urban Affairs, said. "Four cases in the last year and a half—three of them in the last half-year—and before that, zero."

For the poor, on the other hand, action by the Clinton Administration is slower, despite the resolve of top officials.

Last September, Cisneros swooped down on the small all-white town of Vidor, Texas, a longtime Ku Klux Klan stronghold, and with federal marshals took over the Vidor public housing project and forcibly integrated it.

In the intervening six months, 12 black families have moved into the Vidor project, and so far, Achtenberg explained—superstitiously knocking on the wood of her desk—all has gone well. "But our work is not over by a long shot," she said.

That's for sure, civil rights activists say. Vidor is a tiny fragment of a sprawling, 14-year-old segregation case against HUD in East Texas, and Texas is but one small example of a nationwide problem of segregated HUD-owned and subsidized housing for the poor.

In 1980, Dallas lawyer Mike Daniel sued HUD for allowing segregation in public housing projects in 36 Texas counties. HUD and the Justice Department's Civil Division fought the case. Daniel won, but little was done. Now, more than a decade later, Cisneros is trying to remedy the situation and integrate the housing projects. But he's apparently running into as much resistance from the federal bureaucracy as he is from the local segregationists.

Cisneros, for example, formed a federal-local task force to come up with a desegregation plan. The plan used racial data by census tracts, each of which contains about 4,000 people. That might have been a logical desegregation unit in Achtenberg's hometown of San Francisco, where a census tract covers a typical neighborhood, but "in most East Texas towns, a census tract includes the whole town and sometimes extends for 80 square miles out into the country," Daniel explained.

As a result, the housing projects appeared on paper to be a lot less segregated than they really are. "So they could use that analysis to basically say they don't have to do much more," Daniel said. "Declare a victory that HUD housing in East Texas is desegregated."

So Daniel complained and demanded that the plan be based on census blocks, statistical designations that are about the size of city blocks. "The Justice Department lawyers said, with a straight face, that they couldn't get block data and pro-

REVERSAL IN THE SOUTH

Percentage of black students in majority-white schools

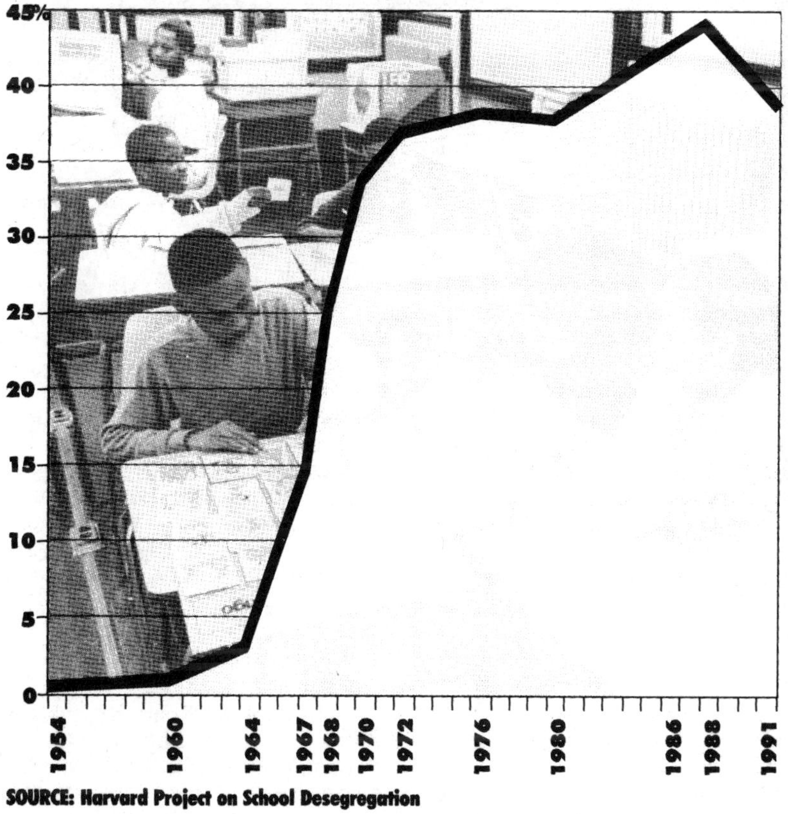

45%, 40, 35, 30, 25, 20, 15, 10, 5, 0

1954, 1960, 1964, 1967, 1968, 1970, 1972, 1976, 1980, 1986, 1988, 1991

SOURCE: Harvard Project on School Desegregation

duced a HUD intellectual who also said it," Daniel said. "I just don't see how anybody who [knows about census data] could possibly fall for that crap."

The complaint eventually reached Achtenberg on a Thursday. On Friday, she ordered that the plans be reworked. But that wasn't the end of the fight, Daniel said. "On Monday, the task force met to discuss *whether or not* to make any changes," he said. "It just goes on and on."

Meanwhile, the Administration's fiscal 1995 budget requests several small pots of money to encourage integration in assisted housing. One proposal seeks $149 million to establish programs, such as the one in Chicago, to help families who live in subsidized housing in inner cities look for apartments in the suburbs. Another would allocate $24 million to demonstrate one-stop shopping for subsidized housing in an entire metropolitan area, merging what are now separate, segregated housing programs for cities and their suburbs.

The Buffalo (N.Y.) metropolitan area, for example, has two housing voucher programs—one for the city and one for all its suburbs. The one for the suburbs has a residency requirement that makes it just about impossible for blacks from the city to get a subsidized apartment in the predominantly white suburbs. Achtenberg acknowledged the problem and said that she is trying to fix it.

"They've taken some fine first steps," said Thomas J. Henderson, the deputy director of the Lawyers' Committee for Civil Rights Under Law. "But we have yet to see whether the folks over there are up to the task of really coming to grips with the terrible legacy of institutionalized segregation that has been built into our housing system."

SEPARATE AND UNEQUAL

Until housing integration is achieved, real school desegregation is unlikely. And so far, the Clinton Administration's education policies don't change the equation.

An end to the institutionalized segregation of education was what much of the civil rights movement was about in the 1960s and 1970s. The civil rights activists won, state-enforced segregation requirements ended and considerable integration took place. *(See chart, p. 765.)*

But that was mostly in the South, where housing generally was less segregated than in the North, and where many school districts covered whole counties, so that a district's school desegregation plan included white suburban students.

The issue is much trickier in the North, where schools have remained much more segregated. In a recent study for the National School Boards Association, for example, Harvard's Orfield found that 50.1 per cent of black students in the Northeast attended schools that were 90-100 per cent minority during the 1991-92 school year; the comparable proportion in the South was 26.6 per cent. For more than a decade, Illinois, Michigan, New Jersey and New York have topped the list of states with the most segregated school systems.

The Supreme Court, which facilitated southern desegregation, complicated northern integration efforts with its 1974 ruling in *Milliken v. Bradley*. Its decision overturned a desegregation plan for the Detroit schools that included busing to the suburbs. Afterward, northern whites found that they could hide from desegregation, and their flight to the suburbs picked up speed.

Richard A. Bloom

William L. Taylor, a Washington civil rights lawyer
"It's yet to be seen what the Clinton Administration will do."

Black families are moving to the suburbs, too, but for black children, that doesn't necessarily mean going to an integrated school. Orfield found, for example, that of 1.3 million black students in the suburbs of the nation's 33 largest metropolitan areas, three-fifths went to predominantly black schools.

Since the 1970s, neither Congress nor five Presidents have done much to integrate the nation's public schools. In 1972, Congress enacted the Emergency School Assistance Act, which pumped billions of dollars into schools undergoing desegregation. But in 1981, at President Reagan's request, Congress abolished the program. Meanwhile, Congress has routinely attached an anti-busing rider to the Education Department's annual appropriation, prohibiting the use of any federal education funds for busing to achieve integration and making it difficult for the department to cut off assistance to schools that don't desegregate.

Nonetheless, the desegregation that was achieved in the late 1960s persisted for nearly two decades, primarily because the courts retained control over the school districts they had ordered desegregated. In the mid-1980s, however, William Bradford Reynolds, then the assistant attorney general for civil rights, intervened in several cases in an effort to remove the school systems from court supervision. Orfield and others attribute the resegregation that began during the Bush Administration partly to Reynolds's move.

What's more, many civil rights activists no longer look to the federal courts for help in achieving school integration. "We are not bringing any new school desegregation cases," said David S. Tatel, a Washington-based civil rights lawyer. "We are spending a lot of time with school districts that are trying to keep [old] desegregation plans going."

So far, the Clinton Administration has been all but mum on the subject of desegregating the nation's public schools, although it has actively promoted the desegregation of institutions of higher learning through lawsuits and minority scholarships. As for elementary and secondary schools, however, about all it has done is to propose, in its fiscal 1995 budget, increasing assistance to magnet schools from $108 million to $120 million. A less controversial alternative to mandatory busing to achieve some integration, magnet schools—often in poor city neighborhoods—receive extra funds to provide special programs to attract students from outside the neighborhood or even outside the city.

"I think it's yet to be seen what the Clinton Administration will do," William L. Taylor, a Washington-based civil rights lawyer, said. "I think it is reasonable to expect that this battering that went on during the Reagan and Bush Administrations will cease, but absent any kind of affirmative policy, I think the trend toward resegregation is likely to continue."

Because the school systems in many of the large old northern cities are predominantly black, the only way meaningful desegregation can occur is to transfer city students to suburban schools and vice versa. Naturally, there is a lot of controversy and considerable disagreement about the value of such transfers.

Orfield and others point to studies that show that poor black students do much better in white suburban schools. James E. Rosenbaum, a professor of education and social policy at Northwestern University, studied children involved in the Chicago program that Irvin runs, for example. That program began in 1976 as the result of a court case, *Hills v. Gautreaux*. In 1989, Rosenbaum compared the records of children who had moved out to the suburbs with those of similar children who had remained in the city. The differences were striking.

Where 20 per cent of the city students had dropped out, only 5 per cent of the suburban students had. A similar pattern prevailed for college attendance. Among those who moved to the suburbs, 54 per cent attended college—and 27 per cent of them a four-year college. The comparable figures for those who remained in the city was 21 per cent and 4 per cent. Of those who didn't go to college, 75 per cent of the suburban students had a full-time job, compared with only 41 per cent of the city students.

But Rosenbaum acknowledged that the dramatic results didn't happen overnight. "We found that suburban movers initially had difficulties adapting to the higher expectations in the suburban schools, and their grades suffered in their first years there," he wrote in an article in the June 1993 issue of the *North Carolina Law Review*.

The same is true for a massive city-suburban magnet program in St. Louis and its suburbs. "I think it's accomplishing a lot," said Susan Uchitelle, the executive director of the Voluntary Interdistrict Coordinating Council, which runs the decade-old program. "But it's going to take more than 10 years" for the impact to show up in test scores.

Under the program, 14,000 young St. Louis residents take buses out to suburban schools while 1,100 suburban youngsters travel in the opposite direction to magnet schools in the city. Tests have shown that the black elementary school students who travel out to the suburbs haven't done much better than children who remain in the city. But by 10th grade, the achievement of the city students begins to decline while that of the suburban students begins to improve.

St. Louis Mayor Freeman R. Bosley Jr., who is black, has expressed his misgivings about this plan in particular and busing in general.

"Even though I appreciate white kids and black kids going to school together, it has not been good for the neighborhoods," he told editorial writers at the *St. Louis Post-Dispatch* last fall. "If you don't have good neighborhood schools, people won't live there. If you live there and send your kids to school somewhere else, there's no sense of commitment."

Bosley also complained about the $25 million that the city must spend to bus its children out to the suburbs. He said he'd rather use the money to improve the city's schools.

Bosley's concerns seem to jibe with the Clinton Administration's policy of putting a high priority on improving schools and saying nothing about integrating them. But the debate continues as to whether that policy can be implemented. Apparently separate but equal was not really decided once and for all in 1954.

A state court judge in Pennsylvania recently ordered Philadelphia's schools to both desegregate and improve the education achievement of poor students. The ruling is the latest development in a case that was brought under Pennsylvania's human relations law in 1970. "It remains the Pennsylvania Human Relations Commission's position that physical desegregation of schools is required," said Michael Hardiman, the lawyer who argued that side of the case. "But it doesn't stop there."

"Our view is that you could stop looking at the issue of mandatory busing and physical integration and start focusing on educational quality issues," responded Michael Churchill, a lawyer for the Public Interest Law Center of Philadelphia, which intervened in the case. "Desegregation is not disappearing as an issue, but it's not going to be the preeminent issue. Quality is going to be."

The prospects don't look good for achieving integration through new plans to bus city students to the suburbs. The Minnesota State Board of Education has recommended doing just that. Minnesota has long been known as the state that can peacefully accomplish the kind of difficult social experiments that would provoke riots in other states. But when the board's plan was announced, there was an explosion of protest. "We took phone calls for two solid days from the community," said Barbara Stillwell, an employee who worked on the plan. "It was quite challenging to sit and listen politely to some of the comments we got."

A color-blind society is still a very long way off. The Clinton Administration seems willing to address the issue of housing integration, but it has done little, if anything, to eliminate school segregation—the condition that started the civil rights movement 40 years ago.

John Eisele

Paul F. Hancock, who heads the Civil Rights Division's housing section at Justice In the past 18 months, his office has sued four lenders and obtained big settlements.

The Wedge Issue

Conservative activists and politicians have declared war on affirmative action, which may well emerge as a potent wedge issue in the 1996 presidential campaign. But civil rights activists aren't standing still for what they see as a perversion of both history and true democratic principles.

ROCHELLE L. STANFIELD

[*In June 1995, the U.S. Supreme Court announced a 5-to-4 decision that could turn out to be a landmark ruling on the issue of affirmative action. In *Adarand Constructors v. Pena,* the divided Court set forth new standards that made affirmative action programs of the national government more likely to be judged unconstitutional. However, the Court left detailed application of the new standards, at least for the immediate future, to lower federal courts. **Editor**]

Clint Bolick sees the fight over affirmative action in stark terms: "Those of us who are arguing for race neutrality," he says, "have really claimed the mantle of the great civil rights advocates from Frederick Douglass to Martin Luther King Jr. and Hubert Humphrey."

Bolick, the litigation director of the Washington-based Institute for Justice, a conservative public-interest law firm, continued in an interview: "Defenders of the status quo have lost the moral high ground. Defending discrimination of any sort is a very treacherous enterprise."

Bolick and his colleagues on the Right are trying to rewrite the dictionary of social issues that liberals compiled over the past 30 years—just in time for use in the 1996 presidential elections.

As part of this exercise, the Right has adopted and adapted much of the rhetoric and many of the tactics that the Left had long employed effectively. For example: cast your arguments in terms of basic constitutional principles and your constituents as the victims of selfish, undemocratic policies.

Affirmative action is a natural starting point for this conservative strategy because it readily lends itself to such a redefinition.

Reduced to the basics, affirmative action policies grant special treatment to certain groups: admissions officers for colleges and universities consider the race, gender and ethnicity of applicants; personnel directors do the same in hiring and laying off workers; government contracts provide set-asides for minorities and women.

It's a small step for opponents of affirmative action to call such treatment "a preference" and not too great a leap to label the preference as discrimination. To drive this message home, they cite a handful of highly publicized legal cases over the years to highlight affirmative action practices that did involve discrimination, the most famous being a quota system employed by the admissions office of the University of California (Davis) medical school that the Supreme Court struck down in 1978 in the *Bakke* case.

In the 1970s and early 1980s, opponents of affirmative action characterized the practice as "reverse discrimination." Today, many conservatives brand affirmative action "discrimination" and suggest that it's the only government-sanctioned kind of discrimination going on.

"Once you discover how pervasive

Richard A. Bloom

Clint Bolick of the Institute for Justice
Defending discrimination is a "treacherous enterprise."

From *National Journal,* April 1, 1995, pp. 790-793.

[affirmative action] really is, it becomes easier to say 'discrimination' as opposed to, 'Well, there's all that other discrimination and then there's this peculiar side area of reverse discrimination,' " said Michael S. Greve, the executive director of the Center for Individual Rights, another conservative public-interest law firm in Washington. "The only legalized discrimination in this country is against whites and males."

Those who hold to the new redefinition of affirmative action find it a tempting wedge issue to maintain the splintering in the 1994 midterm elections of the traditional Democratic Party bases: minorities, women and working-class white men.

That may be why Senate Majority Leader Robert Dole, R-Kan., the acknowledged front-runner in the 1996 Republican presidential sweepstakes, now urges a ban on federal affirmative action programs, which he steadfastly supported throughout the 1980s. Sen. Phil Gramm, R-Texas, who is trying to corner conservative votes for his presidential run, meanwhile, brags that he's consistently opposed affirmative action from the beginning. And Patrick J. Buchanan, who entered the contest on March 20, takes credit for inventing anti-affirmative action as a Republican campaign issue in 1992.

The rhetoric of conservatives already has centrist Democrats scrambling. Sen. Joseph I. Lieberman, D-Conn., the chairman of the Democratic Leadership Council, has lined up with the opponents of affirmative action, labeling it "patently unfair."

And even President Clinton, with a glistening record on the affirmative action front, is searching for a middle road that somehow satisfies both sides. While he wants "to open up more opportunities," Clinton told college journalists on March 23, "I'm against giving people opportunities who are unqualified." Then he repeated a question he often asks: "How do we now go forward?"

Meanwhile, old-line civil rights activists aren't standing still for what they see as the right wing's perversion of both history and true democratic principles.

"When these people say they are the inheritors of Martin Luther King, that is lying and it's just obscene," Roger Wilkins, a friend of King's who helped to plan his funeral, served as an assistant attorney general in the Carter Administration and is now a history professor at George Mason University, said in an interview.

Civil rights activists insist that the basic strategies to undermine affirmative action aren't new. "What's amazing about

It's a small step for opponents of affirmative action to call such treatment "a preference" and not too great a leap to brand it discrimination.

the arguments of the Right on affirmative action is that there's not one new argument," Barbara R. Arnwine, the executive director of the Washington-based Lawyers' Committee for Civil Rights Under Law, said.

But the rhetoric is bolder now, and maybe more telling. The times are particularly propitious for the conservatives' campaign, longtime civil rights activists say. Added to long-standing prejudices—to a large extent driven underground for decades, but once more bubbling up—is anxiety over an increasingly competitive economy where college and graduate school admission, job security and promotions are no longer a sure thing for white men. Although the rhetoric on both sides of the affirmative action battle is aimed at both minorities and women, the real venom is reserved for minorities, especially blacks.

While the tactic of "wrapping resentments in morality" has been tried for decades, Wilkins said, "all of a sudden, you have a potent combination [of prejudice and anxiety], and it is patriotic to be bigoted. It's wonderful mental jujitsu and it's absolutely fraudulent."

SOUNDBITTEN

Redefining affirmative action is especially appealing to conservatives now because the issue is tailor-made for soundbite politics: Affirmative action equals discrimination. Period.

Supporters of affirmative action thus are forced into long, complicated and subtle rebuttals about why the issue isn't that simple. In his 1990 reelection campaign, Sen. Jesse A. Helms, R-N.C., demonstrated how this tactic can work with effective television advertisements that attacked his opponent, Harvey B. Gantt, a black, as favoring quotas.

Public opinion analysts point to an analogy in how questions for polls are framed. Tom W. Smith, the director of the general social survey at the University of Chicago's National Opinion Research Center, explained it in this way: "You get results that run from 80 per cent pro down to 20 per cent pro, depending on what you ask. If you ask about something like 'fighting discrimination,' 'promoting equal opportunity' or 'treating everyone fairly,' you'll get 80 per cent agreed. If you take a vaguer term like affirmative action but don't define it further, you might get 40-50 per cent in favor. But if you shift and say 'special treatment' or 'special preference,' you'll get no more than a third. And if you get even stronger and talk about racial quotas, you'd be lucky to get 20 per cent."

Thus, in response to question No. 67 in a January poll for the *Los Angeles Times*, which asked about "affirmative action programs designed to help minorities get better jobs and education," only 39 per cent of those surveyed said that the programs "go too far," while 32 per cent said that they are "adequate now" and 23 per cent said that they "don't go far enough."

But the following question in the poll, which asked whether Congress should ban "preferential treatment in hiring," found 73 per cent of the respondents in favor and only 23 per cent opposed.

For years, opponents of affirmative action programs argued that they were nothing more than "quotas." That word was especially useful as a wedge between blacks and Jews, many of whom were early supporters of the civil rights movement, because many colleges and universities had employed numerical or percentage quotas until the 1950s to limit their Jewish enrollments.

But supporters of affirmative action easily countered the argument by responding that quotas are illegal and that legitimate affirmative action programs don't use them.

"I will say a thousand times a day that quota situations are illegal under the law, and if people are hiring or admitting strictly by the numbers, rigidly, and not taking into account qualifications, they are in violation of the law," Ralph G. Neas, the executive director of the Leadership Conference on Civil Rights, said in an interview. "The answer is to enforce the law, not to repeal the law."

Supporters of affirmative action seem to have driven this point home. While Gramm still peppers some of his statements with the "Q" word, others have retired it in favor of the all-encompassing and even more emotional tag of discrimination. "My sense is that the word 'quotas' has basically done its duty and will now be discarded," the Center for Individual Rights' Greve said.

Conservatives now tend to target the affirmative action policies of most colleges, universities and graduate schools as automatically discriminatory.

"When we give preferential treatment we are almost by definition discriminating against someone else," Ward Connerly, a member of the University of California Board of Regents and a leader of the fight in California against affirmative action, said on ABC News's *This Week With David Brinkley* on Feb. 26.

Richard A. Bloom

Longtime civil rights activist Roger Wilkins
"All of a sudden, . . . it is patriotic to be bigoted."

In the *Bakke* case, the Supreme Court "said you can put your finger on the scale for race, but admissions policies can't be race-driven," Abigail Thernstrom, a Boston-based senior fellow of the Manhattan Institute, said. "Well, all over this country, admissions policies are race-driven. So it didn't matter—the Supreme Court was talking to itself."

John Eisele

Michael S. Greve, the executive director of the Center for Individual Rights
"The only legalized discrimination in this country is against whites and males."

If admissions policies are indeed so race-driven, there's no evidence of it yet in national college and university enrollment statistics. The annual report on minority enrollment recently issued by the American Council on Education showed that of all 18-24-year-old high school graduates, 42 per cent of whites were enrolled in college in 1993 but only 33 per cent of blacks and 36 per cent of Hispanics. And while blacks and Hispanics constitute about 26 per cent of the college-age population, they account for less than 17 per cent of the enrollment at the nation's 3,600 institutions of higher education.

Nonetheless, college admission is an especially fertile field for opponents of affirmative action because of some highly publicized examples of illegal preferences—often at law schools, ironically—and also because standardized examinations enable simple comparisons between admitted and rejected students.

The hot case now is *Hopwood v. Texas*. In each class it admits, the law school at the University of Texas (Austin) aims for Mexican-Americans to account for at least 10 per cent and blacks at least 5 per cent. As simply a goal, that's perfectly constitutional, Federal District Judge Sam Sparks ruled last fall.

But to achieve that goal, in 1992 the law school used separate admissions committees for white and minority applicants and lowered the numerical cutoff (based on test scores and grade point averages) for minorities by three points. Sparks held those two practices unconstitutional.

Opponents of affirmative action, however, were far from satisfied by Sparks's decision and are appealing the case. By allowing the school to set such a goal, the judge "in effect said, 'Do it in the basement—don't advertise to the world that you have separate cutoff scores,' " Greve, whose Center for Individual Rights argued the case for the plaintiffs, said.

"At some point, we have to come to grips with the fact that whether or not they keep the minority files in separate file cabinets isn't the question," Greve added. "The question is, do you tilt the playing field in such a way and such an extent, in whatever form you do it, that whites with identical qualifications are never compared to blacks or, if they are, they have no chance of getting in?"

Supporters of affirmative action can only argue that it's not that simple. Test scores aren't the be-all and end-all in determining qualification for admission, they say; they're designed only to predict how well an applicant is likely to do as a first-year student, not general competence.

"Critics [of affirmative action] view these scores as talismanic," William L. Taylor, a leading civil rights lawyer in Washington, said. "Though they won't admit it, they treat them as though they are perfect indicators of somebody's competence. Small differences in scores among people who meet basic qualifications may not be that important. That's the important thing."

In general, the schools that rely most heavily on test scores for admissions are the least selective public institutions that admit state residents who are high school graduates and meet minimum test score criteria, Joyce E. Smith, the associate executive director of the National Association of College Admissions Counselors, said. The more selective the school, the more individualized the process. "Many [selective schools] are committed to the idea of having a very interesting composition within their entering classes," she said, recalling her experience as an admissions officer at Amherst College. "So when we talk about diversity, we want want to make sure that we're admitting music students. Geographic diversity is another issue. If you're in New England and you get an application from Hawaii, you're going to look at that kid. And legacy is another factor. If you are the son or daughter of an alumnus, that's something that's important."

When asked about these other kinds of preferences, the Institute for Justice's Bolick replied: "I honestly don't know the extent to which various types of preferences occur. I think it is very legitimate to reexamine any sort of group preference, including those that operate to the disadvantage of outsiders. By the same token, there is no form of discrimination that is as odious as racial discrimination. So, however offensive we might find these other things, the fact that they may exist is not a reason to abstain from prohibiting race as a factor."

How can supporters of affirmative action respond to a statement like that? "By showing that it's just not true," Arnwine said. "Truth still has some power in this world."

John Eisele

Barbara R. Arnwine of the Lawyers' Committee for Civil Rights Under Law "There's not one new argument" from the Right on affirmative action.

WHO ARE THE REAL VICTIMS?

The second part of the conservatives' two-pronged rewrite of the social-issues dictionary is to define their target constituency—white men—as the real victims.

Victimization, in general, has become a potent conservative weapon. Members of the Christian Right, for example, have adroitly cast themselves as the victims of antireligious bureaucrats in the school prayer battle. *(See NJ, 1/7/95, p. 22.)*

Some supporters of affirmative action say that the cries of victimization are an effort to deflect attention from fundamental problems in the economy. "Along come the politicians and say, 'If you're not advancing, don't blame American employers or the economy and don't blame the government, which is supposed to stimulate the economy—somebody else is getting your job and it's that black guy over there,' " Taylor said.

The victimization argument outrages supporters of affirmative action and evokes particularly emotional reactions from many African-Americans.

"You can never have reverse discrimination in this country," said Reginald Wilson, a senior scholar at the American Council on Education who supervised the study of minorities in higher education. "You just need to look at what discrimination was: You had to go to the back of the restaurant, you couldn't ride the bus. Blacks were *lynched* in this country. You just can't compare the treatment of whites to blacks. Whites are never going to have that kind of treatment."

That was then, not now, opponents of affirmative action say. "There certainly is racism in this society, but not at a level at which blacks and Hispanics cannot get ahead," the Manhattan Institute's Thernstrom said. "You cannot seriously say to a black child in elementary school, 'It doesn't matter how hard you work in your science and math courses, you'll never become a doctor.' That's ludicrous. Now, will that same child fail to get a taxi on a street in New York? Sure. But will that stop that child in his or her tracks? No way."

Wilson and others reply that many forms of discrimination, some of them subtle, still stop many black children in their tracks.

"Maybe blacks can go to school with whites, but there's still tracking in the schools," Wilson said. "There's assignment of black kids to special education. There's exclusion and suspension of black kids much more than white kids."

Another element of the victimization strategy is even subtler. By defining affirmative action as discrimination and white men as its victims, opponents of the practice can justify white resentment against blacks—resentment, they say, that could lead to turmoil. The only way to get rid of the resentment and calm down society, the argument goes, is to eliminate affirmative action.

"We do not have a color-blind society," Bolick acknowledged. "The only way we will ever get to a color-blind society is for government, first and foremost, to stop discriminating on the basis of race. A ban on racial preferences will go a long way to remove the venom from race relations."

"Anybody who says that is a liar or utterly stupid," Wilkins responded. "To say that we would have a color-blind society were it not for affirmative action is to ignore two things: human nature and the fact that racism is a central part of this culture."

The real life consequences of doing away with affirmative action are often blurred by the rhetoric. Would America resegregate? Would the courts drown in discrimination cases? Would civil war break out? Or would society make faster progress on the road to color-blindness? These, of course, are questions a war of words cannot answer. *

A SPEAK-NO-EVIL VEIL LIFTED

LOUIS JACOBSON

The debate over the fate of affirmative action may mark the beginning of the end for race-conscious policies in hiring, contracting and education. But such federal policies might not be the only things on the way out. The emergence of a forthright debate over affirmative action may also turn out to be a watershed in the recent history of public discourse about racial matters. After two decades or more in which policy makers and journalists have treaded lightly around sensitive racial issues, the taboos have started to fall with breathtaking speed. Where this may lead is anybody's guess.

Few would dispute that racism still exists in America.

Few would dispute that racism still exists in America. But it is well-established that racism is now more commonly displayed privately, quietly and subtly than it is openly and bluntly. Ever since the heyday of the civil rights movement, many Americans have learned that silence is a safer option than risking the label "bigot" or the ire of minority groups. Whites have often considered frank criticism on racial matters to be impolite.

This isn't to say that, under the surface, whites have been all smiles toward minorities. According to Paul Sniderman, a political scientist at Stanford University, long-term research has found consistent—and massive—antagonism among whites toward preferential hiring and race-based college admissions. Like clockwork, 8 or 9 of every 10 whites have opposed such policies ever since pollsters started asking questions about them in 1982.

Even whites who considered themselves liberal on racial matters—that is, those who expressed support for affirmative action when asked about it directly—tended to reveal substantial reservations when pollsters plumbed their feelings on race-conscious policies in less direct ways. "If you ask it covertly, liberals were just as likely to be angry as conservatives," Sniderman said in an interview. "These are people who were very concerned that things get better for blacks, and were genuine about it. But they suppressed [their misgivings], because who wants to sound like some redneck or some outrageous conservative?"

"Liberals were just as likely to be angry as conservatives."

In the past few months, however, these inhibitions have begun to crumble. Though many liberals (and some conservatives) continue ritual expressions of sensitivity toward minorities, the coast is now clear for critiques of long-off-limits racial policies. The responses may be thoughtful or knee-jerk; what's new and notable is that they're finally being aired in polite company at all.

Sniderman suggests a couple of reasons for this sudden shift. The most obvious is that the Democrats—long the party that defended race-conscious policies, whatever the gut beliefs of its supporters—lost control of the House and Senate. As long as the Democrats controlled Congress, any plan to dismantle race-based policies was effectively dead on arrival. Republicans felt that they had little to gain in pressing the issue (and a lot to lose if the party appeared racist), while dissenting Democrats had little stomach for a potentially explosive internecine struggle.

The other big change has been a shift in political discourse away from elites and toward Everyman. The driving force behind the speak-no-evil consensus came from what social scientists call

No longer contrained by the old consensus, lots of politicians have pushed to roll back affirmative action.

"elites"—politicians, academics and journalists. In 1989, for instance, two-thirds of all references to affirmative action on the evening news and in the big news magazines were favorable—and thus greatly at odds with the public's view, according to the Center for Media and Public Affairs.

Even Republicans abided by this agreement: The Nixon Administration helped to implement many race-based policies, the Reagan Administration refrained from tearing them all

down and Republican leaders such as Sen. Robert Dole of Kansas had kind words for affirmative action. And whatever the feelings people revealed to pollsters, there was no groundswell for eliminating affirmative action.

All that has changed with surprising speed. Maybe it was talk radio, which opened up an outlet for non-elites to hold forth on national issues in a no-holds-barred (and generally conservative) setting. Maybe it was the backlash against the excesses of "political correctness" that made liberal policies fair game. Maybe it was the creeping fear of economic stagnation that prompted Americans to look for scapegoats. Or maybe it was that ideas that used to seem radical had been floating around long enough for even skeptical Americans to become comfortable with them.

With this foundation, only a spark was needed—California's Civil Rights Initiative, which purports to roll back all government-sanctioned discrimination, for and against minorities. The text of the initiative, whose language echoes Martin Luther King Jr.'s vision of a color-blind society, gives Sniderman's worried white liberals intellectual cover. And with the emergence of a citizen-initiated ballot measure, the old elites lost control over the debate. No longer constrained by the old consensus, lots of politicians (including Dole and moderate Democrats) have rushed to roll back affirmative action. After all, if Sniderman's data are correct, it's a big vote-winner.

The new candor might get blacks and whites talking honestly about their differences.

The question now is whether the new frankness is good or bad for America. The benefits of the old, enforced politeness were not trivial: It encouraged Americans to refrain from hurtful comments and to avoid suffusing every event with racial significance. (By and large, many of the blacks and Hispanics in the Clinton Administration who've run into trouble—Ronald H. Brown, Henry G. Cisneros, Joycelyn Elders, Mike Espy, Henry Foster Jr., Federico F. Peña—have been tried in the court of public opinion on factors other than the color of their skin.) By contrast, an unfettered dialogue on race could produce—in addition to the scuttling of some arguably helpful policies—demagoguery that could poison American politics. The recent debate on the House floor over welfare reform—with conservatives likening welfare recipients to alligators, liberals calling conservatives Nazis—does not provide much cause for optimism.

But if there is any reason at all for hope, it's that the new candor might eventually get blacks and whites talking honestly about their differences, shorn of excessive self-censorship, something that until recently had been rare. This, of course, would require patience and understanding on both sides of the racial divide. Is a happy ending too much to hope for?

Crime, Urban Affairs, and Other Domestic Policy Areas

As the first selection in this unit points out, the United States has the highest incarceration rate in the world. That means that a larger percentage of people in the United States are behind bars than in any other country. Not only do we imprison a relatively large segment of our population, we also rank among the most frequent users of the death penalty in the industrialized world. In many countries the death penalty has been abolished altogether.

The United States is also plagued by unusually high rates of crime, especially violent crimes that kill or injure people. Murder and manslaughter rates, assault and battery rates, and rape rates all exceed comparable figures in most other countries of the world. The policy problem to which the foregoing facts point seems clear enough: even though our governments incarcerate a relatively large percentage of the population and use the death penalty with a relatively high degree of frequency, we still live in a society with one of the highest rates of violent crime in the world.

What policies should governments pursue to reduce violent crime in American society? An effective government response to this question would presumably require an answer to a prior question: What causes the high rates of violent crime in the United States? Unfortunately for public policymakers, there is no consensus about what causes violent crime, and, thus, there are many conflicting suggestions about what policies our governments should pursue in response to crime. Some suggest that the criminal justice system needs to apprehend and convict even more criminals and perhaps punish them more severely, and in that way reduce crime. Others think that governments should try to do a better job at rehabilitating

those convicted of crimes, since a large proportion of those leaving prison wind up being convicted again after commission of yet another crime. Still others argue that the relatively low levels of spending on social welfare programs in the United States are the most important cause of crime and that increasing social welfare spending is the best solution to the nation's crime problem.

What all of these proposed policy solutions have in common is that they would cost a great deal of money. Given the financial difficulties that national, state, and local governments in the United States face today (see unit 2), policymakers confronting the crime problem often find themselves between a rock and a hard place, unable to pursue any plausible course of action in a vigorous and coherent fashion. This situation pleases no one, except perhaps proponents of a theory that violence is ingrained in our national character. According to this theory, the level of criminal violence in the United States stems from years of confrontations between Europeans and Native Americans and the generally forbidding western frontier faced by European settlers. That is to say, our violent tendencies have been deeply and perhaps irrevocably embedded in our culture, were later nurtured by racial and ethnic tensions and animosities, and now lie beyond the reach of any feasible public policy.

Nowhere is violent crime more problematic than in our urban areas. The homicide rates—and incarceration rates—among young African American males raised in American cities are astounding. Fear of crime stalks many urban dwellers every day. High unemployment rates, air and noise pollution, poor mass transportation, and a whole host of other problems join the problem of crime in plaguing our cities.

Selections in this unit treat crime and the criminal justice system as well as urban problems. There are also articles on a few other domestic policy areas of note.

Looking Ahead: Challenge Questions

Which of the solutions to the U.S. crime problem suggested in this unit do you think public policymakers ought to pursue? Why? What would you do if you were a criminal justice policymaker faced with absolutely no chance of getting more funds to deal with crime?

What do you think public policymakers ought to do to make our cities more livable? Why? Do you think that the portrait of Washington, D.C., in the year 2016 that is painted in "An Urban Nightmare Come True?" is farfetched? Or do you think that unless public policy comes to grips more effectively with crime and urban problems that what is now a hypothetical portrait will come true?

"Why should we kill people who kill people to show them that killing people is wrong?" So goes one slogan of capital punishment opponents that gives pause for thought. What do you think about capital punishment? Its morality as practiced in the contemporary United States? Its effect on deterring or reducing crime? The tendency for racial minorities and the poor to be disproportionately among those executed, even if they are convicted of the same type of crimes that wealthier white people have committed?

Name some areas of domestic policy that are not treated in this unit or any other unit of the book. Consider the apparent public policy successes and failures there seem to have been in the areas you have identified.

Locked In

An explosion in the nation's prison population is creating a fiscal black hole for state and federal governments. And the boom has created a powerful corporate constituency to protect prison budgets.

W. JOHN MOORE

One million. Justice Department number crunchers guess that the number of inmates in federal and state prisons will reach that milestone around New Year's Day 1995.

No celebration is planned—even by the politicians, Democrats and Republicans alike, who promise that putting enough dangerous people in prison will extinguish America's crime problem. By year's end, the prison system will incarcerate more people than live in Idaho, Rhode Island or any one of eight other states. Imagine guard towers and barbed wire blocking all exits from the city of Dallas.

From 1980-93, the nation's prison population grew 188 per cent, giving the United States the highest incarceration rate in the world. *(See charts, pp. 193 and 195.)* "We have an insatiable lust for locking up people," said Alvin J. Bronstein, executive director of the Prison Project at the American Civil Liberties Union (ACLU) in Washington.

Nor is there an end in sight. The population in federal prisons is growing by more than 700 inmates a month, according to the Justice Department. Over the next decade, the federal and state prison population will rise to at least 2.26 million if Congress enacts a pending crime bill that's designed to force murderers, rapists and robbers to serve at least 85 per cent of their sentences, according to a recent study. The study, by the National Council on Crime and Delinquency (NCCD), a nonpartisan research group in San Francisco, warned that its estimate could be too low because it did not consider the effects of "three-strikes-you're-out" laws that put repeat offenders away for life. Several states have enacted such laws, and there is a three-strikes provision in the pending federal crime bill.

The social costs of putting huge numbers of people in prisons across the nation could be immense. "We will have a nation of gulags," said Jerome G. Miller, founder of the nonprofit National Center on Institutions and Alternatives in Alexandria, Va.

And getting a grip on future prison costs is even harder than keeping track of the number of prisoners. In fiscal 1993, federal and state prison systems spent $21.3 billion, up from $14.8 billion in 1985, according to the Criminal Justice Institute Inc. in South Salem, N.Y. The NCCD study estimated that federal and state governments would need another $351 billion over the next decade to pay for an influx of inmates attributable to provisions in the crime bill.

The tab for prisons will be "astronomical," warned Norman A. Carlson, the former head of the Justice Department's Bureau of Prisons and now criminal justice professor at the University of Minnesota (Minneapolis).

And prison budget figures don't tell the whole story because a growing prison system puts pressure on other government agencies. For example, legal costs stemming from federal prisoners' lawsuits are borne by the Attorney General's office, not by the Bureau of Prisons. Likewise, state attorneys general bear the expense of fighting constitutional challenges brought against their prison systems. Pension benefits for state corrections workers often are paid by other agencies.

Although the swelling prison population hasn't made a dent in the crime rate, it has produced a booming industry. Average daily spending per inmate rose from $43.54 in 1987 to $50.22 in 1992, according to the Criminal Justice Institute. Medical costs are way up. So are starting salaries for correctional officers.

Corporate America gets a big piece of the action: Publications for prison officials feature page after page of advertisements for products ranging from riot gear and uniforms to telephones. The prison boom has created a powerful constituency to protect prison budgets.

If prison spending is becoming a fiscal black hole, politicians do not feel much pressure to address the problem because the biggest part of the bill won't be tallied for years. "It's a win-win situation for legislators," said Marc Mauer, deputy director of the Sentencing Project, a nonpartisan Washington research organization. "You can act tough on crime but not have to face the fiscal consequences. In the long run those costs will be someone else's problem."

Federal and state prison costs are expected to skyrocket as prisoners age and the incarceration of women increases. *(For details on the growing female prison population, see box, next page.)*

Mandatory sentences imposed in the mid-1980s for federal and state crimes are already keeping many prisoners behind bars longer. In 1986, the average sentence for robbery was four years. By 1991, it was seven and a half years. That trend, coupled with three-strikes provisions, will keep many prisoners behind bars after they reach old age. "We'll need bedpans and walkers, not bars and guards," Carlson said.

A SICK SYSTEM?

Carlson likens the prison system to a balloon. What matters is not just the number of prisoners coming into the system, but how long they stay. "There is a cumulative effect of having all those bodies stacked up. That is how you get these tremendous outyear costs."

The prison buildup since the 1980s, coupled with the pending crime bill, add up to "one of the most significant financial commitments the federal government has ever made," Mauer of the Sentencing Project warned. "And the taxpayer will be paying for this for the next 50 years."

In 1992, state and federal governments added 41,886 prison beds at a cost of $1.4 billion. But construction costs are only a down payment. "When a legislature decides to spend, say, $100 million in new construction, it is committing the taxpayers of the state to $1.6 billion in expenditures over the ensuing three decades," according to the Justice Department's National Institute of Corrections.

Some states find that after building a prison, they can't afford to run it. South Carolina, with the nation's third-highest incarceration rate, spent $80 million on two prisons but has not opened them because of projected high costs.

Health care is a big worry. In his stump speeches, President Clinton says that if you want guaranteed health care, "go on welfare, go to jail, get elected to Congress or get rich." It's a good line—and true. After decades of litigation, basic health care is a right for prisoners.

But the cost is enormous. And nobody has examined actuarial tables to estimate how the influx of prisoners will affect future health care costs, said Armand Smart, an expert on prison health care at the University of Wisconsin Medical School in Madison. "These costs are huge. And the costs will be borne by our children."

Richard A. Bloom

In 1992 alone, governments spent $1.4 billion to expand prison capacity.

"Prisoners are a very unhealthy subset of the population," Carlson said. Many have ignored preventive medicine. Some have never visited a dentist. Most smoke. A huge percentage have used dangerous drugs, ranging from marijuana to heroin. Others have the AIDS virus.

Mental problems are acute, with more than 35,000 prisoners enrolled in mental health programs last year and another 12,000 in sex-offender programs, according to the Criminal Justice Institute.

"The lifestyle of someone who ends up in prison is one of self-abuse," Smart said. Many develop ailments prematurely. Forty-year-old male prisoners often have heart trouble. And while mammograms for breast-cancer screening are generally recommended for women in their 40s and older, it's recommended that women inmates get a mammogram at age 35.

Older prisoners are a major drain on health care budgets. Nationwide, 44,300 federal and state prisoners were over 55 years old at the end of 1992. In California, a study showed that the 5,500 state prison inmates age 55 and over have annual medical costs of $60,000-$80,000 each, compared with $20,000 for younger inmates. A state prison in Chino, Calif., has a special block for geriatric inmates—nicknamed the Old Man's Dorm—that has done away with bunk beds because inmates are too feeble to climb to the upper bunk.

The benefits of keeping elderly people incarcerated are minimal, prison experts say. Only 2 per cent of inmates over 55 return to prison after their release, according to the Justice Department.

Women prisoners—the fastest-growing segment of the inmate population—have had a major impact on health care costs because of pregnancy, drug dependency, AIDS and other diseases.

"Managing that patient [with multiple health problems] puts a tremendous demand on resources in terms of providing community standard care," said John H. Clark, chief medical officer for the Los Angeles County sheriff and president of the American Corrections Health Services Association.

AIDS looms as a potentially huge cost

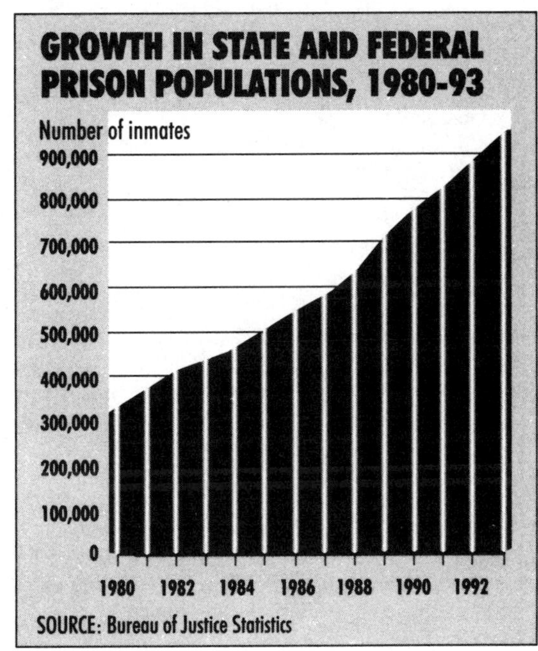

WOMEN BRING PROBLEMS—AND BABIES—TO PRISON

If there is a downside to women's changing role in society, perhaps it can be found in Alderson, W.Va., home of a 1,100-bed minimum-security prison for women.

Built as the first federal women's prison in 1925, this penitentiary in the remote western part of the state is needed now more than ever. From 1987-91, the number of crimes committed by women jumped 16.4 per cent, double the increase in male crime. As a result, the number of women in federal and state prisons surged to 55,365 in 1993, up from 12,200 in 1980.

"Girls and women are casting aside female roles and choosing violent options," Meda Chesney-Lind, a University of Hawaii (Honolulu) criminologist and the author of a recent study on women gang members, told *The Phoenix Gazette*. "The liberation hypothesis includes women who do not operate by a moral code of nice girls."

Richard A. Bloom

Brenda V. Smith of the National Women's Law Center Less judicial discretion means more women behind bars.

Some anecdotal evidence buttresses Chesney-Lind's feminist theory of crime. Floridians were shocked when the cold-blooded killer of a German tourist in Miami last year proved to be a woman. Women have started to play a role in the violence-prone drug trade, according to recent studies.

But Depression-era bank robber Bonnie Parker is hardly a role model for most female inmates. Only 32 per cent of women now in prison were incarcerated for violent crimes. The leading offenses are drug possession, followed by drug sales, prostitution and money crimes. And mandatory minimum sentences have forced judges to punish women as severely as men.

"The same attitude that put women on a pedestal denied them opportunities, but it protected them from some things, including being sent to prison," University of Colorado (Boulder) sociologist Patti Adler said.

"There has been a constricting of judicial discretion, so more women are doing time," said Brenda V. Smith, senior counsel and director of the Women in Prison Project at the National Women's Law Center in Washington.

Many criminologists dismiss as romanticism the notion that the women sent to prison are outlaws who shatter stereotypes just like their counterparts in the corporate suite. Inequality, not liberation, is the culprit, these experts say. Half of women prisoners are black, 43 per cent are victims of physical or sexual abuse and two-thirds had children before they were 18 years old. "The histories of women prisoners are litanies of victimization," said Denise Johnston, director of the Center for Children of Incarcerated Parents in Pasadena, Calif.

Once they arrive in prison, women pose special problems for authorities. Because women inmates are likelier to have abused drugs than male inmates have, and because many have engaged in prostitution or other risky sexual activity, the incidence of AIDS is higher in women's prisons than in men's. Other problems include high rates of sexually transmitted diseases and increased risks of cervical cancer.

According to Justice Department statistics, 8-10 per cent of women admitted to prison are pregnant, which means that the government is going to pick up the childbirth tab. Moreover, corrections officials must decide what to do with the child. In some prisons, the newborn is taken from the mother within hours of birth.

But public-interest groups have increasingly pressed authorities to let women keep their infants, either in prison or, preferably, in community-based facilities. The Taconic Correctional Facility in Bedford Hills, N.Y., has a 23-bed nursery for infants born in prison, costing approximately $80,000 a year. "We look at the long-term savings," Taconic superintendent Bridget P. Gladwin said. None of the approximately 100 women who participated in the program and then were released have returned to prison, she said.

But in most states, the baby is taken from the mother and delivered either to relatives or foster parents.

Infants are only part of the problem in a prison system where 80 per cent of the inmates are mothers, and virtually all of them were the sole support for their children. The current system works on the assumption that a child should not live with a parent who is incarcerated—even in a low-security setting such as a halfway house. Mandatory sentences reduce the chances that mother and child will be reunited. Immigration laws demand that foreign nationals sentenced to more than five years in prison must be deported, with or without their children.

Tracy Huling, a Freehold (N.Y.)-based consultant and an official with the National Network for Women in Prison, says that separating one million children from imprisoned parents will have dangerous repercussions. "There is an intergenerational pattern that we have begun to see that is quite frightening," Huling said. Recent studies show that kids separated from imprisoned mothers are five times likelier to be incarcerated than other children are, she said. "So we are creating a whole new generation at risk."

Demonstration programs in Roxbury, Mass., and San Francisco allowing nonviolent offenders to stay with their children in community-based programs have been effective as lower-cost alternatives to prison. Some of the mothers work, some use food stamps and some collect welfare benefits—all of which cost less than incarceration, Huling said.

Some Members of Congress want to give such programs a shot in the arm. An agreement reached by House-Senate conferees meeting on the crime bill would earmark $22 million over six years to develop a federal program and five state programs similar to the California and Massachusetts experiments. Nonviolent offenders who are their families' primary caregivers could serve their sentences in supervised homes where they could watch their children.

But in a crime bill larded with punitive provisions, the measure could fall by the wayside.

for federal and state prisons. Clark estimated that it would cost $5.3 million annually just to test the 800-1,000 persons a day who are locked up, however briefly, in Los Angeles County. The drugs needed to treat the county's 600 inmates who have tested positive for AIDS have added $150,000 to the county's budget for pharmaceuticals, he added. New York state prisons spent $2 million last year on the anti-AIDS drug AZT.

Future AIDS costs could skyrocket. Of the 5,713 AIDS cases in federal and state prisons on Jan. 1, 1993, almost half were diagnosed in 1992. The number of AIDS deaths in prisons climbed from approximately 200 in 1986 to 702 in 1992.

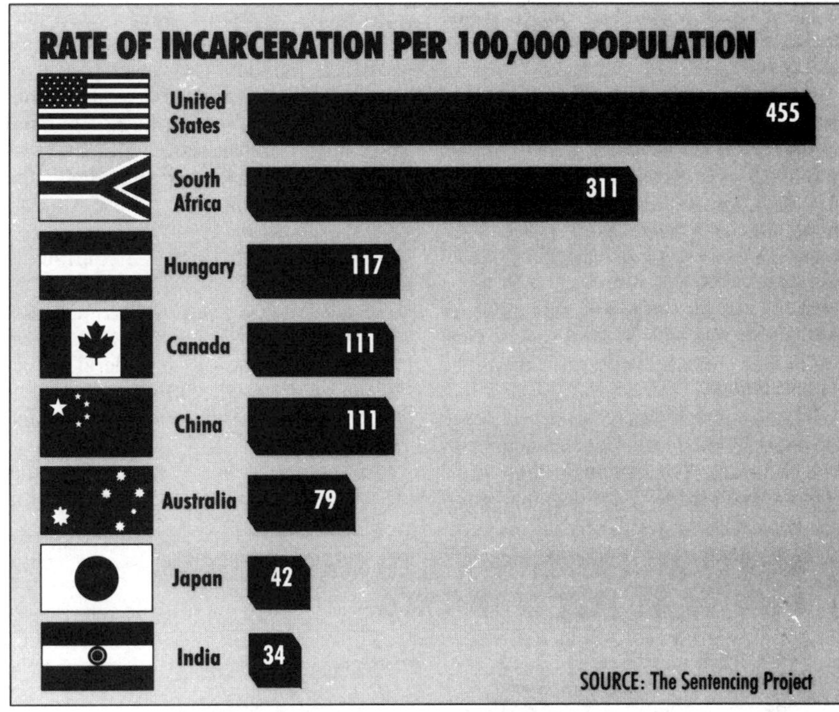

CUTTING COSTS

The incarceration craze has provoked a split between conservatives and liberals. But this time there is a bit of role reversal. Now it is liberals who question what kind of bang for the buck the taxpayer is getting from billions of dollars in government spending. There's been no dent in violent crime, and the proportion of killers, muggers and rapists in the prison population has fallen as the number of nonviolent drug offenders has surged. *(See chart, next page.)* By 1997, it's forecast that 70 per cent of those in the federal prisons will be there for drug offenses.

"Policy makers are going to have to face up to the fact that these are an expensive but not clearly productive use of our resources," said consultant Michael Quinlan, a former head of the Bureau of Prisons.

But conservatives promise results—once their entire plan is implemented. In an influential 1992 article in *Corrections Today*, Eugene H. Methvin, an editor of *Reader's Digest*, promised that doubling the federal and state prison population "to somewhere between 1 million and 1.5 million" while keeping the city and county jail population constant at 400,000, "will break the back of America's 30-year crime wave."

The Clinton Administration has embraced the conservative approach. "Our Administration is committed to pursuing a policy that maximizes the creation of prison space to lock up violent offenders in the most cost-effective and timely manner possible," Bureau of Prisons director Kathleen M. Hawk told the House Judiciary Subcommittee on Intellectual Property and Judicial Administration earlier this year.

The crime bill, now being considered by House and Senate conferees, includes some provisions aimed at underlying causes of crime. But the emphasis is on punishment. The feds would spend $3 billion to build 10 regional prisons that would accept inmates from state prison systems. To be able to send inmates to these prisons, states would have to adopt "truth in sentencing" laws requiring many prisoners to serve at least 85 per cent of their sentences. (The bill would also require certain federal prisoners to serve at least 85 per cent of their sentences.) Proponents argue that this approach, along with three-strikes-you're-out laws, will keep bad guys off the street. In 1992, 400,000 people were released from federal and state prisons.

Liberals have long lamented that state and federal officials choose expensive prison-building schemes over less-costly alternatives. The NCCD's study said that federal and state governments could slash their prison and law-enforcement budgets, boost spending on Head Start and youth job programs, and still save $5.2 billion annually.

Law and order advocates maintain that the benefits of keeping criminals off the street should be deducted from prison costs. Society saves money—everything from insurance to hospital costs—when a dangerous criminal is behind bars.

But conservatives also favor efforts to incarcerate prisoners in the right kind of prison because the costs vary tremendously. The average cost of a bed in a maximum-security prison is $74,862 a year. The price drops to $29,034 for a bed in a minimum-security prison.

John Eisele

Marc Mauer of the Sentencing Project
Politicians like to act tough. But who will pay?

Federal prison administrators have taken several steps to reduce costs, including consolidation of various prison sites. Still, the average cost per inmate inched upward in 1993, primarily because of increased salaries for corrections workers, said Robert Newport, the Bureau of Prisons deputy assistant director for administration.

But it's the states that have faced the

biggest squeeze on their budgets, and they have taken the lead in trying to control costs.

North Carolina, in an effort to see that runaway costs don't wreck its budget, has developed a complicated grid to match prisoners' sentences with available cells. The idea is to release less-violent inmates when prisons become overcrowded, while ensuring that the most-dangerous prisoners stay locked up. Although such a system can reduce costs, a similar effort in Minnesota was junked after several prisoners were released early and committed violent crimes.

Many of the states' costs are imposed on them by the federal government or by the judiciary. The prison systems in 42 states currently are operating under court orders, mandating better health care or reductions in overcrowding.

The pending crime bill would offer states some federal assistance for prison-building—but at a price. "Rather than offering aid to states already facing federal court mandates, . . . [the legislation would require] that states adopt laws that would increase their prison population even further before becoming eligible for federal assistance," the National Conference of State Legislatures complained in a June 8 letter to Senate Judiciary Committee chairman Joseph R. Biden Jr., D-Del. "To be helpful and effective, grants need to be much more flexible."

BENEFITING FROM A BOOM

If prison costs keep rising and the crime rate doesn't plummet, the public may eventually demand a different approach. But by then it could be too late. A network of Wall Street underwriters, architects, builders and developers, corrections officer unions and local communities has developed a huge financial stake in the current system. "Corrections today is a gigantic cash machine," the ACLU's Bronstein said. "There is a correctional-industrial complex."

In fact, some big defense contractors such as Alliant Techsystems Inc., Minnesota Mining & Manufacturing Corp. and Westinghouse Electric Corp. have partially offset the loss of federal spending on weapons by entering the high-technology end of the crime-fighting and prison business.

Every major Wall Street firm has developed a thriving business helping state and local governments finance prison construction.

A perusal of advertisements in the American Correctional Association's 1994 convention guide reveals just how much corporate America is excited by the prospects of prison profits. Architects, builders, divisions of *Fortune* 500 companies including Abbott Laboratories and General Electric Co., food-service vendors such as Canteen Corp., and every major telephone company plugged their wares in the catalog, all hoping for a share of the booty.

Smaller companies hyped their accomplishments. "Over one billion in corrections construction across 12 states currently under way," bragged the Atlanta-based Facility Justice Group, a prison construction company.

Some of the beneficiaries of the prison building craze are protecting their investments with political clout. In 1990, the California Correctional Peace Officers Association, the prison guards' union, contributed $1 million to help Republican Pete Wilson become governor. After his election, Wilson began the most expensive prison construction program that any state has ever undertaken; he also supported the union's quest for better retirement benefits.

In 1992, the union contributed $1 million to political candidates in California, more than the powerful California Teachers Union, which has 10 times more members, and second only to the California Medical Association. This November California voters will vote on a three-strikes-you're-out proposal. So far the guards' union is the initiative's biggest financial supporter, with $51,000 in contributions, according to state campaign records compiled by the California affiliate of the lobby group Common Cause.

In Washington, the high-powered Corrections Corp. of America, with $100 million in sales, keeps a careful eye on the crime bill. The legislation, the company's chief financial officer recently told *The Wall Street Journal*, "is very favorable to us." The company recently tapped former Bureau of Prisons chief Quinlan to monitor the bill.

Communities, often in depressed or isolated areas, have also become aroused over the prospects of luring prisons, with their promise of relatively well-paying jobs. In fact, the old military-industrial complex seems to be melding quite nicely with the prison boom. Since 1989, the Bureau of Prisons has opened prison facilities at 4 active military bases and at 10 closed-down bases. In 1996, the bureau will open a combination prison and hospital for 1,655 inmates at the former Camp Butner in Butner, N.C. And local businessmen cheered when Sen. Edward M. Kennedy, D-Mass., announced recently that the Army's Ft. Devens in Ayer, Mass., would be closed and would become the site of a 1,600-inmate prison.

With civic boosters eager for prison jobs, corporate interests hungering for business and a public outraged over violent crime, it's easy to see why politicians have embraced ever-harsher measures to put criminals behind bars.

And the political volatility of the prison issue makes it even more difficult to predict costs. "What you really end up trying to forecast is how politicians will respond to public opinion polls," said criminal justice expert Douglas C. McDonald, a senior social scientist at Abt Associates, a Cambridge (Mass.) consulting firm. "That is how criminal justice policy gets established, and it is not exactly amenable to scientific projections."

NEW COURT COMMITMENTS TO STATE PRISONS, 1980-92, BY TYPE OF OFFENSE

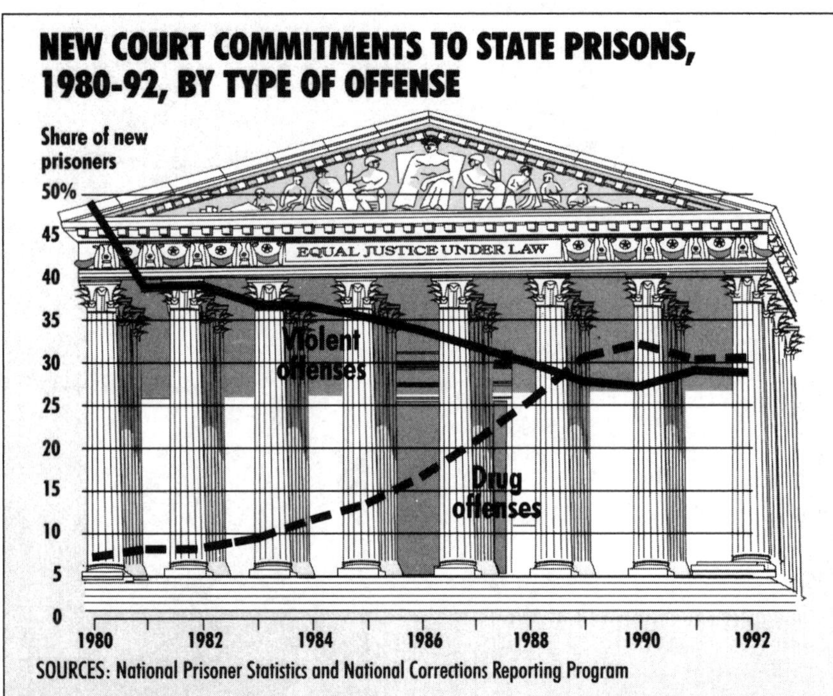

SOURCES: National Prisoner Statistics and National Corrections Reporting Program

PUTTING A PRICE TAG ON DEATH

LOUIS JACOBSON

Death penalty opponents have never been a majority in the United States, but lately they've become an especially lonely bunch. Polls taken by the Gallup Organization Inc. since 1936 show that opposition to capital punishment peaked at 47 per cent in 1966 and dropped off precipitously during the next two decades. The most recent of these surveys, in 1991, showed that 76 per cent of Americans favored the death penalty for murder, while only 18 per cent said they opposed it.

The reasons are easy to fathom: Voters see the death penalty as a way to get tough against a rising tide of violent crime. Appeals to conscience are not passé.

Capital murder cases last longer and cost more than other murder cases do.

Yet people who know the death penalty intimately—judges and law enforcement officials—are rapidly growing skeptical of its crime-fighting value. Their concern: that a rapid expansion of capital punishment is squandering scarce law enforcement dollars that could be put to better use.

The Washington-based Death Penalty Information Center points out that capital murder cases last longer and cost more than other murder cases do, thanks to pretrial motions, additional expert witnesses, jury selection and the need for a separate sentencing proceeding after a defendant is convicted. Factor in the cost of litigating years of appeals, plus incarceration costs for defendants awaiting trial or execution, and the total for each case typically runs into millions of dollars.

With the nation's death row population soaring—from 2,021 in 1988 to 2,870 to this year—a fiscal nightmare could be taking shape.

The burden varies by region, but virtually every study since the late '80s has found that taxpayers get stuck with huge bills for capital cases. Florida was found to spend at least $3.2 million on each death penalty case; California spent $90 million annually on such cases. In 1989, the New York state Department of Corrections estimated that Democratic Gov. Mario M. Cuomo's perennial vetoes of death penalty legislation were saving the state $118 million a year. Esther F. Lardent, a Washington-based consultant to the American Bar Association (ABA) on death penalty issues, says that such estimates are probably low.

In Texas, the state that executes more criminals (at $2.3 million each) than any other, some unlikely people have begun to fret about the cost. Take former state Attorney General Jim Mattox. In the 1990 governor's race, Mattox avidly sparred with his opponents over death penalty bragging rights and ran television advertisements proudly recounting the 32 executions that he oversaw.

But now that he is practicing law in Austin and no longer needs to cater to voters, Mattox takes the view that the death penalty is eating up far more than its share of the state budget. As he pointed out in a newspaper column last year, the money spent on a single Texas death sentence could pay to keep three convicts in maximum security for 40 years. "Prosecutors are beginning to realize how much it costs and that it cuts down on the number of prosecutions that could otherwise be done by the district attorney," Mattox said in a telephone interview.

Court-watchers say that such concerns have spread quickly among lawyers and the judiciary. "I do think it's an emerging consensus," said Bryan Stevenson, executive director of the Alabama Capital Representation Resource Center in Montgomery, a group that assists defendants in death penalty cases.

The money spent on a single Texas death sentence could pay to keep three convicts in maximum security for 40 years.

But could worries about costs reverse public sentiment on capital punishment? Not very quickly. So far, complaints about the impact of the death penalty on law enforcement budgets have come mostly from the legal community. Few politicians have publicly expressed concern. In this year's Texas gubernatorial race, for example, Democratic Gov. Ann W. Richards and Republican George W. Bush are actively backing the death penalty.

And controversy over the expense of death penalty cases could be a Trojan horse for capital punishment foes. If such cases are too expensive, advocates may argue, why not limit appeals and remove statutes that protect defendants? On the other hand, the ABA's Lardent said, even if all death penalty appeals were stopped—a measure that no one is publicly advocating—capital trials would still be considerably more expensive than noncapital trials.

Still, some analysts perceive seeds of doubt in the electorate. Today, 4 in 10 voters doubt that the death penalty deters crime, up from 3 in 10 a decade ago.

And alternative penalties are gaining popularity. In 1993, a survey by the polling firms of Greenberg Research Inc. and the Tarrance Group found that 77 per cent of Americans supported capital punishment and that 57 per cent described their support as "strong." But the numbers changed dramatically when the pollsters offered respondents the option of life imprisonment without parole, with the inmate's prison earnings earmarked for victim compensation. Forty-four per cent said they preferred to impose that sentence, while 41 per cent continued to favor the death penalty.

In 1993, 77 percent of Americans supported capital punishment.

If today's budget cutting mood prevails, and if crime continues to soar, the death penalty's burden on taxpayers might make a good campaign issue one day. Soon, states will be coping with the recently enacted crime bill's three-strikes-you're-out provisions, which penalize states that don't impose life sentences on three-time felons. *(For details, see NJ, 7/30/94, p. 1784.)* Analysts predict that these obligations, coupled with the death penalty, will drain ever-larger shares of state budgets.

Death penalty opponents could try to turn the tables on capital punishment supporters, accusing them of shortsightedly lavishing so much money on executing a few criminals that other criminals are allowed to escape justice. It wouldn't be easy for capital punishment foes—who have traditionally framed their arguments in terms of morality—to present themselves as being tougher-than-tough on crime. But that may be the only way for them to reverse three decades of eroding public support for their cause.

AN URBAN NIGHTMARE COME TRUE?

ROBERT GUSKIND

WASHINGTON, JUNE 18, 2016—An armored personnel carrier bearing the markings of the Army's Urban Defense Force (UDF) rounds a corner in a rundown apartment complex in the Anacostia neighborhood and trains its floodlights on a group of residents.

"You are violating curfew," a soldier's voice booms through a loudspeaker. "Disperse immediately or we will use force. Disperse immediately. . . . "

A few people in the crowd start to walk away. Most glare at the soldiers and jeer. The blazing light from the armored vehicle sweeps in a wide arc, illuminating a wall painted with the insignia of the Homeforce, a gang of former drug dealers and users led by an African-American nationalist who calls himself Brother Khalid. The gang's robberies and shootings have terrorized affluent neighborhoods in the nation's capital and other cities. But support for the Homeforce—whose motto is "Self-Respect + Force + Direction = Destiny"—runs high in Anacostia, where the gang's members are considered heroes because of the housing, schools and social programs that they help finance.

"Disperse," a soldier orders again. The command is greeted by rocks, bricks and bottles hurled by children, teenagers and adults. The crew fires a burst of warning shots. People run into doorways, dive through broken apartment windows and dart down alleys.

It is an average night in the running battle between the soldiers of the UDF and the residents of this sealed-off quadrant. Three years into "the Uprising"—an often violent protest against military control of hundreds of neighborhoods similar to the *intifada* in the Israeli-occupied West Bank more than a quarter-century ago—tension remains high, and there appears no end in sight to either the violence or the poverty and misery afflicting so many cities.

"I hate the soldiers," said 18-year-old Keesha Adams, who had been throwing rocks at the UDF vehicle. "We're trapped here like prisoners behind walls. We can't go nowhere and there's nothing here except Homeforce stuff. There's no stores, no movies, no jobs. Nothing. I feel like there's no future."

The UDF, a million-troop division that polices "urban military zones" sealed off from their surroundings in more than 100 cities and suburbs, is seen by most residents of the neighborhoods as the ultimate affront. For more than a quarter-century, they have known little more than decline, blight and indignity, and they have seen little in the way of government help.

Life in Anacostia has never been easy, but by any measure it's worse than ever: Unemployment stands at 75 per cent, more than 90 per cent of young black males are jobless and 95 per cent of them have been arrested or served time in jail. The poverty rate is 87 per cent. The infant mortality rate is equivalent to Haiti's. The violent crime rate is five times the city average, which itself is triple the national average.

The dire situation has spilled over to the downtown K Street corridor and Georgetown, even though they're separated by walls, barricades and thousands of troops. While Washington, like most cities, still is home to businesses and affluent residents, it resembles a territory under siege. Downtown office buildings are ringed by heavily armed private guards. Employees enter through parking garages or a maze of tunnels built in recent years. In Georgetown, guards outfitted for combat keep watch on bars, restaurants and stores. UDF troops are on 24-hour patrol, manning checkpoints into and out of the neighborhood.

"Damn government sent soldiers and turned us into prisoners," said Wardell Hull, a 60-year-old Anacostia native. "Money was supposed to come. Programs was supposed to come. Housing was supposed to come. Jobs was supposed to come. The children was supposed to have hope."

Hull was talking about the massive federal urban aid program recommended

Richard A. Bloom

The prison population soars—but residents of urban neighborhoods feel like prisoners, too.

Richard A. Bloom

From a distance, American cities appear prosperous and calm. But up close, it's another story.

by the Carter Commission, the panel that studied the causes of a 1999 urban uprising that claimed more than 1,000 lives nationwide and was the costliest disaster in American history. The riots were widely regarded at the time as an opportunity to reassert Washington's role in the nation's cities.

The commission compared American cities at the turn of the century to "pools of gasoline ready to ignite at the slightest spark" and called the violence "sadly predictable." It painted a sobering picture of cities suffering from record middle-class flight—not only by whites, but by minorities. Older inner-ring suburbs were suffering similar problems.

The neighborhoods left behind were depopulated, plagued by rotting infrastructure and shorn of most of their tax base. Even the Carter Commission, however, failed to predict the wholesale abandonment of such cities as Gary, Ind., and East St. Louis, Ill.; the wave of municipal bankruptcies of the 2010s; and the flight of major urban institutions, symbolized by *The Washington Post*'s recent decision to move to Loudoun County, Va.

"The bleak urban future predicted by the Kerner Commission 40 years ago is upon us," the presidential commission said in its widely quoted chilling conclusion. "There are now two Americas, divided, unequal, separated by a dangerous chasm that threatens to undermine our very existence as a nation. One America is white, affluent and suburban. The other America is urban, largely minority, poor, ill-housed, undereducated and underemployed. It is torn by violence. It suffers from frightening levels of drug abuse. Female-headed households are the norm. Health care systems that verged on chaos 20 years ago are now catastrophically close to collapse."

The commission recommended a two-pronged approach to urban revitalization: creation of the UDF to secure troubled neighborhoods and a $50 billion federal "Marshall Plan" for the cities.

The Carter proposal, trimmed to $250 million by President Clinton and Congress for budgetary reasons—was passed by the House but died in the Senate after Jack F. Kemp defeated Vice President Albert Gore Jr. to take the White House in 2000. A small UDF presence in five cities was the only recommendation to survive. It was approved by Congress and signed by Clinton before he left office.

The UDF was expanded by the Gingrich Urban Peacekeeping and Policy Act of 2004—named after Kemp's Vice President. The law also abolished the Housing and Urban Development Department, long plagued by complaints of ineffectiveness and mismanagement, which had its budget severely slashed under the Kemp Administration. (Kemp was HUD Secretary in the Bush Administration.)

Now, the few urban neighborhood programs that residents say are successful are financed largely by the Homeforce. The Homeforce borrows the tactics of the Rio de Janeiro bandit gangs that terrorized affluent neighborhoods in the 1980s and 1990s, blending them with the self-help ideology of African-American nationalist leaders. Discipline is strictly enforced; all proceeds of gang robberies are to be given to poor communities.

Asked what they wanted to be when they grow up, several eighth-graders sitting in Anacostia's Brother Khalid Middle School shouted "Homeforcers" in unison. Some raised their hands in the clenched-fist Homeforce salute. "Without the Homeforce we wouldn't have nothing," a 13-year-old girl said. The school was built largely with money that authorities believe was stolen by the Homeforce, laundered and distributed to residents who donated it to the project.

The Homeforce—which took credit for 990 robberies and 24 murders last year and is blamed by the UDF for another 500 thefts and 200 killings—is believed to have 6,000 members in Washington.

"Twenty-five years ago, if anyone had suggested that things would get this bad and so many parts of so many cities and suburbs would be in such deep trouble, they'd have been written off as crackpots with no faith in this country," Sen. Henry G. Cisneros, D-Texas, said. "But this is what the result of the multibillion-dollar mistakes of the 1960s and 1970s and the nickel-and-dime approach of the 1980s and 1990s turned out to be."

"The shame of it is that we learned what didn't work in the '60s and '70s," Illinois Gov. Richard M. Daley said. "And we figured out what worked in the '80s and '90s, except we weren't willing to spend the money." Now, Daley said, "we're spending $15 billion a year on troops and prisons and nobody much likes the result."

A sprawling federal penal colony in the Arizona desert houses one million prisoners—many of them convicted and sentenced by special federal urban criminal tribunals. The prison, built to "last a century," is so overcrowded that Congress recently voted to expand its capacity to three million.

In Washington last night, UDF troops arrested 375 suspects on charges ranging from armed robbery to murder. The Homeforce claimed credit for 15 break-ins of homes and office buildings. And a pipe bomb planted in an Anacostia parking lot took the lives of five UDF troops and 15 bystanders.

Splitsville

As the debate over the vaunted "information superhighway" rages, smaller cable television and telephone firms—arguing that their interests have been neglected and sometimes thwarted by the huge companies that dominate their trade associations—are increasingly working Washington on their own.

KIRK VICTOR

It was nothing less than a call to arms. Some of the nation's small cable television operators, many of them already on thin financial ice, were mad as hell about the latest government fiat from Washington and weren't going to take it anymore.

Their anger came last year on the heels of sweeping regulations issued by the Federal Communications Commission (FCC) to carry out the 1992 Cable Television Consumer Protection and Competition Act, which reregulated the cable industry. These entrepreneurs, who run companies that serve primarily rural and small-town America, complained bitterly that the FCC's rules would either cripple them or drive them over the brink and into financial ruin.

They criticized Washington policy makers for often lumping them in with huge cable conglomerates, as if the industry were monolithic. Many operators of small cable companies feel so threatened by the combination of recent FCC actions and the momentum in Congress for sweeping telecommunications legislation that they decided they had no choice but to become activists in Washington. Recently, they even formed their own trade association to make sure that their message got across in unalloyed fashion.

Their engagement in the policy process obviously reflected a feeling that the traditional Washington trade groups to which many of them belonged were neglecting them. "Most small operators were attending to their business, thinking one of two things—either all of these new rules and regulations wouldn't apply to them or that the big associations and the big cable operators would handle it," Lynette J. Simpson, a vice president of Pleasanton (Calif.)-based Sun Country Cable Inc., said.

But when the FCC issued hundreds of pages of rules, regulations and forms to implement the law last year, such passivity ended. Two leaders from the small-cable arena—A. Dean Petersen, the president of Southwest Missouri Cable Co. in Carthage, Mo., and Stan Searle, the chief executive officer of Pioneer Cable Inc. in Monument, Colo.—sent out an SOS to their friends and colleagues in the business and asked them to convene for an emergency session in Kansas City, Mo., on May 15 of last year.

The response was enthusiastic. More than 90 cable executives trekked to a hotel near the airport to discuss the impact of the new rules. Late that night, a new group was formed: the Small Cable Business Association (SCBA).

The SCBA's style is captured in a recent newsletter, in which the lead story is headlined "Rules Grow More Punitive, Byzantine and Voluminous." The story began, "Even to those familiar with the labyrinthian and unrealistic nature of many federal regulations, the latest set of cable rules and rate-setting formulae are almost beyond belief."

At a time when cable interests are already represented in Washington by two highly visible trade groups—the National Cable Television Association (NCTA) and the Cable Telecommunications Association (CATA)—the formation of a group to represent the concerns of small companies demonstrates just how high the stakes are.

It also sends a signal to other trade associations that represent companies in the communications arena—and, perhaps, to trade groups across the board—that the days in which they could speak with confidence for an entire industry on contentious issues may well have passed. Executives of smaller companies are more restive than ever and, as the emergence of the SCBA shows, more willing to mount their own lobbying efforts in Washington.

The goal, in part, is to give small operators a greater voice as federal policy is hammered out. "The thing that happens with [established] trade associations is that they lose the grass-roots contact over time," Petersen said in an interview.

"The feeling expressed in Kansas City was that nobody [in Washington] is focused on the problems of small operators," said David D. Kinley, who was drafted by acclamation at the meeting to be the chairman of the new group. "They were not saying that we're not represented, but that the focus gets blurred and lost in the demands and priorities of larger companies. There was a feeling that the big companies, as the largest dues-paying members, controlled the policies of the existing trade associations. It gives the small entities the sense that their focus and their priorities take the backseat, although it doesn't mean that we have been thrown out of the car."

As the debate roils on Capitol Hill and in the Clinton Administration over the rules that will govern the vaunted "information superhighway," the folks who run small cable companies aren't the only communications executives who feel that their interests have been neglected—and sometimes thwarted—by the huge telecommunications companies that have loads of clout within their trade groups.

For example, the CEOs of a group of mostly midsized telephone companies also served notice on their trade group, the U.S. Telephone Association (USTA), that they had needs that are not in sync with the legislative agenda of the seven mammoth regional Bell operating companies (RBOCs)—the so-called baby Bells—a powerful force within the association. They formed a separate group to lobby Congress and to let lawmakers know that the policy agenda of the local telephone industry did not begin and end with the RBOCs.

The message from small and midsized communications firms is that they will no longer passively pony up dues and leave it solely to others to represent their interests. Instead, they'll augment those efforts by jumping into the policy fray themselves as never before.

"They have decided that given the severe damage they have already incurred, the only way to protect their interests is to be marching on Washington," Stephen R. Effros, the president of the CATA, said. He and others in established Washington trade associations profess not to feel threatened by the emergence of new groups to do battle on Capitol Hill and at the FCC.

"Both NCTA and CATA have been telling them for years that no matter how many times the professionals [lobbyists] and lawyers went up there [to Capitol Hill] and said, 'Look, you've got a series of unintended consequences [from legislation] that are going to really hurt people, including your own constituents,' they didn't listen to us," Effros said. "The people whose livelihood is at stake are finally beginning to understand that they have to get personally involved.

"The more you hit somebody with a stick, the more they have a tendency to want to hit back. That's why you have them on everybody's doorstep now—because they are bleeding."

"HOLES IN THE DOUGHNUT"

Despite Effros's effort to put the best face on the increased activism of small-company executives, not all of them buy his notion that the CATA, which had been founded in 1974 principally to be the independent voice for smaller firms, had done everything it could to gin up a more intensive grass-roots effort. Some are even angry about the hits they've taken.

John Eisele

Cable Telecommunications Association's Stephen R. Effros
Why a new trade group? Because his members "are bleeding."

"Steve abandoned us," the president of a small cable firm, who spoke on the condition that his name not be used, said. "It hurts me. I see these guys [cable operators] going under now, and they damn sure should have had the representation they were deserving of when this thing [the 1992 Cable Act] passed. We're struggling to pick up the pieces. I wish things were different."

Such strong feelings aren't confined to the cable industry. As the USTA became active in lobbying for the RBOCs' legislative goals, small and midsized companies that were unhappy with its approach formed the Independent Telephone and Telecommunications Alliance (ITTA). They also retained a high-powered Washington lobbying outfit—Johnson, Smith, Dover, Kitzmiller & Stewart—to provide some firepower.

"Not a single one of us has anywhere near the size or market share of a regional Bell—thus, we should not be regulated as one," said Larry Ross, the chief executive officer of Lufkin (Texas)-based Lufkin-Conroe Telephone Exchange Inc., in a statement announcing the formation of the group in February. "We are smaller companies with a long-standing commitment to serve telephone customers in many of America's rural areas. This responsibility makes it imperative that we not become unintentional victims of legislation or regulation which may impede our ability to continue providing state-of-the-art communications to our communities."

"They were having trouble getting their voices heard within USTA," said Diane Smith, the vice president for federal government affairs of Little Rock (Ark.)-based ALLTEL Corp. "When that seemed to get worse instead of better, we began trying to educate our USTA board members so that they not only heard the Bell company perspective but they heard other perspectives as well. The CEOs at trade association board meetings are very reliant on the staff and briefings that they get. We found those to be very RBOC-driven.

"It became clear that as legislation was percolating more and more over the last couple of years, particularly when it sort of kicked off in 1993, not only were we not getting heard inside the trade association, we weren't getting heard as well as we wanted to by policy makers, who were assuming that USTA was indeed speaking for the entire industry."

The independent companies were especially troubled by the endorsement by the USTA's board of directors of the RBOCs' legislative agenda, which some of them even see as a threat. The baby Bells' game plan has been driven in large part by their desire to be freed from the business restrictions that had been imposed upon them as part of the 1982 court decree—the so-called Modification of Final Judgment (MFJ)—that broke up American Telephone & Telegraph Co. (AT&T).

AT&T's breakup resulted in the birth of the seven RBOCs. For the past decade, they've spent a ton of money—including $11.2 million in political action committee and "soft"-money contributions alone, according to Common Cause—to win legislation that would end the restrictions. They are particularly eager to grab a bite of the biggest plum of all: the lucrative long-distance market. *(See NJ, 3/5/94, p. 526.)*

Unlike the RBOCs, the 17 members of the ITTA were never related to AT&T and aren't subject to the court decree that precludes the baby Bells from entering various lines of business. "The independents didn't have a dog in the RBOCs' fight, even though that fight seemed to be driving so much of the [USTA's] legislative effort," Smith said. "I don't think asking other segments of the industry to sit on the sidelines while the RBOCs pursue their strategy is something that makes sense."

Echoing that view, Richard A. Lumpkin, the chairman and chief executive officer of Mattoon (Ill.)-based Illinois Consolidated Telephone Co., said: "I think that USTA . . . has not been as sensitive as it might be to the needs of medium-sized companies in the legislative effort. We are not getting the focus on our issues, so it has become necessary to mount an independent effort, so to speak. I would be very happy if Congress would leave us alone, [but] that's not going to happen—because we are going to be affected by the same sweeping legislative solutions that are crafted for the Bell operating companies."

When pressed about the impact of a separate alliance of companies to lobby on the hotly debated legislation, Roy M. Neel, who joined the USTA as its president and chief executive officer in January after serving as President Clinton's deputy chief of staff, said: "I take it as a wake-up call to this association. I not only accept that, I think it makes sense for them to do that. From what I've been able to determine, USTA did not do a good job on behalf of these companies. I'm absolutely committed to fixing it."

Neel acknowledged that the smaller companies have a "special problem." At one end of the scale, the very small companies have for some years been represented by the Rural Telephone Coalition, an alliance of the National Rural Telecom Association, National Telephone Cooperative Association and the Organization for the Protection and Advancement of Small Telephone Companies. More than 850 small and rural telephone systems in 46 states are members of one or more of the three groups. At the other end of the scale, all seven RBOCs have extensive resources, Washington offices and a slew of lobbyists.

John Eisele

Diane Smith of Little Rock (Ark.)-based ALLTEL Corp. "The independents didn't have a dog in the RBOCs' fight."

Companies in between the two extremes do not have the deep pockets on the one hand or the established, narrowly focused trade groups on the other. Their association's annual budget of less than $500,000 is dwarfed by the RBOCs' multimillion-dollar lobbying machine in Washington. As a consequence, Neel said, they "do run the danger of falling through the cracks."

Still, Neel is quick to point out that the RBOCs don't have disproportionate clout within the USTA and, even though they contribute about half of the group's dues, have just seven votes on its 40-plus-member board. "They don't dominate USTA's policy making or advocacy agenda," he said. "Every trade association has this problem, where the smaller companies worry about domination by the larger companies and the larger companies are concerned they don't have a [sufficient] say in the association's politics."

Lumpkin and Smith candidly acknowledged that part of the impetus for forming the ITTA was a growing concern that the RBOCs' entry into the long-distance business would constitute new, powerful competition. The baby Bells' local telephone service, when coupled with the ability to offer long distance, Smith said, would enable them to provide the kind of "one-stop shopping capability" that would make them very imposing players, with massive market clout.

"We are holes in the doughnut of an RBOC territory," she said. "Because of the way our territories look, . . . we are surrounded on all sides by this enormous participant in the industry. They possess huge competitive advantages from the front end because of their size and their market presence and their economies of scale and so forth."

Should they be given the go-ahead to leap into long distance, Smith added, the RBOCs will be positioned to come in and pick off the independent companies' most attractive customers.

With that threat looming, the independents decided to formally launch their alliance and work Capitol Hill more aggressively.

Nonetheless, Neel doesn't expect any defections or long-term fallout. "I have talked with just about every one of the CEOs of the companies who are participating in that alliance," he said, "and they have assured me to a person that they have no interest in withdrawing from USTA."

And Jeffrey Ward, the vice president for federal policy of New York City-based NYNEX Corp., one of the baby Bells, had a prediction for those in the telephone business who oppose new entrants into their market: "That perspective will seem as quaint as buggy whips in another few years."

Ward said that at the heart of the sweeping changes in communications law

Richard A. Bloom

Roy M. Neel of the U.S. Telephone Association "You'd have to be Houdini to make [the tensions] go away."

that Congress is considering is a reciprocal opening of markets—a quid pro quo in which the RBOCs agree to competition in their local markets and, in exchange, are given the green light to enter the cable, manufacturing and long-distance businesses.

"For those companies that have arrived at the conclusion that they want to stick with the buggy whips, that is not the policy that USTA has been following for over a year," Ward said. "It's a fundamental split from where most of the industry is because it is a fundamental split of where the political reality is."

Why the emergence of such antagonisms within industries that were once unified? "I think the Association [USTA] is going through a difficult time," Lumpkin said, "in trying to adjust from being an association of noncompetitors to an association of competitors."

Neel agreed. "There are always going to be tensions within the association because these companies are starting to compete with each other," he said. "The tensions are not only between the mid-sized companies and the RBOCs [but also include other] intra-industry tensions based on competitive strategies. That's always going to be with us. . . . You'd have to be Houdini to make those things go away."

Nearly everyone agrees that the stakes have become too high for the smaller companies to stay on the sidelines. "So long as issues weren't as critical, it was a lot easier not to worry about whether your voice was getting heard," Smith said. "But the fact is that policy makers are dealing with issues that will literally dictate and control the way our companies do business over the next years."

THE MORE THE MERRIER?

If the formation of new groups to represent smaller companies is disquieting to them, the chiefs of the two established cable groups aren't letting on.

Decker Anstrom, who became the NCTA's president and chief executive officer in January after serving as its executive vice president for seven years, said that the emergence of such groups as the SCBA sends a message that he takes seriously. "I think it reflects their sense of urgency about how the regulatory and political processes affect their business," he said in an interview. "There is clearly a feeling that NCTA hasn't fully or adequately represented them . . . and that their concerns haven't been fully reflected here in Washington.

"I am not at all threatened by that. The cable industry is a very diverse industry with a lot of voices and a lot of companies that are moving in different directions. NCTA's job is to be like an orchestra conductor."

But conductors abhor cacophony, and the cable arena, like the telephone industry, is made up of companies of such dramatically different sizes that adequately and fairly representing their interests is a herculean—maybe even impossible—challenge.

The numbers tell the story: The nation's top 10 cable companies—led by Denver-based Tele-Communications Inc. (TCI), which has more than 10 million customers, and Stamford (Conn.)-based Time Warner Cable, which has more than 7 million—have signed up more than half of the country's subscribers. By contrast, small cable systems—those with 3,500 or fewer customers—account for more than 70 per cent of the 11,385 systems in the United States but serve only about 10 per cent of all subscribers.

Not being large enough to have Washington offices, the small cable operators relied heavily on others to wage their public policy battles, and some say they felt blindsided when the FCC began issuing what they see as onerous regulations to carry out the 1992 cable law. The law was enacted after a furious lobbying battle, culminating in an override of President Bush's veto—the only instance in which that happened.

Some now concede that they erred by not bothering to present their side to Capitol Hill lawmakers. As a result, they say, the debate was defined mostly by larger companies, many of which have their own retinue of lobbyists to add to the firepower of the trade groups.

A similar scenario had played out in 1990, when a far less burdensome cable bill was considered by Congress but was

Richard A. Bloom

Decker Anstrom of the National Cable Television Association "NCTA's job is to be like an orchestra conductor."

killed partly because of disagreements over strategy between TCI and Time Warner. *(See NJ, 3/2/91, p. 505.)*

In both instances, the small companies "picked their poison by joining forces with the big [operators] against any form of regulation," a congressional aide said. "They never came in and said they would be willing to drop their opposition to the bill in return for an agreement that Congress do some very simple, limited regulation of small companies. If they had done that, they would have won."

Petersen has heard the same thing. "Many legislators have told me that had our little organization existed during the reregulatory effort, this legislation would have taken on a very different form," he said. "In the case of a lot of small businesses, their plight was never taken into consideration when the legislation was being drawn."

Now, as they focus on Washington, some executives of small companies are making it a personal crusade to show the FCC that its new rules are especially burdensome to them.

"If you're Time Warner and you get 196 pages of forms to deal with, you have a phalanx of lawyers that you can hand it to," the CATA's Effros said. "If you're a mom-and-pop cable system of 3,500 subscribers and that 196 pages of forms hits your desk, you're in a markedly different position."

Worse still for small operators has been the impact of a rate freeze that the FCC initially imposed in April 1993 and has subsequently extended three times. Smaller companies rely heavily on subscription fees because they are too small to attract advertising, and so the freeze has had an especially devastating effect on them.

A cable company in Kentucky recently went belly-up, and Effros predicted that more will fall and that the industry will become more consolidated as banks foreclose because prices can't be increased to reflect rising operating expenses.

Even as they decry the impact of the 1992 law and regulations, many cable executives acknowledge that it came about in part as a result of price-gouging by some in their business. But they argue that Congress and the FCC, in trying to check such abuses, have unfairly painted with a broad brush.

"It's absolutely ludicrous to assume every single cable system is charging too much money," said Michael J. Pohl, a senior vice president of Ridgewood (N.J.)-based Douglas Communications Corp. II and a leader of yet another group of smaller companies that have lobbied the FCC. "That's the FCC's premise—that we're all monopolistic monsters taking advantage of the communities we serve. We're penalized for being small."

But Patrick J. Donovan, the acting chief of the FCC's policy and rules division, argued that his agency has "done a lot of things for small systems." He said that systems with 15,000 or fewer subscribers will not be subject to the 17 per cent rate rollback imposed on all other systems until the agency completes a study of the smaller systems.

Donovan also noted that in cases of severe economic hardship, the systems may apply for exemptions. Only five such applications have been received to date, he said.

"They have the agency's ear," Donovan said. "We are trying to balance the rights of subscribers—recognizing that customers of small systems have rights—against the relative difficulties that real small operators will have complying."

Even the SCBA, the new cable group, acknowledges that the FCC must be listening more, because of its recent decision on rate rollbacks. The action was "directly attributable to SCBA's efforts," according to its newsletter, which said that it marked the first time that the agency admitted a need to vary its regulations based on a company's size.

As the regulatory debate continues, smaller cable operators have also increasingly lobbied Congress. They are seeking to expand opportunities for mergers between telephone and cable companies in rural areas. A House proposal would permit mergers in limited circumstances, and they hope to get Sen. Ernest F. Hollings, D-S.C., the chairman of the Commerce, Science and Transportation Committee, to include a comparable provision in his bill.

"We don't think that in these small towns and rural areas that we serve you can sustain two competitive infrastructures," SCBA chairman Kinley said. "You need to allow small cable operators and telephone companies to work together. And if that doesn't make sense, they ought to be able to join together. Otherwise, one bleeds to death."

That's why the smaller operators, many of whose companies are on the financial edge, say that they are determined to head off sweeping laws and regulations that make no distinctions based on company size.

"We've been told how the Washington game works: You have highly paid people who are well connected and spread a lot of money around," cable company official Simpson said. "We can't afford those highly paid people and we don't have the money to spread around, so our members have to depend on themselves."

Call it a grass-roots rebellion, but whatever name you attach to this new group of activists, their heightened visibility and clout in Washington could give the leaders of established trade groups some huge headaches.

John Eisele

Lynette J. Simpson, a vice president of Pleasanton (Calif.)-based Sun Country Cable Inc.
"We don't have the money to spread around, so our members have to depend on themselves."

Try, Try Again

The last time Congress tried to overhaul the nation's labor-management laws, the fight was so fierce that the issue went into the deep freeze for more than a decade. Now there are signs of a thaw. But will it last?

KIRK VICTOR

Veterans of Washington's policy wars know that a bitter political fight is bound to erupt when any effort is launched to reform the laws governing labor-management relations. Battalions of business and union lobbyists go for broke, showing little willingness to seek compromise.

But remarkably, when a blue-ribbon panel recently sent a 163-page "fact-finding" report to President Clinton on this hot-button issue, there was an outpouring of praise from both sides.

"We congratulate the commission for focusing on the adverse consequences of outdated regulations and excessive court litigation," Jerry J. Jasinowski, president of the National Association of Manufacturers (NAM), said after the Commission on the Future of Worker-Management Relations issued its report in early June. "The 150 current laws and regulations governing the workplace do more to impede than help achieve employee participation and productivity."

John J. Sweeney, president of the Service Employees International Union, was equally upbeat. The report, he said, "confirms publicly what we in labor have struggled with for many years: On an unprecedented scale, our outdated labor laws have eroded the balance in employer-employee relations and allowed employers to game the laws in order to defeat union organizing campaigns and pervert the bargaining process."

The commission, led by former Labor Secretary John T. Dunlop, apparently learned a thing or two from earlier reform efforts. The no-nonsense Dunlop, who has a reputation as one of the country's most skilled mediators, has tried to find enough carrots for both sides to avoid a replay of the nasty political wars of the past.

The question is whether the 80-year-old former Ford Administration labor chief, who reportedly has run the panel with an iron fist, can continue to induce unions and management groups to keep their combat fatigues closeted as the commission moves to its next task: recommending whether to revamp the laws that have governed labor-management relations for decades.

The commission's early success stems

Richard A. Bloom

John T. Dunlop, who heads a commission that's reviewing the nation's labor laws A skilled mediator, he's trying to avoid a replay of the nasty wars of the past.

From *National Journal,* July 9, 1994, pp. 1623-1627.

in part from its decision to employ a bifurcated approach: Its fact-finding report is to be followed, within the next six months, by a set of recommendations. "This presents an opportunity for serious dialogue," Dunlop said in an interview. "Nobody has jumped overboard in either the labor or business community—that makes a constructive second stage possible."

Clearly, Dunlop has his eye on history. In 1978, a bloody battle erupted when the Carter Administration offered a sweeping proposal that offered greater protections for union organizing efforts. When that initiative, which was developed largely behind the scenes, was unveiled, the business lobby denounced it as an attempted power grab by organized labor. Six Senate votes were taken to try to end a filibuster against the proposal. When the effort failed, advocates of reform essentially put the issue in deep freeze, where it remained during 12 years of Republican control of the White House.

Malcolm R. Lovell Jr., a top Labor Department official in the Reagan and Nixon Administrations, recalled that the Carter proposal looked so much like a union wish list that it "scared the living bejesus out of every management group in the country." Its defeat "engendered a lot of hard feelings," he said.

"What Dunlop has done is not frighten anybody yet—he's giving six months for everybody to think about it," Lovell added. "He's conditioning the parties in a way that tempers have not flared and there is an opportunity, if everything else goes well—which is very tough and may well not happen—to forge something that when it hits the street will not be treated like the proposal was in 1978."

Rep. Steve Gunderson, R-Wis., a self-described moderate who sits on the Education and Labor Subcommittee on Labor-Management Relations, said that the commission's work provides a real shot at reform. But, he said, "it's very easy to be a pessimist because both labor and business really are on an all-or-nothing mind-set on these kinds of issues."

Richard A. Bloom

Manufacturers' association chief Jerry J. Jasinowski Existing laws "do more to impede than help" productivity.

Still, Dunlop has allayed some early concerns about whether the commission would be evenhanded. Jeffrey C. McGuiness, the president of the Labor Policy Association, which represents more than 200 major U.S. corporations, contrasted the commission's willingness to listen to corporate concerns with the indifference that business often runs into on Capitol Hill on labor-management issues.

"In the legislative process, the issue goes on the table, hearings are held, and by the time we testify, everybody's gone to lunch," McGuiness said. "Nobody gives a damn anyway, and then there's a vote on the floor and the debate ends. All of our arguments are inherently suspect, according to the majority in Congress."

By contrast, he said, "the commission has created a forum in which we can say that we are in the process of re-engineering our companies to adopt very different systems of work, and we need to change employment policy and employment laws to support that reengineering."

But some skeptics doubt that Dunlop will be able to keep the business and labor lobbyists from brandishing their artillery for long. Charles E. Hawkins III, senior vice president of the Associated Builders and Contractors, predicted that the commission would call for a major overhaul of labor laws—and that such a proposal would be followed by "the mother of all wars."

Such a conflict might be averted, Hawkins said, only if the November elections significantly alter the makeup of Congress, giving it a more conservative tilt. In that case, he said, "it's entirely possible that the whole effort could be neutralized."

TO THE BARRICADES?

For the Clinton Administration, the decision to venture into the thicket of labor-management law carried large political risks. Clinton had assiduously cultivated business support during his 1992 campaign. As President, he was intent on pursuing an ambitious domestic agenda and would need the help of his new allies to secure it. *(See NJ, 12/12/92, p. 2829.)* Having won with only 43 per cent of the vote, he could hardly afford to waste political capital on an initiative if it had little prospect for enactment.

But unions had thrown their considerable weight—in manpower as well as political contributions—behind the Democratic ticket in 1992. And Administration officials, congressional Democrats and even some Republicans contend that it is difficult to make the workplace more productive and competitive if workers and managers operate in an atmosphere of hostility and distrust.

"The cost of failure to come up with a new partnership between workers and managers is rising very rapidly. You can see it in terms of rising litigation, higher workers' compensation costs and potential productivity improvements that are not ever fulfilled," Labor Secretary Robert B. Reich said in a recent interview.

"I feel very strongly that this whole issue of the relationship between management and labor lies at the heart of our ability to be productive and to hold our standard of living," House Majority Leader Richard A. Gephardt, D-Mo., said.

Gunderson agreed that U.S. workers and businesses would pay a high price if labor and management continued on a collision course. "If we want to maximize our opportunities internally to improve the quality of living for the American worker in the face of a global economy, we need some kind of a vision and plan that simply doesn't exist with existing law," he said. "In the absence of reform, we will continue to sputter along, by hit and by miss, by one company's success and one company's handicap."

For Administration officials, the quandary was how to avoid appearing so predisposed to an overhaul of labor laws that business groups would take to the barricades, undermining other Administration initiatives.

Ultimately, they settled on one of Clinton's favorite approaches to decision making: Convene a group to solicit the views of all the parties, spend lots of time deliberating and then emerge with recommendations. The commission's 10 members, named in March 1993 by Reich and Commerce Secretary Ronald H. Brown, include business executives, labor leaders and academics. The choice of Dunlop as chairman was a key to the effort, according to several sources. He was viewed as one of the few people who had the mediating skills to avoid yet another bloodbath. To sidestep a collision with other initiatives such as health care reform, the commission was given a year to deliver its findings.

Past efforts to amend the nation's labor laws have succeeded mainly when there is a sense of national urgency or when one side or the other has gained lots of political momentum. But such instances are rare: Congress has enacted only four major labor-management laws in the past 68 years, the most recent in 1959.

The centerpiece of labor legislation, the National Labor Relations Act—commonly known as the Wagner Act—passed in 1935. Nine years earlier, the Railway Labor Act was enacted; it now is applicable to the railroad and airline industries. The so-called Landrum-Griffin Act, which among other things imposed financial reporting requirements on unions, became law in 1959—but only after extensive congressional hearings that exposed the influence of organized crime in some unions.

Those statutes, as well as the 1947 Labor-Management Relations Act—the Taft-Hartley Act—were enacted only after fierce battles. To minimize the fireworks this time, the commission has sought consensus on the facts, without which there will never be agreement on recommendations, said F. Ray Marshall, Labor Secretary in the Carter Administration and a member of the commission.

"What I hope will be different is that we will have much broader political underpinnings, much broader public information, long before any legislation is introduced," Marshall said in an interview. "One lesson I learned [from the Carter effort] is it's hard to get facts out to people during a fight."

"I do not believe that the factual side of this report would have received any significant attention in the relevant communities if I had come out with recommendations at this time," Dunlop said. "People wouldn't give a damn about the facts of the case—they would have just turned to the recommendations and there would have been no opportunity for public or even private discourse on the meaning of the facts, their consequences and so on if you had combined the two."

A CHANGING WORKPLACE

Labor leaders say that the commission's fact-finding report confirmed their view that the country is in a crisis that requires bold governmental action. They point to the panel's finding that a two-tiered labor force has emerged, with a rapidly growing gap between higher-paid, more-educated workers and those with few skills.

Susan M. Muniak

AFL-CIO secretary-treasurer Thomas R. Donahue
A "two-tier" labor force is emerging; "unions are a necessary part of the solution."

The chasm has been exacerbated by the stagnation of hourly wages—and declining real income for male workers over the past two decades—after a 44-year period in which earnings steadily grew. The United States also suffers from a long-term decline in the rate of productivity growth.

These changes have occurred even as the country faces growing pressure from a global economy. "A healthy society cannot long continue along the path the United States is moving, with rising bifurcation of the labor force," the commission's report says. "The changes affect the working lives of nearly all Americans and firms and pose a major challenge to worker-management relations."

Reich and Brown asked the commission to examine three issues: whether new methods or institutions should be encouraged, or required, to enhance productivity through labor-management cooperation and employee participation; what changes, if any, should be made in labor law and collective bargaining to increase cooperative behavior and reduce conflict and delay; and what, if anything, should be done to help resolve workplace disputes without resorting to court or federal agencies.

"You need to look at labor laws in the

Venturing into the thicket of labor-management law carried large political risks for President Clinton. He had courted business leaders during his campaign and needed their continued help. But unions had thrown their weight behind his candidacy, too.

context of a very rapidly changing workplace and an economic structure that is itself undergoing fundamental change," Reich said. "One of the errors made in 1978 with labor law reform, I believe, was looking at labor laws in isolation."

Although there is little dispute over the commission's finding of a growing dichotomy in the labor force, there is hot debate about the causes and meaning of the trend—and whether it warrants government intervention.

Advocates on both sides of the issue are already putting their own spin on the commission's report. AFL-CIO secretary-treasurer Thomas R. Donahue likened the findings to those of the Kerner Commission, which 25 years ago found the country divided racially and moving toward separate, unequal societies.

"I think the Dunlop Commission report has done in the economic arena or the employment arena . . . what the Kerner Commission did in the civil rights arena," Donahue said at a press conference on the day the findings were announced. "To arrest the trend toward a two-tier society, we must assure working men and women of a meaningful opportunity to form unions."

"The commission makes clear that unions are a necessary part of the solution," he added. "[It] points to a dangerous trend where the rights of workers are increasingly violated by employers. The commission finds that 25 per cent of employers, faced with organizing campaigns, illegally fire someone during that campaign and that the risk of being fired for union activity has increased fifteen-fold in the past 40 years."

Douglas A. Fraser, former president of the United Auto Workers and a member of the commission, agreed. "We're facing a tremendous economic dilemma, and I would argue one of the reasons we face this economic problem is the decline of unions," he said.

John Eisele

Rep. Steve Gunderson, R-Wis.
"I'm not willing to say we're in a crisis . . ."

But business advocates argue that there is no need for a massive change in labor laws. "I can cite all these findings and say that the world has changed dramatically, and it just goes to show you that the law is not nearly as important as many of us think it is," said William J. Kilberg, Solicitor of Labor in the Nixon and Ford Administrations. "There are stronger forces—namely, economic—than law."

Although he acknowledges that there is a two-tier labor force, Kilberg said, "changing the National Labor Relations Act will not help that one whit." A deficiency in the commission's report, he said, is that it "starts with a prejudice, and the prejudice is that unionism and unionization is basically a good thing."

The NAM's Jasinowski agreed that there was such a bias. "The report tended to overemphasize the role of organized labor in labor-management relations in general," he said. "The bulk of the evidence that I've seen show that worker empowerment and movement toward a high-performance workplace is often better in nonunion environments, although it is clear that it works in both."

On the other hand, the business community also wants some changes in labor laws, and it views the commission as a vehicle to press for that reform. Business lobbyists argue that recent decisions of the National Labor Relations Board (NLRB) have chilled employers' ability to establish or continue committees in which employers and managers discuss issues ranging from health and safety to increased productivity. The agency has ruled that certain committees are little more than "shams" because they are under management's control. Such "company unions" are banned by the 1935 law.

Business advocates say that the NLRB rulings prevent many types of labor-management cooperation unless employees are first represented by unions. Noting the widespread consensus that employee participation is imperative to achieving a more efficient and productive workplace, they argue that the commission must propose clarifying—or even reversing—the rulings.

"It could very well be that we ought to clarify that, take away the fear that doing something like a safety and health committee would violate the law," Marshall said. But Marshall said he saw little need for a more sweeping change.

The AFL-CIO's Donahue contends that the business lobby is exaggerating the problems caused by the NLRB rulings. He noted that a recent study cited by the commission found an average of about three NLRB decisions a year on labor-management committees during the past quarter-century. "If our evidence was that thin on any [other issue on which] we sought a change in law, I'd be ashamed to offer it," he said.

Labor leaders worry that worker-management committees could become alternatives to unions, enabling management to maintain control while giving workers a sense of empowerment. "When a labor-management cooperation scheme is in a nonunion setting, what you have is an autocratic arrangement because management appoints a committee and management has the final word and can dissolve it," Fraser said. "In a union setting, it is done jointly."

But the commission may have identified the key elements of a potential deal. There is speculation that the gruff, determined Dunlop may try to arrange a swap in which business gains some reassurance on employee participation committees and labor gets some help on the organizing front.

Still, the odds are that the hard-liners on both sides have enough clout to scuttle such a deal. "While we can agree on articulating the problem, I don't think we are anywhere close to a consensus on a solution," Gunderson said. "I'm not willing to say we're in a crisis and that there will be a workplace meltdown in the absence of substantive reform."

Such statements from a person who does not reflexively oppose reform show the magnitude of the job. Still, if anyone might be able to pull off a coup, it's Dunlop.

Foreign and Defense Policy, Trade, and Immigration

The first unit of this book treats policy-making institutions and processes, and units 2 through 9 treat different areas of domestic policy. This unit turns to foreign and defense policy and related matters such as trade and immigration.

The traditional and convenient distinction between domestic and foreign policy is becoming more difficult to maintain, since so many contemporary policy decisions seem to have important implications for both foreign and domestic settings. Examples abound. The well-being of the national economy conditions the government's ability to carry out diplomatic and military initiatives. In addition to affecting the economy, many U.S. environmental and energy policies must be coordinated with the environmental and energy policies of other nations to have any chance of success. Agricultural and food policies often have international ramifications, especially in the area of trade. Civil rights policies can subtly, and not so subtly, affect U.S. relations with African, Latin American, and other nations. The big buildup of the U.S. military establishment in the late 1970s and early 1980s was one cause of the large budget deficits that continue to plague the national government. All these examples suggest the growing links between traditional domestic policies and traditional foreign and defense policies in the American political system. Even so, from the perspectives of both the American public and American policymakers, "foreign policy" and "domestic policy" still constitute recognizably distinct spheres.

For at least three decades the United States and the Soviet Union each had the capacity to end human existence as we know it. Not surprisingly, the threat of nuclear war often dominated American diplomacy and national security policy making. Yet no nuclear weapons have been exploded in warfare since the U.S. dropped two atomic bombs on Japan in the closing days of World War II. Since that time, the United States has used conventional forces in a number of military actions—in Korea, Vietnam, Grenada, Panama, and the Persian Gulf area. In 1991 the Soviet Union dissolved into 15 independent republics. This change left the United States as the world's sole remaining superpower and has greatly affected world politics and U.S. foreign policy. Questions about the appropriateness of U.S. intervention in disparate places such as Bosnia-Herzegovina, Somalia, Haiti, and even Russia itself have been at the forefront of foreign policy concerns since President Clinton assumed office.

Since the end of the cold war and the onset of increasing concern about the national government's budget deficits, the size and shape of the U.S. military forces have come under heightened scrutiny. The balances between conventional and nuclear armaments, between ground, naval, and air forces, and between today's readiness and tomorrow's research and development have all been called into question. There have been criticisms of "hollow forces," a term that implies that the state of U.S. military preparedness is inadequate, as well as accusations of continued and unnecessary overspending in the post–cold war era. Several of the selections in this unit address these general issues, while another one treats the controversial issue of homosexuals in the military and how well the compromise policy that the Clinton administration put into effect during its first year in office is working.

Amidst great fanfare and considerable opposition and at the urging of President Bill Clinton, Congress approved the North American Free Trade Association (NAFTA) in late 1993. NAFTA represented another step in the direction of unrestricted global markets or worldwide free trade. For centuries, trade among nations has been shaped and restricted by tariffs, quotas, and the like. But the advent of increased economic integration of highly industrialized Western European nations through the European Union (originally named the Common Market) has spurred a worldwide movement toward freer international trade. In turn, trade relations and trade agreements loom large in the conduct of relations between and among nations today, and economic interdependence extends beyond commodities to currencies, inflation rates, budget deficits, and the like. One of the selections in this unit focuses on the early 1995 Mexican currency crisis, its implications for one of its major trading partners, the United States, and the sorts of policies that might be put into place to prevent reoccurrences of such problems.

California's passage of its controversial Proposition 187 in 1994 heightened awareness across the nation to a whole range of policy issues related to immigration. The proposition was designed to deny illegal immigrants many government services provided to other residents of California. As the selection on that issue reflects, immigration policy probably cuts across the traditional boundary between foreign and domestic policy as much as any other policy area.

Looking Ahead: Challenge Questions

As the world's leading military and economic power, the United States could try to assert itself in unilateral efforts to make the world a more peaceful, secure place. Or it could pursue the same goals through alliances or through

Unit 10

the United Nations. Or it could sit back and let the rest of the world take care of itself unless U.S. interests were directly and seriously threatened. Which policy does the Clinton administration seem to be following? Which course of action do you think U.S. national government ought to pursue?

One recurrent theme in the U.S. policy process is the struggle between Congress and the presidency over who controls foreign policy. The Constitution gives Congress the power to declare war and makes the president commander in chief of U.S. military forces. According to the Constitution, the president proposes treaties to the Senate, where they must be approved by a two-thirds majority before they take effect. The Constitution contains other provisions that have the effect of sharing the power to make foreign and defense policy between the legislative and executive branches. Who do you think should be in control of fashioning U.S. relations with other nations? Why?

When he took office, President Clinton said that national economic security was fundamentally important to U.S. continuing leadership role in world affairs. For that reason, he said, improving the health of the economy and shrinking the national government's budget deficit had to be given the highest priority. Do you agree that the national economy is a crucial ingredient in the nation's ability to pursue its interests in the international arena? Why or why not?

Ready for What?

Can you really have too much military readiness? Yes, if it's the wrong sort. Under fire from a Republican Congress, the Clinton Administration is stoking near-term, operational readiness at the expense of longer-term, structural readiness—an imbalance that could spell trouble in the future.

DAVID C. MORRISON

In popular mythology, the American military has been ever-ready to charge off to war since the glory days of the Revolution. You know, that Minuteman thing: one if by land, two if by sea, three if by air, four if from space.

While waging more than its share of wars, Washington has actually presented less than the perfect picture of armed vigilance. "Throughout most of its history, the United States proved unready for the wars that it wound up fighting," Columbia University political scientist Richard K. Betts observes in *Military Readiness: Concepts, Choices, Consequences*, an exploration of this much-debated, little-understood issue just published by the Brookings Institution.

"Never again" is the watchword of the day. The long Cold War may be won, but readiness tops the political and planning agenda as never before. Reporting to Congress last February, Defense Secretary William J. Perry pledged "to make readiness the first priority, even at the expense of other important uses for the department's resources."

This intense focus on the day-to-day preparedness to fight of a shrinking military establishment raises a perplexing question, one that might never have occurred to late-1970s critics of the "hollow force" created by the post-Vietnam dip in defense budgets: Is it possible to have too much readiness?

That sounds like wondering about having too much money. But a nation can be overly ready—if it invests in the wrong sort of readiness. Unless defense dollars are unlimited—which they assuredly are not—forces can be kept well-staffed, well-paid, well-trained and well-equipped only by borrowing from future readiness, meaning the procurement of the next generation of weapons and the research on the generation to follow that. As Army Gen. John M. Shalikashvili, the chairman of the Joint Chiefs of Staff, said last year, "Modernization is tomorrow's readiness." *(See NJ, 3/26/94, p. 721.)*

If all of the readiness pots are to be kept at an even simmer, a bewildering array of factors must thus be kept in artful balance and thoughtful tradeoffs made between force structure, training, maintenance and purchases for the future. Whipsawed by partisan defense politics, Washington may be losing that balance.

"The politically potent argument is always readiness," Barry M. Blechman, chairman of the Henry L. Stimson Center, a Washington think tank, said. "I wouldn't be surprised to see a constitutional amendment that all units must be equally ready. It's crazy to keep your active forces at such a high rate of readiness. But, politically, it's very powerful, and nobody will go against it."

Even Senate Armed Services Committee member John McCain of Arizona, who has rung the tocsin about alleged short-term readiness shortfalls louder than any other Republican in Congress, is worried that the preparedness pendulum has swung too far toward the immediate.

"When I started a couple of years ago talking about the issue, I was concerned about a lot of the short-term areas, whether there would be pay raises to keep up [troop] retention, for instance," McCain said in an interview. "My concern is now shifting much more to long-term readiness, which has to do with modernization."

In Washington, the political incentives are usually perverse. President Clinton, a Vietnam-era draft avoider, boasts a defense policy Achilles' heel stretching up to and around his neck. With an ugly reelection drive looming next year, he can ill-afford another contretemps like last November's flap over three Army divisions that were rated unready. With budgets for arms procurement hitting a post-World War II low, moreover, the readiness-modernization imbalance seems unlikely to be redressed any time soon.

Meanwhile, "readiness," has become everyone's hobby horse, a rhetorical bludgeon much as "deterrence" once was. As Ronald V. Dellums of California, the ranking Democrat on the House National Security Committee, commented, "We are going to try to outready each other."

"Unless we begin procurement activity again soon," a group of retired officers recently reported, "our legacy to the next generation will be 45-year-old training aircraft, . . . 25-year-old fighters, 35-year-old trucks and 40-year-old assault helicopters."

Defense Department

In last February's House debate over the defense planks in the GOP's Contract With America, Democrats attacked plans to ramp up missile defense as undermining operational readiness. A Republican then retorted that continental defenses would enhance readiness by assuring troops that their home folks were safe. Lobbyists for a reserve forces tooth-care plan actually refer to "dental readiness."

Enshrining near-term readiness as a golden calf could one day exact a price. "Most of my observations come down to the theme that there is no free lunch," Columbia's Betts said, summing up his 315-page book in an interview. "Our most serious [threats] will come down the road rather than tomorrow morning. Because the worse thing we have to worry about tomorrow morning is North Korea or Iraq, which are not the Soviet Union or Nazi Germany or Imperial Japan. But 15 years down the road, we could face something like those powers—China, perhaps.

"In a perverse kind of way," he added, "it seems that a fixation on retaining readiness now is less attuned to potential worst cases than an approach that limits a concern with immediate readiness and bolsters future readiness."

UNREADY ROUGH RIDERS

Whatever faults critics might find with the current tack toward readiness, U.S. history shows far worse ways to approach the preparedness problem.

When Uncle Sam took on Spain in Cuba and the Philippines in 1898, troops were dispatched to the tropics with winter uniforms and obsolete rifles. Two decades later, many of the two million doughboys drafted to fight Kaiser Bill sat idle in their barracks waiting for enough gear to be ginned up. On the eve of World War II, similarly, GIs were reduced to drilling with wooden rifles.

The Korean conflict provides the most sobering case study for military planners. Task Force Smith, the first Army unit rushed in to block North Korea's assault across the DMZ, was armed with but six rounds of high-explosive antitank ammunition. Its bazooka shells simply ricocheted off Soviet T-34 tanks. After a disastrous July 5, 1950, firefight, fully a fourth of the ill-trained task force's 540 men were dead, wounded or missing.

Besides providing a grim object lesson in the human costs of unpreparedness, Korea ushered a novel phenomenon onto the strategic stage. Henceforth, Washington would maintain a huge, standing force to "contain" a huge, standing threat—the Soviet Union and other Communist regimes.

As the notion of a truly "peacetime Army" became obsolete, so did standards for peacetime preparedness. When war might erupt at any moment with the press of a button or the charge of tanks through Germany's Fulda Gap, readiness became *the* touchstone for defense planners. It also, small surprise, became a political punching bag.

The Kennedy campaign savaged the Eisenhower-Nixon Administration for allowing the Soviet Union to open up a (fictitious) "missile gap." Two decades later, the GOP pummeled President Carter for letting readiness sag in a post-Vietnam "decade of neglect" that actually began under two Republican Presidents.

By 1980, the services *were* in sad shape. More than 60 per cent of all aviation squadrons, divisions and ships were rated marginally or not at all combat-ready. Their woes were epitomized by Desert One, the accident-prone 1980 hostage-rescue attempt in Iran. Although the services were beset by shortages of spare parts and munitions, personnel problems may have been the biggest shovel digging the much-decried 1970s readiness trough.

Following abolition of the draft in 1973, military pay in the all-volunteer force badly lagged behind civilian compensation. The services were unable to attract and retain high-quality troops, and noncommissioned officers fled, until the Navy was bewailing a shortfall of 20,000 petty officers.

After President Reagan rode into town pledging to regird the nation's loins, military spending roughly doubled, pay was boosted and ammo bins began to fill. But not even Reagan could dodge the readiness snipers. A 1983 House Appropriations Subcommittee on Defense report detailing preparedness shortcomings spawned blaring headlines. Democratic candidates in the 1982 midterm election were urged to attack Reagan's bent for "hardware over readiness."

That charge had some merit. But readiness spending had climbed by some 20 per cent—nearly $10,000 per troop. So why did the Joint Chiefs conclude in 1984 that readiness had *declined* across the board, save on Navy ships? Quite simply, the services had lowered the limbo bar.

As assistant Defense secretary for

manpower, installations and logistics, Lawrence J. Korb was the "readiness czar" from 1981-85. "The services were terrified that the Reagan buildup would run out of steam without keeping the pressure up, so they raised the number of supplies you needed to keep on hand to be ready—without even telling us," Korb, now with the Brookings Institution, recalled. "So you'd see things not getting as well as you would have thought."

In time, a rising fiscal tide raises all boats—and tanks and planes. Readiness indicators climbed steadily through the late 1980s, culminating in Desert Storm, the 1991 war with Iraq and the symbolic antithesis of Desert One.

Then came Clinton and a fierce re-eruption of partisan readiness warfare. "Operational readiness is something that's had an enormous amount of focus that it has not had before," Adm. William A. Owens, the vice chairman of the Joint Chiefs of Staff, said in an interview, "in the breadth in which it has been looked at, in the [interservice] jointness in which it's been looked at and in terms of the civilian oversight of it."

Other officials, both uniformed and civilian suits, also testify to the emphasis on operational—or current—readiness. Last June, a Defense Science Board task force chaired by former Army Chief of Staff Gen. Edward C. (Shy) Meyer, who coined the "hollow force" expression in 1980, termed the preparedness of today's forces "acceptable in most measurable areas."

While it found "pockets" of unreadiness, the Meyer report said, "most of these 'pockets' are a result of changes taking place in the armed forces and the turbulence created by these changes."

Outside analysts largely agree. "For the most part, this effort to protect readiness in the short term is succeeding," the Congressional Budget Office (CBO) reported last year. Retired Army Lt. Col. Andrew F. Krepinevich, who directs the private Defense Budget Project, said, "We are much closer to Desert Storm than to Desert One."

Richard A. Bloom

Senate Armed Services member John McCain, R-Ariz. "My concern is now shifting much more to long-term readiness."

BEANS, NO BULLETS

The Republican choir sings a sourer tune. Rep. James M. Talent, R-Mo., has formed a Hollow Forces Update Task Force "to call attention to the effect President Clinton's defense budget cuts are having on our forces' readiness."

In December, Floyd Spence, R-S.C., who chairs the House National Security Committee, put out a report, "Military Readiness: The View From the Field," one of more than a half-dozen statements he had issued on the topic since the November elections. "Virtually every measure of readiness that has surfaced during this exercise seems to confirm the early stages of a long-term systemic readiness problem," the chairman charged.

McCain has issued two fat reports, called "Going Hollow," since 1993. "I believe we are now seeing the beginning of a new hollow force," McCain wrote in last September's edition. "My principal criticism of the military is their reluctance to be candid about their problems," he added.

After presiding over an April 27 Senate Armed Services Readiness Subcommittee hearing where service chiefs were grilled, McCain dropped that charge. "These guys did speak out, I have to hand it to them," he said. "They did it in a way that there was no mutiny or disrespect to the President."

But neither did the chiefs describe a military machine grinding to a halt as decried by those Clinton critics given to overshooting their target. As U.S. forces funneled into Haiti last September, Sen. Hank Brown, R-Colo., went so far as to charge that Army Rangers had been issued a mere 15 rifle rounds each and were thus denied "the ability to defend themselves properly."

Talk-meister Rush Limbaugh then circulated Brown's allegation, leading the brass at Fort Bragg, N.C., to attest that infantrymen in Haiti had been allotted the standard 210 rounds of M-16 ammo.

At McCain's hearing, Gen. Gordon R. Sullivan, the Army Chief of Staff, pegged his readiness at 8 on a scale of 1-10. "We are ready today," Adm. J.M. Boorda, the Chief of Naval Operations, said. The outgoing Marine Commandant, Gen. Carl E. Mundy Jr., said that the corps was not hollow, but "shallow." Short-term readiness was being maintained, he said, echoing the other chiefs, but "I remain concerned about the not-so-distant implications of continuing to defer needed investment in the Marine Corps of the future."

The factors feeding into readiness are far more complex than the often-glib discourse on the subject might suggest. Consider the mounting backlog of weapons and gear waiting at depots for repair and maintenance, often cited by critics as a measure of looming disaster.

"This indicator can be very misleading," the CBO reported last year. "Particularly in the case of the Army—where some of the equipment that is freed up because of the reduced number of active units is being sent to depots for reconditioning—a growing backlog is not a reliable early-warning indicator of future readiness problems."

Another worry is troop quality. Even as the force shrinks from 2.1 million toward 1.4 million, some 200,000 new recruits have to be rounded up every year. "Recruiters must work harder . . . because propensities to enlist are noticeably reduced," Congressional Research Service (CRS) analyst John M. Collins observed. "Prospects of onerous duty in destitute, disease-ridden sites such as Somalia deter some eligibles. Uncertainties concerning assignments, promotion, potential, pay, emoluments and retirement benefits discourage others."

Congress recently boosted recruiting budgets, and the services are hitting their targets, though the quality of those signing up has slipped marginally. In 1980, only 54 per cent of new Army troops had boasted school diplomas. By 1992, that figure had climbed to 100 per cent. Last year, however, high school grads dropped back to 96 per cent of Army recruits. But that hardly portends the fall of the Republic.

The Administration has twice sought to cut fiscal corners by deferring military pay raises to keep up with inflation. Congress has twice mandated fatter pay envelopes. The Administration's belated embrace of competitive military pay has exacerbated longer-term defense budgeting problems, but it has stilled some criticism on near-term readiness.

"The Administration appears to have more robustly funded many readiness accounts than in years past," Spence commented in a recent Heritage Foundation address. But he went on to rap the Administration's many contingency missions, terming them "a $2 [billion]-$4 billion 'tax' on the services' operating budgets."

As seen from this year's tussle over the Pentagon's $2.5 billion fiscal 1995 supplemental spending request, contingencies—unbudgeted missions in Bosnia, Haiti, Iraq, Rwanda, Somalia and other zones of crisis—pose particular problems. Monies for these expeditions must be drawn from a fixed operations budget, which gets mighty tight late in the fiscal year. Unless Congress coughs up supplemental funds ASAP, the price is paid in training schedules slashed and maintenance deferred.

The Pentagon is thus seeking "readiness preservation authority" that would allow it to shift funds at will when an operations spending squeeze arises in the straitened second half of the fiscal year. *(See NJ, 2/18/95, p. 427.)*

"I understand that the Hill might be concerned that if you give this sort of blank check to spend money in the last two quarters because of contingency operations, that it loses ability to then oversee the contingencies," Adm. Owens acknowledged. "But it is very important that we . . . maintain the readiness of American fighting forces. It is just the nature of the way the budget is put together that we have to have this kind of flexibility to deal with the problem."

TEMPEST IN A TANK TURRET

This lack of flexibility generated a rather bizarre flap last November when the Army disclosed that three stateside divisions had been rated C-3, or "marginally unready," under the Status of Resources and Training System, known as SORTS, by which commanders report the preparedness of their units.

Only weeks earlier, then-deputy Defense secretary John M. Deutch, now the CIA director, had declared U.S. forces "more ready and capable than they've ever been," prompting Spence to charge "a disturbing misinterpretation of the gravity of the readiness problem." Deutch and Perry then dove for a foxhole, strangely, even though the C-3 controversy was a tempest in a tank turret—or "a blip on the screen," as an Army general dubbed it.

"That was one of the most ironic things I can think of," Betts scoffed. "Here the Cold War was over and all of sudden we're hysterical because a few Army divisions have fallen to C-3. That's asinine. We never even had that level of readiness for most of the Cold War.

John Eisele

Adm. William A. Owens, vice chairman of the Joint Chiefs of Staff "Operational readiness is something that's had an enormous amount of focus."

"In this kind of world, you should be willing to have some of your forces at lower levels of readiness," he continued. "That flurry of criticism last fall was a symptom of how the politicization of the issue [is] out of touch with a reasonable distribution of readiness levels."

Readiness hawk McCain concurs that the Administration "got a bum rap on the three divisions." For one thing, all were reinforcement units. For another, two of the divisions were slated for imminent demobilization. Finally, SORTS is rife with shortcomings.

Units commanders score their readiness according to three criteria—troop numbers, training and equipment—and on a continuum ranging from C-1, fully ready, to C-4, not ready. The lowest score in any criterion is applied to the whole unit. The rear-echelon Army divisions had simply deferred training because of the fiscal demands posed by overseas contingencies and so were rated C-3.

SORTS "is a snapshot in time and does not predict impending changes," the General Accounting Office noted in a March report. It "does not provide data with which commanders can adequately assess joint [interservice] readiness" and "is based on a commander's subjective assessment of the number of additional training days a unit needs to reach a C-1 status."

The services are developing more-dynamic methods to assess preparedness. Meanwhile, Owens has implemented a joint monthly readiness review, where senior officers "come together to look at how we do war fighting and readiness."

Other measures also sharpen insight into readiness. The Joint Requirements Oversight Council, chaired by Owens and including the vice chiefs of staff of the four services, was once charged only with pondering war-fighting issues. It now "proactively" considers issues of readiness, sustainability and modernization.

A Senior Readiness Oversight Council, co-chaired by Owens and the deputy Defense secretary, also meets monthly, and is underpinned by a Readiness Working Group, co-chaired by the deputy Defense undersecretary for readiness—a new billet—and the Joint Staff operations director.

Don't underestimate the novelty of the exposure that readiness has gained. "I was the readiness czar, and I never even saw the SORTS readiness reports," Korb recalled. "I could go check into them. But nobody ever sent them to me and said, 'Look at these things.' I had the clearances, but it was such a closed system."

The blossoming readiness organizational tree is being amply watered with dollars. Factoring out bucks for such controversial "non-defense defense" items as environmental remediation, spending for "operations and support" is $90,000 per troop this year, the Defense Budget Project reports, compared with $75,000 in fiscal 1980 and $87,000 in 1990.

The CRS, likewise, reports that monies earmarked for operations and maintenance in Clinton's fiscal 1994-99 plan total $535.9 billion, only a few million dollars less than President Bush would have spent on 200,000 more troops.

It seems hard to contend, then, as House Republicans did in the original draft of their National Security Revitalization Act, that "a return to the 'hollow force' of the 1970s has already begun."

Richard A. Bloom

Columbia University political scientist Richard K. Betts
"Our most serious [threats] will come down the road rather than tomorrow morning."

Between then and now, "the biggest difference is standards," Meyer said at a press briefing last July upon release of his readiness report. "What we call an acceptable level of readiness today would in the '70s have been regarded as unattainable pie-in-the-sky, you're-from-some-other-planet. We sent people into combat in Vietnam regularly who the armed forces today wouldn't consider qualified to go to a major training exercise."

A GOOD ARMY OR A LARGE ONE?

The prospects for maintaining long-term readiness by procuring sufficient numbers of new weapons early in the next century does have a pie-in-the-sky quality.

"The thing that's curious to me is we're acting as though near-term readiness is as important today as it was during the Cold War, when we had a commitment to rush 10 divisions to Europe," budget analyst Krepinevich remarked. "We don't have anything like that today, and yet we continue to postpone recapitalization in order to maintain a high level of near-term readiness. It would seem to me that we would want to stress things in the longer-term direction, build in some strategic options for yourself."

In February, McCain published a 72-page readiness report signed by former Air Force Chief of Staff Gen. Charles A. Gabriel and three other retired four-star officers. "Over all, the services have done an effective job implementing the Administration's guidance to maintain *current* readiness as their highest priority," they found.

But, the officers added, "the defense budget has become 'front-end loaded' to support current operations at the expense of future capabilities and readiness. Unless we begin procurement activity again soon, our legacy to the next generation will be 45-year-old training aircraft, 35-year-old bombers and airlifters, 25-year-old fighters, 35-year-old trucks and 40-year-old assault helicopters."

The Pentagon has budgeted $94.9 billion for operations and maintenance this year. Compared with the $96.8 billion devoted to procurement in fiscal 1985, however, only $39.4 billion is earmarked next year, a historic low. Asked at a late-February hearing how they would spend an extra $1.5 billion, the service chiefs each said they would throw it at arms and infrastructure, not readiness.

The weapons-buying budget is to go vertical at decade's end, soaring to $67.3 billion in 2001. But the Pentagon is counting on savings from base closures and management reforms for the extra bucks. Of the $25 billion bonus that Clinton pledged last December to bolster defense, $15 billion must be found just as procurement is slated to jump.

Pulling this off will be a neat trick, one many analysts say is unachievable with political imperatives demanding unprecedented expenditures on daily readiness. "You can't afford to maintain this size of force structure and maintain readiness and modernize without significant budget increases," Korb said. "It's just not going to happen."

Something, somewhere, will have to give. While looking to add $46 billion to Clinton's five-year defense plan, House Republicans also seek to yank the Pentagon off the global cop beat. But Owens denied that overseas contingencies necessarily exact so severe a toll.

"If you look at the numbers involved in 'operations other than war' at any given time, it is about 24,000 . . . out of 1.5 million-plus [troops]," he said. "The numbers are not huge. The issue then is how we manage this level of operations to maintain the readiness to do the first mission—fighting this nation's wars. We think we can do that efficiently."

Two centuries back, Gen. George Washington posited a choice between "a good army rather than a large one." That is the tradeoff now under discussion. The Army already talks of coming to rest at 475,000 troops instead of 495,000.

Slimming down the forces would be facilitated by relaxing the 1993 Bottom-Up Review of post-Cold War defense requirements that the military be able to wage two near-simultaneous major regional conflicts—in the Persian Gulf, say, and in Korea.

"I think the two[-war] planning guideline was a mistake," Betts said. "That we have to meet this criterion, when we probably could never have done it too well even in the Cold War with that huge military establishment, is just too demanding. If we keep it and try to maintain all the necessary divisions, it will have to come out of operational readiness."

That's a specious dichotomy, some Repubiians contend. "We have an unhealthy household that pays only to cut the grass and pay the lights and forgets to fix the roof," Heritage Foundation defense analyst Lawrence T. Di Rita argued. "We take the knuckles-dragging-on-the-ground approach—that we have to do it all. You shouldn't have to make a false choice between operational readiness, force structure and modernization. The government is responsible for the common defense."

At a time when Republicans are also moving to slash middle-class entitlements to balance the federal budget, though, can the Pentagon really do it all? At some point, it seems, all 210 of those standard-issue bullets will have to be bitten and the tough tradeoffs addressed.

Spar Wars

The ballistic missile defense controversy just keeps going and going. As the debate proceeds in a post-Soviet era of fiscal belt-tightening, what was once envisioned by President Reagan as an "impenetrable shield" has increasingly become a tangled web.

DAVID C. MORRISON

Did you really think that the raucous debate over ballistic missile defense (BMD)—aka "Star Wars"—ended two years ago when the Clinton Administration came into office? Guess again, foolish Earthlings.

With the Republican sweep of Congress, BMD is most definitely back on the policy burner. And why not? The desirability—or the danger—of erecting systems to swat down nuclear warheads aimed at the United States has come to be one of those hardy perennials of American strategic discourse.

A much ballyhooed Feb. 15 House vote narrowly approved an amendment pressed by John M. Spratt Jr., D-S.C., that dramatically diluted the already watered-down commitment to push BMD embodied in the House GOP's Contract With America. But the vote has not shelved this issue for good. Far from it.

"We have appropriations bills coming," House Speaker Newt Gingrich, R-Ga., noted after debate on the GOP's National Security Revitalization Act was concluded. "There are many ways to make our point."

As the BMD debate winds through its unexpected twists and turns, however, it can be tough to discern any longer precisely what that point might be. The current round of dispute, in fact, resembles one of those deceptive basing schemes for the since-abandoned MX missile. The chief of the exercise, for many players on all sides, appears to be little more than political posturing.

In his landmark March 1983 Star Wars speech, remember, President Reagan proposed rendering nuclear weapons "impotent and obsolete" by supplanting traditional retaliatory deterrence with a shield against atomic attack. A dozen years and $36 billion after Reagan opened this debate, W. Curtis Weldon, R-Pa., who chairs the House National Security Military Research and Development Subcommittee, has been tapped to captain the GOP's forces in coming battles in the long-running BMD campaign. But Weldon is hardly a dollars-be-damned Star Warrior.

"I'm going to try to be a moderating force in this debate, and not be saying, 'Let's throw $20 billion-$30 billion at this problem,' " Weldon said in an interview. "I'm not in favor of giving a blank check to the [Pentagon]. I think we can be modest in this approach and not go out asking for huge sums of money which will just not be possible in this budget."

That caveat is key. Granted, BMD is an article of faith for true-blue Republicans. But so is balancing the federal budget. Missile defense pits defense hawks against deficit hawks as few other issues do. Two dozen House Republicans, including their leading deficit foe, Budget Committee chairman John R. Kasich, R-Ohio, thus sided with Spratt. Kasich later termed his vote a misunderstanding, but the damage was done.

Spratt's amendment, moreover, hoisted the GOP defense hawks with a petard of their own making. Republicans have vociferously decried the "hollowing out" of U.S. military forces under President Clinton. Spratt's measure placed the deployment of national missile defenses in a third order of priority, after "ensuring operational readiness of the armed forces" and fielding defenses against theater or battlefield missiles.

Military readiness, therefore, became the steed upon which BMD critics rode into the fray. "It will cost megabucks, gigabucks. That will only pull more money from readiness that everybody is talking about in the hollow force," Patricia Schroeder, D-Colo., protested on Feb. 15. "Star Wars II, the Sequel, will not only waste money, it will take away from efforts to enhance military readiness," Gary L. Ackerman, D-N.Y., added.

This putative "Star Wars II" is something of a straw man. Few Republicans talk any longer of a multi-gigabuck Astrodome defense (which then-Vice President Dan Quayle described in 1989 as being merely "political jargon," anyway). With the collapse of the Soviet Union, even the most fervent BMD advocates recognize, the threat of coordinated attack by thousands of sophisticated warheads has largely evaporated. "I am donating $1 to the Science Fiction Writers Foundation for every time [Democrats] mention the term Star Wars," Weldon finally protested on the floor. "It has nothing to do with this debate."

In the final analysis, it's hard to say what that debate did have to do with. In keeping with the ritualistic, Kabuki theater nature of much of the BMD debate this year, the contretemps was probably irrelevant. The Senate shows no inclination to move companion legislation, meaning that the House GOP's defense bill will never become law.

Besides which, the Clinton Administration has threatened a veto if the measure ever does cross the President's desk. But that warning hinges more upon provisions that would erode executive branch foreign policy prerogatives than anything in the bill pertaining to BMD. The final language that emerged from the National Security Committee in late January, after all, merely called for deployment of national missile defenses "at the earliest practical date"—as opposed to the "earliest possible moment," as called for in the original contract. It also gave Defense Secretary William J. Perry 60 days after the bill became law to submit a plan.

"I do not see a clear conflict and could support the language," Perry declared the day before the GOP bill was softened even further by Spratt's amendment on the House floor. That's because, playing to Republican pressure, the Pentagon is already bruiting an "emergency response system" that would place interceptors on 20-50 converted Minuteman intercontinental ballistic missiles stationed at Grand Forks (N.D.) Air Force Base. According to a Feb. 7 memo by deputy Defense secretary John M. Deutch, this scheme would cost $5 billion to deploy within four years.

Some Republican BMD boosters, significantly, have greeted the plan, product of the multiagency Pentagon "tiger team," as adequate, or at least a reasonable starting point for discussion.

"The path the Administration is on is not necessarily inconsonant with" the House GOP language, Sen. Jon L. Kyl, R-Ariz., who ardently pressed for missile defenses during his tenure in the House, said in an interview. "That is not to say that we want a system deployed immediately which is really not that good of a system. So I think it is a matter of working together and devising a national missile defense which would be good enough and can be deployed soon enough to do what we want it to do."

Outside analysts on both sides of the debate deride the emergency response system as something falling far short of

"good enough." It is "junk," Lawrence T. Di Rita, deputy director of foreign policy and defense studies at the conservative Heritage Foundation, scoffed.

"The main threat that the $5 billion system is designed to defend against is an internal fractionation of the Republican Party," John E. Pike, a missile defense critic with the liberal Federation of American Scientists, contended.

"It is better than nothing, so maybe the defense hawks will salute it, and yet it is the smallest, most pathetic and wretched thing they could do, so maybe it will be cheap enough that the deficit hawks won't choke on it," Pike continued. "The problem is that it is pathetic and wretched."

Richard A. Bloom

Rep. W. Curtis Weldon, R-Pa.
"I'm going to try to be a moderating force."

FROM NIKE-X to THAAD

Curiouser and curiouser, however "pathetic," the emergency system would also contravene the Antiballistic Missile (ABM) Treaty, which forbids pressing offensive weaponry, such as the Minuteman missile, into service as defensive interceptors. That would serve BMD advocates, who despise the 1972 pact, just fine. But this Administration has sworn continued fealty to the ABM Treaty.

What was once envisioned as an impenetrable shield, it seems, is increasingly becoming a hopelessly tangled web.

In untangling that web and discerning where the BMD debate might be going, it helps to understand where it has been. The pattern established in successive rounds of this dispute has been one of ever-diminishing strategic and technological expectations for the systems under discussion.

In a 1967 speech, then-Defense Secretary Robert S. McNamara denounced as destabilizing plans then in train to field a robust, ground-based, nationwide missile defense system called Nike-X. Then, oddly, he turned around and announced plans to build a scaled-down system, called Sentinel, ostensibly to defend against Chinese missile attack. ("To my knowledge," Perry let slip in recent House testimony, almost 30 years after Sentinel was proposed, "the Chinese do not have any missiles targeted" on the United States.)

In 1969, President Nixon touted an even more limited system, called Safeguard, designed simply to defend missile silos against Soviet attack. At a cost of $8 billion, a 100-interceptor site was unveiled at Grand Forks Air Force Base in 1975—only to be shuttered as cost-ineffective a few months later.

Eight years further down the road, Reagan made his famous bid for an "umbrella defense" of the United States. After whittling down an earlier plan that would have run some $115 billion, the Pentagon's Strategic Defense Initiative Organization (SDIO) received top-level approval in 1987 for a $69 billion system. To become operational 10 years later, this infrastructure would have had 2,000 ground-based interceptors and 4,000 space-based interceptors.

In 1990, with the Cold War over, the Bush Administration came up with a $40 billion BMD complex dubbed Global Protection Against Limited Strikes, which called for only 1,000 ground-based and another 1,000 space-based antimissile weapons. Unlike in the Reagan years, so-called theater missile defense against shorter-range rockets received considerable attention in the Bush plan, especially after scores of converted Patriot anti-aircraft missiles were fired against Iraqi Scud missiles—with a questionable effectiveness—in the Persian Gulf war.

The global protection scheme seemed to be on a roll in the Gulf war's wake. Congress passed the Missile Defense Act in 1991, which called for fielding a national BMD system by 1996. After the SDIO conceded that 2002 was a more feasible date, Congress's gusto waned markedly. In 1992, lawmakers zeroed out any target date and set to slashing away at the SDIO's budget. BMD spending thus peaked in fiscal 1992, at $4.1 billion. Of $5.4 billion requested in fiscal 1993, only $3.7 billion was approved, a number that fell by another $1 billion the next year.

On moving into the Oval Office, Clinton inherited a glide path under which the SDIO was to have spent $6.3 billion in fiscal 1993 and $40.9 billion from 1995-99. The monies would have been about evenly divided between strategic defenses of the United States and tactical defenses on the battlefield.

Clinton's team dramatically revamped those priorities. Declaring the "end of the Star Wars era," then-Defense Secretary Les Aspin abolished the SDIO in May 1993, replacing it with a downgraded Ballistic Missile Defense Organization (BMDO). Whereas the SDIO reported directly to the Defense Secretary, for instance, the BMDO answers to the Defense undersecretary for acquisition.

Even more painful to the Star Warriors, in the September 1993 Bottom-Up Review of post-Cold War defense needs, Aspin slashed President Bush's BMD spending profile back to $18 billion, $12 billion of which would be consumed by theater missile defenses. Perry's new BMDO budget, submitted in January, eases up even further. It would spend $16.5 billion from fiscal 1996-2001, only some $400 million of which would go each year for national missile defenses.

Although the Marine Corps is also upgrading HAWK anti-aircraft missiles for antimissile purposes, three primary systems lie at the core of the BMDO's effort to fend off such shorter-range theater missiles as the Scud, which are fielded by almost a score of developing nations.

Although called the Patriot Advanced Capability-3, the Army's PAC-3 system is not a Patriot missile at all, but rather what was formerly known as the ERINT, or Extended-Range Interceptor. Production of some 1,500 PAC-3 missiles is slated to begin in 1998.

By pumping up the software and sensors on existing cruisers and destroyers equipped with the AEGIS battle management radar and Standard-IV air defense missiles, the Navy plans to field a lower-tier missile defense system. Some 1,500 of these sea-based antimissile missiles are to flow off the production lines beginning in 1999.

The Army's Theater High Altitude Area Defense (THAAD) missile, finally, is designed to intercept incoming rockets at longer range than the PAC-3. Production of some 1,300 THAAD missiles and

14 associated ground-based radars is slated to begin in 2001.

These so-called core programs will not come cheap. The BMDO projects that fully fielding and operating the PAC-3, THAAD and the Navy's lower-tier effort for 10 years will run more than $25 billion.

The Pentagon is also exploring more-advanced options, such as an upper-tier Navy system, which might incorporate either the THAAD or a new interceptor called the LEAP; an Army and Marine Corps system called Corps SAM,to be developed jointly with the British, Germans and Italians; and a high-altitude, air-launched weapon to be fired by Air Force F-15 and Navy F-14 fighters to knock out missiles in the early, boost stage of flight.

"The bottom line is that we see the threat for the immediate future as theater missiles, and that's where we have the emphasis in the program," Air Force Maj. Tom La Rock, a BMDO spokesman, said. As for national missile defenses, he added, the Pentagon "would prefer to follow the program we have established, laying out the technology, and then, once those systems are developed, make the decision to deploy or not deploy."

WRONG END OF THE STICK?

In the national missile defense arena, $400 million a year will buy a "technology readiness program." That includes research on a ground-based radar system and on a ground-based interceptor, the first of which is to be test-flown in 1998. This work, the BMDO says, is designed to provide "a hedge against the emergence of a ballistic missile threat to the United States." Outside of stray launches by Russia or China, the Defense Intelligence Agency says, such a missile hazard cannot be expected before 2005 "at the earliest."

Challenging that sanguine view of the threat, national missile defense advocates plump for a far more vigorous program. "The Administration is basically saying, 'Look, there's no threat out there today, and we'll wait for one to emerge and then we'll react,' " Robert C. Smith, R-N.H., who chairs the Senate Armed Services Acquisition and Technology Subcommittee, said in an interview. "But you can't react that quickly. This isn't like moving troops to Kuwait. And it's morally wrong to say we're willing to protect troops in the field and our allies, but not citizens here in the U.S."

Yet another example of the odd political disconnects that mark the BMD debate these days can be found in the BMDO's annual report to Congress last July. Some $600 million annually would be needed to field "a single, ABM Treaty-compliant" antimissile site, the BMDO reported then. It discussed and rejected a "program alternative" costing only $450 million per year. "This funding level would seriously damage our [national missile defense] readiness strategy and would likely permit projected Third World threats to the homeland to materialize prior to any viable deployment capability," the BMDO warns. And yet it is locked into a $400 million per year budget for homeland defense.

The technology readiness undertaking, moreover, which Perry has said could cost as much as $10 billion to implement, is distinct from the $5 billion, Minuteman-based emergency response system, for which budget bucks are not yet earmarked. In this climate of comparative austerity, missile defense advocates strive mightily to draw what comfort they can from current Pentagon plans.

"At least you have this Administration saying it could conceivably and responsibly spend at least $5 billion over the next five years deploying an emergency defense capability," Frank J. Gaffney Jr., director of the Center for Security Policy, said in an interview. A Reagan-era Pentagon figure, Gaffney coordinates the Coalition to Defend America, set up last summer to flog interest in missile defenses. "I think it is a very helpful baseline from which to draw out what I'm confident would be a far more capable program," Gaffney concluded.

John Eisele

Defense Secretary William J. Perry
He's dug in his heels in opposition to GOP proposals.

The more capable the program, of course, the more daunting the fiscal, political and diplomatic hurdles to be leaped. An emergency response system "would only be capable of defending against a thin attack," Perry told the House National Security Committee at a Jan. 27 hearing. "On the other hand, if the threat that one wants to defend against is a large-scale threat, then ground-based systems turn out not to be so capable of doing that, and one needs to look alternatively at space-based systems. . . . Now we're talking about many tens of billions of dollars."

Such stratospheric sums aren't even remotely on the table these days. Moreover, the emergency system—not to mention a robust multisite national missile defense infrastructure—would fall well outside the ABM Treaty, which permits no more than the 100 antimissile interceptors fielded at Grand Forks.

Because the 1972 pact doesn't address the issue, the theater missile defense program has wandered into a diplomatic gray area. Since November 1993, the Administration has been holding "demarcation talks" with Moscow, trying to decide how to distinguish between permitted theater and outlawed national defenses. The ball is currently very much in Moscow's court. But the U.S. negotiating stance has been to limit the demonstrated capability of theater defenses, in flight testing, to a capability against missile targets flying no faster than 5 kilometers per second and no further than 3,500 kilometers.

According to the Congressional Budget Office, however, the THAAD missile could potentially protect a limited area, such as a major metropolitan area, against missiles traveling six to seven kilometers per second, the speed of a longer-range strategic missile. The demarcation talks thus alarm arms control advocates, who are keen to press forward with the first Strategic Arms Reduction Treaty, which has just gone into effect, and with START II, which is now up for ratification. Together, the two pacts would dramatically pare back U.S. and Russian strategic warheads.

"These [theater] systems are overdesigned and do in fact have strategic intercept capability and will undermine the ABM Treaty and will put a chill on strategic force reductions," Jack Mendelsohn, the deputy director of the private Arms Control Association, argued. "It doesn't make sense to sacrifice reductions to 3,500 strategic warheads or below in the one nation that you know can really hurt you because you want to protect against a potential rinky-dinky nation that might get a half-dozen short-range missiles. You've got the wrong end of the stick."

"I think it would be serious mistake at this stage to preemptively repudiate the ABM Treaty," John D. Holum, director of the Arms Control and Disarmament Agency, concurred in an interview. "The ABM Treaty is very important to those offensive reductions, and we don't need to endanger [it] in order to defend against theater ballistic missiles." But Holum rejected the thesis that U.S. theater missile defense plans would undermine the treaty.

Those pushing for national missile defenses are just as alarmed by the demarcation talks as arms controllers such as Mendelsohn are. The chaos in Moscow is such that the chances of the Russian parliament ever ratifying START II are slim to vanishing, these critics contend. Anyway, the ABM Treaty is a Cold War dinosaur, they further argue, a relic no longer suited to today's strategic environment. "I think that we need to develop the kind of system that we want, unconstrained by an irrelevant ABM Treaty," Kyl asserted.

John Eisele

Heritage Foundation's Lawrence T. Di Rita His group will take "a stair-step approach."

On Jan. 17, Kyl and 21 other Senate Republicans fired a letter off to Clinton fretting that the talks might foreclose promising theater missile defense options. Following up on language incorporated last year into the fiscal 1995 defense authorization bill, these Senators insisted that "any agreement which 'substantially modifies' the ABM Treaty be submitted to the Senate for advice and consent."

These Senators may not welcome a situation where whatever is decided must also be ratified by the Russian parliament, the arms control agency's Holum noted. "We're beginning from the proposition that the treaty does not limit theater defenses," he added. "But what we've said is that we are prepared to consult with the Senate once we have something."

AN UNHOLY ALLIANCE

Following passage of the Spratt amendment on Feb. 15, House National Security Committee chairman Floyd Spence, R-S.C., sought to play jujitsu with the readiness issue himself. He moved an amendment to establish that "affordable, highly effective" theater and national missile defense systems are "an essential objective" for the Pentagon. What practical effect that narrowly passed measure will have in propelling national defenses down the road remains unclear, but it is likely to be minimal.

Reflecting Gingrich's pledge to press missile defenses in spending bills to come, missile defense fan Gaffney argued that "there will be opportunities, and hopefully soon, for the House of Representatives to revisit this decision and put itself back on track with what it promised the public it would do last November." Should those attempts fail, he conceded, "it will complicate the effort to do much of anything until the next President of the United States arrives on the scene."

Congress is far from being an irrelevant bystander in crafting U.S. defense policy, of course. Indeed, the legislative history of the past three decades has largely been one of lawmakers' wrestling relentlessly for control of the Pentagon helm. "Congress has an ability to steer policy," Sen. Smith insisted. "By funding various specific programs within the missile defense organization, we certainly have that capability." Along those lines, Kyl talks of boosting the BMDO's budget by as much as $1 billion next year.

But, when it comes to implementing major military initiatives, rather than just tinkering on the margins, Capitol Hill's leverage has typically been as a negative force staying the executive branch's hand, rather than a positive push propelling the White House down avenues it resists treading.

Senate opposition thus helped prompt President Carter's decision to withdraw the second Strategic Arms Limitation Treaty in 1980. In 1987, Senate Armed Services Committee chairman Sam Nunn, D-Ga., led a successful campaign to prevent the Reagan Administration from acting upon a controversial permissive reinterpretation of the 1972 ABM Treaty. And, in a battle ranging across the mid-1980s, House Democrats managed to impose a moratorium on anti-satellite missile tests.

It's another story, though, when Congress tries to impel the Pentagon. In 1978, Carter denied the Navy's request for a new aircraft carrier. Amid heated debate about the "decade of decline," carrier money was tucked into the fiscal 1979 defense authorization bill. Carter vetoed that bill—and made it stick.

Clinton has yet to wield a single veto—which is not to say that he couldn't quickly learn to do so. At a Feb. 14 press conference anticipating the House floor debate, Perry firmly dug in his heels in opposition to GOP missile defense proposals. "I believe that the program is a sound one and is tailored approximately to the threats we may see in the future," he insisted. "And I see no national security basis for accelerating or moving that program any faster than we are now going."

As the BMD debate winds on, Perry will confront more than a few plans for acceleration. The most comprehensive of those is likely to be the report due soon from the Heritage Foundation. Under the gavel of Henry F. Cooper, who ran the SDIO under Bush, the foundation has assembled a "Team B" of once-prominent Star Warriors to draft the blueprints for a robust national missile defense.

"It will take a stair-step approach," Heritage's Di Rita said. "This is what you can do under the following assumptions: no treaty, certain restrictions, different funding profiles, based on the most feasible technology. It is truly our intention to get the debate back to dead center."

But, he acknowledged, completing the report in time to affect this spring's defense authorization debate is likely to be the least of the challenges confronting Team B. "People who understand the problem and what needs to be done," he said, "know there will be this unholy alliance of deficit hawks and Democrats out to foil them."

Aiming High

With Republicans in control on Capitol Hill, defense contractors and their allies are mobilizing to seek more money for their favorite weapons systems. But the mission won't be easy.

PETER H. STONE

Shortly before Nov. 8, a group calling itself the Coalition to Defend America launched a radio and television advertising campaign around the country to revive the ballistic missile defense program known popularly as "Star Wars." The coalition, chock-full of Republican Members of Congress, former military men and ex-Reagan Administration bigwigs, asked all congressional candidates to sign pledges supporting its cause; 193 did so.

The group's message dovetailed with a plank in the Republican Contract With America that called for deploying ballistic missile defense systems and for beefing up defense spending generally. Now, with the GOP running Congress, the coalition is moving fast to raise $1 million to help push for funds to build a large-scale missile defense system.

But the mission won't be easy. Even with sympathetic lawmakers and squadrons of industry lobbyists on the coalition's side, it's far from clear that Congress will come up with the money. Boosting spending on the program would have been difficult under any circumstances; the new Republican majority's push to cut taxes and pass a balanced budget amendment make the battle even harder. Backers of other big-ticket weapons systems such as the B-2 stealth bomber, the Comanche attack helicopter and the C-17 transport plane will be competing for the same scarce funds.

Many defense firms have assembled a stable of lobbyists including retired military men and former Capitol Hill heavyweights. They have cemented their ties with the new Republican leadership through generous campaign contributions. And they have lined up ideological support from such conservative think tanks as the Heritage Foundation and the Alexis de Tocqueville Institution.

Besides seeking more money for weapons, industry trade groups and some companies are seeking more government help in the increasingly important foreign sales arena. *(See box.)*

Few industry lobbyists expect a return to the palmy days of the Reagan Administration. "Nobody in the industry is naive enough to believe that we're returning to the numbers that were in President Reagan's defense buildup in the early 1980s," said Thomas Culligan, vice president of government operations for AlliedSignal Aerospace, a major subcontractor on many weapons programs.

In an interview, House National Security Committee chairman Floyd Spence, R-S.C., said that he favored increased funds for ballistic missile defense and for the B-2. But, he said, "it's going to be difficult. When everybody else is trying to cut back, we're asking for more." And, Spence said, President Clinton could wield his veto power to block defense increases.

Late last year, Clinton requested another $25 billion for Pentagon readiness programs over the next six years. But over all, he is expected to propose trimming the defense budget from $252 billion this year to $246 billion in fiscal 1996. The expectation is that the Republicans will try to add more than $10 billion to his request.

The defense contractors' game plan is to try to slash spending for "nondefense" items in the Pentagon budget—such as medical research, environmental cleanup and conversion of abandoned military bases—that consume about $11 billion annually. Some top Republican lawmakers, industry consultants and conservative think tanks are leading a drive to recapture these funds for such traditional defense purposes as weapons systems and readiness.

In a study released in late December, Heritage Foundation defense policy analyst John Luddy found that nondefense spending as a share of the Defense Department budget rose by 238 per cent from 1990-93, while over-all defense spending declined 20 per cent. The study criticized increased spending on such items at a time when the military services have "huge maintenance backlogs and insufficient training funds and are delaying much-needed modernization of weapons and equipment."

Dov S. Zakheim, who was deputy Defense undersecretary for planning and resources during the Reagan Administration and now heads SPC International, an Arlington (Va.)-based defense consulting firm, has also called for cutting back nondefense spending in the Pentagon budget and channeling the savings into readiness programs. He wrote an op-ed article in *The New York Times* in late December arguing for such cuts and recently spoke on the subject at a conference sponsored by the Center for Strategic and International Studies. "I think there's sympathy in both parties for this," he said in an interview. "It's not a partisan issue."

Even if nondefense spending is cut sharply, some industry lobbyists wonder if the money saved would go into procurement accounts, where defense contractors would have a crack at it, or into readiness accounts, where they wouldn't. "Without substantial increases in over-all procurement spending, which means several billion dollars, it's going to be hard to add any programs that haven't already been requested—or even keep programs at their current levels," Culligan said.

The Pentagon must also find cost savings in overhead and other areas, said Richard K. Cook, the chief Washington lobbyist for Lockheed Corp. He estimated that 50 per cent of the current $260 billion Pentagon budget goes to overhead items, ranging from paying for auditors to conducting security clearances.

Cook said that he has had two meetings recently with House Appropriations Committee chairman Bob Livingston, R-La., to discuss the issue and has spoken about it with Defense Secretary William J. Perry as well. "I think there's a unique opportunity here for a Democratic Secretary of Defense to work with a Republican Congress" to cut nondefense spending, he said.

The defense contractors may not get all they want, but they have been generous to some Republican lawmakers whose support could prove essential.

Lockheed is a major employer in House Speaker Newt Gingrich's Georgia district and gave the maximum $5,000 to his reelection campaign last fall. The company also gave $10,000 to the Progress & Freedom Foundation, a Washington-based think tank that helps organize a college course that Gingrich teaches. *(For details, see NJ, 1/14/95, p. 72.)*

Over all, defense industry political action committees (PACs) gave about 60 per cent of their campaign contributions to Democrats in the 1994 campaign cycle through Sept. 30. But defense PACs sharply increased their giving to Spence in 1993-94. He received $59,050 from them through Sept. 30, compared with $32,850 in the entire 1992 cycle.

GENERATING PRESSURE

Besides pushing for over-all budget increases, many defense companies and groups have launched separate lobbying drives for their own pet programs. The most visible battle is over the plank in the Contract With America that calls for the earliest possible deployment of a ballistic missile system capable of defending American troops abroad and the United States against attacks—including accidental or unauthorized launches from Third World nations.

That would be a sharp reversal from the direction that the Clinton Administration has pursued over the past two years. The Administration has stressed the development of systems to defend against missiles in the field, dubbed theater missiles. But it has cut funds for bigger missile defense programs such as Brilliant Pebbles, Brilliant Eyes and National Missile Defense and has rejected ideas such as space-based sensors and firing devices that were part of President Reagan's original Star Wars plan.

The Bush Administration had proposed spending $40 billion on ballistic missile defense programs from 1995-99, but Clinton's "bottom-up" review of defense spending pared that figure to $18 billion, and last August, the Pentagon trimmed another $2 billion. It also renamed what had been known as the Strategic Defense Initiative Organization; it's now called the Ballistic Missile Defense Organization (BMDO).

Enter the Coalition to Defend America, a group set up last summer to push for more ballistic missile defense spending. Spearheaded by Frank J. Gaffney Jr., the head of the Center for Security Policy, a Washington think tank devoted to national security issues, the group has signed up a heavyweight list of sponsors, including Livingston, Senate Republican Whip Trent Lott of Mississippi and former Defense Secretary Caspar W. Weinberger.

The coalition has been been active on several fronts to generate pressure on Congress and the Administration, and Gaffney said that it is well on its way to raising $1 million. Although he declined to identify contributors, the

Northrop Grumman Corp., with backing from a stable of lobbyists and conservative think tanks, is pushing to build more B-2 stealth bombers.

list of coalition supporters includes *Forbes* magazine publisher Malcolm Forbes Jr. and Robert Krieble, the former chairman of Loctite Corp., a manufacturer of adhesives, who is a longtime backer of such conservative groups as the Heritage Foundation.

About 80 per cent of the coalition's budget is slated to go to grass-roots lobbying; the remainder is tentatively allocated for Washington lobbying activities and other programs, Gaffney said. The coalition recently hired Frank Luntz, an Arlington (Va.) pollster who worked with the House GOP on the Contract With America, to conduct polls and focus groups.

The first poll was released at a Jan. 24 press conference attended by Livingston, Spence and other lawmakers. According to Luntz, 88 per cent of a random sample of adults said they were "aware of the dangerous proliferation of ballistic missiles around the world" and 70 per cent said they were "concerned about this trend."

Some observers question whether the poll results were skewed, though. According to *Defense Week*, one of the questions was prefaced by the statement, "The truth is some 25 countries—including Iraq, Iran and North Korea—are acquiring ballistic missiles that can be used in an attack on the United States or its troops and allies overseas." But U.S. intelligence agencies have concluded that the United States will not "face the threat of intercontinental ballistic missiles launched by rogue nations for at least the next 10 years," *Defense Week* said.

During last fall's campaigns, the coalition also ran radio spots in several states. And the group advertised on the conservative National Empowerment Television network. The ads were designed with the help of Forrest Communications, a Chicago-based firm that provided its services free.

Several big defense firms, including Hughes Aircraft Co., Lockheed, Raytheon Co., Rockwell International Corp. and Thiokol Corp., have sizable contracts with the BMDO and are eager for increases in spending. Some of their lobbyists have joined the coalition, including Brian Dailey, who was an aide to then-Vice President Dan Quayle and is now the chief lobbyist for Lockheed Missile and Space Co.; Alison B. Fortier, who served on the National Security Council under Reagan and now runs Rockwell's Washington office; and Tidal W. McCoy, who was an assistant Air Force secretary under Reagan and now heads Thiokol's Washington office.

Lockheed is the prime contractor on the $20 billion Theater High-Altitude Area Defense, the Army's land-based theater missile defense program. Rockwell has been a major contractor on the Brilliant Eyes program, and Thiokol makes the propulsion systems for the standard Navy missiles used in antiballistic missile defenses.

On a related front, the coalition has pressed the Administration to suspend negotiations with Russia and other former Soviet states on the 1972 Antiballistic Missile (ABM) Treaty that bans testing of space weapons systems. The group, which is concerned that the treaty could jeopardize theater missile defense systems, helped organize two letters from Members of Congress to the White House, including one in January from Gingrich, Majority Leader Richard K. Armey of Texas and 15 other House Republicans. They asked that negotiations on the ABM treaty relating to certain technical matters be suspended until the new Congress "has had an opportunity to examine these questions with care."

But supporters of ballistic missile defense programs may be disappointed in their push for more funds. "It's certainly not going to be the El Dorado that some contractors see glittering in their eyes," a Republican congressional aide who deals with defense issues said. The industry will be lucky if it receives another $1 billion for ballistic missile work this year, consultant Zakheim said.

A full return to the Reagan program is unlikely, McCoy of Thiokol said. "Because of a change in the nature of the threat and because of budget considerations, I think industry and the conservatives want to be more selective in the timing and deployment of the missiles." He predicted an effort by the industry and its Republican allies to hike spending from

DRUMMING UP BUSINESS ABROAD

The defense industry is not just fighting for more money on the home front. Leading contractors and industry trade groups are seeking help from the Clinton Administration and Congress to spur U.S. arms sales overseas.

Over the past few years, as the Pentagon budget has declined, big contractors have increasingly looked abroad. With help from the Bush and Clinton Administrations, U.S. arms sales overseas have soared.

Since the end of 1989, when the Berlin Wall fell, U.S. contractors have sold $82.4 billion worth of weapons abroad, compared with $66.8 billion in sales registered by all other nations combined. In 1993, U.S. arms transfer agreements totaled $22.3 billion, dwarfing the $2.8 billion that Russia, the second-leading seller, completed.

But defense companies want more. They have been frustrated in obtaining federal loan guarantees that they say would make their products more competitive internationally because many foreign governments provide similar guarantees.

A handful of weapons exporters, including Raytheon Co., Unisys Corp. and United Technologies Corp., are working closely with such trade groups as the Aerospace Industries Association of America Inc., the American Defense Preparedness Association, the American League for Exports and Security Assistance Inc., the Electronic Industries Association and the National Security Industrial Association to draft legislation that would establish a guarantee program.

Dan Howard, the Washington lobbyist for Unisys who is coordinating the effort, said that his firm has retained the Washington lobbying firm of Capitoline/MS&L to push for the measure. Arch W. Roberts Jr., a former House Foreign Affairs Committee staff member who now works at Capitoline, is the chief lobbyist on the issue.

In the past few years, similar bills have failed, in part because of concerns raised by Democrats and arms control groups. Critics have noted that some U.S. weapons sold abroad have been used against American troops in foreign conflicts and that increased arms sales could undermine politically and economically fragile Third World governments.

But defense contractors argue that foreign arms sales are vital to preserving the country's defense industrial base and boosting U.S. export earnings. They have lined up some key supporters, including Sen. Christopher J. Dodd, D-Conn., who has long championed an export loan program. Dodd has also gone to bat to help Connecticut-based United Technologies obtain loan guarantees from the Export-Import Bank of the United States. Although the Eximbank has historically been barred from providing guarantees for weapons exports, Dodd helped Sikorsky Aircraft, a unit of United Technologies, obtain an exemption in 1992 that enabled it to sell 95 Black Hawk transport helicopters to Turkey.

about $18 billion over six years to about $25 billion over the same period. "Potentially, it would ultimately do the same thing as Reagan had envisioned, but stretched out," he said.

Some Democratic critics are likely to fight hard against more funds, too. "There's no justification for moving quickly to a national missile defense," said Rep. Barney Frank, D-Mass., a leading critic of defense spending. Under the terms of the ABM Treaty, Russia has been dismantling its missiles faster than the United States has, Frank said.

Building the ballistic missile defense system that is being proposed would not only cost tens of billions of dollars, Frank said; it would also entail violating the ABM Treaty. The last time the Senate considered the issue, he said, it voted, 99-0, that the U.S. ballistic missile defense program should comply with the treaty.

THE B-2 BATTLE

Another major war is brewing over the B-2 stealth bomber. Although it was not mentioned by name in the GOP contract, the B-2 enjoys strong support among congressional Republicans, and lobbying for more funds is likely to be vigorous this year. To date, the Pentagon has ordered 20 of the bombers at a total cost of $44.6 billion; an effort to authorize another 20 was killed last year, but the Pentagon budget contained $125 million to keep the program alive.

Many defense analysts have questioned the need for more B-2s because of the high price of the planes and the breakup of their primary target, the Soviet Union.

Northrop Grumman Corp., which makes the B-2, is pressing for another order of 20; it has said that it could produce them for about $11.4 billion, although the Congressional Budget Office has estimated that the cost would be $26 billion.

Northrop Grumman has an impressive stable of lobbyists, including Timmons and Co., a Washington lobbying firm, and Hicks & Associates, a Tysons Corner (Va.)-based consulting firm chaired by Donald A. Hicks, who was Defense undersecretary for research and engineering in the Reagan Administration.

The B-2 has received a boost from conservative thinks tanks as well. In early January, the Arlington (Va.)-based Alexis de Tocqueville Institution's defense unit, the Committee for the Common Defense, which is run by former Rep. Jim Courter, R-N.J., organized a letter to the Administration that was signed by seven former Defense Secretaries, calling for increased production of the B-2.

The campaign had no direct support from the defense industry, according to the Committee for the Common Defense. But Merrick Carey, the president of the de Tocqueville Institution, said that it has received some funds from Northrop Grumman. The institution is working on a study about the need for more B-2s that is due out shortly.

The push for the B-2 also involves subcontractors such as Boeing Co., which makes key components of the plane's fuselage. Boeing's outside lobbyists include Denny Miller, a longtime aide to the late Sen. Henry M. Jackson, D-Wash.

Still, the B-2 faces stiff opposition. One of the lawmakers who helped to kill additional funds for the plane last year is Rep. John R. Kasich, R-Ohio, the new Budget Committee chairman. He has said that he remains opposed to ordering more B-2s.

There's also a dilemma for firms that have a big stake in several weapons systems. AlliedSignal, for example, is a major subcontractor not only on the B-2 but also on the F-18 fighter plane. If funds to build more B-2s are taken out of the F-18 account, that could create problems for AlliedSignal. Northrop has already asked AlliedSignal to help lobby for the B-2, and the firm "will help push the B-2 because we're a player," Culligan said. "But you have to push over-all defense spending up to make it happen."

TILLING THE GRASS ROOTS

Another program whose backers are hoping for better times this year is the RAH-66 Comanche helicopter, made by Boeing and Sikorsky Aircraft, a division of United Technologies Corp.

Representatives of Boeing and Sikorsky have been meeting with their major subcontractors, including AlliedSignal, Allison Engine Co., Harris Corp. and Sundstrand Corp., to devise a strategy to restore $174 million in Comanche research and development funds that were cut out of the fiscal 1996 budget. The companies are also pushing to have production funds that were cut from the fiscal 1997 budget restored. AlliedSignal and Allison are particularly concerned because they have already received government approval for the engines. AlliedSignal estimates that it has invested $150 million-$200 million in the project.

The Comanche has plenty of friends among congressional Republicans. Two days after Election Day, 16 GOP lawmakers, including Gingrich, sent a letter to the White House asking that the program be saved. The letter was organized by House National Security Committee member Robert K. Dornan, R-Calif.

Another lobbying drive is being revved up to support the C-17 transport plane made by McDonnell Douglas Corp. Although the Pentagon has not proposed cutting funds for the plane, Sen. Dale Bumpers, D-Ark., a member of the Appropriations Defense Subcommittee, has introduced a bill to cap production of the C-17 at 40 planes and to modify other aircraft to fulfill its mission. He estimates that such a move would save $20 billion over 25 years.

Richard A. Bloom

Richard K. Cook, Lockheed Corp.'s chief Washington lobbyist
The Pentagon must cut overhead costs, which account for about half of its spending.

John Eisele

Frank J. Gaffney Jr. of the Center for Security Policy
He's spearheading a coalition that's trying to revive the 'Star Wars' program.

McDonnell Douglas has asked key subcontractors to rally their employers in support of the plane. "Our divisions out in the field are getting letters from McDonnell for their support," said Culligan of AlliedSignal, which has contracts worth $2.5 million-$3 million per plane.

AlliedSignal is headquartered in New Jersey and is likely to target the state's Democratic Senators, Bill Bradley and Frank R. Lautenberg, both of whom have signed on to the Bumpers bill. "It's obvious that we need to do some work with them," said Buzz Hefti, AlliedSignal's vice president for legislative affairs. But Hefti said that the company's lobbying will be complicated because only a small portion of the components that it supplies for the C-17 are made in New Jersey.

McDonnell Douglas is expected to deploy some of the same lobbying team that it used last year, when it tapped Burson Marsteller, the public relations giant, to run a grass-roots lobbying effort with its subcontractors, employees and suppliers. The contractor also used the Washington lobbying firm of Cassidy and Associates and two of its affiliates, the public relations firm Powell Tate and the grass-roots lobbying company Beckel Cowan.

Also representing McDonnell Douglas on the C-17 is Carl M. Smith of the Washington lobbying firm of Wunder, Diefenderfer, Cannon & Thelen; he's a former Republican staff director and chief counsel to the Senate Armed Services Committee.

Still another item on the defense contractors' wish list is the F-22, an advanced tactical fighter that Lockheed and Boeing have been developing for the Air Force. Last December, Perry ordered $200 million cut from its fiscal 1996 budget.

Cook of Lockheed said that he's been talking to anyone who will listen about the program's importance. "It's the only aircraft designed to meet the unknown threats of the 21st century," he said. "We're anxious to get the first F-22 flying. We have to maintain the schedule. It's the only really new aircraft in development anywhere."

Bumpers has introduced a bill that would reduce funds for the F-22 by limiting the inventory of planes to 42. He has called the plane another "Cold War system seeking a new justification," and has cited a General Accounting Office study saying that the F-15 will be more than adequate until 2015. Substituting the F-15 for the F-22 would save $6 billion over five years, according to Bumpers.

Despite the industry's lobbying efforts, the outlook for large increases in defense spending remains problematic.

Kasich, the Budget Committee chairman, has said that the Pentagon should be examined under the "same microscope as the rest of the federal government."

And veteran lawmakers such as Rep. John P. Murtha, D-Pa., who used to chair the Appropriations Defense Subcommittee, doubt whether defense contractors will get what's on their procurement wish list when Republicans seem more enthusiastic about spending on near-term readiness. "If you're going to have any kind of impact on readiness, you're going to have to eliminate some of these big-ticket items," Murtha said. "I don't see any way that the money is there" to increase spending on ballistic missile defenses and other major programs.

Some defense industry lobbyists sound pessimistic, too. "I'm one of those who doesn't expect major change," Fortier of Rockwell said. "We're dealing with a Republican Congress that's committed to balancing the budget and tax cuts."

Last November's election may have represented "epochal change," Cook of Lockheed said. "There's been a shift of where the ideas are—from the White House to Congress. The Republicans control the machinery of government." But when it comes to the defense budget, he said, "I don't know if they'll succeed. I think of all the things in the contract, increasing defense spending is the least popular."

Richard A. Bloom

Sen. Dale Bumpers, D-Ark.
He would limit spending on the C-17 and F-22 aircraft.

INTERVENTION V. SOVEREIGNTY

DAVID C. MORRISON

One of the many striking developments in an unexpectedly grim post-Cold War era is the Left-Right switch on the matter of military intervention. Things used to be simple. The December 1989 Panama invasion qua drug bust, after all, was the first major U.S. incursion since World War II that Washington did not justify as a counter to Communist penetration. Even the naval patrols launched in 1987 to fend off Iranian attacks on Persian Gulf oil tankers were sold to Congress, in part, as offsetting the Soviet gains in the Gulf.

When the geopolitical lay of the land is so starkly bipolar, the politics of intervention is no less stark. "In the good old days of the Cold War, the Left had little difficulty with the question of interventionism," Princeton University professor Richard Falk notes in a Dec. 20 *Nation* essay. Opposition to U.S. intervention was argued on grounds of sovereignty and national self-determination. Support for intervention was couched in terms of rolling back Communism. Today, the Soviet Union is but a memory and the rallying cry for military action is "humanitarian intervention." Things are not so simple.

Cases in point: Michael T. Klare, a professor of peace and world security studies at Hampshire College and a Cold War critic of American interventionism, was moved in a recent op-ed piece to bemoan that "with the American public ever more opposed to the United States playing global peacekeeper, Washington is unlikely to respond on its own to fresh atrocities in distant and unfamiliar areas." The Heritage Foundation, a vociferous booster of the interventionist "Reagan Doctrine," meanwhile, argues in a position paper that "using U.S. military forces for vaguely defined humanitarian purposes, and in cases where no U.S. interest is threatened, is unworkable."

Actually, these are both eminently defensible positions—which simply underlines the agonizing dilemmas posed by the world community's ostensible moral duty to march on to the planet's many killing fields and impose peace. The unhappy upshot of a provocative package of essays in the fall 1993 *Harvard International Review* debating the pros and cons of humanitarian intervention is that there is no pat formula for dealing with humankind's innate inhumanity. Nowhere are the quandaries more dismaying than when the carnage is unfolding within sovereign borders—as in such recent interventionary arenas as Iraqi Kurdistan, Yugoslavia and Somalia.

Depending on one's philosophical approach, the U.N. Security Council's passage in April 1991 of resolution 688, authorizing the U.S.-led Operation Restore Hope to protect the Iraqi Kurds, was a red-letter day for humanitarianism or a pratfall down a slippery slope. The U.N. charter insists on the sanctity of sovereignty. But, rather disingenuously, resolution 688 invoked chapter VII of the charter, which permits intervention when a nation's internal affairs pose "a threat to international peace and security."

With U.S. fighter planes still enforcing "no-fly zones" in Iraq, Massoud Barzani, president of the Kurdistan Democratic Party of Iraq, quite understandably has no qualms about the U.N.'s legal legerdemain. "For years," he says in an interview published in the Harvard journal, "dictators have barricaded themselves behind the sovereignty of their states to justify gross human rights violations." The Kurds are proud, Barzani adds, that "they have moved the consciousness of the world to introduce the principle of humanitarian intervention as a precedent in international relations."

And what a precedent: In his 1992 *Agenda for Peace* report, U.N. Secretary-General Boutros Boutros-Ghali insisted that "the centuries-old doctrine of absolute and exclusive sovereignty no longer stands." In February of that year, U.N. "peacekeepers" descended on the former Yugoslavia with the consent of all parties to that grisly conflict. But, Oxford University professor Adam Roberts writes in the *Review*, later U.N. resolutions addressing the Bosnian-Croatian-Serbian bloodfest "were so phrased as to suggest that the U.N. might actually require the states involved to accept the continued presence of peacekeeping forces with a humanitarian role whether they wanted them or not."

Somalia had no functioning government to resist or applaud resolution 794, which authorized outside forces to impose order on that famine and faction-ridden land. With even less justification than in the case of Iraq, resolution 794 ritualistically invoked the threat to international peace and security percolating in Somalia. African nations, significantly, insisted on a preamble that stressed the "unique," "extraordinary" and "exceptional" nature of the Somali situation. "In other words," Roberts writes in the *Review*, "they did not want the invasion of Somalia to be viewed as a precedent for invasions of other sovereign states."

That concern highlights the profoundly problematic nature of humanitarian intervention, at least as a uniform for international action. In an ideal world, powerful and neutral outsiders would shield the defenseless from gross abuses, even when the atrocities are committed by the victims' own government or neighbors. But, in this far from ideal world, who decides when intervention is in order? Suppose that the Security Council voted in the early 1960s to dispatch Somali-piloted AC-130 gunships to the Deep South to defend blacks from segregationist whites? That, of course, could never have happened; the United States is one of five powerful nations that wield a Security Council veto.

That helps explain the idiosyncratic nature of the humanitarian interventions undertaken to date. Why protect Iraq's Kurds but not Turkey's? Why go into Somalia but not Liberia? Why intervene in Yugoslavia, but not the Caucasus? Several of the Harvard essayists argue that consistent guidelines on when to intervene would ease the moral and political dilemmas. But is consistency really the answer? In a world as rent by civil conflict and injustice as ours, to insist that the international community respond to all humanitarian disasters is to ensure that it responds to none.

Tottering Markets

Mexico's currency crisis showed that once the international economic system springs a leak, there's a need for enormous—and fast—financial transfusions. But now that America is no longer willing to be the rescuer of last resort, who'll take the lead?

BRUCE STOKES

Bruce Stokes is a senior fellow at the Council on Foreign Relations.

In the years immediately before World War I, Quincy Gilmore (Gil) Shannon farmed a small plot of land in Connoquenessing, Pa., a few miles north of Pittsburgh. Shannon, a frugal man, kept his accounts in a small ledger, dutifully recording in his cramped penmanship the amount he spent for each new shirt, the repair of a broken plow and, interestingly enough, the purchase of Eastern European bonds.

How, at the turn of the century, an unsophisticated farmer became a speculator on international capital markets is a tale now lost in the cobwebs of family history. Maybe Shannon's local banker pooled depositor resources to play in the big leagues with the Morgans and the Rockefellers. Maybe these paper financial instruments were sold from the back of a wagon by some itinerant stockbroker of the day.

In any event, Shannon was worried about the future. He had six children to feed and educate. There wasn't much money to be made in tilling the thin soil of Butler County. Interest rates at local banks were so low that his savings grew even slower than his crops. The returns offered on securities from exotic lands half way around the world were too good to pass up.

But all too quickly, the value of the bonds vaporized in a financial panic in a country he probably could not find on a map. Soon thereafter, Shannon sold his farm and moved his family to the city. Family mythology has it that he gave up his beloved land so that his children could live closer to schools and churches. But family stories often sugarcoat the truth. Was Gil Shannon forced to sell his farm, a victim of overreaching in pursuit of returns that were, in fact, too good to be true?

If so, Shannon was just one of the many casualties in the collapse of the first golden age of global financial capitalism, a brief period at the end of the Victorian era when international capital flows—foreign direct investment and investments in stocks and bonds—attained a level not again reached until modern times.

The recent Mexican currency crisis "has far more in common with [such] 19th-century financial panics than any recent stock market crash or loan default," said David D. Hale, chief economist at Kemper Financial Services Inc. in Chicago. In recent years, newly emerging market economies—such as Mexico's—not unlike those of many countries in Eastern Europe, Latin America and even the United States three generations ago, have rapidly become dependent upon large infusions of foreign capital. In 1994 alone, offshore cash totaled $178 billion, much of it "hot" money in the form of highly liquid, short-term investments in stocks and bonds by industrial country pension and mutual funds.

And, as in Gil Shannon's time, as apprehension rose about Mexico's ability to meet its international financial obligations—principally about $17 billion in foreign-held short-term government bonds—panic swept through the financial market. Foreign investors, and many Mexicans, pulled their money out of the country. By the end of January, Mexico's foreign exchange reserves had plummeted to $3.4 billion, a sixth of its holdings just a few months before. And fear rapidly infected investors in other emerging market economies. On Jan. 30 alone, the Brazilian stock market declined 8 per cent, Argentina's fell 6 per cent.

Faced with the prospect of a new generation of Gil Shannons—small investors stripped of their savings by the speculative gyrations of foreign financial markets—the possibility of losing thousands of U.S. jobs because of declining exports to Mexico and perhaps a new wave of illegal immigration sparked by a profound Mexican recession, the Clinton Administration finally acted to restore confidence. Stalemated by congressional opposition to a package of $40 billion in loan guarantees for Mexico, President Clinton crafted a Mexican bailout package on his own authority: $20 billion from the U.S. Exchange Stabilization Fund, $17.8 billion from the International Monetary Fund (IMF) and $10 billion from the

Bank for International Settlements (essentially money from the central banks of Europe and Japan).

In early February, the financial markets were calm again. But for how long?

"I think it would be foolish to suppose this would be the last financial crisis," said Lawrence H. Summers, Treasury undersecretary for international affairs. Mexico is not out of the woods yet. And many financial analysts warn that in the years ahead, several of the newly emerging market economies—Argentina, Brazil, Indonesia and Hungary, to name just four—and maybe some more advanced economics—such as Canada, Italy and Sweden—may face economic turmoil.

"It's a global problem of governments that have run up debts from fiscal excess," said Harold B. Malmgren, an international business consultant. "If a really strong country like Mexico is struggling to keep its head above water, then you know the others are drowning."

WATCHDOG WANTED

The global nature of capital markets almost ensures that these troubles will reverberate with grave consequence around the world.

The experience with the Mexican rescue package suggests that the world is ill-prepared for such an eventuality. "We need international financial institutions that are as modern as the problems they face," Treasury Secretary Robert E. Rubin told reporters in a recent briefing. To that end, reform of the IMF, originally a low priority item on the agenda for the June G-7 summit of the major industrial powers in Halifax, Nova Scotia, suddenly has greater urgency and sharper focus.

As yet, however, there is no international consensus, or agreement within the U.S. government for that matter, on such reforms, and many of the proposals under consideration present more questions than answers.

Most analysts agree that sharing information about the fundamentals of the newly emerging market economies has to be timelier. But much such information was available about Mexico, and many investors still failed to act on it.

Even if the IMF or some other international institution is given a greater role in monitoring emerging economies, what real leverage will it have over sovereign nations? An aggressive "watchdog" could end up spooking the market, triggering the very crisis it is attempting to avoid.

Mexico demonstrated that once the international economic system springs a leak, enormous financial transfusions are needed to revive the patient. The United States is no longer willing to be the lender of last resort. So a new international blood bank may be needed for future rescue operations. But a budget cutting U.S. Congress, already distrustful of international institutions, seems in no mood to contribute funds to such an effort. And foreign governments are unlikely to pony up the money if Washington continues to call the shots at the IMF.

As the first line of defense against new financial crises, the governments of emerging market economies will be under increasing pressure to heal themselves. To keep them from simply printing money to solve their problems, countries may be pressed to create currency boards that tie their domestic money supplies to the availability of foreign exchange. To withstand the buffeting of future financial crises, fragile banking systems in several nations may need to be radically restructured. And there is growing discussion about new controls on the movement of capital flowing into emerging markets, controls that would effectively put them on a diet so they don't binge as Mexico did.

Yet no one who has studied the growing complications of this new age of financial capitalism foresees easy solutions. Faced with policy alternatives that may prove half-measures at best, the Clinton Administration and its allies may have little choice but to muddle through.

WHO'LL STUMBLE NEXT?

The 1990s have been a bear market for investment in emerging market economies. Foreign investors more than quadrupled their equity holdings in such countries from 1990–94, topping $81 billion last year, according to estimates by the Institute of International Finance Inc., a Washington-based association of banks and securities firms. As a result, private, potentially short-term capital flows now account for nearly half of all the external financing used by the major emerging market economies.

To provide some sense of the unprecedented magnitude of these capital flows, in 1993 the volume of capital flooding out of the United States to be invested in foreign stocks and bonds equaled 1.7 per cent of the U.S. gross national product, more than America transferred to Europe on an annual basis at the height of the Marshall Plan.

But even before the Mexican crisis, the bloom began to come off this investment rose. Foreign purchases of stocks and bonds in major emerging market economies slipped in 1994, down from their peaks in 1993.

"We are looking at a continued moderation of those flows in 1995," predicted Charles H. Dallara, managing director of the Institute of International Finance. Hale, the Kemper economist, is more pessimistic. He predicts that rising interest rates, thanks to the Mexican crisis, will temporarily halve the flow of funds to emerging markets.

Nevertheless, volatile private capital flows are likely to continue to outstrip more stable lending by commercial banks and international financial institutions. And even Hale forecasts that the flow of funds to emerging markets will bounce back dramatically in 1996. The sheer volume of such transactions, driven by quick-return-oriented investors, technology that permits money to be moved around the world with a single computer key stroke and a multiplicity of investment opportunities, raises the spector of a financial crisis in one emerging market spreading rapidly around the globe.

Administration officials say that it was fear of such contagion that lent urgency to their efforts to stanch Mexico's bleeding. "It is clear that if Mexico had tumbled, there would have been more tumbling," Summers said.

Not all economists subscribe to the theory that another Mexico could lead to a meltdown of the global financial system. In many ways, Mexico's problem may have been unique. During the past four years, Mexico financed only 40 per cent of its current-account deficit through relatively stable, long-term foreign direct investment.

The rest of Latin America bankrolled 80 per cent of its deficit through such investment. Mexico let its reserves slip to a fraction of its current-account deficit. Other allegedly vulnerable economies still have reserves that are several multiples of their annual international deficit. And only Mexico has been so dependent on U.S. capital, which many analysts say may be more skittish than investment by others.

But few politicians are likely to bet their careers on economists' theories that Mexico may have been a one-of-a-kind crisis.

In 1982, when Mexico precipitated a Third World debt crisis by defaulting on its loans, governments and international financial institutions were able to sort out the problem, much as a bankruptcy court would. The debts were primarily owed to banks, all the creditors could be assembled in one room to parse out the pain, U.S. banks were still highly regulated so that Washington had great leverage over them and the banks had commercial interests in Mexico and other debtor countries that encouraged them to ride out the storm.

Richard A. Bloom

Treasury undersecretary Lawrence H. Summers "If Mexico had tumbled," others would have followed.

None of these conditions apply today. Emerging market debt is tilted toward stocks and bonds, the creditors are thousands of small, highly mobile investors and governments have little suasion over their actions. As a result, financial analysts argue, any formal defense against future financial panics may have to be more reactive and at arm's length.

"The only thing we can do is have more fire inspectors and a bigger fire brigade," said Robert D. Hormats, vice chairman of Goldman Sachs International Ltd. in New York City.

RIGGING A SAFETY NET

To that end, the U.S. Treasury, the IMF and other governments are exploring ways of preparing for Mexico-style crises in the future.

The general consensus within the financial community and the Clinton Administration is that investors need an early-warning system. Many analysts say that Mexico's problems crept up on some private investors and government specialists because Mexico did not publish important national financial data in time. And sharing of such information is now a prerequisite for current U.S. aid to Mexico.

But more data are of little use, Dallara said, without a marketplace that analyzes that information and changes investment patterns accordingly. "Investment firms have relied too much on rating agencies, not analysis of the fundamentals," he said.

Firms also need to set investment standards and stick with them. As demarcations between banks and securities firms blur, Dallara said, "firms will need to ensure that they have just as high standards in their underwriting business as they do in their medium-term lending."

Also, implicit in making more information available is the assumption that investors are rational and will act on it. But "financial markets are subject to herd behavior and mood swings," said C. Fred Bergsten, director of the Institute for International Economics, a Washington-based think tank. And the best analysis by the IMF or others is not necessarily going to be read, or understood, by the stock broker in Dubuque under pressure from her clients to get a better return on their individual retirement accounts by investing in emerging market mutual funds.

Several Wall Street veterans suggest that investment firms need to take a hard look at their internal conflicts of interest. Mexico's problems were evident early on to those willing to dig to find them. Yet Wall Street continued to channel money into the country because mutual fund managers and others made good money on such business.

Greater access to information is only half the battle, however. Emerging market governments must be persuaded to change behaviors that are creating the economic instability that leads to financial panics.

Many economists say that this requires greater IMF surveillance: a more rigorous examination of a country's books and a more pointed dialogue about what changes are needed. Even then, an IMF official said, "if you are not borrowing from the IMF, we don't have a lot of leverage. The question is how to make surveillance effective absent borrowing."

One way, a senior executive at a New York City investment house suggested, "is making this timely information available to the markets." The challenge is how to do that without causing panic. "The street-smart way to deal with this is well-planted leaks," he said, "using back-channel, sophisticated ways to get the message across that a country is overspending itself." The problem may be, he complained, that "I don't think the staff of the World Bank and the IMF are hired for their street smarts."

To put greater muscle behind surveillance, to provide a safety net for individual countries and to backstop the international financial system, "you [also] need a lender of last resort," Hormats said, "someone with a lot of money up front that can be mobilized very quickly."

Congress's recent foot-dragging over Mexico suggests that the United States can't be relied upon to play that role. **Last year, IMF managing director Michel Camdessus proposed that a quick-response facility be created at the fund, in essence a separate lending window with its own cash and lending conditions. This facility would be available to all countries facing liquidity problems, including industrial ones.**

But, the IMF official said, "if you are going to give the IMF this role, you have to give it the money to do it." Bergsten estimates such a facility would need $100 billion to be credible. Camdessus has suggested that all member nations ante up more money, what the fund calls a quota increase. But congressional staff aides say that a quota increase is a non-starter on Capitol Hill.

Italian Prime Minister Lamberto Dini will propose in Halifax that the IMF be permitted to raise emergency money in private capital markets. It's a politically attractive option that obviates the need for taxpayers to front the money. But the

scheme wouldn't save taxpayers from holding the bag if some of these loans go bad.

IMF member nations could change the institution's rules to enable it to guarantee loans, which would dramatically expand the amount of capital that could be mobilized. But Administration officials worry that such backing would rapidly get out of hand and that soon no one would lend to the Third World without an IMF guarantee.

Princeton University economist Peter Kenen has suggested that the facility be self-financing. Countries experiencing large inflows of foreign capital would deposit some portion of those funds with the IMF in return for the privilege of borrowing some multiple of their deposit in a crisis. But what if a country refuses to participate? It may still be in the interest of industrial nations to bail it out.

If some such facility is created, Administration officials say, it will have to be structured so that it does not intervene prematurely in support of emerging market economies, thereby short-circuiting necessary economic adjustment. "You don't want to get in the position of defending the indefensible," Summers said. A means of avoiding this may be to make the cost of such help so onerous that countries will be desperate before they ask for a bailout.

Ultimately, reform of the IMF and the establishment of new funds for a safety net will depend on political support in the major member countries, especially the United States.

The first hurdle will be the populist perception now ascendant in America that the Mexican bailout and future such efforts are mostly protections for the rich.

In addition, not everyone agrees that overhauling the IMF will be sufficient. "The IMF has a history of tremendous blunders," said Jeffrey Sachs, a Harvard University economics professor. "It failed in Mexico. Where was its surveillance when it was needed?" Sachs has proposed greater oversight of the IMF, even as the fund increases its surveillance of emerging markets. "The institution is completely unscrutinized," he said. "Transparency is essential for accountability." Such proposals are likely to resonate on Capitol Hill among both left-wing and right-wing critics of the IMF and complicate any IMF reform effort.

European abstentions in the Feb. 1 vote on IMF involvement in the current Mexican bailout suggest a crumbling international consensus on how best to handle these crises. Some European specialists say that future bailouts should be handled through regional development banks. Such thinking reflects major differences among American allies over "burden-sharing" that could have serious repercussions on Capitol Hill.

LET THE MARKETS RULE!

Providing more fire inspectors and a bigger fire brigade, as Hormats urges, won't help much unless the homeowners themselves take more precautions.

Several economists, promoted by the editorial page of *The Wall Street Journal*, longing for the discipline of the gold standard, have suggested the creation of currency boards in emerging markets. A currency board limits a country's domestic money to its supply of foreign exchange. Such constraints curb a government's inflationary impulses and stabilize the exchange rate, easing foreign investors' concerns and presumably avoiding Mexico-style crises.

But a currency board may not be the panacea its advocates imply. "It simply changes the nature of the vulnerability," said Larry Krohn, a senior economist for Latin America with UBS Securities, a New York-City based investment house. "It makes countries more vulnerable to deflation." And, Bergsten said, "it is far from clear that it is in the U.S. interest to have on its border a country committed to severe recession as a form of economic adjustment."

Analysts say emerging market economies must also bolster their chronically weak banking systems. Mexico's banks, for example, may yet prove to be the Achilles' heel of the Mexican bailout. December's peso devaluation and new curbs on government spending and credit creation ensure a dramatic slowdown in Mexican economic growth. Mexican banks already have a high level of nonperforming loans, according to market analysts. If there are corporate bankruptcies, as there almost surely will be, this bad paper will be exposed, possibly leading to bank failures and a new run on the peso.

"One way to make a sick banking system better would be to allow banks to earn juicy spreads for some time," said Gary Clyde Hufbauer, a fellow at the Institute for International Economics, much as the United States did after the savings and loan crisis of the late 1980s. Keeping out foreign competition is a way to do that. But Mexico is committed to financial market liberalization as part of the North American Free Trade Agreement (NAFTA).

Financial analysts say that banks in Argentina, Indonesia and elsewhere suf-

John Eisele

International analyst Charles H. Dallara
Investment firms rely too much on rating agencies.

fer from similar maladies. And any effort to weave an international safety net for these economies without also helping them restructure their banking system could be self-defeating, they add.

Meanwhile, the Mexican crisis has breathed new life into an old idea: controls on the potentially destabilizing free movement of capital. "I think there will be a rethinking of that part of the free-market model," Bergsten said.

Even after the liberalization of capital markets in the 1970s, several European countries have imposed such restrictions in crisis situations. No one is suggesting banning all foreign capital, but controls would limit the inflow of hot money and ensure a certain stability in investment.

Chile, which avoided much of the backwash of the Mexico crisis, already discriminates against short-term portfolio investment by imposing huge penalties on investors who are in for only the short run. Such restrictions could help dampen volatility in other markets.

Many economists question the efficacy of such initiatives. "The question is," Summers said, "can you actually control the flows of capital? I'm skeptical."

The forthcoming U.S. negotiations with Chile over accession to NAFTA could prove a test of the new interest in capital controls. U.S. financial institutions want Chile's controls dropped as a price of admission. But the Mexican crisis could lead both sides to opt for slower liberalization.

The domestic and international pitfalls confronting any orchestrated response to another Mexico-style crisis lead many conservatives to argue that the only effective discipline on greedy investors and profligate governments of emerging market economies is the ruthless punishment meted out by the free market. They contend that bailing out individuals or countries with only reward and encourage intemperate behavior. And many economists agree that without reliance on market forces, government efforts to deal with future crises will be overwhelmed by the shear volume of current capital flows.

But the actions of individual investors can have broad societal repercussions. A "hands-off" stance may be both morally and pragmatically correct. But when markets begin to gyrate, few governments are likely to be able to withstand the political pressures to act. And the economic and social cost of inaction may be just too high.

Of course, all such talk of changes presupposes that Washington and other capitals will be able to maintain their focus on the threat of future financial crises, at least through the Halifax summit in June. Governments are notorious for letting issues drop once they are off the front pages. The flutter in financial markets in early February when Mexico announced a new crackdown on the rebels in Chiapas suggests that inattention may not be a problem this time around.

The Mexican crisis "will have a reverberation that will be with us for a number of years," an Administration official said.

Susan M. Muniak

Kemper Financial Services Inc.'s David D. Hale
The flow of funds to emerging markets will bounce back.

WAITING FOR A NEW CLINTON DOCTRINE

WILLIAM SCHNEIDER

These days, no one much argues with the view that the United States must take an active role in the world to protect its interests. "Pearl Harbor ended isolationism for any realist," Sen. Arthur H. Vandenberg, R-Mich., said during World War II.

He was right. The Chicago Council on Foreign Relations, in its survey last October of Americans' views on foreign policy, found that two-thirds said that the United States should take an active part in world affairs. Fewer than a third said that it should "stay out." Those numbers haven't changed since 1947.

And yet, President Clinton said this month, "there is a struggle now going on between those of us who want to carry on the tradition of American leadership and those who would advocate a new form of American isolationism."

Democrats argue that because Republicans reject multilateralism, they are becoming de facto isolationists. As the President put it, the new isolationists "trumpet the rhetoric of American strength" and then "eliminate any meaningful role for the United Nations," "deny resources to our peacekeepers" and "refuse aid to the fledgling democracies and to all those fighting poverty and environmental problems that can literally destroy hopes for a more democratic, more prosperous, safer world."

Until liberals come up with a rationale, the conservative argument for a foreign policy driven by self-interest will prevail.

Indeed, the Republicans are planning to cut foreign aid, reduce U.S. funds for U.N. peacekeeping operations, require congressional approval for U.S. troops to participate in peacekeeping missions and ban the deployment of U.S. soldiers under foreign command. Clinton has threatened to veto those measures.

Republicans insist that unilateralism is not isolationism. They argue that the United States must determine its own purposes in the world and act on its own interests. *We*, not the U.N., must decide whether it is in our national interest to bring democracy to Haiti or relief to Somalia. *We*, not NATO, must decide whether it is in our national interest to stop the slaughter in Bosnia.

If this were simply an argument about multilateralism, Republicans would lose. In the Chicago council's survey, support for strengthening the United Nations as "a very important foreign policy goal of the United States" was up to 51 per cent, its highest level in 20 years. A majority supported U.S. participation in international peacekeeping forces. Fewer than one in five said that the United States should refuse to take part in such efforts. The public was split over whether Americans should be allowed to serve under a U.N. commander.

Public support for NATO also remained high. A plurality felt that NATO should be expanded to include the Czech Republic, Hungary and Poland, "thereby committing the United States to defend them against attack in the same way we are committed to defending Western Europe."

When it comes to U.S. purposes in the world, however, Democrats have a problem. Since the end of the Cold War, public support for a non-self-interested U.S. foreign policy has dropped sharply.

Support for "protecting weaker nations against foreign aggression" as a very important goal of U.S. foreign policy is down 33 percentage points since 1990, to its lowest level in 20 years. "Protecting and defending human rights in other countries" is down 24 points since 1990, to its lowest level since 1978. "Defending our allies' security" is down 20 points. "Helping to improve the standard of living of less developed nations" is down 19 points, to a level far below the previous low during the economic crisis of the 1970s. And "helping to bring a democratic form of government to other nations"—never a widely supported goal—is down to its lowest level since 1974.

At the same time, self-regarding foreign policy goals such as protecting American jobs, securing adequate energy supplies, preventing the spread of nuclear weapons and even promoting free trade have all gained public support.

Political leaders like to believe that they are all internationalists, arguing about the proper framework for conducting foreign policy, unilateral or multilateral. From the public's point of view, however, the issue is more basic: With the fall of Communism, does America have any purpose in the world beyond promoting its own interests?

Republicans are inclined to say no and accuse the Democrats of multilateralism. Democrats are inclined to say yes and accuse the Republicans of isolationism.

It's interesting that unilateralism is now being called a smokescreen for isolationism. Only a few years ago, multilateralism was considered a smokescreen for isolationism. Liberals critical of U.S. intervention abroad argued that America should act only when there is a clear international consensus behind it, unlike, say, Vietnam.

The conservative model of U.S. intervention is the Persian Gulf war. America was pushed, it rallied the world to its cause and it responded with unstoppable force. According to the Chicago council's poll, George Bush is still given high marks for his foreign policy.

The liberal model of U.S. intervention is Haiti. America acted with restraint, under authorization from the United Nations but not from Congress. Most poll respondents gave the Clinton Administration low marks for its handling of Haiti.

With the end of the Cold War, the world agenda has shifted from containment of Communism to economic development, human rights and democracy—from an East-West to a North-South agenda, generally speaking. As a result, the ideological alignment in U.S. foreign policy has shifted.

Liberals are now the most ardent internationalists. But they have so far failed to communicate a rationale to the American public. Until they do, the conservative argument for a foreign policy driven by American self-interest is likely to prevail.

The last time the country was at this kind of turning point was in 1947. That year, President Truman articulated a rationale for the United States to assume the burden of leading the free world. The country is waiting for the Clinton Doctrine.

Second Thoughts

After Election Day, it appeared the stage was set for a radical overhaul of the nation's immigration policies. Suddenly it's no longer clear that the Republican Party is itching for an inflammatory and partisan confrontation.

DICK KIRSCHTEN

Since Californians voted with such gusto last November to deny public services to illegal aliens, immigration—lawful and otherwise—has become a hot policy topic in Washington. It's also become a hot potato.

At first, the political calculus seemed pretty straightforward. Immigrants are pouring into the United States at a furious pace, and the public, according to opinion polls, wants something done to stanch the flow.

When the voters on Election Day turned control of Congress over to conservative Republicans, the stage appeared set for radical changes: sharp cuts in legal immigration, a major crackdown to rid the country of illegal aliens and tough restrictions—such as denial of welfare benefits—to make the country less hospitable to foreigners who live here in full accordance with U.S. law.

The most dramatic argument for such action came from the nation's most populous state, California. Republican Gov. Pete Wilson had revived a flagging re-election campaign by championing a ballot initiative, Proposition 187, to cut off most state and local benefits, including nonemergency health care and public education, for unlawful immigrants.

"Prop 187" was a roaring sucess. It received nearly 60 per cent approval, and Wilson, who is widely thought to have 1996 presidential ambitions, coasted to a second term with a comfortable 55 per cent of the vote. It should also be noted that San Diego—the site for the 1996 Republican National Convention—is not only Wilson's hometown, but the birthplace of California's grass-roots anti-immigrant protest movement.

Similar initiatives are now being explored in other states that have experienced huge surges in immigration over the past two decades. The six states with the largest foreign-born populations—California, Florida, Illinois, New Jersey, New York and Texas—control 181 electoral votes, two-thirds of the total needed to capture the White House, a fact that has not escaped the notice of political strategists.

Although the nation's unemployment rate recently dropped to a four-year low of 5.4 per cent, concern about foreigners taking jobs away from citizens still runs high. In four of the big urban states most affected by immigrants, the jobless rate remains well above the national average. (In California, it's 7.4 per cent; Florida, 6.3 per cent; New Jersey, 6.1 per cent; and Texas, 6.0 per cent).

GOP congressional leaders, accordingly, are still eager to get credit for enacting tougher and more restrictive immigration laws. But in recent weeks, their rhetoric has a cooled a bit. More care is being taken to differentiate between legal immigrants and illegal ones.

Suddenly it's no longer clear that the Republican Party is itching for an inflammatory and partisan confrontation that might divide the country into pro-immigrant and anti-immigrant camps. Sober second thoughts are being given to the concerns of business interests that rely upon immigrant labor as well as to the risk of alienating rapidly growing Hispanic and Asian voting blocs.

The punitive tone of the California ballot initiative, which among other things would expel many immigrant children from schools and require others to inform against their parents, alarms some members of Washington's Republican elite. Conservatives William J. Bennett and Jack F. Kemp last fall condemned Proposition 187 "as politically unwise and fundamentally at odds with the best tradition and spirit of our party."

In a recent interview, Sen. Alan K. Simpson, R-Wyo., who will spearhead his party's drive for immigration reform, was also cautious. His goal, he said, "is to do something, but do it in a way that will not be ugly, because there are plenty of provisions out there that have an ugliness to them."

Simpson's House counterpart, Lamar S. Smith, R-Texas, who said he regards illegal immigration as "a crisis," added that he hopes a bipartisan legislative solution can be forged so that the immigration issue does not "become entangled with the 1996 presidential race."

At a meeting with lobbyists for the restaurant industry—a major employer of immigrant workers—House Speaker Newt Gingrich announced second thoughts about GOP plans to reduce welfare spending by eliminating benefits for legal immigrants who have not become citizens. Gingrich earlier had received similar advice from several Republican governors.

Even California's Wilson, just 10 days after the Proposition 187 vote, suggested during a Washington appearance that it may now be necessary to enact a new guest worker program to make sure that the seasonal labor needs of his state's growers are met.

BACK TO THE FUTURE

There is a sense of déjà vu about the coming immigration debate in the 104th Congress. Fourteen years ago, the report of a blue-ribbon reform commission raised essentially the same questions that are under consideration today: How many foreigners do we want to let in? How do we keep out the ones we don't choose to admit? What do we do about the millions of illegal aliens already in the country?

Over the ensuing nine years, Congress labored to devise answers. Illegal immigration was addressed in a 1986 law barring the employment of unauthorized aliens. Those already here for some time were granted amnesty and permitted to apply for legal residency. And, at the urging of California legislators—including then-Sen. Wilson—a less-stringent legalization provision was added for farm workers.

As a result of the 1986 law, more than three million unauthorized immigrants became legal residents, 40 per cent of them through the Wilson-sponsored Special Agricultural Worker (SAW) program.

In 1990, despite clear evidence that illegal immigration had not abated, Congress expanded legal immigration quotas to bring in more skilled workers and more immediate family members of immigrants previously admitted or legalized.

Now, as Congress is returning to the drawing board with the report of a new commission in hand, the immigration landscape is strikingly familiar. Only the numbers have changed. Immigrants are now entering the country at a near-record rate, the vast majority of them legally. It's estimated that 1.1 million foreigners comer here to live each year—700,000 as legal immigrants, 110,000 or more as refugees and 300,000 without authorization.

Although the nation's foreign-born population increased dramatically during the past two decades, it remains less than 10 per cent of the current total. Roughly a third are naturalized U.S. citizens, and applications for naturalization are on the increase.

But because 72 per cent of the immigrants, along with their U.S.-born children who are citizens, have congregated, mostly in cities, in just six states, they have elicited a visceral political impact disproportionate to their aggregate numbers.

Illegal aliens are notoriously hard to count, but expert estimates put their number at about four million. In a country of 261.6 million, that represents a scant 1.5 per cent of the population. But that's of little comfort in California, home to perhaps 40 per cent of the nation's illegal immigrants. Taxpayers there have made it clear that they don't wish to be saddled with the costs of educating the children of that youngish, largely Latino population.

"The folks who voted for Prop 187 by 60-40 are not racists or bigots," Simpson said. "They are people who are very concerned about their country and about [public] programs that are being used by people who have chosen to be here illegally."

But Simpson, a longtime advocate of slowing the immigration influx in general, took issue with the focus of the California ballot initiative. "I have a little trouble with saying that someone 7 or 8 years old is, quote, 'deportable,' when we don't even have resources to deport criminal aliens who are in jail."

Simpson also noted that the Supreme Court ruled, in a 1982 Texas case, that children of illegal immigrants have the right to a public education. (Implementation of the California initiative has been blocked pending the resolution of lawsuits that challenge its constitutionality.)

As chairman of the Senate Judiciary Subcommittee on Immigration, Simpson plans extensive hearings, which he said he hopes can be conducted jointly with the House immigration panel that Smith heads. All aspects of immigration law will be on the table, Simpson said.

"We passed a piece of legislation in 1986 that didn't do what it was supposed to do," he said, explaining that "an inundation of fraudulent documents" has made it impossible for employers to deny work to illegal aliens. In addition to seeking tougher penalties for the manufacture and use of forged documents, he said he wants to create some "breathing space" for the country by reducing legal immigrant admissions by at least 25 per cent for five years.

Smith said both topics might be addressed in a

John Eisele

Sen. Alan K. Simpson, R-Wyo., who'll spearhead his party's drive for reforms
"We passed a piece of legislation in 1986 that didn't do what it was supposed to do."

IT'S BEEN RAINING MONEY ON THE INS . . .

At a time when the rallying cry on Capitol Hill is for a smaller and less intrusive government, Doris M. Meissner is a federal official in a rare position. She heads an agency, the Immigration and Naturalization Service (INS), at which even Republicans lawmakers love to throw money.

Prompted by alarm over illegal immigration, Congress last year hiked the INS's budget by 25 per cent, an increase that amounted to roughly $100 million more than the Clinton Administration had requested. The increased appropriation—mostly to beef up border enforcement—was so popular on the Hill that it was approved well in advance of the crime bill provisions that authorized its expenditure.

In the new, Republican-run Congress, the INS budget could rise again. GOP legislators responsible for immigration issues are eager to spend more for speeding the deportation of aliens who are criminals and for weeding illegal immigrants from the workplace. Following are excerpts from a Dec. 21 interview in which Meissner discussed her agency's responses to the attention and money that is being showered upon it.

Q: Given the success last fall of California's ballot initiative—Proposition 187—to deny public services to illegal aliens, do you think anti-immigrant sentiment will emerge as a major political issue in other states?

A: The Califonia election was a surprise to me from the standpoint of how incredibly charged the atmosphere became. . . . I suppose it shouldn't have been a surprise, because [of] the impact of immigration occurring during a terrible, dramatic economic restructuring. But it is our purpose in the immigration service—and it is the broader intent of the Administration—to administer the immigration laws in a way that gives the public confidence that we can manage this problem without going to harsh extremes.

Richard A. Bloom

Doris M. Meissner: California is getting more attention from immigration officials.

Q: Will the additional Border Patrol funds voted by Congress enable you to reassure the public that illegal immigration is under control?

A: By this spring, in California in particular, we will be able to show some very impressive numbers. We are measuring for the first time in the INS's history what the real flow across the border is. We now have all kinds of technology that gives us a way to quantify what we are accomplishing in interrupting the flow. And by the end of this fiscal year, we're going to have a lot more resources out there than we do now.

Q: But by your agency's own estimates, only half of illegal immigrants come in by crossing the U.S.-Mexican border. The other half enter legally and then simply overstay their visas.

A: The most important thing that we have done is to reform an asylum system that until now has invited abuse. . . . There is no question that many people have come on visas—a typical six-months tourist or some other visa—and then filed claims for asylum when the visa expires. They then get to stay for

single bill, but emphasized that "to me, the top priority is illegal immigration." Smith, an advocate of greatly increased patrolling of the U.S-Mexican border, echoed Simpson's concerns about fraudulent documents and rattled off statistics indicating that illegal aliens place a disproportionate financial burden on prisons and public hospitals in states such as California and Texas.

Both legislators indicated support for a national verification system involving tamper-proof documents that would enable employers to screen illegal aliens from the workplace. As in 1986, immigrant advocacy and civil libertarian groups protest that a national identification system smacks of police-state tactics, would be expensive to implement and invites discrimination against individuals who appear to be foreign.

"There won't be a single argument that we haven't heard before," Simpson sighed. "The job is to humanely control immigration to protect our national interests and to do it in a nonnativist and nonracist way."

BEYOND THE BORDER

In response to congressional prodding and a series of crises, the Clinton Administration has scored few points with the pro-immigration groups that Smith derisively refers to as the "open borders crowd." The President has turned away Cuban and Haitian refugees—reversing in the case of the Cubans a U.S. policy of more than 30 years' standing.

Attorney General Janet Reno, a Florida native well versed in the political and social implications of mass movements of migrants, and Immigration and Naturalization Service (INS) commissioner Doris M. Meissner, a respected expert in the field, have brought a degree of professionalism to the issue that was missing in prior Administrations.

Following the 1993 bombing of the World Trade Towers in New York City, a crash effort was undertaken to automate

. . . HERE'S WHAT THE BIGGER BUCKS ARE BUYING

some time longer until we got to their case. Requiring timely application and providing speedy disposition is key to blocking off of a major visa abuse category. The other key is sanctions against those who hire people who aren't authorized to be here. If you do employer sanctions effectively, that's really the proper response to visa abuse.

Q: Since employer sanctions were enacted in 1986, they have failed to deter illegal immigration because aliens easily obtain fraudulent documents. Do you support the recent immigration reform commission proposal to develop a computerized registry for determining who is authorized to work?

A: We are in agreement with the commission that there has to be a much-improved way for employers to reliably know who they are hiring and that it is the government's responsibility to provide a system that will make employer sanctions work. The registry idea is a good one; it will enable employers to make one telephone call and find out from somebody's social security number whether he or she is eligible to work.

Q: Critics on both the left and right contend that the proposal is tantamount to a national ID card requirement. They say that it will be costly to implement, prone to error and subject to abuse by government officials.

A: The commission did not propose an ID card. They are proposing pilot projects to test the idea of a registry or data bank that merges INS information on noncitizens with Social Security Administration records. Their proposal does not rest on a card, it rests on a number. We already verify for states where benefits are concerned.

Q: What would a nationwide verification system cost?

A: The linking of the two databases creates a lot of complexities that we are trying to sort through. There are issues of privacy, of error rates, of cost. The answer is, we don't have a firm cost figure.

Q: Sen. Alan K. Simpson, R-Wyo., has proposed a 25 per cent cut in legal immigration to allow the country a "breathing spell"? Do you agree?

A: First and foremost, we are hoping for bipartisan agreement on legislation. I think we will work most effectively first off with the Senate. We are prepared to make some changes in the legal immigration numbers, but they would not be same ones that Sen. Simpson now has on the table. There can be a reasonable lowering without damaging the basic construct of the 1990 act that established a better balance between employment-based immigration and family-based visas.

Q: How do you explain the Clinton Administration's policy shifts with respect to its handling of would-be refugees from Haiti and Cuba?

Richard A. Bloom

Hoping for a bipartisan agreement on legislation

A: What we did in the Haitian and Cuban situations was to dramatically change policy in a way that averted serious immigration emergencies. I'm not sure the public understands how migration has become a post-Cold War security issue. An unstable country on your border, such as Haiti, gets your attention as a big power because of the ongoing possibility of migration emergencies.

information systems used to determine who gets into the country and to tighten up a much-abused system of adjudicating claims for political asylum.

Meissner's agenda has been dictated largely by Congress, which has given the INS more money than the Administration requested and directed that most of it be spent to beef up the Border Patrol. Reno, in a four-day publicity blitz along the Southwest border, and Meissner, at a Washington press conference, recently boasted that illegal crossings already appear to have lessened and that more manpower and improved technology are on the way.

In a recent interview, however, Meissner cautioned that the INS must maintain a balanced approach. "It is crucially important that prevention at the border succeeds, and I think we are showing results that indicate we are going about that in a better way than ever before," she said.

"But you can't do it all at the border; you can't do it all by just concentrating on the issue of undocumented crossings from Mexico. There is an awful lot of this issue that deals with other nationalities and other ways of entering the country." *(For more on the interview, see box, these two pages.)*

According to INS estimates, only 39 per cent of the illegal aliens now in the United States are from Mexico. The preponderance of undocumented immigrants from other countries are people who entered the country with legal business, student or tourist visas and then simply stayed when their visas expired.

So-called visa overstayers make up 52 per cent of the total illegal population, INS officials say. There are just over two million of them, and for the most part, they have greater economic mobility and are harder for immigration officials to track down.

Most advocates of effective immigration control believe that the only way to attack the problem of visa overstayers is to find a way to deactivate the magnet

At a meeting with lobbyists for the restaurant industry, House Speaker Newt Gingrich announced second thoughts about Republican plans to reduce welfare spending by eliminating benefits for legal immigrants who have not become U.S. citizens.

that attracts them: the propensity of Americans to hire them.

In a September report, the U.S. Commission on Immigration Reform, a congressionally mandated panel headed by former Rep. Barbara Jordan, D-Texas, stressed the need to "deter the employment of unauthorized migrants" by finding a way to breathe life back into the discredited employer sanctions provision of the 1986 immigration reform act.

Her panel concluded that "the most promising option for alleviating the fraud and discrimination found in current verification procedures is a computerized registry based on the social security number." It recommended that pilot programs be begun immediately to phase in and evaluate such a system. The commission estimated the cost of developing the registry and correcting for discrepancies at roughly $125 million with subsequent annual operating costs of $60 million or more.

Susan Martin, the commission's executive director, explained in an interview that the panel had tried to avoid the controversy surrounding the concept of a national ID card. Among the concepts the commission would like to see tested, she said, is a telephone verification system that does not require a document.

Richard A. Bloom

Commission on Immigration Reform's Susan Martin
A telephone verification system is worth trying out.

Under such a system, Martin explained, job applicants would simply supply a prospective employer with a social security number and some simple backup information such as their date of birth and/or mother's maiden name.

The employer, in theory, could then check the accuracy of the information and the validity of the applicant's social security number by making a single 1-800 phone call. Other proposals include a "more secure" social security card that perhaps could be checked electronically the way many stores now verify credit cards.

If the commission thought it was sidestepping controversy, it guessed wrong. More than three-dozen prominent conservatives, ranging from free-market economist Milton Friedman to GOP strategic guru William Kristol, immediately signed a letter sent to Republican Members of Congress. The letter said the cost of a computer registry for all workers would be "perhaps in the billions of dollars" and denounced the concept as "another leap forward in the ever-encroaching police powers of the federal government."

Immigrant rights advocates who oppose the concept of employer sanctions as inherently discriminatory said they have been assured that House Majority Leader Richard K. Armey of Texas will help lead the charge against the ID card/registry proposal.

The Jordan Commission also wants to put teeth in the law that requires sponsors of legal immigrants to keep the new arrivals from becoming public charges. Affidavits of support signed by sponsors currently cannot be enforced. Immigrants, during their first five years in the country, must report their sponsor's income along with their own when applying for public benefits. But sponsors' assets, although "deemed' to be available, are not always shared with immigrants in need.

REALITY CHECK

If immigration has gotten out of hand, why is the U.S. economy humming along so nicely with inflation in check and unemployment rates falling, even in the states glutted with both legal and illegal aliens?

"If you look to identify a single, definable group that has been missing in action in the immigration debate, it is business interests," said Demetrios G. Papademetriou, a Labor Department official in the Reagan and Bush Administrations who now directs immigration studies for the Carnegie Endowment for International Peace, a Washington think tank.

"All the way from the Microsofts and the IBMs, including the universities, down to the farm interests," Papademetriou said, there is great anxiety about the "changing climate" of public opinion toward immigration. Mostly, business leaders have stayed out of the political debate because of "cowardice and to avoid getting dirty," he said, but also because they're not yet sure what the "implications are for their ability to conduct their businesses."

In Papademetriou's estimation, there is

no doubt that attitudes toward immigrants have soured. With the end of the Cold War, refugees from Communism have lost their political cachet. And ordinary citizens, fretting over stagnant incomes and rising tax burdens, are prone to seek out scapegoats.

"The country is not in the business any longer of being magnanimous," he said. "We are now dropping back from the truly progressive principle that said, 'If you bring people here to work, you make that a way station toward full membership in our society.' "

What's needed now, he added, is a realistic look at the pluses and minuses of immigration. "Americans need to get off of this bullshit about illegal immigration and to begin to think about what it means to have a work force which presumably we need in certain industries," Papademetriou said. "We need to think about how we can maintain the advantage it gives us."

In California, farming interests are already worried about maintaining their immigrant advantage. A month after the Proposition 187 vote, a meeting of Western growers' representatives was held in Sacramento, Calif., to discuss strategy with Washington lobbyist Monte B. Lake, counsel for the National Council of Agricultural Employers (NCAE).

In a Washington interview, NCAE executive vice president Sharon M. Hughes said that even though the number of seasonal farm workers legalized under the 1986 SAW program greatly exceeded expectations, many of those laborers have not stayed in agriculture. The vacuum has been filled, she said, by what growers refer to as "illegally documented" workers.

Under the 1986 law, employers must fill out forms attesting that they have been shown appropriate work authorization documents but are not held responsible for determining their validity.

Richard Matoian, president of the California Grape and Tree-Fruit League, attended the Dec. 20 meeting of growers in Sacramento. He noted that the producers he represents are part of an "$8 billion" sector of the state's over-all $20 billion a year agriculture industry.

Matoian said any changes in immigration policy can affect his members. He added that the Proposition 187 vote was a cause of concern to growers "because they employ people who sometimes would be targeted by Proposition 187 whether they are legal or not."

Perhaps because of loyalty to Wilson, California's growers mostly stayed on the sidelines during the ballot initiative debate. "Growers tend to be Republican and conservative, but all of the ones I've talked to voted against Prop 187," Matoian said. "Most of the ag groups were neutral on Prop 187, and some actually opposed it. There was no group that was in support of it."

California growers know that when the border gets tight, pickers can become scarce. Last year, the INS assigned 300 new Border Patrol officers to the state; 200 more are to be added this year. Agency officials say that apprehensions of illicit border crossers declined 32 per cent in the last quarter of 1994.

That statistic doesn't surprise Harry Kubo, president of the Nisei Farmers League, a large growers' association headquartered in Fresno, Calif., some 300 miles north of the border. Kubo said that the labor pool in the San Joaquin Valley shrank by 25 per cent last fall, causing uninsured losses that will run "well into the millions" for farmers who were unable to complete the time-sensitive harvest of their raisins.

In an interview, Kubo, the son of Japanese immigrants, said he is all in favor of controlling the border, but said he was frustrated that U.S. citizens and even some immigrant groups that are here legally have no interest in agricultural work. He said attempts to recruit Southeastern Asian refugees for work in the fields fell flat because refugees, unlike most other legal immigrants, are immediately entitled to public assistance.

If Republican plans to radically overhaul the welfare system come to fruition, the potential pool of low-skilled native-born workers could increase markedly. But no one is sure that they will replace the immigrants who now hold down low-wage jobs not just in agriculture, but in the hotel and restaurant, garment and meat-packing industries and as janitorial and household help.

John Eisele

Carnegie Endowment for International Peace's Demetrios G. Papademetriou
American business interests have been mostly missing from the debate over immigration policy.

The Carnegie Endowment's Papademetriou believes that a transition program for undocumented workers may be needed to assure that U.S. labor needs are met while efforts are made to generally upgrade working conditions and pay standards. Such a program, he said, might also smooth ongoing U.S.-Mexican negotiations on migration issues.

As of now, U.S. workers simply aren't applying for many menial jobs. According to California growers' representative Matoian, "It's not so much the pay scales, which are well above minimum wage; it's because the season is short, it's generally dirty work, and because the welfare system is in place."

That's why California Gov. Wilson is once again talking about a guest worker program. Immigrant labor comes in handy when the state's crops are ready to be harvested.

NOT ASKING OR TELLING: NO REMEDY?

DAVID C. MORRISON

If President Clinton harbors any delusions that the policy of "Don't Ask, Don't Tell, Don't Pursue" promulgated a year ago rang down the curtain on the raging gays-in-the-military controversy, he is, well, deluded. Not only have military discharges of homosexuals continued unabated, but so have the legal challenges and political jockeying that prompted eruption of this issue even as Clinton was moving into the Oval Office.

The controversy promises to be a matter of contention in the 1996 presidential race. Clinton asserted last month that the issue blew into a major flap in early 1993 only because a politically motivated Sen. Robert Dole, R-Kan., pushed it to the forefront. (In fact, Clinton had pledged in the 1992 campaign to lift the gay ban by executive order.) A March 20 *Washington Times* story reports that religious conservatives fret that Dole, now the Majority Leader and a front-runner for the GOP presidential nomination next year, sounded too soft on the ban in a recent *New York Times* interview.

"Sexual orientation is a personal and private matter," the new formula, which went into effect on Feb. 28, 1994, states. Military officials would not be required to ask—nor those serving under them to tell—about sexual orientation. But, should a soldier engage in "homosexual conduct, he or she is subject to administrative separation."

Is Clinton happy with implementation of the policy over the past year? "He is," White House spokesman Michael McCurry said at a March 13 briefing. "Military commanders in the field are satisfied with it, and the number of expulsions clearly is declining. So . . . we're satisfied that the policy is working well and we ought to proceed with it."

NATIONAL SECURITY

In absolute terms, gay-related expulsions are down. In 1991, 949 troops were discharged on grounds of homosexuality. That fell to 708 in 1992, and to 597 last year. At the same time, though, total troop numbers have also dropped steadily since 1991. Proportionately, gay-related separations have remained a constant 0.04 per cent of the active force.

Those who seek to overturn the military's gay ban are thus far from satisfied. The Servicemembers Legal Defense Network marshals 200 lawyers nationwide to assist soldiers targeted for expulsion. In a Feb. 28 one-year-later report, the network charged that "a pattern of violations . . . often renders the policy little more than 'Ask, Pursue and Harass.' " Cited are 340 abuses of the protection that the Clinton policy seemed to afford actual or accused gays in uniform.

"I don't paint the military with a broad brush," network co-director C. Dixon Osburn said in an interview. "Some commanders use their discretion widely, so gays serving under them are better off. But many find themselves no better off, and others are even worse off. You have service members who are doing things, thinking they are protected. And, then, when their commanders come down on them, they realize that it was a trap."

A young sailor is being discharged because he truthfully answered a direct question about his orientation, the network reports, even though the Navy has admitted that the question violated the new policy. Military psychologists have been instructed to turn in soldiers seeking counseling about their sexual orientation. At a minimum, the Clinton policy was designed to end anti-gay "witch-hunts." From March-June 1994, however, 21 marines at Camp Hansen on Okinawa were called in and grilled about their sexual orientation and conduct.

Throughout the services, the network reports, "commanders and inquiry officials routinely seize personal diaries, private letters, address books, personal computers, erased computer files, photos of friends, copies of popular gay-themed books and videos like *Torch Song Trilogy*, HIV pamphlets, academic notes from classes on human sexuality and, in one serviceman's case, even a pair of men's platform shoes."

The Pentagon has yet to respond formally to the network's report. But its spokespeople have termed the findings "exaggerated" and contend that purported violations are "isolated" instances. In any event, no commander has yet been disciplined for infringing upon the "Don't Ask, Don't Tell, Don't Pursue" rules.

Those who fervently agree with the military's stance that "homosexuality is incompatible with military service" are no happier with the Clinton policy than gay-rights advocates are. Speaking for the Center for Military Readiness, a Livonia (Mich.)-based group favoring the gay ban, Elaine Donnelly recently told *Army Times* that she wants Congress to toughen things up this year, eliminating the "artificial dichotomy between homosexual status and conduct."

That fine distinction has fostered its share of legal perplexity. Three of 20 service members who have admitted to being gay but have denied the presumption that they thus engage in homosexual conduct, have managed to stay in the service. In an opinion last November upholding the 1987 expulsion of Joseph C. Steffan from the U.S. Naval Academy, however, the U.S. Court of Appeals for the District of Columbia Circuit ruled that "when an individual's statement can reasonably be taken to evidence a propensity to engage in certain conduct, the military may certainly take that individual at his word."

At least 15 openly gay troops continue to serve. Ruling that the gay ban was "grounded solely in prejudice," a federal judge last June ordered the reinstatement of Army National Guard Col. Margarethe Cammermeyer, whose expulsion was the subject of a recent NBC television movie. In November, the Justice Department abandoned efforts to press Petty Officer Keith Meinhold's expulsion through the courts because the Navy proceedings had originated under the pre-Clinton policy.

In the first unambiguous legal challenge to the new policy, a judge for the U.S. District Court for the Eastern District of New York is slated to rule by the end of this month on a suit brought by six active-duty and reserve soldiers contending that "Don't Ask, Don't Tell" violates constitutional guarantees of free speech and equal protection.

The ambiguities riddling the new policy have sparked some bizarre incongruities—especially in view of the widespread presumption that the rank and file are invariably hostile to their gay comrades. Petty Officer Mark Phillips was presented with a chocolate cake by crew members on the first anniversary of his coming out to his unit, the network reports. And, on Feb. 28, the first anniversary of the Clinton policy, Lt. Tracy Thorne, facing expulsion for having declared his homosexuality, was awarded a Navy Achievement Medal for "superior performance" of his duties.

"My commanding officer said, 'What are we doing here? On the one hand, we're kicking you out. On the other, we're giving you a medal,' " Thorne said. "I'm still befuddled by it all."

Credits/ Acknowledgments

Cover design by Charles Vitelli

1. Institutions and Processes

Facing overview—Capitol Building photo by K. Jewell.

2. The Economy, Taxing, Spending, and Budgeting

Facing overview—EPA-Documerica photo.

3. Agriculture and Food

Facing overview—United States Department of Agriculture photo.

4. Environment and Energy

Facing overview—Alcoa photo.

5. Health Care

Facing overview—EPA-Documerica photo.

6. Safety Net Programs

Facing overview—United Nations photo by P. S. Sudhakaran.

7. Schooling, Children, and Child Care

Facing overview—United Nations photo by Milton Grant.

8. Civil Rights

Facing overview—AP/Wide World photo by Mark Lennihan.

9. Crime, Urban Affairs, and Other Domestic Policy Areas

Facing overview—Criminal Justice Publications photo, New York.

10. Foreign and Defense Policy, Trade, and Immigration

Facing overview—U.S. Air Force photo.

PHOTOCOPY THIS PAGE!!!*

ANNUAL EDITIONS ARTICLE REVIEW FORM

■ NAME: ______________________ DATE: ______________________

■ TITLE AND NUMBER OF ARTICLE: ______________________

■ BRIEFLY STATE THE MAIN IDEA OF THIS ARTICLE: ______________________

■ LIST THREE IMPORTANT FACTS THAT THE AUTHOR USES TO SUPPORT THE MAIN IDEA:

■ WHAT INFORMATION OR IDEAS DISCUSSED IN THIS ARTICLE ARE ALSO DISCUSSED IN YOUR TEXTBOOK OR OTHER READING YOU HAVE DONE? LIST THE TEXTBOOK CHAPTERS AND PAGE NUMBERS:

■ LIST ANY EXAMPLES OF BIAS OR FAULTY REASONING THAT YOU FOUND IN THE ARTICLE:

■ LIST ANY NEW TERMS/CONCEPTS THAT WERE DISCUSSED IN THE ARTICLE AND WRITE A SHORT DEFINITION:

*Your instructor may require you to use this Annual Editions Article Review Form in any number of ways: for articles that are assigned, for extra credit, as a tool to assist in developing assigned papers, or simply for your own reference. Even if it is not required, we encourage you to photocopy and use this page; you'll find that reflecting on the articles will greatly enhance the information from your text.

We Want Your Advice

Annual Editions revisions depend on two major opinion sources: one is our Advisory Board, listed in the front of this volume, which works with us in scanning the thousands of articles published in the public press each year; the other is you—the person actually using the book. Please help us and the users of the next edition by completing the prepaid article rating form on this page and returning it to us. Thank you.

ANNUAL EDITIONS: AMERICAN PUBLIC POLICY 96/97

Article Rating Form

Here is an opportunity for you to have direct input into the next revision of this volume. We would like you to rate each of the 64 articles listed below, using the following scale:

1. Excellent: should definitely be retained
2. Above average: should probably be retained
3. Below average: should probably be deleted
4. Poor: should definitely be deleted

Your ratings will play a vital part in the next revision. So please mail this prepaid form to us just as soon as you complete it.
Thanks for your help!

Rating	Article	Rating	Article
	1. Do We Ask Too Much of Presidents?		33. Burial Insurance
	2. When There's Too Much of a Good Thing		34. Unmanaged Care?
	3. Still Trying to Reinvent Government		35. Managed Medicare
	4. Going to Extremes, Losing the Center		36. No Strings Attached
	5. Their Turn		37. A Medicaid Miracle?
	6. The V-Word		38. Long-Term Problem
	7. Return to Sender		39. Straining the Safety Net
	8. The *New* Federalism		40. Legitimate Questions
	9. The New Fixation of Federalism		41. Test Drive
	10. Who's Being Egregious Now?		42. The Good, the Bad, and the Ugly
	11. The Dawning of the Making-Do Decade		43. Big Money in Low Rents
	12. The Economy You Can't See		44. Vouching for the Poor
	13. The Downside of Downsizing		45. Reform by the Book
	14. Critics Down on This Levy		46. Price War
	15. Takin' on the Bacon		47. The Kiddie Card
	16. A Capital Idea, or a Fiscal Sand Trap?		48. When a Penny Saved Is a Dollar Spent
	17. Market Basket Mixup?		49. The Split Society
	18. Weak Link		50. The Wedge Issue
	19. Thrift Begins at Home		51. A Speak-No-Evil Veil Lifted
	20. Rethinking Worker Retraining		52. Locked In
	21. Unequal Shares		53. Putting a Price Tag on Death
	22. The Visible Hand		54. An Urban Nightmare Come True?
	23. A New Way to Budge the Budget		55. Splitsville
	24. Genes in the Bottle		56. Try, Try Again
	25. Food Fight		57. Ready for What?
	26. The Big Harvest		58. Spar Wars
	27. Plowing a New Field		59. Aiming High
	28. The Greening of Environmental Regulation		60. Intervention v. Sovereignty
			61. Tottering Markets
	29. This Land Is Whose Land?		62. Waiting for a New Clinton Doctrine
	30. The Conquered Coalition		63. Second Thoughts
	31. Cutting the Strings		64. Not Asking or Telling: No Remedy?
	32. A New Shade of Green		

(Continued on next page)

ABOUT YOU

Name_______________________ Date_________

Are you a teacher? ☐ Or student? ☐

Your School Name _______________________

Department _______________________

Address _______________________

City _______________ State _________ Zip _________

School Telephone # _______________________

YOUR COMMENTS ARE IMPORTANT TO US!

Please fill in the following information:

For which course did you use this book? _______________________

Did you use a text with this Annual Edition? ☐ yes ☐ no

The title of the text? _______________________

What are your general reactions to the Annual Editions concept?

Have you read any particular articles recently that you think should be included in the next edition?

Are there any articles you feel should be replaced in the next edition? Why?

Are there other areas that you feel would utilize an Annual Edition?

May we contact you for editorial input?

May we quote you from above?

No Postage Necessary if Mailed in the United States

ANNUAL EDITIONS: AMERICAN PUBLIC POLICY 96/97

BUSINESS REPLY MAIL

First Class Permit No. 84 Guilford, CT

Postage will be paid by addressee

Dushkin Publishing Group/
Brown & Benchmark Publishers
Sluice Dock
Guilford, Connecticut 06437